JOURNAL FOR THE STUDY OF THE OLD TESTAMENT SUPPLEMENT SERIES
266

Editors
David J.A. Clines
Philip R. Davies

Executive Editor
John Jarick

GENDER, CULTURE, THEORY
7

Editor
J. Cheryl Exum

Sheffield Academic Press

D0898548

Biblical Studies/ Cultural Studies

The Third Sheffield Colloquium

edited by
J. Cheryl Exum and
Stephen D. Moore

Journal for the Study of the Old Testament
Supplement Series 266

Gender, Culture, Theory 7

Copyright © 1998 Sheffield Academic Press

Published by Sheffield Academic Press Ltd
Mansion House
19 Kingfield Road
Sheffield S11 9AS
England

Printed on acid-free paper in Great Britain
by Bookcraft Ltd
Midsomer Norton, Bath

British Library Cataloguing in Publication Data

A catalogue record for this book is available
from the British Library

ISBN 1-85075-965-0
ISBN 1-85075-970-7 pbk

CONTENTS

LIST OF ILLUSTRATIONS

ACKNOWLEDGMENTS

We would like to acknowledge the British Academy for a grant supporting the travel expenses of four of the North American participants in the Colloquium. Special thanks are due to Gill Fogg and Alison Bygrave, Secretaries in the Department of Biblical Studies, for their considerable help in the organization of the Colloquium. Thanks are also due to Vicky Acklam of Sheffield Academic Press for her labours on behalf of this volume.

ABBREVIATIONS

AB	Anchor Bible
ABD	David Noel Freedman (ed.), *The Anchor Bible Dictionary* (New York: Doubleday, 1992)
ANRW	Hildegard Temporini and Wolfgang Haase (eds.), *Aufstieg und Niedergang der römischen Welt: Geschichte und Kultur Roms im Spiegel der neueren Forschung* (Berlin: W. de Gruyter, 1972–)
BBB	Bonner biblische Beiträge
BHS	*Biblia hebraica stuttgartensia*
BibInt	*Biblical Interpretation: A Journal of Contemporary Approaches*
BJRL	*Bulletin of the John Rylands University Library of Manchester*
BJS	Brown Judaic Studies
BKAT	Biblischer Kommentar: Altes Testament
BN	*Biblische Notizen*
BNTC	Black's New Testament Commentaries
BTB	*Biblical Theology Bulletin*
BZAW	Beihefte zur *ZAW*
CBQ	*Catholic Biblical Quarterly*
CurTM	*Currents in Theology and Mission*
EHS	Europäische Hochschulschriften
ETL	*Ephemerides theologicae lovanienses*
FAT	Forschungen zum Alten Testament
FOTL	The Forms of the Old Testament Literature
FzB	Forschung zur Bibel
HBS	Herders Biblische Studien
HTR	*Harvard Theological Review*
ICC	International Critical Commentary
IDB	George Arthur Buttrick (ed.), *The Interpreter's Dictionary of the Bible* (4 vols.; Nashville: Abingdon Press, 1962)
Int	*Interpretation*
JAAR	*Journal of the American Academy of Religion*
JAOS	*Journal of the American Oriental Society*
JB	*Jerusalem Bible*
JBL	*Journal of Biblical Literature*
JHS	*Journal of Hellenic Studies*
JJS	*Journal of Jewish Studies*
JNES	*Journal of Near Eastern Studies*
JSJ	*Journal for the Study of Judaism in the Persian, Hellenistic and Roman Period*

JSNT	*Journal for the Study of the New Testament*
JSOT	*Journal for the Study of the Old Testament*
JSOTSup	*Journal for the Study of the Old Testament*, Supplement Series
JSP	*Journal for the Study of the Pseudepigrapha*
JTS	*Journal of Theological Studies*
KAT	Kommentar zum Alten Testament
LCL	Loeb Classical Library
NCB	New Century Bible
NEB	Neue Echter Bibel
NRSV	New Revised Standard Version
NTS	*New Testament Studies*
OTL	Old Testament Library
OTS	*Oudtestamentische Studiën*
PAAJR	*Proceedings of the American Academy of Jewish Research*
PMLA	*Proceedings of the Modern Language Association*
SBB	Stuttgarter biblische Beiträge
SBM	Stuttgarter biblische Monographien
SBS	Stuttgarter Bibelstudien
SJT	*Scottish Journal of Theology*
SNTSMS	Society for New Testament Studies Monograph Series
TDOT	G.J. Botterweck and H. Ringgren (eds.), *Theological Dictionary of the Old Testament*
TPQ	*Theologisch-praktische Quartalschrift*
VT	*Vetus Testamentun*
WBC	Word Biblical Commentary
WUNT	Wissenschaftliche Untersuchungen zum Neuen Testament
ZAW	*Zeitschrift für die alttestamentliche Wissenschaft*

NOTES ON CONTRIBUTORS

Alice Bach teaches at Stanford University. She is the editor of *Biblicon*, a journal of Bible, media and culture, and is the author of *Women, Seduction and Betrayal in Biblical Narrative*. She has edited a number of volumes, including *Women in the Hebrew Bible: A Reader* and *Biblical Glamour and Hollywood Glitz*. In an earlier life, she wrote more than 20 books for children, including the novels *Mollie Make Believe*, *Waiting for Johnny Miracle* and *When the Sky Began to Roar*. A member of the Catholic Worker community, she possesses the secret of cooking thick soup from tired vegetables to serve 500 people.

Fiona C. Black is completing a PhD thesis entitled 'The Grotesque Body in the Song of Songs' at the University of Sheffield. Her article, 'Scholars Amazed! *Weekly World News* and the Bible', is forthcoming in *Semeia*, and her essay, 'Unlikely Bedfellows: Feminist and Allegorical Readings of Song of Songs 7.1-8', is forthcoming in Sheffield Academic Press's Feminist Companion to the Bible (second series). She is also co-editing a Festschrift for Robert Culley, which will appear in the Semeia Studies series.

Athalya Brenner is Professor of Hebrew Bible/Old Testament in the Department of Theology and Religious Studies at the University of Amsterdam. She is the editor of the Sheffield Academic Press series A Feminist Companion to the Bible (in 11 volumes, with a second series pending). Her latest book is *The Intercourse of Knowledge: On Gendering Desire and 'Sexuality' in the Hebrew Bible*.

Robert P. Carroll is Professor of Hebrew Bible and Semitic Studies at the University of Glasgow. He is the author of *When Prophecy Failed*; *From Chaos to Covenant*; *Jeremiah*; *Jeremiah: A Commentary* and *Wolf in the Sheepfold*. He is co-editor with Stephen Prickett of *The Bible: Authorized King James Version* in the Oxford World's Classics series.

David J.A. Clines is Professor and Head of the Department of Biblical Studies at the University of Sheffield. He is a former President of the Society for Old Testament Study. His books include *The Theme of the Pentateuch*; *What Does Eve Do to Help?*; *Interested Parties: The Ideology of Writers and Readers of the Old Testament*; *The Bible and the Modern World*; *Ezra, Nehemiah, Esther*; and *Job 1–20* (he is currently working on the second volume). He is editor of *The Dictionary of Classical Hebrew*, four volumes of which have appeared. He and Philip Davies edit the *Journal for the Study of the Old Testament* and its Supplement Series. He is also Publisher and Director of Sheffield Academic Press.

Margaret Davies is Senior Lecturer in Biblical Studies at the University of Sheffield. She is the author of *Matthew*; *Rhetoric and Reference in the Fourth Gospel* and *The Pastoral Epistles*, and is co-editor of *The Bible in Ethics*. She is co-author (with E.P. Sanders) of *Studying the Synoptic Gospels*. Most recently she has published *The Epworth Commentary on the Pastoral Epistles*. She is now working on a book on New Testament ethics.

Philip R. Davies is Professor of Biblical Studies at the University of Sheffield. His books include *IQM: The War Scroll from Qumran*; *Qumran*; *The Damascus Document*; *Daniel*; *Behind the Essenes*; *In Search of 'Ancient Israel'*; *Whose Bible Is It Anyway?*; *Sects and Scrolls*; and *Scribes and Schools*. He is co-author with John Rogerson of *The Old Testament World*. He and David Clines edit the *Journal for the Study of the Old Testament* and its Supplement Series. He is also Publisher and Director of Sheffield Academic Press.

Philip F. Esler is Dean of Divinity and Professor of Biblical Criticism at the University of St Andrews. He is the author of *Community and Gospel in Luke–Acts: The Social and Political Motivations of Lucan Theology*; *The First Christians in their Social Worlds: Social-Scientific Approaches to New Testament Interpretation* and *Galatians*. He is the editor of *Modelling Early Christianity: Social-Scientific Studies of the New Testament in its Context* and *Christianity for the Twenty-First Century*.

J. Cheryl Exum is Professor of Biblical Studies at the University of Sheffield. Her books include *Tragedy and Biblical Narrative: Arrows of the Almighty*; *Fragmented Women: Feminist (Sub)versions of Biblical Narratives*; *Plotted, Shot and Painted: Cultural Representations of Biblical Women* and *Was sagt das Richterbuch den Frauen?* She is editor of the journal *Biblical*

Interpretation, and of the Sheffield Academic Press series Gender, Culture, Theory. She is Co-Chair of the Bible and Cultural Studies Section of the Society of Biblical Literature.

Yael Feldman is Associate Professor of Hebrew and Comparative Literature at New York University. She is the author of *A Woolf in the Holy Land: Israeli Women Novelists* and a co-editor of *Teaching the Hebrew Bible as Literature*. Currently she is working on a book tentatively entitled *The Psycho-Political Narrative in Hebrew Literature*, of which her essay in the present volume is a chapter. She is an Associate Editor of *Prooftexts* and Cultural Editor of *HaDo'ar*.

Jennifer A. Glancy is Associate Professor of Religious Studies at Le Moyne College in Syracuse, NY. She has published on gender studies, cultural studies, ideological criticism, and the representation of slaves and slavery in biblical texts. Currently she is working on a book on slavery and the New Testament.

Jan Willem van Henten teaches Bible and Second Temple Judaism at the University of Amsterdam and is Director of the Netherlands School for Advanced Studies in Theology and Religion at Utrecht. He is the author of *The Maccabean Martyrs as Saviours of the Jewish People*, and has also published on Jewish and Christian views about noble death, on Jewish inscriptions, and on apocalyptic literature.

David Jasper is Professor of Literature and Theology and Director of the Centre for the Study of Literature and Theology at the University of Glasgow. He is the author and editor of many books. For ten years he was Senior Editor of the journal *Literature and Theology*, and is Series Editor of the Macmillan Press series Studies in Literature and Religion. Apart from his work on Turner, he has also published on Rembrandt and American Abstract Expressionism.

Francis Landy is Professor of Religious Studies at the University of Alberta. He is the author of books on the Song of Songs and Hosea, and is currently at work on a book on Isaiah. He is married and has a three-year-old son, Joseph, who has contributed greatly to his interest in cultural studies, and participated on the sidelines of the colloquium. He also has two cats, seven fish, and some stick-insects. The cats contribute to the writing from time to time.

R. Barry Matlock is Lecturer in Biblical Studies at the University of Sheffield. He is the author of *Unveiling the Apocalyptic Paul: Paul's Interpreters and the Rhetoric of Criticism*. Currently he is working on two further books, one a volume on Galatians, the other a study of the Pauline expression πίστις Ἰησοῦ Χριστοῦ. He serves on the editorial board of the *Journal for the Study of the New Testament*.

Stephen D. Moore is Senior Lecturer in Biblical Studies at the University of Sheffield. His publications include *Literary Criticism and the Gospels*; *Mark and Luke in Poststructuralist Perspectives*; *Poststructuralism and the New Testament* and *God's Gym: Divine Male Bodies of the Bible*. He co-authored and co-edited *The Postmodern Bible*, and co-edited *Mark and Method*. He is editor of the *Journal for the Study of the New Testament*, and chair of the Hermeneutics Seminar of the British New Testament Conference.

Hugh S. Pyper is Senior Lecturer in Biblical Studies at the University of Leeds. His publications include *David as Reader: 2 Sam 12:1-15 and the Poetics of Fatherhood* and articles on the literary study of the Bible. Before turning to biblical studies, he studied and taught biology and maintains an active interest in the interface between science and religion.

John W. Rogerson is Professor Emeritus and former Head of the Department of Biblical Studies at the University of Sheffield. His main publications have centred on the history and assumptions of Old Testament interpretation, and the use of the Bible today. They include *Myth in Old Testament Interpretation*; *Anthropology and the Old Testament*; *Old Testament Criticism in the Nineteenth Century: England and Germany* and *The Bible and Criticism in Victorian Britain*. His *Atlas of the Bible* has been translated into six languages.

William T. Scott is Head of the Department of Language and Media at Glasgow Caledonian University, where he teaches courses in linguistics and semiotics. He is the author of *The Possibility of Communication* and various papers, particularly on aspects of legal semiotics, with deceit and misrepresentation as major concerns.

Regina M. Schwartz is Professor of English at Northwestern University and Director of the Chicago Institute of Religion, Ethics, and

Violence. She is the author of *Remembering and Repeating: On Milton's Theology and Poetics*, which won the James Holly Hanford Book Award from the Milton Society of America, and *The Curse of Cain: The Violent Legacy of Monotheism*. She is also editor of *The Book and the Text: The Bible and Literary Theory*, and co-author of *The Postmodern Bible*.

Erich Zenger is Professor of Old Testament Literature at the University of Münster. He is the author of *Das Erste Testament: Die jüdische Bibel und die Christen*; *Am Fuß des Sinai: Gottesbilder des Ersten Testaments*; *Die Nacht wird leuchten wie der Tag: Psalmenauslegungen* and *The God of Vengeance: Understanding the Psalms of Divine Wrath*; and the co-author of *Die Psalmen: Psalm 1–50*; *Neue Wege der Psalmenforschung*; *Der Gott Israels und die Volker: Untersuchungen zum Jesajabuch und zu den Psalmen* and *Als Anfang schuf Gott: Biblische Schöpfungstheologien*.

Biblical Studies/Cultural Studies

J. Cheryl Exum and Stephen D. Moore

This book originated in an international colloquium on 'Biblical into Cultural Studies' held at the University of Sheffield in April of 1997 under the auspices of the Centre for Biblical and Cultural Studies. The colloquium, the third in a series of interdisciplinary colloquia sponsored by the Department of Biblical Studies,[1] took as its starting point the premise that the practice of cultural studies offers critical tools for analysing the Bible's position of privilege in the Western canon and provides a theoretical perspective from which to look not only at the production of meaning in the past but also at ways the Bible and contemporary culture mutually influence each other. The participants, scholars from various disciplines but mainly from within the field of biblical studies, were invited to write on a topic of their choice relating to the intersection of cultural studies and biblical studies. The result was a series of stimulating discussions, leading to further reflection, revision, and a cultural product: the following, and we believe fascinating, mix of essays. It is not the intention of this volume to try to define the emerging area of biblical cultural studies—even if that could be done—but rather, in these early stages of what promises to become a significant development in biblical studies, to provide a sense of the possibilities a cultural studies approach to the Bible opens up and to indicate some of the directions it might take. Since cultural studies is relatively new on the biblical horizon, we begin with a brief sketch of how cultural studies has developed, which we hope will help to situate the present project in its larger academic and cultural context.

---

1. For the proceedings of the first two colloquia, held in 1990 and 1995, see Loveday C.A. Alexander (ed.), *Images of Empire* (JSOTSup, 122; Sheffield: Sheffield Academic Press, 1991), and John W. Rogerson, Margaret Davies and M. Daniel Carroll R. (eds.), *The Bible in Ethics: The Second Sheffield Colloquium* (JSOTSup, 207; Sheffield: Sheffield Academic Press, 1995).

The Story of Cultural Studies

There is a 'received history' of cultural studies, a fairly tightly plotted narrative of ascent and decline, which generally begins with the work of Richard Hoggart and Raymond Williams in the 1950s, continues through the founding and flowering of the Centre for Contemporary Cultural Studies at the University of Birmingham in the 1960s and 1970s, and culminates in the internationalization, institutionalization—and domestication—of cultural studies in the 1980s and 1990s.

This historical recital customarily commences with verbal portraits of the founding fathers. The first depicts Hoggart clutching a copy of his 1957 book, *The Uses of Literacy*.[2] Hoggart's quirky book, with its affectionate ethnographic attention to such mundane matters as English working-class speech patterns, living-room decor, eating habits, motherhood, fatherhood, neighbourhoods, and so on, proceeding to a critique of popular magazines, songs, newspapers and pulp fiction, anticipates what British cultural studies would become—pre-eminently the study of British working-class culture and popular media.

The second founder figure, Raymond Williams, is, like Hoggart, customarily portrayed clutching a book to his breast, in this case *Culture and Society*.[3] In certain respects, *Culture and Society* anticipates the subsequent agenda of British cultural studies less markedly than *The Uses of Literacy*, being a historical study of the emergence and evolution of the modern notion of culture. Yet Williams's legacy to cultural studies consists precisely in his intense attention to the concept of culture itself (a concept everywhere evoked but nowhere defined in *The Uses of Literacy*). In *Culture and Society* and its successor volume, *The Long Revolution*, Williams shifts the definition of culture away from 'the best that has been thought and said' to 'a whole way of life'. 'The analysis of culture, from such a definition...will...include analysis of elements in the way of life that to followers of the other definitions are not "culture" at all: the organization of production, the structure of the family, the structure of institutions which express or govern social relationships, the characteristic forms through which members of the

2.   Richard Hoggart, *The Uses of Literacy: Aspects of Working-Class Life, with Special Reference to Publications and Entertainments* (London: Chatto & Windus, 1957).

3.   Raymond Williams, *Culture and Society: 1780–1950* (London: Chatto & Windus, 1958).

society communicate.'[4] In sum, *Culture and Society*, and *The Long Revolution* which builds upon it, can be read as a sustained historical and theoretical argument for a paradigmatic shift of attention from an *aesthetic* to an *anthropological* study of culture—the culture in question, however, not being the 'primitive' or 'exotic' cultures beloved of ethnographers but the culture(s) of industrial societies instead—just as *The Uses of Literacy* can be read as the first instalment of this improbable fieldwork, an ethnography of English working-class culture.

Much more could, and perhaps should, be said about the primaeval history of cultural studies, in particular Hoggart's and Williams's debts to the educational philosophy of F.R. Leavis,[5] but let us press on. A third figure is often pushed on stage at this point in the story, also bearing a book—indeed, a little flushed with the effort of holding aloft his thousand-page tome, *The Making of the English Working Class*. This is E.P. Thompson, and his book is commonly regarded as exemplary of cultural history 'written from below'.[6] Far more significant than Thompson, however, for the subsequent development of British cultural studies is a fourth figure (a fourth evangelist?), Stuart Hall.

In 1964 the Centre for Contemporary Cultural Studies (henceforth, CCCS) was established at the University of Birmingham as a graduate annex of the English Department with Hoggart as Director and Hall as Deputy Director. In 1968 Hoggart left for Paris to take up a position with UNESCO. For the next 11 years, first as Acting Director, and then, from 1972, as Director, Hall ran the Centre. This period is generally seen as the 'golden age' of British cultural studies.

The 1970s was also the Marxist phase of CCCS. The influence of Marxism on British cultural studies is regularly emphasized (and often exaggerated). 'All the basic assumptions of cultural studies are Marxist', claims John Storey. 'This is not to say that all practitioners of cultural studies are Marxists', he continues, 'but that cultural studies is itself grounded in Marxism'.[7] Richard Johnson draws up a checklist of three

---

4.   Raymond Williams, *The Long Revolution* (London: Chatto & Windus, 1961), pp. 57-58.

5.   On Leavis and cultural studies, see Fred Inglis, *Cultural Studies* (Oxford: Basil Blackwell, 1993), pp. 35-46.

6.   E.P. Thompson, *The Making of the English Working Class* (London: Gollancz, 1963).

7.   John Storey, 'Cultural Studies: An Introduction', in John Storey (ed.), *What Is Cultural Studies? A Reader* (London: Edward Arnold, 1996), pp. 1-13 (3).

Marxist premises that have informed cultural studies: the first is that cultural processes are intimately connected with social relations, especially with class relations and class formations; the second is that culture involves power and helps to produce asymmetries in the abilities of individuals and social groups to define and realize their needs; and the third, which follows from the other two, is that culture is neither an autonomous nor an externally determined field, but a site of social differences and struggles.[8]

The cultural studies to which Storey and Johnson refer is primarily that which was forged at CCCS.[9] It was not until 1970-71, however, that Marxism took centre stage at CCCS: 'We chose as a coherent theory one the Centre had not previously analysed, that of Karl Marx'.[10] But which interpretation of Marxist theory would CCCS endorse? By 1973 the Marxism of French structuralist Louis Althusser had come to dominate the agenda at the Centre.[11] This is also the period when explicit concern with ideology comes to the fore at CCCS—so much so, indeed, that at least one commentator would later suggest that 'British cultural studies could be described just as easily and perhaps more accurately as ideological studies'.[12] This is, in fact, the most conspicuous point of convergence beween cultural studies and recent biblical studies (we speak, of course, of that ever-expanding body of biblical scholarship now commonly termed 'ideological criticism').

Central to Althusser's system was the concept of *ideological state apparatuses* (ISAs). This rather inelegant term designated a disparate group of relatively autonomous but functionally interlocking social institutions,

8. Richard Johnson, 'What Is Cultural Studies Anyway?', in Storey (ed.), *What Is Cultural Studies?*, pp. 75-114 (76).

9. Another locus for British cultural studies in the 1970s was the group centred on the influential film studies journal, *Screen*, on which see Ioan Davies, *Cultural Studies and Beyond: Fragments of Empire* (London: Routledge, 1995), pp. 89-93.

10. Anon., *Centre for Contemporary Cultural Studies Report: 7.1969–12.1971* (Birmingham: University of Birmingham, 1971), p. 10, quoted in Colin Sparks, 'Stuart Hall, Cultural Studies and Marxism', in David Morley and Kuan-Hsing Chen (eds.), *Stuart Hall: Critical Dialogues in Cultural Studies* (London: Routledge, 1996), pp. 71-101 (81).

11. See Louis Althusser, *For Marx* (trans. Ben Brewster; London: Penguin Books, 1969), and *Lenin and Philosophy and Other Essays* (trans. Ben Brewster; London: New Left Books, 1971).

12. James W. Carey, 'Overcoming Resistance to Cultural Studies', in Storey (ed.), *What Is Cultural Studies?*, pp. 61-74 (65).

such as the family, the media, and the educational and political systems. ISAs were to be distinguished from *overtly* coercive social institutions, such as the army, the police, and the legal system. By *covertly* inducing people to behave in socially acceptable ways, as though they were free agents, ISAs do the subtle work of ideology. Ideology, in Althusser's celebrated definition, 'represents the imaginary relationship of individuals to their real conditions of existence'.[13]

The Althusserian Marxism in vogue at CCCS was by no means unadulterated, however. Althusser's concept of ideology, in its details, seemed to lack nuance. Very soon, leading CCCS members such as Hall were attempting to synthesize the more persuasive features of Althusser's system with other concepts drawn from the Italian Marxist Antonio Gramsci, and subsequently, in the 1980s, from the poststructuralist Marxist Ernesto Laclau.[14] Other influences on British cultural studies from the late 1970s onwards included the French theorists Pierre Bourdieu, Michel de Certeau, and Michel Foucault.[15] Althusser's enduring legacy to British cultural studies, however, has consisted in inducing it to make ideology, viewed as housed especially in the mass media, in state institutions, and in language itself, a central focus of attention.

Additionally during the 1970s, British cultural studies began to forge a style of analysis of social institutions and cultural products that is best termed 'semiotic'—a decoding of 'surface' features designed to reveal underlying meanings, and ideological meanings in particular. The most notable precursor for this sort of work was the Roland Barthes of *Mythologies*, and the most celebrated example of it to emerge from CCCS

13. Althusser, 'Ideology and Ideological State Apparatuses (Notes towards an Investigation', in *Lenin and Philosophy*, pp. 127-86 (153).

14. See Antonio Gramsci, *Selections from the Prison Notebooks* (ed. and trans. Quintin Hoare and Geoffrey Nowell-Smith; London: Lawrence & Wishart, 1971), *idem, Selections from the Political Writings* (ed. and trans. Quintin Hoare; London: Lawrence & Wishart, 1978), and *idem, Selections from Cultural Writings* (ed. David Forgacs and Geoffrey Nowell-Smith; London: Lawrence & Wishart, 1985); also Ernesto Laclau, *Politics and Ideology in Marxist Theory* (London: New Left Books, 1977), and Ernesto Laclau and Chantal Mouffe, *Hegemony and Social Strategy: Towards a Radical Democratic Politics* (London: Verso, 1985). On Hall's appropriation of Gramsci see his 'Gramsci's Relevance for the Study of Race and Ethnicity', in Morley and Chen (eds.), *Stuart Hall*, pp. 411-40; and on Hall's appropriation of Laclau see Sparks, 'Stuart Hall, Cultural Studies and Marxism', pp. 89-95.

15. On this see Simon During, 'Introduction', in Simon During (ed.), *The Cultural Studies Reader* (London: Routledge, 1993), pp. 1-25 (10-13).

was Stuart Hall's 1980 essay, 'Encoding, Decoding'.[16] As Hall's essay is heavy on theory but light on application, however, we shall attempt to convey the flavour of the eclectic cultural critique—Marxist, ideological, semiotic—that characterized CCCS in its heyday with reference instead to another influential essay, one by Richard Johnson, who succeeded Hall in 1979 as Director of the Centre. At one point in his essay, Johnson homes in on the Mini-Metro,

> a pretty standard late twentieth-century capitalist commodity that happened to carry a particularly rich accumulation of meanings. The Metro was the car that was going to save the British car industry, by beating rivals from the market and by solving British Leyland's acute problems of industrial discipline. It came to signify solutions to internal and external national threats. The advertising campaigns around its launching were remarkable. In one television ad, a band of Mini-Metros pursued a gang of foreign imports up to (and apparently) over the White Cliffs of Dover, whence they fled in what looked remarkably like landing craft. This was a Dunkirk in reverse with the Metro as nationalist hero. Certainly these are some of the forms—nationalist epic, popular memory of World War II, internal/external threat—that I would want to abstract for further formal scrutiny. But this raises interesting questions too about what constitutes a 'text' (or raw material for such abstractions) in these cases. Would it be enough to analyse the design of the Metro itself as Barthes once analysed the lines of a Citroën? How could we exclude ads and garage showroom displays? Shouldn't we include, indeed, the Metro's place in discourses upon national economic recovery and moral renaissance?
>
> Supposing that we answered these questions affirmatively (and gave ourselves a lot more work) there would still be some unposed questions. What was made of the Metro phenomenon, more privately, by particular groups of consumers and readers? We would expect great diversity of response. Leyland workers, for example, were likely to view the car differently from those who only bought it. Beyond this, the Metro (and its transformed meanings) became a way of getting to work or picking the kids up from school. It may also have helped to produce, for example, orientations towards working life, connecting industrial 'peace' with national prosperity. Then, of course, the products of this whole circuit returned once more to the moment of production—as profits for fresh investment, but also as market researchers' findings on 'popularity' (capital's own 'cultural studies'). The subsequent use, by British Leyland

---

16. Roland Barthes, *Mythologies* (trans. Annette Lavers; London: Jonathan Cape, 1972); Stuart Hall, 'Encoding, Decoding', in During (ed.), *The Cultural Studies Reader*, pp. 90-103.

management, of similar strategies for selling cars and weakening workers suggests considerable accumulations (of both kinds) from this episode. Indeed the Metro became a little paradigm, though not the first, for a much more diffused ideological form, which we might term, with some compression, 'the nationalist sell'.[17]

CCCS members published little in the 1960s and early 1970s. Beginning around the mid-1970s, however, a succession of highly significant publications begin to issue from the Centre. The first was *Resistance through Rituals*, edited by Stuart Hall and Tony Jefferson.[18] That it was a collectively authored work, like several of its immediate successors, was itself not without significance. Michael Green has noted how CCCS was concerned 'to democratise academic knowledge forms', and has provided an account of the key role that group work played in research and pedagogy at the Centre.[19] *Resistance through Rituals* consists of ethnographic explorations of the relations between British youth subcultures (ranging from teddy boys to skinheads) and the dominant ideologies of British society, complex relations of contestation and compromise. This preoccupation—a pervasive one at CCCS through the 1970s—received its definitive expression in Dick Hebdige's *Subculture*.[20] The positive significance ascribed to subcultural speech, hairstyles, dress, music and dance by Hebdige and his CCCS colleagues (*Subculture* focuses especially on punks) suggested the distance that the study of working-class culture had come from Hoggart's *The Uses of Literacy*, which took an unremittingly negative view of popular culture and (then nascent) youth subculture. Paul Willis's *Learning to Labour*, another CCCS product from the 1970s, is also much preoccupied with strategies of resistance to state power employed by the relatively powerless, while John Clarke, Chas Critcher and Richard Johnson's *Working Class Culture*, with its Althusserian and Gramscian subtexts, further suggests the rift that had opened up between the first and second generation of cultural studies scholars.[21] (E.P. Thompson's *The Poverty of Theory* from

17. Johnson, 'What Is Cultural Studies Anyway?', pp. 83-85.

18. Stuart Hall and Tony Jefferson (eds.), *Resistance through Rituals: Youth Subcultures in Post-War Britain* (London: Hutchinson, 1976).

19. Michael Green, 'The Centre for Contemporary Cultural Studies', in Storey (ed.), *What Is Cultural Studies?*, pp. 49-60 (54-56).

20. Dick Hebdige, *Subculture: The Meaning of Style* (London: Methuen, 1979).

21. Paul Willis, *Learning to Labour: How Working Class Kids Get Working Class Jobs* (Farnborough: Saxon House, 1977); John Clarke, Chas Critcher and Richard

1978 is principally a denunciation of the Althusserian Marxism that seduced the second generation.[22]) The first major studies of television to emerge from CCCS were Charlotte Brunsdon and David Morley's *Everyday Television: 'Nationwide'* and Morley's *The 'Nationwide' Audience: Structure and Decoding*—the 'Nationwide' of the titles being a popular BBC news-magazine show—followed by Dorothy Hobson's *'Crossroads': The Drama of a Soap Opera*.[23]

There were at least two 'interruptions' (as Hall would later put it) in the work of the Centre during the 1970s, 'the first around feminism, and the second around questions of race'.[24] When feminism broke into CCCS's agenda, Hall recalls, it was as a 'thief in the night… The title of the volume in which this dawn-raid was first accomplished—*Women Take Issue*—is instructive: for they "took issue" in both senses—took over that year's book and initiated a quarrel'.[25] The feminist intervention at CCCS, which began at least as early as 1974,[26] yielded, in addition to *Women Take Issue*, a number of other significant publications.[27] The feminist intervention exposed the androcentrism, not just of

Johnson, *Working Class Culture: Studies in History and Theory* (London: Hutchinson, 1979).

22. E.P. Thompson, *The Poverty of Theory and Other Essays* (London: Merlin Press, 1978). Hall addresses the rift in his own way in 'Cultural Studies: Two Paradigms', *Media, Culture and Society* 2 (1980), pp. 57-72.

23. Charlotte Brunsdon and David Morley, *Everyday Television: 'Nationwide'* (London: British Film Institute, 1978); David Morley, *The 'Nationwide' Audience: Structure and Decoding* (London: British Film Institute, 1980); Dorothy Hobson, *'Crossroads': The Drama of a Soap Opera* (London: Methuen, 1982).

24. Stuart Hall, 'Cultural Studies and its Theoretical Legacies', in Lawrence Grossberg, Cary Nelson and Paul Treichler (eds.), *Cultural Studies* (New York: Routledge, 1992), pp. 277-94 (282).

25. Hall, 'Cultural Studies and its Theoretical Legacies', p. 282. See Women's Studies Group, Centre for Contemporary Cultural Studies, *Women Take Issue: Aspects of Women's Subordination* (London: Hutchinson, 1978). For a detailed account of the 'quarrel' to which Hall refers, see Charlotte Brunsdon, 'A Thief in the Night: Stories of Feminism in the 1970s at CCCS', in Morley and Chen (eds.), *Stuart Hall*, pp. 276-86.

26. See Helen Butcher *et al.*, *Images of Women in the Media* (Stencilled Occasional Paper, 34; Birmingham: Centre for Contemporary Cultural Studies, 1974).

27. E.g. Angela McRobbie, *Jackie: An Ideology of Adolescent Femininity* (Birmingham: Centre for Contemporary Cultural Studies, 1978); Angela McRobbie and Trisha McCabe (eds.), *Feminism for Girls* (London: Routledge & Kegan Paul, 1981); Hobson, *'Crossroads'*; Charlotte Brunsdon (ed.), *Films for Women* (London: British

the first generation of cultural studies scholars, but frequently of the second generation as well, notably its failure to engage critically with the sexism and misogyny of many of the youth subcultures it analysed, coupled with its neglect in its media studies of genres such as soap operas, perceived as 'feminine', in favour of 'masculine' genres such as news and current affairs shows.[28]

With regard to the second 'interruption', Hall (himself of black Jamaican extraction) recalls that 'getting cultural studies to put on its own agenda the critical questions of race, the politics of race, the resistance to racism...was itself a profound theoretical struggle, a struggle of which *Policing the Crisis* was, curiously, the first and very late example'.[29] *Policing the Crisis*, collectively authored by Hall, Chas Critcher, Tony Jefferson, John Clarke and Brian Roberts, is often regarded as CCCS's most impressive product, a multifaceted analysis of the emergence of a New Right in 1970s Britain.[30] The trajectory it represented was extended in subsequent works such as CCCS's *The Empire Strikes Back* and Paul Gilroy's *There Ain't No Black in the Union Jack*.[31] Of the hard-won emergence of race and ethnicity as objects for cultural analysis (as a result of which cultural studies forefathers such as Hoggart and Williams now seemed not only narrowly androcentric in their concerns, but narrowly anglocentric as well), Hall notes: 'It represented a decisive turn in my own theoretical and intellectual work, as well as in that of the Centre'.[32]

A third defining trait of British cultural studies in its formative period, in addition to its fundamental preoccupations with contemporary

Film Institute, 1986); Janice Winship, *Inside Women's Magazines* (London: Pandora, 1987).

28. See Elizabeth Long, 'Feminism and Cultural Studies', in Storey (ed.), *What Is Cultural Studies?*, pp. 197-207 (198).

29. Hall, 'Cultural Studies and its Theoretical Legacies', p. 283.

30. Stuart Hall *et al.*, *Policing the Crisis: Mugging, the State, and Law and Order* (London: Macmillan, 1979).

31. Centre for Contemporary Cultural Studies, *The Empire Strikes Back: Race and Racism in '70s Britain* (London: Hutchinson, 1982); Paul Gilroy, *There Ain't No Black in the Union Jack: The Cultural Politics of Race and Nation* (London: Hutchinson, 1987).

32. Hall, 'Cultural Studies and its Theoretical Legacies', p. 283. As examples of Hall's numerous essays on race and ethnicity, see 'New Ethnicities' and 'What Is This "Black" in Black Popular Culture', in Morley and Chen (eds.), *Stuart Hall*, pp. 441-49, 465-75.

culture and with ideology, was its anti-disciplinary inclinations. This was bound up with a distrust of academic disciplines, specifically of their tendency to turn inwards, to become esoteric dialogues between experts conducted in the pages of technical journals and scholarly monographs read only by professional scholars or scholars-in-training (a distrust that also crops up in some of the essays in the present volume, notably Alice Bach's). Hall remarks of CCCS, 'there is no doubt in my mind that we were trying to find an institutional practice in cultural studies that might produce an organic intellectual'.[33] The term 'organic intellectual' is drawn from Gramsci (on whom see further Jennifer Glancy's essay in this volume). The organic intellectual 'must work on two fronts', explains Hall.[34] First of all, he or she must be at the cutting edge of intellectual work.

> But the second aspect is just as crucial: that the organic intellectual cannot absolve himself or herself from the responsibility of transmitting those ideas, that knowledge...to those who do not belong, professionally, in the intellectual class. And unless those two fronts are operating at the same time, or at least unless those two ambitions are part of the project of cultural studies, you can get enormous theoretical advance without any engagement at the level of the political project.[35]

Of CCCS in the 1970s Michael Green recalls: 'Inside the Centre, groups attempted to think of their work in relation to the problems of the nearest appropriate constituency, which might not always be that of teachers in higher or secondary education'; instead it might be media workers, alternative publishers and bookshops, or working-class teenage girls.[36]

In the 1980s and 1990s, British cultural studies became increasingly occupied with matters of race and ethnicity,[37] of gender and sexuality, of nationalism and postcolonialism, and also with postmodernism, which became the great challenge for cultural studies in the 1980s just as

33. Hall, 'Cultural Studies and its Theoretical Legacies', p. 281.
34. Hall, 'Cultural Studies and its Theoretical Legacies', p. 268.
35. Hall, 'Cultural Studies and its Theoretical Legacies', p. 268. Cf. Hall, 'Gramsci's Relevance for the Study of Race and Ethnicity', pp. 432-33.
36. Green, 'The Centre for Contemporary Cultural Studies', p. 57. Brunsdon, too, offers a description of this 'outreach' ('A Thief in the Night', p. 281).
37. See Houston A. Baker, Jr, Manthia Diawara and Ruth H. Lindeborg (eds.), *Black British Cultural Studies: A Reader* (Chicago: University of Chicago Press, 1996).

Marxism had been its great challenge in the 1970s.[38] This realignment of interests actually created the conditions for cultural studies' 'internationalization'.[39] Analyses of racism, sexism, nationalism and (post)-colonialism, coupled with debates on and with postmodernism, possessed a cross-cultural appeal and trans-Atlantic transposability (at least for academics) that ethnographic analyses of British working-class culture did not possess, analyses that often seemed arcane, or merely parochial, to non-natives.

In the 1980s cultural studies began to take off, in Britain but in other countries as well, notably the United States. First and foremost, this was a curricular boom, linked, in Britain at least, with the 1980s bust in higher education. The curricular dissemination of cultural studies in Britain resulted from the widespread modularization of degree courses in response to the crisis in higher education; the eclectic combinations of subjects that students now routinely chose were conveniently labelled cultural studies in many institutions. Similarly, in the United States, the dismantling and reassembling of media-based programmes by cost-cutting administrators could be justified in the name of 'cultural studies'.[40]

The 1980s and 1990s saw the establishment of a remarkable number of cultural studies journals. The first was the *Australian Journal of Cultural Studies*, founded in 1983,[41] which, in keeping with the 'internationalization' of cultural studies then underway, was retitled *Cultural Studies* in 1987 (and its headquarters relocated to the United States shortly thereafter). Other cultural studies journals founded in the past 15 years in the United States, Canada, Britain or Australia have included *Cultural Critique, Social Text, Arena, Borderlines, New Formations, News from Nowhere,*

---

38. See, e.g., Morley and Chen (eds.), *Stuart Hall*, Part II, 'Postmodernism and Cultural Studies: First Encounters'; Lawrence Grossberg, *It's a Sin: Essays on Postmodernism, Politics, and Culture* (Sydney: Power Publications, 1988); *idem, We Gotta Get Out of This Place: Popular Conservatism and Postmodern Culture* (London: Routledge, 1992); Angela McRobbie, *Postmodernism and Popular Culture* (London: Routledge, 1994); Davies, *Cultural Studies and Beyond*, pp. 149-55; John Fekete, 'Postmodernism and Cultural Studies: On the Utopianization of Heterotopia', in Martin Kreiswirth and Thomas Carmichael (eds.), *Constructive Criticism: The Human Sciences in the Age of Theory* (Toronto: University of Toronto Press, 1995), pp. 201-19.

39. See During, 'Introduction', p. 15.

40. See Brundson, 'A Thief in the Night', p. 277.

41. Although the first cultural studies journal per se was CCCS's house journal, *Working Papers in Cultural Studies*, founded in 1971, of which ten issues appeared.

Theory, Culture and Society, and *parallax*. Additionally during this period new professional associations for cultural studies were formed, notably the Cultural Studies Association and the Group for Early Modern Cultural Studies, and international conferences were staged.

The first book-length introductions to cultural studies did not appear until 1990, somewhat surprisingly—Patrick Brantlinger's *Crusoe's Footprints* and Graeme Turner's *British Cultural Studies*—although a host of other introductions followed hard on their heels.[42] As the 1990s

42.   Patrick Brantlinger, *Crusoe's Footprints: Cultural Studies in Britain and America* (New York: Routledge, 1990); Graeme Turner, *British Cultural Studies: An Introduction* (Boston: Unwin Hyman, 1990; New York: Routledge, 2nd edn, 1996). Other volumes, too, showcased national (or, in one instance, ethnic) traditions in cultural studies: John Frow and Meaghan Morris, *Australian Cultural Studies: A Reader* (St Leonard's: Allen & Unwin, 1993); Rob Burns (ed.), *German Cultural Studies: An Introduction* (Oxford: Oxford University Press, 1995); Neil Campbell and Alasdair Kean, *American Cultural Studies: An Introduction to American Culture* (New York: Routledge, 1997); Baker, Diawara and Lindeborg (eds.), *Black British Cultural Studies*. Several other readers appeared. One of the earliest was Martin Barker and Anne Beezer (eds.), *Reading into Cultural Studies* (London: Routledge, 1992), largely a series of excerpts from the 'golden age' of British cultural studies (the prototype for this collection was CCCS's own 'reader', Stuart Hall *et al.* [eds.], *Culture, Media, Language: Working Papers in Cultural Studies, 1972–79* [London: Hutchinson, 1980]). This was followed by Simon During (ed.), *The Cultural Studies Reader* (London: Routledge, 1993), which roped into the cultural studies corral thinkers as diverse as Theodor Adorno, Roland Barthes, Teresa de Lauretis, Michel de Certeau, Michel Foucault, Jean François Lyotard, Gayatri Spivak, Cornel West, Eve Kosofsky Sedgwick, and Pierre Bourdieu (although the collection's excessive eclecticism is offset by During's excellent introduction). Also eclectic (comprising 31 selections from Williams to Bourdieu and beyond) was Ann Gray and Jim McGuigan (eds.), *Studying Culture: An Introductory Reader* (London: Arnold, 2nd edn, 1997 [1993]). John Storey published *An Introductory Guide to Cultural Theory and Popular Culture* (Hemel Hempstead: Harvester Wheatsheaf, 1993; London: Prentice Hall, 2nd edn, 1998) and a companion volume, *Cultural Theory and Popular Culture: A Reader* (Hemel Hempstead: Harvester Wheatsheaf, 1994; London: Prentice Hall, 2nd edn, 1998). Especially useful, however, is Storey's other reader, *What Is Cultural Studies?*, 22 essays focused (more or less) on the title question. Also indispensable is the 800-page mega-collection modestly entitled *Cultural Studies* (ed. Lawrence Grossberg, Cary Nelson and Paula Treichler; New York: Routledge, 1992), if only to demonstrate the astonishing range of cultural studies in the 1990s. Notable among the other introductory volumes that appeared were Antony Easthope, *Literary into Cultural Studies* (London: Routledge, 1991); Inglis, *Cultural Studies*; Davies, *Cultural Studies and Beyond*; Morley and Chen (eds.), *Stuart Hall* (a mine of information on the history and present state of cultural studies); and two glossy undergraduate

progressed, more and more publishers began to converge on cultural studies, with Routledge leading the pack. In spring 1995 Routledge even began publishing a promotional 'newspaper', *The Cultural Studies Times*, targeted especially at booksellers. Mimicking the masthead of *The New York Times*, the 'Late Edition' produced in time for the 1995 American Booksellers Association convention in Los Angeles carried a 'weather box': '*Today*, clearing minds. *Tomorrow*, clearing shelves. *Monday*, creating *cultural studies* sections in your bookstore'. Even casual observers could hardly fail to be struck by 'the contradictions of pushing ostensibly radical critique like so much laundry soap'.[43]

Cultural studies' stunning success, especially in the United States, is causing considerable concern, and in two very different camps. On the one hand, traditionalists in literature departments especially are alarmed at the spectacle of faculty and graduate students in apparent flight from the classics of the literary canons to analyse music videos or shopping malls instead. But cries of alarm can also be heard in the cultural studies camp itself, warning that cultural studies' connections with its political and activist roots are being cut, that it is being declawed and domesticated in the process of being institutionalized—even that it is now deceased, having been 'dead on arrival in the United States'.[44]

In 1990, at a high-profile international conference on cultural studies, Stuart Hall expressed the fear that if cultural studies managed to achieve an institutionalization in the United States equivalent to that earlier achieved by deconstruction, 'it would, in rather the same way, formalize out of existence the critical questions of power, history, and politics'.[45] Yet the 'Birmingham experiment' in cultural studies can hardly be repeated in the United States. For one thing, as Alan O'Connor observes, 'the relative absence of a Left intellectual tradition' in the US—not to mention a Left political party of any standing—has significant repercussions for the way in which cultural studies is there

textbooks, Paul du Gay *et al.*, *Doing Cultural Studies: The Story of the Sony Walkman* (London: Sage Publications, 1997), and Stuart Hall (ed.), *Representation: Cultural Representations and Signifying Practices* (London: Sage Publications, 1997).

43. Rick Perlstein, 'Funny Doctor, I Don't *Feel* Antidisciplined: Cultural Studies as Disciplinary Habitus (or, Reading *Cultural Studies*)', *parallax* 1 (1995), pp. 131-42 (141 n. 31).

44. Neil Nehring, untitled letter, *PMLA* 112 (1997), p. 264. Nehring's letter was one of 32 selected and published in this issue of *PMLA* in response to a call for comments on the actual or potential relations between cultural and literary studies.

45. Hall, 'Cultural Studies and its Theoretical Legacies', p. 286.

understood. In the States, cultural studies 'is being sponsored by scholars who rarely have any connection to existing political and cultural movements and are somewhat surprised that this might even be possible'.[46] On a similar note, Ioan Davies complains that cultural studies is almost always perceived as an *academic* phenonenon in the US as opposed to a political or publicly situated one, 'forgetting that many of the debates in Britain took place in the pages of *New Left Review*, *Marxism Today*, and a host of non-academic magazines and journals'.[47] And Cary Nelson has prophesied bitterly that 'of all the intellectual movements that have swept the humanities in America since the 1970s, none will be taken up so shallowly, so opportunistically, so unreflectively, and so ahistorically as cultural studies'.[48]

We find this a bit unfair, however. Why should cultural studies in the US strive to reproduce faithfully the elements of its British roots? (The 'War of Independence' or 'Revolutionary War', depending on how you look at it, might serve as an interesting analogue here.) Like the appropriation of the Bible by different interest groups, with which the present volume is very much concerned, the transmutation of cultural studies is inevitable, and trying to proscribe how it should be done, and according to whose agenda or 'original intentions', is unlikely to make much of a difference. Nonetheless, some may feel that Nelson's allegations are not without substance, and biblical scholars who are beginning to apply the convenient label 'cultural studies' to their own work might do well to consider them seriously. We leave the last word to Hall, however, who, at a high-profile conference at Nelson's home campus in 1990, refused to play the professorial policeman: 'I don't want to talk about British cultural studies…in a patriarchal way, as a keeper of the conscience of cultural studies, hoping to police you back into line with what it really was if only you knew'.[49] Still, it cannot hurt to know.

46. Alan O'Connor, 'The Problem of American Cultural Studies', in Storey (ed.), *What Is Cultural Studies?*, pp. 187-96 (190). See also Joel Pfister, 'The Americanization of Cultural Studies', pp. 287-99 in the same volume. A section of Pfister's essay is titled 'Americanization: Towards a Post-Political Cultural Studies'.

47. Davies, *Cultural Studies and Beyond*, p. 158.

48. Cary Nelson, 'Always Already Cultural Studies: Academic Conferences and a Manifesto', in Storey (ed.), *What Is Cultural Studies?*, pp. 273-86 (274).

49. Hall, 'Cultural Studies and its Theoretical Legacies', p. 277. Entitled 'Cultural Studies Now and in the Future', the conference was held at the University of Illinois at Urbana–Champaign and its proceedings were published as Grossberg, Nelson and Treichler (eds.), *Cultural Studies*.

Cultural Studies as Biblical Studies

No one doubts the immensity of the Bible's influence on the Western tradition, yet the ways it continues to affect contemporary culture are only beginning to be explored. One place where discussion of the issues can be found these days is at the annual meetings of the Society of Biblical Literature, which have provided an important and congenial forum for testing new approaches and presenting experimental studies that draw on cultural criticism. There is a programme unit of the SBL devoted specifically to 'The Bible and Cultural Studies', and other programme units, such as 'The Bible in Ancient and Modern Media', 'Semiotics and Exegesis' and 'Reading, Theory and the Bible' welcome papers taking a cultural studies slant. The 1998 annual meeting in Orlando, Florida, may well prove to be a biblical–cultural phenomenon in itself, offering an irresistible opportunity for looking at such bizarre cultural developments as the 'Disneyfication' of the Bible.[50] If, indeed, papers presented at the SBL represent the latest trends, developing methodologies, and cutting-edge work-in-progress in biblical studies, then the future promises to see an ever greater attention to cultural constructions of the Bible, ancient and modern.

There is now a biblical journal devoted to cultural criticism, *Biblicon*, founded in 1997, edited by Alice Bach, and published (not insignificantly we think) by Sheffield Academic Press. Scholarly articles that either self-consciously identify themselves as cultural studies or that draw on cultural studies models can be found in the pages of *Biblical Interpretation* and *Semeia*, and both these journals have published thematic issues that would fall under the rubric of cultural studies.[51] Other works in the broad area of cultural studies and the Bible that come to mind include Mieke Bal's important contributions to biblical studies,[52] Alice Bach's

50. Several of the programme units both in the SBL and in the American Academy of Religion (which meets jointly with the SBL) have invited 'Disney' offerings in their official 'Call for Papers'.

51. See Alice Bach (ed.), *The Bible and Popular Culture* (*Biblical Interpretation*, 2.1; Leiden: E.J. Brill, 1994); J. Cheryl Exum (ed.), *The Bible and the Arts* (*Biblical Interpretation*, 6.3 and 4; Leiden: E.J. Brill, forthcoming); Alice Bach (ed.), *Biblical Glamour and Hollywood Glitz* (Semeia, 74; Atlanta: Scholars Press, 1996); Stephen D. Moore (ed.), *In Search of the Present: The Bible through Cultural Studies* (Semeia; Atlanta: Scholars Press, forthcoming).

52. Especially relevant in connection with cultural studies are her *Lethal Love:*

recent book in which she traces the cultural history of Salomé,[53] Fernando Segovia's self-conscious intercultural readings,[54] Itumeleng Mosala's CCCS-inspired study in black South African hermeneutics,[55] diverse cross-cultural experiments by George Aichele, Roland Boer and Tina Pippin,[56] and we would also include our own work here.[57] The present volume is intended as a contribution to this developing area of inquiry, and the range of topics it includes reflects the fluidity, breadth and interdisciplinarity of cultural approaches to the Bible. It is concerned with the Bible as culture and the Bible in culture, ancient and modern. While some of the contributions, such as Robert Carroll's and Hugh Pyper's, foreground the role of the Bible in modern Western culture, others, like Philip Esler's and David Clines's, are concerned with the ancient cultural context of the Bible and the ways we investigate, or construct, that context, and interact with it, from our distinct and distant cultural location. It is characteristic of the approach

Feminist Literary Readings of Biblical Love Stories (Bloomington: Indiana University Press, 1987), and '*Myth à la lettre*: Freud, Mann, Genesis and Rembrandt, and the Story of the Son', in Shlomith Rimmon-Kenan (ed.), *Discourse in Psychoanalysis and Literature* (New York: Methuen, 1987), pp. 57-89. Bal's *Reading 'Rembrandt': Beyond the Word–Image Opposition* (Cambridge: Cambridge University Press, 1991) is also important for cultural readings of Rembrandt's biblically inspired works.

53.   Alice Bach, *Women, Seduction, and Betrayal in Biblical Narrative* (Cambridge: Cambridge University Press, 1997).

54.   See, e.g., his several contributions to Fernando F. Segovia and Mary Ann Tolbert (eds.), *Reading from This Place*. I. *Social Location and Biblical Interpretation in the United States*; II. *Social Location and Biblical Interpretation in Global Perspective* (Minneapolis: Fortress Press, 1994–95). Segovia was one of the first biblical scholars to apply the term 'cultural studies' to his work.

55.   Itumeleng J. Mosala, 'Race, Class, and Gender as Hermeneutical Factors in the African Independent Churches' Appropriation of the Bible', *Semeia* 73 (1996), pp. 43-57. As far as we know, Mosala was the first biblical scholar to draw on the work of the Birmingham school. He is followed by Ralph Broadbent in 'Ideology, Culture, and British New Testament Studies: The Challenge of Cultural Criticism' (forthcoming in *Semeia*).

56.   See, e.g., George Aichele and Tina Pippin (eds.), *The Monstrous and the Unspeakable: The Bible as Fantastic Literature* (Playing the Texts, 1; Sheffield: Sheffield Academic Press, 1997); Roland Boer, *Novel Histories: The Fiction of Biblical Criticism* (Playing the Texts, 2; Sheffield: Sheffield Academic Press, 1997).

57.   J. Cheryl Exum, *Plotted, Shot, and Painted: Cultural Representations of Biblical Women* (JSOTSup, 215; Gender, Culture, Theory, 3; Sheffield: Sheffield Academic Press, 1996); Stephen D. Moore, *God's Gym: Divine Male Bodies of the Bible* (New York: Routledge, 1996).

to cultural studies reflected in this volume that no fixed boundary is observed between ancient and modern culture; indeed, the transgression of such boundaries is the aim of many of the contributors.

The title of this volume, *Biblical Studies/Cultural Studies*, rather than, say, 'Biblical Studies and Cultural Studies' or 'Cultural Studies and Biblical Studies', is another attempt to blur boundaries, as well as a refusal to legislate the particular nature of the relationship between these areas of inquiry or to prioritize one over the other. (The title layout on the jacket of this book is designed to represent this refusal in a way that standard typeface does not allow.) Biblical Studies/Cultural Studies is not just the Bible influencing culture or culture reappropriating the Bible, but a process of unceasing mutual redefinition in which cultural appropriations constantly reinvent the Bible, which in turn constantly impels new appropriations, and biblical scholars find themselves, in their professional capacity, haunting video stores, museums, and other sites of cultural production.

A number of shared assumptions and common interests characterize these essays. They are interdisciplinary, reflecting their authors' suspicion of the way the codes or discourse of a discipline function to limit and define the kinds of interpretative questions that it may 'legitimately' consider. A topic repeatedly addressed at the Colloquium and running through these essays is the appropriation of the Bible by various groups to serve ideological purposes—an appropriation that derives its efficacy from the authority ascribed to this book by so many social and religious constituencies. Many of the contributors share a suspicion of this authority and the hegemonic ideologies it undergirds. But they are also keenly aware of the ideological character of their own interpretations, and that there is no neutral place from which interpretation may occur, that social locations are always interpreted, not given. As we noted earlier, this preoccupation with ideology, which the contributors to this collection share with an ever-increasing number of biblical scholars, marks the most readily apparent point of convergence with the British tradition of cultural studies, epitomized by the work of the Birmingham Centre.

A common denominator among the contributors is the recognition of the Bible's status as cultural icon. This special status is addressed directly in the essays by Robert Carroll and Hugh Pyper. Carroll deals with the Bible as a commodity in the consumer-oriented capitalist society of the West (mainly the US and the UK), taking us on a Dantesque tour through a dizzying variety of Bibles and the subsidiary market of Bible paraphernalia available to the consumer who will perforce want to own a Bible though not necessarily to read it. If the Bible is subject to the law of supply and demand, then translation, mass production and certain profit ensure a steady supply, while the cultural status of the object in question, coupled with the packaging targeted to specific consumer groups, create the necessary desire and demand. 'Productions of the Bible', observes Carroll with a nod to Hugh Pyper's thesis, 'are one of capitalism's many ways of advancing capitalist objects and values'.

The spread of the Bible throughout the world is intimately linked with the spread of Western culture, a culture the Bible has helped considerably to shape and support (notwithstanding its non-Western origins). This theme echoes throughout the volume. Pyper puts it provocatively—'Western culture is the Bible's way of making more Bibles'—and draws an analogy between biological evolution and the development of culture in order to sketch out a novel account of the Bible's influence, pervasiveness and resilience. He posits a kind of DNA-model of the Bible as an 'active replicator' that works on its environment—human communities—to increase its chances of being copied and disseminated. This amounts to the 'survival of the fittest (of texts)', and one reason the Bible has survived so well, Pyper surmises, is because it successfully transmits to its readers the message that their survival and that of their community depend upon *its* survival. The Bible is adaptable—astonishingly so—and the fact that its contents are so diverse that almost anyone can find something to their liking within them has certainly contributed to its survival. While a number of other contributors are uneasy about the (mis)uses this adaptability encourages, Pyper proposes that this diversity can function for us as a 'cultural memetic reserve'—a potential resource of cultural variety and richness.

The symbiotic relationship of the Bible and Western culture and the fact that wildly disparate meanings are constantly being attached to biblical texts as they enter and re-enter the culture is another concern of the cultural studies project represented in this volume. As an example of the Bible's malleability, Pyper notes in passing its capacity to sustain both sides of the apartheid debate in South Africa. Jennifer Glancy, in her article on the appropriation of biblical texts about slavery in American politics, draws attention to the dangers inherent in such adaptability. Her point of departure is a recent speech by a southern legislator defending slavery, reported in *The New York Times*, which she uses to illustrate the way the cultural authority of the Bible is invoked to manipulate public opinion. Criticizing the Bible and its moral and cultural authority is tantamount to political suicide in the current American political climate, she notes (significantly, *The New York Times* found the speech morally reprehensible, but did not question the authoritative status of the Bible). There are serious ethical implications for the guild of biblical scholars. For example, a current trend in biblical studies affirms the 'legitimacy' of the interpretations of 'ordinary readers' from different social locations and seeks to encourage and promote such readings. What would happen, Glancy asks, if such a stance were taken in the case of a 'real reader' like the racist Senator Davidson? An uncritical biblical pluralism that defers to popular readings without taking account of the social and political effects of those readings, she cautions, is likely to repeat and reinscribe the liabilities of the readings. Glancy thus advocates a more pragmatic approach, one that focuses on the consequences of adopting a particular interpretation and also questions the consequences of relying on biblical authority in political discourse. Glancy's essay also highlights the difficulty of effectively challenging an ideological apparatus like the Bible in the first place, as do other essays in this volume.

Alice Bach is another reader who is critical of the privileging of the Bible in Western culture and, in particular, of what has traditionally been promulgated as *the canon*. She asks us to ponder the curious process by which the god of ancient Israel became the God of European civilization. Using the debate within classical studies over Martin Bernal's *Black Athena* as as a resource, she criticizes the ideological hegemony of Euro-American academic discourse that has led, among other things, to the privileging of the biblical god over all others. It is, moreover, testimony to the disciplinary compartmentalizing of knowledge, which constitutes part of the problem, that the Bernal-versus-the-classicists debate has had virtually no impact on the field of biblical studies, only a stone's throw across the Mediterranean. All too often scholars read only through the codes or conventions of their specialized disciplines, and whereas codes make interpretation possible, they also control and delimit it. When readers encounter the biblical god, Bach observes, they resort to the theological code to explain his behaviour, and frequently end up being his uncritical, pious defenders. When they read about Greek or ancient Near Eastern gods, in contrast, they employ a literary code that allows them to dismiss not only their behaviour but the gods

themselves as mere mythical creations. As a counter-strategy, Bach proposes an intercultural comparison of the god Dionysus in Euripides'
Bacchae with the biblical god in the book of Judges that takes seriously as
its point of departure Dionysus's status as a god.

Bach's caveats about reading the Bible through the theological code
and Greek myths through the literary code finds an interesting counter-
point in Yael Feldman's criticism of the scholarly, but also popular, habit
of reading the Bible through the lens of Freudian psychology and its
Greek foundations. In particular, an interpretation of the Aqedah, the
story of the binding of Isaac in Genesis 22, in terms of the Oedipal
conflict imposes upon the biblical text psychological dynamics that are
culturally alien to it. In the Bible, where sibling rivalry plays a much
larger role than generational conflict, fathers and sons do not fit the
Freudian masterplot. In spite of fundamental differences, however, the
Aqedah, as a central text in contemporary Israeli culture, has become
the equivalent of the Oedipal scene in Freudian psychology, and Feldman examines the complex psychological dynamics that have contributed to its power as a cultural paradigm: the ability of the story to
accommodate interpretations ranging from passive victimhood to stoic
heroism, ideological martyrdom, and even fanatic aggression.

The Bible is cultural property. While Feldman looks at transmutations
of the Aqedah, Francis Landy, in his contribution to this collection,
tackles transmutations of the flood story. Beginning with the biblical
version, with its two intertwined narrative strands that stand in tension
yet are indispensable to each other, Landy examines the flood as a
source of anxiety in the Bible. He then moves on to trace echoes and
appropriations of its themes of dissolution and concord (symbolized in
the ark) in midrashic interpretations, mystery plays, novels, children's
Bibles (considered also by Robert Carroll in his survey of Bibles aimed
at specific consumer groups), and even children's toy arks (which calls to
mind as well the religious paraphernalia of which Carroll is so critical),
coming to rest on Hilary Mantel's 1989 novel, *Fludd*.

Erich Zenger, in his study of David as musician and poet, is also concerned with cultural transmutations; in this case, with the history of the
reception of the motif of David as musician and poet. After a survey of
how the motif finds expression in the Bible and the non-biblical literature of early Judaism, Zenger turns his attention to the reception of the
motif in selected examples from the visual arts: the murals in the synagogue of Dura-Europos, the sequence of reliefs on the door of the

basilica of San Ambrogio in Milan, the *Psalterium aureum* of St Gallen, the Bamberg Psalm commentary of Peter Lombard, and, lastly, portrayals of David by Rembrandt and his school. His analysis demonstrates dramatically what cultural studies emphasizes about appropriations of the Bible: they take on a cultural and political significance of their own independent of the biblical context. The paintings, he stresses, are not *supposed* to be interpretations of specific biblical texts; rather they function to create a particular religious, cultural, anthropological or political horizon for their viewers.

Culture in this volume, as we noted above, refers to both ancient and modern culture. While some of the contributors focus more on one than the other, all are keenly aware of the kinds of interaction that take place between the contemporary interpreter and the biblical text as the product of a culture quite alien to our own modern or postmodern one, in spite of the manifold ways it has been Westernized. Philip Esler stresses the importance of giving the biblical culture its due by asking how the portrayal of Saul's madness in 1 Samuel might have been understood by its original ancient audience. In considering a typical scholarly view that Saul's suffering is best understood theologically, Esler exposes the limitations imposed by the disciplinary codes that Bach warns us about in her essay. Esler's reading of the narrative through the anthropological code demonstrates its obvious advantages over the theological code. His reading of Saul's madness in a cultural perspective involves three stages: analysis of the narrative within the framework of ancient Mediterranean culture, with its orientation of social relations around the group rather than the individual, its notions of honour and shame, and of 'limited good'; consideration of Saul's condition in relation to both emic and etic frameworks of health, illness and disease (drawing on insights from cross-cultural health care); and a reading of two paintings of David playing the lyre for Saul from the Rembrandt school (paintings also discussed by Zenger) as an intercultural exercise that seeks to bring insights gained about the ancient culture into a creative tension with the interpreter's own cultural context.

Margaret Davies, in her essay on cultural stereotyping in New Testament times and ours, has a similar concern for ancient literary conventions and the way ancient audiences would have understood them. Focusing on the depiction of the Pharisees in the Gospel of Matthew, she highlights three features that distinguish biblical characterization from that familiar to modern readers: simple rather than complex characterization, group rather than individual characterization, and the attribution of distinctive cultural traits to a particular group. The Pharisees are depicted in Matthew as the inverse of Jesus; they provide the negative stereotype that clarifies the positive and sets it in sharp relief. Against the background of Matthew's culture-bound stereotypes, Davies asks us to examine our own and their potential political and ethical ramifications.

Another contributor who focuses primarily on the ancient context is David Clines, who examines the cultural construction of masculinity as represented in the figure of Jesus in the Gospels. In theorizing about biblical characters—be it Saul, the Pharisees or Jesus—neither Esler nor Davies nor Clines is interested in the historical figures that assumedly underlie these characterizations. But whereas Esler defines his task as historical in the sense of interpreting the textual evidence in the light of our reconstructions of the ancient cultural context, Davies and Clines pursue a decidedly literary approach. Unlike Davies, who tacitly acknowledges the singularity of the Matthaean picture of the Pharisees, Clines is interested in the composite picture of Jesus, for it is the composite picture that has become a cultural property, and few outside the biblical field would bother to distinguish between the Jesus of Matthew or Mark or Luke or John. Is it Clines's own identity as an Old Testament scholar that emboldens him to violate this most sacred taboo of New Testament scholarship, the sharp separation of the four canonical portraits of Jesus? Jesus is portrayed in traditional male categories, Clines concludes, and he proceeds to evaluate these categories against modern constructions of masculinity in order to highlight significant differences. To speak simply and unreflectively of Jesus as human, as is customary in traditional theological discourse, he cautions, is to ignore his limitations as a traditional man.

The importance of the cultural location of the interpreter stressed in so many of the essays presented here is forcefully illustrated in Barry Matlock's contribution on Paul. Not unexpectedly for students of culture, but not evident to all of its practitioners, the 'new perspective' discussion in Pauline studies is as embedded in its own cultural trappings as the old perspective it seeks to overturn. For example, the 'new perspective' Paul, like so many moderns, is less concerned with sin, guilt and forgiveness than with community, and reconstructions of Paul's relation to his Jewish tradition are subtly—or not so subtly—shaped by a contemporary renewed interest in Jewish–Christian dialogue. The Paul of the 'new perspective' is the construction of contemporary Protestant interpretation, and thus the vexed question of Paul's continuity and discontinuity with his nomocentric Jewish tradition plays a central role in the debate, with Judaism now being evaluated positively whereas earlier it was assessed negatively. The position of Judaism in the equation may have shifted from one side to the other, notes Matlock, but the same set of values are still brought to bear in the calculation. Into this equation Matlock introduces a potentially destabilizing variable, Daniel Boyarin's cultural reading of Paul in *A Radical Jew*.

A number of the essays in this volume deal with the appropriation of the Bible in the visual arts. We have already mentioned Zenger's study of the motif of David as musician and poet in artistic representations through the ages, and Esler's intercultural engagement with two paintings from the Rembrandt school. David Jasper, in a discussion of the artist J.M.W. Turner as an interpreter of the Bible, draws attention to the habitual refusal of art to understand itself as derivative. Biblically inspired art can claim a cultural life of its own, an independence that enables it to take the role of an equal partner in a critical dialogue with the Bible. Turner's utter lack of concern with biblical accuracy—even when bestowing very precise titles on biblical paintings—is an illuminating example of the way cultural appropriation works in general and in the realm of the arts in particular. In Turner's art, Jasper finds a radical refiguring of Scripture based not on history or even on narrative but rather on colour and light, a 'reading' of Scripture with fascinating epistemological implications, which Jasper proceeds to unpack. What Zenger observes of the artistic representations of David is, if anything, still more true of Turner: his works are not supposed to be 'interpretations' of biblical texts, at least not in any conventional sense.

The two-way dialogue between the Bible and artistic representations of it that Jasper speaks about is precisely the focus of Fiona Black and Cheryl Exum, and also of Athalya Brenner and Jan Willem van Henten in their respective essays in this volume. Using the specific example of a stained-glass window representing the Song of Songs by the pre-Raphelite artist Edward Burne-Jones, Black and Exum ask not simply how the Bible has influenced art but also how art can influence biblical interpretation. They note the way that key issues in the interpretation of the source text—questions about its unity and plot—reappear when one starts to interpret the window, and they apply to the biblical text some of the insights gained from answering these questions in relation to the window. Among other things, Burne-Jones's foregrounding of the only disturbing aspects of the Song (in particular, the scene in which the woman is beaten by the watchmen) leads them to reconsider features of the biblical text that scholars typically gloss over, and to ask what would happen if these aspects were given a greater role in the interpretation of the biblical text.

The visual arts serve as only one of the sources used by Brenner and van Henten in their essay, which emerged out of a course they jointly offered on the story of Potiphar's wife in Genesis 39. They describe how they focused on gaps, ambiguities and repetitions in the story, and on the ways these are dealt with in a range of Jewish, Christian, Islamic and non-religious sources from different times and cultural locations and reflecting different ideologies. They trace out the implications of various readings—central among them, a reading of the narrative as a story of gender relations—noting the way certain elements reappear in criss-cross fashion across the spectrum of sources, both visual and literary (the literary texts ranged from early postbiblical sources to Thomas Mann's novel, and also included scholarly commentary). Not only do Brenner and van Henten provide a helpful resource for the venturesome teacher who might want to try something similar in the classroom, they also sketch out how such a course might be conducted.

The other essay that deals directly with pedagogy is that of Regina Schwartz, who reflects on the challenge of teaching the Bible, a body of literature that, on the one hand, enjoys such cultural currency, and, on the other, is considered to be something more than literature—something sacred, indeed—by many of its readers. Her essay resonates with others in this book, with Alice Bach's reflections on the elevation of the biblical god to the position of 'real' god and on the status of canons, and with other contributors' emphasis on Western culture as responsible for the hegemony of biblical 'truths'. Schwartz's discussion of fruitful juxtapositions of texts and traditions and of the kinds of questions about meaning, interpretation, and, yes, truth that lead to a genuine learning experience for student and teacher alike directs our attention to that one sphere where most of us with a professional stake in teaching and writing about the Bible have the best chance of influencing the culture at large—the classroom.

Music, which throughout the ages has been an important means of keeping the Bible alive in culture, is represented in only one essay in this volume, John Rogerson's study of the use of the Song of Songs in

Bach's Church Cantatas. Rogerson's examination of the way the Song figures in the work of one composer, and the cultural context in which it was performed, provides a complement to Black and Exum's discussion of the Song in the work of one particular artist. What music is uniquely able to represent is the mutuality some commentators find in the Song, for in music it is possible to have two voices simultaneously singing different words set to different melodic lines, and, as Rogerson shows, Bach exploits this potential beautifully. And, like the Bible, Bach's works have been able to survive transplantation into a world in which culture has become increasingly commercialized and the secular has largely displaced the sacred.

Curiously enough, given the important role it plays in cultural studies of the Bible, film, too, is central to only one of the essays in this collection, in Philip Davies's review of a movie you either love or hate, *Life of Brian*. One strongly suspects that Davies himself loves it; certainly he finds it a much more informed and incisive biblical film than much of the bland fare Hollywood has cooked up for the mass audience, and he offers illustrations of its sophistication that might well surprise Monty Python 'himself'. Brian's singular characteristic is that he is not Jesus. Or is he? Davies suggests that Monty Python has parodied Christian theology's concept of the dual nature of Jesus by using the Jesus character to represent the divine and Brian, the human. This device, he notes, no doubt contributed to the success of the film by allowing it to escape charges of blasphemy. And while the film may seem like an iconoclastic romp, it nevertheless manages to affirm its own set of values, which are resolutely different from those of conventional Christian piety.

Pious images of Jesus, and their subversion, are also of concern to Stephen Moore in his essay. Moore is intrigued by the fact that whereas fewer and fewer people know what Jesus is supposed to have said, most remain reasonably confident that they at least know what he looked like. But does Jesus' physical appearance play any role in the current quest for the historical person? To discover the answer, Moore proceeds to read a number of scholarly Jesus books by their covers, all of which feature surprisingly specific images of the elusive Nazarene, images that almost invariably depict him as exceptionally handsome. To what extent do popular representations of Jesus as physically well-favoured buttress the oppressive age-old equation of beauty with virtue? asks Moore. Might not the socially subversive Jesus sketched out by leading contemporary Jesus scholars be in need of an ill-favoured face and form?

Something about the Identikit sketch of 'Bible John', discussed in William Scott's essay on the media coverage of a series of murders in Scotland in 1969, looks suspiciously like the kind of book-jacket Jesus that caught Moore's attention. Was the shadowy suspect's similarity to Jesus suggested purely by his propensity to quote the Bible? If so, the sketch is an excellent example of the power of suggestion that Scott is concerned with in his analysis of cultural relativism. Like other contributors to this volume, Scott stresses the importance of context, of social location, for the production of meaning. His case study, like Glancy's, is one drawn from the media. Analysing the factors that made a murder suspect popularly dubbed 'Bible John' into a media figure in the late 1960s, Scott shows how changing cultural conditions made it impossible for a 1990s audience, when the case was resurrected, to have the same reactions as viewers only a generation earlier. Not only would the earlier, moralizing manner of reporting be quite unacceptable now, but the media could no longer take for granted its audience's familiarity with the Bible and a commonly shared cultural attitude towards it.

In some respects, Scott's study, centred as it is on the mass media (not entirely unexpectedly, since the author teaches in a Language and Media Department), is closest of any of the essays in this collection to the 'classic' cultural studies tradition, which, as we saw earlier, was much preoccupied with the media as mediators of ideology. Few of the essays in the volume borrow directly from nonbiblical cultural studies (Glancy's being the main exception; her debt to the cultural studies 'tradition' is actually more explicit than Scott's). For although there is a 'received history' of cultural studies—witness our recital of it earlier in this introduction—biblical cultural studies seems to have sprung up entirely independently of this history, especially of its first two phases, the early period associated with Hoggart and Williams and the middle period associated with CCCS. (The third phase in this potted history, it will be recalled, is the period of international and transdisciplinary dissemination.) Biblical cultural studies seems to have emerged instead out of that subspecialization of religious studies known (especially in the US) as 'arts, literature, and religion', specifically, the analysis of how biblical scenes, themes and stories have been represented in the traditional arts (especially painting) and modern media (especially cinema). With the recent dissemination of the term 'cultural studies' in the humanities, it is not surprising that this handy label should come to be applied to a disparate body of work in biblical studies that is otherwise difficult to categorize. But it is also probable that, as biblical cultural studies advances, more and more of its practitioners will turn to the history and practice of nonbiblical cultural studies as a source of challenge and an impetus for innovation. We eagerly wait to see what this yet to be written chapter of biblical cultural studies will bring.

Lower Case Bibles:
Commodity Culture and the Bible

Robert P. Carroll

Capitalism is a parasite of Christianity. Capitalism is a religion of pure cult with dogma. Capitalism has developed as a parasite of Christianity in the West... until it reached the point where Christianity's history is essentially that of its parasite—that is to say, of capitalism... The Christianity of the Reformation did not favor the growth of capitalism; instead it transformed itself into capitalism.

Walter Benjamin[1]

God's too little acre: People on Holy Island have objected to a bid to open a new Bible shop on the grounds that 'saturation point' has already been reached.[2]

The dialectical critic of culture must both participate in culture and not participate.

Theodor W. Adorno[3]

Let's start with culture: 'Culture is a set of common understandings, manifest in act and artifact. It is in two places at once: inside somebody's head as understandings and in the external environment as act and artifact.'[4] It matters little whether we think of culture as being an upper case phenomenon—Culture—or as a lower case matter.[5] As a cultural

---

1. Walter Benjamin, 'Capitalism as Religion', in Marcus Bullock and Michael W. Jennings (eds.), *Walter Benjamin: Selected Writings*. I. *1913–1926* (Cambridge, MA: The Belknap Press of Harvard University Press, 1996), pp. 289-90.

2. Item on p. 1 of *The Guardian* 'Society' section for 16 July 1997.

3. Theodor W. Adorno, 'Culture Criticism and Society', in Adorno, *Prisms* (trans. S. and S. Weber; London: Neville Spearman, 1967), pp. 15-34 (33).

4. Paul Bohannan, *How Culture Works* (New York: The Free Press, 1995), p. 47.

5. For arguments against making any distinction between upper case Culture and lower case culture, see the work of Pierre Bourdieu, especially the section on 'The Field of Cultural Production', in P. Bourdieu, *The Field of Cultural Production: Essays on Art and Literature* (ed. Randal Johnson; Oxford: Polity Press, 1993), pp. 27-141. In more general terms see Clifford Geertz, *The Interpretation of Cultures: Selected*

object the Bible reflects the ancient cultures from which it was produced, yet as a much translated entity it also represents a transcultural object at home in many different cultures. As such, the Bible is an ideal subject for commenting on in any discussion of culture, and its study and production may be freely consigned to the category of Cultural Studies. It is, however, far too big and complex a topic for the average biblical scholar to be able to cover all the aspects of treating the Bible as part of the cultural productions of human societies. How and where to begin? There are simply far too many bibles in production for me to give anything approximating to a competent survey of the Bible in culture. Difference and variety dominate the production of bibles. Nor can I possibly begin at the beginning because in the beginning there was no Bible as such—to rephrase the ancient Christian theologians, there was a time when the Bible was not. So regarding the basic questions of *when*, *where* and *how* does the Bible begin to be treated in culture *as a bible*, the wise cultural commentator will have to admit to a fair amount of ignorance. Nor would I wish to start with the productions of parts of the Bible such as the Book of Kells, the Book of Durrow or the Lindisfarne Gospels either, because I am not competent to deal with such mediaeval illuminated manuscripts. So, given the framing discourses of Cultural Studies, I shall just have to focus my attention on the subject of the Bible as a *material–cultural object* in the capitalist period of Western civilization, especially in relation to the commodity culture of the consumerist society in which we in the West all live now.[6]

I shall begin then with an observation on the production of bibles in the years following the Gutenberg revolution which gave rise to the era of print capitalism.[7] This was the age of the 'discovery' by the Old World

Essays (New York: Basic Books, 1973); Homi K. Bhabha, *The Location of Culture* (London: Routledge, 1994); Bohannan, *How Culture Works*; E. Doyle McCarthy, *Knowledge as Culture: The New Sociology of Knowledge* (London: Routledge, 1996); and Paul du Gay (ed.), *Production of Culture/Cultures of Production* (London: Sage Publications and the Open University, 1997).

6.   On the historical background to the period when the Bible began to emerge as a vernacularized cultural object in human history, see Norman Davies, *Europe: A History* (Oxford: Oxford University Press, 1996), pp. 469-507; John M. Roberts, *A History of Europe* (Oxford: Helicon Publishing, 1996), pp. 220-33.

7.   On the complex subject of print capitalism, see Lucien Febvre and Henri-Jean Martin, *The Coming of the Book: The Impact of Printing 1450–1800* (ET; London: New Left Books, 1976); see also Elizabeth L. Eisenstein, *The Printing Revolution in*

of the so-called New World,[8] the age of travel and voyages of discovery
by European navigators traversing the (un)known world, the period
when the mediaeval Church fragmented in the schismatic conflicts of
the Reformation and the Counter-Reformation period and when widespread literacy began to be developed among people other than the
clerics and the ruling classes. As it would take a whole book to do an
adequate introduction to a cultural–materialist account of the history of
the Bible in English (not to go any further among the vernaculars of
Europe), I shall start with a quotation from Lisa Jardine that reflects on
the phenomenon of the production of what Jardine calls 'extravagant
Bibles':

> When Borso d'Este travelled to Rome in 1471 to be invested with his
> dukedom by the Pope, he included in his luggage his two-volume, lav-
> ishly decorated Bible (total weight, 34 pounds), to be displayed alongside
> the tapestries and furnishings which also went with him on the trip.
> Burso's Bible had cost him the enormous sum of 2200 florins and
> included more than a thousand miniatures by Taddeo Civelli and Franco
> di Rossi. To enhance its beauty further Borso had it specially rebound for
> his triumphal visit to the Vatican. A sumptuous Bible was the centrepiece
> for any respectably magnificent collection and patrons borrowed each
> other's copies on short-term loan to give their own miniaturists inspira-
> tion (Borso d'Este borrowed one which had belonged to the first Mar-
> quis of Ferrara, Nicolo III).[9]

The average person would not have been able to afford such luxury
goods as bibles—ordinary people have never been able to afford the
luscious, extravagant bibles that have almost always existed for the rich,
the powerful and, of course, the religiose. Indeed, when the King James
Bible was first published in 1611 it cost about the same as a farm labour-
er's annual wages, so peasants simply could not buy bibles—even had

---

Early Modern Europe (Cambridge: Cambridge University Press, 1983), esp. pp. 159-
86, 271-78.

8.   I enter the world of politically correct discourses here and freely acknowledge that as a European academic writer I necessarily take a Eurocentric perspective—I cannot imagine or afford *the view from nowhere* (to use Thomas Nagel's
phrase)—when writing about the trips Columbus made to 'India'. But I make absolutely no apologies for recognizing my own ethnic specificity (white, male, Irish-
European) nor do I for a moment imagine that the Europeans 'discovered' an empty
America. They did however discover *for themselves* a world they had never imagined
existed before that fatal landfall.

9.   Lisa Jardine, *Worldly Goods* (London: Macmillan, 1996), p. 205.

they been able to read or had wished to own such an obscure object of desire. Yet the wonders of capitalist development, especially in the early stages of print capitalism, were such that when the Geneva Bible was produced in 1560 it appeared in an edition small enough for it to be carried in the pocket of those who could afford it. Today if I enter a bible shop or some such religious book repository, I can still find examples of massive, expensive, ornate bibles such as *The Holy Bible with Illustrations from the Vatican Library*.[10] This is a luxurious, and splendidly illustrated, but rather large, production of the bible as a Family Bible. Its price tag of £95 ($150) is far beyond what the average book buyer or even religious person is usually prepared to pay for a book or even for a bible. So from Borso d'Este of Ferrara's wonderful bible to the great ornate Vatican Family Bible of today, the Bible has been an object of ostentatious display, indicating the wealth and status of its individual owners. It has also been an object very much constructed in relation to and reflecting the cultural values of capitalist practices. Indeed, one might go so far as to say that capitalism is the Bible's way of making more bibles or, for postmodernists, productions of the Bible are one of capitalism's many ways of advancing capitalist objects and values. In short, the Bible is one means of reproducing capitalist culture.[11]

The Bible in Western Culture

It would take a book-length treatment to provide an adequate cultural–materialist account of the Bible by way of cultural background to this study. While I only want to focus on the Bible as a consumer good in contemporary commodity culture, it should be recognized that the current commodification of the Bible is the result of centuries of preoccupation with the Bible when the Book was a formative influence in the construction of Western culture (a predominantly White-Anglo-Saxon-Protestant culture wherever English was spoken, but not exclusively so). Even today when so many people are happy to talk about postmodern society, we still live ostensibly in a culture where there are (strong) resonances and traces of a past shaped by the Bible. In courts of law people still swear on a bible. It may be a non-postmodern irony that the very book which contains the prohibition against all such swearing should be the object upon which such swearing is done, but, whatever

10. London: HarperCollins, 1996.
11. See Hugh Pyper's paper in the present volume.

its iconic status, cultural uses of the Bible are not themselves irony-proof. Some people still talk about 'swearing on a stack of bibles', but most quasi-literate folk today would be hard put to distinguish the Bible from Shakespeare—insofar as random quotations from either work were proposed for source identification. The term 'bible' is also used to refer to any *vade mecum*. Some of the more serious broadsheet newspapers still print a biblical verse every day, reflecting the piety of a bygone age. Wayside posters bearing biblical verses can still be seen outside funda-mentalistic churches. At major sporting events, especially American football and World Cup soccer matches, large banners proclaiming the reference John 3.16 can be spotted around the sports ground.[12] Open a drawer in a hotel room and a Gideon Bible is likely to be detected. The walls of religious goods shops are often covered with pictures of small or charming furry animals with biblical texts extruding from their rear ends. It is said that Orange Order Marches (the occasions of much vio-lence in Northern Ireland) used to form up behind a person carrying an open Bible on a cushion and march off down the street in defence of the Protestant Faith typified by that open Bible. Among controversialists of a Protestant fundamentalist streak, the Bible was (perhaps still is) a favourite object for hurling at other Protestants considered by the Bible-chucking devotees to be heretics, or at ecumenically minded clerics, or even at visiting priests who had strayed from their own sacred enclaves into Protestant churches. Manifold are the cultural uses of a bible—a thousand-and-one uses of a bible—but it would take yet another book to delineate them all and to produce a serious account of their cultural contextualization.

There are, of course, much subtler and more dynamic ways of analy-sing the Bible as an object in the cultural formation of the West, but to attempt to describe them would be to take this study very far from its much more modest aim of focusing on the Bible as a commodity in a consumer culture. In the many representations of cultural piety in the past, the Bible occupies a mythic place. I will not here analyse again that famous Victorian painting of Queen Victoria presenting a bible to an African (Indian?) prince (?) which so epitomizes Victorian imperial piety, but it is typical of nineteenth-century English chauvinistic views

---

12. An extension of this curious obsession with the late mediaeval division of biblical texts into chapters and verses, especially as focused on the reference grid of 3.16, is nicely illustrated by Donald E. Knuth, *3:16: Bible Texts Illuminated* (Madison, WI: A-R Editions, 1990).

of the Bible.[13] On the other hand, Robert Burns's famous poem 'The Cotter's Saturday Night' (1785) has also been read as typifying ancient Scottish piety's deep treasuring of the Bible. Those well-known lines, 'The sire turns o'er, wi' patriarchal grace,/The big ha'bible, ance his father's pride', have tended to be generalized by readers of Burns and writers on Burns to such an extent that they have been made a universal characteristic of the deep Bible-based piety of all Scots of the past. Such a reading is more characteristic of late nineteenth-century 'kailyard' mythmaking ('kailyard' is a Scottish word meaning 'cabbage-patch') than it is a true representation of 'Scottishness' in Burns's time.[14] But this phenomenon of the cultural transformation of the particular into the general is endemic in popular religious treatments of the Bible as a cultural entity and its supreme value in the past.

It is as an object of desire and a thing of delight for every consumer wishing to possess one that the Bible owes much of its appeal today as a commodity in modern times. Apart from the huge world of Christian piety and Western fundamentalism where the Bible is a religious fetish, icon and image, it is essentially as a consumer good in a commodity culture that the Bible *now* flourishes in contemporary society. As I shall only be interested in looking at bibles as material entities in such a commodity culture in this study, I shall not devote time to asseverations about the importance of bibles as values beyond the level of commodity goods. I will attempt to catalogue this feature of the Bible as a consumerist commodity and to offer some observations on what I would regard as an aspect of the Bible in contemporary society which generally is little stressed in current biblical studies, especially among the scholars of the Academy.

13. The painting of Queen Victoria presenting a bible is by T. Jones Barker (1861) and is to be found in the National Portrait Gallery in London. Its popularity was such that it was also frequently used on Orange Order banners too. As a painting it constitutes an iconic representation of the Bible as a key semiotic element in Victorian culture. For further comment on it see my book (in preparation), *The Bible as Cultural Icon* in the Gender, Culture, Theory series (Sheffield Academic Press).

14. For the poem see 'The Cotter's Saturday Night', in J. Logie Robertson (ed.), *The Poetical Works of Robert Burns* (repr.; London: Open University Press, 1963 [original edition 1904]), pp. 26-31; the lines cited are on p. 28. On the 'kailyard' aspect of the poem's later reception, see Andrew Nash, 'The Cotter's Kailyard', in Robert Crawford (ed.), *Robert Burns and Cultural Authority* (Edinburgh: Edinburgh University Press, 1997), pp. 180-97.

That Obscure Object of Desire

By way of preparation for this paper I did some limited market research
by going into the city centre of Glasgow, to the bible shops there and
also to some of the commercial bookshops, in order to see what bibles
were commercially available in our consumerist society. This research
was in no sense comprehensive. For such a task I would need to have
had the time, funds and energy to have travelled to the Bible Belt states
in the United States, where I would have encountered a very different
world of bibles galore in all their finger-licking glory—Bibles-R-Us
shops! But what I saw in the centre of Glasgow proved to be more than
adequate for my purposes. To be honest, there were in fact *far too many
different versions of bibles* for me to be able to do justice to the subject of
the Bible as cultural object and commodity. The sheer number of different editions and translations of the Bible, not to mention the varieties of
size, shape, colour and price, defeated me and frustrated any attempt to
provide a comprehensive schema of the matter. In what follows I will
attempt to outline some of my responses to the things I found in my
search for the Bible as a commodity among the commodities of the
market as we know it today. I was surprised, bemused, amazed and a
little shaken by the sheer range of bibles for sale in these shops.[15]

Such amazement was especially generated by the sections devoted to
children's bibles, where there appeared to be yet a further range of
objects for sale. Such a cornucopia of bibles left me gasping open-
mouthed at the variety and inventiveness of the publishers. Here I must
also confess to operating out of *ignorance reinforced by prejudice*. All my
working adult life—that is, since I was a graduate student more than 30
years ago—I have tended to think of the Bible as 'an adult book written
by adults for adults'. The notion of a 'Children's Bible' has always struck
me as being an oxymoron or a curiously attentuated notion of what a
bible might be. Of course I am familiar with those Ladybird books

15. Here I should record my gratitude to those students who were in the
Workshop for my Biblical Studies Level One course in the University of Glasgow
(session 1996–97) and who so enthusiastically participated in going around the shops
cataloguing the range, price and details of the bibles on sale there. They provided
greater depth to what I had found out for myself in the visits to the shops preparatory to the Workshop project. I should also admit to experiencing something akin
to 'cultural dissonance' (Paul Bohannan's phrase) in my encounter with so many
bibles which were such tawdry items in a consumerist culture.

devoted to extracts of the Bible and those Lion books which produce a similar set of books using pictures and biblical narratives to provide children with 'bible stories'. But the idea of a whole children's bible is not something I had ever given much thought to, nor, had I thought about it, would I have imagined that such books often consisted of the Bible as adults know it but modified a little for children and accompanied by pictures. Yet this is precisely what I did encounter in the shops: adult bibles with the words 'for children' stamped across the cover. Of course there were also some bibles which had been constructed for children in the sense that such bibles had been reduced to narratives retold in whatever kind of language was deemed to be suitable for children (Lion and Ladybird selections of biblical stories come to mind here). On the other hand, to encounter American editions of the Bible for children which had colour insets of American television cartoon figures reinforcing the imagined moralities of biblical stories surprised me more than I can say. Not knowing these cartoon figures, I cannot comment on the connotations they may have had for non-American kids reading such books. I suspect that this is a form of cultural imperialism whereby American cultural values are mediated to the world via bibles. I know they conveyed nothing to me, except to stimulate the reflection that it was highly unlikely that the watered-down bourgeois message these cartoon figures appeared to be peddling bore much relationship to the stories in the Bible. But they did constitute very colourful insets in the bibles. This factor seemed to me to make the books much more attractive as objects worth purchasing. The words remained very much the words of whatever adult edition of the Bible was being used by the publishers (most often the NIV), only the cartoons made any concessions to facilitating infantile understandings of the book. Of such, no doubt, is the kingdom of heaven!

I should perhaps add the following observations about the phenomenon of 'the Bible as a book fit for children to read', especially because I have always thought of the Bible as having had at least the one redeeming feature of being adult literature beyond the reach of the childish mind.[16] A recent version of the Bible known as The Contemporary English Version of the Bible (CEV) has as one of its selling points that it 'can be understood by five-year-olds'. What can I say? The

---

16. See Ruth B. Bottigheimer, *The Bible for Children: From the Age of Gutenberg to the Present* (New Haven: Yale University Press, 1996).

notion of an adult book that is on the same level as that of the understanding of a five-year-old kid frightens me. What kind of reductionism
is this? Is it part of the banalization of culture so typical of late capitalist
consumerism? Does the infantilization of the Bible represented by such a
selling point carry the implicature that only infantile adults should read
the Bible or that the understanding of a five-year-old is all that is necessary for understanding the Bible? Of course I realize that it is only
advertising copy (it is only a recommendation from some academic or
other, a plug on the back cover), but the mind behind such a claim is
what frightens me. This is not only the commodification of the Bible, it
is also the infantilization of the community of Bible readers. The commodity culture renders the Bible infantile as well as a commodity. What
you see is what you get! Such are the values of the market and it is as
such a material object in the market that the Bible functions in a commodity culture. The market determines the demand for such bibles and
shapes the production required to meet such a demand. No consumerist
culture could dare to be without commodities directed towards meeting
the imagined needs of children, so an endless production line of children's bibles (whether adult bibles stamped 'for children' or the genuine
childish object itself) will provide more than adequate supplies for all the
retail outlets for such objects.

The Bible as Bestseller

> Popularity became confused with universality. If the Bible was truly an
> inspired Great Book, it must have something to say to everyone; by a
> quaint reversal, it then became axiomatic that anyone could understand
> the Bible. In the twentieth century our highest praise is to call the Bible
> 'The World's Best Seller'. And it has come to be more and more difficult
> to say whether we think it is a best seller because it is great, or vice
> versa.[17]

Market values are the determinant of the phenomenon known as 'the
bestseller'. A bestseller is a category of book that everybody buys
because that is what makes it a bestseller. Religious consumerists who
boast about the Bible being 'the world's greatest bestseller' are using the
discourse of the market and give ample testimony to the role of the
Bible as a book in the commodity culture. It is at this very point that

---

17. Daniel J. Boorstin, *The Image or What Happened to the American Dream* (New
York: Atheneum, 1962), pp. 121-22.

high culture and low culture merge into one in the matter of the Bible. Given its origins in the shaping epoch of European civilization, the Bible has always had claims to belong to high culture. Given its role in the cheap printing processes and ideological missionary work of the nineteenth century and in the great mission campaigns of fundamentalistic forms of religious activity in the twentieth century (typified by the Billy Graham organization), the Bible has also always participated in low (brow) culture. Thus it is as an ideal form of cultural entity that the Bible participates in both high and low cultures—a very postmodern thing.[18] Yet as a bestseller it also partakes of all the negative connotations of being such a consumer good: everybody buys it but few people read it, it belongs to the 'shop till you drop' kind of consumables and loses forever any claim to be taken seriously because bestsellers are constantly renewable (exchangeable) commodities. Bestsellerdom is a statistical phenomenon and represents the lowest possible denominator of book evaluation. The sales figures for bibles may make it a statistically significant commodity as far as such sales go, but that is all that a bestseller need be. Bibles sell for many different reasons, whether as cheap and nasty paperbacks or as objects for smuggling into Russia—a lost cause now that the Berlin Wall has come down and communism in Russia has collapsed—or as gifts for the rites of passage of religious folks. But whether the Bible sells well because it is a bestseller or is a bestseller because it sells well, who can tell? The category of bestseller is one that can only compound the confusion that abounds in accounting for the Bible as an object in the commodity culture of late capitalism.

The phenomenon of multiple translations of the Bible, with which Western culture is awash, may be considered under the subcategory of bestseller or in terms of the necessary proliferation of versions of the Bible entailed in the activity of each publisher having to produce their own translation in order to own and possess copyright to the printing and production of bibles. Originally produced under licence, the antique famous versions of the Bible (such as The King James Bible or, as it became better known, The Authorized Version) are not available to most publishers. If publishers wish to have the bestselling Bible on their stocks, they must acquire a version for themselves that they can sell

---

18. In spite of its advocacy of popular culture, *The Postmodern Bible* volume does not in fact devote a chapter to such popular and populist readings and uses of the Bible nor does it pursue a populist approach at all to its subject. See The Bible and Culture Collective, *The Postmodern Bible* (New Haven: Yale University Press, 1995).

freely. So the cultural activity of translation, in particular translation of the Bible, has a part to play in the proliferation of bibles and the swamping of the market (see second epigraph to this study for an expression of the problem of the saturated market). Among the purposes of such translations must be the values and demands of the market. That is, the production of translations to suit every taste and to mirror every ideological demand of the receiving communities for specific translations of the Bible. Denominationalism plays a great part here, as it is very rare for one specific translation of the Bible to be acceptable across the board of denominational differences (the RSV Common Bible is one of the few exceptions to this general rule). Thus in a good Protestant Bible shop it will be much more difficult to acquire copies of the Douai or Jerusalem Bible than it will be in Catholic repositories (and vice versa with regards to the Authorized Version). Culture, ideology and market forces work together to meet the varying needs of different collectivities of consumers as a form of modern consumerist trinity.

The Bible in Planet Hollywood

One aspect of the Bible as part of a commodity culture that deserves considerably more attention than I shall give it here is that of the Bible in relation to Planet Hollywood. What I have in mind here is not so much the larger subject of the actual films made about the Bible or parts of it, but more the kind of cack-handed representations of the Bible using Hollywood values. It would require a full study to do justice to this issue, so I shall only touch on a couple of points here in order to draw some attention to certain cultural aspects of filming the Bible. Filming the Bible in Hollywood has tended to reflect the phenomenon of the most inappropriate castings and absurd representations of biblical stories and characters. I could therefore imagine a film version of the Life of Jesus (or Moses, for those of a different persuasion, but with *mutatis mutandis* adjustments[19]) made under current Hollywood values in which Madonna or Demi Moore would be cast as the Virgin Mary, with Elizabeth Taylor or Shirley Maclaine as the Virgin's mother, Holly Hunter as the baby Jesus and Winona Ryder or Michael Jackson as John

---

19. Although very different characters would need to be represented in a filmic Life of Moses, the plague of Hollywoodism would remain the same. Cecil B. DeMille's *The Ten Commandments* is adequate proof of that contention.

the Baptist.[20] It would not suprise me in the least to discover that such a film had been planned or even released. On the other hand, it would not be appropriate for this study to analyse high culture appropriations of the Bible in such films as Bunuel's *Nazarin*, Pasolini's *The Gospel According to Saint Matthew*, Arcand's *Jesus of Montreal* and (perhaps) the Monty Python film *Life of Brian* as being more characteristic of the kind of film which *in my opinion* constructively and creatively transforms the Bible into genuine filmic discourses without imposing Hollywood values on the material. I shall resist the temptation to develop either approach (high or low culture and the Bible) here because I think such film criticism deserves a separate study.[21] As a bestseller the Bible has inevitably provided many plots and narratives for Hollywood and some of the most famous films ever made have been of stories from the Bible. Often these films have become legendary as examples of *Kitsch*. Indeed, it would be fairer to say that many of these films pose the problem for modern viewers of determining whether *Kitsch* or *Schlock* is the correct category for cataloguing such films. But *Kitsch* and *Schlock* are exactly the values one expects to find in the bestseller category and therefore we should not be surprised that the Bible, as a bestseller, is so easily represented as *Kitsch* and *Schlock* by the expert producers of such cultural entities.

The Bible and Family Values

The survival of that older phenomenon of 'The Family Bible' as a special production aimed at reflecting and reinforcing old-fashioned family values surprised me because I had imagined that modern so-called secular culture would have made greater inroads on the commercial

20. This imaginary scenario reflects the kind of inappropriate casting so typical of current film making in Hollywood where the bankable star determines the shaping of a film much more than the dynamics involved in making such a film. Nothing is sacred in Hollywood, save dollars and celebrities. My discursive approach here also reflects something of the style of film criticism perfected by Joe Queenan; see his *If You're Talking to Me, Your Career Must Be in Trouble: Movies, Mayhem, & Malice* (London: Picador; New York: Hyperion, 1994).

21. Fortunately Philip Davies's contribution to this Colloquium includes a focus on the film *Life of Brian*, so my self-denying ordinance against doing film criticism here will not leave an unfilled gap in the coverage of the Bible from the cultural point of view. For a serious treatment of the Bible in film see the extensive works of Alice Bach and Cheryl Exum.

performances of the bible industry (what my students call 'Bible capitalism'). I well remember that kind of bible from my youth: too large and
heavy, too expensive and too important for regular use—the terror
induced in me by the thought of accidentally tearing one of its precious
pages while reading it remains with me to this day. It was kept safely in
a cupboard somewhere else in the house and contained pictures that
reflected very little of biblical culture but everything of that imagined
biblical culture constructed by Victorian imperializing ideology. But its
current survival as an object in contemporary culture surprised me
because we live in an age of single people, gay groups, divorced persons
and broken and abused–abusive families. The least I would have expected from such family bibles would have been an updating of cultural
relevance by the provision of further spaces for divorces, remarriages
and the names of step-parents, half-siblings and significant others. But I
saw no such provision of additional spaces. Perhaps separated parents
tear their family bibles in half or perhaps one partner gets the family
bible and the other (separating) partner has to buy a new one. Or it may
be the case that nowadays prenuptial marriage contracts carry a clause
determining who gets the family bible in the eventuality of the breakdown of the relationship. Who knows what goes on in contemporary
culture in the matter of separating families and their bibles? But it would
be very interesting to hear further on this matter from the States, where
such commercial matters are both more advanced and better handled
than in the United Kingdom and Europe.

Another commodity which I came across in my research travels was
the phenomenon of what is called 'The Marriage Bible'.[22] Once again
that prejudice-reinforced ignorance of mine was shaken to find such
things as bibles in white covers entitled 'Marriage Editions'. While I am
sure that there are stories of marriages contained in the Bible, I do not
recall that such stories are in any sense either a dominant feature of the
Bible or reflect any form of advocacy. If asked about how I might
summarize the Bible in a few words or describe its contents briefly,
advocacy of marriage would not appear in any of the few words chosen
by me. Indeed, from a traditional Christian point of view I would have
to regard the deep hostility of Jesus *as represented in the Gospels* to marriage and family matters to be a serious challenge to this kind of consumerist stuff. I am also conscious of the long-standing advocacy of

22. For example, The NIV *Marriage Edition Bible* (London: Hodder & Stoughton,
1990).

chastity and celibacy in Christian theology, so I would be absolutely amazed to find that some Christian publisher had produced such a marriage bible. Here I must speculate that it is the culture that drives the production of bibles and not the other way around (cf. Boorstin on the notion of 'the Bible as bestseller'). Current right-wing ideology in Britain and the United States is driving this kind of propagandistic use of bibles. Few if any references to the advocacy of marriage or command-ments about the importance of getting married seem to have survived in the bibles that have been produced over two millennia of Western cul-ture, so to find such a focus on marriage and the Bible in contemporary Bible shops was to encounter the real consumerist thrust of contempo-rary bible production.

What gave one marriage edition of the Bible its added value dimen-sion was the inclusion of a short collection of love poetry at the end of the book (poems of love by such famous Christians as Shakespeare, Elizabeth Barrett Browning, Bernard of Clairvaux).[23] Had a market researcher stopped me in the street and put to me the question 'What would you understand by the term "Marriage" edition of the Bible?', I would have laughed loudly and checked the date (could it possibly be April the first?). Then, having ascertained that the question was a gen-uine one and that such a product did exist, my personal opinion would have been to suggest to the researcher that a 'Marriage' edition of the Bible would have consisted solely of the Song of Songs, Genesis 24, Psalm 45 and perhaps Jn 2.1-11 and whatever other passages might be judged to reflect narratives about weddings and metaphors of that ilk that may be found scattered around in parts of the Bible. At best that would only have entailed a modest, slim volume product. To find *a whole bible between white covers* masquerading as a marriage bible is aston-ishing and a great tribute to market values. Whatever will they think of next? A Bible for Divorced Couples? Why not? After all, divorce is as much a biblical practice and custom (see the Torah) as polygamy, con-cubinage, marriage or that strange biblical practice of giving one man's

---

23. This specific bible is the one referred to in the previous footnote. The selec-tion of love poetry is taken from *Classic Love: Timeless Wisdom from Classic Writers* (compiled by Robert Backhouse; London: Hodder & Stoughton, 1995). There is a high degree of abstract idealism inherent in this curious supplementation of the words of Scripture with such a brief extract from world literature on the topic of human love. The absence of any serious erotic poetry in the supplementation is typical but hardly justifiable.

wife to another man (see Judg. 14.20; 1 Sam. 25.44). Perhaps a Bible for Abusing, Abusive and Abused Couples and for Violent Marriages or even a Bible for the Baptized Dead (cf. 1 Cor. 15.29) would also be appropriate! I guess the market determines everything, so that whatever will sell gets produced. Given the pervasiveness of such market values, I can see that there are yet many more different editions of the Bible to be produced by the ever-watchful Bible publishers. When the market drives, there are no limits to human folly or to the production of what will sell, and, in this world without boundaries or limitations, bibles will continue to be produced in whatever forms are dictated by the consumerism of a commodity culture. The commodification of culture inevitably includes the sacred books of antiquity, and some of the finest displays of late capitalist consumer goods are to be found among the proliferation of bibles in the bible shops of the Western world.[24]

The marriage edition of the Bible is not only a good example of the commodification of the Bible, it also represents the role of commercial bible production as part and parcel of Western ideology, especially in relation to the ideological aspects of modern socio-religious pressure groups. In current right-wing ideology in the West, notions about marriage and the family have suddenly come to the fore as absolute values to be enforced on people. I caught something of this aspect of the implication of bible production in cultural struggles when I came across yet another edition of the Bible, this time of the common type of bibles that have lists of verses and passages inside the front cover whereby readers are given guidance for all of the exigencies of life imaginable to such Bible readers. This particular version started off with a sheet of biblical references to the subject of 'Abortion'. Never in my wildest dreams did I imagine that abortion could ever appear as one of the lead topics in any version of the Bible. Of course there are one or two references to abortions in the Bible, but they are of the kind of thing illustrated by Job 3.10-19 and Jer. 20.14-18: the 'would-to-God-I'd-been-an-abortion-myself' type of lament that is uttered by a speaker in the depths of despair. Needless to say, neither of those two references appeared in the list of readings suggested by what I shall choose to refer to as 'The Abortion Bible'. All the references were of that bland pietistic kind that referred to the LORD (Yhwh) as the giver and protector of life (but not the Lord who is the killer of life as in 1 Sam. 2.6). So this

---

24. On the general phenomenon of the commodification of culture, see McCarthy, *Knowledge as Culture*.

particular edition of the Bible was designed as a weapon for the Pro-Life party in the States in their ideological war against the 'Right to Choose' party. To pious women reading their bibles for (moral) guidance on the matter of their pregnancy and whether they should have an abortion or not, this edition of the Bible will prove to be utterly useless. It will just be counterproductive and will reinforce the anti-abortion side of that struggle, but without presenting either argument or guidance for making a choice. Here the Bible has been recruited as an ideological weapon *on one side* of a complex argument in the socio-political struggles of modernity.[25] But, of course, political and ideological elements have never ever been far from the surface in the production of bibles as consumables in the commodity culture of late capitalism. All too often, however, they have just not been recognized as weapons in such ideological struggles (the Bible and instrumental reason).

The Gideon Bible

Perhaps the best example of the Bible as an ideological tool (weapon) in contemporary society is that strange phenomenon of Hotel-land, the Gideon Bible. All across the world, in lonely hotel bedrooms are to be found, tucked into a drawer somewhere, Gideon Bibles. You have to be one real sad *barstad* to find them, but they are there. On occasion, when the company in the hotel room has been less exciting than toying with a Gideon Bible, I have read the wretched things! Of course, nobody ever reads one of these things right through. Only the introductory 30-odd pages have anything to do with Gideonness, the rest is a normal bible of some description or other. This Introduction, in the most recent edition I read, is called 'An Instructor's Manual Approach'.[26] How very New Age and trendy it all is. Who the Instructor of Bibles (how Gogolesque)

25. I should make it clear that while I am inclined to think that reading the Bible for guidance in matters having to do with contemporary social issues is probably a foolish practice, I would equally want to stress the point that the Bible contains such a wide range of contrary points of view that it cannot in any sense be monopolized by any one side in such debates. Cultural transformations of selected parts of the Bible are too multitudinous in contemporary culture for the practice of using the Bible to be either approved of or ruled out of order, but the practice requires a serious application of cultural hermeneutics.

26. The Gideons International Organization will supply such 'Bible Helps' booklets, but the discourses used require considerable literacy in fundamentalist-speak.

might be was not declared in the version which I leafed through, just an address for The Gideons International in the British Isles—but no reference to Interpreter's House. Further information told me that the Gideons International was started in the States in 1899 and developed a British branch in 1950. Apparently the organization has distributed worldwide some 325 million Scriptures—now that is a lot of greenbacks, however you slice them. The cheap bibles phenomenon of the early nineteenth century has certainly been capped by the Gideon phenomenon of distributing bibles to hotels free of cost.[27] Of course nothing is free in a capitalist world, so such public generosity reflects an ideology of indoctrinating mission backed by commercial and moneyed interests. Business people put up the money in order to encourage the dissemination of such capitalist values in an imperializing form of religious literature. Ideology and religion are nicely married in this testimony to capitalism as the most dominant form of the Protestant religion (see Benjamin epigraph).[28]

In contemporary society there is a tendency for the bible attached to the Gideon Introduction to be the NIV (with some delicate little changes to reflect Received Text prejudices). The NIV has become the new bestseller bible in English, replacing the Authorized Version (still the all-time bestseller). The use of the NIV helps to underline the fact that the theopolitical nature of the Gideon International Organization is very much that of American fundamentalism. The Notes are deeply fundamentalist in tone and discourse and *in my opinion* more 'untruths' are told about the Bible in the space of less than 40 pages than could be imagined in such a short space. For example, the statement 'all parts agree in doctrine, teaching and prophecy' (p. 9) is plainly false about the Bible. It is just fundamentalist propaganda. It is also a good example of the need for paying attention to the fundamental principle of any commercial operation—*caveat emptor*—let the buyer beware! Consumers of Gideon Bibles have everything to lose and nothing to gain by consuming the instructions to Gideon Bibles. There are also many things in this Introduction that are just plain silly. For example, the representation of Jn 3.16 in 'twenty-five of the best-known world languages' is just plain silly (in my opinion) because among those 'best-known world

27. See Leslie Howsam, *Cheap Bibles: Nineteenth Century Publishing and the British and Foreign Bible Society* (Cambridge: Cambridge University Press, 1993).

28. See also Bhabha's discussion of the introduction of the Bible into Indian culture in his *The Location of Culture*, pp. 102-22.

languages' are *classical* (!) Hebrew and *Welsh*! Neither of these languages could under any circumstances be justifiably described as a world language or as best-known, and classical Hebrew is not a currently spoken world language at all (if it ever were a real or spoken language in the past). This is just the typical hyperbolic overkill of contemporary advertising values reflective of rampant consumerism run riot. The ideological prejudices of American fundamentalists are to be found on every page in the Introduction. This is nothing more than consumerism in the service of fundamentalist ideology. It may be a manual of instruction, but it is only such for Christians of a fundamentalistic persuasion who will be instructed by it because they already believe it (a redundant activity)—all other readers of the Bible will be left unimpressed by such do-it-yourself ideological banalities. The fundamentalist Christian prejudices of the writers fail inevitably to take the true measure of the Hebrew Bible, but then in an age of consumerism there is no place for accuracy, integrity, complexity or truth. Gideon Bibles are the religious equivalent of Coca-Cola or chewing gum and reflect that American imperialist inculturation of the known consumer world that seems to have swept away local values and practices wherever its goods have been distributed in the markets of local cultures. Such bibles are also prime examples of the theory and practice of the production of bibles as consumer goods for a commodity culture. At the same time, they are relatively harmless cultural objects as only insomniacs or those who have chosen to share a hotel room with a rather boring person are likely to have had to have recourse to leafing through such ubiquitous objects concealed in the drawers and cupboards of hotels.

Infrastructure of Bible Culture

The invention of the internal combustion engine and its incorporation into vehicles transformed the modern world from a culture of horse-drawn cabs into the automobile universe. The car brought with it a huge infrastructure that was utterly unimaginable before the production of actual automobiles. With the car came roads, freeways, motorways, *Autobahnen*, slip-roads, roundabouts, garages, repair shops, tyre manufacturers, lock-ups, petrol suppliers and the great oil industries and a thousand-and-one other auxiliary systems necessary for the maintenance of cars and the car culture. Another paper would be required to spell out all the material consequences of the invention of the car, but here it will do just to draw people's attention *by way of analogy* to the similar fallout from the production of bibles as consumer objects in a commodity culture. The great power of capitalism in its consumer mode is that entities are multiplied beyond necessity on a daily basis.

Walk into any bible shop and look around the place. Not only are there bendy bibles everywhere, but the walls are covered with banners, posters, pretty pictures (mostly of animals and little children) and flags featuring texts as slogans drawn from the Bible. Dozy gorillas peer across biblical texts at the viewers, cuddly koala bears clutch textual extracts in their furry paws, snooty giraffes peer over biblical phrases and complacent rhinos illustrate the power of God unto salvation. Apart from the collections of videos and tapes of famous people reading or acting out parts of the Bible, there are endless items of everyday use which have biblical texts and slogans engraved or painted on them: cups and saucers, bowls and goblets, pens and pencils, boxes and ornaments, tags and bottle-openers all declare the glory of God. Leather containers for bibles come in every size, shape and price. In Scotland the tartan cover makes a particularly attractive addition to every bible. There is a size, quality and material of bible-holder for every purse's capacity and a wealth of variety and choice to keep any consumer society ecstatic with the promise of fulfilled desire. Bookmarks, pulpit falls, tapestries and crocheted cloths illustrate all the bits of the Bible that are fit to be quoted in public places and among mixed genders (so much of the Bible is entirely unsuitable for any such quotation usage). While I have not yet found them, I can imagine *a world of fridge magnets* featuring biblical texts or pictures imagined from the Bible. Every time I go into such shops I am staggered by the range and variety of tasteless objects produced to adorn, illustrate or enhance bibles. In my opinion this is the *Schlock* end of *Kitsch*. True to the best values of consumerism this kind of thing has succeeded in reducing the Bible to the level of *Kitsch* (God's *Kitsch*) or even *Schlock*. But just as the car trade has engendered a world of car accessories—everything for your car—so the bible trade has created a world of bible accessories—everything for your bible. A do-it-yourself world of bibled New Age spirituality indeed has dawned for the consumers of such a commodity culture. Here is where fundamentalism and its twin sister, evangelicalism, merge into the consumerist world so devoted to the production of an infinite variety of New Age type commodity-based spiritualities.

On the more positive side of the infrastructure of bible production there are all the different kinds of bible that may be purchased for con-siderable sums of money, bibles that enhance a room, study or the working habits of religious folk. For example, loose-leaf, study edition bibles such as the boxed volume of *Holy Bible: NIV Prepunched Pages* (Cambridge: Cambridge University Press; £45 [$70])—sold under the logo 'Create Your Own NIV Study System'—or *The Comparative Study Bible: KJV, Amplified, ASB, NIV* (Grand Rapids: Zondervan, 1984; £70.50 [$110]) will provide students of the Bible who lack any knowl-edge of Aramaic, Hebrew or Greek with the means for second guessing the translators.[29] There is also *The Personal Growth Study Bible: New KJV* (London: Thomas Nelson; £44.99 [$70]) which has a nice, consumerist 'New Age' ring to it. Endless versions of study bibles, interleaved bibles, interlinear bibles, bibles with pictures, and every other sort of bible imaginable (and then some unimaginable) to some producer somewhere are to be found among endless shelves of bibles in these bible shops. My students reported back from their trips to town, for the Level One Workshops, of their incredulity at the sheer range, numbers and prices of the bibles available in each bible shop. They were simply shocked at the vulgarity of it all—a good example, I think, of cultural dissonance on their part.[30]

Although English is usually written in forms that are not especially beautiful or attractive, and nothing like as aesthetically pleasing as, say, Arabic—all those wonderfully calligraphic Qur'ans to which the classical Arabic script lends itself so freely—it is still possible to produce English type in different and pleasing fonts. A good example of how the vari-eties of this kind of printing may produce the most handsome of selec-tions of texts from the Bible may be found in Donald E. Knuth's fascinatingly curious book *3:16: Bible Texts Illuminated*. This represents the art of calligraphers in the service of texts, and the end result is most appealing. A volume such as Knuth's book does much to restore faith in

29. Before the great age of print culture, the Polyglot Bible was the kind of multilingual resource available to the scholarly mind. Today, given the crisis of liter-acy in the West, the closest most people are likely to get to such polyglottism is the multiple *English* translations Bible typified by this kind of *Comparative Study Bible*—a monoglot form of the ancient polyglot phenomenon!

30. For the notion of cultural dissonance, see Bohannan, *How Culture Works*, pp. 133-43. Bohannan's notion relates to dissonant interactions between two groups, whereas I am using his phrase here more in relation to his sense of dis-sonance 'between generations in times of very rapid social and cultural change' (pp. 135-36).

human culture as an aesthetic endeavour after the encounter with so much of the *Kitsch* and *Schlock* goods that dominate the shelves of the average Bible shop.

Then there are the atlases, the concordances, the dictionaries, the encyclopaedias of the Bible, all devoted to explaining to modern readers what they cannot get from the text itself. Back-up for reading the Bible comes in endless forms of commentaries, Scripture Reading Notes, selections of favourite bits of the Bible, diaries and 'a-text-a-day' material, not to mention all the photographic volumes on the Bible, written by such outstanding and world famous scholars as John Drane and John Rogerson. A veritable alembic of the cognoscenti! There is no end to the production of this kind of stuff, and only a serious decline of capitalism will make a dent in this market. On the other hand, it should be noted that the newspapers reported in 1996 that a serious decline in bible sales had been registered for that year.[31] Publishers of bibles appeared to be of the opinion that growing illiteracy in the West and the so-called decline in morality had contributed greatly to a decline in bible reading or buying. The two activities of buying and reading bibles should, however, always be differentiated. There may be no necessary connection between the two activities. If the Bible is to be categorized as a 'bestseller'—a consummately consumerist evaluation, but one much loved by fundamentalists—then we must judge it to be a book more often bought than read. Hence the well-known phrase, 'lovers of the Bible, not readers of the Bible'.[32] Of course it is a more often bought book because so many people buy a copy of the Bible as a gift for somebody else on such occasions as their cultural norms determine bible-giving is the socially correct thing to do. How many of those gifted bibles are also read bibles is a matter for market research and therefore beyond the scope of this writer's attentions in this study.

Economic explanations could be provided for the decline in the annual \$200 million US Bible market (£125 million). Explanations that need have no necessary reference to any imagined decline in morality or materialist refusal of things spiritual. If the economy of a country is not doing well, if workers are being laid off and industries closed down, then there is going to be far less money available for expending on such luxury goods as expensive bibles. Downsizing inevitably affects the sales

31. See the report on 'Bible Sellers Take a Bashing' in *The Times* (29 October 1996), p. 13.

32. For further discussion of this notion, see my *The Bible as Cultural Icon*.

of bibles too. As consumer goods in a commodity culture, bibles cannot hope to avoid the consequences of fluctuations in the market. It may also be the case that there are far too many bibles already on the market (hence the second epigraph to this study). The bewildering variety of different versions of bibles flooding the market today must militate against the sales prospects of any one version of the bible. Buying and stocking so many different translations and versions inevitably increases booksellers' costs and also clutters their shelf space, so intelligent stockists are bound to be cutting back on their purchases and even returning unsold loads of KJVs. While I am greatly comforted to hear that that *plonkingly awful translation* which we know as the King James Bible (perhaps better known to American readers as the Saint James Bible) is being rejected by the public, I suspect that the real reason for its unsaleability has to do with illiteracy and the economy rather than a growing maturity among the great American reading public.[33] While I am not *au fait* with the average American family's purchasing strategies, it would be my guess that if members of the family had been laid off from work and if the cost of living was steadily rising, then the purchase of fewer bibles might just be one of the more obvious savings they could factor into their budgets. It is just a guess, but there might be something in it. As a commodity in a consumerist society, the Bible must inevitably reflect the fortunes of the market. If the market downsizes, then expect bible sales to go into decline. Once the market regains its buoyancy, perhaps bible sales may rise again. On the other hand, if the market has been saturated with too many bibles, then the demand for bibles will inevitably continue to decline—whatever the state of literacy or morality may be. Also it should be remembered that in an audio-visual culture the demand for reading material is bound to be less than what it once was.

33. Having spent a considerable time working on English Bibles, especially the KJV, when editing the World's Classics *The Bible: Authorized King James Version* with my Glasgow colleague Stephen Prickett (Oxford: Oxford University Press, 1997), I write here with feeling. I should also remind readers that the King James Bible is a strange kind of translation in that it is much more an intertextual fusion or palimpsest of previous English translations than an honest translation in its own right. Past translations have corrupted its integrity and rendered it virtually unreadable today—hence my view of it as a 'plonkingly awful translation'. On the other hand, it is a wonderful example of the cultural, the political and the ideological fused together into one commodity in competition with other similar commodities (bibles) in the seventeenth century.

Conclusion

My initial explorations of the topic of the Bible as a material object in a commodity culture are at an end. I have chosen a number of aspects of the topic in order to be able to lay out some of the issues involved in analysing the notion of the Bible as a cultural object, reflecting the material conditions of all such cultural productions. The rampant consumerism of bible production, allied to those other features of bible productions akin to New Age self-development obsessions so characteristic of the consumerist world of late capitalism (do-it-yourself spirituality), will have to serve as the base material for theorizing the matter in relation to the framework of Cultural Studies. Theorizing is currently neither my hermeneutic strength nor my prime object in discussing the various matters raised in this paper. It would need somebody of the calibre of Yvonne Sherwood to do a proper job of theorizing the above discussion.[34] What I have presented here is certainly capable of being theorized, but should be seen first of all as constituting the basis for such a further analysis along theoretical lines. Thus I might subsume the data under a theoretical account of how the production of bibles in the West can be seen as an instrument of white cultural hegemony via the commodity culture of the West. This beginning of a theorizing of the subject would feed into an account of cultural production in the West and contribute something to contemporary accounts of post-colonial theory and praxis. Also, the production and sale of such cultural objects as bibles must be regarded as reflecting not only the market values of a commodity culture, but as contributing something to a comprehensive account of the relations between religion and capitalism. As Walter Benjamin observed, 'The Christianity of the Reformation did not favour the growth of capitalism; instead it transformed itself into capitalism'. The role played by productions of the Bible as part agent, part object in that transformation should be obvious. In the commodity culture of late capitalism at the end of the twentieth century, there is a near infinity of bibles designed to meet the consumerist needs of every pocket, class, gender and desire. In this culture, bibles function, among

---

34. See, e.g., her *The Prostitute and the Prophet: Hosea's Marriage in Literary-Theoretical Perspective* (Gender, Culture, Theory, 2; JSOTSup, 212; Sheffield: Sheffield Academic Press). For a very useful approach to theorizing such matters as cultural studies see Barbara Adam and Stuart Allan (eds), *Theorizing Culture: An Interdisciplinary Critique after Postmodernism* (London: UCL Press, 1995).

so many things, as items in a museum culture, as tokens of affluence and cultured leisure, as icons, as fetishes and even as idols. Such cultural resonances are capable of considerable theorizing in relation to cultural theory, but let that activity be for a second paper. If my starting point for framing this paper was Walter Benjamin's observations on the close connections between capitalism and religion (and, in my opinion, a visit to any Bible shop in any of the shopping malls of the West would confirm the good sense of Benjamin's analysis and illustrate the point made by him), then I have also ended this paper with a reference back to Benjamin's observation. So in my beginning was my end.[35]

35. This paper is perhaps more confessional than cultural studies orientated, but confessionalism is currently fashionable in Biblical Studies—see Janice Capel Anderson and Jeffrey L. Staley (eds.), *Taking It Personally: Autobiographical Biblical Criticism* (Semeia, 72; Atlanta: Scholars Press, 1972)—and registering the impact on oneself of cultural developments in contemporary society is a good way to start to address the subject of the Bible and cultural issues (for oneself).

The Selfish Text: The Bible and Memetics

Hugh S. Pyper

According to the collective authors of *The Postmodern Bible*, it is a 'truism' that the Bible has exerted more influence on Western culture than any other book (The Bible and Culture Collective 1995: 1). In art, literature, politics and religion, biblical thought forms, narratives and quotations are all-pervasive. As Western culture becomes globalized, so too does the Bible. It is said that between a quarter and a third of all Japanese households possess a Bible, in a country where only one or two percent of the population have any Christian adherence. This is because it is regarded as essential background for a proper understanding of Western culture. One effect of the spread of Western culture through trade and conquest as well as missionary activity has been the spread of a collection of ancient Hebrew and Greek texts to every corner of the globe. Where Western culture goes, the Bible goes too.

Simply in terms of the number of copies currently in existence, the Bible represents one of the most successful texts ever produced. Whereas other great texts of the ancient world have either been lost or else exist only in a relatively small number of copies, the Bible is ubiquitous. It exists in over 2000 different languages and in many of those languages it exists in multiple translations. Something identifiable with the Bible in its present form has existed for nearly two millennia and some of its components for much longer. If 'survival of the fittest' has any validity as a slogan, then the Bible seems a fair candidate for the accolade of the fittest of texts.

The purpose of this essay is to explore more fully how the biblical texts have achieved this remarkable success and what this reveals about the culture in which they are embedded. It will be obvious that the model by which I intend to do this is a Darwinian one. Indeed, I propose to turn for this to one of the fiercest contemporary critics of the biblical worldview, Richard Dawkins. His book *The Selfish Gene* (1976 and 1989), itself a runaway bestseller, has popularized the admittedly controversial idea that human beings, indeed all living organisms, can be construed as the 'survival vehicles' for their genetic material.

This claim is a variant on Samuel Butler's well-known description of a hen as 'an egg's way of making another egg'. An organism is a gene's way of making another gene. More pertinent to our purposes is Dawkins's further claim that there is a strict analogy between the processes of biological evolution and the development of human culture. This idea has been taken up by Daniel Dennett, who adapts Butler's epigram to read, 'A scholar is just a library's way of making more libraries' (1991: 202). It is the following further adaptation of this slogan that forms the proposition that this paper will discuss: *Western culture is the Bible's way of making more Bibles*.

In an attempt to see if and how far this rather bold assertion can be defended, I shall analyse in more depth the nature of the analogy that can be drawn between biological and cultural evolution and in particular the usefulness of Dawkins's concept of the 'meme' in this context. In the process, however, it will become apparent, I hope, that the literature of popular Darwinism is itself a cultural product, affected by the very phenomena, including the prevalence of the Bible, that it tries to analyse. My contention overall will be that any attempt at a reductive reading of the Bible in terms of some metanarrative of biological determinism or a postmodern analysis of cultural relativism may find itself hoisted with its own petard.

Genes, Memes and Texts

In *The Selfish Gene* (1976), Dawkins contends that just as biological evolution can be studied at various levels—the gene, the genome, the individual, the gene pool or the species—so cultural evolution can be looked at in multiple levels, from the spread of the simplest catch-phrase to the rise and dominance of the great civilizations of China or the Islamic world. In terms of evolutionary biology, the main point he argues in the book is that the clearest way to think about evolution is to work from the point of view of the smallest replicating entities, in the case of genetics, the gene. By analogy, studies of cultural evolution in Darwinian terms will proceed best by examining the smallest replicating units in culture. It is these that he designates as 'memes'.

He illustrates the concept as follows:

> Examples of memes are tunes, ideas, catch-phrases, clothes-fashions, ways
> of making pots or building arches. Just as genes propagate themselves in

the gene pool by leaping from body to body via sperm or eggs, so memes propagate themselves in the meme pool by leaping from brain to brain via a process which, in the broad sense, can be called imitation (1976: 206).

Later, however, Dawkins becomes concerned to distinguish between a meme as a unit of information lodged in a brain and the phenotypic effects of that meme, such manifestations as the tune or the idea (1982: 109).

Definitions are difficult, to say the least, in these areas. What exactly constitutes a meme or a culture defies classification and the recent literature on memes is bedevilled by shifting definitions and unsupportable generalizations and comparisons. Extravagant claims for the explanatory power of this concept have been made, including claims that the key to human self-understanding is in the new 'science' of memetics. As the originator of the concept, Dawkins has been far more modest in his assessment of its value. Dennett, who as a philosopher has written with more rigour on the subject than most, elaborates the concept of the meme in Chapter 12 of his *Darwin's Dangerous Idea* where he defines memes as 'self-replicating complex ideas which form *distinct memorable units*' (1995: 344). Even so, the concept remains notoriously fluid and therefore liable to abuse. How could it be applied to the Bible? The Bible, if anything, seems more like a repository of memes than a meme itself or even a 'meme complex'. In the ensuing argument, I shall at times be using the term 'meme' for its convenience and its heuristic power in applying Darwinian insights to cultural developments, but always with a weather eye on its slippery nature.

The Bible as Replicator

At this point, however, I want to turn to a more fruitful line of enquiry provided by Dawkins's later, more rigorous discussion of another concept, that of the *replicator*. This he defines as follows: 'A replicator is anything in the universe of which copies are made' (Dawkins 1982: 83). At a banal level, that is a claim that can undeniably be made for the Bible and so it may be of interest to explore the ramifications of this analogy.

Note, first of all, that Dawkins carefully does not say that the replicator must be *self*-replicating. There is a fundamental point here that has often been missed. DNA is sometimes described as a 'self-replicating' molecule. In one sense this is true. Given the right environment, a molecule of DNA is capable of acting as a template so that an exact copy of itself is produced. The important point is that it needs the right environment. DNA on its own cannot reproduce itself; it needs a complex of enzymes which will guide and manage the process. In fact, it is only at the level of the cell that we find a replicating structure that can produce copies of all its parts from raw materials in a simple environment.

In that sense, the Bible is no different from DNA. Shut a Bible, or even two, in a cupboard and you will certainly not find more Bibles when you come back. Leave a jar of DNA on a shelf, however, and it will not increase either. Only in the context of a cell, of a 'survival machine', will we find DNA reproducing. Likewise, Bibles can only reproduce through the agency of a human reader, who then takes steps to ensure that more copies are produced.

The crucial point that lifts all this from the level of a truism is the way in which Dawkins then refines the concept of the replicator. He distinguishes between an *active* replicator, the nature of which has some influence over the probability of its being copied, and a *passive* replicator, the nature of which is immaterial. DNA, the replicating molecule that encodes genetic information in cells, is an example of the first, in that it exerts phenotypic effects on the environment through the protein synthesis it enables. These effects in turn influence whether it will be copied.

Active replicators modify their environment in such a way as to enhance their own reproductive capacity. To illustrate this, Dawkins makes a particular study of the interactions between parasites and hosts. For example, at a simple level, a gall wasp larva will carry genes that encode for the synthesis of chemicals that mimic the growth hormones of an oak tree, inducing the tree to grow an unusual structure that serves to protect and feed the wasp larva. Here the wasp genes are acting on the phenotype of the oak tree, not the wasp, in a way that enhances the wasp's reproduction but which may have a deleterious effect on the tree. The relevance of this parasite–host model for the consideration of the Bible will become clearer as the discussion develops.

Unfortunately for my purposes, Dawkins's example of a passive regulator is a sheet of paper which is Xeroxed. On the face of it, this undercuts any analogy between the genetic material and the Bible. He goes on, however, to concede that some pieces of paper are much more likely to be copied than others because of what is written on them. They then become active replicators as they convey information that acts on the reader and her environment in such a way as to induce her to copy the text. The argument I shall pursue is that in this sense the Bible is indeed an active replicator, one which alters its environment so as to increase its chances of being copied. The intriguing questions then become how the Bible does this and why it has been so conspicuously successful.

Dawkins goes on to discuss other aspects of active replicators. It is a fundamental point in his argument that no process of replication is infallible. Strikingly, a favoured metaphor to illustrate this in popular genetic texts is the variability of the biblical text in different translations or through processes of copying. Robert Pollack in his *Signs of Life*, for instance, sets out six English versions of Jas 4.5 to illustrate the phenomenon of alleles, the existence of variant forms of the same gene within a population or indeed an individual genome (1994: 38). Dawkins himself uses the 'mistranslation' of the Hebrew for 'young woman' as 'virgin' in the Septuagint version of Isa. 7.14 as an example of the potentially enormous phenotypic effects of a small change in DNA. He also provides a footnote explaining the Hebrew and Greek texts complete with citations in Hebrew, remarking that 'I suppose the scholars of the Septuagint could at least be said to have started something big' by this (1989: 16). This infiltration of biblical examples into the texts of popular genetics is an intriguing phenomenon to which I shall return.

The crucial consequence of this variation is that, when it occurs, some replicators may turn out to be less efficient than others at replication and so will tend to be replaced by the more successful replicators. For active replicators, whose nature affects their success in achieving replication, such variation may have a remarkable effect on their reproductive ability. Those that replicate most efficiently will, if all else is equal, come to predominate in the population.

Yet variability in itself is not enough; it must be coupled with stability. If 'successful' variants are to survive and out-compete the others, they must be conserved over time. Dawkins sets out the conditions for a successful replicator in the following slogan: longevity, fecundity and fidelity. The replicator must last long enough to reproduce, it must be capable of producing a sufficient number of copies, and these copies must be accurate. To ensure accuracy, the genetic material has a whole complex of 'editor enzymes' which repair and correct copying errors in

DNA. So too the biblical text has become sacrosanct with a premium put on its accurate reproduction. The great complexes of the Masoretic apparatus and the libraries of biblical criticism that have sought to preserve the text in its 'original' form are the evidences of this.

The stability of a particular text or a particular DNA sequence, what Dawkins calls its 'longevity', is an important factor. The replicator must maintain its identity over time. Equally important, however, is its capacity to throw up variants which, when conditions change, may confer an advantage on the organisms that bear them. It is this balance between the ability to reproduce faithfully a particular variant but also to be able to produce variation if the circumstances favour it that confers reproductive success on any replicating system.

The Cell and the Community

The Bible, then, operates as a replicator in a way analogous to DNA. Like DNA, it stores information which can be read and translated and which contributes to its own reproduction. This, however, requires the action of another level of agency. In the case of DNA, this agent is the cell, where the information contained in DNA is translated into proteins that both structure and control the host of chemical processes that are necessary to sustain the life of the cell, and therefore the reproduction of DNA. In the case of the Bible, the agency is a human community that will recopy and disseminate the text.

The crucial question then becomes how the active effect of the cellular DNA on the constitution of the cell or organism which is its 'survival vehicle' is paralleled in the case of the Bible. That a case can be made is evident from the fact that the analogy has been pursued in the opposite direction, notably by Robert Pollack. In his book *Signs of Life* he explicitly embraces the analogy of DNA as text.

> … I have organised this book around the notion of DNA as a work of literature, a great historical text. But the metaphor of the chemical text is more than a vision: DNA is a long skinny assembly of atoms similar in function, if not form, to the letters of a book, strung out in one long line. The cells of our bodies do extract a multiplicity of meanings from the DNA text inside them, and we have indeed begun to read a cell's DNA in ways even more subtle than a cell can do (1994: 5).

Molecular biology is shot through with metaphors of reading: translation, transcription, reading enzymes and the like. Pollack extends this metaphor by suggesting that the genome is like an encyclopaedia, where the volumes are represented by the chromosomes, the articles by the sets of genes encoding for a particular character, the sentences by the genes themselves. Words are domains and letters are base pairs (1994: 21).

Nor is he alone in drawing such comparisons. Dawkins himself speaks of the tempting analogy of seeing DNA as a 'family Bible' (1995: 39), a record of our ancestry slightly different for each one of us, although he quickly goes on to point out flaws in this metaphor. Dennett makes the point that the strict analogy between genes and memes can be maintained on the ground that they are both 'semantic entities', by which he means that they constitute information that can be variously encoded. A gene is not simply a piece of DNA, although to be effective it has to be expressed as such. It could equally be said to be encoded in a sequence of letters on a page, just as a meme may be contained in the pages of a book.

But as texts, both DNA and the Bible have to be read. In the case of DNA, this is a matter of the synthesis of RNA and, through it, of particular amino acid sequences in cellular proteins. In the case of a text such as the Bible, the analogous process, in Dennett's view, is that its memes influence a human mind and so influence a common meme pool so as to ensure the physical survival of the text. Dennett expresses this as follows: 'memes still depend at least indirectly on one or more of their vehicles spending at least a brief pupal stage in a remarkable sort of meme nest: a human mind' (1995: 349).

Mere reproduction of a text as a physical artefact is not enough to ensure its continued survival as Dennett makes explicit. Copies of books will only endure so long, and the relative youth of even the earliest complete manuscripts of the Bible bears this out. He quotes an analogy from Manfred Eigen, who points out that a Mozart symphony cannot be said to survive as a living cultural entity unless it is played and replayed and checked for continuing value against other compositions. The Bible must be read and must make itself read if it is to be reproduced. Its success in achieving this is what makes it an example of a highly adaptive active replicator.

In this view the biblical reader, then, acts as the site of transfer of the information contained in the text to the meme pool in which he or she operates. The book itself encodes memes which once active in the mind lead the human agents of that meme pool to produce more examples of the text. But like all memes, in Dennett's view, they encounter competition. People have a lot of other things to do with their time and energy besides copying Bibles, indeed a lot of other texts to read. What has led to the particular success of the Bible in this competition for mental space?

The Viral Bible

Controversially, this can best be looked at under the rubric of its 'infectivity'. In a paper entitled 'Viruses of the Mind', Dawkins gives an account of the propagating power of what he calls a mind virus (Dawkins 1993). By this term he means a piece of information that ensures its own duplication without regard to the survival of the system it exploits. Viruses are propagated differently from the genes of their hosts. For instance, influenza viruses spread by coughs and sneezes rather than by being incorporated into a viable embryo for the next genera-tion. This means that, unlike host cells, whose genes will only be propa-gated by the reproduction of the organism of which they are part, viral genes and viruses have no vested interest in the reproductive success of their host.

So, how would a successful 'mind-virus' operate? The problem for a virus is that it must be incorporated into the replicative machinery of its host. What is the parallel mechanism among viruses of the mind? Such a meme will have to instil in the host a mechanism for conserving the meme, and a mechanism for propagating it. It would ideally act like the gall wasp to divert the host's energies to its own reproduction. It would also, however, be well advised to have a mechanism for conserving its variability so that any changes in the environment, including the intru-sion of other foreign memes, and in particular any developments in the host's own immune system, can be either countermanded or else outflanked.

My tentative suggestion is that the Bible instils a meme in its readers which aligns its own survival with that of the reader and his or her community. 'Your survival depends on mine' is the message that the Bible gives. If the primary evolutionary drive is for survival, then a virus or a meme that 'persuades' its host that it is necessary to the host's own survival, and therefore conveys a reproductive advantage, will have an instant welcome into the replicatory machine. The virus becomes a symbiont, an organism that cooperates to mutual benefit with its host, rather than a parasite.

Of course, it is only in hindsight that the nature of the association can be known with certainty. It is quite possible that an organism will live quietly as a symbiont and then suddenly turn on its host at a later stage. Images of John Hurt and the parasitic alien bursting out through his body wall are only too apt in this connection, but the process may be a much quieter one. It may be that a false offer of reward to the host is never cashed out. From the invader's point of view, this matters little as long as it achieves its goal of its own reproduction.

Strategies of Survival

What the Bible has to offer the communities that it needs in order to reproduce is the unique variety of powerful strategies of survival it enshrines. Dawkins and other writers on memetics frequently cite the example of the 'God-meme' as a meme which has a powerful record of propagation across time and space. From a theological point of view, of course, the reduction of the complexity of human accounts of God to a single meme is a gross oversimplification. What seems to be implied is rather a meme that predicates human survival on something other than purely biological grounds, that offers a space not only for bodily survival but for memetic survival.

This has resonances with the account that Zygmunt Bauman offers of the whole enterprise of human culture (Bauman 1992). Culture, he claims, is a human construct designed to fend off the threat of death. It is a survival mechanism that finds a way of promising a form of survival in the face of the inevitability of individual death. For Bauman, the Jewish tradition is the clearest case of the subsuming of individual death in communal survival. The individual may die but his or her genes and memes will carry on. The duty of the individual, then, in the sense of his or her best survival strategy, becomes one of ensuring the survival of the group, not of prolonging his or her own life. Christianity has adopted the alternative strategy of a promise of immortality, in that the believer's death is caught up in the context of the resurrection of Jesus. Both genetically and memetically, the afterlife of the believer is strictly irrelevant except in so far as belief in personal immortality acts to sustain the continuity of the meme pool.

Both of these strategies are offered to the reader of the biblical text, together with stern warnings of the likely outcome of failing to abide by the word of the text. This is also aligned to a particular set of strategies that reinforce the integrity of the biblical text. In order to maintain continuity and identity, any organism or any gene pool has to be able to filter out undesirable interlopers.

Again, a cunning usurper will both penetrate these defences but also quickly turn them to its own advantage, keeping out competitive genes and installing itself as the object of the host's attention. On an organismic scale, the efforts of a baby cuckoo to throw the host species' own eggs and chicks out of the nest combined with its success in subsequently subverting the host's nurturing instincts to its own development are a classic case. The cuckoo succeeds in deflecting to its own benefit the mechanisms of rearing the young which have evolved for the vital task of reproducing the host species.

The Bible contains powerful instructions as to its own unique worth and the limits to be placed on the infiltration of foreign information or texts into the communities that propagate it. Transgression of these limits will lead, so it warns, to communal disaster, which must be avoided by rooting out any alternative ideology. The whole process of canonization reveals a complex interaction between text and community that serves, for example, to oust the fledgling apocrypha and turn the community's attention to the ever-growing task of copying and commentating on the biblical text with an increased sense of its importance and of the need for its conservation.

The propagation of the text and the founding of new communities are also linked to the survival of the reader and his or her community, or meme pool. The Hebrew Bible is full of admonitions about the duty to hand down its teaching, and, by implication, the text, to the next generation. In addition the text contains a strong message of evangelization which encourages the recruitment of new transmitters of the tradition. The survival of the reader's community, so the Bible intimates, depends on the production of new copies of the texts and new communities. This complex of memes and of strategies forms a powerful ensemble to ensure the accurate transmission of the text.

Biblical Variation

If the Bible thus encodes strategies to ensure its longevity and accuracy, what then of biblical variability? Superficially, of course, Bibles show variation. The physical appearance of the Bibles on our shelves is very different from that of the scrolls found at Qumran, an evolution that has something to do with ease of reading, portability and changes in the mechanics of reproduction. In another obvious sense, the Bible has evolved out of its component parts, which themselves have undergone a long process of development. It now exists in a number of forms: the Tanakh, and the various canons of the Christian churches.

Despite this variation it might be argued that within each community it has on the whole developed a fixed form. However, that form itself preserves a great variety of strategies of survival. There is an analogy here perhaps in the way in which variant genes can be maintained in a population even if they have no particular advantage, or are perhaps deleterious.

In many organisms, chromosomes and the genes they contain are carried in pairs. This means that an individual may carry two different variants of any gene, such variants being termed alleles. In most cases, one of the alleles is dominant, so that in an individual which carries two copies of the gene, only the dominant characteristics are expressed. The consequence of this is that the individual may carry without any disadvantage another allele which could, if expressed, have a deleterious effect, but might also, in changed circumstances, turn out to confer an advantage. The sexual process leads to the constant reassortment of alleles, which means that the population will be able both to express the alleles of the gene but also to carry them under the cloak of the dominant phenotype.

It is tempting to speculate whether some of the redundancies and doublings in the biblical text may have a similar function in that they can preserve maverick readings. These can be ignored by the mainstream interpreters, especially if an interpretative parallel to the dominance mechanism is in play, whereby an anomalous or redundant verse or passage can be 'corrected' by appeal to other verses in Scripture, or the perceived overall theological thrust of the material. The day may come, however, when the suppressed alternative reading may prove of interest or use to a particular interpretative community, which then propagates the Bible on the basis of that alternative reading.

Furthermore, even in its canonical form the Bible can still generate variety. The information contained between the covers of any given edition of the Bible varies and develops, especially in terms of marginalia and commentary, which may, at times, have outweighed the biblical text in terms of importance. It is only necessary to count the number of editions of the Bible currently available to realize how, in adapting to the needs of different communities, cultures and age groups, the contents of the physical entity called the Bible can vary widely. These variations serve to widen its appeal, or, in other words, to enable it to gain entry to and propagate itself in a whole variety of new environments.

In this connection, one of the most obvious sources of variation and adaptive strategies that the Bible has is its translatability. Translation is a good trick for increasing the number of Bibles—I certainly possess at least 17 versions of the Scriptures and I suspect that most regular biblical readers, let alone scholars, possess more than one version, something which would be unlikely for many other books in their libraries. From the blindly functional point of view, there is paradoxical advantage for a text in being written in a dead language once it has achieved a cultural dominance in another language group. It can potentially always be re-translated because the precision of the match between the words and the meanings cannot be guaranteed in the way that the text itself insists is important. It is more open to revision than a text inscribed in the native language of a culture, except in rare instances where a text preserves an older form of the evolving tongue. It is possible, for instance, to find modern language paraphrases of Shakespeare, but there is a great resistance to producing new English versions of his works, whereas once the interesting conservatism over the Authorized Version was broken, the floodgates of new biblical translations opened. Additionally, there is implicit permission for the text to be translated into the vernacular language of any community that uses the book, again increasing both its diversity and adaptability but also the sheer numbers of copies in existence.

This is by no means a one-way process. The success of the Bible in reforming the communities into which it moves through translation is also striking. As Carroll and Prickett observe in their introduction to the World Classics edition of the Authorized Version,

> What we *can* observe is that it was not just the Bible that was transformed in the course of successive reinterpretations. The Vulgate, a single, authoritative, monolingual instrument for the entire Western Church, was the instrument of the new imperial power of the Roman Church. Luther's Reformation translation of the Bible was to change the German language for ever; his commentary on Romans to set the agenda of theological debate for centuries. Tyndale's translation of the New Testament, on which the Authorised Version was to be so closely modelled, did the same if not more for English (Carroll and Prickett 1997: xiv-xv).

Communities based on the Bible may have a strong interest in conserving it unchanged. From the point of view of the Bible, however, its ability to adapt to new communities is an essential part of its success. The fact that much human ingenuity has been expended on ensuring that the Bible does *not* change and that such mutations have at times been physically rooted out merely goes to show the strong pressure on the text to mutate and its potential for evolution. As we noted before, the interests of the text and those of its nurturing community may not coincide.

This leads to the conclusion that when another champion of scientific realism, the astronomer Carl Sagan, lays into the Bible in his attack on what he conceives of as superstition in his recent book, *The Demon-haunted World*, he in fact reveals one source of its reproductive success. Contrasting the love of one's enemy enjoined in the Gospels with the celebration of holy war of Joshua, he writes, 'The Bible is full of so many stories of contradictory moral purpose that every generation can find scriptural justification for nearly any action it proposes, from incest, slavery and mass murder to the most refined love, courage and self-sacrifice' (1996: 275). Indeed, and this has surely contributed to its survival. A book to which both the apartheid regime in South Africa and its most fervent opponents can turn to justify their position may not offer simple moral precepts, but does ensure that both sides will own their own copies. For the survival of the *book*, its amazing capacity to sustain opposing camps is a very successful strategy.

Part of its success is its very diversity, but also the fact that diversity can be differently enacted. As is well known, every cell in the human body contains the same genome, but this is differently expressed in different tissues to give cells that vary radically in form and function. The difference lies in the particular portions of the genome which are read. So, too, the Bible contains more information than any one community can readily assimilate, especially as it may seem mutually contradictory or impossible to apply in a given situation. What then happens so often is the formation of a canon within the canon, where the community opts to read and follow a particular smaller set of instructions, read with a particular interpretative slant. This may change over time, giving a flexibility and yet continuity to the community. Biblical communities themselves show a capacity for survival that consists in a knack for maintaining continuity through change.

Biblical Advantage

It was allegedly the physician to Frederick the Great who, when asked by that monarch to give a proof of the existence of God, replied, 'The continued existence of the Jews'—an existence bound up with the identity, adaptability and continuity that the Bible confers. In a more theoretical vein Sir Peter Medawar attributes the biological success of human beings as a whole to a new form of inheritance: exogenetic or exosomatic heredity. 'In this form of heredity, information is transmitted from one generation to the next through non-genetic channels—by word of mouth, for example, and by other forms of indoctrination; in general by the entire apparatus of culture' (1977: 14; quoted in Dennett 1995: 342). Henry Plotkin, in his *Darwin Machines and the Nature of Knowledge*, cites the Bible and the Koran as just such devices of exosomatic storage. He speculates on the selective advantage of such texts to the cultures that retain them by drawing on Bartlett's work on the degradation of oral narratives, which implies that over time any group will retell a tale in such a way as to bring it into line with accepted norms. Plotkin argues that the 'exosomatic storage of memes' in the Bible may have preserved 'richness subtlety and beauty' in cultures which possess the book (1994: 220).

That continuity is bound up with the continued existence of the Bible. The community of readers sees it as its duty to ensure the survival of the book. More than this, it sees the book as the guarantor of its own continuity and survival. The book itself contains a whole plethora of strategies for survival, and, in particular, is the record of an amazing feat of cultural continuity, as the diaspora communities of Jews manage to retain a sense of themselves as Israel, as members of one 'meme pool' of cultural exchange, protected by firm filters from external memetic contamination. The fact that historians might take leave to differ over the actual continuity of the community and its immunity to outside infection is surely a proof of the power of the meme complex in question. Despite the available evidence of all that might have led to its dissolution and disappearance, the community is maintained, and the text is preserved.

Even more amazing is the development of communities of those supposedly excluded by the text, the Gentiles, who find ways of identifying themselves as Israel and arrogating to themselves both the promises and the duties imposed by the text, chief among which is the duty to ensure the perpetuation and dispersal of the text. Here the 'gene pool' of Judaism, with its claim of descent from Abraham's seed, is replaced by a 'meme pool', a claim of descent from Abraham's faith, a line of argument already presaged in the Old Testament itself.

This is an astonishing success and one of crucial importance to the propagation of the text. The consequence of its incorporation into the canon of the Christian Bible is an exponential leap in the number of copies produced. However, it may also be true that the text turns against the communities that have sustained it if that is to its advantage.

The horrid record of Christian anti-Semitism shows the consequences of the filter mechanisms for memetic purity being turned against the original host community, as the Bible takes on a new existence as Christian Scripture. The mechanisms that served to exclude 'Canaanite' memes from the community now act to exclude Judaism. A prime exemplar of such 'selfishness' of the text might be seen in the Reformation, where the text operates to cause a major breach and disruption in the community that sustained it in order to take advantage of the new technology of printing. It achieves this through the propagation of a meme that removed the authority of interpretation from the institution to the individual and to the possibilities of reproduction within vernacular language communities. The peril of too close an association with the host community may be that the text will fall with the community that guards it. The success of the Bible has been predicated on its ability to 'jump ship' when necessary.

The paragraph above is an obviously self-parodic example of the prevalence of the intentionalist fallacy in the discussion of Darwinian replicants. It is patently a fallacy to argue that the Bible provoked the Reformation in order to increase its own population, but the facts remain. Whatever damage the Reformation did to the church and to the victims of the religious wars that accompanied it, it was certainly good for the Bible.

The Survival of the Bible

What then of the Bible in late twentieth-century society, where the traditional communities of interest in the Bible may be thought to be in danger of collapse? Selection is a cruel business, as many species and their DNA find every day. Surviving intact for a hundred million years is no defence when your habitat is suddenly filled with industrial pollutants. The best that can be said for any replicator is that it has survived *so far*. Tomorrow is another day and will perhaps bring an insurmountable challenge.

Even if the worst comes to the worst in terms of a diminishing community of biblical readers, the important thing for the text in a memetic view is not that it be read but that it be copied. By achieving an iconic status within a culture, the text can relieve itself of the pressure of seducing readers. The baptismal Bible or wedding Bible may be a gift that is never read, and no one is likely to open the pages of the court room Bible on which oaths are sworn, but they must be complete, as the community is well endowed with reverence for the canonical text that is either all or nothing: an incomplete Bible is not a Bible. This may work more powerfully for the New Testament than the Old, as the New circulates independently, but it nonetheless still allows for the reproduction of redundant, unread material within the New Testament. For the sake of iconic completeness, it may even extend to the replication of the even less appealing Old Testament.

This too has a biological analogy. One of the more unexpected findings of molecular biology is that a large proportion of the DNA in any genome is seemingly also redundant, consisting of simple repeating sequences that do not encode any gene. Opinion is still divided as to the function of this material. It may have structural or geometrical implications. This redundant DNA is, however, copied and transmitted to the next generation as faithfully as any other. Analogously the Bible carries a great deal of seemingly redundant information: the detailed instructions for the construction of the tabernacle, for instance. As long as there is some commitment to a notion of completeness, however, this seemingly irrelevant material will be replicated. This means that the Bible can survive to a remarkable extent even on the vestiges of a culture which valued it.

However, the situation for the Bible is by no means as gloomy as that. As I was finishing this paper, by coincidence two documents arrived together in my pigeonhole. One was a copy of a review of several modern popular debunking biographies of Jesus, which finished by quoting Lord Gowrie's admission that A.N. Wilson's version 'sends us scurrying back to the gospels' (Stanford 1997: 3). The second was a leaflet from the National Bible Society, urging donations for the despatch of Bibles to the displaced and starving population of Zaire.

Whatever one thinks of the anti-biblical polemics of an A.N. Wilson and the response of the Bible Society to the disasters of war, there is a common feature to these documents: both seem to serve to increase the sale and distribution of the Bible. The Bible Society can still launch an appeal to increase the number of Bibles in the belief that the Bible will contribute uniquely to the survival of the people of Zaire. A.N. Wilson, who seeks to debunk it and would no doubt pour scorn on the Bible Society's work, finds himself both propagating biblical memes in his own texts and sending his readers back to consult the original text. The biblical text is not affected by the fact that the person who reads it is only doing so to refute it as long as there is a sufficient cultural community or meme pool to maintain the argument and therefore sustain the need for the text.

Yet the Bible has always shown an astonishing facility in generating communities that will see it as worth transmitting. What memetic pull is it that brings together a group of scholars of diverse backgrounds and beliefs to Sheffield to discuss the Bible and culture, for instance? Has the Bible 'succeeded' in making a bid beyond its native environment of the religious community, one which may be severely threatened in a new memetic ecology? Is it now able to persuade communities of readers to consider it as a cultural artefact, using the same memetic appeal as Homer and Plato? If so, what a tribute to the extraordinary staying power of the particular combination of memes that the text and the communities it builds around itself enshrine. Having formed communities about itself for 2000 years, often by coopting its enemies, is the Bible proving able to do this again by infiltrating not religious but cultural discussion?

A telling example of this ability of the biblical text to infiltrate the most unlikely communities is the very genre of popular genetic writing of which Dawkins is the most celebrated practitioner. For someone who evinces such a suspicion of the influence of the Bible, he makes a surprising number of references to it. His main rival, both as a best-selling writer of popular genetics and as an advocate of what to Dawkins seems a 'heretical' view of Darwinism, is Stephen Jay Gould, whose books are shot through with biblical allusions. Another populist geneticist's recent book, Stephen Jones's *In the Blood: God, Genes and Destiny*, a companion to a television series, is an interesting case in point. In it he covers such topics as the Lost Tribes of Israel and the concept of Armageddon, in the process alluding to a large number of biblical texts and outlining many biblical stories. It would be ironic, would it not, if we were to conclude that Dawkins himself has become a 'survival machine' for the

Bible, a 'meme nest' for its dispersed memes, which may induce readers who would otherwise leave their Bibles unread to go back to the text.

Dawkins, however, is merely one articulate representative of a much wider conversation in a global gene pool that could loosely be designated as 'Western culture'. Insofar as we have seen that the survival of the Bible seems to be predicated on the persistence of its peculiarly effective set of memes, which induce reading communities to propagate it, it is Dawkins's inescapable cultural environment that is in evidence here.

But are we then simply the victims of the Bible? Dawkins ends *The Selfish Gene* with a rallying cry: 'We are built as gene machines and cultured as meme machines, but we have the power to turn against our creators. We, alone on earth, can rebel against the tyranny of the selfish replicators' (1976: 215). Is he actually a witness that we may think we can rebel against biblical memes, but that such replicators have an uncanny power to survive all our efforts? The telling passage in his *River out of Eden* (the title itself needs no comment) on the 'ravishing' poetry of the Authorized Version of the Song of Songs, and the 'lifetime's repetition' which has given it its own haunting appeal despite the possible inaccuracy in translation (1995: 40) argues that aspects at least of the Bible have succeeded in inserting themselves into the 'meme nest' of Dawkins's mind in such a way that they are transmitted, if not replicated.

Dennett comments on Dawkins's challenge to the power of the memes, 'This "we" that transcends not only its genetic creators but also its memetic creators is…a myth' (1995: 366). His own writings show also the power of persistence of the biblical tradition. He ends his 1995 book with an ambivalent plea for the preservation of meme complexes such as religions for their cultural enrichment. 'I love the King James Bible', he declares. 'My own spirit recoils from a God Who is He or She in the same way in which my heart shrinks when I see a lion pacing neurotically back and forth in a small zoo cage. I know, I know, the lion is beautiful but dangerous; if you let the lion roam free it would kill me; safety demands that it be put in a cage' (1995: 515).

This is a rather extraordinary paragraph which is somewhat baffling in its uncharacteristic ambiguity and its implications. What is it that distresses Dennett so much? Is it the use of gendered language of God, rather than the idea of God? Is the King James Bible the cage, in which case what is the love he bears it, or is its place in the cage with the lion because of its dangers?

My own view, and no doubt I here manifest symptoms of my own freight of memetic viruses, is that the Bible has so firmly entrenched a place in our culture that it is ineradicable. It is not a parasite but a constituent part of the great complex of meme complexes that can be designated 'Western culture', part of the exosomatic genome of that culture's members. More than that, I see it, in Plotkin's terms, as an indispensable source of what might be called 'memetic diversity'. In agricultural genetics, one of the most worrying trends has been the loss of diversity from the appellations of food plants and animals. There are obvious superficial gains, not least to seed companies and fertilizer manufacturers in growing vast tracts of pure stands of the 'best' varieties, the judgment of 'best' depending on the particular values of the grower or the market. Ease of marketing may well win out against nutrition. However, there is a potential disaster looming if the super variety is suddenly attacked by a pathogen or if there is a major climatic shift. A variety may be fit for the purpose and the conditions of the moment, but what if conditions change?

Here it becomes vitally important to maintain a 'gene pool' of wild relatives of the crop plants, which may themselves have all sorts of drawbacks from the point of view of the technology of farming, but which have shown themselves able to fend for themselves in this competitive world over time. Such wild populations contain a huge diversity of genetic material maintained over time and a vast potential for diversity and for change. Can we view the Bible as a sort of cultural 'memetic reserve'? Parts of it may seem irrelevant, redundant, even detrimental to our survival, but it has kept going. As Medawar and Plotkin indicate, it may serve to maintain a memetic richness and complexity, an inexhaustible source of variety which may contain the unexpected counter to forces that threaten to impoverish our cultural lives.

But Dennett's rather inarticulate declaration of love for the Bible suggests other possibilities. This paper has, of course, taken a slightly wry look at a provocative rereading of the dynamics of cultural development. Nothing in the theory of memetics can help us to establish the truth or falsity of a meme, it can only deal with its frequency and prevalence. Questions of reference are not raised. Indeed, the practitioners of memetics have erected some pretty formidable filters to debar any such questions. Methodologically, this may be necessary to prevent muddled thinking, but methodology is not truth despite its strong tendency to become so. The easiest way to filter out a proposition is to declare it to be either meaningless or false. A very different account could have been given on the premise that the Bible reflects the encounter of God with the complex web of human culture and individuality, a premise which *methodologically* Darwinism cannot entertain. The attempt, however, to follow through such a methodology is a discipline that I hope has brought to light intriguing connections which any account of the relations of the Bible and culture might need to take on board.

More radically, however, is survival, as Darwinism must have it, really the primary value, or is it in turn a methodology that has become a truth? The lion may be dangerous, and human culture, as Bauman argued, may well have been a device to keep it caged and to ensure survival, just as the wild lion has been confined practically to game reserves. The beauty of the cage, then, is in some sense engendered by the lion. Letting the lion out would have disturbing implications for culture as well as for scientific method.

But is there no other model of co-existence between human and beast, between human beings, the Bible, and the God which it cages and displays? Here I want simply to recall that Isak Dinesen has a won-derful account in her book, *Shadows on the Grass*, of the mutual respect between the hunter and the lion which grows from the fact that each knows that the other is hunter as well as prey: 'a lion hunt each single time is an affair of perfect harmony, of deep, burning, mutual desire and reverence between two truthful and undaunted creatures on the same wavelength' (1985: 305). Somewhere in this may be a dynamic that can lift us beyond the mechanisms of the meme and into true encounter.

BIBLIOGRAPHY

Bauman, Z.
    1992   *Mortality, Immortality and Other Life Strategies* (Cambridge: Polity Press).
Carroll, R.P., and S. Prickett (eds.)
    1997   *The Bible: Authorised King James Version with Apocrypha* (Oxford: Oxford University Press).
Dawkins, R.
    1976   *The Selfish Gene* (Oxford: Oxford University Press).
    1982   *The Extended Phenotype* (Oxford: Oxford University Press).
    1989   *The Selfish Gene* (Oxford: Oxford University Press, new edn).
    1993   'Viruses of the Mind', in B. Dahlbom (ed.), *Dennett and his Critics: Demys-tifying Mind* (Oxford: Basil Blackwell): 13-27.
    1995   *River out of Eden: A Darwinian View of Life* (London: Weidenfeld & Nicholson).

Dennett, D.C.
    1991   *Consciousness Explained* (London: Allen Lane).
    1995   *Darwin's Dangerous Idea* (London: Allen Lane).
Dinesen, I.
    1985   *Out of Africa/Shadows on the Grass* (Harmondsworth: Penguin Books).
Jones, S.
    1996   *In the Blood: God, Genes and Destiny* (London: HarperCollins).
Medawar, P.
    1977   'Unnatural Science', *The New York Review of Books* 3 (February): 13-18.
Plotkin, H.
    1994   *Darwin Machines and the Nature of Knowledge: Concerning Adaptations, Instinct and the Evolution of Intelligence* (London: Penguin Books).
Pollack, R.
    1994   *Signs of Life: The Language and Meanings of DNA* (London: Penguin Books).
Sagan, C.
    1996   *The Demon-Haunted World: Science as a Candle in the Dark* (London: Headline Book Publishing).
Stanford, P.
    1997   'Jesus Christ's Smarter Brother', *The Guardian* 2; 25 February: 2-3.
The Bible and Culture Collective
    1995   *The Postmodern Bible* (New Haven: Yale University Press).

Whatever Happened to Dionysus?

Alice Bach

Once again, in the earliest ideas of Europe, we find an emphasis on what is human over and above what is, at one moment or another, held to be divine. Gods may come and gods may go, but we, with any luck, go on forever.

Salmon Rushdie, New York Times, 14 February 1997

'We must remember that until very recently Nigeria was British,' said Miss Spurgeon. 'It was pink on the map. In some old atlases it still is.' Letty felt that with the ways things were going, nothing was pink on the map any more.

Barbara Pym, Quartet in Autumn (London: Macmillan, 1977)

I have been thinking about God lately, that is, the god of Israel. He is the only divinity who frightens my students. Their literary ability does not extend to analyzing his behavior in the biblical narratives we read in class. They are quite skeptical of the idiosyncratic Zeus, sardonic about Inanna and her manipulations of Gilgamesh; but they, of course, are not gods, but merely literary figures in Greek or ancient Near Eastern myths. Attracted by Nietzsche's penchants for abstractions, students write romantically but definitively of the chaotic world of Dionysus and the rational universe preferred by Apollo. But when it comes to considering the god of Israel as the master of the chaos in the book of Judges they fall silent. Goaded by my improper questions, they switch roles, from suspicious readers of literary texts to pious protectors of the god of Israel. Perhaps he needs their earnest protection. He is after all the only god left in Western culture. Why are my students never drawn to the ebullient, dancing and drinking Dionysus, so much more like themselves than the celibate isolated god of Israel?

A cultural analysis of the canonization of 'God' within the mythos of Greece and Rome, the Mediterranean roots of European culture, allows the biblical scholar to assume a perspective in respect to divinity that has been denied us. My own reasons for reading Greek texts against biblical ones stem from the same inclination as classical scholar and Chair in

Comparative Studies of Ancient Religions at the Collège de France Jean-Pierre Vernant more than 25 years ago discussing the perspectives provided by classical texts:

> The works ancient Greece created are different enough from that of our mental universe to give us a sense of disorientation from ourselves, to give us, along with the feeling of a historical distance, the consciousness of a change in the person. At the same time they are not foreign to us as others are. They are transmitted to us without a loss of continuity. They are still living in the cultural tradition to which we remain attached.[1]

I would extend Vernant's position to the works of the ancient Near East and Egypt, most particularly the biblical narratives that reflect a religion that is remote to us but provides the roots of the Western religious traditions that involve us today. This Eurocentric viewpoint is further emphasized by the lack of scholarly interest in pursuit of the connection between the singular Egyptian god Akhenaten and the figure of Moses. The examination of a Moses–Egypt discourse has been approached by figures as different as Freud and Bernal, but in general scholars of classics and of the Bible are comfortable to blur if not ignore the basic distinctions that were symbolized by the antagonistic constellation of Israel and Egypt.[2] While those who argue for a Moses–Egyptian connection are aware of the vast differences between biblical religion and Egyptian religion, there are important similarities between Moses' construction of Israelite religion and the religion of Aten. As Assmann notes in analyzing Freud's argument for the connection between the two, 'he [Freud] takes the "long way" of comparing the religions involved and shows quite convincingly that Akhenaten's revolutionary religion meets all of the requirements of Biblical anti-Eyptianism'.[3] The basic principles of similarity are (1) the stress upon ethical requirements upon the individual, (2) exclusion of magical rituals, and (3) a lack of specific concepts of an afterlife. Both stress the mortality of the human being and both are aniconic.

---

1.   Jean-Pierre Vernant, *Mythe et pensée chez le Grecs* (1965), p. 10; *Myth and Thought among the Greeks* (ET; London: Routledge & Kegan Paul, 1983).

2.   The basic points of antagonism between Egyptian and Israelite religion are the biblical condemnation of magic and images, the negation of a pantheon of deities and its concomitant insistence on only one god, and the emphasis on ethical as opposed to ritual purity.

3.   Jan Assmann, *Moses the Egyptian* (Cambridge, MA: Harvard University Press, 1997), p. 153.

Crossing those mental boundaries that have discouraged a comparative study of Yahweh and Aten, biblical religion with the religion of Aten, like the study of Dionysus and his cult in relation to the study of Yahweh and Israelite religion, is fraught with landmines. For the most part, the practice of disciplinary essentialism has kept traditional biblicists behind their borders, following only one trajectory, the one that 'God' took, north through Europe.[4] In spite of the special affinity between the Greek tradition and the biblical one, the fear of disciplinary border crossings is not surprising. For any biblicist tempted to try such peri-Mediterranean comparisons, the contempt sprayed upon the efforts of W. Robertson Smith and Sir James Frazer to compare biblical and classical texts acts as a scholarly slap in the face.[5] Since 'God' is the only deity in the canon, 'God' has provided the model of what the category of God should look like. This category of one is supported and reflected in the first commandment: 'You shall have no other god before me'. Of course in ancient cultures, other gods did exist, only a few miles away. Thus, believers had a real choice to make. What Western cultural memory seems to have erased is the monotheistic period in Egypt in the figure of Akhenaten. The problem of course is that such a 'Moses as Egyptian' discourse benefits neither Jewish nor Christian biblical claims, and would require a reinscription of the myth of Western civilization. Freud himself seems to have been resigned to the erasure of Egypt. First, he raises the question, 'Why did nobody among those who identified

4.   Henry Louis Gates points out the continuing problems of imagining our disciplinary boundaries as hermetic in *Loose Canons: Notes on the Culture Wars* (New York: Oxford University Press, 1992). Gates points out the irony in departments called comparative literature, when the literatures under investigation are French, German, Italian, but not the languages and literatures of Yoroba, Urdu or Arabic (pp. 116-17).

5.   The devaluing of scholarship that goes against the agenda of those scholars who control a discipline is not unusual. See comments later in this essay about the Lefkowitz series of essays excoriating the project of Martin Bernal, which is certainly a clear-cut example. See Mary R. Lefkowitz and Guy MacLean Rogers (eds.), *Black Athena Revisited* (Chapel Hill: University of North Carolina Press, 1996). See also Mary R. Lefkowitz, *Not Out of Africa* (New York: Basic Books, 1996). When Elaine Pagels first published her popular edition of some Nag Hammadi texts, *The Gnostic Gospels* (New York: Random House, 1979), the scholarly buzz among those in control of New Testament scholarship was that Pagels's Coptic was weak. Her translations were inaccurate. See especially Raymond E. Brown, *New York Times Book Review* (June 1979).

the Egyptian etymology of the name Moses consider the possibility that Moses was an Egyptian?', and then eventually he rejects the Egyptian heritage of Moses with a 'strange note of resignation'.[6] Freud sets up a straw-dog argument, stating that the Bible itself proves the lack of Egyptian lineage since there is no exact date of Moses' birth (in Egypt) nor a historical account of the Exodus from Egypt to be found there. Therefore, 'the publication of all further conclusions that could be drawn from the fact that he was an Egyptian has to stop'.[7] However, the proof or proclamation of Moses as an Egyptian is quite a different argument from what the biblical writers claimed that Moses taught about religion.[8]

Following Freud's decision to stop being tempted by the Egyptian possibilities, I shall focus in this investigation upon the trajectory of Yahweh and the religions and culture rooted in the western Mediterranean world. Thus, I shall be carried along the current of cultural studies, in arguing that the pull of pan-European beginnings that awarded cultural priority and privilege to ancient Greece over Egypt and the Near East became a proxy fight for cultural prestige, one that continues to be waged in certain academic circles. The triumph of the classical Greek civilization in the name of an eternal 'West' has resulted in a rewriting of history that has united a mythic unified Greek civilization with its equally mythic 'Judeo-Christian' religion. Within the cultural reinscription of ancient history, Israel is not part of the Afro-Asiatic landscape. Politics has overdetermined cultural geography and presented us with a schoolroom cultural cliché: a singular focus on the double cradle of democracy and Christianity.

By following the scholarly dedivination of Dionysus, I hope to catch scholars in the act of unmasking Dionysus, and return the 'man masquerading as a god masquerading as a man' of Euripides' play *The Bacchae* back to divinity status—if only for the duration of this essay. For it is only when the reader has a sense of Dionysus as a divinity that a

---

6.   Assmann, *Moses the Egyptian*, p. 150.

7.   Assmann, *Moses the Egyptian*, p. 150.

8.   The temptation remains to follow a line of argument in which Moses is translating and making overt what has been preserved under cover of the hieroglyphs in the Egyptain mystery cult. For further discussion of Freud's Egyptomania, see Peter Gay, *A Godless Jew: Friend, Atheism, and the Making of Psychoanalysis* (New Haven: Yale University Press, 1987); and Yosef Yerushalmi, *Freud's Moses: Judaism Terminable and Interminable* (New Haven: Yale University Press, 1991).

comparison of the god Dionysus in Euripides' *Bacchae* with the Yahweh god in the biblical book of Judges can occur. Ordinarily a contemporary reader uses a theological code to read the character of Yahweh God and a literary code for the pagan gods in peri-Mediterranean texts. This overpowering of the literary code in relation to Yahweh with the theological code and the insistence upon using the attributes of Yahweh God as the model for 'proper' divinity are two major elements in the dedivinizing of the Greek gods in literary analysis.

Through the miracle of nineteenth-century cultural transcriptions and recreations of the glories of Greece and Rome, whole continents were turned into slave continents. At the same time that Victorian England was inscribing its colonial empire, Victorian artists and poets in connection with their infatuation with ancient Greek culture struggled with the figures of the Greek gods. Dionysus does not play the powerful role that he had in former times. Indeed, most of the figures from classical epics are now located in the world of metaphor rather than in the external, visible, literal world. By the beginning of the twentieth century, the influence of Freud and Jung had spread, until readers and literary theorists alike forced the epic inward. The *Odyssey* abandoned Homer's islands and seas to become Joyce's *Ulysses*, a journey of the psyche which took place within a single town on a single day. Long before this moment, Zeus had ceased to hurl his thunderbolt. But the suggestion of a continuum of sensibility plunges us into the period's dominant cultural milieu. And so I urge my students and myself to think of the Greek gods as divine, at least long enough to compare their behavior—scurrilous, bumptious, erotic, sly—with similar qualities revealed in the actions of Yahweh God.

From Plato to NATO

Since one of my concerns in this investigation is to understand how the God of ancient Afro-Asiatic Israel got to be the God of European civilization, I need to glance at the axis east–west. Like its orientalizing counterpart the 'East', the 'West' is a fictional construct embroidered with myths and fantasies.[9] Israel is seen as a Western country, while

9. In a geographic sense, too, the concept is relative. What the West calls the Middle East is from a Chinese perspective Western Asia. Situated in California, one refers to the Far East, which lies a few thousand watery miles to the west. In Arabic, the word for west (*magreb*) refers to North Africa, the westernmost part of the Arab world, in contrast to the *mashreq,* the eastern part. For a history of the way the term

Turkey (much of which lies to the west of Israel), Egypt, Libya and
Morocco are all 'Eastern'. My point here is to call attention to the arbitrariness of the standard cartographies of identity because they influence
designations of readings of literary pantheons and theological texts.[10]

If Edward Said in *Orientalism*[11] points to the Eurocentric construction
of the East within Western writing, others, such as Martin Bernal, point
to the complementary Eurocentric construction of the West via the
obliterating or 'writing out' of the East (and Africa). Bernal describes the
process in relation to Africa in *Black Athena*:

> If it had been scientifically proved that Blacks were biologically incapable
> of civilization, how could one explain Ancient Egypt—which was incon-
> veniently placed on the African continent? There were two, or rather
> three solutions. The first was to deny that the ancient Egyptians were
> black; the second was to deny that the ancient Egyptians had created a
> civilization; the third was to make doubly sure by denying both. The last
> has been preferred by most 19th and 20th century historians.[12]

Bernal distinguishes between the 'Ancient model', which simply assumed
classical Greek civilization's deep indebtedness to both African (Egyptian
and Ethiopian) and Semitic civilizations, and the 'Aryan model', which
developed in the wake of slavery and colonialism. Evidence for the
Ancient model appears in 'a mass of literary and artistic circumstantial
evidence' suggesting that the Ancient model existed in Archaic (776–
550 BCE) and possibly Geometric times (950–776 BCE).[13] The early

'West' becomes overlaid, see Raymond Williams, *Keywords: A Vocabulary of Culture
and Society* (New York: Oxford University Press, 1976).

10. There is of course a north–south axis, to which the Victorians adhere, contrasting their own cold, pragmatic north with the sunny, erotic Mediterranean,
where the Greeks disported. Dickens uses two schools to show the contrast: Grad-
grind's school is characteristic of northern England—scientific, utilitarian, factual—
while down in Sussex Dr Blimber offers a wholly classical training to the children of
the upper middle class. 'Mrs. Gaskell's contrast of south and north is a contrast
between gentry and bourgeoisie, between leisure and industry; but it also marks the
opposition between past and present, between ancient Greece and Victorian England' (Richard Jenkyns, *The Victorians and Ancient Greece* [Oxford: Basil Blackwell,
1980], p. 48). See further *idem, Dignity and Decadence: Victorian Art and the Classical
Inheritance* (London: HarperCollins, 1991).

11. New York: Pantheon Books, 1978.

12. Martin Bernal, *Black Athena: The Afroasiatic Roots of Classical Civilization*. I.
The Fabrication of Ancient Greece 1785–1985 (London: Free Association Books,
1987), p. 241.

13. Martin Bernal, *Black Athena: The Afroasiatic Roots of Classical Civilization*. II.

dating for this model allows Bernal to argue for the advantage of the Ancient model having existed nearer the period it concerned than the Aryan model.

Another aspect of Bernal's project to undermine the originality of Greek culture is his focus upon Hermetic practice, once again insisting upon an early dating to give the Hermetic material chronologic priority over the other contemporary syncretic religious movements, Neo-Platonism and Gnosticism. This move allows Bernal to argue Egyptian influence and primacy over the Greek, emphasizing the heavily Egyptian nature of Hermetism over the more Hellenistic qualities of Neoplatonism and Gnosticism. This dating squabble involves the Hermetic texts that developed from the blend between the Egyptian deity Thoth and the Greek Hermes. Most scholars agree that the manifestation of this commingling—the god Hermes Trimegistus—was worshipped in rituals that drew upon both Greek and Egyptian practice. As Fowden points out, 'the Olympians seemed out of place on the banks of the Nile. Even in areas that had a large Greek population, the immigrants were often happy to attach themselves to the dominant local gods'.[14] The conflict arises from Bernal's habit of taking a position of scholarly agreement (the syncretistic nature of the Egyptian–Greek rituals, particularly in Alexandria) and pushing the argument, in this case by following Flinders Petrie's dating of parts of the Hermetic literature as early as the sixth century BCE. By traveling back in time, back to the work of Petrie, who seems to have been discounted by Eurocentric scholars, Bernal is able to continue his push toward an Egyptocentric and often explicitly Hermetic view of early modern European thought.

The Aryan model, established in the Victorian era, had to perform ingenious acrobatics to 'purify' classical Greece of all African and Asian contaminations. It had to explain away Greek homages to Afro-Asiatic cultures, such as Homer's descriptions of the 'blameless Ethiopians' and the frequent references to the *kalos kagathos* (handsome and good) Africans.[15] Not surprisingly the scholars structuring the Aryan model

The Archaeological and Documentary Evidence (London: Free Association Books, 1991), p. 4.

14. Garth Fowden, *Egyptian Hermes: A Historical Approach to the Late Pagan Mind* (Cambridge: Cambridge University Press, 1986), pp. 19-20.

15. Another cultural blur occurs in the representation of Africa as a sub-Saharan area of the continent, sustaining the artificial gap between European civilization and the strange Other. The American film factory turned out the Tarzan films in the

sought to justify European and American imperialism and colonialism, which was at its highest tide from 1880–1940. Since this was also a period in which humanist scholars—and I include here archaeologists, classicists, and biblicists—wished to appear scientistic, they did not indulge in speculative theories, but were rather more comfortable with the pointillism of arguing small details. Since sweeping theories can result in charges of speculation or irresponsibility, scholars took the safer route and juggled theories of dating and provenance for ancient activities.

Bernal proposed to replace the Aryan model with the Revised Ancient model, which would accept that Egyptians and Phoenicians settled in and had a massive influence upon ancient Greece, while considering the fact that Greek is fundamentally an Indo-European language. In the conclusion to Volume 1, Bernal writes that the

> conception in sin or ever error [of the Aryan Model] does not necessarily invalidate it. Darwinism, which was created at very much the same time and for many of the same 'disreputable' motives, has remained a very useful heuristic scheme. One could perfectly well argue that Niebuhr, Muller, Curtius, and others were 'sleep-walking' in the sense that Arthur Koestler used the term—to describe useful 'scientific' discoveries made for extraneous reasons and purposes which are not accepted in later times. All that I claim for this volume is that it has provided a case to be answered. That is, if the dubious origin of the Aryan Model does not make it false, it does call into question its inherent superiority over the Ancient Model.[16]

One flaw in Bernal's system enters with the suggestion that the Ancient model is innocent. He indicates this position by interpreting the ancient texts at face value, avoiding a critical analysis of traditions, conferring on myths the value of true history.[17] This concept of a serene core of cultural values at the center of Western civilization is of course false. Part of

---

thirties, in which the colonial clash between the European and the African was evaded, but continued to mythify the Eurocentric view of the African–European relationship. Later action films such as *Stanley and Livingstone* (1939), *Mogambo* (1953) and *Hatari* (1962) continued the double-edged process of mythification and defamation that had operated in relation to African cultures and the African continent.

16. Bernal, *Black Athena*, I.

17. In the view of Mario Liverani, 'hardly a single chapter (or even page) of *Black Athena* escapes the blame of ignoring correct methodology, adopting old-fashioned explanations, and omitting relevant data and literature'; Liverani, in Lefkowitz and Rogers (eds.), *Black Athena Revisited*, p. 425. I cite Liverani, rather than other contributors to this volume, because I believe his article to be calmer and freer of the classical frisson that many of his colleagues exhibit in this collection.

this construction has been generated by his misreading of ancient literary and historical texts as a bias-free mirror of what happened. Bernal adds more motives to the mix in claiming that the men who established the Aryan model were racists and anti-Semites. While Bernal claims to promote Africa, he remains Eurocentric in approach and method. He neither attempts to show that the values or achievements of African societies are independent of the West or superior to it. Rather, his argument is temporal, concerned with establishing that African achievements were anterior to those of classical and later Western civilization and that these achievements were subsequently diffused to much of the world.

Those scholars who argue for a linear production of *Wissenschaft* seem to think that our job as scholars is singular: to transmit knowledge, not to create it. If, however, one of our tasks is to understand what we ourselves are about when we create history, the mirror is cracked. In fending off an attack on his own 'ideologic readings of biblical history', Thomas Thompson has drawn a line in the sand with which I am comfortable. While defining what he understands as his role as a historian of ancient history, he writes,

> In no way would I restrict the kinds of questions to be asked of the past. Rather I address the code of our discipline in answering questions in a disciplined and critical way, beginning from within the grounds of what we, in fact, know about the past and addressing that much greater world of the unknown and the not yet known.[18]

While Thompson presents a sharp critique of the politics of present-day Euro-American academia, it must be said that he is just to the West of disingenuous when he ignores the politics of his own Hellenistic dating of the Hebrew Scriptures. While he and his colleagues Philip Davies and Niels Peter Lemche have suggested to biblicists the importance of looking at ancient Israelite history as it is inscribed in the Bible as a nationalist literary fiction (my term, not theirs), they omit the parallel notion of what Mikhail Bakhtin has defined as 'chronotypes', mediating between the historical and the discursive, providing fictional environments where historically specific constellations of power are made visible. Like Bernal, Thompson and Lemche have been pilloried by members of the academy, although it seems to me that there is nothing inherently sinister in their project—except that it may be deployed

18. Thomas L. Thompson, *JBL* 114 (1995), p. 683.

asymmetrically, to the advantage of some national and ethno-racial imaginaries and to the detriment of others. They have not to my knowledge tried to close off or write out the work of other scholars, to put an intellectual lock on certain forms of discourse.

It seems clear from the attacks upon Afrocentrism in general and the passionate depths of the hostility toward Bernal's *Black Athena*,[19] by Mary Lefkowitz (and some of the other classicists she has gathered together in *Black Athena Revisited*), however, that these scholars assume that the classical world has already revealed its secrets, and they need not inhabit a position that considers 'addressing that much greater world of the unknown and the not yet known'.

In *Not Out of Africa* Lefkowitz argues for a clear-eyed view of ancient Mediterranean history—her own:

> It is another question whether or not diversity should be applied to the truth. Are there, can there be, multiple, diverse 'truths'? If there are, which 'truth' should win? That one that is most loudly argued, or most persuasively phrased? Diverse 'truths' are possible only if 'truth' is understood to mean something like 'point of view' ... The notion of diversity does not extend to truth.[20]

Throughout her polemic, Lefkowitz assumes for herself the power to define: to define the role of the academy, scholarship and the ideological stance of *other* scholars.[21] She does not accept that setting critical

---

19. In the Preface to Volume 2 of *Black Athena*, Bernal writes of 'one Indo-European linguist who compares my work—in private conversation—to that of the 'revisionists' who deny that the Holocaust ever took place' (p. xix). Another example, in my opinion, of scholars attempting to create a battle where none should exist. Many of the blustery attacks on Bernal have the fictive flavor of accusing him of scandalous behavior and threatening to horsewhip the fellow on the steps of a London club.

20. Lefkowitz, *Not Out of Africa*, p. 162.

21. An additional power is illustrated by Lefkowitz's book, the power to publish with a mainstream press. Her book is published by Basic Books, a division of the megalith Murdoch-owned HarperCollins, while many of the Afrocentrist books she critiques are available through such publishers as Africa World Press in Trenton, NJ; Alkebu-lan Books in New York City; and Black Classic Press in Baltimore, MD. The power of the press brings along with it the money for media-savvy advertising and promotion campaigns, an extensive sales force for wide distribution and the capital and warehouse space to keep the book in print. For positive versions of Afrocentrism, see Innocent Chilaka Onyewuenyi, *The African Origin of Greek Philosophy: An Exercise in Afrocentrism* (Nsukka, Nigeria: University of Nigeria Press, 1993); C. Tsehloane Keto, *Vision, Identity, and Time: The Afrocentric Paradigm and the*

standards for scholarly competence is a value-laden process. Lefkowitz critiques the scholars whose 'motivation and identity have been taken as the equivalent of professional credentials'.[22] She is referring to Afro-centrists, attaching motives to their scholarship that she does not attri-bute to her own. That her agenda is to protect and promote the classics as prime Eurocentric currency is apparent to this reader if not to her. The effect of her bristling diatribe is to proclaim that the properly trained academician is the keeper of the keys of knowledge. Through their interpretations such scholars resist the winds of change and offer a timeless ideal, guaranteeing that the Eurocurrency will not be devalued.

What Bernal shares with most of his critics is the lack of an examina-tion of the constructedness of the basic concept of race. Acknowledging the slipperiness of defining race, Bernal reminds his scholarly audience that for the past 7000 years the population of Egypt has been a mix of African, South-West Asian, and Mediterranean types, but the civiliza-tion was fundamentally African.[23] It is with his use of the word *African* that one runs into difficulty, since the term seems as constructed and as full of myth as either *European* or the binary *white/black*.[24] Often he uses

Study of the Past (Dubuque, IA: Kendall/Hunt Publishing Co., 1995).

For Afrocentric interpretations of Christianity, see Glenn Usry and Craig S. Keener, *Black Man's Religion: Can Christianity Be Afrocentric?* (Downers Grove, IL: InterVarsity Press, 1996); Cheryl J. Sanders (ed.), *Living the Intersection: Womanism and Afrocentrism in Theology* (Minneapolis: Fortress Press, 1995).

22. Lefkowitz, *Not Out of Africa*, p. 166.

23. Bernal, *Black Athena*, I, p. 242.

24. For detailed whitewashing of the issue of who was black in the ancient Mediterranean world, see Frank M. Snowden, *Blacks in Antiquity: Ethiopians in the Greco-Roman World* (Cambridge, MA: Belknap Press of Harvard University Press, 1970); *idem, Before Color Prejudice: The Ancient View of Blacks* (Cambridge, MA: Har-vard University Press, 1983). In this earlier work Snowden claims that 'in spite of the association of blackness with ill omens, demons, the devil, and sin, there is in the extant records no stereotyped image of Ethiopians as the personification of demons or the devil', p. 107). It seems to be a thin argument, since connecting blackness with ill omens, demons, the devil and sin appears to me to be clearly the kind of negative stereotype that Snowden wants to deny.

A decade later, in *Black Athena Revisited*, Snowden attempts to be one of the boys, arguing, 'Many Afrocentrists, however, continue to reject valid criticism of their inaccuracies and denounce their critics as Eurocentric racists if they are white, and as dupes of white scholarship and traitors to their race if they are black. It is neither racist nor traitorous, however, to insist upon truth, scholarly rigor, and objectivity in the treatment of the history of blacks' (p. 117). Note that in his recent work (*Before*

the terms 'black', 'Egyptian' and 'African' interchangeably. Thus, Bernal shoots himself in the foot by generalizing about Eurocentric cultural politics, and maintaining a monolithic focus upon European imperialistic agendas. Therefore, Bernal's focus, like a monolithic focus upon any class or ethno-racial group, approaches a racist position—at the same time that it tries to decry Eurocentric racial supremacy.

In the first volume of *Black Athena*, Bernal traces the historiographic scholarship that resulted in the creation of the discipline of Classics as we know it today. He dates the finished product of Classics with precision: 1815–30, the period of the Greek War of Independence, when Christian Europe united against the traditional Islamic enemies from Asia and Africa.[25] First, it is ironic that Bernal, questioning the bias of cultural nationalism, goes back to the canon to establish historic credentials. Secondly, as he freely admits, he is more interested in exploring a 'sociology of knowledge' than in *proving* distant linguistic connections. In his claim that such proof is impossible, he clearly provokes those linguists who interpret their research as exactly that.

I do not want to leave the reader with the idea of a totally polarized scholarly discussion between Bernal on the one side and all classicists on the other. Each side occupies a sharply angled polarity of its own. Acknowledging the importance of Bernal's work for his insights about 'the biased approaches of former (and present) classical scholars',[26] Italian classical historian Mario Liverani agrees with his colleagues in the field of classics that Bernal's major difficulty lies in his lack of historical methodology and control of primary sources. Liverani is more even-handed, acknowledging the messiness of Bernal's work (his dismissing as biased the racist approaches of European scholars of past centuries, without understanding the rules these same scholars established in the areas of philology, etymology and comparative linguistics, and religio-historical method investigating the nature of myths and legends), but at the same time recognizing the importance of the larger questions that Bernal has raised, the questions that have become such irritants within the academy. Thus, Liverani does not try to blind the reader to the fact

Color Prejudice) Snowden introduces a political and ideological argument on the part of Afrocentrists and then allies himself with the objective, non-ideologic classicists who deal in fact and truth rather than ideology. Yet in his earlier work his examples show the color prejudice his argument tries to hide.

25. Bernal, *Black Athena*, I, pp. 440-41.
26. Liverani, in Lefkowitz and Rogers, *Black Athena Revisited*, p. 417.

that Bernal, like most of us, is both salt and wound.

What I find most interesting about this Bernal versus Classicists argument, which has taken on a life of its own, is simply that. Ordinarily, a book so riddled with errors involving basic philology and reading of myth as history would not have caused more than a ripple on the literary and scholarly landscape. But *Black Athena*, first published in England and then in the US by Rutgers University Press, a small publisher by any standards, has generated an industry: several major colloquia at national scholarly meetings; special issues of scholarly journals, more than 50 articles, the major scholarly collection, *Black Athena Revisited*, cited frequently in this essay, as well as Mary Lefkowitz's frequent protestations about the arguments and expertise of Bernal. The field of biblical studies, scarcely a stone's throw across the Mediterranean from classics has been uninterested in the Bernal debate—at least as far as I can tell. This silence reflects more of a disciplinary myopia, in my opinion, than a disinclination to deal with the subject of race within biblical literature. Bernal is classics' problem; 'we' have to struggle with the Jesus Seminar's obsession with the actual words Jesus spoke. The compartmentalism of knowledge that the scholarly disciplines exhibit in the case of Bernal versus the academy the need for a blending of approaches. The first tentative steps in this direction have been taken by scholars proposing interdisciplinary programs such as peri-Mediterranean studies.

Canon as God, God as Canon

As a cultural critic, I always keep one eye on 'the canon', the system through which my students learn about Western culture. According to a contemporary high priest of the religion of the Western canon, former US Secretary of Education William Bennett, one's responsibility to that iconic canon is to transmit Western (read 'European') culture intact from one generation to the next. Just as in the scholarly position argued by Lefkowitz, Bennett and his neoconservative ally, Allan Bloom, favor an imagery of purity and 'standards', of ancient fortresses defended against barbarian sieges.[27] Another 'eternalist', American historian

---

27. I suspect what Lefkowitz, Bennett and other neoconservatives find most threatening about multiculturalism is the intellectual and political regrouping by which different 'minorities' become a majority seeking to move beyond being 'tolerated' to forming active intercommunal coalitions.

Arthur Schlesinger invokes culinary language—'the melting pot' of American culture—and cooks up other culinary metaphors, such as the 'ethnic stew, tossed salad, gumbo, bouillabaisse, stir-fry'. This group of American public intellectuals encodes multiculturalism to mean 'progressive or left opposition' and 'people of color', both ideal scapegoats now that the Cold War has ended. Leaping from their frying pan of universalism into the fiery marinade of multiculturalism that results from attempting to situate a narrative within two cultural groups, I am brought back to the central concern of my investigation: if Bennett's privileged canon has been transmitted to us, whatever happened to Dionysus? How did the gods of Greece and Rome dissolve and the god of Israel become the only God awarded divine status in the canon?

While a superficial answer might begin with the observation that Constantine Christianized the Roman Empire in 333, and thus, the Greco-Roman gods lost their state power, that would imply that cultural change can occur within an instant. What would one do with the medieval habit of using typology to perform biblical exegesis? In such works there were frequently parallels between classical 'myth' and the Bible; Deucalion is taken to correspond to Noah, Hercules to Samson, the gods' overthrow of the giants is compared with the destruction of the Tower of Babel. An example of the survival of the Greco-Roman gods is found in Dante's *Inferno*, which describes Charon ferrying souls into a Christian Hell. More intricate parallels occur in Canto 12 of the *Purgatorio*, where classical and biblical mortal figures coexist in lyrical pairs:

> O Niobe, with what grieving eyes did I see you traced on the roadway between seven and seven children slain! O Saul, how upon your own sword did you appear there dead on Gilboa, which never thereafter felt rain or dew! O mad Arachne, did I see you already half spider, wretched on the shrouds of the work which to your own hurt was wrought by you! O Rehoboam, there your image does not seem to threaten now, but a chariot bears it off full of terror, and no one is in pursuit![28]

While Niobe and Arachne are not divine, their memorable challenges to proudful but vindictive goddesses determine their literary immortality. It is not within the scope of this investigation to argue the negative qualities of divinity possessed by the classical gods compared with the high Christology found in Dante's works, or to investigate why the Greek

---

28. Dante, *The Divine Comedy*, *Purgatorio*, XII, ll. 37-48.

mortals are paired only with Old Testament figures, but rather to indicate that there is not a specific cultural moment in time at which the Greek gods ceased to be divine, or that Western writers cased to weave Greek literary figures into Christocentric texts.

Nevertheless, the desire to pinpoint the moment of the death of various gods persists. Classicist A.H. Henrichs has argued widely that the modern tendency to understand the Greek god as a personification of powers located within the human being was first exemplified by Nietzsche in *Birth of Tragedy* (1872).[29] Tracing the cultural landslide that 'destroyed Dionysus as a god even as [Nietzsche] preserved him as a concept', Henrichs notes that Nietzsche transplanted the fertility god from the natural world first onto the tragic stage and from there directly into the human psyche.[30] But while Nietzsche argued that Dionysus was the antithesis to the Apollonian figure of order—flute to lyre, music to sculpture—he seems to have honored the powers of these gods within the ancient world to be mediators between the humans and the abyss. He warns the too casual reader, 'Whoever approaches these Olympians with another religion is his heart, searching among them for moral elevation...will soon be forced to turn his back on them, discouraged and disappointed. For there is nothing here that suggests asceticism, spirituality, or duty'.[31] In spite of his weighing down these gods with abstractions, Nietzsche's recognition of 'another religion' seems to suggest at least a residual respect for the divine element in their makeup. And more important for this investigation is Nietzsche's intuitive focus upon a connection between Dionysus and the Christian god (the heir of Yahweh).

29. F. Nietzsche, *Birth of Tragedy* (New York: Vintage Books, 1967). Note especially A.H. Henrichs, 'Greek Maenadism from Olympias to Messalina', *Harvard Studies in Classical Philology* 82 (1979), pp. 121-60; *idem*, 'Greek and Roman Glimpses of Dionysus', in C. Houser (ed.), *Dionysus and his Circle: Ancient through Modern* (Cambridge, MA: Fogg Art Museum, 1984); *idem*, 'Loss of Self, Suffering, Violence: The Modern View of Dionysus from Nietzsche to Girard', *Harvard Studies in Classical Philology* 88 (1990), pp. 205-40; *idem*, 'Between Country and City: Cultic Dimensions of Dionysus in Athens and Attica', in Mark Griffith and D.J. Mastronarde (eds.), *Cabinet of the Muses: Studies in Honor of T.G. Rosenmeyer* (Atlanta: Scholars Press, 1990).

30. A.H. Henrichs, 'He Has a God in Him: Human and Divine in the Modern Perception of Dionysus', in T.H. Carpenter and C.A. Faraone (eds.), *Masks of Dionysus* (Ithaca: Cornell University Press, 1993), pp. 13-43.

31. Nietzsche, *Birth of Tragedy*, p. 41.

In comparing the Christian god as a figure of death and sacrifice who led to eternal hope, Nietzsche argues that the Greek gods were reminders of life, amid the sure knowledge that finality awaited. In describing a Greek festival, Nietzsche writes, 'only the curious blending and duality in the emotions of the Dionysian revelers remind us—as medicines remind us of deadly poisons—of the phenomenon that pain begets joy, the ecstasy may wring sounds of agony from us'.[32] How different is this lush emotional landscape from the lifeless Christianity he decries.

> Behind this [Christian] mode of thought and valuation, which must be hostile to art if it is at all genuine, I never failed to sense a *hostility to life*— a furious, vengeful antipathy to life itself: for all of life is based on semblance, art, deception, points of view, and the necessity of perspectives and error. Christianity was from the beginning, essentially and fundamentally, life's nausea and disgust with life, merely concealed behind, masked by, dressed up as, faith in 'another' or 'better' life. Hatred of 'the world' condemnations of the passions, fear of beauty and sensuality, a beyond invented the better to slander this life . . .'[33]

Along with the hostility to life that Nietzsche identifies in Christianity, there is a tension within the creative human mind between the Dionysian and Apollonian impulses. Clearly this pattern has been of major influence in the discourse of aesthetics and literature in the twentieth century. It is interesting that Freud's thought follows similar patterns, although the lines of influence between Freud and Nietzsche are blurred. Nietzsche's ideas of tragedy were partly dependent upon Wagner, and Wagner claimed that his idea of music drama descended from Aeschylus and the Greek stage. These cases suggest to me that the ancient classical world had indeed played a part in forming some of the most distinctively modern aspects of twentieth-century culture. But the influence appears to be Greek rather than Roman.[34] The strongest comparisons and classical reflections for the British came in the connection between the British and Roman empires. Pater had envisioned both Greek and Roman influence knit into the tools of British civilization. There was for Matthew Arnold a sense that the British and the Romans

32. Nietzsche, *Birth of Tragedy*, p. 40.
33. Nietzsche, *Birth of Tragedy*, p. 23.
34. The heavily Greek influence can also be seen in the early anthropology of Frazer, who begins his search for the golden bough in a dark corner of Italian religion, the grove of Nemi, where the priest was an escaped slave who came to office by murdering his predecssor. And one must admit to the influence amid the Decadents of Apuleius's *Golden Ass*, found in Gautier, Pater, Huysmans.

were the only two capable governing nations. And of course in the opening of Henry James's *The Golden Bowl* (1904), Prince Amerigo, an Italian whose views are more American than continental, remarks that he envisions himself 'one of the modern Romans who find by the Thames a more convincing image of the truth of that ancient state than any they have left by the Tiber'.[35]

Rather than choosing between the Greeks and the Romans, their gods and the God of the Empire, Matthew Arnold tried to portray a harmonized version in *Culture and Anarchy*. In trying to move between his own schematized poles of Hebraism and Hellenism, he defines the poles using a racial theory of history: 'Hellenism is of Indo-European growth. Hebraism is of Semitic growth; and we English, a nation of Indo-European stock, seem to belong naturally to the movement of Hellenism.'[36] Who would believe, Arnold asks, 'that the delicate and apprehensive genius of the Indo-European race will find its last word on the subject of sexual morality in the institutions of a Semitic people, whose wisest king had seven hundred wives and three hundred concubines?'[37] Disabling Hebraism as a moral system of conduct and obedience, he portrays God as a governess, perhaps a British nanny, ordering the children of Israel by a series of moral commands. He goes on to remove Christ from Christianity, by presenting it not as a saving gospel but as a moral code: 'Christianity... occupied itself, like Hebraism, with the moral side of man exclusively... and so far it was but a continuation of Hebraism.[38] Like Freud, he dismisses the authority of Scripture as the diminished voice of memory.

As can be seen from the tone of Arnold's work, the construction of Hellenism was changing in character. Greek ideals and Greek art were characterized as pure and clear and calm. The Victorian notion of Greek life was becoming 'less an active enquiry into the past and more a symbol for a certain type of aesthetic ideal which aimed at calm, balance, and proportion, or at any rate celebrated these qualities in the art of the past'.[39] Classics were becoming more and more associated with

---

35. Henry James, *The Golden Bowl* (London, 1904).

36. Matthew Arnold, *Culture and Anarchy and Other Writings* (ed. Stefan Collini; Cambridge: Cambridge University Press, 1993), Chapter 4.

37. I have created this sentence from fragments of Arnold's prose from Chapters 4 and 7 of *Culture and Anarchy*.

38. Arnold, *Culture and Anarchy*, p. 95.

39. Jenkyns, *Victorians and Ancient Greece*, p. 275.

opposition to political and social reform. Jenkyns characterizes the idealization of Hellenism in the classical education of the elite as

> a tendency towards hero-worship; among old-fashioned dons and school-masters this tendency was worsened by a fear of conceding anything to the enemies of classical education, among the aesthetes by Pater's rhapsodic account of antiquity, which collapsed unless the Greeks were assumed to be virtually without fault.[40]

A fictional account of the antipathy between modernism and classics can be seen in Sir Compton MacKenzie's novel *Sinister Street*:

> 'You stinking Modern beasts! Classics to the rescue!'—and physics and chemistry textbooks scattered in the corridors. Then again there was the Classical v. Modern rugby match: 'Into that game Michael poured… detestation for everything that the Modern side stood for… They were at Thermopylae, stemming the Persian charges…[41]

When in the 1920s Virginia Woolf caricatured the lofty world of classics and canon, she added the element of gender, firmly nailing in place the connection between the male desire for control of education and the method that had been employed. In her novel *Jacob's Room*, Woolf describes both a male and a female don at Cambridge:

> Sopwith went on talking, talking, talking—as if everything could be talked—the soul itself slipped through the lips in thin silver disks which dissolve in young men's minds like silver, like moonlight. Off, far away they'd remember it, and deep in dullness gaze back on it, and come to refresh themselves again.[42]

---

40. Jenkyns, *Victorians and Ancient Greece*, pp. 275-76. Jenkyns also reminds us of another side of the classics for the elite at British public schools: 'At Harrow [Byron] has been amused to be given an expurgated edition of Martial, in which the objectional epigrams were removed from the main text and printed together at the back, so that the smutty schoolboy was spared the trouble of reading the whole volume' (Jenkyns, *Victorians and Ancient Greece*, p. 280). In a similar vein, in George Eliot's *Middlemarch*, Lydgate is described as having enough of a classical education to read the indecencies in each book. The classics were clearly a male preserve, and the naughtiness of the authors of the ancient world were an added incentive to study them. George Eliot herself was a classicist, who even turned to the Greeks when she was ill. Referring to his partner's fixation upon the ancient world, Henry Lewes wrote, 'She sits up in bed and buries herself in Dante or Homer' (Jenkyns, *Victorians and Ancient Greece*, p. 113).

41. Compton MacKenzie, *Sinister Street* (London: Martin Secker, 1913), Ch. 4.

42. Virginia Woolf, *Jacob's Room* (London: Hogarth Press, 1929).

But language is wine upon his lips. Nowhere else would Virgil hear the like. And though as she goes sauntering along the Backs, old Miss Umphelby sings him melodiously enough, accurately too, she is always brought up by this question as she reaches Clare Bridge: 'But if I meet him, what should I wear?'—and then, taking her way up the avenue towards Newnham, she lets her fancy play upon other details of men's meeting with women which have never got into print. Her lectures, therefore, are not half so well attended as those of Cowan, and the thing she might have said in the elucidation of the text for ever left out.[43]

It must be emphasized that these changes of perspective were cultural rather than linear. In spite of the British upper-class Victorian reveling in the world of Greek myth, narrative, architecture and vase paintings, it was the *flavor* of Greece, its thought rather than its religion, that the British admired. Thus, we are no closer to pinpointing a cultural moment at which Dionysus lost his divinity than Miss Umphelby was to filling the seats of her lecture hall.

But that desire to dwell in the mythic clouds of Olympus is still warm, if not hot. Like the biblical characters who populate the unconscious of Western civilization, even for nonbelievers, Greek mortals and immortals still shadow our literary lives. It is the need to sing them melodiously, without the mediation of the highly structured scholastic's canon, that might restore Dionysus and his kind to their divine state—if only for a moment in scholarly time. For the postmodern reader, Dionysus is particularly attractive. Blurring the boundaries between God and human, between human and beast, between visible and invisible, Dionysus tempts the reader to infuse text with a divinity that is so immanent as to be sometimes undetectable. And thus, a literary character is quantified and analyzed, and a deity flickers and fades.

'Zeus is just a story now', writes Salman Rushdie in the *New York Times*, reflecting the same perspective as my students. 'He is powerless, but Europa is alive'.[44] Simultaneously with demoting Zeus from divinity to protagonist, he recalls the myth that brought mythic Europe into being. As Italian novelist Roberto Calasso puts it, 'Europe began with a bull and a rape'.[45] Traveling back through time along mythic roads, back to the archaic world, we encounter the Asian maiden Europa, who

43. Woolf, *Jacob's Room*.

44. *New York Times*, 14 February 1997.

45. Roberto Calasso, *The Marriage of Cadmus and Harmony* (translated from the Italian by Tim Parks; New York: Alfred A. Knopf, 1st American edn, 1993).

became the beloved of Zeus. Europa was abducted by Zeus (who changed himself into a white bull for the occasion) and held captive in a new land that came, in time, to bear her name. The prisoner of Zeus's unending desire for mortal flesh, Europa has been avenged by history, enshrined in the canon. But the stop-time of the literary canon is enlivened by the movement of history. Rushdie wants history to be more powerful than the canon, envisioning history as human and the canon as the discarded divine. At the very dawn of the idea of Europe is an unequal struggle between human beings and gods and, for Rushdie, an encouraging lesson: 'While the bull-god (Zeus) may win the first skirmish, it is the maiden-Continent (Europa) that triumphs in time'.[46] The object of a *fatwa* proclaimed by the Ayatollah Ruhollah Khomeini eight years ago, Rushdie claims that we live in the time when the tyranny of the gods should be vanquished. 'The loss of the divine places us at the center of the stage', Rushdie insists.[47]

The 'us' provides a clue to Rushdie's angst. It is little wonder that when people sought to wrest control of their persons and lands from imperialists and colonizers, they should begin by claiming the right to represent themselves. But like Bernal, Rushdie is caught between the worlds of black and white. His 'us' is a hybrid; his perspective a mirror of Bernal's. As a colonized person, he is seemingly outside the traditional European story, yet it is within the Western world that he found his own place in the sun as a writer and public intellectual. Reading Rushdie's 'Indian–Anglian' work made clear to me the fragility of identity. As he observes rather tartly about criticism of his own work from the Indian subcontinent,

> the ironic proposition that India's best writing since independence may have been done in the language of the departed imperialists is simply too much for some folks to bear. It ought not to be true, and so must not be permitted to be true.[48]

I find it odd that Rushdie can write with such surety of the death of god while writing of the necessity of his own dodging of Khomeini's thunderbolts. What sort of bravado has lulled him into thinking that history has indeed subsumed the theological canon? Rather history has enshrined one god within the canon, and expelled all others. What

46. *New York Times*, 14 February 1997.
47. *New York Times*, 14 February 1997.
48. *The New Yorker*, 23 and 30 June 1997.

Rushdie has been experiencing is the outrage of one who has observed the overturning of the natural order of things: Eastern thunderbolts permeating the privileged protected Western landscape. As he has acknowledged in writing about the minor arrows that have been aimed at him 'from home' about his own work written in English, 'One's man's ghetto of privilege is another's road to freedom'.[49]

The God of Epiphanies

It is smack in the middle of the Western cultural landscape that we find God, our God, who sprang from Yahweh, the god of Israel, without history or family, autochthonous. While the privileging of our God occurred centuries before nineteenth-century reconstructions of classicism, the theological focus on God by faithful interpreters resulted in apathy toward comparing our established God with any of the former Gods of the Mediterranean world. The anti-Semitism of classicists, which embraced Greek civilization and rejected the ancient Near East, allowed these excellent scholars to overlook the Semitic influences on the Aegean trading partners, influences that provided both alphabetic writing and iron technology as well as many foundational myths to the Western Mediterranean world. Liverani sees other important cultural trends that moved from the area west of the Euphrates and north of the Sinai (Palestine, Syria, Cyprus, Anatolia) to the Aegean and Greece: 'aristocratic governments in the city-states and national feeling in the new states of tribal origin, more equitable relationships between town and countryside, an economy less dependent on palaces'. Because of the growth of empires in Mesopotamia (Assyria, Babylon) and later in Persia, the situation changed after 750 BCE—'urbanization and state structures spread toward Europe and the central Mediterranean, so that Greece became part (a preeminent part) of a so-called western world'.[50]

Another discarded Greek divine was a child of Zeus, one who was nurtured in the father god's loins before birth. A god who appears in human disguise, Dionysus has captured the poetic imagination of artists and philosophers from the time of Euripides and Ovid to the modern intellectual categories of Nietzsche and the embodiment of structural polarities of the French cultural critics Vernant and Detienne. In a variety of ways, these modern interpretive works show the tendency to

---

49. *New York Times*, 14 February 1997.
50. Liverani, in Lefkowitz and Rogers, *Black Athena Revisited*, pp. 426, 427.

treat Dionysus as a cluster of abstractions, to treat the figure as if he were anything except a god. The modern attempt to locate Dionysus within the internal dimensions of the human psyche has rendered the god an intellectual Other. Imposing a human face upon the many masks of Dionysus results in a literary figure lacking divinity, and thus powerless to shed light upon the divinity of the Israelite god Yahweh.

While it is beyond the scope of this investigation is to follow the current state of scholarship with regard to the historical cult of Dionysus in Athens and in the Greek world, I want to emphasize the importance of reading Euripides' play as an account of *an aspect* of the cult of Dionysus. Albert Henrichs has pointed out the dangers of conflating the Dionysus myth, as depicted in *The Bacchae* and in other literary works with the actual Dionysian cult.[51] Even the cult itself has been constructed by modernists, who have harmonized the god's facets, symbols and cults into a metanarrative. 'Dionysus had no central priesthood, no canonical books, and not even a panhellenic shrine of his own. His cults were regional and emphasized different aspects of the god.'[52] In following Heinrichs instead of Dodd, who assumed that the play was continuous with real cultic practices, I am also pleading a kind of ahistoricity, in using the general figure of Dionysus as a god to be compared with the ahistorical Yahweh, as he appears in the book of Judges. In both of these cases, an argument can be made for the deity to be understood in a particular way, following those believers or spectators from the region and time of the construction of the literary work under consideration.

In Hebrew myth Yahweh controls procreation, not merely in creating both male and female figures, but also in assigning and erasing barrenness from mortal women. In Greek myth and philosophy the cosmic symbol of the female sexual role is also passive, that is, the earth, while male sexuality is represented sometimes by water, sometimes by fire, and sometimes, by a combination of the two.[53] Thus philosophers from

51. See A.H. Henrichs, 'Greek Maenadism from Olympias to Messalina', *Harvard Studies in Classical Philology* 82 (1979), pp. 121-60.

52. Henrichs, 'Greek Maenadism', pp. 151-52.

53. The fructifying rain that falls from the sky (Sky God Uranos) falls upon the earth goddess. This symbolism is vividly expressed in a fragment of the lost *Danaides* of Aeschylus: 'Eros makes holy Sky lie with Earth; Earth makes Eros want to lie with Sky. Rain falling from Sky's coming makes Earth pregnant . . . ' Jones suggests that there is an association between the Greek noun *ouranos* and the verb *ourein* (to

Anaximander and Keraklitos to Protagoras and Theophrastos spoke of fire as the generative element in nature, often in the context of an activating principle working on an otherwise inert mixture of earth and water. Aristotle's comment that the hot and cold are active whereas the wet and dry (i.e. water and earth) are passive finds an interesting parallel in the myths that attribute the creation of the first humans from earth and water to the work of the fire god Hephaisatos or Prometheus.[54]

The idea of the male procreator is emphasized clearly in the myth of Dionysus and his most unusual gestation.

> Zeus fell in love with Semele and went to bed with her behind Hera's back. But she was deceived by Hera and, when Zeus agreed to do whatever she asked, she asked him to come in the same way he came when he was courting Hera. Zeus could not refuse, and so, arriving at her bedroom in a chariot, accompanied by thunder and lightning, he threw a thunderbolt. *Semele died of fright* and Zeus, seizing the six-month-old fetus from the fire, sewed it in his thigh. When Semele died, the other daughters of Cadmus began a rumor that Semele had had an affair with some mortal, had blamed it upon Zeus, and for this reason had been incinerated. But in due time Zeus undid the stitches and gave birth to Dionysus, whom he gave to Hermes.[55]

A reading of the phallic code emphasizes the use of Zeus's lightning bolt as the possession that establishes and ensures his rule over gods and humans. That the lightning ultimately represents Zeus's overwhelming sexual power can be seen more clearly in the traditional version of the myth, found in Hesiod. Tricked by Hera into demanding that her lover Zeus have sex with her in the same way he had made love to his divine consort, Semele is instantly incinerated by the force of Zeus's lightning bolts. In Apollodorus's retelling, the mortal woman Semele (whose name means earth) dies of fright, thus watering down the fiery sexual

urinate) which can be found in the unconscious connection in many folk religions where urine symbolizes semen. Thus, the paternal sky god Uranos could be translated 'He who urinates'. (E. Jones, *Essays in Applied Psychoanalysis* [London: Hogarth Press, 1951] pp. 443-44.) Compare Asiatic myths, such as Ras Shamra: El (*Marzeah*) text, where urination is a sign of male impotence, a leaking of semen. Babylonian *Enuma Elish* has both male and female water gods (Apsu and Tiamat).

54. *Metaphysics* 278b22.

55. *Apollodoros* 3.4.3; emphasis mine.

image of Zeus bursting through her door hurling lightning bolts. Euripides intertwines both myths in *The Bacchae*, with Dionysus proclaiming the version in which his mother is incinerated and Pentheus the other. Tiresias offers a third possibility:

> Hera wanted to throw the child from heaven, but Zeus, in his godly wisdom, countered her. Breaking off a fragment of the ether the world floats in, he made a doll, a Dionysus-doll, that he showed Hera. But men confused the words; they garbled 'showed' to 'sewed' and made the story up about his having 'sewed' the god in his thigh to hide him from Hera.[56]

While Zeus makes a doll to trick his jealous wife, his action is intended to protect his child from female wrath—and perhaps to punish Hera for tricking Semele in the first place. As Tiresias's speech indicates, it was mortal men who got the story wrong, comically through a play on words, confusing 'showed' and 'sewed'. The male narrator certainly does not want the head of the Gods to be doing women's work, that is, gestating a baby, a partially mortal one at that. Might this ambiguity of language surrounding the circumstances of Dionysus's birth be a foreshadowing of the ambiguities of his identity?

And what was this Dionysus doll, this odd combination of child born of the violent conjoining of earth and the most august of gods? This godling who was gestated by a male, this Dionysus who is to become the god of madness, of frenzy, of disorder—the very female characteristics that set him apart from the Apollonian male gods of deliberation, of rational thought. But once born of Zeus, he is to be carefully nurtured by the feminine; he is shown in opposition to the rational male deity. If one traces Dionysus's fall from the loins of Zeus to the fringed feminized god who attracts women as nurturer-protectors, one can appreciate the chasm between the Greek Dionysus and the Israelite Yahweh, that of birth and history. So gender is at the heart of the ambiguity of Dionysus's life. His world seems bound by women, unlike Yahweh. Women awaken Dionysus and accompany him wherever he appears. Although Yahweh speaks to women such as Sarah, Hagar, and Hannah, the action

---

56. While this particular passage (ll. 300-305) is difficult (the entire manuscript is corrupt), the general sense of Zeus fooling Hera is not in dispute. The quotations from *The Bacchae* in this paper have been taken from C.K. Williams's lyrical translation (New York: Farrar, Straus Giroux, 1990). Another superior translation is Donald Sutherland, *The Bacchae of Euripides* (Lincoln: University of Nebraska Press, 1968). Both translators take some license in restoring the lacunae from the very problematic Greek text.

is annunciatory rather than erotic, and is a solitary appearance. Yahweh punishes Miriam directly for her boldness, and supports the warrior women in their victories in the name of Israel; he does not elicit the tumultuous eroticism of women followers, the maenads, that Dionysus can claim. But unlike Yahweh, Dionysus is never a god of birth. In his myth there is no normal birth, and he has no connection to normal childbearing. Rather he is connected with the feminine roles of nurse and maenad, with the milk and physical energy of women.[57]

A final difference between Yahweh and Dionysus illustrates the difference between a monotheistic world of a god who neither sleeps, takes lovers, or dies, and the randy Dionysus, whose narrative history involves all the life stages of mortals, that is, a birth story, a history involving mortals and other gods in various cities in the ancient Mediterranean, a violent death, dismemberment, and a trip through the underworld. Like Baal recovered from the entrails of Mot, Dionysus continues to reappear, to live after his death. Like Mot, a god after being ground to powder by Anat, Dionysus continues his appearances at festivals. The closest similarity to Mot (and the dismembered Osiris) is the Orphic doctrine in which the Titans eat the pieces of Dionysus, except for one piece—the heart. A parallel tradition has Apollo gathering the pieces of Dionysus and burying them on Mt Parnassos.

The Apollo–Dionysus connection leads back to the Nietzschean connection between the dark maddened god and the luminous god of reason, the connection that made a god into an adjective, Dionysian. The celebration of a god became, through the interpretation and romanticization of Nietzsche, a moment in the history of ideas. As Kerenyi and others have argued, it was the Nietzschean path that led away 'from a true understanding of the Dionysian religion'.[58] Nietzsche creates a fairy-tale god, whose power to enchant has become rather a fixed enchantment.

> In song and in dance man expresses himself as a member of a higher
> community; he has forgotten how to walk and speak and is on the way

57. I follow Kerenyi in this interpretation which extends to the festivals of Dionysus, in which only women participate (pp. 131-33). Kerenyi argues that the ecstatic festivals are more connected to the woman's greater visionary capacity than to the allied tropes of childbearing and nursing as the sphere of Dionysus. Carl Kerenyi, *Dionysus: Archetypal Image of Indestructible Life* (trans. Ralph Mannheim; Princeton, NJ: Bollingen Books, 1976).

58. Kerenyi, *Dionysus*, p. 134.

toward flying into the air, dancing. His very gestures express enchantment. Just as the animals now talk, and the earth yields milk and honey,
supernatural sounds emanate from him, too; he feels himself a god, he
himself now walks about enchanted, in ecstasy, like the gods he saw
walking in his dreams. He is no longer an artist, he has become a work of
art. In these paroxysms of intoxication the artistic power of all nature
reveals itself to the highest gratification of the primordial unity.[59]

The erotic influences of the maenads, the frenzied connection to
woman, hallmarks of the divine Dionysus, are turned into artistic frenzy
through Nietzsche, into a primitive tune, a profession of faith in intoxication that is Dionysian. What is lacking in this portrait of enchantment, both of the god and of the artist, is the ongoing life of the god.
His power to enchant, his power to command the erotic liquidity of
women, have turned into a static enchantment. And thus Dionysus dies,
giving way to a Dionysian abstraction.

59. *Birth of Tragedy*, p. 37, quoted in Kerenyi, *Dionysus*.

Flood and Fludd

Francis Landy

Let us tell the toledot of the Flood story, the literary and imaginative genre, in Midrash, mystery play, novel, children's Bibles, in Noah's Arks, the ephemeridae of the toy industry, the Ark adrift from any placement in the Bible, a floating signifier of human and animal concord, of the world in miniature. And *Fludd* by Hilary Mantel, one of the great novels of Catholic disenchantment, named after the Elizabethan alchemist, a novel of transformation, dissipation and pre-Vatican II premonition. The echoes of the Flood and its transmutation are my theme, in the context of the loss of faith, and truth, and all those things that make the ground seem solid.

The Flood story is, like our ancestor, a wandering Aramean, finding its way into the Bible as it did into Gilgamesh, and thence into the Western canon. That it is grafted into our text makes its inherence questionable; it is always something of a stranger, infusing its foreign provenance into the host text, so that the Bible itself is disrupted, pervaded with the theme of its own dissolution into the world's texts and narratives.[1] Avivah Zornberg argues that Noah is a latecomer, who differs from Adam in his knowledge of the past: 'The difference between Adam and Noah is precisely this—that Noah has Adam's text to decipher' (Zornberg 1995: 70).[2] The Flood story, as David Damrosch shows, is central to the Primeval narratives of Genesis 1–11 (Damrosch 1987: 122). But it also points elsewhere, to a different narrative domain. Noah's memory, enclosed in his silence, is of his Mesopotamian

---

1.   Of course, no text in the Bible is 'original', in that the Bible was not a preexistent entity into which its constitent parts fitted. For the role of chance in canon formation, see Davies (1997). In that sense, every constituent is a wandering signifier.

2.   For the modelling of Noah on Adam see also Sarna (1989: 49-50) and Steinmetz (1994).

precursors and cousins.[3] Intertextuality, the rooting of texts in other texts, and the interplay between them, is ever at odds with the text's struggle for autonomy. Damrosch claims that the whole of the Primeval narrative is a duplication of, and comment upon, that of Gilgamesh (119-20). But if so, the transformation is also the site of repression, marked, according to Damrosch, by the elimination of interiority, of conflict in the divine world and the netherworld (122-25).

If the Flood story is central to the Primeval narratives, it is also a parenthesis, as has been pointed out, for instance, by Ellen van Wolde. God decides to destroy the earth, because 'every form of their heart's planning was only evil all the day' (Gen. 6.5);[4] in 8.21, he renounces destruction, 'since what the human heart forms is evil from its youth'.[5] Nothing changes; humanity will be as evil as before. God's destructive and salvific programs coexist, without apparent interference or conflict (van Wolde 1994: 80). On either side of the divide we have Kenites,[6] Nephilim, and the same assessment of the human condition. We begin

---

3.   Whether the writers of the biblical story knew the Mesopotamian texts directly, that is, whether the knowledge was conscious or unconscious, is, of course, imponderable. Damrosch notes that copies of Gilgamesh have been found in Palestine, and could have been known to the biblical writers (1987: 120 n. 23). A further argument for direct transmission is the closeness of the connections. Damrosch assumes a Palestinian rather than Babylonian composition for the text. For a derivation from non-royal versions of the Flood story, see Davila (1995).

4.   Biblical references for the Pentateuch are taken from *The Schocken Bible: A New Translation with Introductions, Commentary, and Notes* (New York: Schocken Books, 1995).

5.   Sarna (1989: 59) sees in the repetition a modification, suggesting that the evil is neither all-inclusive nor innate. Zornberg (1995: 69) cites Rabbenu Bahya, quoting *Gen. R.* 38.4, as holding that evil is the result of separation from the womb. The word יער otherwise occurs only in Deut. 31.21, though it is the basis for the rabbinic concepts of the יער הטוב and יער הרצ, the good and evil inclinations, in contradiction to our passage. Interpretations of *yeṣer* differ. Sarna (1989: 47) translates 'product'; Westermann (1984: 410) holds that it is a virtual synonym of 'thoughts'. But the parallel with the verb יער, 'form, shape, mould', used of the creation of the human being in Gen. 2.7, suggests an intrinsic structure or pattern from which the thoughts arise, as well as divine responsibility.

6.   Westermann (1984: 333) states categorically that there is no connection between Cain and the Kenites; similarly, Sarna (1989: 36, 39) holds that the Cainite line passes into oblivion. However that may be—and the case is unargued—the incidence of the name on either side of the Flood narrative produces a mirroring effect.

with the descendants of Noah (5.31; 6.10) and we end with the descendants of Noah (9.18; 10.1), picking up, as it were, where they left off, with the serious business of begetting and dying. And with the rhythm of the seasons, and of day and night.

Noah 'sees a new world' (Zornberg 1995: 70), one continuous with ours. Steinmetz argues that the story of Noah's drunkenness is a paradigmatic illustration of the difference between the postdiluvean and antediluvean ages, the increase in human responsibility and autonomy, for instance. Whether it is better or worse, however, is indeterminate; the decline in longevity and alienation from the animals (9.2) is compensated for by the revocation of the curse on the earth in 8.21.[7] The earth will still be full of violence; whether the formulation of inveterate human evil in 8.21 differs significantly from that in 6.5, as Sarna argues, is imponderable,[8] and does not override their conspicuous similarity. Likewise, the reduction in longevity has already been determined before the Flood, and foreshadows its ineffectiveness.

The newness of the world does not necessitate essential difference, *apart from the experience of the Flood*. The permanent legacy of the Flood is a covenant, and a constraint on human and animal behaviour. The covenant is both a guarantee and renders life insecure, since we know that the temptation to destroy has not disappeared and the violence that provoked it subsists. The Flood is a trauma whose repetition is always deserved, and withheld through an effort of memory. The rainbow mediates between God and humanity (9.13, 16, 17); it is seen, by God and humans (9.14); and what is seen is that God looks upon it (9.16).[9]

---

7.   Harland (1996: 114-18) argues, on the basis of the position of the word עוֹד, 'further', that Yahweh simply promises not to add to the curse on the earth, but not to revoke it. Harland, in my view, minimizes the importance of the paronomasia between אָדָם and אֲדָמָה, with its reference to 3.17-19, and to Lamech's naming of Noah in 5.29.

8.   The issues are whether 'every form' in 6.5 differs significantly from 'form' in 8.21, since both seem to be generalizations about the human condition, and whether 'all day long' implies greater temporal inclusiveness than 'from his youth'. Likewise, Harland (1996: 55) argues for a difference between the two occurences.

9.   Batto (1987: 196-97), following a long critical tradition, holds that the rainbow is God's warbow, which he hangs up in the sky as a token of peace. Similarly, Marduk, after his victory over Tiamat, hangs up his bow as the bowstar. Westermann (1984: 473) rejects this explanation, citing Benno Jacob's observation that there is no evidence of a cosmic fight in the narrative. He holds that the P author is citing a popular etiology of the rainbow, which is found in other Flood traditions.

The Flood is further disturbed as an integral part of the biblical narrative by the uneasy coexistence in it of two narrative strands. Each casts doubt on the other; there is no true story. The duplication inserts the intertextuality and distantiation that Damrosch finds between the Primeval History and Gilgamesh into the text itself. The effect is stranger than the juxtaposition of the two creation stories. There at least there is the appearance of two complete stories. Here each story is interrupted, asserts its separate identity, and cannot but be drawn into and contribute to the reading of the other. It resembles a text such as Derrida's *Glas*, or a poem consisting of two parallel columns, that complement or negate each other. Between the two stories there is not so much an aporia, pointing to the constructedness of all memory, as subversion or upstaging. For instance, 6.9 is an evident beginning of the story—אלה תולדות נח, 'These are the generations of Noah'. We look back, however, and see that it has already begun with 6.5, or perhaps 6.1, and that the details of Noah and his progeny are repeated from 5.32. The beginning is no beginning, and suggests an instability in the foundations of story, in the anchorage in a starting point. The beginning of the story merges with the climax of the previous one, 'the book of the generations of Adam'. The overlap, like the much larger one between the beginning and end of the story, produces an effect of parenthesis. Between the first mention of Noah's seed and the second, almost identically worded, there are inset the story of the sons of God

The only example he gives, however, is Peruvian, which does seem somewhat remote from our text. Harland (1996: 138) likewise argues against the identification with the warbow (which seems to be based on simple homonymy) and argues that the rainbow is a representation of the firmament that holds back the celestial waters. Harland (1996: 139) also stresses the community of seeing between humanity and God. Murray (1992: 187 n. 22) also expresses doubts.

The only other instance of the rainbow in the Hebrew Bible is Ezek. 1.28, where likewise it appears in a cloud. There it is likened to the splendour (נגה) that surrounds the appearance of fire (כמראה אש), which is what Ezekiel sees of the divine body, 'from the thighs downwards' (1.27). The mystical experience—dissimulated further by its characterization as simile and likeness—deflects the gaze from God's nakedness, and the phallic energy it represents. In Gen. 6, divine sexual desire, projected onto the sons of God, and violence are both enacted; the rainbow in Gen. 9 inhibits his destructiveness. The rainbow, as the spectrum of colours, kabbalistically represents the sefirot, through which the divine being is refracted and made accessible to humanity. In particular, it is one of the many symbols for the Shekinah, that encloses and neutralizes the divine phallus, the *berit*, identified with the Sefirah Yesod.

and the account of God's decision to blot out humanity. The parenthesis is of course preparatory;[10] it opens a gap between one story and the other, illustrates the corruption of the earth, and finally explains why Noah was chosen.[11] The linear and rhetorical progression is undercut by simultaneity; while Noah was blithely producing heirs, these other things were happening. The asides not only provide background for the ongoing story; they illustrate the parenthetic proclivity of narrative, including biblical narrative, for instance, the immense digression of the sojourn in Egypt. Thereby it acquires thickness, by which I mean a sense of the complexity and multiplicity of lives, and that we live on several planes at once.[12]

My interest is in the afterlife of the text, and in the two versions of the Flood story not in terms of priority but of tension and mutual implication.[13] Each produces an effect of correlation, of anteriority and

10. I am indebted for some of this discussion to my student, Benjamin Berger.

11. There are still problems. Does the miscegenation of divine beings and humans constitute חמס, 'violence'? If so, are humans blamed for divine desire? What is the relationship between Noah's righteousness (6.9), and the 'favour' (*ḥen*) he paronomastically receives in God's eyes in v. 8, between desert and arbitrary preference (cf. Zornberg 1995: 40-42)? Intertestamental readings, such as *1 Enoch* (6-10), covered their tracks by attributing the Flood both to the sexual sin of the sons of God and to the consequent violence; cf. also Rashi. Cassuto (1984: 52-53) argues that חמס is a term for wickedness in general. Harland (1996: 25) rejects any direct connection between the story of the giants and the Flood; it is merely 'an isolated unit of obscure meaning'. He identifies חמס with 'violence' and specifically murder (37-40). However, Harland is too categorical in his judgment. He ignores the contrast between the 'sons of God' and God, denies that the divine limitation of the human lifespan implies any condemnation (25), does not refer to the function of the keyword בשר, 'flesh', and in his brief account of later exegesis omits entirely the widespread identification of חמס with polymorphous sexuality in the Pseudepigrapha and Midrash.

12. Gen. 6.1-4 compounds the parenthetical effect by adding the note about the Nefilim in 6.4. It is not clear whether they were the offspring of the sons of God and daughters of human beings (cf. Westermann 1984: 366; Kunin 1995: 170). Others, however, identify the Nefilim unambiguously with the גברים in the last part of the verse as the descendants of that union (e.g. van Wolde 1994: 74; Sarna 1989: 46).

13. Van Wolde (1994: 75) discusses the issue succinctly. Critiques of traditional documentary theory are too numerous and familiar for rehearsal. For a good account, see Davies (1992) and Whybray (1989). Harland attempts to read the two sources separately and then to combine them. His approach, however, is overly concerned, in my view, with the resolution of tension.

revision. For instance, P—in traditional parlance—begins in full knowledge that J has preceded him, or vice versa: J adds his bit in spite of P's
opening. The claims to originality and the last word, two opposite
modes of authority, occupy the text. Each, however, is indispensable to
the other, not only as master and slave, nor in the ways I have outlined—that 6.1-8 provides a dark background to the introduction of the
story in 6.9, that the two accounts of the earth's and human evil provide
multiple perspective—but in their discontinuity, their suggestion of a
breach of cosmic and narrative order. Repetition, as when we return to
the scene of Noah's procreating,[14] testifies to the disruption of narrative,
that linkage does not link. Return to the matrix is invested with horror,
given the negative connotations that accumulate round the word בשׂר,
'flesh' (6.3, 12), a metonym in context for the semen that reproduces
flesh, that transmits the essence of the human body.[15] God's disgust must
at least complicate our implication in Noah's sexuality. Déjà vu is ironic,
since we hear in it, regressively, Lamech's voice of celebration at Noah's
birth and with it the hope for the reversal of the terrestrial curse (5.28-
31), the rounding off of the primal story.[16] The revisited mother's body
has become the source of death instead of life, especially since the

14. Procreation in the text is a purely male affair; father emits son through a
textually absent womb. The repression of maternity is one of the elements that
destabilizes the narrative, since it maintains its patrilineal purity only through ever-
repeated denial, as well as the creation of textually redundant daughters. Davies
argues that the story reflects the late emergence of a strictly patriarchal monotheism,
which could not mingle with human nature (1993: 200); similarly, Nancy Jay sees in
the genealogy an attempt to assert 'unilineal continuity' (1992: 98). Ilana Pardes
(1992: 56), like Jay, contrasts J and P, and thinks that P misreads J in the genealogy.
Her reason for assuming the priority of one over the other is unclear (as indeed is
the assumption of misreading as opposed to revision).

15. The same verb שׁחת that is used for all flesh corrupting its way on the earth
in 6.12 denotes Onan's spilling his seed in Gen. 38.9 (ושׁחת ארצה).

16. Lamech is another instance of duplication in the text, given the two
Lamechs and their contrasting speeches at the end of the Kenite and Sethite
genealogies. A long line of critics transfers Lamech's speech to the end of ch. 4
(Vermeylen 1991: 177). Vermeylen suggests that Noah was originally the son of
Enosh, and that P inserted his genealogy, based on Mesopotamian prototypes, into
the original Sethite lineage. In any case, the symmetry of the two Lamechs, and
indeed of the two genealogies, is evident and frequently observed, and does not
have to be explained by the poverty of P's imagination, as Vermeylen supposes
(1991: 184). Damrosch sees in Lamech's naming an echo of the creation of human
beings in Atraḥasis (1987: 125).

human mother is absorbed as matrix into the figure of the earth, which is 'corrupted before God' (6.11). It is thus uncanny, in the Freudian sense, a place where we cannot be, and cannot but be, at home. The double vision, the two unsynchronized voices, the double act of generation, decompose time. Noah is a belated Adam; if his fault, as Zornberg suggests, is that he misreads Adam's text, this is a consequence of his lateness (1995: 70). And this, according to Zornberg (71), is the precondition of his humanity.[17]

Style, vocabulary, and vision cross over between the apparently discontinuous narrative strands. This may be—and usually is—interpreted in terms of adoption or intrusion.[18] P, for instance, lays her eggs in J's nest. From a literary point of view, however, each voice becomes complex and intertextual. Each may be informed by the other, either dialogically and agonistically, or as opening up the possibility of transformation, that one may become the other. Two examples will suffice. J's preface embeds the following divine determination: ויאמר ה' אמחה את־האדם אשר־בראתי מעל פני האדמה מאדם עד־בהמה עד־רמש ועד־עוף השמים, 'YHWH said, "I will blot out humankind, whom I have created, from the face of the soil, from human to animal, to crawling thing and to the fowl of the heavens"' (6.7). As has frequently been pointed out (Westermann 1984: 406-407), the verb ברא, 'create', as well as the taxonomy of living creatures, recalls the P account of creation in Genesis 1 as opposed to the J account in Genesis 2. The juxtaposition of the two accounts results in intensification: YHWH's grief[19] in his heart in 6.6 is aggravated by his acknowledgment that he 'created' (בראתי) human beings, and by the recollection of the perfectly ordered hierarchy of Genesis 1. The two voices could be seen as dialogic, between God's assessment of the evil in the human heart and his memory that humans were created in the divine image. The citation of P also anticipates and

---

17. Zornberg's discussion is complex and repays close reading. She relates Noah's misreading to Winnicott's theory of transitional space. Only through our misreadings—what Winnicott calls 'apperception'—of our cultural heritage can we create our own version of it.

18. For a critique of this procedure, see Tigay 1985: 170.

19. YHWH's grief (ויתעצב) is matched in 5.29 by Lamech's prediction that Noah will relieve the 'pains of our hand' (עצבון ידינו) in another cross-over between sources. Again, the phenomenon is erased by many critics through attributing this verse to J (or D, in the case of Vermeylen 1991: 188): 'This verse is almost unanimously ascribed to J' (Westermann 1984: 359).

pre-emptively disabuses us of the rhetorical strategy of the introduction
to the P story, in which the narrator repeatedly absolves God from responsibility, since God is presented, and constructs himself, as purely passive, merely watching the earth's self-destruction: 'Now the earth had
gone to ruin before God... God saw the earth, and here: it had gone to
ruin... God said to Noah: An end of all flesh has come before me'
(6.11-13), before finally confirming his own part in the process: 'here, I
am about to bring ruin upon them' (6.13).[20] P is then used against P. It
is equally important to note, however, that J transforms itself into P,
adopts a P persona, that one vision is metaphorically related to the
other.

The second example, which requires much less elaboration, is 7.22, in
the midst of the P account of the rising of the waters and the destruction
of all life. Suddenly we hear, כל אשר נשמת־רוח חיים באפיו מכל
אשר בחרבה מתו, 'all that had rush or breath of life in their nostrils, all
that were on firm ground, died'. The phrase נשמת־רוח חיים באפיו recalls
YHWH's creation of the human being in Gen. 2.7, ויפח באפיו נשמת
חיים, 'he blew into his nostrils the rush of life'.[21] As with בראתי, 'I
created', in 6.7, it reminds us of God's creation, and his immanence in
humanity. The Flood is also God's self-destruction. Here the external,
slow progression of P is transformed into the interior perspective of J: P
reveals J at its core. This is emphasized by the convergence and near
synonymity of נשמה and רוח at its centre.

The Flood is the paradigmatic breach of cosmic order, the ultimate
threat to the creation and the biblical narrative. If the Flood had succeeded there would have been no story. That one side of God saves the
human race while the other destroys it is the evidence, the straw, on
which we can pin our hopes. The dissociation within God is manifested
in the narrative through the rhythm of forgetting and remembering:
God conveniently forgets Noah while allowing his destructive impulse
full sway; his returning memory in 8.1 causes him to pass a wind/spirit
over the waters, and the waters to recede, in a palpable reminiscence of

---

20. For this reason, Murray must surely be overstating when he claims that the
Flood is never presented as God's actual work (1992: 35).

21. The combination of נשמה and רוח is unique, and accounted for in different
ways. Westermann (1984: 439) predictably sees in רוח an addition, possibly for the
sake of harmonization. Sarna (1989: 56) holds that it emphasizes the totality of the
extinction.

Gen. 1.2. The Flood is then associated with unconsciousness and chaos, the memory with creation, order and consciousness.

Robert Murray has seen in the sequence creation–uncreation–recreation a basic pattern in the Hebrew Bible, which is adumbrated in what he calls the cosmic covenant, which God makes not only with Israel and with individuals, but with all creation. The covenant at the end of the Flood story (9.8-17) is between God, humans and animals, suggesting a repetition of the order of creation established in Genesis 1. It conflicts, however, with the violence and terror institutionalized between humans and animals in 9.2-6. Murray (1992: 34) notes the contrast, without developing it, between biblical realistic and paradisal visions. Their coexistence in the same divine discourse indicates that the covenant persists, despite, or on condition of, its breach, through displacement to the far future or the primordial past.

It exists, however, in the central image of the Flood story, the Ark. The Ark is a microcosm of the world, that which preserves God's creation in the midst of his amnesia. In it the harmony between humans and animals projected in Genesis 1 and intimated as a dissonant possibility in Genesis 2 is ideally realized. Zornberg (1995: 57-64) discusses the Midrashic tradition that Noah's feeding the animals was his transformative experience (59), that made him, retrospectively, into a *tzaddik* (58).[22] Holloway has argued that the Ark is modelled on Solomon's Temple;[23] it would be more accurate to see both as belonging to the same set of representatives of a blissful enclave in a hostile world. It is the Ark, I think, that makes the story so popular for children, replicated by the toy industry. It is not very different from Fisher-Price farms and zoos, symbolizing what Winnicott calls the 'play space', the contained environment in which the child learns to relate to objects, the dramas and dangers of the world, creatively and safely. The play space for Winnicott is the foundation for cultural experience, for the knowledge of space and time. The Ark is both isolated from the world before and after, and prepares us for it. Violence ceases; if wild animals incarnate ferocity and intractability, here they are incorporated into the human

---

22. See also Murray (1992: 101 and 198 n. 10), with an interesting contrast of Jewish and Christian traditions.

23. Cf. Blenkinsopp (1977: 64), who holds that the account of the building of the Ark is paradigmatic for P's account of the building of the sanctuary in Exodus.

domain. As Murray (1992: 103-105) shows, the Ark foreshadows the peaceful dominion of Isaiah 11.[24]

Noah is notoriously silent in the biblical story, as are all the other human personages (van Wolde 1994: 77). Compared to its Mesopotamian precursors, it is remarkable for its total flattening of character and exclusive concentration on the enormity of the disaster. Noah's silence has been the subject of much negative comment, exemplified, intrabiblically, by Abraham's challenge to God on behalf of the inhabitants of Sodom. Zornberg (1995: 58) thinks that it is symptomatic of the disease of his time, that none cared for or were curious about the other.[25] Within the narrative, however, it corresponds to God's lapse of memory. God's repression, the parenthesis in which the world and all its signifiers is negated, is matched, on Noah's side, by a failure of language. We follow Noah, his family, and all the creatures, through the building of the Ark, the preparations, embarkation, the rain and flood. We can imagine what they might feel, not feel, and refuse to acknowledge. The silence may be a pall over the Ark, the womb–island–prison; the claustrophobia of the inhabitants is the subject of many metatexts. It may also be a sign of traumatic shock, the inability to speak the unspeakable.

Noah 'walks with God' (6.9), but what kind of God does Noah walk with? The metaphor suggests that they walk in tandem, into the Flood and out again. The complicity with the nihilistic, self-destructive God, who represses his memory, implies a parallel process in the human being. But Noah walks also with God against God, building an Ark, for instance, against destruction. Noah then represents God's ambivalence.

Murray pursues the theme of the cosmic covenant throughout the Hebrew Bible, and we need not retrace his steps. It is remarkable, however, how little impact the Flood apparently has on the rest of the Hebrew Bible. It is subject to amnesia, or perhaps tactful silence. There are three direct references. One is particularly apposite to the cosmic covenant: כִּי־מֵי נֹחַ זֹאת לִי אֲשֶׁר נִשְׁבַּעְתִּי מֵעֲבֹר מֵי־נֹחַ עוֹד עַל־הָאָרֶץ כֵּן נִשְׁבַּעְתִּי מִקְּצֹף עָלַיִךְ וּמִגְּעָר־בָּךְ, 'For these are the waters (or days)[26] of

---

24. A few weeks ago my two-year-old Joseph lost the chicken from his Fisher-Price farm, and has been plaintively talking about it ever since. It seems to me that it is less that he is actually grieving over the chicken than practising the sensation of grief.

25. See also Fish (1989–90: 75).

26. Murray (1992: 37, 187 n. 25) and Batto (1987: 190) read 'as the days of', following the Septuagint (Batto) and understood, according to Murray, by Jerome

Noah to me. Just as I swore never to pass the waters of Noah over the earth again, so I have sworn not to be angry with you or rebuke you' (Isa. 54.9). Here the Flood is clearly a metaphor for the Exile. The reference is followed by one to a ברית שלום, a covenant of peace, which will be more stable than the hills and mountains (54.10),[27] and which is linked, as Murray (1992: 37) shows, with the ברית עולם, 'the eternal covenant', God makes with the prophet's potential audience in Isa. 55.3, and which clearly corresponds to the ברית עולם, the eternal covenant, in the Noah story. The reference participates in the complex chains of association and correlation that constitute the metaphoric structure of Second Isaiah: the eternal covenant in 55.3 is immediately identified with the covenant with David, which in turn is subsumed into the mission of the prophet/Israel,[28] transposed onto the ambiguous figure of Cyrus, and so on. The Flood, as a figure for the Exile, presages the crossing of the Red Sea in Isa. 51.10, reenacts the defeat of Rahab and Sea in 51.9, and is ultimately interlinked with the barrenness of Sarah's womb in 51.2 (and 54.1) and the bereaved mother/daughter of Zion. Cosmic, Davidic and national covenants intersect; the promise given to David (חסדי דוד) is transferred to the world. The oceanic immersion of the world and God in the Flood story is the restless sea of nations among which Israel is adrift and the matrix in which it was miraculously born. Two points in particular may be made. The first is that the evocation of the Flood in 54.9 is preceded by another reference in 54.8: בשצף קצף הסתרתי פני רגע ממך ובחסד עולם רחמתיך, 'In a flood of anger I hid my face momentarily from you, but with eternal *ḥesed* I have compassion upon you'. Here the deluge is identified with God's wrath, and is immediately dissimulated as divine self-concealment. If in the Flood story God disclaims responsibility, here the violence is not the earth's but God's, and is manifested and simultaneously retracted through the denial of God's presence, his non-relation, as communicated through the expression 'his face'. Absence and violence are metaphorically correlated. The rhyme בשצף קצף compresses the intimations

and the Targumist. Both are equally possible, and, in any case, as Murray points out, there is probably a pun between ימי, 'days of', and מי, 'waters of'.

27. The nearest analogue is Ps. 46. The shaking and moving of hills and mountains are among the epiphenomena of theophany (e.g. Judg. 5.5; Ps. 68.9). That the ברית שלום does not move suggests that it is the one thing that is not cowed by the advent of God.

28. For these interconnections, see Murray (1992: 37-38).

of flood and wrath, so conventionally associated with combustion. Wrath, according to the metaphor, inundates God's personality, and indeed threatens to wash it away. But there is a second, less dominant, significance. קֶצֶף, in Hos. 10.7, means something flimsy, like straw, that is borne away on water. This reinforces the instantaneity insisted on by רֶגַע, 'momentarily', and that contrasts with God's eternal *ḥesed*. God's wrath then is the Flood and is borne away by the Flood, which is aligned with God's everlasting compassion. The relation of the Ark— the world in miniature—to the Flood is reversed; the Flood itself is surrounded by God's compassion, and becomes a metaphor for it.

The second point is that, as Murray shows (1992: 36), the recollection of the Flood occurs at the centre of a long apostrophe to the female persona of Israel, Jerusalem, as widowed, bereaved, abandoned and sterile wife and mother. Jerusalem, stereotypically, is imagined as tent, ship, and temple, and is metonymically related to the prophet and David as the new Noah, and hence the new Ark. The marriage metaphor here encloses God's destructive memory. The poem is about God's desire, etherealized as it is through metaphor, wish-fulfilment and dream, and haunted by the past. The union of God and Israel recalls that of the sons of God and daughters of human beings that precipitates the Flood. God takes on the role of the sons of God, who fulfil his desire at one remove.

A second reference is Ezek. 14.12-23, in which Noah is grouped with Daniel and Job as three righteous men whose virtue would save them in catastrophe, but who would not be able to save their children.[29] The

29. Most critics identify the Daniel here with a traditional non-Israelite legendary hero, evidenced in the Ugaritic epic of Aqht as well as Ezek. 28.3, rather than with the biblical character (Greenberg 1983: 257-58; Allen 1994: 218; Craigie 1983: 101; Wevers 1982: 91-92; Eichrodt 1975: 189; Zimmerli 1979: 315). Dressler (1979) and Wahl (1992), however, argue in favour of the canonical figure. See, however, the responses to Dressler by Day (1980) and Margalit (1980), as well as Dressler's counter-argument (1984). Against Wahl as well as Dressler, it may be advanced that the biblical Daniel saves neither land nor people, and that the land in question in 14.13 appears to be any land. Wahl's (1980: 551) argument that the composition of the Flood narrative, Job, Ezekiel and the tales of Daniel can be dated to approximately the same era (fifth century BCE), and reflects a cultic and wisdom concern with the correspondence of righteousness with fate seems unduly limited; surely, the whole of the Hebrew Bible, and ancient Near Eastern literature generally, is preoccupied with this issue.

Aqht is incomplete, and hence its relevance is uncertain. Day (1980: 179-80)

passage is a non sequitur, whose strangeness is magnified by the formu-laic repetition of the protasis. Four times we hear that if a land were to sin and commit sacrilege against Yahweh, not even Noah, Daniel and Job would be able to save their children from one of Yahweh's destruc-tive agencies; finally all four converge on Jerusalem, where, however, sons and daughters do survive, to exemplify through their wickedness Jerusalem's just fate.[30] The climax is thus a reversal, or a transformation.

Noah here is clearly the opposite of the Noah of the Flood story.[31] The Noah of the Flood story did save his children through his righ-teousness, and if he had not, there would have been no point, and no one to write it. The coupling with Job is equally peculiar. Job is like Noah as the one perfect human being; he, however, suffers for his righ-teousness, and his children die, not because of their wickedness, but vicariously for their father.[32] If 14.12-20 schematically illustrates Ezekiel's theme of individual responsibility, Job is a precise contradic-tion of that claim.

Secondly, the survival of the children is justified, in 14.22-23, as a 'consolation', using the verb נחם, 'repent, change one's mind, comfort', that pervades the Flood story and provides Noah with the etymology of his name.[33] As Greenberg (1983: 261) points out, נחם is a metathesis of

argues strongly in favour of the supposition that Daniel restored his land to fertility and obtained the resurrection of his son. He also suggests connections between the Phoenician legend and the biblical narrative. It is not clear, of course, what version of the legend lies behind our text.

30. For this reason, Wevers (1982: 91) and Pohlmann (1992: 8-11) see it as a supplement. Greenberg (1983: 262) notes that such inconsistency is characteristic of prophetic writings generally; similarly, Zimmerli (1979: 313) argues that the two parts are necessarily connected. Hals (1989: 97) remarks that in contrast to vv. 12-20, vv. 22-23 speak only of 'survivors', but not of deliverance. Finally, Joyce (1989: 74-76) holds that vv. 21-23 introduce a reality sense. There will, inevitably, be sur-vivors, but their escape will have nothing to do with their own or their parents' righteousness.

31. See Joyce (1989: 72). Eichrodt (1975: 189) thinks that the reference is to Noah's curse of Ham/Canaan, without supporting evidence (cf. Joyce 1989: 149 n. 48).

32. Spiegel (1945: 329) hypothesizes an original form of the Job story in which his children were restored to him. This, however, eliminates the contrast that is the point of my argument.

33. Zimmerli (1979: 315, 316) argues that vv. 22b-23a have been inserted in the interests of seeing God's inexorable judgment as consolation, since it breaks up the

חנם, '(not) for nothing', that immediately follows it. This is a pointed reversal of the Job story, in which Job was afflicted, God admits, חנם, 'for nothing' (Job 2.3); it also replicates the ambivalence of the Flood story, the left hand of God not knowing what the right is doing. God's change of mind can always mitigate Jerusalem's deserved destruction.[34]

In Ezekiel 14, then, dissonance between the hypothetical fates of the three righteous men and the narratives they evoke is projected into that between Jerusalem and other lands, and thus confirms the ideology that Ezekiel supposedly condemns.

Ellen Davis (1989: 117) has commented on the role of marginality in Ezekiel's citation of narrative. 'The margins are the place of the social critic.' Noah, Job and Daniel are idealized figures, far away and long ago, who establish a universal rule; the land that sins is any land, and, in the case of Noah at least, the whole earth. The personification of the four instruments of death and the stylized repetitiveness of the entire passage compounds its distantiation and hence its parabolic quality. The failure to draw the logical consequence is thus a symptom of poetic alienation, between the ideal and the actual, the mythical imagination and its application. Correspondingly, the ambivalence and questioning of divine justice in the Noah and Job narratives cast doubt on the efficacy and validity of the divine judgment on Jerusalem, and thus on the schema on which the prophetic book is based.

The third possible reference is Ps. 29.10: ה' למבול ישב וישב ה' מלך לעולם, 'YHWH was enthroned over the Flood, and YHWH is enthroned as king for ever'.[35] Most critics think that מבול here refers only to the celestial ocean (e.g. Gerstenberger 1988: 131; Girard 1984: 237 n. 8), and has no connection with the Flood story, the only context in which the word otherwise occurs.[36] However, the parallels between Psalms 29 and 114[37] suggest that, like Psalm 114, Psalm 29 alludes to Israel's wilderness experience, and thus the Flood too could refer to the

formulaic, 'And you shall see... and know.' His case does not seem very strong, and has received little support.

34. In contrast to Zimmerli, Allen (1994: 220) sees the consolation as mitigation.

35. Avishur (1994: 48-49, 102-103) discusses attempts to emend or provide a different meaning for מבול, concluding persuasively that they have little justification.

36. Blenkinsopp (1997: 170 n. 36) does, however, hold that it refers to the Flood.

37. The principal parallel is between the images of the cedars and mountains of Lebanon dancing like calves in vv. 5-6 and the almost identical simile in Ps. 114.4 and 6. The role of the Flood in Ps. 29 is perhaps that of the Sea in Ps. 114.3 and 5.

biblical narrative. 'The wilderness of Qadesh' in v. 8, for instance, recalls the location of Israel's 40-year sojourn.[38] Marc Girard (1984: 238, 240) has proposed that the ten occurrences of YHWH in vv. 3-9ab, the central section of the Psalm, correspond to the Decalogue. If so, the wilderness is antonymic to the Flood, as two opposite kinds of desolation, and, as we have seen above, a metaphor for it.

Psalm 29 is complex,[39] and v. 10 has two primary structural relations. The first is with v. 3: קול ה׳ על־המים אל־הכבוד הרעים ה׳ על־מים רבים: 'The voice of Yahweh is over the waters, the God of glory thunders, Yahweh over many waters'. The waters are both equivalent to the Flood, especially as a conventional symbol for chaos, yet not identical with it. The Flood isolates in the past what the waters are in the present; it recollects the sea's moment of total prevalence. The second is with vv. 9c and 11 in the final section of the Psalm.[40] Verse 9c reads: ובהיכלו כלו אמר כבוד, 'And in his Temple everything says "Glory"',[41] while v. 11 has ה׳ עז לעמו יתן ה׳ יברך את־עמו בשלום, 'YHWH will give strength to his people, YHWH will bless his people with peace'. The reference to the Flood is then enclosed between two to the Temple,[42] where everything says 'Glory', and from which YHWH gives strength and blessing to his people. These in turn correspond to the summons of the divine beings to worship in vv. 1-2.

Psalm 29 is characterized by sound, energy and violence. The first moment of silence is v. 10, when the voice of YHWH, as well as of

---

38. Avishur (1994: 46-48) cites and criticizes proposals to situate the wilderness of Qadesh elsewhere, especially in Syria, in support of the hypothesis that Ps. 29 was originally a Canaanite composition, whose geographical reference is predominantly northern. Avishur (47-48, 71) holds that Lebanon, Sirion, and the wilderness of Qadesh evoke the northern and southern extremities of the land of Israel in the period of the early monarchy, which is entirely pervaded by the presence of God.

39. For the complexity, see Girard (1984: 234-41, esp. 240).

40. My divisions are those of Girard (1984: 235). Others divide it slightly differently (e.g. Gerstenberger 1988: 131).

41. Freedman and Hyland (1973: 240, 253), following a suggestion by Margalit (1970: 303), divide the verse after אמר, 'for metrical and other reasons'. Their proposal has not been otherwise adopted, and obscures the parallel between v. 1, in which the divine beings praise Yahweh's 'glory', and v. 9 (cf. Girard 1984: 235).

42. Girard (1984: 235, 237) and Kraus (1988: 350) assume that this is the heavenly Temple. But see Gerstenberger (1988: 131), who thinks that here the Psalm is brought down to earth. There seems to be no reason not to identify the היכל with the earthly Temple, especially in view of the evocation of the people.

everything saying 'Glory', is stilled, and action comes to rest in the verb ישׁב, 'was enthroned, dwelled'. Only YHWH ruled over the Flood, when nothing else was. The Flood is paralleled in v. 10b by עולם, 'eternity'. The voices of the Psalm, and the liturgy of the Temple, contain the moment of silence and annihilation, project it into eternity, and transform it into blessing and peace.

Despite the paucity of direct references, the Flood is a persistent source of anxiety in the Hebrew Bible, evoked in every threat of annihilation. There are traces of allusions in the prophets (e.g. Hos. 4.3; Zeph. 1.2-3),[43] references to a primaeval destruction of the wicked in Job (22.15; 38.13-15), vague implications of Flood imagery in visions of apocalyptic destruction (e.g. Isa. 24.18).[44] However, it virtually disappears from biblical narrative, with the exception of two stories, both of which carry their own train of intertextual associations, but are nonetheless isolated, displaced, or accomplishing a displacement, within the narrative.

The first is the destruction of Sodom and Gomorrah in Genesis 18–19.[45] They are already characterized as being reminiscent of antediluvian time on their first appearance in Gen. 13.10, where they are described as being 'like the garden of Yahweh'. But they are very wicked and sinful (13.13); God destroys them, rescuing the one righteous man, Lot, and his family, with one unfortunate exception. The episode of the sons of God and the daughters of human beings is repeated, and travestied, in the attempted rape of the angels; similarly, the concluding scene of Noah's drunkenness and Ham's transgression recurs in the incestuous union of Lot and his daughters, transposing heterosexuality for homosexuality, generation for the intergenerational curse.

43. Cf. Landy (1995: 54), de Roche (1980, 1981), and critical comments in Ben-Zvi (1990: 55-58). Berlin (1994: 81-83), however, endorses de Roche's approach to Zeph. 1.2-3, and expands on it.

44. See the discussions in Wildberger (1989: 938-39) and Kaiser (1980: 191), and, generally, Lewis (1978: 8).

45. The most exhaustive account of the parallels is provided in tabular form by Fisch (1988: 69-71), with further discussion on pp. 74-75 and 78. Fisch adds Deut. 32 and Isa. 1 to the intertextual weave, noting however that the destruction of Sodom and Gomorrah is much more evident in the latter than the Flood. He mentions the comparative rarity of references to the Flood in the Hebrew Bible, omitting, however, Ezek. 14. There is also a discussion in Alter (1996: 88), who points out that Lot's daughters think that the catastrophe has been global (Gen. 19.31). See also Alter (1990: 153), Letellier (1995: 219, 226, 232) and Zornberg (1995: 54).

There are other differences. Most obviously, it substitutes fire for flood. Fire and flood are opposite modes of destruction; whereas flood merges all distinctions, corresponding to the heterosexual conflation of divine and human beings and closing the gap between upper and lower waters, fire dematerializes, creating a dry and lifeless space,[46] transforming the Sodomites' metamorphic desire into destructive divine knowledge (18.21). Sexuality becomes a vehicle for disjunction, sterility, and aversion, blinding, or petrifaction of the eyes. However, fire and flood metaphorically converge, since 'Yahweh rained on Sodom and Gomorrah sulphur and fire' (Gen. 19.24), in an apparent reference to the Flood (Alter 1996: 88). The destruction of Sodom is a parody flood, that has turned into its antithesis.

Secondly, the figure of the righteous man is distributed between Abraham and Lot. Abraham articulates Noah's failed protest, in an implicit critique, while Lot develops his comic aspects. The bifurcation of the hero, giving him a voice, launches the narrative on its Midrashic career.

The story of Sodom and Gomorrah has echoes throughout the Bible, notably in Judges 19 (Lasine 1984; Niditch 1982), and the stories of Tamar and Ruth (cf. Fisch 1982). Accordingly, the Flood has attenuated recurrences, for instance in the deaths of Er and Onan, and the famine and mortality at the beginning of Ruth.[47]

At the same time, the story is a displacement, an aside, from the main Patriarchal narrative. The covenant is here given to Abraham in the previous chapter; the annunciation of Isaac takes the place of the celebration of Noah's birth in Gen. 5.29. Lot's issue remains marginal, and ambivalently charged with exclusion and kinship.

The second story that repeats elements of the Flood narrative is that of Moses's birth in Exodus 1–2, as part of a detailed recapitulation of the Primeval History (Ackerman 1974).[48] The Israelite male children are threatened with death through drowning; Moses survives in an ark on

---

46. See the discussion of the contrast between myths of fire and flood in Sullivan (1989: 57-72).

47. Other intertextual connections are suggested by Penchansky (1992) and Hawk (1992).

48. In 2.15-22, there is also a recollection of the 'betrothal' type scene from the Patriarchal narratives; as a shepherd, Moses relives the occupation of his ancestors.

the river, and ultimately God 'remembers' his covenant (2.23-25). The word for ark (תבה) is the same as that used in the Flood story, and occurs nowhere else.[49] The repetition is satirical; the pharaoh is an anti-God, whose Nile is a diminished cosmic inundation, and who is defeated by an infant Noah.[50] The motif of sin is accordingly absent; like the gods in Atraḥasis, the pharaoh is troubled by the Israelites' fecundity, their response to the divine blessing of Genesis 1. Behind the allusion to the Flood story is that of immersion and enslavement in Egypt; behind the pharaoh is God. The pharaoh is displaced as master of events by his own daughter, who takes on the salvific aspect of God; Moses is entirely passive, except for his capacity to weep, cared for and protected by his mother and sister (Exum 1994a: 52). His mother and sister then adopt the role of Noah. The men in the narrative, such as Moses' father, are impotent or nonentities. The dominance of women permits the transformation. In the Flood story, the attractiveness of women blurs divine–human boundaries and is antecedent to the Flood. Lot's daughters conceive from their father through rendering him powerless and unknowing.[51] Here the activity of women changes the fear of castration, and corresponding suppression of women, into a transference of power, from Egypt to Israel, from masters to slaves, from men to women, if only for the moment.[52]

David Damrosch (1987: 272-73, 292-95) traces in detail how the Moses birth story becomes the prototype for his entire life, and the

49. Cassuto (1983: 18-19); Damrosch (1987: 272-73); Exum (1994a: 54). Damrosch points out that Moses' mother caulks the Ark to seal it (Exod. 2.3), just as Noah is instructed to do (Gen. 6.14), though the materials differ.

50. See Damrosch (1987: 287) for a general tracing of this motif in the Exodus story. Satire against the divine pretensions of kings is a commonplace in the Hebrew Bible e.g. Ezek. 29.1-16; Isa. 14.4-27. See also Weems (1992: 31).

51. The common biblical use of the verb ידע, 'know', for sex is pointedly reversed in the repeated insistence that Lot 'did not know' that his daughters lay with him (Gen. 19.33, 35), thus emphasizing the castration theme.

52. Exum (1996: 94-98) discusses how women's power in these chapters is endorsed, but also tamed, through diffusion among several female characters, and by subordinating them to socially sanctioned male interests. She also suggests that the prominence of women in the initial chapters of Exodus is a form of compensation for their almost total exclusion from the rest of the Pentateuchal narrative. Cf. Exum (1994b), of which her chapter ('The Hand that Rocks the Cradle') in Exum 1996 is an expansion. Weems (1992: 32-33) describes how the narrative simply reinscribes ideological differences.

consequent parallels between Israel's journey through the wilderness and the Flood. According to Damrosch, for instance, the jewels on Aaron's breastplate correspond to the rainbow, and the spies to the raven and dove.[53] Moses is the great intercessor, who, unlike Noah and even Abraham, saves his people from annihilation.

Yet he is also alien, floating between his birth mother and his foster mother, between Israel and Egypt, his task and his frustration. Moses, and the Moses lineage,will remain marginal in Israel. The wilderness and the Flood are emblematic, according to Damrosch (1987: 295), of the exile in which we, and all narratives, find ourselves.[54]

In the Hebrew Bible, then, the Flood articulates a foundational instability,[55] with its alien origins, its unintegrated narrative voices, its conflict between the divine nihilism and commitment. We have found various responses: transformation into compassion and rebirth, containment, subversion. The text tends to grow, to bifurcate, and to develop new possibilities; the silence of Noah becomes voluble. Thereby it becomes Midrash.

Midrash[56] on the Flood narrative incorporates two interpretative strategies, one supportive of the biblical text, the other subversive of it. The narrative is thus elaborated and unravelled at the same time. None of the premises of the story remains intact and unquestioned, but it still retains its overarching structure. The dissolution of the causal network stated so clearly in the source text (violence > judgment > retribution >

---

53. Pardes (1994: 10) discusses the *unheimlich* quality of the reversion to the antediluvian Nefilim in the story of the spies. The spies see in the land not continuity with their ancestors, but the paradigmatic discontinuity of the Flood.

54. See also Blenkinsopp (1977: 65), according to whom the 'P-edited deluge story [is] a kind of parable of the inundation of Israel by the nations resulting in exile from the land'.

55. Cf. Levenson (1988: 18): 'the [Flood] story itself manifests a profound anxiety about the givenness of creation, a keen sense of its precariousness'.

56. Neusner, in several works (e.g. 1985: ix; 1990: 15; 1992), insists on the literary and ideological autonomy of each Midrashic collection, and polemicizes against those who treat Midrash as a whole. Clearly, a millennial tradition will exhibit some evolution and change (Rubenstein). Nonetheless, Neusner overstates his case, largely through extreme selectivity; the difference between the collections does not override their marked similarities, in hermeneutic technique, style, and material. For a critique of Neusner, see Boyarin (1992). In the following discussion I will focus on the presentation of the story in *Genesis Rabbah*, much of which is repeated in later collections. As ever, I have found Zornberg's reading of the Midrash invaluable.

salvation) exposes the underlying chaos, the rupture of all meaningful connections, that the narrative relates. The generation of the Flood was evil indeed—and the Midrash expatiates on its wickedness[57]—but less so than the ten tribes, or Judah, or even the contemporary inhabitants of the coastal regions. The latter subsist because of the merit of one Gentile, one Godfearer, among them; if so, the Flood generation too should have been spared (*Gen. R.* 28.5).[58] Similarly, one point of view maximizes the righteousness of Noah,[59] and another minimizes it. R. Hanina claims that he did not have an ounce of merit (*Gen. R.* 29.1); he only survived for the sake of Moses (*Gen. R.* 26.6),[60] or because of God's arbitrary decision (*Gen. R.* 28.9; 29.1; 31.1).[61] God remembered him (Gen. 8.1) because he fed the animals in the Ark, or because of their merit (*Gen. R.* 33.3). His righteousness was especially praiseworthy in the context of his generation, or else he would have been a nonentity in any other generation (*Gen. R.* 30.9).

The Flood was not necessarily global; some hold that the land of Israel was spared, and thence the dove brought the olive leaf; another view is that it came from the Garden of Eden, which likewise, presumably, was not inundated (*Gen. R.* 33.6).[62] In that case, the olive leaf was not a sign

57. The Midrash disagrees also on the nature of its crimes. One line of interpretation emphasizes indiscriminate sexuality, while another stresses robbery. A passage that holds that they were guilty of theft beneath legal consideration (*Gen. R.* 31.5) is juxtaposed with another that accuses them of every possible transgression (*Gen. R.* 31.6).

58. Likewise, R. Abba bar Kahana holds that the ten tribes survived because of the merits of the righteous men and women who were descended from them.

59. This is most notably evident in the pseudepigrapha (e.g. *1 En.* 106–107; cf. Lewis 1978: 20-35). In *Genesis Rabbah* we find that Noah's true generations were his good deeds (30.6). It redounds to God's credit that he wasn't jealous of Noah's righteousness (32.2). Noah exemplifies the dictum that the righteous person is the foundation of the world (30.1). Zornberg (1995: 60) discusses his 'God-like role in "feeding the creatures"'.

60. In *Gen. R.* 29.5, R. Simon holds that Noah is saved because of the merit of his descendants.

61. Another Midrash is that Noah was a man of little faith, who only entered the Ark when the Flood reached his knees (*Gen. R.* 32.6). In 32.1, Noah himself admits that he was no different from the men of his generation, and was only saved through God's special dispensation.

62. In 32.10, however, R. Jonathan's ass-driver refutes a Samaritan who claims that Mt Gerizim alone was spared the Flood by arguing that since the text states that the high mountains were covered (Gen. 7.17), the low mountains were also.

that the Flood abated. Likewise, not all creatures outside the Ark perished. The Re'em was attached to the Ark by its horns, since it was far too big to enter it (31.13); according to another view it stayed in the land of Israel.[63] Og, future king of Bashan, sat on top of the Ark and was fed by Noah daily.[64]

Others stress the totality of the Flood. Even the otherwise indestructible 'almond bone' of Adam was pulverized, according to R. Yohanan (*Gen. R.* 28.3). R. Huna and R. Jeremiah say that three handbreadths of topsoil were removed (*Gen. R.* 31.7). The victims were boiled as well as drowned (*Gen. R.* 28.9);[65] their obliteration, according to *m. Sanh.* 10.1, extends to their not being resurrected for judgment.[66]

Opposing views may converge on the same point. For instance, in *Gen. R.* 30.9 the phrase 'righteous, perfect he was in his generations' (Gen. 6.9) produces symmetrically opposed interpretations. R. Judah holds that in any other generation he would have been unremarkable, while R. Nehemiah claims that he was especially laudable because of the unpropitious moral climate.[67] This is followed by a discussion of the

According to this argument, the land of Israel would not have escaped either. In *b. Zeb.* 113b the view that the land of Israel escaped the Flood is attributed to R. Yohanan, and that it did not to Resh Lakish.

63. *B. Zeb.* 113b. Another view is that only its young entered the Ark (*Gen. R.* 31.13; *b. Zeb.* 113b). The immensity of the Re'em, and even of its young, is the subject of considerable discussion (*b. Zeb.* 113b; *Gen. R.* 31.13).

64. *B. Zeb.* 113b. According to *Pirke de Rabbi Eliezer* 23, Og stayed on a rung of a ladder of the Ark, and had sworn perpetual servitude to Noah's descendants.

65. Cf. also *b. Sanh.* 108b; *b. Zeb.* 113b. According to *Tanḥ. Noah* 7 and *Tanḥ. Buber* 2.10, the giants were too tall to be drowned by the Flood, and consequently were destroyed by fire. Another view is that they stopped up the springs of the great deep with their children, and thus God had to resort to a flood from above.

66. Nor is their soul restored to its sheath (*b. Sanh.* 108a; *Gen. R.* 26.6).

67. In *b. Sanh.* 108a, these views are attributed to R. Yohanan and Resh Lakish respectively. The construction of the argument is much less elegant. The care with which the arguments are rhetorically balanced is evident. Each supports his position with two matching similitudes. R. Judah says that in the market of the blind the one-eyed man is clear sighted, and that in a cellar of vinegar indifferent wine smells sweet, while R. Nehemiah claims that Noah was like a bag of balsam in a graveyard or a virgin in the market of prostitutes. Each sets up the generations of Moses and Samuel as an ideal (tongue-in-cheek?). According to R. Judah, Noah would have been held of no account, while R. Nehemiah argues *a fortiori* that how much more righteous he would have been. Fish (1989–90: 75), in her citation of this passage, only mentions the negative interpretation, but not the positive one. A flaw in her

succeeding phrase, 'with God walked Noah', in which the same argument is used to support opposite positions. R. Judah holds that it was a sign of Noah's moral weakness that God had to take him by the hand, while R. Nehemiah contends that it was out of love for him that God led him through the quagmire of his era. Both contrast Noah's virtue to the superior righteousness of Abraham, whom God told to 'walk before me' (Gen. 17.1). R. Nehemiah, however, reverses the relationship between God and the righteous man. Here it is God who is in a dark alley, and Abraham who illumines the way for him. In both cases, one figure is lost or stuck in the mire, and the other assists him, suggesting the mutual partnership of God and humanity, and their joint difficulty in finding their way through the perplexing world.

The contrary readings may be mutually reinforcing. Noah may have been an unexceptional man, whose creation God regretted with that of all the rest of humanity;[68] but insofar as he was righteous, indeed the paradigmatic righteous man of his generation, it suggests that God's revulsion encompassed good and evil alike. Behind the Midrashic account of the Flood, as Avivah Zornberg (1995: 44) points out, is the spectre of indiscriminate slaughter, which the Midrash calls *andro-lemousia*,[69] of which the prototype is the destruction of the Temple. This may be dissimulated through parable, as in *Gen. R.* 32.8, in which God's action is like 'a governor who decrees a general massacre (*dro-lomousia*)[70] in his province, and takes his beloved and binds him in a prison', to protect him.

In another parable (*Gen. R.* 29.4), the relationship of God and Noah is compared to that of a man who comes across another on the way, grows attached to him, and gives him his daughter in marriage. The

article in general is that she seeks to establish unambiguous and uniform interpretations for Midrash and Jewish exegesis, vis-à-vis its Muslim and contemporary counterparts.

68. This interpretation is arrived at through a daring rereading of Gen. 6.8-9, trespassing across the verse divider: כי נחמתי כי עשׂיתם ונח, 'For I regret that I made them and Noah' (*Gen. R.* 28.9; 29.1; 31.1; *b. Sanh.* 108a). *Tanhuma Re'eh* 3 cites the rabbis, on the contrary, as suggesting that there were many worthy people at the time of the Flood who were wiped out by it. Individual reward and punishment only began with the giving of the Toarh at Mt Sinai. I owe the reference to Zornberg (1995: 42).

69. See Jastrow (1971: 81), who holds that it is a popular pronunciation of ἀνδροληφία.

70. A variant of *androlomousia* (Jastrow 1971: 321).

daughter, Zornberg suggests (1995: 41), is wisdom, manifested, in the Midrash immediately following, by the discernment of when and how to feed the animals. The disturbing aspect of the parable, as Zornberg points out, is the randomness of the encounter. Noah 'found favour' in God's eyes (Gen. 6.8) for no special reason—'favour' has no reasons—and the arbitrariness of God's choice corresponds to the arbitrariness of the destruction.

Similarly, the exposition of the enormity of the dereliction of the generation of the Flood combines with that of its minuteness and with comparison with the sins of other generations, to infect our everyday actions with hyperbolic evil. R. Hanina distinguished violence (חמס) from robbery (גזל) by its imperceptibility. 'Violence refers to that which is worth less than a *perutah*, robbery to that which is worth a *perutah*' (*Gen. R.* 31.5).[71] Violence, on this view, is beneath the threshold of consciousness and legal accountability. Violence here may refer to legal chicanery,[72] or to a pervasive and diffuse propensity.[73]

Noah 'saw a new world' (*Gen. R.* 30.8), and in this he is linked to Joseph, Moses, Job, and Mordechai.[74] Zornberg (1995: 59) remarks that in the latter cases the new world is metaphorical, while in Noah's it is real. She then reverses the direction of the metaphor by suggesting that just as in the other instances the transformation is subjective, so Noah could not but be 'profoundly changed' by his experience. The Midrash is a comment on the word היה, 'was', in 'perfect he was in his generations' (Gen. 6.9). In each case, the Midrash claims, the word היה,

71. A *perutah* was the smallest coin.

72. R. Hanina's dictum is illustrated by an anecdote in which in the antediluvian age a farmer would bring a basket of lupines to market, and people would steal less than a *perutah*'s worth, until he had none left.

73. Zornberg (1995: 52) identifies 'violence' (חמס) with 'rapacious egotism', which may include amoral sexual possession, with a fundamentally colonialist attitude towards the world (53); cf. also Fish (1989–90: 75).

74. Another interpretation is that these five figures were exemplars of providing for others; היה refers to the capacity to give and maintain existence. Joseph sustained his family, Moses the generation to the wilderness, Job nourished the poor, while Mordechai, in a Midrash that caused even the audience to laugh, suckled Esther when he could not find a wet nurse. Noah's care for the entire animal kingdom is implicitly equated with charity for the poor and the exigencies of the Diaspora. This interpretation achieves an at least notional (or rhetorical) authority through being attributed to the rabbis. In *Tanh. Noah* 5, the paradigm of those who saw a new world consists of Noah, Daniel and Job, just as in Ezek. 14.

'was', refers to a decisive rupture in a person's life; it denotes a 'before' and 'after'. היה, another Midrash affirms, expresses continuity; Noah was consistently righteous from the beginning to end of his life (*Gen. R.* 30.8). Yet another view is that היה refers to an absolute past; God had foreordained Noah's perfection and survival. In God's predetermination all events have already happened; the narrative is foreclosed before it has begun. God's arbitrary choice of Noah is on a plane with that of all human destiny. The gap between past and present, total foreknowledge and utter singularity, synchronic history and diachronic discontinuity, between humans acting out their preassigned roles and the indeterminacy they experience, is mediated through imagination, parable, anecdote, and typology.[75] Noah and God may walk together; but God does not move, and for Noah one step is irretrievably distant from the other. Noah A and Noah B have only the obscure quality of righteousness in common. The Midrash is a long attempt to explore the distance, in all its many forms, and give it life, through imagination and illustration.

The Midrash fills the gap between the old and new worlds with domestic detail: what did they eat? when did they sleep (if they did)? how many cells were there? The noise, smell, even the cold, of life on the Ark are minutely related.[76] There are moments of pathos, such as a

75. Space precludes detailed elaboration. Parables are stereotyped, folkloric and timeless; while they appear to be illustrations of the source text, in fact they assimilate the text to underlying archetypes (Boyarin 1989: 80-92; Stern 1991). At the same time, they permit subversion at one remove. Stern (1991: 12) writes illuminatingly about the metonymic character of Midrash, and its mediation between straightforward illustration and occult subversion (51). The conventional figure of the king, for instance, reflects the ambivalence associated with human monarchs back onto the deity. The oddity of some parables exposes the oddity of the text. Similarly, the anecdotes about sages, or even figures such as Alexander the Great, with which the exegesis is interwoven, break down the breach between the biblical age and that of Midrash. (On this divide, see Kugel [1986: 90], who states that 'there is no bridge between the Bible's *time* and our time'.) If Midrash mythologizes the past, making it wondrous, the effect of the parenthetic narratives is to make the current age miraculous. It is also the occasion for ideological transfers, for example, from the idea of the deliverance of the righteous from evil to that of his suitability for suffering (e.g. *Gen. R.* 32.2, 34.2). Typology, likewise, eliminates particularity. Noah, Joseph, Moses, etc., are all members of same paradigm; history endlessly repeats itself.

76. For the number of cells, see the discussion between R. Judah and R. Nehemiah (*Gen. R.* 31.10). Some hold that all the animals lived off dried figs; others that Noah fed each animal with its normal diet (*Gen. R.* 31.14; cf. *Sanh.* 108b). In *Tanh.*

description of a lioness who brought her cubs to the Ark and stayed behind while they entered (Ginzberg 1928: I, 157, citing *Yashar Noah* 15a-16a), of danger,[77] and of comedy,[78] but these barely interrupt the overwhelming drudgery,[79] exhaustion and claustrophobia.[80] The effort of memory, which in the Midrash is echoed by Abraham's servant Eliezer asking Shem to recall life on the Ark, recapitulates God's act of recollection. God remembers Noah, as do we, and through our capacity to invent, imagine, and recreate, we cross and hold open the distance between ourselves and the other.[81]

Mediaeval miracle plays introduce new elements into the story: a liturgical dimension within the Corpus Christi cycle from Creation to the Last Judgment; a relation to non-elite culture, manifest in performance by the various guilds; and the interposition of comic episodes, principally Mrs Noah's refusal to enter the Ark.[82] Within the drama of salvation, of which the deliverance of Noah and his family is the prototype, pleasure may be contained and validated. Ritual action is transferred from the clergy to the laity, and expressed through the dissonant, sometimes farcical, vernacular. Mrs Noye is a misogynist stock figure, like the Wife of Bath (Storm 1987), and like her, represents potential resistance to dominant values. Her representation differs, however, in

---

Noah 7 and *Tanh*. *Buber* 2.2, 14, Noah and his sons did not sleep for the whole twelve months in the Ark, because of the animals' different feeding schedules. Other sources report that Noah suffered from the cold, as indicated by the particle אַךְ, 'only', in 7.23, which is a sign of diminution, and onomatopoeically represents his cough (or else a groan) (*Gen. R.* 32.9; *Tanh. Noah* 9).

77. There are several accounts of Noah being attacked by the lion. In some, this occurs at the exit from the Ark (*Gen. R.* 30.6, 36.4), and is unmotivated; others recount that one day Noah was late in feeding it (*Tanh. Noah* 9; *Tanh. Buber* 2.14). This is an alternative explanation of Noah's groan.

78. I am thinking especially of the dialogue between Noah and the raven, in which the raven accuses Noah of having designs on his wife! (*b. Sanh.* 108b).

79. Cf. Shem's account in *b. Sanh.* 108b.

80. Zornberg (1955: 63) notes that the prayer, 'Release my soul from prison' (Ps. 142.8), is a leitmotiv in the *Tanhumas*. According to *Tanh. Noah* 11, this was his constant prayer (cf. *Tanh. Buber* 2.17).

81. Zornberg (1995: 70-71) interprets this distance as a 'transitional space'—borrowing Winnicott's terminology—in which Noah and we are free to create and imagine our new world.

82. In the N-Town play, the motif of Mrs Noah's reluctance is missing. Instead, blind Lamech's killing of Cain provides the comic subplot. In my discussion, I have not referred to the Newcastle play, for reasons of space.

each of the main versions. In the Towneley cycle, the tension is most extreme between the framing narrative and the inset comedy. As in the Second Shepherds' Play, the writer cultivates laughs, at the expense perhaps of the integrity of the drama (Jack 1989). Mrs Noye enacts, however, the possibility of metanoia, as, once she is in the Ark, she becomes as articulate in her praise of God and in her initiative as she was in carping at Noah. Noah and his wife match each other in blows and invective, but also in a certain affection despite conflict, as when they agree to pray for each other (ll. 238-43). They respond to their children's plea to suspend their quarrels. The family provides the underlying community within which conflict arises and is resolved.

In both the York and the Chester plays, Noah's wife expresses pity and grief over the victims. In the York play, she weeps on the exit from the Ark over 'all our kin and company' (ll. 269-71), and, in her very last words, over the future devastation of the world by fire (ll. 303-305). She wishes to rescue her co-mothers and cousins (l. 143), and grieves over her friends (l. 151). This motif is mingled with others, such as the charge that Noah should have consulted her (ll. 113-16), that she needs time to prepare (ll. 109-10), and the understandable suspicion that Noah might have gone mad (ll. 89-92). She is depicted, traditionally, as a gad-about: 'Come, bairns, and let us truss to town' (l.81). However, the conflict is not as intense as in either the Towneley or Chester cycles, since she is not forced aboard, and since she is motivated less by antagonism than by concern, confusion, and pity.

The Chester play, perhaps the last to be written (Mills 1994: 109), articulates her resistance most clearly, against a background of familial harmony established through her cooperation with Noah, together with her sons and daughters-in-law, in building the Ark, and her participation in their celebration of the entrance of the animals (ll. 173-76). Her refusal to enter the Ark is unambiguously a choice not to sail without her 'gossips', or else to die with them. Uniquely among the characters in the plays, she opposes female (or human) solidarity to divine judgment, embodying an evident, if not explicit, protest on behalf of her friends. Unlike her counterparts in the York and Towneley cycles, she remains obdurate; compelled on board by her son Japheth, she slaps Noah and does not say another word for the rest of the play.[83] The motif of solidarity, moreover, is transferred to the 'gossips', who 'drinke or we

---

83. Marx's (1995: 120) insistence that she does undergo a transformation at this point seems to me to be entirely unfounded.

depart' (l. 229), the only time in the plays we hear the voice, and at least fleetingly embrace the consciousness, of the condemned, who are not so much perverse, it seems, as bibulously jolly.[84] The clash of values is not clearcut; they represent a subversive anti-authoritarianism, in contrast to the colourless conformity of Noah's sons and daughters-in-law. In the Chester play, the stock figure of Noah's wife acquires more serious dimensions, evidenced also by the reduction of conventional stereo-typing.[85]

I had hoped to discuss the Flood motif in fiction, both as a figure of eschatological closure, and as an instrument for rewriting the Bible, and with it the Western tradition. In George Eliot's *Mill on the Floss*, the flood, of which there have been intimations throughout the novel, breaches the conventions of nineteenth-century realist fiction, the expectation that life goes on, that loose ends will be resolved, that our affairs have significance. Maggie and Tom die in each other's arms, their estrangement suspended, in the womb of the flood. The Flood is unsat-isfactory, but its irrelevance, its disruption of the entire fabric of the novel and of life, produces one of the rare, pure moments of jouissance and absurdity in the classic novel.

Sandra Birdsell's haunting first novel, *The Missing Child* (1989), is about a small Manitoba town about to be swept away by the melting of an underground glacier. As the signs of the impending catastrophe mul-tiply, so cracks appear in the surface of the town's streets and in its soci-ety, a child disappears, and the conventions, cruelties, and struggles of normality shift. The flood here becomes a symbol for the sense of pre-monition, of flimsiness, in the prairie novel, in which the history of European settlement merges with the flatness of the landscape, the mirages, the possibility of inversion.

In Gabriel Garcia Marquez's epic, *Cien Años de Soledad (Hundred Years of Solitude)* (1969), the Flood is much more closely related to biblical and apocalyptic themes, as well as to South American mythology. Finally, Timothy Findley's *Not Wanted on the Voyage*, with its dying Yahweh, its patriarchal monomaniac Noah, and the helplessness of all its sympathetic

84. Note also that they are characterized as 'good gossips'.

85. Noah's wife is not, for example, habitually shrewish, as apparently is the case in the Towneley play (ll. 186-89), nor is there any conventional warning to prospective husbands, as in Towneley ll. 397-400. The only evidence of misogyny I detect is that gossips like to drink.

characters, is a terrifying parable on the legacy of shame, guilt and despair in the apparent safety of the Ark.

In children's bibles and children's Arks, the narrative becomes part of children's culture, adrift from its biblical moorings.[86] When my child carries around a cloth Noah's Ark, or inserts the pieces in a Noah's Ark jigsaw, or reads a Noah's Ark pop-up book, comments on Noah's long beard, identifies the animals, the thunder and lightning, and so on, the implied narrative has little to do with the biblical terror and promise. Indeed, the figure of Noah and his Ark may be a pretext for the child's drama of possession, control, identification and wonder: the child's mastery of language, of his or her body, and the opening to the world which the pop-up book enacts. When I read these books, I ignore the incomprehensible and rudimentary text, as, I suspect, do most parents. Of course, as the child grows older, so the relationship with the text changes, but without necessarily displacing the primary association with play. The narrative enters a different canon (alongside Thomas the Tank Engine, Curious George, Mother Goose), and while it may come fraught with sacred associations, reciprocally it stamps the Bible as children's literature. The ambiguity, as we have seen, is characteristic of the entire tradition, in which the Flood story is both integral to the Bible and alien to it.

Children's bibles are frequently imaginatively disappointing, whether or not they simply reproduce or paraphrase the text, as Robert Carroll points out in his contribution to this volume. They perpetuate the fallacy that the Bible is children's literature, which may lead to the assumption that it is not properly serious. Midrashic elaboration is transferred to the illustrations, some of which emphasize the realism of the narrative, while others diffuse it. Tomie de Paola's version (1995), for instance, strives towards an iconographic and typological effect. While the text, taken from the NIV, reinforces the sacrosanct particularity of the story, the illustrations suggest that it is timeless and ethereal, for instance through the elimination of perspective. The final epiphany frames Noah and his family in an ecclesiastical setting, perhaps a basilica, with

---

86. Fish's is the only contribution I know to relate the Noah of children's books to the Noah of the Midrash and the Bible. As elsewhere, she tends to polarize, contrasting the wish-fulfilment and happy ending characteristic of children's versions with the realism and moral sobriety of the biblical and Midrashic narrative. The history and ideology of children's Bibles is very complex, and has been undergoing rapid change. See in particular Bottigheimer 1996: esp. 206-15.

mediaeval (Romanesque?) overtones; the rainbow forms the cupola, separated from the family by a frieze of arches, under which they are enclosed in an alcove or niche, just as icons often provide saints with architectural background (Fig. 1). The family itself schematically constitutes a sacred tableau. Noah's arms are outstretched, presumably in blessing, while he is flanked by two boys holding olive sprigs, like YHWH in Zechariah 4. The grouping of the figures, the positioning of hands, the doleful expression of the woman on the right, the dove held by Mrs Noah on the left, compound the iconographic association: it could be a saint with donors, or the women at the cross. A hand from heaven indicates the rainbow, while leading back metonymically to the invisible deity, again reminiscent of mediaeval convention. A composition of two cats and two kittens stares out from the left-hand corner, communicating domesticity, and perhaps a sense of mystery and grace. On the entrance to the Ark, Mrs Noah is foregrounded with the same two cats, but without the kittens. The cats may represent the continuity of life, as well as proliferation in the Ark,[87] but they also serve as emblems for Mrs Noah, evocative of the wifely domain of home and kitchen.

The *Reader's Digest Bible for Children* (Delvall 1995), on the other hand, depicts people climbing onto rooftops, embracing, weeping, clinging to logs, and clambering onto protruding rocks, as they watch the Ark sail away (Fig. 2). In an earlier picture, passers-by are puzzled by the Ark's construction. The horror of the scene is distanced by the simplification of the features of the characters, their primitive clothing, and the impressionistic merging of sea, rain and mountains. A starker, lurid realism is to be found in the immensely popular *The Golden Children's Bible* (anon.): rushing highlighted waters, terrified animals, elephants or perhaps mammoths[88] trumpeting at the skies, two men dressed in what look like teatowels staring at the Ark in anger or regret, one of them incongruously stroking the head of a kid. The effect is

---

87. In Jewish sources, life on the Ark was celibate, a rule broken by only three creatures: the dog, the raven, and Ham (*b. Sanh.* 108b). Note also that in Christopher Smart's *Jubilate Agno*, the Israelites left Egypt accompanied by their cats (not to speak of Cecil B. DeMille's *Ten Commandments*).

88. The divide between prehistoric and modern fauna seems to be that between Gen. 1 and Gen. 2 in *The Golden Children's Bible*. Nonetheless, the elephants in this illustration seem to have woolly coats, though this may also be the effect of the rain. Perhaps, unlike the Re'em in Midrash, the mammoths became extinct because there was no room for them on the Ark.

Figure 1. 'The Rainbow', in Tomie de Paola, *Book of the Old Testament*
(illus. Tomie de Paola; New York: Putnam's Sons, 1995)

Figure 2. 'The Rising Waters', in Marie-Hélène Delvall, *Reader's Digest Bible for Children: Timeless Stories from the Old and New Testaments* (illus. Ulises Wencell; n.p.: Joshua Morris Publishing, 1995)

cinematic—one suspects the influence of Bible movies—and difficult to take seriously, whether because of stylization or exaggeration.[89]

Some versions paraphrase the biblical text, to explore the depths of the narrative, to ask its questions, to bring it to life, or to introduce a particular twist. Bach and Exum, for instance, draw attention to Noah's silence, through repeating three times that he did not respond; in fact, neither he nor any other human character says a word throughout the narrative. We do not know why this is; Bach and Exum are entirely non-judgmental. The silence is subsumed unobtrusively in the life of the Ark and the exit from it. In this Bach and Exum are faithful to the biblical narrative, as they comment in their note to the story. The characters, and the animals, are vividly imagined, through non-verbal interactions (Noah and Noah's wife smile at each other when the sun emerges), thoughts, and activities. We see the world for the last time, before it is inundated. Noah's sons are reluctant to brings turnips, sprouts and kohlrabi, because they do not like them—a comic detail that opens up the realm of idiosyncracies. The animals are realized in their fear, depression, and pleasure, as the sun warms their fur on the deck. As one might expect, Bach and Exum attempt to shift gender boundaries. Whereas version after version simply reinscribes traditional gender roles,[90] Bach and Exum distribute roles equally and without apparent reason. It is not clear, for instance, why the sons should gather grain and the daughters-in-law fruit and leaves. Noah's wife takes the initiative in smiling at Noah. Another example of paraphrastic retelling is Scholem Asch's delightful version in his collection *In the Beginning*. Asch draws on Midrash for much of his detail, for instance the jewel that illumined the Ark or Noah's objection that he is not a hunter. Asch's Noah is much wryer and more bad-tempered than those in most conventionally pious readings, and certainly than Bach and Exum's Noah. When his contemporaries mock him, he says to himself, 'Laugh all you wish; I know

89. The problem of taking the Flood seriously is, I think, pervasive in the literature. Norman Cohn (1996) traces in fascinating detail how the problem of the veracity of the Flood stimulated the development of geology and the dissolution of biblical cosmology.

90. Frequently, Noah and his sons are depicted building the Ark, while their wives are cooking meals beside it. In Lorimer's *Noah's Ark* (1978), the men build the Ark, while the women harvest the grain and other food products. See also Baynes (1988). This suggests the influence of popular anthropological studies on the division of labour in traditional societies.

what I know'. Driven to distraction on the Ark, he curses, scolds and strikes the animals. The animals themselves spend their time spreading scandal. The shtetl has come to the Ark; the Ark is the shtetl. And like the shtetl, it is not a benign world, but it does have vitality. And it is this world that is redeemed.

A more radical Midrashic reading is to be found in Marc Gellman's immensely popular *Does God Have a Big Toe?* (1989). Gellman devotes three stories to the Flood. In the first, all the animals seek God to inter-cede with him to avert the Flood. Only the fish, however, realize that he is everywhere, and thus only they are entirely saved. In the second, Noah cannot bring himself to tell his friends about the impending Flood, while in the third the rainbow is preceded by a rainbow of birds, who have come to look for their friends, the raven and dove. The sec-ond story ends with Noah expressing his grief to two of his friends, who have tried to sneak into the Ark by dressing in a zebra suit. 'My dear friends, I don't know how I can live without you. The world was not this bad when God gave it to us. I don't know why God is saving me. Maybe God needs somebody to tell the story of how we all messed up the world... I love you. I am sorry for you, sorry for the animals, sorry for me, and sorry for God.' It is the only point I have found in the entire tradition in which Noah addresses, and identifies with, all that has been lost. In a truly sublime Midrashic touch, Gellman concludes: 'Then the great rains came and flooded all the earth. Some say it was just rain, but others say it was God's tears.'

Hilary Mantel's novel, *Fludd*, is not about the Flood, though it does have a few references to it. It is about the disintegration of a world, the mouldering sacred canopy of an imaginary Catholic community on the moors in the 1950s, ruled by the fearsome and sadistic Mother Perpetua at the convent, and the kind, weak, sceptical and resourceful Father Angwin in the presbytery, Mother Perpetua's perpetual antagonist. The bishop invades this backwater in the first chapter, bringing tidings of modernity, ecumenism and the vernacular Mass ('There are men in Rome who think of it'), and threatening Father Angwin with a curate. On the bishop's instructions, the plaster saints are removed from the parish church and buried. One wet and windy night a man arrives at the presbytery, introducing himself as Father Fludd, and is assumed to be the new curate, the bishop's spy. In fact, he is Robert Fludd, the alchemist, who revisits the world, with other members of his fraternity, to effect its transformation. Father Angwin stays up all night with Father

Fludd, drinking whisky, and telling him about his loss of faith ('The curate spoke in his light, dry voice: "In considering the life of Christ, there is something that has often made me wonder: did the man who owned the Gadarene swine get compensation?"'). Father Angwin has to consider the vacuity of his life for the first time, becoming older, feeling himself as paralysed as Father Surin, and yet suddenly capable of action. A young Irish nun, Sister Philomena, feeds him with questions of marvellous abstruseness in the confessional ('"If it is a fast day, and you are taking your morning collation, eight ounces that is, can the bread be toasted?" "Oh yes, it may." "But then it would shrink up, Father. Perhaps it might weigh less. So then you could have an extra slice"'). He looks forward to these sessions, and in them one can feel both the impoverishment of his intellectual life, the seduction of theological detail, and his avoidance of—and entrance into, precisely through these questions—the real questions of his life (and her life).

Sister Philomena is the centre for the novel's alchemical project of transformation, not only for herself but for all, or at least most, of the characters.[91] Sister Philomena has arrived at the convent and the religious life through a combination of social pressure and mischance (a nervous rash is mistaken for the stigmata); in the novel she achieves a realization of the hopelessness of her situation and a sexual awakening. At the end she escapes with Father Fludd, and is last seen choosing a new life for herself, at random, at Manchester railway station.

The Flood story begins and ends with the evil in the human heart, emphasized with the totalizing על and the concatenation of יצר and מחשבת. It seems that there isn't any room for human imagination and creativity, and that any pensive activity is inherently suspect. Noah's silence, and God's choice of him, is perhaps not to be explained by his exemplary conduct, as a *saddiq*, 'a righteous person', but by witlessness. The various rereadings enact a certain rehabilitation of human thought and imaginative empathy, for instance in the Midrashic narrative of Noah's care for the animals, which, as Zornberg says, is also care of the self, or in the resistance to Noah and all he stands for in *Not Wanted on the Voyage*. In *Fludd*, thought is not merely evil and suspect, it is profoundly antisocial, associated as it is with class privilege. The grammar

91. Some of them remain mysterious, in particular Judd McElvoy, the tobacconist, a clearly alchemical figure who comes to Sister Philomena/Roisin O'Hallaran's rescue at the very end, and may or may not be responsible for Mother Perpetua's igneous apotheosis.

school children walk armed and in grim phalanx against the attacks of the kids of less ambitious parents. Atheism in fact is a curious synonym for social ostracism (one of the grammar school boys says regretfully, 'We are atheists'). The women of the community, who are in charge of its morals and its serious discourse, are on the lookout for any deviation, of mind or body. They were 'unforgiving about any aberration, deviation, eccentricity, or piece of originality' (Mantel 1989: 14). The maternity of the Church, personified in Mother Perpetua (universally known as Mother Purpit), sees its main task and certainly gains its greatest pleasure from the beating of children and the bullying of adults. The bishop, with somewhat greater civility, has the same objective and the same gratification: 'he liked nothing better than to tear around the diocese in his big black car' (1).[92]

Into this world Father Fludd irrupts, with his message that we are free, that we can make choices. We live on many levels at once, physically and emotionally, but also symbolically and anagogically. Shortly before she leaves, Sister Philomena has a vision of her life if she stays in the Order: 'If every day from now on was to be the same, why have the days at all?' The timelessness that is at stake in the Flood story is now horror: 'whoever regulates my future steals it from me'. Repetition does not open the space of a parenthesis, the comfort of the cosmic covenant; instead the blankness of the interval, the emptiness of a church where there is no room for the 'imagination of the human heart', which, at the beginning of the novel, is crammed with plaster saints, is transmuted into its opposite: that nothing ever repeats. Transubstantiation passes from the institution—the church's work of petrifying humanity—to the imagination of the human heart. One of the many ironies is that Father Fludd enjoys being a priest, and is very good at it, especially in administering the sacraments. The alchemist is the true expert at transubsantiation, at effecting the birth of the divine–human. He describes being a priest as a secret ambition (105). The church itself undergoes a process of death and resurrection, as the saints are buried and then restored. We last hear of them on their plinths, newly washed, polished and buffed (170); more important, the work of disinterment, through a synchronous collective inspiration, is the founding event of the subversive community that forms at the institutional core of the novel and precipitates the denouement. For Father Angwin, its significance is not so much an

---

92. Almost the same sentence is repeated at the end of the novel, with relation to the Chief Constable.

act of defiance of the bishop and the church as a claim to faith, in himself if nothing else, even if it means joining the devil's party.[93] For Sister Philomena it means a recognition of her desire and needs, and an escape from the convent into the nocturnal air—as well as into value.

The beginning of the novel, like that of the Flood story, tells of the descent of the sons of God and their mating with the human daughters. In *1 Enoch*, the sons of God transmit esoteric knowledge. The motif of the sons of God is transferred to the priesthood, but in particular to the alchemists, whom the book imagines as a mystical, sempiternal fraternity, like Wim Wenders' angels. Fludd transmits strange knowledge, marvels such as melon, which Sister Philomena (or Philly)/Roisin O'Halloran experiences somewhat unpleasantly as like 'flesh dissolved in water' (177). But—like a fallen angel—he also acquires knowledge. Alchemists, so we are told, have always avoided sex and women: 'to him it had always seemed as if women were leeches of knowledge, sappers of scholarship' (164-65). We do not know how Fludd has been transformed by his encounter with Featherhoughton, the fabled setting for the novel. But we know that he has been, that he fears this is his nigredo, his dissolution, and that Philly has also redeemed him.

As with the story of the Flood, the novel concludes with the discovery of wine: 'a sweetish, straw-coloured wine, the first she had ever tasted' (1989: 169). And as with that story, drunkenness is an uncovering of flesh. But it is not disgusting; rather it is the element of transformation. Philly/Roisin reflects that virginity is 'a wound that opens with every casual knock from casual passers-by', and that with its loss one grows a new skin.

There is also silence, not Noah's silence, but the silence necessary for change. Fludd, on their last evening, refuses to tell Roisin's future, because 'the art requires the whole man… And then, when all of these are brought together, there must be one further thing… silence' (179).

The Renaissance, and Fludd with it, saw the human condition as one of infinite possibility, and that is the point of cultural studies, and our discourse with the Bible.

---

93. In the midst of this strange parody of a witch's Sabbath, Judd McElvoy, whom Father Angwin regards as the devil, appears with a dish of fish and peas. In one of the few direct biblical references, Angwin wishes vaguely to himself 'whether the curate might effect some sort of multiplication. After all, there was a precedent for it' (139).

BIBLIOGRAPHY

Ackerman, James S.
  1974   'The Literary Context of the Moses Birth Story (Exodus 1–2)', in K.R.R.
              Gros-Louis, James S. Ackerman and T.S. Warshaw (eds.), *Literary Interpre-
              tations of Biblical Narratives* (Nashville: Abingdon Press): 74-119.
Allen, Leslie C.
  1994   *Ezekiel 1–19* (WBC, 28; Dallas: Word Books).
Alter, Robert
  1990   'Sodom as Nexus: The Web of Design in Biblical Narrative', in Regina
              Schwartz (ed.), *The Book and the Text: The Bible and Literary Theory*
              (Oxford: Basil Blackwell): 146-60.
  1996   *Genesis* (New York: W.W. Norton).
Anon.
  n.d.   *The Golden Children's Bible* (New York: A Golden Book).
Asch, Scholem
  1966   *In the Beginning* (trans. Caroline Cunningham; New York: Schocken Books).
Avishur, Yitzhak
  1994   *Studies in Hebrew and Ugaritic Psalms* (Jerusalem: Magnes Press).
Bach, Alice, and J. Cheryl Exum
  1989   *Moses' Ark: Stories from the Bible* (illus. Leo and Diane Dillon; New York:
              Doubleday).
Batto, Bernard F.
  1987   'The Covenant of Peace: A Neglected Ancient Near Eastern Motif', *CBQ*
              49: 187-211.
Baynes, Pauline
  1988   *Noah and the Ark* (London: Methuen).
Beadle, Richard
  1982   *The York Plays* (London: Edward Arnold).
Beadle, Richard, and Pamela M. King
  1984   *The York Mystery Plays: A Selection* (Oxford: Oxford University Press).
Ben-Zvi, Ehud
  1990   *A Historical-Critical Study of the Book of Zephaniah* (BZAW, 198; Berlin: W.
              de Gruyter).
Berlin, Adele
  1994   *Zephaniah* (AB, 25a; New York: Doubleday).
Blenkinsopp, Joseph
  1977   *Prophecy and Canon: A Contribution to the Study of Jewish Origins* (Notre
              Dame: University of Notre Dame Press).
Bottigheimer, Ruth
  1996   *The Bible for Children* (New Haven: Yale University Press).
Boyarin, Daniel
  1990   *Intertextuality and the Reading of Midrash* (Bloomington: Indiana University
              Press).
  1992   'On the Status of the Tannaitic Midrashim: A Critique of Jacob Neusner's
              Latest Contribution to Midrashic Studies', *JAOS* 112: 455-65.

Cassuto, Umberto

1983	*A Commentary on the Book of Exodus* (trans. Israel Abrahams; Jerusalem: Magnes Press).

1984	*A Commentary on the Book of Genesis, Part Two: From Noah to Abraham* (trans. Israel Abrahams; Jerusalem: Magnes Press).

Cohn, Norman R.C.

1996	*Noah's Flood: The Genesis Story in Western Thought* (New Haven: Yale University Press).

Craigie, Peter C.

1983	*Ezekiel* (Philadelphia: Fortress Press).

Damrosch, David

1987	*The Narrative Covenant: Transformations of Genre in the Growth of Biblical Literature* (San Francisco: Harper & Row).

Davies, Philip R.

1992	*In Search of 'Ancient Israel'* (JSOTSup, 148; Sheffield: JSOT Press).

1993	'Women, Men, God, Sex and Power: The Birth of a Biblical Myth', in Athalya Brenner (ed.), *A Feminist Companion to Genesis* (The Feminist Companion to the Bible, 2; Sheffield: Sheffield Academic Press): 194-201.

1997	'Loose Canons: Reflections on the Formation of the Hebrew Bible', *JHS* 1.

Davila, James R.

1995	'The Flood Hero as King and Priest', *JNES* 54: 199-214.

Davis, Ellen F.

1989	*Swallowing the Scroll: Textuality and the Dynamics of Discourse in Ezekiel's Prophecy* (JSOTSup, 78; Sheffield: Almond Press).

Day, John

1980	'The Daniel of Ugarit and Ezekiel and the Hero of the Book of Daniel', *VT* 30: 174-84.

Delvall, Marie-Hélène

1995	*Reader's Digest Bible for Children: Timeless Stories from the Old and New Testaments* (n.p.; Joshua Morris Publishing).

Dressler, Harold H.

1979	'The Identification of the Ugaritic Dnil with the Daniel of Ezekiel', *VT* 29: 152-61.

1984	'Reading and Interpreting the Aqht Text: A Rejoinder to Drs J. Day and B. Margalit', *VT* 34: 78-82.

Eichrodt, Walther

1975	*Ezekiel* (OTL; Philadelphia: Westminster Press).

Exum, J.Cheryl

1994a	'You Shall Let Every Daughter Live: A Study of Exodus 1.8–2.10', in Athalya Brenner (ed.), *A Feminist Companion to Exodus to Deuteronomy* (Feminist Companion to the Bible, 6; Sheffield: Sheffield Academic Press): 37-61. Reprinted from *Semeia* 28 (1983): 63-82.

1994b	'Second Thoughts about Secondary Characters: Women in Exodus 1.8–2.10', in Brenner (ed.), *A Feminist Companion to Exodus to Deuteronomy*: 75-87.

1996   *Plotted, Shot, and Painted: Cultural Representations of Biblical Women* (JSOTSup, 215; Gender, Culture, Theory, 3; Sheffield: Sheffield Academic Press).

Fisch, Harold
1982   'Ruth and the Structure of Covenant History', *VT* 32: 425-37.
1988   *Poetry with a Purpose* (Bloomington: Indiana University Press).

Fish, Varda
1989–90   'Noah and the Great Flood: The Metamorphosis of the Biblical Tale', *Judaica Librarianship* 5: 74-78.

Fishbane, Michael
1985   *Biblical Interpretation in Ancient Israel* (Oxford: Clarendon Press).

Fox, Everett
1995   *The Five Books of Moses* (The Schocken Bible, 1; New York: Schocken Books).

Freedman, David Noel, and C. Franke Hyland
1973   'Psalm 29: A Structural Analysis', *HTR* 66: 237-56.

Gellman, Marc
1989   *Does God have a Big Toe? Stories about Stories in the Bible* (illus. Oscar de Mejo; New York: HarperCollins).

Gerstenberger, Erhard S.
1988   *Psalms: Part 1 with an Introduction to Cultic Poetry* (FOTL, 14; Grand Rapids: Eerdmans).

Ginzberg, Louis
1928   *The Legends of the Jews* (trans. Henrietta Szold; Philadelphia: Jewish Publication Society of America).

Girard, Marc
1984   *Les Psaumes: Analyse Structurelle et Interpretation: 1–50* (Montreal: Bellarmin; Paris: Cerf).

Greenberg, Moshe
1983   *Ezekiel 1–20* (AB, 22; New York: Doubleday).

Hals, Ronald M.
1989   *Ezekiel* (FOTL, 19; Grand Rapids: Eerdmans).

Happé, Peter (ed.)
1975   *English Mystery Plays: A Selection* (London: Penguin Books).

Harland, J.
1996   *The Value of Human Life: A Study of the Story of the Flood (Genesis 6–9)* (Leiden: E.J. Brill).

Hawk, L. Daniel
1992   'Strange House Guests: Rahab, Lot, and the Dynamics of Deliverance', in Danna Nolan Fewell (ed.), *Reading between Texts: Intertextuality and the Hebrew Bible* (Louisville, KY: Westminster/John Knox Press): 89-97.

Holloway, Steven W.
1991   'What Ship Goes There: The Flood Narratives in the Gilgamesh Epic and Genesis Considered in the Light of Ancient Near Eastern Temple Ideology', *ZAW* 103: 328-55.

Jack, R.D.S.
1989   *Patterns of Divine Comedy: A Study of Mediaeval English Drama* (Cambridge: Brewer).

Jastrow, Marcus
    1971   *A Dictionary of the Targumim, the Talmud Babli and Yerushalmi, and the Midrashic Literature* (New York: Judaica).
Jay, Nancy
    1992   *Throughout your Generations Forever: Sacrifice, Religion, and Paternity* (Chicago: Chicago University Press).
Joyce, Paul
    1989   *Divine Initiative and Human Response in Ezekiel* (JSOTSup, 51; Sheffield: Sheffield Academic Press).
Kaiser, Otto
    1980   *Isaiah 13–39* (trans. R.A.Wilson; OTL; London: SCM Press, 2nd edn).
Kraus, Hans-Joachim
    1988   *Psalms 1–59: A Commentary* (trans. Hilton C. Oswald; Minneapolis: Augsburg Press).
Kugel, James L.
    1986   'Two Introductions to Midrash', in Geoffrey H. Hartman and Sanford Budick (eds.), *Midrash and Literature* (New Haven: Yale University Press): 77-103. Reprinted from *Prooftexts* 3 (1983): 131-55.
Kunin, Seth Daniel
    1995   *The Logic of Incest: A Structuralist Analysis of Hebrew Mythology* (JSOTSup, 185; Sheffield: Sheffield Academic Press).
Landy, Francis
    1995   *Hosea* (Readings; Sheffield: Sheffield Academic Press).
Lasine, Stuart
    1984   'Guest and Host in Judges 19: Lot's Hospitality in an Inverted World', *JSOT* 29: 37-59.
Letellier, Robert Ignatius
    1995   *Day in Mamre, Night in Sodom: Abraham and Lot in Genesis 18 and 19* (Leiden: E.J. Brill).
Levenson, Jon D.
    1988   *Creation and the Persistence of Evil* (San Francisco: Harper & Row).
Lewis, Jack
    1978   *A Study of the Interpretation of Noah and the Flood in Jewish and Christian Literature* (Leiden: E.J. Brill).
Lorimer, Lawrence T.
    1978   *Noah's Ark* (New York: Random House).
Mantel, Hilary
    1989   *Fludd* (London: Viking).
Margalit, Baruch
    1970   'A Ugaritic Psalm (RŠ 24.252)', *JBL* 89: 292-304.
    1980   'Interpreting the Story of Aqht', *VT* 30: 361-65.
Marx, William G.
    1995   'The Problem with Mrs. Noah: The Search for Performance Credibility in the Chester *Noah's Flood* Play', in John A. Alford (ed.), *From Page to Performance: Essays in Early English Drama* (East Lancing: Michigan State University Press): 109-26.

Midrash Tanḥuma
   1989   *Midrash Tanḥuma* ((S. Buber Recension. I. Genesis; trans. John T. Towns-
               end; Hoboken: Ktav).
Mills, David
   1992   *The Chester Mystery Cycle: A New Edition with Modernised Spelling* (East
               Lancing: Colleagues).
   1994   'The Chester Cycle', in Richard Beadle (ed.), *The Cambridge Companion to
               Medieval English Theatre* (Cambridge: Cambridge University Press): 109-
               33.
Murray, Robert
   1992   *The Cosmic Covenant* (London: Sheed & Ward).
Neusner, Jacob
   1985   *Genesis Rabbah: The Judaic Commentary to the Book of Genesis. A New
               American Translation* (Atlanta: Scholars Press).
   1990   *The Canonical History of Ideas: The Place of the So-Called Tannaitic Midrashim*
               (Atlanta: Scholars Press).
   1992   'Intertextuality in Judaism: The System and the Canon, the Word and
               Words', *Conservative Judaism* 45: 53-65.
Niditch, Susan
   1982   'The "Sodomite" Theme in Judges 19–20: Family, Community, and
               Social Disintegration', *CBQ* 44: 365-78.
Paola, Tomie de
   1995   *Book of the Old Testament* (New York: Putnam's Sons).
Pardes, Ilana
   1992   *Countertraditions in the Bible* (Cambridge, MA: Harvard University Press).
   1994   'Imagining the Promised Land: The Spies in the Land of the Giants', *His-
               tory and Memory* 6: 5-23.
Penchansky, David
   1992   'Staying the Night: Intertextuality in Genesis and Judges', in Fewell (ed.),
               Reading between Texts: 77-88.
Pirke de Rabbi Eliezer (trans. Gerald Friedlander; New York: Benjamin Blom, 1971).
Pohlmann, Karl-Friedrich
   1992   *Ezechielstudien* (Berlin: W. de Gruyter).
Roche, Michael de
   1980   'Zephaniah I 2-3: The "Sweeping" of Creation', *VT* 30: 404-409.
   1981   'The Reversal of Creation in Hosea', *VT* 31: 400-409.
Rubenstein, Jeffrey, L.
   1996   'From Mystic Motifs to Sustained Myths: The Revision of Rabbinic
               Traditions in Medieval Midrashim', *HTR* 89: 131-59.
Sarna, Nahum
   1989   *Genesis* (The Torah Bible Commentary; Philadelphia: Jewish Publication
               Society of America).
Spector, Stephen
   1991   *The N-Town Play*. I. *Introduction and Text* (Oxford: Oxford University
               Press).
Spiegel, Shalom
   1945   'Noah, Danel, and Job', in *Louis Ginzberg Jubilee Volume* (New York:
               American Academy for Jewish Research): 305-55.

Steinmetz, Devora
    1994   'Vineyard, Farm, and Garden: The Drunkenness of Noah in the Context
                of the Primeval History', *JBL* 113: 193-207.
Stern, David
    1991   *Parables in Midrash* (Cambridge, MA: Harvard University Press).
Storm, Melvin
    1987   'Uxor and Alison: Noah's Wife in the Flood Plays and Chaucer's Wife of
                Bath', *Modern Language Quarterly* 48: 303-19.
Sullivan, Lawrence
    1989   *Icanchu's Drum: An Orientation to Meaning in South American Religions*
                (Chicago: Chicago University Press).
Tigay, Jeffrey
    1985   'The Stylistic Criterion of Source Criticism in the Light of Ancient Near
                Eastern and Postbiblical Literature', in Jeffrey Tigay (ed.), *Empirical Models
                for Biblical Criticism* (Philadelphia: University of Pennsylvania Press): 149-
                73.
Vermeylen, Jacques
    1991   'La Descendance de Caïn et la descendance d'Abel (Gen 4,17-26 +
                5, 28b-29)', *ZAW* 103: 175-93.
Wahl, Harald-Martin
    1992   'Noah, Daniel und Hiob in Ezechiel 12–20 (21–3): Anmerkungen zum
                traditionsgeschichtlichen Hintergrund', *VT* 42: 542-53.
Weems, Renita J.
    1992   'The Hebrew Women Are Not Like the Egyptian Women: The Ideology
                of Race, Gender and Reproduction in Exodus 1', *Semeia* 59: 25-34.
Westermann, Claus
    1984   *Genesis 1–11* (trans. John J. Scullion; Minneapolis: Augsburg Press).
Wevers, John W.
    1982   *Ezekiel* (NCB; Grand Rapids: Eerdmans; London: Marshall, Morgan &
                Scott).
Whybray, R.N.
    1989   *The Making of the Pentateuch: A Methodological Study* (JSOTSup, 53;
                Sheffield: JSOT Press).
Wildberger, Hans
    1989   *Jesaja 13–27* (BKAT, 10.2; Neukirchen–Vluyn: Neukirchener Verlag).
Winnicott, Donald W.
    1971   *Playing and Reality* (London: Tavistock).
Wolde, Ellen van
    1994   *Words Become Worlds: Semantic Studies of Genesis 1–11* (Leiden: E.J. Brill).
Zimmerli, Walther
    1979   *Ezekiel. I. A Commentary on the Book of the Prophet Ezekiel Chapters 1–24*
                (trans. Ronald E. Clements; Hermeneia; Philadelphia: Fortress Press).
Zornberg, Avivah Gottlieb
    1995   *Genesis: The Beginning of Desire* (Philadelphia: Jewish Publication Society
                of America).

Isaac or Oedipus?
Jewish Tradition and the Israeli Aqedah

Yael S. Feldman

Pre-Preface: Cultural Studies?

Cultural Studies presents challenges to literary studies... Its most significant challenge, radical contextualization, has been explicit or implicit
in many of the methods literary studies has adopted...

It is not in the best interest of the discipline to replace Shakespeare
with music videos...

Cary Nelson

Psychoanalysis is a prime example of how and why cultural studies and
the literary are not mutually exclusive.

Marcia Ian

[T]he formalist reading of the high literary text, which many of us were
trained to do... is a recent, technicist aberration and certainly not a pedigree vocation of long standing.

Andrew Ross

The above is but a small selection from about 30 pages of a Forum on
'the relations between cultural studies and the literary', published in
PMLA shortly before our meeting at Sheffield.[1] For me, this Forum
provided a confirmation of something I have suspected for some time,
namely, that—somewhat like Molière's comic character, Monsieur Jordan—I woke up one morning and realized I had been 'doing' cultural
studies all along...

Indeed, if 'the discipline' is not limited to the decentering of the
'Euro-American canon, the ideology of high culture, and other privileged forms of textuality', as categorically declared in the same forum by
other practitioners of the field (e.g. Rolf Goebel in *PMLA* 112.2: 260),

---

1. *PMLA* 112.2 (March 1997): 257-86. The quotes appear on pp. 276, 279,
286, respectively.

then there is room in cultural studies for my kind of scholarship. Preferring (by training? by proclivity? who can tell today...) 'the high literary text', and refusing 'to replace the Bible [!] with music videos', I am nevertheless delighted to supplement them with *any* cultural production—be it popular or scientific, discursive or visual. 'Radical contextualization' has long complemented my 'formalist technicity', as the culture I was raised in (and which is my main object of study) has still to learn to divorce its letters from politics, and its psychology from ideology (see Feldman 1985; 1989b). Finally, as the Hebrew Bible is unambiguously alive in the education, psychology and politics of modern Israel, any inquiry into its contemporary functioning is a cultural probe by default.

Preface

The question posed in my title has been simmering in my mind for some time now, bringing together several areas of interest and making them overlap in unexpected ways.[2] But what brought it to a boil was a challenge raised by the foremost Israeli author, A.B. Yehoshua, the 1995 recipient of the prestigious Israel Prize. Following the publication of his masterful yet controversial novel *Mr. Mani* (1990), Yehoshua declared a personal vendetta against Genesis 22, namely, 'the Aqedah'. In public lectures, delivered at American universities and elsewhere, he claimed that the memory of Abraham's knife throughout Jewish history has become too close for comfort. We can never be sure, he argued, that the knife will continue hovering in mid-air and not strike home instead; one should therefore prevent the Aqedah from fully materializing by exorcising the myth from the very core of Jewish culture.

Yehoshua left it to his listeners to interpret the meaning of his

---

2.   My earliest thoughts on this subject were presented at the New York University Conference on 'Myth and Ritual in Judaism', 23-24 October 1994; at the Gruss Colloquium in Judaic Studies at the Annenberg Center for Judaic Studies, University of Pennsylvania ('Historical Memory and the Construction of Tradition'), 30 April–2 May 1995; and at the New York University Faculty Colloquium on Psychoanalysis and the Humanities, 7 December 1995. Special thanks to the members of the latter for their insightful debate and helpful suggestions. The present version, however, came into being during my instructive and productive tenure as a Koerner Fellow at the Oxford Centre for Hebrew and Jewish Studies in Winter 1996 (and was presented as work-in-process at the University of Cambridge Centre for Modern Hebrew Studies, 31 January 1996). My thanks to Geza Vermes and Martin Goodman for their help and encouragement.

startling use of the biblical story; nor did he tell us exactly how he thought such cardinal surgery could be carried out; except, of course, for the clues offered in *Mr. Mani*, the novel that constituted the topic of his lecture. It is this novel, which appeared in English translation in 1992, that serves as one of my guidelines in the attempt to gauge and historicize the latest transformations of the Aqedah narrative in Israeli culture. But before we approach this heavily loaded subject, another question is in order: Should we accept Yehoshua's unequivocal premise about the central place occupied by the Aqedah in Jewish tradition?

Here I must confess that, growing up in Israel, I had no trouble recognizing in Yehoshua's flat statement a truism on which we were all raised. Indeed, to anyone familiar with modern Hebrew culture, *motiv ha-akeda* (the motif of the Aqedah) has been a major theme in poetry, drama and prose fiction, and in the visual arts as well, almost since its inception. What is precisely meant by it—passive victimhood, stoic heroism, ideological martyrdom, or fanatic aggression (the range is rather broad!)—is quite another question, one that will concern me soon. But for the moment, let me say that only after hearing the objection raised by one of my colleagues at the lecture did I begin to doubt my Israeli perspective on the Aqedah. Arguing *mi-de'oraita*, namely, from the biblical text, that colleague challenged Yehoshua's assumption, suggesting that the Exodus, for one, is much more prominent in Jewish collective memory. Not only is the Aqedah never alluded to in the biblical corpus outside of Genesis; it is read only on the High Holidays, whereas it is the Exodus that is referred to on a daily basis in the prayer service. Making the Aqedah the centerpiece of Judaism is therefore a gross exaggeration.[3]

At the time, neither Yehoshua nor I had a convincing counter-argument. Yehoshua went on to write his own defence, which has subsequently appeared as a postscript to a collection of critical essays about

3. This argument apparently disregards the fact that Gen. 22 is also included in the daily morning service for the reason that it is not 'really read' in the daily *shaharit* prayer. A similar qualification may be found in Levenson (1993), who concludes his chapter on 'The Rewritten Aqedah of Jewish Tradition' with the following 'warning': 'Nor should our choice of topics mislead us into imagining that the aqedah alone occupied center stage in the theology of the periods discussed. This was, instead, an honor it shared with a number of other Pentateuchal episodes—the splitting of the sea, for example, or the revelation at Sinai, the incident of the golden calf...' (1993: 199).

Mr. Mani ('Undoing the Aqedah by Acting It Out' [1995]). As for myself, I have embarked on an odyssey that led me from an analysis of the uses of Genesis in *Mr. Mani* (also featured in that collection [Feldman 1995]) to an exploration of the Aqedah in postbiblical retellings. To say that what I have so far discovered is a drop in the ocean is not a mere figure of speech. It is to convey my sense that despite surface appearances, measurable and quantifiable in the corpus of the prayer ritual, the postbiblical Aqedah has had a life of its own, spreading and branching into several related yet differentiated areas of human behavior.

The wording of this last statement is not arbitrary. It reflects my own understanding of the attraction of this myth not only for early and late midrashists and medieval *paytanim* (liturgical poets), but for modern scholarship as well. And I suspect that it is the *nature* of this attraction, its mytho-psychological quality, if you will, that has also aroused the defences of *other* scholars. The latter range from Abraham Geiger, the nineteenth-century rationalist and reformist, who used the Aqedah as a foil in his critique of the Babylonian Talmudists, to contemporary scholars of similar persuasion. For Geiger, the absence of 'Aqedah merit' from the Mishnah proper was sufficient proof of its Syrian church origins, leading him to conclude that it is 'a notion in flat contradiction of the whole spirit of Judaism and is completely opposed to every one of its fundamentals'.[4] This objection notwithstanding, interest in the postbiblical vicissitudes of the Aqedah has continued to grow, becoming especially vigorous in the second half of this century.[5]

Inter-Cultural Identifications: Isaac/Jesus/Oedipus

In hindsight, this interest followed two courses: the principal course was signaled by Shalom Spiegel's classic Hebrew study *Me'agadot ha'akedah* (1950), which had been largely overlooked by general scholarship until its publication in English, in 1967, as *The Last Trial*. The other line of inquiry was ushered in by Wellisch's book, *Isaac and Oedipus* (1954). The divergence between the two titles strikes the eye at first glance:

---

4.   Quoted in Spiegel 1979: 87. All subsequent quotations from Spiegel are from this English version.

5.   Spiegel documents earlier responses to Geiger, notably Israel Levi (1912, French), and M. Robinson (1911, Hebrew). On the timing of Spiegel's treatise as a response to the Holocaust see Band 1996.

Spiegel's exploration, under the Hebrew subtitle, 'A Liturgy by Rabbi
Ephraim of Bonn about the Slaughter of Isaac and his Resurrection',
appears to be directed internally, toward the Jewish tradition, while
Wellisch's gaze is clearly directed outward, toward a comparative cultural context. A closer look reveals, nevertheless, that this divergence is
somewhat misleading. Despite the ostensibly internal gaze of Spiegel's
intent, it does much more than trace the transformation of the Aqedah
into a proof text of *medieval* martyrdom. Although Spiegel's comparative
framework is not as obvious as that of Wellisch's, his study is nonetheless heavily involved in an argument precisely over the question of origins and of interfaith contact. His anti-Geiger position, arguing that
postbiblical rewritings of the Aqedah derive more from ancient Canaanite rituals (mostly child sacrifice) than from Christianity, their contemporary rival, established the major terms of a debate that was to continue
for the rest of this century. The first phase of this debate is represented
by Geza Vermes's polemical study of the shape of the Akedah in *early*
Jewish lore. In his 'Redemption and Genesis 22' (1961), Vermes traces
the metamorphosis of the figure of Isaac from the passive, sacrificial victim of Genesis 22 to a willing self-immolator, fully cognizant of his role
as a redeemer. Tracing this evolution back to second- and first-century
sources such as the Palestinian Targumim, and before them, to Josephus,
4 *Maccabees* and *Pseudo Philo*, Vermes upholds Spiegel's denial of
Geiger's hypothesis of Christian influence. Although Vermes's historical
reconstruction has been severely critiqued by a line of scholars, culminating in 'A Revised Tradition History' put forward by Davies and
Chilton (1978), a recent discovery of a similar version of Isaac as a willing sacrifice in a Dead Sea Scroll fragment (4Q225) allowed him to date
this tradition to the first century BCE, thereby vindicating his 'time-
table'.[6]

The comparative framework of the second line of inquiry pursued in
the last half century is indicated by the subtitle of Wellisch's book, 'A
Study in Biblical Psychology of the Sacrifice of Isaac, the Akedah'. Following J.G. Frazer's worldwide anthropological survey of child sacrifice
(of the firstborn in particular; see *The Golden Bough*, Ch. 6, Pt. 3, 'Sacrifice of the King's Son'), Wellisch places the Aqedah in that context,

6.   For the debate that raged throughout the 1970s and 1980s, see Levenson
1993: Ch. 14, 245 n. 2. For Vermes's recent rejoinder, based on Qumran
manuscript 4Q225, see Vermes 1996. I was privileged to hear an oral presentation of
this rejoinder at an Oxford seminar on 23 January 1996.

while at the same time also subjecting it to a classical Freudian analysis. The main thrust of his analysis is the moral and behavioral import of the Aqedah for the ubiquitous problem of intergenerational conflict, namely the Oedipus Complex. It is the resolution of this Complex, the conquering of the 'Oedipal hatred' (Wellisch 1954: 95), that Wellisch locates in the differences between the Greek and Hebrew narratives. With this, he established the Aqedah as one of the major attractions for the then young field of the psychoanalytic study of religion. His interest was subsequently appropriated by psychologists of different persuasions, among them the Israeli Shlomo Shoham, to whom I shall return.[7]

By the 1990s, however, these separate lines of inquiry seem to intersect. Two recent studies, published almost concurrently, update and elaborate in great detail on data collected by their precursors. Both focus on intergenerational conflict as the psychological significance of the historical context of child sacrifice. Martin Bergmann's *In the Shadow of Moloch* (1992) is a work of applied psychoanalysis; Jon Levenson's *The Death and Resurrection of the Beloved Son* (1993) is a textual probe into the history of religion. However, despite differences in method and scholarly rigor, they share two essential features: a reliance on child sacrifice as an *aetiological* context, and a *teleological* concern with intercultural relations in general and with the Judeo-Christian construct in particular. Bergmann's book is subtitled 'The Sacrifice of Children and its Impact on Western Religions'; Levenson's 'The Transformation of Child Sacrifice in Judaism and Christianity'. Published within the space of a single year (and featuring on their covers the same painting by Rembrandt!), these books may explain the almost sinister attraction that the elliptic narrative of Genesis 22 exerts on contemporary readers: Whether read for its *pshat* (plain sense) or counter to it, this text bristles with questions about submission versus aggression, hierarchy and domination, fatherhood versus sonship, surrender or free choice. And although the appeal of these universal issues is age-old, as attested by the rich postbiblical and medieval literature they have spawned, their prominence has greatly grown in a generation marked by psychological consciousness on the one hand, and historical relativism on the other.

To read that 'Abraham's willingness to sacrifice Isaac symbolized

7.   For an earlier history of scholarship on the Aqedah see Eli Yasif (1978). The second wave of psychological interest in the topic took place in the 1970s, as we shall see below; for a summary of this literature, see Elitzur 1987: 308-28. Cf. Bergmann 1992: Ch. 9, 219-43, 'Mythology and Religion: The Psychoanalytic View'.

victory of his sonhood over his fatherhood' (Bergmann 1992: 299) gives one pause; the same goes for the argument that the relationship between the two traditions, Judaism and Christianity, 'usually characterized as one of parent and child, is better seen as a rivalry of two siblings for their father's unique blessings' (Levenson 1993: 232). Although the latter was 'practised' in a way by Christian art and exegesis throughout medieval times, heavily colored by partisan bias (for example, Rachel versus Leah as Christianity versus Judaism),[8] it is the stamp of contemporary scholarship that transforms this perception from a partisan representation to an 'objective' observation, with no value judgment attached. The well-known stylistic paucity (inscribed in one of the foundational texts of the literary approach to the Bible, Auerbach's *Mimesis*) that had in the past invited rereadings and counter-readings in consonance with Jewish history (Spiegel and Vermes) has now opened up the text to psychological encoding and to new-historicist sensibilities. To paraphrase Levenson, 'nowhere is the stark contrast between the utter absence of direct references to the binding of Isaac anywhere else in the Hebrew Bible, and its extraordinary prominence in Rabbinic Judaism' (1993: 173) as obvious as in its afterlife in one offshoot of rabbinic tradition, namely, Christianity. And although the impulse to *deny* the retrospective effect of this development on later Judaism is no doubt one of the major subtexts of Spiegel's fascinating treatise,[9] it is to my mind the less convincing part of his argument. Whether rooted in pagan myth (as claimed by Spiegel) or not, it is clear that the renaissance of 'Akedah merit' in rabbinic and later Judaism was at least partly inspired by the polemic with Christianity. Thus, while Spiegel argues, contra Geiger, that 'the Akedah has no quarrel with Torah and the commandments' (1979: 116), that it was precisely the Church's emphasis on the 'atoning power of the blood' that caused Israel 'to blur more and more the remnants of similar ancient beliefs from pagan times' (1979: 117), he

8.   I thank Edward Greenstein for this example, as for his thorough reading of an earlier version.

9.   See, for example, Spiegel 1979: 86: 'The question therefore is only natural: Did this idea reach us and Christianity from a common pagan source, an inheritance from the remote past before Scripture came into being; or did it reach us from Christianity, from direct contact with it and under its influence?' And cf. Spiegel 1979: 97: 'As regards the Akedah, there is nothing singular about Babylonia, and these ideas did not spread over Judaism because of contact with Syrian Christians...in Palestine early Amoraim no less than late ones were all ears for the thought of the Akedah Merit'. See also pp. 113, 116 and passim.

is finally compelled to conclude that 'it was the peoples of Christendom who retrieved it [the pagan Canaanite inheritance] for them [the Israelites] from oblivion' (1979: 119).[10]

Ironically, the dynamic of this 'retrieval' is now being analyzed with the aid of psychological insights that one may adduce from the very narrative over which the struggle has been raging. For to suggest that the rivalry between Judaism and Christianity should be viewed as fraternal rather than filial, as Levenson does in the *last paragraph* of his book, is not only to suggest a new historical perspective; it is also to acknowledge, albeit indirectly, the psychological specificity of the Hebrew Bible, its difference from our Western perspective.

What is implied in my statement is a critique, which I have adumbrated elsewhere (1989a, 1994), of the habitual reading of the Hebrew Bible through the lens of Freudian psychology and its Greek foundations. This reading has resulted in the imposition on biblical narrative of psychological dynamics that are alien to it, or, at best, secondary within its system. My argument is that in contrast to Greek mythology, the majority of biblical fathers and sons are not made for the Freudian master plot. Rarely expressing aggression, they seem to avoid conflict rather than arouse it.[11] This does not mean, of course, that aggression totally disappears. As observed by Bergmann (1992: 71), it is re-created in the relationship between the siblings, on what I call the 'horizontal' level.[12] Indeed, from a psychological point of view, the family narrative of Genesis may be seen as a chain of sibling rivalries that is only once disrupted in a major way—by the father-and-son scene of Genesis 22. Although on the face of it, the dynamic of this scene is totally different from what we generally label as Oedipal (namely, patricidal)—as often

10. Vermes's recent vindication of the pre-Christian dating of some of the elements of the Aqedah merit does not greatly detract from the recognition that this 'retrieval' was taking place under Christian influence.

11. I demonstrate my critique with the most extreme case of Zeligs (1974); but even Elitzur (1987), who is aware more than most of the divergence, finally falls into similar traps. For a different aspect of this divergence see Rotenberg 1978.

12. As far as I can tell, Bergmann is the first psychoanalyst to acknowledge this divergence between biblical narrative and the Freudian Oedipal 'narrative'. I have developed a similar argument independently (see Feldman 1989a), delineating the psychological difference between the oedipal and the sibling plots in my 1994 essay. Steinmetz (1991) also highlights this narrative feature, placing it, however, within an anthropological rather than a psychoanalytic context.

noticed by the psychoanalytic literature[13]—its unique status in the text has turned it into a Hebraic equivalent of the Oedipal scene in Freudian psychology. It is this confluence, I would suggest, that has made the Aqedah such a central text for *Israeli* culture, particularly during the last couple of decades.

In contradistinction to what I would label the intercultural or new-historicist interest in the Aqedah, in its foreign relations, if you wish, of Anglo-American scholarship, Israelis have channeled into this meta-narrative all their internal turmoil. It would seem that for a generation imbued with Freudian psychology—apparently an obligatory link in its process of Westernization—the need for a myth of intergenerational aggression was too strong to resist. We should not be surprised, then, that in the Israeli ethos, the Aqedah has come to symbolize all the tensions associated with the generational gap. 'The story of the Aqedah', as a recent literary critic (Weiss 1991) reflects, 'is perhaps the main code through which Israeli society converses with itself. It is perhaps no exaggeration to note that there is not one work of prose fiction in which father–son relations do not refer, directly or indirectly, to the *topos* of the Aqedah' (Weiss 1991: 36; my translation).[14] Similarly, an earlier overview of the recurrences of the ''*Akedah* Theme in Israeli Literature' (Nash 1977), smoothly shifts from a discussion of the Aqedah as the metaphor for an ideologically inspired sense of self-sacrifice in the *palmaḥ* generation (namely, the fighters for Israeli independence in the 1940s, such as the author Moshe Shamir) to the Aqedah as an expression of a generational conflict (as in the work of the young A.B. Yehoshua in the 1960s). Although there is an awareness here of the shift (the latter use is labeled 'Akedah in reverse', Nash 1977: 34), there is no questioning of the meaning of this reversal, or of the changing position of the speaking subject it implies. That the biblical *topos* could have become synonymous with the Oedipal conflict without arousing any questions is undoubtedly one of the ironies of literary transmission. Yet it is in this guise that the Aqedah has recently gained its prominence in Israeli culture, and it is as such that it aroused the startling declaration of

13. See Wellisch 1954; Reik 1951; Bakan 1966; Schlossman 1972.

14. Weiss was preceded by many, not all of whom are cited by him. See Margot Klauzner 1949(!); Baruch Kurzweil 1959; A. Eli 1970; Hillel Barzel 1972; Arie [Leon] Weinman 1977; Stanley Nash 1977, 1986; Israel Cohen 1981; Moshe Steiner 1982; Gideon Ofrat 1979, 1983; Ruth Kartun-Blum 1988; Yair Mazor 1989; and Glenda Abramson 1990, among others.

Yehoshua, the point of departure of the present enquiry. For the identification of the Aqedah with the primal scene of Freudian psychology strains to its breaking point not only the Hebrew myth with all its transformations, but also some basic premises of core Zionist narratives.

The Gender and Psychology of Sacrifice: Victim or Martyr?

Permit me to explain. The first stage in the history of what I call the 'foreign relations' of the Aqedah is Philo's defense of 'Father Abraham' vis-à-vis contemporary Greek culture. The spokesmen of that culture, apparently conditioned by their own tradition, were critical of the Jewish apotheosis of a non-, or aborted, sacrifice. Following Philo's *De Abrahamo*, Spiegel's first contextualization of the biblical story is by a comparison not with the familiar Near Eastern *cultic* analogues (the cult of Moloch, for example), but rather with a number of Greek *narratives* in which a ritual of child sacrifice is carried out by loving fathers for 'the good of the fatherland'. Moreover, like Isaac in our earlier sources, going all the way back to Josephus's *Jewish Antiquities* (first century CE) and also, as shown recently by Vermes, to the Dead Sea Scrolls (4Q225),[15] some of those children 'volunteer for the sacrifice', even rejoice in it, being 'of one mind and singleminded, the father rejoicing to slay, the children rejoicing to be slain' (Spiegel 1979: 10).

However, if truth be told, Spiegel's formulation sounds suspiciously similar to several of the Jewish sources. One of them is Philo's interpretation of *yaḥdâw* ('together', Gen. 22.6, 8), which Spiegel himself quotes as 'they walked with equal speed of mind rather than body' (Spiegel 1979: 10 n. 6). Another is Josephus, whom Vermes paraphrases (1961: 198) in the following fashion: 'Josephus tells how Abraham...informed his son that he was to be the victim. Isaac heard his father's words *with joy and ran to the altar*' (*Ant.* 228–29, 232; my emphasis. For a full quotation see Levenson 1993: 191). The closest is the Fragmentary Targum,

---

15. Cf. G.F. Moore's statement that 'In the Rabbinical literature, however, the voluntariness of the sacrifice on Isaac's part is strongly emphasized' (1932: 539). Vermes, who cites this in support of his thesis of the transformation of Isaac in his 1961 essay (p. 196), will later antedate this to the earlier Dead Sea fragment which preserves a trace of Isaac's request to be bound so he would not involuntarily spoil the offering—a request common in the Palestinian Targumim two centuries later (Vermes 1996). Cf. Bergmann 1992, Ch. 5, 'From the Sacrifice of Isaac to the Sacrifice of Christ', and Levenson 1993, Pt. III, 'The Beloved Son between Zion and Golgotha'.

quoted also in Vermes (1961: 194-95): 'In that hour the angels of heaven went out and said to each other: Let us go and see the only two just men in the world. *The one slays and the other is being slain. The slayer does not hesitate, and the one being slain stretches out his neck'* (emphasis added). In other words, Spiegel's description of his Greek 'prooftexts' may be nothing more than retroactive inscription, having his Greek models speak the language of the Hebrew sources.

This linguistic quibble notwithstanding,[16] Spiegel is on target as far as the spirit of his Greek analogues, which these clearly share with the postbiblical retellings of the Aqedah. There is only one striking difference—their gendered construction. For of all the stories cited by him, only in one case is it a son who is involved in a sacrificial narrative (Phrixus, son of Aeolos, who escaped the knife with the help of a ram, just as biblical Isaac did; 1979: 11); all the others are daughters. Iphigenia is, of course, the notorious case, but she is not alone in this role; in Spiegel's text, she is joined by the daughters of Aristodemus and Leos, to whom others could be added, such as the Trojan princess Polyxena, the daughter of Priam and Hecuba, the young virgin who was sacrificed so that the Achaens could sail back home from Troy. In other words, in order to preserve an aura of cooperation and voluntariness—Leos's daughters' *spontanea morte*, as Jerome defined it (Spiegel 1979: 10)—Greek myth structures ritual sacrifice around the stereotypic female attribute, submission. 'Indeed,' says Spiegel, 'the maids of Leos became in time a model example of love for the fatherland' (1979: 10). That precisely this 'model example' would be criticized in recent feminist scholarship for its idealization of female submissiveness should come as no surprise. Thus, both Keuls (1985: 137-52) and Loraux (1987), for example, refuse this proposition. Loraux even insists that the *difference* between the ways in which Greek tragedians kill off their male and their female protagonists (keeping alive distinctions among sacrifice, suicide and murder) has clear implications for the value judgments attached to each. A more severe critique has been recently put forward by Nancy Sorkin Rabinowitz, who argues that by the time of Euripides, the virgin victim was given 'the illusion of her individuality, but the only action she can perform is that of submission' (1993: 40). Paradoxically, a traditional classicist like Mary Lefkowitz, on the other hand, interprets precisely the same role as the 'most active' in Greek women's repertoire,

16. More work is needed to clarify this point, such as a textual checking of the Greek sources to which Spiegel refers (but does not cite).

comparing it favorably with the later tradition of Christian female martyrdom (1986: 95-111). Finally, a recent study on Greek heroine cults
sheds light on these contradictory interpretations by suggesting that in
spite of superficial similarities, Iphigenia and the groups of heroic, vir-
ginal sisters (usually the king's daughters), 'represent two separate traditions, in terms of both story pattern and social utility' (Larson 1995:
101), the difference between them focusing on the issue of willing
martyrdom (by the sisters, 'the ultimate example of civic virtue' [101]),
versus Iphigenia's unwilling sacrifice (106).

   This controversy no doubt strikes a familiar chord. There is a certain
analogy between the diverging interpretations of Greek female roles and
the historical evolution of Isaac's role. This analogy unwittingly emerges
from reading Bergmann together with Levenson, namely, the former's
chapter, 'The Transformation of Human Sacrifice in Greek Tragedy'
(Ch. 2), and the latter's chapter, 'The Rewritten Aqedah of Jewish
Tradition' (Ch. 14). Oblivious to feminist critiques of the last decade,
Bergmann follows the classicist script, trying to pin down the moment
in which a historical transformation took place from viewing the vir-
ginal sacrifice as an apprehensible victim to representing her as an active
agent, choosing to die of her own free will. Thus, while in the opening
of Aeschylus's *Agamemnon* the chorus recalls Iphigenia's death as 'a
cursed unhallowed sacrifice' (Bergmann 1992: 54), Euripides turns both
Iphigenia and Polyxena (in *Iphigenia in Aulis* and *Hecuba*, respectively)
into martyrs, the former for patriotic reasons ('Our country—think, our
Hellas—looks to me, on me the fleet hangs now, the doom of Troy';
Bergmann 1992: 58), the latter for royal pride ('so slay me, that death
may find me free; for to be called a slave amongst the dead fills my royal
heart with shame'; Bergmann 1992: 61).[17] Similarly, the drama of the
metamorphosis of Isaac is convincingly described by Levenson as the
subtle but steady transformation of the Aqedah 'from the story of
Abraham's offering of his son into one of Isaac's self-sacrifice in the
service of the God of his father' (1993: 187).

   Although there is perhaps a hint of a generational agon in Levenson's
startling conclusion ('Eventually, it became possible to allude to the
aqedah without mention of the hero of the biblical story, Abraham'

---

17. For a diametrically opposite view of this ostensible act of free choice, see
Rabinowitz 1993: 40: 'By willingly sacrificing herself, Iphigenia seems to avoid her
passive status as sacrificial object... In the course of the play, she is both subject and
subjected; in fact, she is subjected by her desire for subjectivity.'

[1993: 199]), the following statement ('Isaac bound himself and offered himself upon the altar') forecloses the possibility of any Oedipal interpretation. Clearly, Isaac does not partake in the function usually preserved for male characters within the orbit of Greek culture—the notorious aggressive struggle with their (respective) fathers or sons, a domestic gendered 'rehearsal' of the military role awaiting them. We could say, then, that among its other transformations of pagan myth, the biblical Aqedah substitutes male for female without, however, changing the psychological structure of the narrative.[18] Isaac fulfills the role of a female, as the troublesome story of Jephtah's daughter should undoubtedly remind us.[19] In this scenario, so diametrically opposed to the Oedipal plot, in any of its versions, there is no room for conflict. In Bergmann's aphoristic formulation, 'Sonhood overcomes fatherhood'. Isaac is not the only obedient son; so is Abraham, who forfeits his fatherhood to remain himself an obedient son to his God.[20] Moreover, the postbiblical narratives that imagine Isaac as a young adult, apparently responsible for his choice to volunteer to martyrdom, only enhance the psychological dynamics outlined in Genesis. From this perspective, the question of whether Isaac was or was not actually sacrificed that has so preoccupied our sages (see Spiegel 1979: Chs. 6, 9; especially 80 [*Gen. R.* 55.5]) is of little import. The same goes for the question of whose sacrifice it really was, Abraham's or Isaac's (see Spiegel 1979: 100, and Vermes 1961: 198).[21] Even Levenson's startling conclusion, cited above,

18. Cf. Jacob as a substitute for the female in the ancient androgynous symbol of opposite-sex twins, in my 1994 essay, 'And Rebecca Loved Jacob, but Freud Did Not'.

19. The literature on Jephtah's daughter is too vast to be recorded here. For the comparison with Isaac, see Leach 1969; Davies and Chilton 1978; Marcus 1986. For a summary of recent feminist scholarship, see Exum 1992: 65-69, and especially her comparison with Iphigenia 'because she does not fight her fate, she does not attain the kind of tragic stature that we find, for example, in the Iphigenia of Aeschylus' (58).

20. 'In both the Isaac and Christ myths there is no hint of rebellion or aggression. The relationship between father and son is played out entirely in the sphere of of love and submission to God's will', says Bergmann (1992: 300). I have argued as much in an earlier essay, 'Towards a Psychoanalytic Approach to Biblical Narrative' (1989a: 79): 'Abraham was just as "bound" by his heavenly father as Isaac was'. It should be noted, however, that Bergmann does inscribe the self-sacrifice of Iphigenia within the dynamics of the Oedipus complex, calling it 'a masochistic variant' on the complex.

21. See Spiegel 1979: 102-103: 'For the most part, it was Abraham's merits they

does not change the psychological content of the plot: The hierarchy of power, the curbing of male aggression takes place there in either case, for both of them together (*wayyēlkhû šenēhem yaḥdāw*).

True, an attentive reading may discern a feeble echo of tension in Isaac's questioning of his father (particularly if he is not a child but a man in his twenties or thirties, as different retellings remind us; and cf. Davies and Chilton: 521-22); but whatever conflict-ridden sediments are still there, they are repressed by the narrative only to be almost drowned out by later canonization. There is no trace of it in the *Zikhronôt* (Memorials) prayer of *Roš Hašanah* (New Year), where it is the father who has the last word. Most instructive in this respect is a variant reading, which did *not* make it into the canon. In this version, Abraham did not 'suppress his compassion for his only son in order to perform God's will', but rather 'he suppresses his impulse to retort to God, to hurl accusations upward' (Spiegel 1979: 90-93). The Abraham of this midrashic version, more in line with the Abraham who argues with God over the destruction of Sodom, is *not*, let me reiterate, the one that entered our collective memory via the prayer book. 'No rabbinic authority casts the slightest doubt upon Abraham's absolute obedience to God', says Yaakov Elbaum in a structural study of some Midrashic versions of the Aqedah (1986: 108).

I have dwelt at length upon this point to demonstrate to what extent the spirit of the Aqedah, even throughout its permutations, is not amenable to Oedipal interpretation (and not only because of the absence of the maternal link in the famous triad!). Neither the father nor the son expresses any rebelliousness toward their respective authority figure. The Freudian model that would better fit here is the one labeled 'negative Oedipus'—the phase or aspect of feminized submission and homoerotic identification. I have elsewhere named this feature of biblical psychology after Isaac's son Jacob, although Isaac would have fit the bill just as well.[22] Isaac, however, is unfortunately (and inappropriately!) already 'occupied' by the 'Isaac Syndrome', Shlomo Giora Shoham's

---

magnified, especially in the Middle Ages. But in an ancient source, in the Memorials prayer of Rosh ha-Shana, it is said: "And in compassion do Thou recall today unto *his* seed Isaac's Akedah."' Beyond the question of Christian influence, there is an intriguing distinction here, that still needs interpretation, between a (medieval) identification with the father and an (earlier) identification with the son (supported also by Vermes's findings).

22. Feldman 1995.

reformulation of psychoanalysis's 'Laius Complex', to which I shall soon return. For now, let me note that despite the 'negativity' attached to the 'Negative Oedipus' by Freud (because of its homoerotic deviation from the heterosexual norms of his general psychology), it may have some positive ramifications for the construction of gender, given our contemporary valorization of a more flexible conceptualization of gender roles. It is the transposition of aggression from the generational to the sibling axis, resulting in the playing down (if not the repression, or perhaps the resolution, as argued by Wellisch) of Oedipal conflict, that allows biblical narrative to cross 'Western' (= Greek?) gender boundaries, creating 'androgynous' males (Isaac, Jacob) and females (Rebecca).[23] We should not be surprised to realize, however, that it was precisely the 'femininity' (namely, 'passivity') of the 'male' in this psychological archetype (cherished today at least in some intellectual quarters) that aroused the ire and derision of nascent Zionism.[24] The new ideal was Gideon or Shimshon, Yiftah (Jephtah), and even Cain— *rak lo' Yitzhak*.[25] The Zionist revolution was also a Freudian revolution, substituting a Hebrew (aggressive) Oedipus for a Jewish (submissive) Isaac.[26]

23. See Feldman 1994. For a different interpretation see Schwartz 1997: 106-19.

24. The 'gender' implications of this aspect of the Zionism versus Judaism dichotomy, and its antisemitic roots, has been recently researched and documented, most notoriously in the work of Sander Gilman. See also Harrowitz 1994. On the Israeli reception of Otto Weininger's infamous *Sex and Character* (1903), one of the foundational texts of this orientation, see Yehoshua Sobol's 1982 play, *The Soul of a Jew*. By contrast, recent scholarship in Israel has focused on the political adaptation of the myth of power within Zionist ideology; see Shapira 1992. For the unravelling of 'virility' in recent Israeli fiction, see Hoffman 1992: 199.

25. 'Except for Isaac'; I pun here on Ben-Gurion's notorious *rak lo' Herut* ('except for Herut'), an objection to include the right-wing party in any governmental coalition, which he reiterated throughout his long tenure as the Prime Minister of Israel.

26. The 'Oedipalization' of the Zionist revolution was 'codified' only by the late 1970s in A.B. Yehoshua's notorious essay, 'The Diaspora: A Neurotic Solution'. In literature, however, Oedipal conflict has been a longstanding mode of representation of the Zionist metanarrative; see Feldman 1989b; for a recent summary see Schwartz 1995.

Zionist Paradoxes: Postbiblical Martyrology Resurrected

Yet in Hebrew literature, and particularly in poetry, this was not the case. Despite the overt secularization of this literature (Kartun-Blum 1988), the early poetry of the first pioneers and throughout the War of Independence is filled with self-immolating Isaacs, rather than with wrestling Shimshons or even Jacobs.[27] Ironically, these Isaacs are direct descendants of their Midrashic (rather than biblical) prototypes. That this point is missed by most Israeli studies of the Aqedah may attest to the measure of their authors' implicit loyalty to the Zionist narrative that has made the Bible its foundational text, while demoting postbiblical literature to the cultural margins. The fact is, however, that by 1930, contemporary Isaacs were said to 'stretch their necks silently on the altar' (Yitzhak[!] Lamdan, 'On the Altar') in an almost verbatim quotation of the Fragmentary Targum I cited above.[28] A quarter of a century later, around the same time that Spiegel published his monumental study of the twelfth-century Aqedah liturgy by Rabbi Ephraim of Bonn, *palmaḥnik* (namely, a member of the pre-State military units that had the lion's share of Israel's struggle for independence in the 1940s) Haim Gouri wrote in his famous poem *Yerushah* ('inheritance') that Isaac's progeny are born with the (sacrificial) knife in their heart (*hem noladim uma'akhelet belibam*).[29] What exactly is meant by this startling image, and who is the carrier of the (ritual) knife, is a question that has never been directly faced by the critics.[30] It was left to A.B. Yehoshua (in the

27. This ironic imbalance was redressed only in 1971, with Benjamin Tamuz's novel, *Yaakov*. Paradoxically, this novel constituted a turning point in this late author's worldview, moving from extreme Israeli/Canaanite nativism to Jewish cosmopolitanism. For more on this point, see my 'Back to Vienna' (1989b): 321, 328.

28. The poem was published in *Baritma hemeshuleshet* (*The Triple Harness*), 1930: 80; quoted here from Lamdan 1973: 119. Cf. Vermes 1961: 195: 'The slayer does not hesitate, and the one being slain stretches out his neck.' See also Spiegel 1979: 85: '*Lamb* sacrifice came to be interpreted as signs and reminders for Heaven, "the merits of *that sheep bound* on the altar who bared his throat for the sake of Thy Name"' (*Targum Jonathan* and *Targum Jerusalem ad* Lev. 22.27).

29. Published in *Shoshanat haruḥot* 1960: 28. For an English translation see Gouri 1996: 27. See Appendix for the full text of this poem.

30. If Gouri 'echoes' Natan Alterman's earlier poem in which the same ritual knife, *ma'achelet*, strikes a Holocaust victim ('*Al hayeled 'Avram*, 1944–45), as suggested by Kartun-Blum (1988), the question is how this intertextual echoing

postscript mentioned above), to make this image the cornerstone of his own filicidal interpretation of Jewish history. Although this charge was categorically denied by Gouri, who in a recent reading at New York University (Fall 1996), disavowed any such misreadings, it is clear that the poem itself does not 'judge' the historical necessity it depicts in the glowing terms used by some of Gouri's peers, all veterans of the 1940s wars. In contrast to novelist Moshe Shamir, for example, who openly praised Abraham for his willingness to give up his son (comparing him favorably to Oedipus in an essay devoted to this theme), or to Yigal Mossinsohn, who dramatized this necessity in his play about the War of Independence, *Be'arvot hanegev* ('On the Plains of the Desert')—Gouri evoked a latent intergenerational conflict: 'The boy unbound saw his father's back'. It is this faint indictment of 'the father' that may have been seized upon by Yehoshua in his quasi 'post'-Zionist critique of the Aqedah. Yet for Gouri himself, as for his generation in general, this indictment was not part of their mental world, at least not consciously so. Being born with a knife in one's heart was unconflictedly accepted as a dire fact of life, with no blame openly apportioned.

In other words, despite the ideological rejection of what was perceived as an 'effeminized' biblical-diasporic psychology of submission, these writers (the biological 'sons' of their era) continued the traditional representation of the Aqedah as a nonconflictual mission carried by father and son together, just as it had been seen by earlier and later midrashists and *paytanim*, as documented by Spiegel, Vermes, Davies and Chilton, and Levenson.

This continuity at the heart of the 'Zionist revolution' is not accidental. Despite appearances, the major turning point in Israeli culture would come only in the late 1960s. The founding fathers, as well as the *palmaḥ* generation, renegade sons as they were, had completely identified with the martyrological position of the *post*biblical Isaac. Willingly binding

functions. Something important has changed between Alterman's historically defined (World War II) 'Aqedah' of the mother(!), which—in contrast to Scripture—is *followed* by the *lekh lekha* command to the son(!) Avraham, who is optimistically imagined as making his way to the promised land, and Gouri's wistful image of an unbroken chain of unredeemable Jewish destiny. It is this subtle shift that the present analysis attempts to address. The use of the Aqedah as a metaphor for the Holocaust is beyond the parameters of this essay. See also Band's recent suggestion that Spiegel's treatise itself is a response to the Holocaust. For the use of the Aqedah/Shoah metaphor in the construction of Israeli Arab identity see my forthcoming essay on Anton Shammas's *Arabesques* (1999).

themselves, so to speak, they preserved the memory of the Aqedah intact by substituting national ideology for divine decree, and contemporary political expediency for historical religious persecution. Lamdan's *Massada* (1927) served as the model for this metaphor, and more: it also supplied an unconflicted 'proof text' for the usurpation of Ishmael's narrative role by the present-day Isaacs. If Islamic thought made Isaac's sacrifice its own by attributing it to its (biblical) Father, Ishmael, modern Zionism took back Ishmael's original (biblical) 'sacrifice', thereby 'doubling' the weight of its own self-immolation:

> Beneath the orphaned bush in desert refuge
> Not the son of the Egyptian woman has been thrown away—
> Here in thirst is Isaac swooning,
> Abraham and Sarah's seed (Lamdan 1966: 134).

'The Isaac Syndrome' or the Laius Complex?
Israel's Wrestling with its Aqedah

To be sure, dissenting voices existed as early as the 1940s (if not earlier). Although S.Y. Agnon, the Nobel Laureate 'revolutionary traditionalist' of Hebrew belles-lettres,[31] has perhaps supplied the first ironic comment on the sacrificial posture of the pioneers,[32] an open Oedipal revolt against the memory of the received Aqedah took place within the corpus of S. Yizhar, the arch-individualist of the *palmah* generation. Whereas in his early stories he invoked the iniquities of Sodom, in his sprawling 1958 novel *Yemei Ziklag* (*Days of Ziklag*) he has one of his 1948 fighters confront 'our father Abraham' in a way that anticipates the changes that would take place later (see, on this point, Nash 1977; Ofrat 1988). Yet this confrontation is ideological rather than representational. It is framed within the dialogue of the novel but is not yet internalized into psychological characterization or plot structure. The latter materializes in the early work of A.B. Yehoshua, who seems to have taken up Yizhar's challenge by daringly *replacing* the Aqedah with an Oedipal plot, though not without some disguise: Having Mrs Ashtor (echoing

31. See Gershon Shaked's study of Agnon by this name.
32. See the ironic representation of Isaac(!) Kumer, the pioneer-turned-sacrifice anti-hero of Agnon's *Temol Shilshom* (1945). For a possible antecedent see Y.H. Brenner's ambivalent allusions to the myth of Christ's sacrificial act in *mikan umikan* ('From Here and from There', 1911 and *Shekhol vekishalon*, 'Breakdown and Bereavement', 1914).

the pagan Astarte) bury the old man alive (*Mot hazaken* [*The Old Man's Death*], 1962) was correctly perceived as a Canaanite call for an Oedipal rebellion, despite its gender substitution. Camouflaged by its allegorical style, this feminized version of the Oedipus myth signalled both an appropriate 'catching up' with some deep structures of the Zionist master plot,[33] as well as some limits imposed by these very structures, namely, an unarticulated interdiction against a straightforward representation of the classically Freudian filial patricide.

Yet this was not the direction in which this intergenerational crucible was to evolve. As early as 1972 (and some say even earlier), Yehoshua himself returned to the psychological dynamics of the Aqedah proper, in his controversial novella *Early in the Summer of 1970*.[34] A secularized, modern replica of the biblical plot, this narrative nevertheless exploded the generational agreement and cooperation of the ancient model.[35] Although the son here returns from his academic sojourn in America to participate and almost be killed in 'his father's' war, his heart and mind are with the peace movement of the 1960s—an ideology that totally alienates him from the historical world of his father, the old Bible(!) teacher. In that, Yehoshua may have joined the (by then) young playwright Hanoch Levin (the 1995 recipient of the Bialik Prize), whose scathing satirical review, *The Queen of the Bathtub* (1970), caused public scandal. At the core of this scandal was a poem addressed by a 'victim/sacrifice' (no lexical distinction in Hebrew)[36] to his 'dear father'. Taken

33. Canaanism was an ideological position that called for a total breach with the Jewish Diaspora and the creation of a 'New Hebrew', anchored in the geo-political Middle East. While generally seen an an extreme form of Zionism, some see Zionism and Canaanism as binary opposites rather than a continuum (Hever 1995).

34. According to literary critic Mordechai Shalev, the dynamics of the Aqedah permeate the earlier story, 'Three Days and a Child' (1968), an argument repeated by I. Cohen 1981: 59. (For a later version of Shalev's essay, see *Bakivun hanegdi*.) From my perspective, however, the broader cultural ramifications of this early story become apparent (if at all) only via an allegorical interpretation, while the latter engages them directly.

35. A milder version of this 'explosion' was already sketched out in Amos Oz's critical representation of a founding father of the kibbutz and his intolerance of his son's poetic, feminized features; see *Derekh haru'ah* ('The Way of the Wind/Spirit') in *'Artzot Hatan* (*Lands of the Jackal*) (1963), and analyses by Barzel and Mazor.

36. This curious absence of lexical distinction between the concepts of 'sacrifice' and 'victim' in Hebrew may be responsible for the centrality of the notion of 'sacrifice' in the mind of Hebrew speakers; I thank Baruch Levine for this suggestion, as

out of context, this poem may be seen as transposing the biblical particularity into universal archetypes, as it bypasses any traces of the original narrative (neither biblical names nor plot are in evidence). This is not, however, the way it was perceived by the Israeli authorities and audiences at the time. Taken in the context of the review and its open political challenge, and aided by a prose dialogue on the Aqedah proper, it was correctly understood to be pointing a blaming finger at (Israeli) sacrificing fathers, namely, the political leadership. As shown by both Gideon Ofrat and Ruth Kartun-Blum, the ideological ramifications of this transformation further reverberated in the 'public debate' carried on in the pages of *Shdemot* (the literary magazine of the kibbutz movement), where the Aqedah was discussed (for the first time in Israel's history) from the perspective of the *dead* Isaac.[37] Finally, this process of rewriting reached its apex in 1975, when one of Israel's *bêtes noires*—controversial writer, criminologist, mythologist and social critic Shlomo Giora Shoham—fixated the Aqedah as a universal psychological complex, the 'Isaac Syndrome'.

Published in the daily *Ha'aretz* (1975), in *American Imago* (1976) and as a chapter in his Hebrew book *Halikhei Tantalus* (1976; published in English as *The Myth of Tantalus* [1979]), this guilt-ridden essay by a bereft father of the Yom Kippur war (1973), is an outright indictment of 'the Fathers' as the perpetrators of aggression in the name of various sites of power, whether religious, national, or statist. This political conclusion is not immediately apparent, however. For Shoham starts with what seems to be the first synthesis of the two strands of interest in the Aqedah that we have been following: the textual-historical and the anthropo-psychological. Relying heavily on both the Spiegel–Vermes and Wellisch–Bakan arguments, he nevertheless rejects the latter's acceptance of Freud's core configuration of the resolution of the Oedipus Complex. Shifting emphasis from the son's Oedipalism to the father's 'negativistic deprivational attitude toward the son' as 'a prime archetypal dynamism of the human family' (Shoham 1979: 299-316

---

well as for his meticulous reading of and enlightening comments on an earlier version of this eassy.

37. This was a rather ironic 'sequel' to their *Siaḥ Loḥamim* (*The Seventh Day*), conducted among young kibbutz soldiers after 1967. The gap between the ideological consensus of the first conversation and the despair and doubt of the latter marks the beginning of the so-called *post*-Zionist revolution of Israeli culture. Cf. Ofrat 1979, 1988; Kartun-Blum 1988; Abramson 1990.

[302]), he chooses to name the latter not after the father in Freud's Greek text, Laius, as post-Freudians have habitually done (Wellisch and Bakan, cited by Shoham; cf. Bergmann 1992: 298-301), but rather, after—and here is the paradox—the *son* of the biblical story, Isaac. A justification for this renaming is never brought forward. Rather late in the essay, a possible reasoning is advanced:

> The separant Isaac Syndrome, as well as the participant Oedipal pressures, are not 'resolved' into another dynamic, as believed by Freud and Wellisch. These two are kept in a dialectical balance by their constantly opposing and contradictory pressures... When this dialectical balance is severely disrupted, a predisposition to crime, deviance, or madness might ensue. Consequently, it is superfluous to argue, as Wellisch and Bakan do, as to whether the Isaac Syndrome (they call it the Laius Complex)[*sic*] precedes or follows the Oedipus Complex (Shoham 1979: 305-306).

Possibly, Shoham's disagreement with his predecessors' Freudianism is at the core of his shift to another model. But why name it after the object of aggression rather than after its imputed perpetrator? Why not make Abraham the counterpart of the 'Medea Complex', 'the infanticidal urges of the mother toward her children' in Shoham's own scheme (1979: 303)?

In the absence of an explanation, we may conclude that an unresolved tension underlies this renaming, perhaps the one between the son–father identifications of the writer, himself both a veteran of the 1948 War of Independence and a bereft father of a later war, who now carries the first name of his late son. Indeed, the equivalence between the Laius Complex and the Isaac Syndrome notwithstanding (see above), Shoham may be betraying the deep motivation of his construct when he elaborates on 'the willful victim', which he perceives as a *deviant complement* of the Isaac Syndrome, namely, 'the son who accepts willfully, and many times enthusiastically, the burdens of the separating social norms' (1979: 307). (Interestingly, there is no mention here of a possible precurser, Erich Neumann's 'Isaac Complex', which interpreted the biblical Isaac as a Jungian universal archetype of passivity, but also singled it out as a 'Jewish trait'; Neumann 1954: 189.) Although the craving for the ostensible universality of anthropo-psychological explanation is still palpable here, adducing (in the spirit of Frazer's *The Golden Bough*, no doubt) tribal examples that range from South Africa to the Eskimo, and placing Jesus Christ in a safe central position (Shoham 1979: 307), a contemporary subtext clearly emerges: 'The paradox is even more accentuated in modern times…the basic incompatibility between the individual and the normative system of the group: the death of a son in war, for instance' (309). A long passage follows, a barely disguised personal attempt to work through, in the guise of scientific objectivity, the 'white-hot fury', the 'stale emptiness', the consuming grief of a bereaved father, the 'abysmal guilt that may plague him for the rest of his days', in the face of 'the worthless verbiage' of 'the glorified idealization of his sacrifice by the group' (309). It comes as no surprise then, that a few pages later, Israel surfaces as the paradigm of the modern state, sacrificing its young to the Moloch of (ideological) wars (p. 311). It is this deep trauma, after all, that Shoham shares with his contemporaries. But it is his personal grief that makes his critique that much more severe.[38]

Revisiting certain passages of *Midrash Rabbah* that Spiegel, for one, cited without so much as batting an eyelash,[39] Shoham makes Abraham the archetype not of checked aggression, as Spiegel, following the biblical conclusion, would have it, but of actual filicide. By so doing, the newly coined concept, evoking the name of Isaac, preserves the memory of the old Aqedah while actually invalidating its original perspective. It goes without saying that, although he pays homage to both Spiegel and Vermes, Shoham's indignant value judgment of the Midrash is light years apart from Spiegel's valorizing conclusion. For Spiegel, 'clearly then, the Midrash again and still again emphasizes … that Abraham was categorically and in no uncertain terms forbidden from heaven so much as to touch Isaac with evil intent, or remove from him even one drop of blood' (1979: 46). For Shoham, on the other hand, Abraham's insistence (in *Midrash Rabbah*) on his mission is 'the image of the pious doctrinaire turned into a compulsive normative ritualist' (1979: 313). Furthermore, the Midrashic devil who tries to stop Abraham from acting out God's command may be speaking 'the voice of the subconscious dynamism, which identifies the absolute command of God with

---

38. The painfully autobiographic motivation behind Israeli representations of the Aqedah, especially (but not only—see, for example, Yigal Mossinsohn) in the visual arts, is clearly recorded in Ofrat's pioneering study (1988) with reference to Abel Pan, Shraga Weill, Naftali Bezem and Moshe Gershuni.

39. 'Why did the angel refer to the hand and not to the knife?…Said Abraham: Perhaps (this has happened because the lad) is not fit to be a sacrificial gift. May I strangle him, may I burn him, shall I cut him up in pieces before Thee? Said He to him: "Lay not thy hand!" [etc.]' (Spiegel 1979: 45-46).

the covert infanticide wishes of the father' (Shoham 1979: 313).[40]

It is this last image of filicide that has recently moved from the controversial margins to the mainstream of Israeli prose fiction. By the 1980s, Hebrew literature had been infiltrated by realistic, though heavily metaphorical representations of families in conflict. In these novels, which I have analyzed in detail elsewhere (Feldman 1989b), the knife is not only a poetic metaphor for Jewish history, or Israeli contingencies, or even the European enemy: it is a knife lifted by a father—against a son, in a transparently symbolic dream (Amos Oz, *A Perfect Peace* [1982]); displaced to the spouse, in a psychological semi-fantasy (Yehoshua, *A Late Divorce* [1982]); or it is directed against an innocent bystander, a substitute victim—a dog, for instance (Yaakov Shabtai, *Past Continuous* [1977]). Behind the knife there is an aggressive father, a real flesh and blood father, whose aggression is matched by his ideological self-righteousness, by his unbending principles (what used to be called *devekut ra'ayonit*, 'unwavering adherence to ideology'). Wreaking havoc around them, these fathers destroy their families, sacrificing them on the altar of their own grandiose ideology.

But what about the sons? If we are to accept the encoding of these narratives as the Akedah of a disillusioned generation, we have to realize that Jewish literature has never known such conflicted Isaacs. The principle of mutuality, even non-aggression underlying the memory of the traditional Akedah, in any of its permutations, does not hold here any more. With the loss of a 'supreme fiction' of any kind—religious, national or other—the demand to surrender one's priorities loses its power. This Isaac is definitely not interested; yet he cannot be Oedipus, either. He is never portrayed as taking up the knife himself—not against his father. (Ironically, the only representation of an oedipal son in those years belonged to the translated play *Sunset* by Russian–Jewish playwright Isaac[!] Babel, performed to great acclaim by *Habimah* National Theatre.) The sons of these novels just turn inside, ready to give up

---

40. In the last page of this chapter, Shoham briefly alludes to a theory he develops fully in a later book, *Valhalla, Calvary, and Auschwitz* (1995). Here he reinterprets the self-immolating Isaac of the early retellings of the Aqedah (*pace* Vermes) not only as the prefiguration of Jesus, but as the anticipation of the 'total acceptance of the role of the victim' by German Jews under Nazism. Interestingly, the direct reference to Israel and to the tragedy of bereaved fathers is not included in his rehearsing of the 'Isaac Syndrome' in this book (Shoham 1995: 111-18), a sign of the times, as the Holocaust takes over the 'local' Israeli trauma in Israeli culture.

their inheritance altogether. Like Melville's Bartleby, they would prefer not to participate in the game.

We have come full circle to the proximity of the knife against which Yehoshua declared his vendetta. Although published only in 1990, *Mr. Mani* was conceived in the early 1980s and is clearly anchored in the despair and fatigue of the post-Lebanon war against which Yehoshua was defending the Israeli collective psyche. By that time the Aqedah had been taken over by the 'protest poets' (see Milman 1991), who, helped along by the visual arts (see Ofrat [1988] on Tomarkin, Gershuni, Ofek, and especially Menashe Kadishman's sculptures [1984, 1985]), turned on its head any residue of the transmitted narrative. Yitzhak Laor, for example, openly challenges Isaac's submission, inciting him to an Oedipal revolt, 'to kill him, to lock up his father, his only one, [his] Abraham, in prison in an asylum in a cellar lest he be slaughtered...' ('Hametumtam hazeh Yitzhak' ['This dolt Isaac'], 1985: 70; see appendix for full text). Laor's warning reverberates in the surprisingly political conclusion of another work, an otherwise straightforward scholarly (psychoanalytic) study of the Bible (and Judaism), published in 1987. For more than 400 pages of *Lifnai velifnim*, the author, Avshalom Elitzur, manages to suppress any extra-scholarly motivation. Three pages, however, before the end of his book, Elitzur betrays his 'scientific objectivity', letting his psycho-political anxieties escape his control: 'Whoever agrees to the banishment of Ishmael, even against his will, will end up binding Isaac' (1987: 433).[41]

It is against this background that one should read the much debated last chapter of *Mr. Mani*, Yehoshua's rendition of the Aqedah as the primal scene (and sin) of Jewish history.[42] This is not the place to

41. A surprisingly different closure is to be found in the catalogue accompanying the two exhibits on the representaions of the Aqedah in Israeli art (Ofrat 1987, 1988); this fascinating cultural compendium requires a separate treatment. On the influence of Shoham on the writer Shulamith Hareven, see my forthcoming *A Woolf in the Holy Land: Gender and Nation in Israeli Women's Fiction* (New York: Columbia University Press, 1999). As this essay goes to print, 'the aqedah of Israel' has moved to the cultural center with Hanoch Levin's play *Murder* (December 1997).

42. This Israeli tendency to 'filicidize' the Aqedah has recently branched into another area—the interpretation of Midrash itself. As I was preparing the final draft of this paper I discovered in the 1995 issue of *JJS* (a special issue commemorating Geza Vermes's twenty-fifth year as its editor), a new psychoanalytic reading of *Genesis Rabbah*. Following Shoham, whose 'Isaac Syndrome' relies on *Genesis Rabbah* more than on Gen. 22, M.R. Niehoff reads this midrash for its 'mythical and

explore the complex ways in which Yehoshua 'undoes the Aqedah by acting it out' (his wording), transforming it once again beyond recognition. Suffice it to point out that Avraham Mani not only acts out the sacrifice that was prevented in Genesis 22; he also gets involved ('for the good of the family/future/ *'am Israel*', no doubt) in a quasi-incestuous relationship. With this coupling of filicide and incest, Yehoshua came as close as a Hebrew text can come to an Oedipal script, all the obvious differences notwithstanding.[43] In that, he was no doubt responding to well-known political trends, along the way dramatizing the dangers of the 'Isaac Syndrome': the self-destruction inherent in any *idée fixe*, the risk that the perpetration of aggression in the name of various sites of power may get out of hand.[44] Furthermore, by entrusting this manic binding to the hands of the Ishmaelite (Muslim) guards on the grounds of the Dome of the Rock, the imputed site of the biblical 'Aqedah', Yehoshua may be echoing Laor's unorthodox remembrance of sins past ('Isaac, Isaac, remember what your father has done to Ishmael your brother'),[45] again shifting the terms of the argument.

Ironically, neither Laor nor Yehoshua (nor Shoham) anticipated that, before long, the tradition of the Jewish Aqedah as they knew it would come to an aggressive end—and not in the manner about which they were apprehensive. Indeed, on that tragic night in November 1995, the knife that came down—albeit in the form of a gun—on Yitzhak (Isaac) Rabin, Israel's prime minister, then on the brink of rehabilitating

---

psychological' contents (without the benefit, however, of the two American studies [Levenson 1993 and Bergmann 1992] that address precisely these issues). Just like Shoham before her, Niehoff ignores the obvious dissimilarity between Isaac and Oedipus and is content to base her psychoanalytic reading on partial findings—the 'murderous inclinations' of Abraham. By so doing, she has joined (perhaps unwittingly) the politically-charged Israeli climate of 'father bashing'. What is still left unanswered, however, is the historically challenging question about the reasons for the shift from the depiction of Abraham in the earlier Midrashim (from *Jubilees* to Josephus) to that of *Genesis Rabbah*.

43. For a fuller analysis see Feldman 1995 (1997 is an English summary); cf. Nash 1993, Shalev 1995.

44. Recently the popularization of this metaphor has reached new heights in Neil Gordon's international thriller, *Sacrifice of Isaac* (1995), whose protagonists are contemporary Israeli representatives of the biblical scenario, with no ram substitute. A Hebrew translation has already made its appearance in Israel.

45. Laor's inverted allusion to the decree against forgetting the 'sins of 'Amalek' complements the Oedipal inversion of the Aqedah.

Ishmael, violently broke with the Isaac of Jewish tradition. With this new Israeli Oedipus, Israel's process of (Freudian) Westernization seems to have reached a new height. An ironic difference nevertheless remains: for this new Oedipus sees himself as the savior of the very tradition whose foundations he has so recklessly destroyed.

APPENDIX

חיים גורי
יְרֻשָּׁה

Haim Gouri
Inheritance

הָאַיִל בָּא אַחֲרוֹן.
וְלֹא יָדַע אַבְרָהָם כִּי הוּא
מֵשִׁיב לִשְׁאֵלַת הַיֶּלֶד,
רֵאשִׁית־אוֹנוֹ בְּעֵת יוֹמוֹ עָרַב.

The ram came last.
And Abraham did not know
it was the answer to the boy's question,
the boy, first issue of his vigor in the
twilight of his life.

נָשָׂא רֹאשׁוֹ הַשָּׂב.
בִּרְאוֹתוֹ כִּי לֹא חֲלָם חֲלוֹם
וְהַמַּלְאָךְ נִצָּב—
נָשְׁרָה הַמַּאֲכֶלֶת מִיָּדוֹ.

He lifted his hoary head.
When he saw it was no dream and the
angel stood there—
the knife slipped from his hand.

הַיֶּלֶד שֶׁהֻתַּר מֵאֲסוּרָיו
רָאָה אֶת גַּב אָבִיו.

The boy unbound
saw his father's back.

יִצְחָק, כַּמְסֻפָּר, לֹא הֹעֲלָה קָרְבָּן.

Isaac, we're told, was not offered up in
sacrifice.

הוּא חַי יָמִים רַבִּים,
רָאָה בַּטּוֹב, עַד אוֹר עֵינָיו כָּהָה.

He lived long,
enjoyed his life, until the light of his
eyes grew dim.

אֲבָל אֶת הַשָּׁעָה הַהִיא הוֹרִישׁ לְצֶאֱצָאָיו

But he bequeathed that hour to his
progeny.

הֵם נוֹלָדִים
וּמַאֲכֶלֶת בְּלִבָּם.

They are born
with a knife in their heart.

יצחק לאור
המטומטם הזה יצחק

לִרְחֹם עַל הָעוֹלָה? לְמִצְווֹת? עַל חֲמוֹר?
בְּצַיְתָנוּת כָּזֹאת? מֵהַנֶּגֶב עַד הַמּוֹרִיָּה לְהִזָּבַח?
לִסְמֹךְ עַל אַבָּא כָּזֶה? שֶׁיַּשְׁכִּים לַהֲרֹג שֶׁיִּכְלָא אֶת אָבִיו אֶת
יְחִידוֹ אֶת אַבְרָהָם בְּבֵית סֹהַר בְּבֵית מַחְסֶה בְּמַרְתֵּף הַבַּיִת וּבִלְבַד שֶׁלֹּא
יִשְׁחָט. יִצְחָק, יִצְחָק, זְכֹר אֶת אֲשֶׁר עָשָׂה אָבִיךָ לְיִשְׁמָעֵאל אָחִיךָ

Yitzhak Laor, 'This dolt Isaac' (1985)

To pity the offered up? Who goes up to [be confirmed in] the commandments? On a donkey?

So obediently? From the South to Mount Moriah to be sacrificed?

To rely on such a father? Let him rise up first to kill him, let him lock up
his father, his

only one, [his] Abraham in a prison in an asylum in a cellar lest he be
slaughtered. Isaac, Isaac, remember what your father did to Ishmael your
brother.

(My translation.)

BIBLIOGRAPHY

Abramson, Glenda
    1990   'The Reinterpretation of the Akedah in Modern Hebrew Literature', *JJS* 41: 101-14.

Agnon, S.Y.
    1945   *Temol shilshom* (*Yesterdays*) (Jerusalem: Schocken).

Auerbach, Erich
    1957   *Mimesis: The Representation of Reality in Western Literature* (trans. Willard R. Trask; Garden City, NY: Doubleday).

Bakan, David
    1966   *The Duality of Human Existence* (Chicago: Chicago University Press).

Band, Arnold
    1996   'Scholarship as Lamentation: Shalom Spiegel on "The Binding of Isaac"' (Stanford University, 14 May [unpublished paper]).

Barzel, Hillel
    1972   *Shiva'a mesaprim* (*Seven Fiction Writers*) (Tel Aviv: Yachdav).

Bergmann, Martin S.
    1992   *In the Shadow of Moloch: The Sacrifice of Children and its Impact on Western Religions* (New York: Columbia University Press).

Cohen, Israel
    1981   'Ha-Aqedah in Modern Hebrew Literature', in *idem, Beḥevion hasifrut ha-'ivrit* (*Within the Depth of Hebrew Literature: A Jungian Probe*) (Tel Aviv: Eked): 55-74.

Davies, P.R., and B.D. Chilton
    1978   'The Aqedah: A Revised Tradition History', *CBQ* 40: 514-46.

Elbaum, Yaakov
    1986   'From Sermon to Story: The Transformation of the Akeda', *Prooftexts* 6: 97-116.

Eli, A.
    1970   'Lay Not Thine Hand upon the Lad', in Ehud Ben Ezer (ed.), *Sha'ananim be-Zion* (Tel Aviv: Am Oved, 1986): 189-208 (ET *Unease in Zion*; New York: Quadrangle Books, 1974): 121-42.

Elitzur, Avshalom C.
    1987   *Lifnai velifnim* (*Into the Holy of Holies: Psychoanalytic Insights into the Bible and Judaism*) (Tel Aviv: Yarom).

Exum, J. Cheryl
    1992   *Tragedy and Biblical Narrative* (Cambridge: Cambridge University Press).
Feldman, Yael S.
    1985   'Poetics and Politics: Israeli Literary Criticism between East and West',
                PAAJR 52: 9-35.
    1989a   'Recurrence and Sublimation: Towards a Psychoanalytic Approach to
                Biblical Narrative', in B.N. Olshen and Y.S. Feldman (eds.), *Approaches to
                Teaching the Hebrew Bible* (New York: MLA Publications): 78-82.
    1989b   'Back to Vienna: Zionism on the Literary Couch', in R. Kozodoy,
                D. Sidorsky and K. Sultanik (eds.), *Vision Confronts Reality: Historical Per-
                spectives on the Contemporary Jewish Agenda* (London and Toronto: Asso-
                ciated University Presses): 310-35.
    1994   '"And Rebecca Loved Jacob", But Freud Did Not', in P. Rudnytsky and
                E. Handler Spitz (eds.), *Freud and Forbidden Knowledge* (New York: New
                York University Press): 7-25.
    1995   'Back to Genesis: Towards the Repressed and beyond It in Israeli Iden-
                tity', in N. Ben Dov (ed.), *Bakivun hanegdi: Selected Essays on Mr. Mani*
                (Tel Aviv: Hakkibutz hameuchad): 204-23 (Hebrew).
    1997   'Identity and Counter-Identity: The Sephardi Heritage in Israel', *Mid-
                stream* 43: 17-20.
    1999   'Postcolonial Memory and/or Postmodern Intertextuality: Anton
                Shammas's "Arabesques" Revisited', *PMLA*.
Fisch, Harold
    1984   *A Remembered Future: A Study in Literary Mythology* (Bloomington: Indiana
                University Press).
Frazer, J.G.
    1900   *The Golden Bough: A Study in Magic and Religion* (London: Macmillan).
Gilman, Sander
    1986   *Jewish Self Hatred* (Baltimore: The Johns Hopkins University Press).
    1993   *Freud, Race, and Gender* (Princeton, NJ: Princeton University Press).
Gordon, Neil
    1995   *Sacrifice of Isaac* (New York: Random House).
Gouri, Haim
    1996   *Words in my Lovesick Blood* (trans. Stanley F. Chyet; Detroit: Wayne State
                University Press).
Harrowitz, Nancy
    1994   *Antisemitism, Misogyny, and the Logic of Cultural Difference: Cesare Lombroso
                and Mathilde Serao* (Lincoln, NE: Nebraska University Press).
Hever, Hannan
    1995   'Territoriality and Otherness in Hebrew Literature of the War of Inde-
                pendence', in L. Silberstein and R. Cohn (eds.), *The Other in Jewish
                Thought and History* (New York: New York University Press): 236-52.
Hoffman, Anne Golomb
    1991   'Constructing Masculinities in Yaacov Shabtai's *Past Continuous*', *Prooftexts*
                11: 279-95.
    1992   'Oedipal Narrative and its Discontents: A.B. Yehoshua's *Molkho* (Five
                Seasons)', in N. Sokoloff *et al.* (eds.), *Gender and Text in Modern Hebrew*

and Jewish Literature (New York: Jewish Publication Society of America Press): 195-216.

Kartun-Blum, Ruth
    1988   ' "Where Does This Wood in my Hand Come from?" The Binding of Isaac in Modern Hebrew Poetry', *Prooftexts* 8: 293-310.

Keuls, Eva C.
    1985   *The Reign of the Phallus: Sexual Politics in Ancient Athens* (Berkeley, CA: University of California Press).

Klauzner, Margot
    1949   'The Aqedah Motif and [the play] *Be-'arvot ha-negev'*, *Molad* 4: 379-80 (Hebrew).

Lamdan, Yitzhak
    1927   *Massada* (Tel Aviv: Sifriyat Poalim).
    1966   '*Ba-ḥamsin*', excerpt from 'Massada', in *Modern Hebrew Poetry: A Bilingual Edition* (trans. Ruth Feiner Mintz; Berkeley: University of California Press).
    1973   *Kol shire* (*Collected Poems*) (Jerusalem: Mossad Bialik).

Laor, Yitzhak
    1985   *Rak haguf zocher* (*Only the Body Remembers*): *Poems* (Tel Aviv: Adam).

Larson, Jennifer
    1995   *Greek Heroine Cults* (Madison, WI: University of Wisconsin Press).

Leach, Edmund
    1969   *Genesis as Myth and Other Essays* (London: Jonathan Cape).

Lefkowitz, Mary R.
    1986   *Women in Greek Myth* (Baltimore: The Johns Hopkins University Press).

Levenson, Jon D.
    1993   *The Death and Resurrection of the Beloved Son: The Transformation of Child Sacrifice in Judaism and Christianity* (New Haven: Yale University Press).

Loraux, Nicole
    1987   *Tragic Ways of Killing a Woman* (trans. Anthony Forster; Cambridge, MA: Harvard University Press).

Kurzweil, Baruch
    1959   'Nosse ha-aqedah be-sifrutenu ha-ḥadashah' ('The Theme of the Aqedah in Our Modern Literature'), *Davar,* 2 October (Hebrew).

Marcus, David
    1986   *Jephtah and his Vow* (Lubbock, TX: Texas Tech Press).

Mazor, Yair
    1989   'Not Like the Wind and with No Perfect Peace' (Hebrew), *Moznaim* 5–6: 176-81.

Milman, Joseph
    1991   '"Remember What your Father Did": The Binding of Issac—The Components of its Meaning in the Biblical Story and in Contemporary Protest Poetry' (Hebrew), in Zevi Levi (ed.), *Ha-aqedah vehatoḥeha* (Jerusalem: Magnes Press): 53-72.

Moore, G.F.
    1932   *Judaism in the First Centuries of the Christian Era*, I (2 vols.; Cambridge, MA: Harvard University Press).

Nash, Stanley
    1977   'Reflections on Israeli Literature Based on Recurrences of the *'Aqedah* Theme', *Edebiyat* 2.1: 29-40.
    1986   'Israeli Fathers and Sons Revisited', *Conservative Judaism* 38: 28-37.
    1993   '*Mar Mani* and the Akedah: Perusing the Fourth and Fifth Conversations of a Novel in the Counter Direction', *HaDoar* 72: 19-21 (Hebrew).
Neumann, Erich
    1954   *The Origins and History of Consciousness* (Princeton, NJ: Princeton University Press).
Niehoff, M.R.
    1995   'The Return of Myth in Genesis Rabba', *JJS* 46: 69-87.
Ofrat, Gideon
    1979   'Aqedat Yitzhak ba-drama ha-yisraelit' ('The Binding of Isaac in Israeli Drama'), *Moznayim* 49: 345-52.
    1983   'Aqedat Yitzhak ba-omanut ha-yisraelit' ('The Binding of Isaac in Israeli Art'), a sketch for a forthcoming exhibition, *Iton* 77: 42-44.
    1987, 1988 Curator. *Aqedat Yitzhak in Israeli Art* (Ramat Gan Museum, exhibition catalogue).
Rabinowitz, Nancy Sorkin
    1993   *Anxiety Veiled: Euripides and the Traffic in Women* (Ithaca, NY: Cornell University Press).
Reik, Theodor
    1951   *Dogma and Compulsion: Psychoanalytic Studies of Religion and Myths* (trans. Bernard Miall; New York: International Universities Press).
    1961   *The Temptation* (New York: Braziller).
Rotenberg, Mordechai
    1978   *Damnation and Deviance: The Protestant Ethic and the Spirit of Failure* (New York: Free Press).
Schlossman, H.H.
    1972   'God the Father and his Sons', *Americam Imago* 29: 35-51.
Schwartz, Igal
    1995   'Israeli Fiction: The Age After', *Efes Shetaim* 3: 7-15 (Hebrew).
Schwartz, Regina M.
    1997   *The Curse of Cain: The Violent Legacy of Monotheism* (Chicago: University of Chicago Press).
Shaked, Gershon
    1989   *S.Y. Agnon: A Revolutionary Traditionalist* (trans. Jeffrey M. Green; New York: New York University Press).
Shalev, Mordechai
    1995   'The Mark of the Akeda in "Three Days and a Child", "Early in Summer 1970" and *Mr. Mani*', in N. Ben Dov (ed.), *Bakivun hanegdi* (Tel Aviv: Hakibutz hameuchad): 339-448.
Shamir, Moshe
    1959   'Oedipus and Avraham', in *Bekulmus Mahir* (Tel Aviv: Sifriyat Poalim [1957]): 329-33.
Shapira, Anita
    1992   *Herev hayona* (Tel Aviv: Am Oved).

1992   *Land and Power: The Zionist Resort to Force 1881–1948* (trans. William Templer; New York: Oxford University Press).

Shoham, S. Giora
1976   'The Isaac Syndrome', *American Imago* 33: 329-49.
1979   *The Myth of Tantalus* (St Lucia, Queensland: University of Queensland Press).
1995   *Valhalla, Calvary, and Auschwitz* (Cincinnati: BCAP Inc.).

Spiegel, Shalom.
1950   'Me-'agadot ha-akedah', in *Sefer ha-yovel le-Alexander Marx* (New York: JTS Press): 471-547.
1979   *The Last Trial* (trans. Judah Goldin; New York: Behrman House [1967]).

Steiner, Moshe
1982   *Haṭḥiya ha-le'umit be-sifrutenu (National Revival in our Literature)* (Tel Aviv: Cherikover).

Steinmetz, Devorah
1991   *From Father to Son: Kinship, Conflict, and Continuity in Genesis* (Louisville, KY: Westminster/John Knox Press).

Vermes, Geza
1961   'Redemption and Genesis 22: The Binding of Isaac and the Sacrifice of Jesus', in *idem, Scripture and Tradition in Judaism* (Leiden: E.J. Brill): 193-227.
1996   'New Light on the Binding of Isaac from 4Q225', *JJS* 47: 140-46.

Weinman L.J.
1977   'The Akeda Motif in the Modern Hebrew Story' (PhD dissertation; Los Angeles: University of California Press).

Weiss, Hillel
1991   'Comments on "Akedat Yitzhak" in Contemporary Hebrew Prose', in Zevi Levi (ed.), *Ha'akedah vehatokheḥa* (Jerusalem: Magnes Press): 31-52 (Hebrew).

Wellisch, E.
1954   *Isaac and Oedipus: A Study in Biblical Psychology of the Sacrifice of Isaac, the Akedah* (London: Routledge & Kegan Paul).

Yasif, Eli (ed.)
1978   *Aqedat Yitzhak: Studies in the Development of a Literary Tradition* (Jerusalem: Makor) (Hebrew).

Yehoshua, A.B.
1980   'The Diaspora: A Neurotic Solution', in *Between Right and Right* (New York: Schocken Books): 27-74.
1990   *Mar Mani* (Tel Aviv: Hakkibutz hameuchad).
1992   *Mr. Mani* (trans. Hillel Halkin; New York: Doubleday).
1995   'Postscript: Undoing the Aqedah by Acting It Out', in N. Ben-Dov (ed.), *Bakivun hanegdi: Selected Essays on Mr. Mani* (Tel Aviv: Hakkibutz hameuchad): 394-98.

Zeligs, Dorothy
1974   *Psychoanalysis and the Bible* (New York: Bloch).

Teaching the Bible 'as' Literature 'in' Culture

Regina M. Schwartz

There are days when teaching the Bible feels like being a prophet: you are slow of speech like Moses, you want to escape to the ends of the earth rather than convey certain messages like Jonah, you feel alone like Amos (who was not in one of the professional bands of prophets) as you forge ahead, interpreting the Bible without the authorization of a church community, and you feel persecuted by everyone—by those who think you ought to be teaching the canon of Western literature and by those who wonder why you are not doing something hip and non-canonical rather than the Bible, so in general you often wish you had never been born, like Jeremiah. But there are also days when you do feel inspired like the prophets, not because the word of God has been conveyed to you, but because you have to rise to the challenge of making the most familiar myths of Western culture, stories like the creation, the fall, and the flood, unfamiliar to students, and because you must face the challenge of making unfamiliar stories, like the rape of the concubine in Judges 19, alien purity laws in Leviticus, horrific curses in Deuteronomy, sound less strange. There are freedoms gained by teaching narratives that enjoy such cultural currency. First, the chances are good that nothing that your students say has not been said before. When a timid student ventures 'I know this is going to sound stupid, but what if', and what follows is a wacky interpretation of Mark 14, you can respond to that student by saying, 'no, that does not sound stupid, as a matter of fact, that is precisely what Zwingli, one of the leaders of the Reformation who changed history, said about the passage'. Your student is empowered, and the whole class loosens up. There are other benefits of that cultural currency. In our efforts to make the literature we are teaching pertinent to the present, we often come up with embarrassing analogies: comparing The Faerie Queene to *Star Wars*, for instance. But because the Bible is so alive in our culture, we can cull examples of its uses and misuses directly from the presidential addresses of Lincoln or Clinton, paintings of Giotto or Rembrandt, Christmas carols or operas, political rhetoric from South Africa or Israel, films like *Salome* or *The Last Temptation of Christ*, to say nothing of the literary legacy, in Milton, Blake, Melville, Faulkner, Zora Neale Hurston, or just about anything else students read in their Western culture classes.

The other challenge arises because this text is held to be sacred by the living breathing faith communities of Christianity and Judaism, and not just literature. How does that impact the classroom? I raise that very question, early in the course, and the Babylonian creation story affords a good opportunity for my students to consider it. The *Enuma Elish* (literally, 'when on high', the opening words of the narrative, as Genesis is 'in the beginning' [1.1]) was once held to be sacred, by those who believed that Marduk was their god, that he created the heavens and the earth (in the same order that Genesis 1 describes it), and who turned to the creation story for explanations of how the cosmos was constituted and governed. In ancient Babylonia, where it was held to be sacred truth, there was an organized religion, a priesthood, and rituals, and this narrative of the defeat of chaos and the creation of the cosmos, of Marduk assuming lordship, was at their center, authorizing all that activity and belief, just as it was authorized by the priesthood. But now, the Babylonians have disappeared and what is left of their culture is no longer believed by a faithful community. Those with faith commitments to Judaism or Christianity would say that this is because the Babylonian story was partial and imperfect and was supplanted by a greater truth, the truth of how the real God—Yahweh, not Marduk—really created the world—not by dividing the body of the Goddess of the waters of the Deep, Tiamat, but by dividing the waters of the Deep, Tehom. For secular students, the Babylonian creation narrative teaches a different lesson: not that an inferior religion has been displaced by a superior one, but that what is deemed sacred is contingent upon a living community with the authority to make the claim that it is sacred stick. According to this logic, if Babylonians were still around and had managed to keep their hegemony, Marduk would still be worshipped, and the Babylonian creation story would still be deemed sacred—not relegated to the status of an ancient epic that is often compared to Genesis in the spirit of comparative literature.

This same logic could be deployed to re-situate works of literature. If *Paradise Lost* had a cult and a priesthood (say, the members and officers of the Milton Society of America), and if it had a liturgy (say, the weekly recitation of the poem), and if it claimed that it was a divine revelation made to Milton (who regarded himself as a prophet of God), and if a community believed that *Paradise Lost* described God as he really is and events as they really occurred, and that all of human history derives its meaning from the sacred history of redemption contained therein, and if the text were ceaselessly interpreted so that a revered tradition of interpretations could be consulted, then it too would qualify as a sacred text. But of course, as students hasten to point out, Milton *did* claim to be a prophet, the text *is* recited weekly in the context of an institution that *does* authorize it and ceaselessly interprets it. And this is not only true of *Paradise Lost*; there is a reason why the *Norton Anthology of English Literature* and the Bible are both called canons. Perhaps the *Norton Anthology* is held to be sacred too, by some, and its editors regarded as the scribal priests who mean to pass that sacred tradition on to future generations of believers. Perhaps, too, the virulence of the attack upon this sacred literary canon is evidence of its religio-cultural authority, one that many want to call into question. But isn't this analogy becoming exaggerated, for isn't one text, the Bible, *really* the word of God and the other, the *Norton Anthology of English Literature*, *really* the word of men and (in more recent editions) women? Aye, there's the rub. Who is to say? Some say men and women wrote the Bible too. Who do we believe?

At this point, I would intervene in this imaginary dialogue to point out that whatever communities may believe about them, sacred texts are, like any works of literature, *representations*, caught in the fallen realm of language. Even if the answer to why the story of Joshua's conquest of Jericho is held to be sacred—but the story of Aeneas's siege of Troy is not—lies outside the text, in the beliefs of communities with authority; nonetheless, the two stories themselves share the same power and the same limitation: language. And whether your theory of signs is informed by Augustine, Derrida, or whoever, these texts are *representations*, and as such, only approximations, not unmediated truth. How can we speak of God when language cannot adequately signify him? Augustine, following Paul, explained that ever since the fall, we are condemned to a realm of interpretation, one in which our interpretations are decidedly limited. For if we inhabit a realm of signs that must be interpreted, behind them await truths that are independent of these signs (for believers, that is). By the Reformation, a theory of accommodation had become current, wherein God had tailored signs, accommodating them to fallen, human understanding.

Immediate are the Acts of God, more swift
Than time or motion, but to human ears
Cannot without process of speech be told
So told as human notion can receive.
    John Milton, *Paradise Lost*, VII.176-79

My students who have deep faith commitments are already equipped with this intuition long before they come to college (even if they could not articulate it), and so the versions of God they encounter in biblical narratives rarely lead to a crisis of faith. One might expect that prolonged looks at portrayals of God as threatening his people with all manner of abuses if they don't obey him—portrayals of the deity as exclusive, possessive, tyrannical and violent—could challenge their convictions. One might even expect that classes on the Bible as literature could easily turn into virtual dens of heresy. It does not happen. My students' intuitive Augustinianism kicks in, and these depictions of God immediately strike them as inadequate representations, portrayals that are drawn more in the image of *man* than in the image of God. They will grant that God is often depicted as a punitive parent in Deuteronomy, a glory-seeking tyrant in Exodus, a vindictively jealous husband in Hosea, a blood-thirsty conqueror in Joshua, but these depictions—I call them the dark side of monotheism—are in the all-too-human image of man, reflecting his preoccupations with possessing women, possessing land, and possessing power—preoccupations that are projected onto the deity who in turn is supposed to authorize these all-too-human ideologies of possession and domination.

On the day that the veil lifts, and students have read enough portrayals of monotheism to assume that humans have not adequately portrayed their God, they also understand that the Bible is not only a sacred text but also a work of literature, deeply embedded in our immanent culture—and not, in any simple sense, a transparent window onto transcendence. They stop asking questions like, why did God accept only one sacrifice when both Cain and Abel offered sacrifices, and instead they ask, why does the narrative *describe* God as only accepting one sacrifice? Why does the narrative *depict* God as demanding allegiance to himself alone—'I am a jealous God, you will have none before me'— and why does it *depict* him as conferring favor on one alone—'God looked with favor upon the sacrifice of Abel but not on the sacrifice of Cain'. And then they are ready to explore the vast political and cultural legacy of such a narrative: the real-world violence that is perpetrated by the elect under the banner of divine wrath against the infidel—the slaughters by Crusaders, the exiles by Inquisitors, the conquest of the New World, the hate crimes of the Christian Identity movement, and the ongoing legacy in the secularized versions of racial and ethnic supremacy—genocide throughout Europe, in Bosnia and in Rwanda. Are we the heirs of Cain because we murder our brothers? Students discover, as they read biblical narratives, that the violent rivalry that breaks out between the first brothers is repeated, *ad nauseam*, among the sons of Noah, the sons of Abraham, the sons of Isaac, the sons of Jacob, and even the sons of David, where murder erupts again. But the longer they look, the more they note the variations on that theme. Sometimes the rivalry issues in murder, sometimes not. Sometimes the parents, human or divine seem at fault; sometimes not. Sometimes the motif of sibling rivalry raises its ugly head only to be resolved. Joseph painfully and painstakingly teaches his brothers that they must be responsible for one another rather than murderous rivals. Before the sons of Israel are qualified to be forged as a nation, they must learn the lesson so dramatically denied by Cain: that they are their brothers' keepers. Even my most cynical students cannot get away with claiming that the dark side of monotheism is the only side. The political afterlife of biblical narratives and the ensuing discussion of the 'dark side' of monotheism are elaborated more fully in Schwartz, *The Curse of Cain: The Violent Legacy of Monotheism* (Chicago: University of Chicago Press, 1997). The brighter side of monotheism—its emphasis on charity and plenitude—is the focus of my current work.

Amid all the variety of representations of God, two poles of monotheism can be discerned. One depicts God as infinitely charitable, infinitely giving, with blessings for all. In the other, divine favor and blessings are scarce, inspiring deadly rivalries, like Cain and Abel's, in which some are blessed and some are cursed. As a drunken Cassio puts it in *Othello*, 'God's above all, and there be souls that must be saved and there be souls must not be saved' (Act 2, Scene 3, ll. 99-101). And as an anguished President Lincoln put it in his Second Inaugural Address, 'Both sides read the same Bible, both pray to the same God, and each invokes his aid against the other'. Why does monotheism so often suggest that a people can only prosper at the expense of the Other? Remarkably, Esau is given that very question.

> After Isaac finished blessing him and Jacob had scarcely left his father's presence, his brother Esau came in from hunting. He too prepared a meal

and brought it to his father for his blessing. His father Isaac asked him.
'Who are you?' 'I am your son', he answered, 'your first-born, Esau'.
Isaac trembled violently and said, 'Who was it then, that hunted game
and brought it to me? I ate it just before you came and I blessed him and
indeed he will be blessed.' When Esau heard his father's words, he burst
out with a loud and bitter cry and said to his father, 'Bless me—me too,
my father'. But he said, 'Your brother came deceitfully and took your
blessing'. 'Haven't you reserved any blessing for me?' Isaac answered
Esau, 'I have made him lord over you and have made all his relatives his
servants and I have sustained him with grain and new wine. So what can
I possibly do for you, my son?'

And then Esau asks that profound question, 'Have you only one blessing, my father? Bless me too, my father'. And Esau wept.

There will be no blessed future for the sons of Esau, for the Edomites,
a people who will be portrayed as the enemies of Israel. What if the
narrative had depicted the Edomites and Israelites enjoying equally
blessed futures? Or the Moabites and the Israelites? Would the cultural
legacy of the Bible have been a less violent one? Would it have been
more difficult to use the Bible as a weapon to degrade those who have
strayed from the one jealous God, peoples who have been classified as
infidels, pagans and idolaters? Surely, we would still have had the Crusades, the Inquisition, the Christian Identity movement, but would
these perpetrators have had to look elsewhere in their cultural legacy,
other than to representations of the will of God as recorded in his
authorized text, to authorize their hate crimes?

In the book of Exodus, before a whole host of laws are enumerated to
curb the aggression induced by a world of scarcity, a moving version of
paradisal plenitude is offered. It is, to be sure, a fallen paradise. This is
the wilderness and not the garden, the children of Israel are not as innocent as the children of Eden, having just escaped the bonds of slavery in
Egypt. But here, God is not depicted as withholding, but as providing.
When he offers bread from the heavens, he asks the receivers to count
on his sustenance, to live with the assumption—despite all the evidence
of their experience to the contrary—that there is enough to go around,
that each will have his or her basic needs met. And it is this glimmer of
ideal plenitude, and not the prevailing real-world scarcity, that is
intended to school the ancient Israelites in ethics.

'That', said Moses to them, 'is the bread Yahweh gives you to eat. This is
Yahweh's command. Everyone must gather enough of it for his needs.'
When they measured in an omer of what they had gathered, the man

who had gathered more had not too much, the man who had gathered
less had not too little. Each found he had gathered what he needed
(Exod. 16.15-18).

Any who fail to accept this divine distribution of wealth, succumb to
greed. And when they hoard their food, it rots and rots them.

> Moses said to them, 'No one must keep any of it for tomorrow'. But
> some would not listen and kept part of it for the following day, and it
> bred maggots and smelt foul; and Moses was angry with them (Exod.
> 16.19-20).

Reading selectively, the way biblical interpretation has always proceeded, can produce a Bible that fits a particular ideological or theological agenda. The manna story can offer up a vision of a generous
egalitarian God and it can suggest the economy of a divine dispensation
of charity. To bolster that case, we can add Deutero-Isaiah and many
other passages: 'The poor and the needy ask for water, and there is
none, their tongue is parched with thirst. I Yahweh will answer them, I
the God of Israel will not abandon them… In the wilderness I will put
cedar trees, acacias, myrtles, olives. In the desert I will plant juniper,
plane tree, and cypress side by side (Isa. 41.19)'. The miracle of the
loaves and fishes revisits this motif of a miraculous generosity, a transcendent generosity, one elaborated recently in philosophy by Jean-Luc
Marion and in theology by Hans Urs von Balthassar. But—and as teachers of literature who highlight the mechanisms of interpretation, it is
important to point this out—even these passages can be interpreted not
to endorse an ethic of charity, but its complete opposite, greed. An editorial written by a spokesman for the Italian right shows how easily the
Bible can be used in culture for any purpose, turning the sentiment of
charity around 180 degrees, all the while invoking biblical authority:
'We can offer them a plate of pasta but not open the cafeterias. Even
Jesus who multiplied bread and fishes did not open trattorias. He transformed water into wine, but, it seems to me, only once, and even then,
for a wedding. Albania, like Bosnia, is not our problem, but the problem of Europe.' It is the cultural appropriations, the acts of interpretation, like this, and not necessarily the narratives themselves, that turn the
Bible into a weapon.

On the question of the Other, the foreigner, the narratives are decidedly inconsistent. If the book of Ezra recommends separation from the
Other, advising the Israelites to put away their foreign wives acquired
during their exile, in contrast, the book of Ruth embraces a foreign

wife—Ruth the Moabite—and gives her the honorific role of progenitor in King David's lineage. If the book of Exodus depicts wrath against the Other, plagues against the first-born Egyptians, drowning of Pharaoh's army and all the while a hardening of his heart, the book of Jonah depicts such forgiveness of the Other, such compassion for the people of Nineveh—Israel's historical enemy—that the prophet is furious with God for being so merciful. And if the God who curses with dearth and with death is depicted in Amos and Deuteronomy, in Genesis we are offered a God who blesses the creation with fecundity, enjoining all created things to be fruitful and multiply and fill all the earth. Even the God of Cain and Abel, who accepts one sacrifice but rejects another, and the God of Jacob and Esau, who has only one blessing, is also challenged by the God of Exodus, who rains manna from heaven, enough for everyone. For the closer we look at these narratives, the more difficult it becomes to name the Other and so to hurt the Other. Who is an insider and who is an outsider is perpetually negotiated and these are not the only options: there are also 'outsiders within' or outcasts who are not altogether cast out. Divine fidelity and sexual fidelity are homologous throughout the biblical narratives (according to the prophet, because David has committed adultery with Bathsheba, the kingdom of ancient Israel unravels when it is at its height). Students typically ask, isn't God overreacting? But then we point out that the king has violated all the commandments and that the promise of the kingdom depends on obeying them. These preoccupations with fidelity are preoccupations of a narrative that tends to construct identity as someone or some people set apart, with boundaries that could be mapped, ownership that could be titled: 'you are my people, my very own'. But the parameters of 'the people' are always shifting and blurred: a people who are bound by a law they refuse to obey, a people defined by their nomadism but who are promised a land, a people who remember (or adopt) a shared history only constantly to forget it.

How do students, with their youthful craving for certainty, react to all this uncertainty? How do they negotiate blatantly conflicting interpretations? No sooner do they open the Bible than they are confronted with two different stories of the creation, one that begins with God creating 'the heavens and the earth', the second reversing that word order to the 'earth and the heavens'; one in which a universe of waters must be divided to create the dry land, another in which sweet waters flow in rivers through the land to irrigate it; one that articulates an entire cosmos, with the sun, moon, and stars, before human beings are created—last of all—another in which man is created first, and the garden is articulated around him and for him. And what about David, the heroic vanquisher of Goliath, the godly fugitive from the disfavored and tormented Saul, who becomes in other narratives an abuser of power who lolls about at home at the season when kings are to lead their troops to war, ravishing his loyal servant's wife and then murdering him to try to cover his crime? The Bible harbors both a narrative in which a powerful woman uses her sexuality as a deadly weapon to defeat ancient Israel's enemy— Judith seducing Holofernes so effectively that he literally loses his head—and a narrative in which an unnamed hapless woman is a sexual victim, gang-raped, left for dead, and then hacked into pieces. And it harbors a God whose prophet announces that he will punish Israel mercilessly—'For the three crimes, or four of Judah I have made my decree and will not relent' (Amos 2.4)—and a god whose prophet is angry that justice is not satisfied by divine universal mercy—so angry that he tries to escape his prophetic commission to warn Ninevah to repent, only to wind up belched ashore from the belly of a whale, commissioned to deliver his message.

If, for some students—believers—these conflicting versions confirm the sense that God cannot be adequately represented, for others—who are secular—truth does not lurk beneath or behind signs, separable from them. For those students, it is signs all the way down. Conflicting interpretations do not signal that a single inviolate truth has been poorly conveyed; rather, these conflicts confirm their sense that the notion of 'one truth' is a fiction, carrying the potential tyranny of certainty—'my truth must be your truth or you are an infidel'—and to their surprise, they come to appreciate the Bible, relieved that it is not just full of pious Sunday-school injunctions they rejected in their childhood, but full of narratives recounting the grittiness of peoples struggling to find their identity in a world of violent competition for scarce resources. They note how the experiments with social order keep being provisional— that a tribal confederacy gives way to judgeship, that when that fails, the experiment of kingship follows, that the monarchy is critiqued by the prophets, that the prophets are reinterpreted in the New Testament in a new light as fulfilled, and that after all the experimentation to achieve a social order, from the military leadership to kings and priests and prophets, in the end, justice doesn't reign in this world at all—but in a new heaven and a new earth where the rivers that once watered an earthly paradise now become the rivers of eternal life in a heavenly paradise—and that vision is not about our political order at all, for it is utopian. They do not experience this multiplicity and provisionality as a Satanic plot against the One Truth; the conflict of interpretations does not lead them into spiritual angst, moral turpitude, and emotional despair. If God is depicted as excluding and unforgiving in some narratives and including and forgiving in others, the students find that discrepancy allows them to make value judgments, and they discover that they respond to biblical narratives, like other literature, with values that are already in place, with the human sympathy and compassion they have derived from other cultural sources, a sympathy that makes them worry about the Egyptians and the Canaanites. For these students the sacred peeps out of the nooks and crannies of narratives chiefly preoccupied with power and greed and lust and violence in small acts of kindness, forgiveness, sympathy or charity, in sporadic efforts to rise above humanity's worst instincts with compassion and thanksgiving. Not only the social dimension but also the philosophical dimension offers such glimpses, for the Bible poses profound questions about divine justice. For such students, if the Bible is a sacred text, calling evil into question rather than assuming its unavoidability, so too is *Paradise Lost*, so too is the *Divine Comedy*, and so too is *Star Wars*—not because they are authorized by a community of believers, but because they take up a sacred question: how to live justly in a world of injustice. For such students, the question we face is less how to teach sacred texts as literature than how to teach literature as sacred texts.

Of course, students do not always divide neatly into these two broad categories, 'religious' and 'secular'. Actively engaged in the process of self-discovery, most are in the midst of defining their religious commitments. They know what their families have asked them to believe, to do, and even to think, but in college they are constantly either altering, confirming or rejecting those childhood injunctions. Nonetheless, teaching the Bible in literature courses with these heuristic poles in mind helps to move students from both fundamentalist extremes toward a less certain middle, one in which signs are not always readily transparent to divinity on the one hand but in which they do not refer, in an archly secular way, only to their own referentiality either. The philosopher Jean-Luc Marion offers a key to this middle realm with his helpful distinction between the idol and the icon. The idol—and this can include any object of knowledge, a concept, a word—stops the gaze for it satisfies its aim; there is no reason to go beyond. If we see the divine in the idol (meaning *as* the sign) it is according to the measure of our own gaze. The icon, in contrast, points beyond itself, to the invisible, the unthinkable, the unutterable. As a sign, the icon neither refers naively to its signified, nor does it arrest the gaze. Rather, it points beyond itself to an immeasurable source: 'The icon recognizes no other measure than its own and infinite excessiveness [demesure]; whereas the idol measures the divine to the scope of the gaze of he who then sculpts it, the icon accords in the visible only a face whose invisibility is given all the more to be envisaged that its revelation offers an abyss that the eyes of men never finish probing.'[1] In this middle realm, one in which signs do not just coldly denote or fail to denote, but mysteriously reverberate, echoing mysteries, we interpret the immanent and its vexed relation to transcendence, albeit variously understood and represented, but we do not just use one to decode the other. Am I suggesting that a person's theory of signs is an index to his or her theology? Absolutely, and any theologians worth their theology would agree. Either the bread is God, stands for God, or is bread. But not necessarily *mere* bread— rather, a 'saturated phenomenon', as the philosopher Jean-Luc Marion would say, or even a resonant cultural inheritance, as in 'bread and circuses', or 'bread and chocolate', or 'loaves and fishes'. Students gradually learn that the very activity they are engaged in—interpretation—can be a sacred one, for it has been, not only the privileged job of English professors, Bible scholars, lawyers and leaders in all religious traditions, but also one shared by all human beings in the world.

And so, while students may find themselves abandoning the hankering for the depiction of one truth, one version, one ideology, one theology, one access to the sacred, their sense that the Bible is a sacred text is rarely sacrificed in the process of discovering these conflicts. To the contrary, I sense from their papers that their understanding of the sacred

---

1.   Jean-Luc Marion, *God without Being* (trans. Thomas Carlson; Chicago: University of Chicago Press, 1991), p. 21. Originally published as: *Dieu sans l'être: Horstexte* (Paris: Librairie Autheme Fayard, 1982). As a phenomenologist in the wake of post-structuralism, Marion recently made important distinctions about signification and the impossible in a debate with Jacques Derrida (forthcoming in a volume tentatively titled *Religion and Postmodernism* [eds. John D. Caputo and Michael J. Scanlon; Indiana University Press, 1999]). See also Phillip Blond (ed.), *Post-Secular Philosophy* (London: Routledge, 1998).

becomes more capacious, and less fragile, as the term proceeds. For some, the sacred emerges in the biblical ideals of social justice, despite all the evidence to the contrary of real injustice. By the end of the term, they are pointing to the way Amos insists that greed is appalling, citing the injunctions against Israel for 'selling the righteous for silver and the needy for a pair of shoes', the generosity of Boaz to Ruth and Naomi, Jeremiah's impatience with social injustice and ritual hypocrisy in his warnings to corrupt worshippers on the steps of the Temple. For this sense of the sacred, they could also turn to Erasmus, who, in his humanist version of a critique of identity politics, was impatient that monks worried too much about the color of their habits and not enough about feeding the poor, or to Matthew Arnold, who defined religion as heightened ethical sensibility. The sacred also emerges from the aesthetic, from the spare haunting verses of the sacrifice of Isaac that Erich Auerbach so brilliantly contrasted with Homeric verse in *Mimesis*;[2] for this, they could also turn to George Herbert or Mark Strand. Or the sacred emerges from the uses of a metaphor like the parting of waters, as it accrues its penumbra of referentiality, from the parting of waters at creation to the parting of the Red Sea to the parting of the Jordan to baptismal waters; for this, they would also turn to Mozart's *Magic Flute* or Lincoln's address at Gettysburg. For others, the sacred emerges from the sheer effort humans make with language to represent what is beyond language—transcendence. Somehow, the ancient peoples who wrote these texts managed to convey a sense of wonder, a sense that something transcends themselves and their immanent concerns even if it defines them and circumscribes them, and this is reflected in portrayals of a deity who creates humankind, yes, but also a whole cosmos; for this, we could also turn to Blake's *Book of Urizen* or the film *2001*. When we return to the creation story after the book of Revelation on the last day of my Bible class (like Milton's Angel sent to teach Adam, I want to leave students not with the conclusion that this world is to be destroyed but that it is newly created), students are frankly amazed—and moved—that the Bible includes narratives of creation at all. Since the Hebrew Bible tells the story of a people's struggle, why not begin with the father of those people, the call to Abraham in Genesis 12? Since the New Testament is devoted to the redemption from sin made possible by the incarnation and sacrifice, why not begin with the first sin of

2.   Erich Auerbach, *Mimesis: The Representation of Reality in Western Literature* (Princeton, NJ: Princeton University Press, 1953).

humankind? The creation story is incredibly evocative of humanity's wonder before the cosmos and of a sense of the sacred, with its blessings of proliferation—to be fruitful and multiply—even if they do quickly degenerate into the first brothers committing the first fratricide. But the blessing to all creation stands alongside the curse of Cain; a transcendent generosity flows in the face of human violence.

Vested, as we inevitably are, with the responsibility to ask students to forge their ethics, often in the face of the monolithic institutions that are only too happy to hand them one of self-aggrandizement, I have come to believe that teachers of literature, whether that literature is *officially* deemed sacred or not, are purveyors of the sacred. 'Woe is me, for I am ruined!' said Isaiah,

> Because I am a man of unclean lips,
> And I live among a people of unclean lips
> For my eyes have seen the king, the Lord of hosts.

> Then one of the seraphim flew to me, with a burning coal in his hand which he had taken from the altar with tongs. And he touched my mouth with it and said,

> 'Behold, this has touched your lips;
> and your iniquity is taken away, and your sin is forgiven' (Isa. 6.5-7).

While some days teaching the Bible feels like you are walking on hot coals, on others, it feels like a hot coal is pressed against your lips.

Madame Potiphar through a Culture Trip, or, Which Side Are You On?

Athalya Brenner and Jan Willem van Henten

It is sometimes worthwhile to have a look at the Hebrew Bible (HB) from a cultural-historical perspective. The ambiguous significance the Bible assumes in most Western, contemporary, multicultural communities is reason enough for doing that. Traditional, not to say orthodox, readers might feel uncomfortable with such a perspective. On the other hand, the retelling of biblical stories is at the core of the arts, literary and visual and plastic, that we consume and have consumed for hundreds of years.[1] The importance of the HB even in today's post-Christian, post-Jewish cultures remains great: in previous times it was even greater. A newly fostered interaction between biblical scholars and scholars of literature and art might yield interesting results that are as relevant to the understanding of contemporary life and the cultural scene as to that of the HB text itself, not to mention the process of reading. It is especially important, we feel, to introduce cultural angles into the HB classroom: especially, but not only, if the students come from fundamentalist backgrounds—be they Christian, Jewish, Muslim or of other convictions.

The Framework

In 1994–95, therefore, we gave an experimental course, based on these views, at the University of Amsterdam. We chose Genesis 39 as our prooftext. Our initial objective was to go through a cultural-historical analysis of the biblical text and its afterlife in Jewish, Christian, Islamic

---

1. For analyses of the Bible's retellings in art see, for instance, M. Bal, *Reading 'Rembrandt': Beyond the Word–Image Opposition* (Cambridge: Cambridge University Press, 1991); or for the Bible's political and cultural significance: M. Bal, *Death and Dissymmetry: The Politics of Coherence in the Book of Judges* (Chicago: University of Chicago Press, 1988); or M. Bal (ed.), *Anti-Covenant: Counter-Reading Women's Lives in the Hebrew Bible* (Sheffield: Almond Press, 1989).

and non-religious sources. In 'sources' we included literary texts as well as paintings, drawings, illustrations, carpets, scholarly articles—in short, everything that might constitute a commentary or a reading.

Why Genesis 39? We wanted to focus on a well-known story, well-known in the sense that it provoked many retellings. The choice itself was almost incidental but influenced by certain factors. We preferred a complete, not too long story, well connected to its context yet relatively independent, in which some gender questions could be seen to operate. Genesis 39.1-20 (or 23) is such a story, a complete episode whose first and last verses remind us of previous (ch. 37, Joseph is sold and taken to Egypt) and later developments (Joseph is in prison, again a metaphorical pit, waiting). There is no dearth of Jewish postbiblical retellings of the story, which was another requirement. Its afterlife in Islamic traditions is also quite well documented. If 'ancient sources' are (should they be?) privileged as interpretations in biblical scholarship, we have a plentitude of them for Genesis 39. We were hoping the story would capture our students' imagination as well.

We knew of Kugel's book,[2] in which most of the relevant (read 'midrashic') literary Jewish materials are discussed, together with some Islamic ones, but were critical of it. The course was taught in Amsterdam: some Dutch secondary literature on the topic had recently become available.[3] Alice Bach had written a dissertation, then an article, on the chapter, with special emphasis on *Testament of Joseph* and Jewish midrashic materials.[4] Mieke Bal had written an article on myth, Genesis 39, a 'Rembrandt' representation and a relevant chapter from Thomas Mann's *Joseph und seine Brüder*.[5] In other words, we had some feminist critiques of the story.

---

2.   J. Kugel, *In Potiphar's House: The Interpretive Life of Biblical Texts* (Cambridge, MA: Harvard University Press, 2nd edn, 1994).

3.   For instance H.A. Brongers, *De Jozefgeschiednis bij Joden, christenen en moham-medanen* (Wageningen: Veenman en zonen, 1962); K. Wagtendonk, 'Van de bijbelse Jozef tot de Joesoef van de Islam', in K.A. Deurloo and F.J. Hoogewoud (eds.), *Beginnen bij de letter Beth* (Kampen: Kok, 1985), pp. 131-38.

4.   A. Bach, 'Breaking Free of the Biblical Frame-Up: Uncovering the Woman in Genesis 39', in A. Brenner (ed.), *A Feminist Companion to Genesis* (Feminist Companion to the Bible, 2; Sheffield: Sheffield Academic Press, 1993), pp. 318-42.

5.   M. Bal, 'Myth à la Lettre: Freud, Mann, Genesis and Rembrandt, and the Story of the Son', in S. Rimmon-Kenan (ed.), *Discourse in Psychoanalysis and Literature* (London: Methuen, 1987); repr. in Brenner (ed.), *Feminist Companion to Genesis*, pp. 343-78.

The art side was also relatively easy to assemble. An exhibition at the Israel Museum in Jerusalem about the Bible in Islamic art[6] provided a beginning for insight into the Islamic materials. An Israeli friend[7] went through some materials and found several intriguing representations of the story in European and Jewish paintings and drawings. In short, there was recent interest in the subject and some material collected, on which we could base our work.

We had about 20 students, mostly in their third and fourth year of theological or Semitic philology studies. Almost all could read Hebrew; several could read Greek. We met ten times over so many weeks; each session lasted for three hours.

The Procedure

We started by reading the Hebrew text (as in *BHS*) together with Meir Sternberg's formulation of textual gap filling and its place in the process of reading.[8] Briefly stated, Sternberg argues that literary texts are full of 'holes', in the sense that the readers are required to supply the missing information. In the HB, where most narrative styles are frugal and extremely spare, readers contribute to the process even more than usual. Gaps and ambiguities on the one hand, doublets and repetitions on the other hand, are dealt with by readers according to their own phantasy of the text. This is done mostly automatically and unconsciously, and is necessary for the understanding of a text as it unfolds during a reading. Therefore, the reading process and, consequently, textual 'meaning' are largely determined by readers' filling of gaps and the way they deal with repetitions and ambiguities. The reader's position, location, experience and other life factors largely condition this process, in their turn.

We therefore read our story, applying to it the usual tools of philology, linguistics, semantics, text criticism and literary criticism. Throughout the reading we asked the students, again and again, to construct

6. N. Brosh, *Biblical Stories in Islamic Painting* (catalogue; Jerusalem: Israel Museum, 1991).

7. Yaffah Englard of the Gordon College, Haifa, who—among Bible scholars— has one of the more sophisticated HB-related art slides collections that I am aware of. I am much in her debt, for art works found and supplied as well as for other things (AB).

8. M. Sternberg, *The Poetics of Biblical Narrative* (Bloomington: Indiana University Press, 1985), Chapter 6.

three lists: one of lacunae in the story; one of doublets/repetitions; and one of ambiguities. Here are some of the findings:

1. Gaps. How old is Joseph? How old are Potiphar and the wife, for that matter? What does Joseph look like—hair, height, skin, eye colour, etc.—beyond being doubly beautiful (like his mother Rachel, v. 7)? Is he aware of his beauty, does it determine or influence his behaviour? What does the wife look like? Why is she nameless? What is her emotional motivation for attempting to seduce Joseph—lust, or love, or both? Is he tempted, does he fancy her? What does he do in the house when all other persons are gone? Why does he go in, especially since he knows how the woman pursues him? Why are the 'people of the house' gone, how and why do they come back suddenly? Which garment, outer garment or a more intimate one, did the woman get off Joseph? After the woman tells her husband her version, whom does he believe? Why does Joseph refrain from defending himself? Why is he put in prison for further treatment and not killed? What happens to the woman?

2. Repetitions. Joseph is twice 'good looking', יפה תאר ויפה מראה. He finds favour in God's and his master's eyes at least twice, and so, at the end, in the eyes of the prison's master. 'Master', 'his [Joseph's] master' (אדוניו, אדון), 'house' (בית) and 'house and field' (בית ושדה) are repeated many times. The woman tells her version three times—to the 'people of the house', to her husband, and this is mentioned again; all in all, then, we readers 'see' it four times—but do we know what actually happened? Which leads us to the next list.

3. Gaps and lacunae are ambiguous and breed further ambiguities, not to mention ambivalence. The demarcation line between 'gap' and 'ambiguity' is therefore not very firm. Nevertheless, some linguistic usages can denote ambiguity by their very existence in a text. Potiphar is presented as a סריס—eunuch, or [military] official? He is שר הטבחים—military leader, or a chief meat cook? From v. 1, then, the Potiphar character is established as ambiguous.

Other points: Why is Joseph loved by all who come into contact with him; is it just his looks, or other things as well? In what way can Joseph's garment serve as evidence for the woman's claim? Finally, if the woman is such a negative character, why is she given so many lines to speak in the story?

Our working hypothesis included the obvious recognition that we were not the first interpreters to have noticed these gaps, ambiguities and repetitions. Therefore, part of our task consisted of tracing the answers to the questions we posed in all the sources at our disposal. Those sources were understood as retellings conditioned by their creators' location, time, temperament and ideologies. This journey was the real business of the course. The fuller lists (the ones here are abbreviated), then, served as our guides on that journey. We proceeded to read the relevant materials in *Jubilees* (39.5-8), the books of Maccabees (1 Macc. 2.53; *4 Macc.* 2.1-4), Wisdom of Solomon (10.10-14), *Testament of Joseph*, Josephus Flavius's *Antiquities* (2.4.1–2.5.1) and Philo's *On Joseph* (Greek sources). We then moved to the Targums (Aramaic: *Onkelos, Pseudo-Jonathan*) and Midrash, earlier *(Genesis Rabbah,* esp. 87-89) and later (*Abot deRabbi Nathan,* ch. 16; the old *Tanḥuma,* not the Buber [Vilna] edition, where this material is absent; the Yemenite *Midrash Ha-Gadol; Sefer Ha-Yashar* [ch. 14], *Midrash Sekel Tov, Yalkut Shimeoni, Chronicles of Yeraḥme'el* and others, including talmudic passages and a Shavu'ot poem from the Vitry Maḥzor [Aramaic and Hebrew]).[9] A reading of Islamic sources, mostly the Joseph *sura* (*sura* 12) of the Qur'an, represented for us Arabic sources. This was followed by an analysis, in groups, of several (Christian) Western paintings, Jewish paintings and Islamic works of art (see below). The artifacts viewed were products of a long period, from the twelfth to the nineteenth century. Readings of some passages from Thomas Mann's novel (German) and *Hippolytus and Phaedra* were then succeeded by a survey of modern secondary literature, especially Bach and Bal. By the time we came back to the HB text and summarized our findings, a major shift had occurred for most of our students. They had begun to identify more and more with the narrated woman who, to begin with, they had seen as the evil mover of the plot. This by-product of the journey was undoubtedly caused by the heightened awareness of how they—and other commentators, in all mediums, through the ages—had filled in the textual gaps and dealt with the ambiguities and redundancies of Genesis 39.

9.   In this stage, Kugel's book (*In Potiphar's House*) was of the greatest assistance for orientation in the field, although it became apparent very early on that his analysis of the Jewish sources was not necessarily the only plausible analysis. Nowadays, of course, students would be required to find the relevant Jewish retellings on the Bar-Ilan *Responsa CD-ROM*, at the very least, before sailing into library work and acts of interpretation.

One Narrative, How Many Stories? Some Reflections

Genesis 39 can be read in several ways. It can be read as a story of ethnicity *and* difference, the tension between the 'we' (Hebrews) and the 'they' (Egyptians). It can be read as a story of education, whose chief figure—indeed, Joseph—undergoes a process of personal development. It can be read as a story of Yhwh's grace in dealing with an individual and, consequently and beyond this episode, with Jacob's sons and their families. It can and should be read, however, as a story of gender relations or, at the very least, with special attention to its love/erotic contents and the narrative figures' roles concerning that issue. (This was in fact done by Thomas Mann in his retelling. Mann, in his own way, combines the motifs of ethnic tension and erotics.) The gaps, ambiguities and—to a lesser extent—repetitions make two readings possible.

In the one, this is a story of Joseph's trial by seduction and temptation, a trial which he withstands with flying colours. This position is apparent, for instance, in two visual art renderings: Joseph escapes from the woman in Orazio Gentileschi's (1563–1638) painting[10] (Fig. 1) and the Golden Haggadah[11] (Fig. 2). In the other, this is a dramatic, impossible story of mutual love and attraction: so for instance, in two Islamic works, from the eighteenth (Fig. 3)[12] and late sixteenth (Fig. 4)[13] centuries.

We may follow the one or the other reading. In each case, though, we shall do so by making certain readerly decisions. For instance, we may decide that Joseph, in an uncomplicated and straightforward manner, refuses the woman out of a sense of duty and righteousness—whether he reciprocated her feelings or otherwise. Examples for such an understanding/retelling of the narrative are many. In Jewish and Christian texts of the Roman period, Joseph is a model figure for self-control and self-restraint. *4 Maccabees*, a philosophical Jewish work of about 100 CE, names Joseph as one of the exemplary instances in the history of Israel. He is used as one of the proofs for Israel's obedience to God and

10. M. Rosci, *Orazio Gentileschi* (I maestri del colore, 83; Milan: Fabbri, 1965).

11. B. Narkiss, *The Golden Haggadah* (London: British Museum, 1997).

12. Joseph chases Zuleika (which is the name given to the woman in some Islamic renderings, and in the Jewish *Sefer Ha-Yashar*). Illustration in a Persian manuscript by Jami, Kashmir, India (Brosh, *Islamic Paintings*, p. 57).

13. Zuleika and her maidservant looking with sorrow at Joseph, who sits in the prison. Iran, Khorasan, Gouache on paper (Brosh, *Islamic Paintings*, p. 71).

Figure 1. Orazio Gentileschi (1563–1638), *Joseph and Potiphar's Wife* (ML 501 HC 165 405477; The Royal Collection © Her Majesty Queen Elizabeth II)

his Torah commandments, in stark contrast to the loose ways of the Hellenistic world (*4 Macc.* 2.1-4). This ideal portrait appears also in some rabbinic texts, in keeping with the dictum put forth in *m. Ab.* 4.1:

איזהו גבור? הכובש את יצרו

Who is a hero? He who controls his libido.[14]

Figure 2. Bezalel Narkiss, *The Golden Haggadah*
            (by permission of the British Library; R97/E2425)

_____

14. For want of a better single term, the Heb. יצר (desire, sexual and otherwise, in both the positive and negative senses, sexually and otherwise) is here translated as 'libido'.

Figure 3. Israel Museum, *Joseph Pursuing Zuleika*
          (Persian manuscript by Jami, Kashmir, eighteenth century)

Figure 4. Israel Museum, *Zuleika Staring at the Imprisoned Joseph*
            (Khorasan, late sixteenth century)

But self-restraint does not necessarily preclude temptation; on the contrary, perhaps. In *Genesis Rabbah*, some sages envisage Madame Potiphar as young, good-looking and attractive, all the more so for allowing Joseph a real triumph over his desire and thus emphasizing their hero's victory of mind over matter, rational over emotional behaviour. The Jewish philosopher Philo of Alexandria, of the first century CE, develops this theme too. He views this episode as a necessary station in Joseph's trajectory to the Egyptian court and being worthy of his political destiny of leadership on two counts: that of avoiding inter-racial sexual relations (see Deut. 23.18) and adultery (Philo, *Jos.* 42-43).

The *Testament of Joseph* within the *Testaments of the Twelve Patriarchs*, a Christian work of the second century CE whose origin is certainly Jewish, is focused on the episode of Genesis 39. On his deathbed Joseph, of all his 'trials', remembers the temptation presented by Madame Potiphar as the most difficult he had to withstand (*T. Jos.* 12.1).[15] Here the narrator pays extraordinary attention to the woman, although she remains nameless. She is extremely good-looking (9.5), and undeniably attractive. He has to fight her advances (2.2). As in some Midrashim, he nearly capitulates (see 2.7; 3.8; 8.1). This picture of Joseph as a self-controlled hero and leader-to-be, obtainable in this work as in Josephus Flavius's self-serving account of the same episode, is largely determined by the interpreter's (or reteller's) ideological need, in each case, to make Joseph worthy of a leadership position. The affirmation of Joseph's chastity is a call for the reader to join the author's perspective and choose Joseph's side. Thus Madame Potiphar's figure and role, although much elaborated upon in comparison to the terse depiction in the biblical narrative, remain a foil of immorality, anonymous otherness and foreignness, with no regard for convention and propriety—all the more to emphasize Joseph's virtues.

But the *Testament of Joseph* is nevertheless far from straightforward. Questions of gaps and ambiguities are relevant to its reading too, and subvert any unidirectional interpretation. Why does Joseph let the woman go that far—for instance, why does he let her come to his room so many times? The woman does not only want to go to bed with him, as implied by Genesis 39, she *loves* him to death (ch. 7) and thinks that Joseph loves her in return. Do we find traces here of the possibility that this is a love story, perhaps the story of a forbidden or impossible love?

15. Bach, 'Breaking Free'.

The much repeated designation, in the HB text, of the woman's status as 'his [Joseph's] master's wife' (אשת אדוניו) may facilitate such a reading. Unlike Potiphar and Joseph, she is nameless: this absence of a name must be considered with regard to authorial intention.

The identities of many women in the HB are relational to the men in their lives: they themselves remain anonymous.[16] Samson's mother (Judg. 13) and the raped then murdered woman in Gibeah (Judg. 19) are relevant examples. Their namelessness indicates that, whatever their significance, their functional role in the narrative is that of an object of male actions and male desires. Potiphar's wife remains nameless in the Genesis story, in keeping with the absence of any other information about her looks, age and temperament. Is she good-looking, ugly, or just plain? Is she old, young, middle-aged, just a few years older than Joseph, about whom we at least know that he is around seventeen years old (Gen. 37.2) and good looking in a general way (39.6).

These gaps can be variously filled, and in visual renderings they must be filled. A few examples will suffice. Applying a name to the woman solves the name problem. In *Sefer Ha-Yashar*, as in certain Islamic traditions (but not in the Qur'an), she is called Zuleika. Bach calls her Mutem-emet, following Thomas Mann. And how is the age and looks question resolved? In a painting by Raphael (1483–1520), Madame Potiphar is young and fair; the same vision characterizes Tintoretto's work (1518–95). Rembrandt (1601-69), in an etching,[17] has her as at least middle-aged and ugly; in another work, showing the final confrontation between Potiphar, his wife and Joseph, Rembrandt has the woman younger and better looking, certainly not evil looking (Fig. 5). Needless to say, the choice of presentation, be it on the older/plain to ugly or the beautiful/young to mature side, echoes and is echoed in the different choices made by midrashic retellings, as is the case with other visual features. The bed introduced into most of these works, the colour red that features largely in them, the uncertain feeling of 'before' or 'after', the erotically charged atmosphere, Joseph's apparent ambivalence as his legs lead him out but his eyes linger on the woman—the variations are individual attempts, freely executed, to fill gaps and iron out

---

16. C. Meyers, 'Hannah and her Sacrifice: Reclaiming Female Agency', in A. Brenner (ed.), *A Feminist Companion to Samuel and Kings* (Feminist Companion to the Bible, 5; Sheffield: Sheffield Academic Press, 1994), pp. 93-104.

17. See Bal, 'Myth'.

ambiguities. But, of course, such attempts only manage to fill certain gaps and resolve certain ambiguities by creating fresh gaps, inconsistencies and ambivalences.

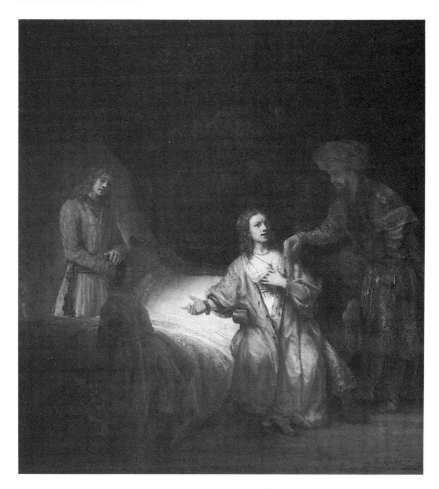

Figure 5. Rembrandt, *Joseph Accused by Potiphar's Wife*
(Andrew W. Mellon collection, © 1998 Board of Trustees,
National Gallery of Art, Washington, DC)

What is Genesis 39, then—a story of love or of lust, of unilateral female attempt to seduce a righteous man or of mutuality? Let us return for a moment to Potiphar, the סריס (v. 1). In the Septuagint he is a eunuch, one of the possible translations. This interpretation by translation is highly significant for constructing the rest of the story: if Potiphar is a eunuch, a castrato, then we can feel more sympathy for his wife and her behaviour.[18] Even so, we still are not sure of Madame's motivation. Is it love, is it lust, is it both? The narrator lets us hang. And Joseph? In his refusal (vv. 8-9) he does *not* claim that he does not find the woman attractive; it is up to the reader to speculate on this point. Why does he come into the house when all other people are away? (Where? See *Genesis Rabbah*, Josephus and others for a solution: by the Nile, for a religious celebration. Why do they all return suddenly at a moment convenient for the woman? A further complication is created by gap filling.) And why does he not defend himself against her accusation, while his silence can cost him his head? Love for the woman, a wish to spare her, can be a motive for his behaviour. And does Potiphar act out of love in dealing leniently with his wife, or with Joseph (see the Rembrandt painting of the romantic triangle, and the *Pseudo-Jonathan Targum* and *Yalkut Shimeoni* for suggestions of his homosexual love for Joseph)? Whose side is Potiphar on?

However the story is constructed in literal or visual retellings, a feature worth noting is that, in all of them and regardless of their individual emotional positions against or for her, Madame Potiphar's role is enlarged and substantiated. En route she gains a name, motivation, voice, depth, emotions, looks and so on. It seems obvious that, in most Jewish and early Christian texts, this substantiation is not motivated by the retellers' wish to dwell on her for her own sake, but as a foil to Joseph. If she is beautiful, his refusal to succumb is seen as more heroic. If he desires her, the same is true. If she nags him, ditto. And so forth. If she is old, older and ugly, then his refusal is less than surprising and his saintly stature diminished. And so on.

Zuleika in Islamic Art

How do Islamic sources retell Zuleika's story? Madame Potiphar has a special place in Islamic letters and visual arts, from the classical commentaries on the Qur'an onwards. Several Persian and Turkish collections are organized around cycles of episodes from Joseph's life.[19] Some of these works were transmitted in beautifully illustrated manuscripts. The poems as well as their illustrations make it clear that love is the

18. As in the story about Yousuf and Ra'il (Zuleika) by al-Thal'abi (before 1035).

19. The Persian poets Firdawsi (beginning of the eleventh century) and Jami (1483); the Turkish poet Hamdi; see Brosh, *Islamic Paintings*, p. 52.

motivation driving Zuleika. In some of these texts, Joseph and Zuleika marry at the end, after she converts to his religion (a reminiscence of *Joseph and Aseneth*, certainly).

The Qur'an inspired these poems greatly. Joseph is the only HB figure to have received a whole *sura* (chapter) to his name. In this *sura*, *sura* 12,[20] many of the HB lacunae and ambiguities are systematically filled. For instance, the type of garment the woman takes off Joseph, and its worth as evidence, are comprehensively treated. The story's events are reshuffled; Joseph goes to prison before his confrontation with the woman, and so on.

One of the interesting features of *sura* 12 is the inclusion of the extrabiblical scene dubbed by Kugel 'the Ladies' Party' (vv. 30-31). In this extrabiblical scene—versions of which are told in the *Tanḥuma, Midrash Ha-Gadol, Sefer Ha-Yashar* and in Thomas Mann's retelling[21]— the woman invites her friends home so as to explain her infatuation and love (yes!) for Joseph: she has to combat female gossip about her falling for a Hebrew slave. She orders Joseph to serve them. Upon his appearance, while they hold fruit knives in their hands, the women are so taken by his beauty that they cannot take their eyes off him, cut themselves and agree that he is like an angel of God, and that the woman's love for him can and should be understood.

Kugel, Bal and Bach—not to mention Thomas Mann—have already contributed to our knowledge and evaluation of this scene. The nature of the links between the Arabic/Islamic versions of it and the Jewish ones is far from clear, in spite of Kugel's conclusion in favour of the relevant Jewish texts' originality.[22] Rather than draw historical conclusions, we can stop at this point and look at some visual renderings of the scene: three representations from nineteenth-century Iran illustrate the scene well, each in its own way. Details differ: the fruit is oranges, other citrus fruit, or apples; the women faint and collapse, or they cut their hands so that blood streams down (as in Thomas Mann). However, in all these renderings Zuleika is as young and beautiful as Joseph is; it can easily be imagined that Joseph will return her love. This scene, of a very handsome man as the object of a group of pretty women's gaze, a sort of

---

20. A convenient translation can be found in the Penguin edition (trans. N.J. Dawood; London: Penguin Books, 1995).

21. See Bal, 'Myth', for the relevant text as well as a brilliant analysis of this scene.

22. Kugel, *In Potiphar's House*, pp. 26-85.

clothed and haloed 'Full Monty' Chippendale guy, is recurrent in nineteenth-century Persian art, no doubt because it was loved for its own
sake, for the human interest element. But, also, it was told and retold in
paint and word because in Sufi mysticism the story of Madame Potiphar
and Joseph has come to symbolize a love relationship between the
human and the divine. The story has become a religious symbol: the
woman had to be reinstated. And she was.

Some Conclusions

Genesis 39, the proof text, is Joseph's story first and foremost. The
woman fulfils the role of a cipher, a negative reflection of Joseph's
extraordinary virtues. The author focalizes Joseph and his righteousness.
One of the narrative techniques employed is to supply more information about Joseph, whereas the other figures are relatively less well
defined. However, this narrative choice for omission has some interesting results. Some readers will search for a vindication of the woman,
about whose person and motives we know so little. Because the woman
is presented as Joseph's foil, the flatter her portrait the more it detracts
from Joseph's own credibility. The gaps concerning her, or her husband,
open new ones concerning Joseph. The story begs to be fleshed out.
This has been done over the centuries, in various mediums. We saw
that, to a large extent, stereotypes have played a role in the readerly
reconstruction, or retelling, of the text; this is how the woman was
made into a beautiful, loving, young figure. As a by-product of this,
Joseph's figure acquired further dimensions and depth.

Methodologically, we mixed languages, sources, artistic mediums,
religious beliefs, times and locations. To begin with, we followed
chronological, spatial, stylistic, religious, generic and other frameworks.
We soon found out that such divisions could be, and were, superseded
by isoglosses that run across them. Retellings from Renaissance art
agreed with items in *Genesis Rabbah*; Josephus and Philo would be
echoed by the Qur'an and by Dutch art works of the late sixteenth and
early seventeenth centuries about certain points, such as variations on
Joseph's chastity. Gaps, ambiguities and repetitions that we listed had
been noticed by retellers as well as professional commentators, and dealt
with in different or crisscross fashions. The question of art as interpretation, and of its worth and links to HB and other religious texts and their
criticism, leads to a discussion of privileged critical discourse as against
other kinds of discourse.

Finally, a postscript. A student of ours is planning to write a PhD dissertation on the Jewish sources of Genesis 39 as compared with references to it in early Christian (patristic and other) literature, an aspect relatively neglected in our own journey. We are planning to run an introductory course for the HB and NT that will be divided between so-called 'classical' Bible criticism and film/art/literature retellings. We could not have contemplated that without running the Genesis 39 course first. This is especially important in our corner, since we are now a department within a large faculty that also includes comparative literature, Dutch literature, languages, history, media studies and philosophy. Cooperation with other departments is a matter of university policy and structure. We might even write a book about this course. And we enjoyed it, as did the students, and fun was had by all.

The Madness of Saul: A Cultural Reading of 1 Samuel 8–31[1]

Philip F. Esler

Introduction

Madness, which I will loosely define as a serious impairment of a person's mental and emotional connection with everyday reality accompanied by various forms of exaggerated affect, is not a very prominent phenomenon in the Old Testament. Yet it was known in ancient Israel. This emerges unambiguously in the famous incident when David flees from Saul to Achish, king of Gath, where he is recognized as the slayer of tens of thousands and becomes greatly afraid:

> So he changed his behaviour before them; he pretended to be mad when in their presence. He scratched marks on the doors of the gate, and let his spittle run down his beard. Achish said to his servants, 'Look, you see the man is mad; why then have you brought him to me? Do I lack madmen, that you have brought this fellow to play the madman in my presence? Shall this fellow come into my house?' (1 Sam. 21.14-16, NRSV).

The last three references to madness in the passage employ forms of the stem *šg'*, which does seem to refer directly to the phenomenon of madness. This word occurs ten times in the Hebrew Bible, seven times as a verbal form and three as a substantive.[2] It has cognates in Arabic and Assyrian that indicate various noises, and this may suggest that its sufferers were characterized by the production of animal sounds (Sussman

1. I am grateful for comments on this essay received at the Biblical into Cultural Studies Colloquium in the University of Sheffield in April 1997, and for further comments received from members of the the Context Group (especially Dennis Duling, K.C. Hanson, Bruce Malina and Gary Stansell) and from Robin Salters of St Mary's College, none of whom, however, is responsible for the views here expressed.
2. As a pual participle at Deut. 28.34; 1 Sam. 21.16; 2 Kgs 9.11; Jer. 29.26 and Hos. 9.7; in the hithpael at 1 Sam. 21.15 and 16; and in substantival form at Deut. 28.34; 2 Kgs 9.20 and Zech. 12.14.

1992).[3] Another instance of madness is that of Nebuchadnezzar in Daniel 4. The king is driven out of human society to live like a wild animal and feed on grass, his hair and nails growing very long, until his reason returns (Dan. 4.25-34).

The most important section of the Old Testament in relation to madness, however, is the story of Saul in 1 Samuel 8–31, even though the word *šg'* is not used in connection with him. For this text both depicts someone suffering from a major form of psychological disorder and also integrates the phenomenon into the heart of the narrative. The madness of Saul in 1 Samuel 8–31 is central to his character and to the movement of the plot. In addition, the text not only provides details of the disorder, but it also offers a causal explanation and prescribes a form of therapy (Rosen 1968: 28).

In this essay I will set out a 'reading', which I will define broadly as an attempt to make sense of the narrative as a narrative. In this case, my reading will seek to demonstrate the extent to which the development of the plot and of Saul's character is related to what we moderns would call his abnormal psychological state, his psychopathology. I am not interested in how what is recounted in 1 Samuel 8–31 correlates with the historical facts of the newly emergent Israelite monarchy. That is to say, I do not claim to be investigating a particular historical figure, Saul, but rather I seek to make sense of his character as presented in a specific narrative which itself presupposes a particular cultural context. My focus is squarely on the narrative, rather than on any actual historical circumstances that arguably 'lie behind' the narrative.

On the other hand, since one of my principal concerns is to understand the narrative in 1 Samuel 8–31 in a manner roughly similar to that of its original audience in ancient Israel, the reading offered here is still historical. It is inaccurate to suggest, as Francis Watson has recently done (1994), that interpreting a biblical text to determine historical facts underlying it constitutes the sum total of historical interpretation of the Old Testament. My reading is historical because it is cultural in the first

---

3.   The Hebrew expression in 1 Sam. 21.14 translated here as 'pretended to be mad' is a hithpael form of *hll*, a word of obscure etymology, which is usually pejorative in meaning and denotes irrational, uncontrolled, feigned or exaggerated behaviour of various sorts, as at Jer. 25.16; 46.9; 50.38 and 51.7, and not simply madness (Cazelles 1978). As a hithpael, its literal meaning is reflexive, 'made himself mad'.

of three senses that I will now introduce as a basis for more detailed exploration in the bulk of this essay.

First, this reading seeks to do justice to the fact that 1 Samuel is a product of an ancient Mediterranean culture very different from our North Atlantic modern, or postmodern one. In this respect my reading differs from other types of readings that have been published in recent years (Humphreys 1978, 1980, 1982; Gunn 1980; Exum 1992). Any attempt to situate a narrative in a cultural context that is distant from us in time, in this case by some three millennia, is necessarily historical—not in the sense of seeking to make out precise correlations between the narrative and the facts of the early Israelite monarchy, but rather in setting the text within the broad shape of ancient Israelite society, which at a certain level of abstraction shares many cultural features common to the ancient Mediterranean.[4] These include the orientation of social relations around the group (especially the family) rather than the individual, the importance of honour as a pivotal social value (together with related issues such as the extent to which those lacking honour felt envy toward those who possessed it and the strength of the desire for vengeance where honour was besmirched), and the fact that all goods were considered to exist only in finite quantities, a phenomenon referred to as the notion of 'limited good'. I will cite two Old Testament examples of 'limited good', given the importance of this feature in the narrative of Saul's madness, as I will explain below. First, Isaac only has one blessing to give, as Esau learns to his cost (Gen. 27.30-40). Secondly, that there is only so much honour to be won from defeating Midian and the fact that Yahweh prefers that he wins it, and not Israel, is offered in Judges 7, for example, as the explicit justification for his requiring Gideon to reduce his army from 32,000 to 300, the remnant who drink in the (dishonourable) manner of dogs:

> There are too many people with you for me to put Midian into their power; Israel might claim the credit for themselves at my expense: they might say, 'My own hand has rescued me' (Judg. 7.2, JB).

Yahweh's motivation for his actions in this incident makes little sense in modern Northern European or North American culture, where the

---

4.   I fully recognize that the various peoples scattered around the ancient Mediterranean exhibited rich cultural diversity; on the other hand, when one moves to an appropriate level of abstraction, they can be seen to share certain common elements, as discussed in the text.

notion of an expanding gross national product, in vogue since the days of Adam Smith, has rendered obsolete previous acceptance of the finite nature of goods, but it made good sense in the ancient biblical world.

These features of Mediterranean culture, identified mainly by anthropologists in the last 40 years, have been admirably modelled as far as the New Testament is concerned—and I mean modelled, not nomothetically prescribed[5]—by Bruce Malina in *The New Testament World* (1993). Gary Stansell has recently taken up the issue of honour and shame in relation to certain narratives concerning David (1 Sam. 18.23; 20.30-34; 25; 2 Sam. 6; 10.1-6; 19.1-9; 13 and 16.20-23) in an essay that offers new and culturally realistic interpretations of these texts (1992).

No apologies are offered for the fact that such an approach involves the explicit use of theories and models. The main alternative approach, the interpretivism of Clifford Geertz, which is not concerned with models, is impractical in relation to societies remote from us in time, since it involves total immersion in the foreign culture to generate a 'thick description' of its complex webs of significance. A further problem with interpretivism in this context is that in seeking to offer a largely emic account of the culture, it fails to provide a conceptual apparatus for making desirable cross-cultural comparison (Esler 1995; *contra* Garrett 1992).

Yet there is a second sense in which this reading is cultural, or rather cross-cultural. It is sometimes said that readings of the Bible which stress its social alienation from us create an unbridgeable gap between the biblical texts and the present and prevent them speaking to us here and now. This is a misconception. The simple fact is that people who do embed themselves in a foreign culture, which means making a deliberate and socially sensitive effort to understand its social script, frequently return to their homelands. When they do, they will generally seek to explain what they have learned about the foreign culture to the members of their own. To do this, they will need to be able to translate from the foreign culture into the local one in language and concepts that will be understood. This is the cross-cultural stage in the meeting of cultures, which necessarily involves a process of translation. Where the translation moves from the culture of an indigenous, pre-industrial people to a modern post-industrial one informed by social-scientific analysis of social realities, the movement is from what has become usefully

---

5. See my discussion in Esler 1995.

described as the 'emic' to the 'etic' levels (Headland, Pike and Harris 1990). In the last two decades the cross-cultural study of health, including mental health, and illness has become an important field at the intersection of a number of areas in medicine and the social sciences. In recent years John Pilch has indefatigably sought to bring to the attention of biblical scholars the importance of this research for their own work (1981, 1985, 1986, 1988 and 1991).

Thirdly, a reading like this could aim at being 'intercultural', although the space constraints of this essay will only permit a brief exemplification of this idea at the conclusion of my argument. Once people who have habituated themselves to a foreign culture come home and engage in the process of translation, they tend to find that they now stand with their feet in both cultures and are able to assess and interpret each with respect to the other. This mediating experience can be a very rich one, although it will vary from individual to individual. Those who have it may be called 'intercultural'.[6] To become intercultural means both to have sought to penetrate the strangeness of the foreign culture in the first place, to have set indigenous (or emic) meanings within more generalized (or etic) conceptual frameworks and then to have brought the understanding so garnered into active relationship and tension with one's own cultural context. There is a growing literature on this notion of interculturalism, although its application to the realm of biblical criticism is just beginning (see Esler 1998).

An inchoate form of interculturalism predates the recent theorizing devoted to it. For every artist who has tried to employ biblical traditions in the production of paintings, sculptures or films without anachronistically or ethnocentrically erasing all vestiges of the Mediterranean social script in which they are written (a process which can be seen in Western artistic depictions of the infancy narratives, as Neyrey [1990] has shown) will be engaging in what is at least a proto-intercultural exercise, even if lacking the anthropological perspectives needed for modern North Atlantic readers to make a better fist of comprehending biblical culture. Whereas biblical scholars may claim to do work that is wholly historical, completely tied up with ancient realities, that can never be the case with an artist who must attune the nature of his or her productions or performances to the sensibility of a contemporary audience. Thus, the way in which Rembrandt dealt with the incident of David playing his lyre to Saul in two paintings, one to be dated to about 1629/30, showing the

6.   See the discussion in Gudykunst and Kim 1992.

king glowering at David, and one dated about 1655-60, which has a very different ethos, repays examination as an intercultural exercise, as I hope to show in the last section of this essay.[7]

The Madness of Saul in 1 Samuel 8–31:
The Narrative in its Cultural Context

Saul's Early Career

Honour upon his House. Samuel (acting on Yahweh's behalf) anointed Saul as the prince (*nāgîd*) over Israel, the man who would defeat the enemies who were surrounding them (1 Sam. 10.1). This had been the main reason that the people had asked for a king (1 Sam. 8.19-20), a reason approved by Yahweh (1 Sam. 9.16). But there was more to being king than this. After all, Samuel had already warned the Israelites of the onerous tithes and services which a king would demand from them (1 Sam. 8.11-17) and had later given Saul himself a glimpse of this side of kingship before he anointed him:

> As for your asses that were lost three days ago, do not set your mind on them, for they have been found. And for whom is all that is desirable in Israel? Is it not for you and for all your father's house? (1 Sam. 9.20, NRSV).

It is important to note that in the group-oriented Mediterranean, where the family is the most important group of all, individual members share any success or good fortune they enjoy with their relatives. Thus, in Isa. 22.23 the appointment of Eliakim to high office means that he has become 'a throne of honour for his father's house', while in Joshua 7 the sin of Achan in keeping something which was under the ban results in disaster not only for him but for his whole family (Josh. 7.15, 24). Accordingly, not just Saul, but his father's house will gain access to the wealth of Israel. Moreover, in a society which believed in the finite nature of all goods and which was characterized by very little social mobility, where individuals and families were expected to remain in the same social position and rarely enjoyed sudden accretions of wealth and honour, Samuel's suggestion was truly surprising for the reason clearly apparent in Saul's reply:

---

7.   See Hoekstra 1990: 110-13 for coloured reproductions and brief discussion of these two paintings. They are also in Bredius 1936: 490 and 526.

> Saul answered, 'I am only a Benjaminite, from the least of the tribes of
> Israel, and my family is the humblest of all the families of the tribe of
> Benjamin. Why then have you spoken to me in this way?' (1 Sam. 9.21,
> NRSV).

In Yahweh's choosing a son from the lowest family among Israel's lowest tribe—and later selecting the youngest son among the sons of Jesse to
replace his first choice—the reader learns—and not for the last time in
this narrative—that Israel has a God who subverts the local honour code
to work his purposes in his own way. Indeed, one cannot appreciate the
gratuitous nature of God's action without paying regard to the cultural
context in which it occurs.

Saul the Individual. But what of Saul the individual? Although the individualism which has become characteristic of North Atlantic culture,
especially in North America, during the last century or so was unknown
in the ancient Mediterranean world, individuality most certainly was
not. Great individuals did appear, and the prevalence of strong group
bonds (especially within the family) and social immobility made their
achievements all the more striking. Often outstanding individuals fell
foul of the system, as illustrated most graphically by the fate of Socrates
and Jesus. Prior to his anointing we do learn a little about Saul. In a
culture that assessed persons primarily with respect to their group
affiliation and group prestige, he enters the narrative as a member of the
tribe of Benjamin and the son of Kish, a *gbr ḥyl*, a man of honour and
wealth (1 Sam. 9.1). Oddly, in view of instances such as 1 Sam. 1.1 and
Judg. 13.2 and the general Mediterranean habit of assessing persons by
their place of origin, the Massoretic text does not mention where he
lives, and this induced Wellhausen (followed by many commentators[8])
to propose the plausible insertion of 'from Gibeah' after 'There was a
man' at the start of 1 Sam. 1.1, even though there is no textual warrant
for this. We discover later, in any event, that Gibeah was Saul's home
town (1 Sam. 10.26; 11.4; 15.34), probably the modern Tell el-Fûl
(Driver 1913: 69). We also learn something of his appearance, that he
was the most handsome and tallest man in Israel (1 Sam. 9.2). Thirdly,
he is presented as a dutiful and obedient son, who obeys without question his father's direction that he and a servant go off and find some

8.   Smith 1899: 59-60; Driver 1913: 68-69; McCarter 1980: 167. The amendment of 'from Benjamin' to 'from Gibeah of Benjamin' also removes the oddity of
Saul's Benjaminite descent being mentioned twice in the first verse; Smith 1899: 60.

donkeys that have strayed. In so doing Saul dutifully honours his father and shows that he, too, is a man of honour. But Saul goes beyond this, in his concern that his father will begin to worry about them when they do not return (1 Sam. 9.5). Here we gain a glimpse of the warmth and intimacy that characterizes healthy relations among family members in the Mediterranean, a glimpse that is somewhat unusual in a culture that usually focuses on external, even stereotypical, features (such as those just mentioned) in describing persons. Even this feature, however, would have characterized most sons who loved their fathers in this culture and it tells us very little that is unique about Saul as an individual. The manner in which he is described reveals how different were ancient Mediterranean ways of portraying persons, which focused on the external and the stereotypical,[9] compared with modern modes of description, where the aim is to bring out someone's unique identity, especially through development of a sense of psychological inwardness.

Saul the Prophet. It is only after his anointing that a truly distinctive aspect of Saul's personality does emerge. Samuel foretells that he will go to Gibeah-of-God, a city with a Philistine garrison, and, as translated by nearly all the versions, meet a group of *prophets* coming down from a high place, with harp, tambourine, pipe and lyre, and they will be *prophesying* and 'then the spirit of Yahweh will rush upon you, and you will *prophesy* with them and you will be turned into an another man' (1 Sam. 10.6). The Hebrew word translated as 'prophesy' in relation to the prophets and Saul is the hithpael of *nb'*. The Hebrew Bible uses this root in a verbal sense only in the niphal and the hithpael and it is often difficult (for example, at 1 Sam. 19.20) to establish a semantic distinction between the two forms (Wilson 1980: 137), although the hithpael has traditionally been thought by Old Testament scholars to have a closer connection with ecstatic behaviour (Wilson 1980: 138). Many years ago Driver proposed that the hithpael form functioned to denote playing or acting the prophet to the accompaniment of manifestations of physical excitement, like the dervishes of fairly recent times (1913: 81), although this is only one example of a common enough phenomenon.

Wilson prefers a more nuanced approach, whereby the niphal meant 'to prophesy', 'to deliver a prophetic oracle', while the hithpael meant

9. See Malina and Neyrey 1996, who offer an illuminating exposition of ancient Mediterranean ways of presenting personality in relation to texts concerning Paul, yet through insights capable of much wider application.

'to act like a prophet', 'to exhibit the behaviour characteristic of a *nâbî*', with the precise characteristics in question to be determined by an examination of the prophet in question (Wilson 1980: 138).

Yet a question of critical importance squarely posed by Parker (1978), and noted by Wilson (1980: 138), is whether we should use the word 'prophesy' at all with respect to the behaviour which Samuel foretells (as well as in relation to the actual incident itself at 1 Sam. 10.10-12 and a later occurrence of contagious 'prophesying' at 1 Sam. 19.20, where the niphal and the hithpael forms appear). Parker suggests that the reference here is to ecstatic behaviour, or trance, to what those drawing on the research of Erika Bourguignon now call 'altered states of consciousness', when the person concerned loses contact with everyday reality, often in association with startling kinetic effects and various types of utterance.[10] As Wilson points out, the behaviour of the band Saul encounters is not specifically described, although the fact that those he meets are pictured as playing musical instruments suggests that trance may have been involved, since music is often used to induce trance (1980: 176; also Lindblom 1962: 59).

Bourguignon distinguishes two types of altered state of consciousness: the first, 'possession trance', where the state is due to possession by spirits and, the second, trance not so interpreted, involving visions or hallucinations. The instances just mentioned in 1 Samuel are of the former type. Moreover, possession trances may either be mediumistic, where they mediate a message from the spirit world to an audience, or personal to those involved. In the latter case they either provide subjective compensation for personal or social stress or an objective compensation through an enhancement of status that results from social recognition accorded the phenomenon. None of the three instances in 1 Samuel are mediumistic and this prompts Parker to suggest that it is inappropriate to employ the word 'prophesy' in relation to the Hebrew root *nb'*. Parker argues that God does make his will known in 1 Samuel, through Samuel and with the use of lots for example, but he never does so by means of forms of this root. The latter aspect of Parker's view runs aground on 1 Sam. 28.6 and 15 where the *nᵉbî'im* are viewed as one

---

10. For recent appropriations of Bourguignon's work in discussion of New Testament material, see Esler 1994 and Pilch 1993 and 1995. Also see Lewis 1986 and 1989 for further discussion of ecstatic religion. For an older approach to this issue, without the benefit of recent social-scientific research, see Lindblom 1962: 47-65.

possible way for Saul to learn Yahweh's will. Nevertheless, Parker's argument is probably plausible as far as the experience of Saul is concerned, so that 'fell into a possession trance' is a better translation than 'prophesy', although it is probably worthwhile persisting with the use of 'prophet' because of the possibility of a mediumistic role as in 1 Sam. 28.6 and 15.

The phenomenon of possession trance in this case seems to function to extend subjective rather than objective compensation, since there is no sign that it produces increased status; indeed, the reverse is the case.[11] The first evidence for this comes in the statement at 1 Sam. 10.6 that Saul would turn into another man. Wilson considers that this is a positive experience for Saul, since it is a sign of divine election (1980: 176). Yet there is reason to doubt this assessment. It is more likely that Saul's transformation would have been regarded as particularly ominous in a cultural context which (unlike the case with modern Northern European and North American cultures) treasured social stability, as achieved through the maintenance of established roles and statuses. The verb used, *hpk*, is a particularly strong one, meaning 'to overturn, to destroy, to transform radically'. It is employed in relation to the destruction of Sodom and Gomorrah (Gen. 19.21, 25, 29; Hos. 11.8; Lam. 4.6), the transformation of the rod into the serpent and water into blood in Exodus 7 (vv. 15, 17, 20), the transition from plague-affected or unclean flesh to healthy flesh (and vice versa) in Leviticus 13 and the alteration of a stream of water into pitch in Isa. 34.9. These examples indicate how often the verb itself denotes change of a deleterious, even dangerous, type, and when it designates alteration in a person's social role and character the effect is very negative indeed. Seybold comes reasonably close to this view in the following comment on the passage:

> With reference to the ecstasy described in vv. 9ff., *hpk* in the niphal (like the qal in v. 9) is meant to represent the resulting change as a perversion of what is normal (1978: 426).

If Saul is about to be transformed into another person, he is heading for a serious diminishment of the regard in which he is held by those who know him. Now this view can co-exist with the position being quite

---

11. This is not to deny that the fact that someone has received the spirit of God may result in their status and personal effectiveness being enhanced; such was the case, for example, with Gideon in Judg. 6.34-35, where there are no other complicating factors. But Saul's experience is very different.

different in Yahweh's eyes. Commentators, like Hertzberg (1964: 85), who think the alteration fits Saul out to be God's instrument miss the negative social implications of this development, against which the divine initiative is all the more striking. This irony is seen most graphically in the stately paraphernalia of drawing lots for the king, which ends with Saul, Yahweh's anointed, being pulled out of the baggage where he had hidden himself (1 Sam. 10.23) and the fact that some in Israel still refuse to accept him (1 Sam. 10.27).

The second indication that Saul's status is not promoted by his going into a trance comes at 1 Sam. 10.7, where Samuel says that, when he encounters these signs, of which the third and the last will be his experience with those in possession-trance at Gibeah, he should do whatever his hand finds to do, for God is with him. This type of reassurance implies a split between how such behaviour might be viewed by observers and what it really entails—the presence of God. Just as God can subvert the local social order by choosing someone from the lowest family of the lowest tribe to be his king, so too he can be present in exhibitions of exaggerated behaviour which are susceptible of another explanation.

Thirdly, since later in the narrative the hithpael form of the root *nb'*, used here at 1 Sam. 10.6 of possession trance, occurs in relation to one of the occasions when Saul is afflicted by the evil spirit of God (1 Sam. 18.10), it has the capacity to denote something personally dysfunctional; we are not just dealing with some status-enhancing eccentricity.

A Prophet in his Home Town. As Samuel had predicted, so it came to pass:

> When they were going from there to Gibeah, a band of prophets met him; and the spirit of God possessed him, and he fell into a possession trance along with them. When all who knew him before saw how he fell into a trance with the prophets, the people said to one another, 'What has come over the son of Kish? Is Saul also among the prophets?' A man of the place answered, 'And who is their father?' Therefore it became a proverb, 'Is Saul also among the prophets?' (1 Sam. 10.10-12, NRSV, slightly modified).

This incident is of critical importance in establishing Saul's character and in paving the way for the manner in which the plot will evolve. We must initially assume that Saul's behaviour in this incident involved his transformation into a different person as predicted by Samuel, with the negative connotations just explored, an experience rendered even more problematic by the narrative's perspective on this experience as potentially dysfunctional that will emerge later. Yet the specific location of this event means that it has a far more precise significance within the narrative. This place, the Gibeah-of-God where Samuel had foretold that Saul would meet the prophets, is probably identical with the Gibeah mentioned as his home in 1 Sam. 11.4 and 15.34, and even at 9.1, if Wellhausen's amendment is correct.[12] Saul encounters the prophets in his home town, or at least in a town containing people who know him (10.11), which is all that is necessary for the argument here.

The extent to which scholars usually misinterpret the local reactions is a sign of their failure to read this text in its Mediterranean context. Thus we find some suggesting that the point of the story is to explain the unlikely fact that a well-placed person such as Saul would begin to prophesy (Smith 1899: 71; McCarter 1980: 183-184), or that it offers an etiology of the proverb, 'Is Saul also among the prophets?', or that it contradicts traditions that denied the prophetic spirit to Saul (see Klein 1983: 92). Hertzberg at least recognizes that the observers are dubious about Saul, although his explanation of their attitude is anachronistic: 'How does a reasonable man, well placed in civic life, come to be in this eccentric company?' (1964: 86). None of these explanations touches the meaning of the incident within Mediterranean culture nor picks up the extent to which it is central to an understanding of Saul's character and the onward movement of the narrative.

It is important to realize that what we learn about Saul here does not resound to his credit, just the reverse. The sting of the account lies in the way in which local observers who know Saul interpret the possession trance that comes upon him. The two questions they ask ('What has come over the son of Kish? Is Saul also among the prophets?') actually constitute a grievous insult; they do not reflect 'amazement and wonder' at his transformation (Klein 1983: 93). In this culture, people

12. Some commentators reject the identification, but the reasons for it are strong. The strongest is that 1 Sam. 10.11 states that people who had known him previously were there (McCarter 1980: 182). Moreover, as Smith notes (1899: 68), Saul goes directly home after meeting the prophets. Thirdly, the parenthetical expression at 10.5, 'where there is a Philistine garrison' (or possibly prefect or pillar), seems to point ahead to 13.3, where the city is probably Gibeah of Benjamin.

were expected to remain in the roles into which they were born; as Proverbs states, 'Instruct a child in the way he should go, and when he grows old he will not leave it' (22.6, JB), Social mobility is a common feature in modern North Atlantic cultures but should not be anachronistically and ethnocentrically imputed to the ancient Mediterranean world. In the latter culture, after all, children were expected to follow the ways and adhere to the authority of their father and their mother. If they did not, both they and their families, their fathers above all, were gravely shamed:

> A discerning son is he who keeps the Law; an associate of profligates brings shame on his father (Prov. 28.7, JB).

This was a matter of great moment, given that honour was the pre-eminent social good:

> A good name is more desirable than great wealth, the respect of others is better than silver or gold (Prov. 22.1, JB).

It is in keeping with such views that Jesus' relatives thought he was mad (Mk 3.20-21), presumably because they could conceive of no other reason for the shameful way he was acting. In the present case, the local townsfolk are suggesting that Saul has stepped out of his usual role as the dutiful son of Kish, where he looked after affairs on the family estate, and this brings disgrace to Saul and his family, particularly to Kish, who has plainly not managed to control his son as a respectable father would.

This interpretation is confirmed by the next question: 'And who is their father?' According to McCarter 'this cryptic question has no obvious meaning' (1980: 184) and Klein finds it 'quite obscure' (1983: 93). Yet its meaning is hardly so opaque. One of the greatest insults which could (and can) be uttered to a person living in the Mediterranean region is to cast doubt on his lineage. Usually this suggestion implies that the mother of the person concerned was a prostitute, although sometimes it is a way of denigrating the son in relation to the father who is actually known (for which see Jn 8.31-59). In either case, the point of the remark is to convey that children of doubtful parentage are beyond the bounds of respectable society. In the present case the text raises just such insinuations in relation to the prophets and also suggests that Saul has come to share in this grossly dishonourable condition by joining them. Hertzberg is the rare exception among recent commentators who comes close to seeing the point, when he suggests that the question is meant as a contemptuous aside in reference to people who have no father, who come from anywhere (1964: 86), although some of the older scholarship came nearer the mark.[13]

Eppstein (1969: 298) rejects the suggestion that the question, 'who is their father?', is an expression of contempt by reason of the description of events later in the narrative when David has gone to the camps[14] in Ramah with Samuel to escape from Saul, where an alternative explanation is offered for the saying 'Is Saul also among the prophets?':

> Then Saul sent messengers to take David. When they saw the company of the prophets in a frenzy, with Samuel standing in charge of them, the spirit of God came upon the messengers of Saul, and they also fell into a prophetic frenzy. When Saul was told, he sent other messengers, and they also fell into a frenzy. Saul sent messengers again the third time, and they also fell into a frenzy. Then he himself went to Ramah. He came to the great well that is in Secu; he asked, 'Where are Samuel and David?' And someone said, 'They are at the camps in Ramah'. He went there, toward the camps in Ramah; and the spirit of God came upon him. As he was going, he fell into a prophetic frenzy, until he came to the camps in Ramah. He too stripped off his clothes, and he too fell into a frenzy before Samuel. He lay naked all that day and all that night. Therefore it is said, 'Is Saul also among the prophets?' (1 Sam. 19.20-24, NRSV, except 'camps' for *nāwyōt*).

Of the six references to 'frenzy' or 'prophetic frenzy' in this translation, the first represents the niphal of *nb'* and the remaining five the hithpael of that root.[15]

The passage reveals the highly contagious nature of the possession states of the people in the camps.[16] Eppstein argues that since 'so exalted a personage' as Samuel himself is reported as being with, and in a position of authority over, the prophets, the earlier question, 'who is their father?', at 1 Sam. 10.12 should not be treated as contemptuous

---

13. Budde said it implied that 'no one knows to whom they belong; they are stray vagabonds without name or pedigree' (1899: 96).

14. See McCarter (1980: 328) for this translation of *nāwyōt*. For a discussion of the groups of prophets in ancient Israel, see Lang 1983: 94-95.

15. Targum Jonathan alters the words *nb'ym* and the two forms of *nb'* to 'scribes' and 'praising' (see Gordon 1987: 48) and this may suggest an unease with the unruly picture these expressions convey. For the Aramaic text of this Targum, see Sperber 1959, and for an English translation, see Harrington and Saldarini 1987.

16. See Lindblom (1962: 47-65, especially 48), whose treatment, while thorough for his time, looks rather dated now in view of recent advances in social-scientific research on altered states of consciousness.

(1969: 298). This objection is unconvincing. First, if one reads 1 Samuel as a narrative, it is a long wait from the tenth to the nineteenth chapter to learn how one should interpret the issue concerning the parentage of the prophets. Secondly, Samuel does not himself take part in the possession trance. His being in authority could be a way of keeping their behaviour under some control; indeed, the location of the prophets apparently in camps away from permanent human habitations may emphasize that these people have thrown off the usual social conventions and domestic economy of village and town in a way that would not have been well received by those who had not. Thirdly, the description of Saul's actions, including the shameful fact of his nakedness for a day and a night, is hard to reconcile with anything other than a very negative view of the cause of such a condition.[17]

Saul's situation bears a striking (although perhaps hitherto unnoticed) similarity to that of Jesus in the synagogue in Nazareth, especially in the Lukan version (Lk. 4.16-30). Like Saul, Jesus abandons his traditional role in his home town to take on a prophetic one and, as in Saul's case, observers note that he is the son of a local man: 'Is this not Joseph's son?' (Lk. 4.22). As Richard Rohrbaugh has proposed in a convincing exposition of Lk. 4.1-30, this question is an insult because in 'antiquity persons were expected to act in accord with birth status and anyone who did not represented a troubling social anomaly' (1995: 186); to ask such a question was an effective way of ridiculing someone, as Cyril of Alexandria noted in relation to the Lukan passage long ago (Rohrbaugh 1995: 194).[18] Exactly equivalent is the question asked of Saul by the people of Gibeah: 'What has come over the son of Kish?' The extreme difficulty of escaping the force of the conventions that kept one tied to the family and the role into which one was born provides the context for Jesus' remark, 'Truly, I say to you that no prophet is acceptable in his hometown' (Lk. 4.24), although the Markan version puts it more completely: 'A prophet is not without honour (*atimos*) except in his

17. Targum Jonathan is sensitive to the embarrassment of Saul's nakedness and renders *'rm* ('naked') in v. 24 by *barsan*, which Gordon seeks ingeniously to interpret as meaning 'afflicted by meningitis' (1987).

18. There is an interesting parallel in traditional Scottish society, where to say 'Ah kent his feyther' ('I knew his father') is a derogatory way of referring to a man who presumes to act in a way inconsistent with the character of his father. I am indebted to Dr Robin Salters of St Mary's College, in the University of St Andrews, for alerting me to this usage.

hometown, and among his relatives and in his own house' (Mk 6.4).
Precisely the same sentiment could have fallen from Saul's lips.

Considerations such as this help explain the next event in the
narrative:

> When his prophetic frenzy had ended, he went home. Saul's uncle said
> to him and to the boy, 'Where did you go?' And he replied, 'To seek the
> donkeys; and when we saw they were not to be found, we went to
> Samuel' (1 Sam. 10.13-14, NRSV, with one amendment[19]).

That it should be his uncle and not his father who speaks to Saul has
been found almost inexplicable by commentators, at least the ones who
even notice the point as an issue.[20] One plausible explanation is based
on the socially realistic scenario that the local gossip networks had
swung into action and that Kish had soon learnt of the disgraceful way
his hitherto dutiful and considerate son had behaved in public. In such
circumstances, a rupture between father and son would be a likely consequence. Kish would either have it out with Saul very dramatically or
simply cut him off. That it is Saul's uncle who speaks to him on his
return suggests that latter alternative may have come to pass. Given that
it would be odd if the uncle had not heard that the son of Kish had disappeared while searching for donkeys, the question he asks Saul and his
servant: 'Where have you been?' can be read as an accusation: 'What
have you been up to?' and Saul's reply, focusing on the donkeys and
Samuel, not his activity with the prophets, is an exercise in prevarica-
tion, which he continues in reply to his uncle's equally blunt, 'Tell me
what Samuel said to you', by restricting his answer to the issue of the
donkeys (1 Sam. 10.15-16).

Accordingly, by the time that Saul's original and secret anointing as
king is confirmed publicly following the drawing of lots at Mizpah
(10.17-24), the reader knows that question marks hang over him, for
not only has he shown a dangerous lability of character by indulging in
trance states, he has done so publicly, to his family's shame.

19. The Massoretic text has in v. 13, 'he went to the high place (*hbmh*)', which
makes no sense, and Wellhausen proposed the generally accepted amendment to
hbyt, followed here. Also see Josephus, *Ant.* 6.58.

20. 'It is surprising to find Saul's uncle here instead of Kish, his father'
(McCarter 1980: 184).

Saul Sins before Yahweh

The doubts that surround Saul's character are strengthened later in the narrative by the two occasions on which he angers Yahweh. He knew that he had incurred Yahweh's displeasure, initially because he had not obeyed Samuel's command to wait for him at Gilgal. On this occasion Samuel had told him that his dynasty would not endure and that Yahweh would seek out a man after his own heart and appoint him as leader over the people (1 Sam. 13.13-14). This meant that he had endangered his own authority and also the honour of his family which depended on it. Then Saul had compounded the offence by not obeying the order to put all of the Amalekites under the ban (1 Sam. 15.3), in that he spared their king Agag and the best of their livestock. As a result, Yahweh explicitly told Samuel that he had turned against Saul (1 Sam. 15.10) and Samuel conveyed this news to the king (1 Sam. 15.23), together with the fact that God had rejected him as king of Israel and would choose a better man in his place (1 Sam. 15.28-29). Saul acknowledged his sin, but successfully sought to have Samuel minimize the shame he must endure before Israel (1 Sam. 15.30-31). These incidents set the scene for the first report of Saul's disorder, in the very next chapter of the text.

Saul's Evil Spirit and David's Lyre

As noted above, anthropologists employ the idea of limited good to refer to the fact that all aspects of life in the Mediterranean are thought to exist in finite quantities, and there are unambiguous biblical examples of this outlook. The notion of limited good also forms an indispensable feature of the narrative concerning the onset of Saul's condition and the curative powers David's lyre-playing has in relation to it.

1 Sam. 16.1-13 recounts the way in which David came to be anointed as king of Israel, beginning with Yahweh's asking Samuel how long he will go on mourning for Saul, whom he has rejected as king of Israel (16.1), continuing through the method of selection (16.6-12) and concluding with the anointing itself:

> So Samuel took the horn of oil and anointed him in the midst of his brothers; and the spirit of Yahweh fell upon David from that day onwards (16.13, my translation).

The understanding of the finite nature of all aspects of life in the Mediterranean means that if David now has the spirit of Yahweh upon him, then it can no longer be on Saul. This is precisely spelled out in the first clause of the next verse, when the narrator states: 'The spirit of Yahweh left Saul'.

This is not all, however, for the verse continues: 'and an evil spirit from Yahweh repeatedly terrified him' (16.14). It is important to note here that the primary meaning of *b't* is 'to alarm', or 'to terrify', although often this point is missed in the versions. The word occurs sixteen times in the Old Testament and always with this meaning.[21] Hertzberg plausibly suggests that the force of the consecutive perfect form of the verb used in v. 14 is to give the verb a sense of continual activity (1964: 140), as reflected in the translation just given. When this is combined with the picture in 16.16, which envisages that Saul will be afflicted on multiple occasions, it becomes clear that the attacks of the evil spirit are intermittent but persistent. This seems to be the dominant feature of Saul's condition from the perspective of the indigenous observer, although it is closely linked with the perceived cause of the problem. Within the emic perspective of the narrative, Saul has suffered a double catastrophe; not merely abandoned by Yahweh's spirit, he also repeatedly experiences the terror caused by an evil spirit actually sent by Yahweh. Saul's servants share the narrator's understanding of his problem: 'An evil spirit of God is terrifying you', with the verb *b't* again appearing, as a piel participle (16.15). They recommend a form of treatment, that Saul should obtain a skilful lyre player, so that when the evil spirit comes, he will play and Saul will get well (16.16).

Saul agrees, yet who should be chosen as lyre player? Few verses in the Bible are as poignant as the one which answers this question:

> One of the young men replied, 'Look, I have seen a son of Jesse the Bethlehemite, who is skilful in playing, a brave man, a warrior, prudent in speech, and a man of good presence; and Yahweh is with him' (16.18, my translation).

David Gunn has perceptively noted that there is 'no flabbiness in the narrative at this point', since the introduction of the spirit besetting Saul leads directly to David's entering Saul's life. Yet, writing at a time before Mediterranean anthropology had been brought to bear on biblical texts, Gunn misses the logic of the narrative:

---

21. Niphal: Est. 7.6; Dan. 8.17; 1 Chron. 21.30; piel: 1 Sam. 16.14, 15; 2 Sam. 22.5; Isa. 21.4; Ps. 18.5; Job 3.5; 7.14; 9.34; 13.11; 13.21; 15.24; 18.11; 33.7. The substantival form, meaning 'terror', appears at Jer. 8.15 and 33.7.

> By the cruellest of fate's tricks no sooner is David anointed and Saul
> unwell...than his own servants are recommending David as the cure for
> his sickness (1980: 78).

David's introduction is not a trick of fate but rather rests on the social
reality of the limited good in circumstances known to the narrator and
the readers of the text: the spirit of Yahweh which Saul has lost is now
with David and therefore in all of Israel only David will be able to help
him. On the lips of the servant who recommends David, however, the
recognition that 'Yahweh is with him' is richly ironic; unlike the reader,
the servant (treated here as a character in the narrative) has no idea of
the precise accuracy of what he has said.

   Yet the narrative develops this irony with an intensity that is almost
painful, for, when David is brought to the king, Saul loves him greatly
(16.21). Does not Saul, his life accelerating on its long slide to ruin, see
in David his old best self? Does he not sense in David a divine presence
which has now forsaken him? No wonder that David can help Saul:

> And whenever the evil spirit from God was upon Saul, David took the
> lyre and played it with his hand; so Saul was refreshed, and all was well,
> and the evil spirit departed from him (16.23, my translation).

Saul Turns against David
While the narrative of 1 Samuel after the defeat of Goliath is largely
propelled by the violent antipathy that Saul generates towards David,
the intertwined dynamics of character and plot by which this is achieved
give a central place to Saul's condition. To explore this issue, however,
we must initially examine the way in which the narrator develops the
theme of the king's madness in its narrative context.

   David's effectiveness on the lyre is followed by the narrative that
recounts his victory over Goliath (1 Sam. 17). In the Massoretic text
there are signs of unskilful blending of the tradition of David's lyre
playing and his role as a warrior in Saul's need to ask the name of
David's father at the conclusion of the Goliath episode (17.58), even
though he had learned this earlier (16.18-22). Nevertheless, thereafter
the narrator manages closely to integrate these strands and the continuing tale of Saul's decline. The deft and compressed way in which these
themes are developed indicates a high degree of narrative artistry. Thus,
after introducing the love between David and Saul's son Jonathan (18.1-
4), the narrative proceeds in a sentence full of tragic potential:

> David went out and was successful wherever Saul sent him; as a result,
> Saul set him over the army. And all the people, even the servants of Saul,
> approved (1 Sam. 18.5, NRSV).

There is something profoundly disordered in Saul appointing David to
this post. One of the main reasons for which he had been made king
was to lead Israel to war:

> But the people refused to listen to the voice of Samuel; they said, 'No!
> but we are determined to have a king over us, so that we also may be like
> other nations, and that our king may govern us and go out before us and
> fight our battles' (1 Sam. 8.19-20, NRSV).

Yahweh himself had endorsed this rationale for kingship:

> When Samuel had heard all the words of the people, he repeated them in
> the ears of the LORD. The LORD said to Samuel, 'Listen to their voice
> and set a king over them' (1 Sam. 8.21-22, NRSV).

By delegating military responsibility to David, Saul has eschewed a critical element in the responsibilities that had initially impelled Israel to
seek a king. An ancient reader would understand that it is likely to lead
him into trouble, just as surely as David later succumbed to disaster
when he tarried in Jerusalem during the Ammonite war, at the time of
the year *when kings go out to battle* (2 Sam. 11.1).

Trouble does not take long to arrive. Saul has given David an arena
where he will be able to win great honour for himself and, in a culture
where all goods, honour included, exist in finite quantities, it is inevitable that David will do so at Saul's expense. Later on Joab managed
to persuade David to leave Jerusalem and assume command of his army
in capturing the Ammonite town of Rabbah only by threatening to take
the town and name it after himself (2 Sam. 12.26-29). So it is not surprising that the ominous note of the universal approval for David's
acquisition of command in 1 Sam. 18.5 is immediately followed by
events surrounding the return of David from slaying the Philistine:

> As they were coming home, when David returned from killing the
> Philistine, the women came out of all the towns of Israel, singing and
> dancing, to meet King Saul, with tambourines, with songs of joy, and
> with musical instruments. And the women sang to one another as they
> made merry, 'Saul has killed his thousands, and David his ten thousands'
> (1 Sam. 18.6-7, NRSV).

In the context of Mediterranean culture, where honour is both a claim
to worth and the public concurrence in that claim, Saul has been

grievously shamed. His social inferior has been very publicly awarded a much higher share of honour than he has. The usual response to such a process in the Mediterranean world is for the one shamed both to envy the person honoured and also to seek vengeance against him. The activation of envy and the desire for vengeance is often associated with the phenomenon of the evil eye, a pervasive phenomenon in the Mediterranean area from at least the time of Hammurabi and even earlier, as Elliott has demonstrated in a number of important articles on the subject (1988, 1990, 1991, 1992, 1994). This is why victorious Roman generals, enjoying their triumph, carried amulets to ward off the consequence of the evil eye which the envy generated by their success was expected to arouse in onlookers.

For these reasons Saul's response is entirely expected:

> Saul was very angry, for this saying displeased him. He said, 'They have ascribed to David ten thousands, and to me they have ascribed thousands; what more can he have but the kingdom?' So Saul eyed David from that day on (1 Sam. 18.8-9).

Some of the more astute commentators note that Saul's eyeing David in v. 9 is a reference to the evil eye (McCarter 1980: 312-13) that is generated by envy,[22] an aspect of the text magnificently brought out in Rembrandt's earlier Saul and David painting (Bredius 1936: 490; Hoekstra 1990: 111), which I discuss in the final section of this essay.

Compounding the fact that he has won far less honour, moreover, is the additional risk, now perceived by Saul for the first time, that David represents a threat to his kingship. 1 Samuel 18–31 frequently emphasizes that David himself harboured no ambitions for the kingship nor animosity towards Saul, but, in the fiercely competitive world of the ancient Mediterranean, Saul's fear, when faced with a potential rival ranked so much higher than him in national esteem, was not entirely an unexpected one.

More important than this, however, is the fact of Saul's distinctive personality, which the narrator has been at pains to point out. Not only is he prone to the attacks of possession trance characteristic of prophets in this culture, but he is also afflicted by an evil spirit from Yahweh.

---

22. For the fundamental (although infrequently noticed) distinction in the biblical world between envy (meaning a negative disposition toward one who has a singular possession) and jealousy (meaning great attachment to and concern for what is exclusively one's own), see Malina and Seeman 1993.

These facts lay the foundation for the way in which the impact of the song sung by the women concerning David and Saul is so dramatically greater than what might have been expected:

> The next day an evil spirit from God rushed upon Saul, and he raved (hithpael of *nb'*) within his house, while David was playing the lyre, as he did day by day. Saul had his spear in his hand; and Saul threw the spear, for he thought, 'I will pin David to the wall'. But David eluded him twice (1 Sam. 18.10-11, NRSV).

Reading 1 Samuel within its Mediterranean cultural context strongly suggests that the narrator of the Massoretic text has deliberately created the impression that Saul has been so shaken by his public shaming on the previous day that he has now lost control completely, even to the extent of his trying to kill David with a spear! The two aspects of Saul's instability, the evil spirit which comes upon him, bringing terror (although that particular element is not mentioned here), and his raving like one of the prophets at Gibeah (evoked by use of the hithpael of *nb'*), are now brought explicitly into conjunction. This is a point of major breakdown in his life, triggered by the degradation of his status that he has just experienced. Yet for commentators like McCarter, writing before Mediterranean anthropology had made an impression on biblical criticism, the crucial role of this passage in the narrative is simply missed. McCarter's view on 1 Sam. 18.10-11 is that this 'duplicate of the incident in 19.9-10 seems out of place at this point' (1980: 305)!

The presence of Yahweh with David, which had previously brought Saul relief, is not enough to keep at bay the violent anger that he now aims at David. Indeed, it features as its cause. For it must be at David that Saul's anger is directed, since in his torment of envy he has come to realize that the one person in Israel with the power to soothe his spirit has become the rival who might take his place as king. The full implication of what it meant for Yahweh's spirit to rest upon David, closely implicated in the notion of limited good, has become all too clear, as the text states:

> Saul was afraid of David, because the LORD was with him but had departed from Saul (1 Sam. 18.12, NRSV).

Saul's Subsequent Career

Although space is lacking to offer a detailed consideration of the narrative in 1 Samuel until the death of Saul, it is worth noting a few features that indicate the extent to which his personality has been unhinged as a result of his condition and the manner in which this fact propels the plot forward. From the time when Saul first raises his spear to David (1 Sam. 18.10-11), his attitude toward him is essentially negative, indeed homicidal, with occasional remissions, as after the two opportunities David has to kill him but does not (1 Sam. 24 and 1 Sam. 26.7-25). There is a further occasion when Saul attempts to kill David when he is playing his lyre for him at a time of affliction by the evil spirit (1 Sam. 19.9-10), which is all the more dramatic since it occurs just after Saul has promised his son Jonathan not to seek to kill David (1 Sam. 19.6). Again and again David tries to persuade Saul that he is not bent on treason but Saul is unable to accept this, except for occasions of the sort just mentioned. The full extent of his hostility emerges in the terrible slaughter of the priests of Nob, and every living thing in the town, in revenge for their having harboured David (1 Sam. 22.18-19).

Yet nothing could more express the desolation of Saul toward the end of the narrative than his night-time visit to the witch of Endor (1 Sam. 28.7-25). Samuel is now dead and buried, and the sight of the Philistines who have encamped against him at Shunem has struck Saul with terror (1 Sam. 28.4-5), somewhat reminiscent of the effect produced on him by the evil spirit, although different Hebrew expressions are used of his fear. The extent to which God has abandoned him is manifest in the fact that he will not answer him by dreams, nor Urim, nor prophets. To whom can Saul turn? Only to the witch of Endor, a trafficker in spirits and ghosts of the very kind whom Saul himself had previously banished (1 Sam. 28.3). He has her call up the ghost of Samuel who has for Saul only the worst of news: that Yahweh, who is now his adversary, will take the kingdom away from him and give it to David, and that Israel and he himself will be defeated by the Philistines. The message overpowers him with fear. But eventually he recovers enough to eat and in due course engages the Philistines and meets his fate with dignity and courage (1 Sam. 31).

Saul's Madness in Cross-Cultural Perspective

Cross-Cultural Health Care

P. Kyle McCarter, writing in one of the main commentaries on 1 Samuel, offers the following view of Saul's plight:

> We may speak of mental illness if we want—Saul manifests some symptoms of paranoia, others of manic-depressive illness—but surely Hertzberg is correct to stress the fact that 'Saul's suffering is described

theologically, not psychopathetically or psychologically'. The evil spirit is 'from Yahweh' and will play its part in the working out of the divine plan (1980: 280-81).

McCarter seems to be suggesting here that modern psychiatric accounts are largely irrelevant to understanding Saul and that what really matters in the narrative is the divine origin of Saul's problem and the importance of Yahweh's spirit in determining his fate. For this reason the appropriate designation for Saul's suffering is 'theological'.

Views such as these, hardly uncommon in biblical interpretation, represent a high degree of theoretical confusion and misunderstanding of the dynamics of plot and characterization in the narrative of 1 Samuel. At the centre of the fog lies a failure clearly to distinguish the various perspectives with which one might view the phenomena of Saul's 'madness', coupled with an attempt to give central place to one inadequately formulated perspective over others. In the present instance, the approbation which Hertzberg and McCarter express toward a non-defined 'theological' viewpoint seems transparently a function of their ascribing to a particular approach to biblical interpretation rather than necessarily telling us anything about 1 Samuel.

In reading 1 Samuel 8–31, a product of a culture alien to ours, the disciplined investigation of foreign cultures conducted by modern anthropologists reveals that the fundamental distinction which must be drawn in such a case is that between the understanding of Saul's condition that would be entertained by one of its original readers (which is the 'native', 'indigenous' or 'emic' perspective) and that of a modern observer, trained in social and medical sciences and even in post-Enlightenment theology (the 'etic' perspective). Unless we outline both emic and etic positions, which involves doing justice, after all, to the *cultural* experience of both the ancient readers and of ourselves, it will be impossible to engage in *cross-cultural* comparison or to arrive at the next stage in the process, the development of genuinely *intercultural* insights and discernment.

We must always be aware of the difficulties inherent in an attempt to apply etic psychiatric perspectives to a narrative text from another historical epoch. Some of the problems emerged in the discussion which followed the publication in 1958 of Erik Erikson's *Young Man Luther: A Study in Psychoanalysis and History*. The principal problem is the lack of the abundant data that modern modes of psychiatric analysis utilize. Nevertheless, we should not overemphasize the difficulties. Just as there is nothing to prevent someone today giving a very cautious diagnosis (no doubt hedged about with appropriate qualifications) on the strength of a brief written report of the condition of a patient in a non-Western context, so too there is no reason in principle why we cannot try to do the same in relation to the written record of the condition of a person from another age, even if we are dealing with a literary figure (who has presumably been portrayed in accordance with prevailing social scripts) rather than a historical personality. It is encouraging to see the approbation Roger Johnson gave to Erikson's attempt to do this for Luther in spite of criticism Erikson had attracted (1977: 1-18).

In dealing with Saul's condition, our primary point of reference will be the fairly new field of cross-cultural health care and medical anthropology. One of the early milestones in this area, *Patients and Healers in the Context of Culture*, was published in 1980 by Arthur Kleinman, a psychiatrist trained in anthropology, who did extensive fieldwork in Taiwan, where modern Western and a variety of types of traditional Chinese medicines and therapeutic practices exist cheek by jowl. Although much subsequent research on cross-cultural medicine and psychiatry has been published in the last two decades, Kleinman's work stands out for the clarity with which he addresses the central issues.

According to Kleinman, the single most important notion for cross-cultural studies of this kind is that in all societies health care activities are closely interrelated. Each society has a health care system, which is a *cultural system* of symbolic meanings anchored in particular arrangements of social institutions and patterns of interpersonal relations. Such a system, which is a conceptual model not an ontological entity, encompasses descriptions of illness, beliefs about causation of illness, norms governing choice and evaluation of treatment, socially legitimated statuses, roles, power relationships, interaction settings and institutions. Patients and healers are the basic components and they are embedded in specific sets of cultural meanings and social relationships. The pronounced cultural orientation of the notion of a health care system radically distinguishes it from the biomedical model favoured by most health carers in North Atlantic contexts, in which biological processes alone constitute the reality addressed and are the central focus of diagnosis and therapy (1980: 24-25). It is Kleinman's view that the biomedical model rests upon Western scientism and ethnocentrism (1980: 32).

In a modern context it is possible to distinguish three broad sectors in a health care system. The first is the popular sector, which comprises various levels such as the individual, family, social networks and community beliefs and behaviour and which around the world handles most illness episodes. Normally disease is first encountered in the family and then a number of steps are taken: symptoms are experienced and perceived, the disease is labelled and evaluated, a particular kind of sick role is sanctioned, decisions are taken as to what to do, even to the extent of engaging in specific health care-seeking behaviour, treatment is applied and evaluated and other therapy may be sought from other sectors in the health care system. The second sector is the professional one (usually meaning scientific medicine, although there are some pre-modern examples), and in some contexts this sector has been quite successful in driving out other types of health therapies, towards which it tends to have extremely negative views, labelling them as 'irrational' and 'unscientific'. Thirdly, there is the folk sector, comprising non-professional and non-bureaucratic specialists. In nearly all premodern societies the popular and folk sectors comprise the entire health care system. Folk healing can be sacred or secular, though this distinction is often difficult to maintain in practice. It covers phenomena such as shamanism, herbalism, and traditional surgical and manipulative treatments, such as bone-setting (Kleinman 1980: 49-60). Traditional Islamic medicine represents a mixture of the popular and folk sectors, but also a movement toward a professional sector (Ullmann 1978).

A central feature of cross-cultural health care is the distinction between two aspects of sickness: disease and illness. *Disease* refers to a malfunctioning of biological or psychological processes, while *illness* refers to the psychosocial experience and meaning attached to the perceived disease. Illness includes secondary personal and social responses to a primary malfunction in the individual's physiological or psychological condition or both. But it also has significant social dimensions, involving communication and interaction within the ill person's family and social network. In this light, illness means the shaping of disease into behaviour and experience. Health care systems have a vital cultural function of creating illness from disease and this, paradoxically, is actually the first stage of healing. Illness so understood is an adaptive response to disease (Kleinman 1980: 72). It goes without saying that similar underlying diseases may be configured quite differently as illnesses in different cultural settings. A disease tends to have a typical course independent of setting, whereas an illness is always unique (Kleinman 1980: 77). The Western biomedical model of health care tends to focus on the disease aspect, which its methodology is well adapted to diagnose and treat, whereas the health care system model sees both elements as essential.

As far as therapy is concerned, Western medicine is primarily interested in dealing with the underlying physiological cause of the disease, whereas in non-Western contexts therapeutic efficacy is sought through treatment of the psychosocial and cultural aspects of the illness.

Saul's Madness in the Context of Mediterranean Culture

These insights from cross-cultural health care provide a useful framework for examining Saul's condition and the way it was treated. We must face up to the initial hurdle—that we have only a tiny amount of evidence upon which to reach any view, as compared with the abundant empirical data available to researchers into similar phenomena in foreign cultures today.[23] Nevertheless, inspired by Kleinman, there are still interesting issues to pursue. First of all, we must consider the health care system in operation, which comes into view at 1 Sam. 16.14-23. As usual in a preindustrial agrarian society, there is no professional sector, yet rather more surprisingly there is no folk sector in view either. The treatment of Saul's condition is left entirely to the popular sector. Here this is not composed of Saul's family (neither his wife, Ahinoam, nor his sons, Jonathan, Ishyo and Malchishua, nor his daughters, Merab and Michal [1 Sam. 14.49] play any part) but rather of the social network consisting of his courtiers and soldiers (whom it would not be unreasonable to regard as his fictive kin) and one of his subjects, David, together with a body of beliefs and behaviour thought to be efficacious. Furthermore, the process described above certainly takes place. Saul's symptoms, especially his terror, are noted and socially interpreted, with the problem being attributed to possession by an evil spirit, a particular role is envisaged for him—that he will receive therapy inside his house but will otherwise continue as king—and a decision is made to find a fine lyre player who will be able to give him relief.

It is also possible to distinguish disease from illness in relation to Saul. The 'disease' consists of some physiological or psychological malfunction that manifests itself in attacks of extreme dread. I will consider the possible nature of this disease from a modern psychiatric perspective further below. On the other hand, Saul's 'illness' refers to the cultural complex

---

23. We also have more data available with respect to other historical periods. There is, for example, a reasonable amount of information available on the notion of 'melancholia' in traditional Islamic society; see Ullmann 1978: 72-78.

that develops around this phenomenon, including the communication and interaction on the matter between himself and his servants, the interpretation attached to it as a visitation by a spirit and the behaviour expected of Saul while he is receiving therapy.

It is often possible to build up very full profiles of 'illnesses' in contemporary foreign cultures because of the availability of informants who may be interviewed and examined. Three examples featuring anxiety states (chosen because they have some similarities to Saul's condition) are worth mentioning. In Chinese culture there is an illness known as *koro* that is characterized by a fear of death. Its victims fear that their penis will retract into their abdomen and ultimately cause their death and they therefore take steps to prevent this happening. Belief in being afflicted by *koro* intensifies ordinary guilt over sexual excess and produces panic and depersonalization of the genitals. The illness occurs most frequently in immature, anxious persons who have been exposed to a sudden fright (Kiev 1972: 66). Secondly, *susto* (or *espanto*) is an anxiety illness that occurs in Spanish–American culture and is believed to be caused by a sudden fright, evil eye, black magic or sorcery, all of which are thought to produce 'soul loss'. Associated with it are irritability, anorexia, insomnia, phobias, reduced libido, nightmares, trembling, sweating, tachycardia, diarrhoea and so on. Traditional cures are prescribed to coax the souls of those affected back to their bodies (Kiev 1972: 69-70). In both *koro* and *susto* the element of environmental stress is perceived as a significant causative factor. Thirdly, there is 'falling-out', a seizure-like disorder apparently connected with anxiety states that occurs among black Americans, Bahamians and Haitians who live in Miami and which manifests itself as a state in which a person collapses without warning and for some time thereafter retains the capacity to hear and understand, while not being able to see or move (Weidman 1979).[24]

It is quite possible that the malady that the ancient Israelite readers of 1 Samuel thought afflicted Saul was a well-known phenomenon within their culture such as *koro*, *susto* and 'falling-out' are within the modern cultures in which they occur. Unfortunately, there is simply insufficient information in the text to develop a profile of Saul's illness in anything like the detail possible with examples known to us from actual case studies. Nevertheless, an important feature distinguishing the Israelite

24. I am indebted to Bruce Malina for drawing this condition to my attention.

condition is the centrality of possession by God's evil spirit to the analysis of the condition, and here we are able to consider comparative material. Murdock's useful worldwide survey of theories of illness points to a basic distinction between natural and supernatural theories of causation (1980: 8). The phenomenon of spirit possession or spirit aggression, defined as 'the attribution of illness to the direct, hostile, arbitrary, or punitive action of some malevolent or affronted supernatural being' (Murdock 1980: 20), and quite separate from magical causation where the supernatural being acts as the agent of a human aggressor, is actually the most common of all types of supernatural causation. Of 139 cultures surveyed by Murdock, spirit aggression was the most common cause of disease in 78 and an important secondary cause in 40 others (1980: 20). Belief in spirit aggression as a cause of illness is almost universal.

Accordingly, there is nothing particularly surprising about the attribution of Saul's illness to possession by a spirit from Yahweh. There is controversy over whether the 'evil spirit from Yahweh' had a status independent of God and was sent by him, or whether it was an aspect of his divinity (Kuemmerlin-McLean 1992: 139). Either way, the phenomenon is readily comprehended within the prevailing emic understanding of illness, which included firm belief in the existence of a God who would deal with his human subjects in this way, just as in other cultures there is no doubt of the existence of spirits who cause illness. For this reason, it is submitted that we may regard Hertzberg's proposal that the spirit's divine origin means Saul's suffering is described 'theologically' as an anachronistic and ethnocentric imposition of a modern viewpoint on an ancient text.

Saul's Madness in a Modern Context
The cross-cultural approach also demands that we consider the phenomena under examination from a modern position informed by the social and medical sciences. We need to ask how we, as post-industrial inhabitants of the North Atlantic culture zone, might conceptualize the full range of Saul's experience. This means that we must explore the nature of Saul's *disease* (since the notion of *illness* still sits more comfortably with the emic perspective I have just examined).

We lack sufficient evidence to make a firm diagnosis concerning Saul; all that we can do is to exclude conditions for which there is no support in the text and fix upon one which is at least possible. If we had more symptoms described, other diagnoses would be possible. According to

McCarter, as noted above, Saul exhibits some symptoms of paranoia, others of manic-depressive illness. Yet while Saul does in due course display arguably paranoid reactions toward David, to which I will return below, there is little support in the text for a manic-depressive diagnosis. Although depression is common to many cultures, Saul does not manifest its symptoms, such as sadness, hopelessness, lack of pleasure with the things of this world and with social relationships (Kleinman and Good 1985: 3). Moreover, the absence of thought disorders in the form of visual or auditory hallucinations seems to exclude schizophrenia as a diagnosis.

The dominant feature of Saul's condition to the extent that it is dysfunctional is the repeated incidence of terror, as shown in the use of the word *b't* in connection with it (16.14, 15). As noted earlier, the use of the consecutive perfect form of this root at 16.14 suggests repetition of the experience. This is a very significant indication of the nature of Saul's problem, and when Rosen wrongly suggests that 'there is no direct information on his subjective condition when he was tormented' (1968: 29), he may have been misled by versions that mistranslate the Hebrew verb without reference to terror. Within a psychiatric framework, one plausible diagnosis allowed by the evidence—and others might be available if we had more information—is that Saul suffers from an anxiety disorder featuring panic attacks; these occur frequently, perhaps once weekly or more often; usually last minutes, rarely hours and are sometimes linked to specific situations (Davison and Neale 1990: 146). In Saul's case we are dealing with neurosis rather than psychosis. In such a disorder there is a sudden and inexplicable attack of a host of jarring symptoms—laboured breathing, heart palpitations, chest pain, feelings of choking and smothering, dizziness, sweating and trembling, and intense apprehension, terror and feelings of impending doom. All of this is very different from the sadness and sense of meaninglessness characteristic of depression. In other words, Saul was too scared to be depressed! Where a panic attack occurs in the course of a chronic anxiety neurosis, the acute anxiety is manifested in part by rapid heart rate, and perception of the rapid heart rate is a feature of the illness experience; the tachycardia exerts a positive feedback on the anxiety, significantly worsening it (Kleinman 1980: 78). In this context it is interesting that at Isa. 21.4 the word *b't* is used in connection with what may be pounding of the heart. More compelling, however, is that the Septuagint, Josephus and Pseudo-Philo all interpret Saul's malady as choking or suffocation, and thus seem to fix on one well-known feature of anxiety states.[25]

Some instances of panic disorder have physiological explanations. In many cases it is caused by a cardiac malfunction in the form of a mitral valve synapse which can produce symptoms very similar to a panic attack. The alarm of patients at the palpitations they experience for this reason can cause their symptoms to escalate. Another possible physiological cause (disputed by some) is overactivity in the beta-adrenergic nervous system that controls the activity of many of the organs that are affected in a panic attack, and drugs that block the activity of this division of the nervous system (beta-blockers) do reduce anxiety (Davison and Neale 1990: 146).

Yet it has not been shown that physiological causes explain all panic attacks. Environmental pressures seem to be of great significance in some cases. Thus, the individual with an anxiety disorder of this type is chronically and persistently anxious and this is commonly linked to life-situations, for example chronic terror concerning a possible accident to a child or persistent worries about financial difficulties. Feelings of not being in control and helplessness are common to those with anxiety disorders (Davison and Neale 1990: 148).

It is important to note that an anxiety neurosis can be chronic and yet also have recurrent acute episodes, often as a result of psychosocial stress; indeed, in some cases the level of dysfunctionality manifested by the person may merit application of the term 'decompensation', or breakdown. Kleinman came upon several such cases in Taiwan (1980: 123). He cites, for example, the case of a Taiwanese man with an acute anxiety neurosis which was usually quiescent but at times became so severe as to suggest the diagnosis of 'acute decompensation due to psychosocial stress' (1980: 357). In highlighting the significance of stress, such as that arising from financial or business concerns in a patient's life (1980: 343), Kleinman is opting for one explanatory model among several offered by Western psychiatry. On the other hand, a behavioural model will stress current environmental and psychological contingencies reinforcing the deviant behaviour, while a psychobiological one will fix upon neurobiological processes (Kleinman 1980: 131).

---

25. See *pnigô* ('choke') in the LXX at 1 Sam. 16.14, while Josephus uses *pnigmoi* ('choking') and *straggalai* ('suffocation') in this place of Saul's experience (*Ant.* 6.166), and Pseudo-Philo employs the word *prefocare* ('to choke', *LAB* 60.1).

Other psychological features can accompany an acute anxiety state, such as delusions of persecution and violent behaviour in response, together with beliefs in spirit possession. All of these were observed by Kleinman in a Taiwanese woman (1980: 167-68).

As with the explanatory model selected, so too the treatment prescribed for persons with anxiety disorders largely depends on the conceptual framework of the therapist. Psychoanalysts view the disorder as resulting from unresolved conflicts and try to help their patients to confront the true sources of these conflicts. Behavioural clinicians adopt different approaches depending on how they construe the anxiety. If the anxiety can be resolved into a number of specific phobias, they might seek to employ desensitization treatment to them. However, where it is difficult to differentiate specific causes of anxiety, they might prescribe more generalized treatment, such as intensive relaxation training (Davison and Neale 1990: 150-52).

We will now consider Saul's case within this framework, meaning the case of a character in a narrative that presumably made cultural sense to the ancient Israelites for whom it was written, since I am not presuming to say anything whatever in relation to a possibly historical figure called Saul. His recent history was one of great stress. He knew that he had incurred Yahweh's displeasure, initially because he had not obeyed Samuel's command to wait for him at Gilgal and then by failing to put all of the Amalekites under the ban. He was threatened with the loss of the kingdom. Although it is uncertain whether Saul took these predictions with complete seriousness, we can assume that they would have caused him acute and on-going concern. Although he is portrayed as primarily interested in his own position, that was not all that was at stake, for there was also the well-being of his whole family, whose wealth and honour it was his duty to maintain, as he makes clear later in the narrative (1 Sam. 20.31). There can be little doubt, moreover, that Saul would have regarded himself as helpless before Yahweh and his prophet. The narrative makes psychological sense if we interpret the shock of these events—on a character whose propensity to possession states had already revealed a personality less tied to everyday reality than some—and the continuing apprehension that Yahweh was going to give his kingship to another as precipitating an anxiety disorder with associated panic attacks.

The first onset of the condition is recorded at 1 Sam. 16.14-23. Its repeated nature, shown by David's frequently being invited to play, suggests the regularity typical of any panic disorder. The inexplicable nature of a panic attack would constitute a good reason for the emic interpreter to see in its presence a spirit from God. Extremely interesting, however, is that the therapy chosen, the skilful playing of the lyre, is recognizably similar to the intensive relaxation treatment recommended by behavioural clinicians in cases such as this, where there is a generalized anxiety syndrome.

The subsequent course of the disorder can also be accommodated to this diagnosis. Saul's first attack on David, at 1 Sam: 18.10-11, which signals the beginning of paranoid hostility toward him, correlates quite closely with the Taiwanese case cited by Kleinman where delusions of persecution and outbreaks of hostility were associated with an anxiety condition. Yet the violence with which Saul turns against David justifies our referring to this incident as 'decompensation', breakdown, in this instance triggered by the extreme stress of the day before, when Saul had been publicly dishonoured by the women's unfavourable comparison of him with David. Saul's sensitivity to his honour, which is quite typical of this culture, has already been established at 1 Sam. 15.30-31. For this reason it is noteworthy, yet not surprising, that it should be the damage sustained to his honour that induces the psychosocial stress, pushing an already chronic anxiety condition into a dangerously acute phase. Thereafter, although there are times when Saul is able to attend to the voice of reason of those around him or to relent of his hostility in the face of extraordinary displays of devotion by David, in general his anxiety condition is characterized by a paranoid and indeed homicidal attitude toward his erstwhile favourite.

One tragic consequence of this rejection of David is that the forces that would be available to wage war against the Philistines are hopelessly split. So it happens that at the last battle, when Israel is routed and Saul and his sons are killed by the Philistine host on Mount Gilboa (1 Sam. 31), David and his soldiers are campaigning against the Amalekites (1 Sam. 30), having previously offered their services to the Philistine king Achish against Israel (1 Sam. 28.1-20), although perhaps hoping that circumstances would see them dispensed, as indeed they were (1 Sam. 29).

An Intercultural Conclusion

Reading the narrative of Saul's madness in a cultural perspective of the sort attempted in this essay involves three stages of exploration. The first is the analysis of the narrative itself within a fairly generalized framework of Mediterranean culture to determine how it might have been interpreted by its ancient readers. The second is the cross-cultural process of considering Saul's condition in relation to both emic and etic frameworks of health, illness and disease. Kleinman's concept of a health care system allows us to value both emic and etic approaches to the madness of Saul. The third, which is an experiential as much as a cognitive process, means acquiring an intercultural stance that mediates between the emic and etic positions and draws on each to create a new and enriched mode of understanding. I will now briefly take up this third stage in reference to certain artistic productions relating to Saul and his plight.

There are two paintings attributed to Rembrandt which have David playing his lyre to Saul as their subject. We should bear in mind their broad context of composition within seventeenth-century Dutch society, which was experiencing rapid commercialization through successful international trade and the change in emphasis from older rural, face-to-face groups sharing a common tradition to more modern urban modes of socialization, which was the type of development sociologically formulated by Ferdinand Tönnies in the transition from *Gemeinschaft* to *Gesellschaft* (1887). The earliest, dated to about 1629/30 (Fig. 1; Bredius 1936: 490), which is 'undoubtedly authentic' according to Bruyn *et al.* (1982: 260), has Saul in the centre of the painting and occupying most of the canvas. He is sitting upright, his right hand firmly clasping the long shaft of an almost vertical object, the head of which remains hidden, leaving us uncertain if it is a spear or sceptre, while he looks severely at David, who is playing the lyre, with only his head (turned away from the viewer) and hands being visible as he concentrates on the strings. The source of the light in the painting is to the centre left, between Saul and David. The painting depicts a scene in which the two persons are tied together by the force of the gaze that Saul directs toward David. The second painting is dated to about 1655 (Fig. 2: Bredius 1936: 526) and some critics regard it as executed by a pupil of Rembrandt, although possibly to his design, and not the artist himself. Here we have Saul on the left, sitting in a slightly humped fashion, with the shaft of some object resting loosely under his arm, considerably inclined from vertical, while his other arm, invisible to the viewer, apparently pushes a velvet curtain to wipe his left eye, also invisible, as his right eye gazes into the distance out of the picture, oblivious to David's presence. Indeed, the position of the curtain means that he

Figure 1. Rembrandt, *David Playing the Harp before Saul*
            (Städelsches Kunstinstitut Frankfurt, © Ursula Edelmann)

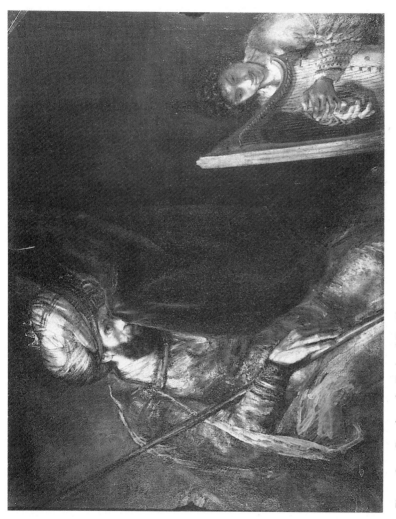

Figure 2. Rembrandt, *Saul and David*
(© Foundation Johan Maurits van Nassan, Mauritshuis, The Hague, Holland)

cannot see David, nor David him. The curtain between Saul and David visually enacts a severance of connection between the two of them. Meanwhile, David plays the lyre in the lower right-hand corner of the painting, his gaze aimed downward, and not on his playing, and away from Saul. He is also thinking his own thoughts. The character of Saul's gaze may bear some relationship to David's playing, but the king is paying no attention to the person of the player. The light in the painting seems to be shining in from the vantage point of the viewer and illuminating the two of them equally. Saul is now no longer the central focus of the scene.

To consider how Rembrandt has mediated the culture of these texts and that of his own time and place, we must begin with the biblical pre-text of each of the paintings. There can be no doubt that Figure 1, the earlier painting, has 1 Sam. 18.10-11 for its pre-text. The envious eye that Saul turns on David just prior to this incident (1 Sam. 18.9) is the focal point of the painting. David is caught in the gaze of Saul, who has been grievously shamed by the women who have praised David more than him and is on the point of attempting to spear his rival. The artist has composed the painting as a study in furious envy. It is done with great power, if not much subtlety. This interpretation finds strong support in an etching of the painting completed no later than 1638, which was inscribed with a Latin poem by the Amsterdam poet Cornelis Gijsbertsz Plempius, a section of which reads as follows:

> Felle tument oculi; mala mens et amara Sauli est:
>   Livida quin putridus viscera rancor edit.
> Non videt ergo suum, iuvenum fortissime, regnum;
>   Carpitur et regnum trux videt ille tuum.[26]

All this suggests that, in Holland in the first half of the seventeenth century, dangerously unbalanced envy was as well understood as it had been in the biblical world. This consideration rather lessens the cultural distance that might otherwise exist between pre-text and painting and thereby diminishes the scope for intercultural enrichment. That is to say, this early Rembrandt, although visually successful, represents a fairly wooden translation of the biblical situation rather than a more decisive

---

26. See Bruyn *et al.* 1982: 263-64 for the details and Latin text. I translate it as follows: 'His eyes bulge with envy. Wicked and bitter is the mind of Saul. Yes, putrid rancor devours his envious bowels. Accordingly, he does not see his own kingdom, O bravest of youths. It is snatched away and, grimly, he sees yours.'

reworking which brings its features into creative tension with the artist's own culture. In this respect Figure 2 is very different.

What, firstly, is its biblical pre-text? Mieke Bal sees in this later Rembrandt (or painting by someone connected with the Rembrandt school) 'antagonism between Saul and David', with Saul's 'melancholia' being 'related to, although not caused by, his fear of David's rivalry' (1991: 355-56). Although she does not mention the precise reference, these views necessitate that she has in mind 1 Sam. 18.9-11, or perhaps 19.9-10, as the pre-text, since these are the two passages giving expression to Saul's animosity toward David. While the point is an important one, Bal is probably in error here. There is nothing in this painting to suggest that Saul has begun to nourish feelings of hostility towards David. Her suggestion that the curtain between them represents a 'narrativized lack' that brings out the antagonism between them (1991: 355) is unconvincing. As we have seen in Figure 1, enmity is more likely to produce—and to be portrayed by the artist—as a focused concentration on the person of the enemy; it is a state in which the persons concerned are all too closely interconnected. Bal's own recognition that the 'rivalry is not represented in any obvious way' (1991: 356) has unfortunately not led her to see that the actual biblical pre-text for the painting is 1 Sam. 16.14-23 and to enlist her subtle interpretation of its visual cues in relation to the connection it has with that text. For the painting fixes upon the happier time before David has won military success and has acquired a name as a victor in battle greater than that of the king among the people of Israel, before the pressure of this circumstance has preyed on Saul's tortured psyche to push him over the edge into homicidal aggression.

In this light the painting reveals a remarkable intercultural richness. Upon the humped yet untensed figure of Saul with his unfixed single eye, Rembrandt has unloaded the full weight of his poignant situation in 1 Samuel 16. Abandoned by God's spirit (1 Sam. 16.14), who has actually transferred to David (1 Sam. 16.13), Saul is both tormented with terror produced by an evil spirit (1 Sam. 16.14) and yet at the same time seems to be moving toward a more quiescent state as a consequence of David's playing. On this 'reading', the curtain that makes David invisible to the king is a visual emblem of his lack of understanding that in all of Israel the very person who has supplanted him in the fickle affections of his God is the one whose playing provides the balm to his spirit, the one whom he loves (1 Sam. 16.21). He cannot see who it is who is temporarily assuaging his troubled spirit. For his part, David, in spite of his youth, is characterized by his self-possession. Neither attentive to the king nor concentrating on his playing, David's mind is elsewhere. His well realized portrayal on the other side of the curtain discloses the solidity of a status independent of the king and underwritten by his position as God's anointed in Israel. The brightly lit front of David's lyre, which juts upwards, thereby suggesting to Bal the inevitable phallic symbol (1991: 355), provides a powerful visual contrast with the flaccid and inclined spear or sceptre held by Saul. The two objects are emblematic of the respective destinies of those holding them. Rather than the tight personal interconnection on the theme of envy in Figure 1, here we have a portrayal of a theme much more at home in modern culture, with its decline in the older group solidarity, of *Gemeinschaft*, namely, mutual obliviousness, or disconnection. For the artist drives homes the pathos and poignant tragedy of a physical closeness which at the same time discloses a personal distance between two individuals moving in entirely opposite directions. The conjunction of a notional intimacy derived from the biblical text and an isolation related to early modern individualism offers a potent intercultural moment and space.

But, to conclude, I will leap from seventeenth century Holland to our own epoch and let Elie Wiesel have the last intercultural word, for few recent commentators have matched his passionate appropriation of Saul's plight. Writing from a personal history in which nocturnal processions must forever connote columns of children marching to their deaths in the flare of the ovens at Auschwitz (Wiesel 1981b), Wiesel develops his account of Saul in relation to his journey with two companions by night to visit the witch of Endor (1 Sam. 28.8). For Saul's

> is the story of a journey filled with melancholy, solitude, and anguish. It is a heartbreaking story dealing with all the elements and themes that make up the fabric of life and literature: prophecy and madness, friendship and betrayal, jealousy and acceptance, military adventure and secular ambition, poetry and thirst for power… The isolation of a king, the first and last of a dynasty; the fall of a kingdom, the birth of another; the deterioration of a dream and a friendship: one leaves this tale overwhelmed by grief (Wiesel 1981a: 69).

BIBLIOGRAPHY

Bal, Mieke
      1991   *Reading 'Rembrandt': Beyond the Word–Image Opposition* (Cambridge:
                   Cambridge University Press).
Bredius, Abraham
      1936   *The Paintings of Rembrandt* (Vienna: Phaidon).
Bruyn, J., B. Haak, S.H. Levie, P.J.J. van Thiel and E. van de Wetering, with the collabo-
                   ration of L. Peese Binkhorst-Hoffscholte
      1982   *A Corpus of Rembrandt Paintings* (trans. D. Cook-Radmore; Stichting
                   Foundation Rembrandt Research Project; The Hague: Martinus Nijhoff).
Budde, Karl
      1899   *Religion of Israel to the Exile: American Lectures on the History of Religions*
                   (New York: Putnam's Sons).
Cazelles, H.
      1978   '*hll*', in *TDOT*, III: 411-13.
Davison, Gerald C., and John M. Neale
      1990   *Abnormal Psychology* (New York: John Wiley & Sons).
Driver, S.R.
      1913   *Notes on the Hebrew Text and the Topography of the Books of Samuel, with an
                   Introduction on Hebrew Palaeography and the Ancient Versions and Facsimiles of
                   Inscriptions and Maps* (Oxford: Clarendon Press).
Elliott, John H.
      1988   'The Fear of the Leer: The Evil Eye from the Bible to Li'l Abner', *Forum*
                   4: 42-71.
      1990   'Paul, Galatians, and the Evil Eye', *CurTM* 17: 262-73.
      1991   'The Evil Eye in the First Testament: The Ecology and Culture of a Per-
                   vasive Belief', in D. Jobling, P.L. Day and G.T. Sheppard (eds.), *The Bible
                   and the Politics of Exegesis: Essays in Honor of Norman K. Gottwald on his
                   Sixty-Fifth Birthday* (Cleveland, OH: Pilgrim Press): 147-59.
      1992   'Matthew 20:1-15: A Parable of Invidious Comparison and Evil Eye
                   Accusation', *BTB* 22: 52-65.
      1994   'The Evil Eye and the Sermon on the Mount: Contours of a Pervasive
                   Belief in Social Scientific Perspective', *BibInt* 2: 51-84.
Eppstein, Victor
      1969   'Was Saul Also among the Prophets?', *ZAW* 81: 287-304.
Erikson, Erik
      1958   *Young Man Luther: A Study in Psychoanalysis and History* (New York:
                   W.W. Norton).
Esler, Philip F.
      1994   'Glossolalia and the Admission of Gentiles into the Early Christian Com-
                   munity', in *idem*, *The First Christians in their Social Worlds* (London: Rout-
                   ledge): 37-51.
      1995   'Introduction: Models, Context and Kerygma in New Testament Inter-
                   pretation', in Esler (ed.) 1995: 1-22.
      1998   *Galatians* (London: Routledge).

Esler, Philip F. (ed.)
    1995   *Modelling Early Christianity: Social-Scientific Studies of the New Testament in its Context* (London: Routledge).
Exum, J. Cheryl
    1992   *Tragedy and Biblical Narrative: Arrows of the Almighty* (Cambridge: Cambridge University Press).
Garrett, Susan
    1992   'Sociology of Early Christianity', *ABD*, VI: 9-99.
Gordon, Robert P.
    1987   'Saul's Meningitis According to Targum 1 Samuel XIX 24', *VT* 37: 39-49.
Gudykunst, William B., and Young Yun Kim
    1992   *Communicating with Strangers: An Approach to Intercultural Communication* (New York: McGraw–Hill, 2nd edn).
Gunn, David M.
    1980   *The Fate of King Saul: An Interpretation of a Biblical Story* (JSOTSup, 14; Sheffield: JSOT Press).
Harrington, Daniel J., and Anthony J. Saldarini
    1987   *Targum Jonathan of the Former Prophets: Introduction, Translation and Notes* (The Aramaic Bible, 10; Edinburgh: T. & T. Clark).
Headland, Thomas N., Kenneth L. Pike and Marvin Harris (eds.)
    1990   *Emics and Etics: The Insider/Outsider Debate* (Frontiers of Anthropology, 7; London: Sage Publications).
Hertzberg, Hans Wilhelm
    1964   *I & II Samuel: A Commentary* (London: SCM Press).
Hoekstra, Hidde
    1990   *Rembrandt and the Bible: Stories from the Old and New Testament, Illustrated by Rembrandt in Paintings, Etchings and Drawings* (Utrecht: Magna Books).
Humphreys, W. Lee
    1978   'The Tragedy of King Saul: A Study of the Structure of 1 Samuel 9-31', *JSOT* 6: 18-27.
    1980   'The Rise and Fall of King Saul: A Study of an Ancient Narrative Stratum in 1 Samuel', *JSOT* 18: 74-90.
    1982   'From Tragic Hero to Villain: A Study of the Figure of Saul and the Development of 1 Samuel', *JSOT* 22: 95-117.
Johnson, Roger A. (ed.)
    1977   *Psychohistory and Religion: The Case of* Young Man Luther (Philadelphia: Fortress Press).
Kiev, Ari
    1972   *Transcultural Psychiatry* (New York: Free Press).
Klein, Ralph W.
    1983   *1 Samuel* (WBC, 6.110; Waco, TX: Word Books).
Kleinman, Arthur
    1980   *Patients and Healers in the Context of Culture: An Exploration of the Borderland between Anthropology, Medicine, and Psychiatry* (Comparative Studies of Health Systems and Medical Care, 3; Berkeley: University of California Press).

Kleinman, Arthur, and Byron Good (eds.)
    1985   *Culture and Depression: Studies in the Anthropology and Cross-Cultural Psy-chiatry of Affect and Disorder* (Berkeley: University of California Press).
Kuemmerlin-McLean, Joanne K.
    1992   'Demons (Old Testament)', *ABD*, II: 138-40.
Lang, Bernhard
    1983   *Monotheism and the Prophetic Minority: An Essay in Biblical History and Sociol-ogy* (The Social World of Biblical Antiquity Series, 1; Sheffield: Almond Press).
Lewis I.M.
    1986   *Religion in Context: Cults and Charisma* (Cambridge: Cambridge University Press).
    1989   *Ecstatic Religion: A Study of Shamanism and Spirit Possession* (London: Rout-ledge, 2nd edn).
Lindblom, J.
    1962   *Prophecy in Ancient Israel* (Oxford: Basil Blackwell).
Malina, Bruce J.
    1993   *The New Testament World: Insights from Cultural Anthropology* (Louisville, KY: Westminster/John Knox Press, rev. edn).
Malina, Bruce L. and Jerome H. Neyrey
    1996   *Portraits of Paul: An Archaeology of Ancient Personality* (Louisville, KY: Westminster/John Knox Press).
Malina, Bruce J., and Chris Seeman
    1993   'Envy', in John J. Pilch and Bruce J. Malina (eds.), *Biblical Social Values and their Meaning: A Handbook* (Peabody, MA: Hendrickson): 55-59.
McCarter, P. Kyle, Jr
    1980   *I Samuel: A New Translation, with Introduction, Notes and Commentary* (AB; Garden City, NY: Doubleday).
Murdock, George Peter
    1980   *Theories of Illness: A World Survey* (Pittsburgh: University of Pittsburgh Press).
Neyrey, Jerome H.
    1990   'Maid and Mother in Art and Literature', *BTB* 20: 65-75.
Parker, Simon B.
    1978   'Possession Trance and Prophecy in Pre-Exilic Israel', *VT* 28: 271-385.
Pilch, John
    1981   'Biblical Leprosy and Body Symbolism', *BTB* 11: 119-33.
    1985   'Healing in Mark: A Social Science Analysis', *BTB* 15: 142-50.
    1986   'The Health Care System in Matthew: A Social Science Analysis', *BTB* 16: 102-106.
    1988   'Interpreting Biblical Healing: Selecting the Appropriate Model', *BTB* 18: 60-66.
    1991   'Sickness and Healing in Luke–Acts', in Jerome H. Neyrey (ed.), *The Social World of Luke–Acts: Models for Interpretation* (Peabody, MA: Hen-drickson): 181-209.
    1993   'Visions in Revelation and Alternate Consciousness: A Perspective from Cultural Anthropology', *Listening: Journal of Religion and Culture* 28: 231-44.

1995   'The Transfiguration of Jesus: An Experience of Alternate Reality', in
            Esler (ed.) 1995: 47-64.

Rohrbaugh, Richard
1995   'Legitimating Sonship—A Test of Honour: A Social-Scientific Study of
            Luke 4:1-30', in Esler (ed.) 1995: 183-97.

Rosen, George
1968   *Madness in Society: Chapters in the Historical Sociology of Mental Illness*
            (Chicago: University of Chicago Press; repr. Phoenix, 1980).

Seybold, K.
1978   '*hpk*', in *TDOT*, III: 423-27.

Simon, Bennett
1978   *Mind and Madness in Ancient Greece: The Classical Roots of Modern Psychiatry*
            (Ithaca, NY: Cornell University Press).

Smith, Henry Preserved
1899   *The Books of Samuel* (ICC; Edinburgh: T. & T. Clark).

Sperber, Alexander
1959   *The Bible in Aramaic. II. The Former Prophets According to Targum Jonathan*
            (Leiden: E.J. Brill).

Stansell, Gary
1992   'Honor and Shame in the David Narratives', in Frank Crüsemann,
            Christof Hardmeier and Rainer Kessler (eds.), *Was ist der Mensch...?*
            Beiträge zur Anthropologie des Alten Testaments (Munich: Chr. Kaiser Ver-
            lag): 94-114.

Sussman, Max
1992   'Sickness and Disease', *ABD*, III: 6-15.

Tönnies, Ferdinand
1955   *Community and Association* (trans. and supplemented Charles P. Loomis;
            London: Routledge & Kegan Paul [*Gemeinschaft und Gesellschaft*, 1887]).

Ullmann, Manfred
1978   *Islamic Medicine* (Islamic Surveys, 11; Edinburgh: Edinburgh University
            Press).

Watson, Francis
1994   *Text, Church and World: Biblical Interpretation in Theological Perspective*
            (Edinburgh: T. & T. Clark).

Weidman, Hazel Hitson
1979   'Falling-Out: A Diagnostic and Treatment Problem Viewed from a Trans-
            cultural Perspective', *Society, Science, and Medicine* 13b: 95-112.

Wiesel, Elie
1981a   *Five Biblical Portraits: Saul, Jonah, Jeremiah, Elijah, Joshua* (Notre Dame:
            University of Notre Dame Press).
1981b   *Night* (London: Penguin Books).

Wilson, Robert R.
1980   *Prophecy and Society in Ancient Israel* (Philadelphia: Fortress Press).

David as Musician and Poet: Plotted and Painted*

Erich Zenger

King David has inspired the biblical tradition as no other figure has. Moses, the central human figure of the Torah, is of course more important in theological terms. And he alone has received a biblical tribute that distinguishes him in an unsurpassable way from the other personalities of Israel: 'Never since has there arisen a prophet in Israel like Moses, whom the Lord knew face to face. He has no equal' (Deut. 34.10). It is true that Moses is not a figure who founded a religion, but he is the decisive figure to whom Israel attached its canonical history of origin. At the same time it is conspicuous that the Hebrew Bible shows little interest in the biography and family history of Moses. His birth and childhood, his wife and children, his brother Aaron and his sister Miriam are indeed talked about, and his death is recorded as well. But these biographical and family aspects *as such* are not the subjects of a broader discussion. Rather than elaborating upon a life story of Moses, the tradition was more interested in the words revealed to him by Yahweh and in his task which he had to accomplish with and for Israel. This task is circumscribed in many ways. The tradition brought together in Moses almost all the functions and offices that were part of Israel's history—with *one* exception: royal traits were never ascribed to Moses, although these would certainly have been suggested by his role as 'lawgiver', 'commander' or 'leader of the people'. Israel reserved the royal title *and* the royal ideology for its God and for its kings. By so doing, Israel acted, on the one hand, in accordance with its political and cultural surroundings. On the other hand, Israel created a 'founder personality' with the figure of its first king, David,[1] who appeared next to

---

* Translated by Martha Matesich.

1. According to the historical view of the Bible, David is the *prime* king of Israel, the founder of the Davidic dynasty, and as such the initial figure who is relevant in royal–theological terms. The fact that, historically speaking, Saul was the first 'king' is not decisive; also, the northern kingdom did not shape tradition as the Davidic kingdom did.

Moses in a tense relationship and, in the postexilic period, progressively advanced to the position of 'figure of the future'. As a 'messianic' figure David then also inspired and not insignificantly influenced early Christianity and its institutional entry into political history.

Unlike the way it deals with Moses, the biblical tradition has given the life story of David a broader treatment. Granted, there is no account of the birth and boyhood of David. Instead, the tradition reflects the issues of how David became *king*, how he lived *as a king* and how things would continue with *his kingdom* after his death. Since David, unlike Moses, was linked with the 'historical' culture of Israel and in particular with Zion/Jerusalem, David (together with his son Solomon) rose to the position of cultural model. On the one hand, this function befits a king a priori in societies that are constituted monarchically and aristocratically. On the other hand, however, in the cultural interplay of king and society it is fascinating to see which royal traits have been selected as culturally dominant in each case.

In what follows I would like to investigate the peculiar phenomenon that, in early Judaism, David was progressively promoted to the figure of royal musician and poet and that he, as such a cultural model, was subject to a diverse reception in the postbiblical period. Understandably, in this study I can only trace a few examples of this multiform reception. And yet I believe that the examples chosen permit some conclusions concerning the role of the Bible in establishing cultural and religious identity.

1. *The Literature of Early Judaism*

The biblical and nonbiblical literature of early Judaism provides a complex picture of David as a musician and a poet. The starting point for this motif in terms of tradition history obviously lies in the composition of the books of Samuel. The small shepherd boy David is already depicted here as an exceptionally gifted musician at his first appearance. His skill at playing the lyre is so well known that he is brought to Saul's court so that he may expel Saul's evil spirit with his music (1 Sam. 16.14-23). And the mysterious power of his music becomes apparent twice when the spear of the jealous king, which he throws at David to kill him, does not strike him. According to the account of the narrator, this is obviously the case because at the time David is playing his lyre (1 Sam. 18.10-11; 19.9-10). David's music is thus assigned a healing and saving power. The tradition presents David as a poet when it has him speak two poetic elegies, one for Saul and Jonathan (2 Sam. 1.17-27) and one for Abner (2 Sam. 3.33-34). When the Ark is retrieved from the control of the Philistines, it is not explicitly stated in 2 Sam. 6.5 that David joins in playing one of the instruments named there, but the general remark nevertheless includes him: 'David and all the house of Israel were dancing before Yahweh with all their might, with singing and lyres and harps and tambourines and castanets and cymbals' (2 Sam. 6.5). And finally, the redaction of the books of Samuel lets David 'speak' a psalm as a summary of his life in 2 Samuel 22 and also lets him recite a poem as his last words before his death (2 Sam. 23.1-7). Based on the redactional linkage of 2 Sam. 22.1-51c and 23.1, as well as the interpretation of David's words in 2 Sam. 23.2 as a gift of Yahweh's spirit, the following three points can be made with a view toward establishing the picture of David as musician and poet:

1. The introductory formula in 2 Sam. 22.1 designates the psalm (2 Sam. 22 = Ps. 18) explicitly as שִׁיר. Since v. 50 describes the psalm by means of the verb זמר as recited words with musical accompaniment, David is also portrayed here as a musician and a poet. Unlike the 'youthful tradition' of David, it is now no longer the shepherd boy, but the king, who writes poetry, sings and plays the lyre.

2. The last words of David in 2 Sam. 23.1-7 depict David's music and poetry as both a prophetic and wisdom-related talent given to him as the anointed king. The fact that the poetic words of David go back to the רוח יהוה, as 2 Sam. 23.2 emphasizes, refers the compositional curve back to 1 Sam. 16.13 on the one hand, but also suggests prophetic ideas on the other. Prophetic charism is also expressed when, in the closing note v. 51c, this redaction places Nathan's prophecy in the mouth of David, who is singing the psalm in 2 Samuel 22. David presents himself as an inspired wise man when, in 2 Sam. 23.3c-4, he proclaims a wisdom saying which has been revealed to him by God himself and then applies it poetically to the subsequent history in 23.5-7.

3. David's musical and poetic charism is part of his God-given talent to fight against evil, to stand under God's special protection in this fight and to become the deliverer of his people as the rescued one. This is already obvious in the composition 1 Samuel 16–17, which opens the beginning of the David 'biography', and it is expressly formulated at the end in 2 Samuel 22 = Psalm 18.

As M. Kleer has convincingly shown in his Münster dissertation, 'Der liebliche Sänger Israels' ('The Sweet Singer of Israel'), this conception of the books of Samuel was the impulse for the explicit, multi-stage 'Davidization' of the Psalter, which cannot be traced here in detail.[2] The notion stemming from the books of Samuel that it is, above all, David, persecuted, yet at the same time standing under God's protection, who composes psalms—whether it be in the conflict with Saul or as king in confrontation with his enemies and, particularly, on the run from his son Absalom—continues to have an effect in particular in the 13 biographical headings of the Hebrew Psalter. Whereas David is certainly still presented as a 'historical' figure in the biographical headings of the first three books of psalms, the David who sings and writes the psalms of the fourth and fifth books of psalms is a future ('eschatological') David figure, who is to be understood in the context of early Jewish hopes for salvation—and who will nevertheless prove his identity through the charism of music and poetry.

The David of the books of Chronicles differs from the picture of David in the books of Samuel in that David himself does not appear as a musician or a poet, nor even as one who prays or sings the psalms. In Chronicles David is the founder and organizer of temple music and probably even the inventor of instruments. He himself does not compose, but commissions the writing and musical performance of the psalms.

Both portraits are then brought together in Sir. 47.1-11.[3] It is David's twofold talent as hero and composer of song texts that predisposes him for being king. And as an anointed king he then distinguishes himself by inventing instruments and melodies for Temple music and by acting as a

---

2.   Cf. M. Kleer, *'Der liebliche Sänger der Psalmen Israels': Untersuchungen zu David als Dichter und Beter der Psalmen* (BBB, 108; Bodenheim: Philo, 1996). Concerning David as musician and poet and the phenomenon of Davidization, cf. also J.L. Mays, 'The David of the Psalms', *Int* 40 (1986), pp. 143-55; E. Ballhorn, 'Um deines Knechtes Davids willen (Ps 132,10), Die Gestalt Davids im Psalter', *BN* 76 (1995), pp. 16-31; J. Becker, *Wege der Psalmenexegese* (SBS, 78; Stuttgart: KBW Verlag, 1975), pp. 99-111; N. Füglister, 'Die Verwendung und das Verständnis der Psalmen und des Psalters um die Zeitenwende', in J. Schreiner (ed.), *Beiträge zur Psalmenforschung: Psalm 2 und 22* (FzB, 60; Würzburg: Echter, 1988), pp. 368-79; M. Millard, *Die Komposition des Psalters: Ein formgeschichtliche Ansatz* (Forschungen zum Alten Testament, 9; Tübingen: J.C.B. Mohr, 1994), pp. 230-34.

3.   Concerning Sir. 47.1-11, cf. also J. Marböck, 'Davids Erbe in gewandelter Zeit (Sir 47,1-11)', *TPQ* 130 (1982), pp. 43-49 = J. Marböck, *Gottes Weisheit unter uns: Zur Theologie des Buches Sirach* (HBS, 6; Freiburg: Herder, 1995), pp. 124-32.

'cantor' of God's praise. At the same time, Ben Sirach paints *his* ideal picture of the king in a modification of Deut. 17.14-20. 'It could be formulated pithily: it is not the Torah scroll in his hand, but the psalms on his lips which reveal the ideal king. The true king is the one who sings and prays the psalms.'[4]

The significance of David's musical and poetic talent is intensified once more in Psalm 151A and B and in the 'David Compositions' from Qumran. If one follows the compositional-critical analysis of Kleer, who has shown that 11 QPs[a] is first of all framed by Psalm 101 at the beginning and 2 Sam. 23.1-7 (DavComp) at the end, and has its midpoint in Psalm 119,[5] then it follows that this collection is designed as a *Davidic* collection of psalms,

> which David writes and sings as sovereign (thus a different biographical situation than in Ps. 151A). The framing psalms span the reign of the 'historical' David, beginning with the sovereign's resolutions in Ps. 101 up to his 'last words' in 2 Sam. 23.1-7; moreover, they already allude to the possibility of an 'eschatological' David. As the framing psalms show, besides and prior to passing judgement on the evildoers, his reign consists in singing and playing to Yahweh with the aid of his psalms. Because he sings to Yahweh he himself will receive integrity of heart and thus reign and judge justly.[6]

In the four psalms following DavComp, namely Psalms 140, 134, 151A and 151B, which are to be read as one composition and (analogous to the final Hallel of the canonical psalms 146–50) constitute the programmatic close of 11 QPs[a] (or of the entire psalter certified by 11 QPs[a]), it is once again the small shepherd boy David who—as the slayer of lions and Goliath and as the gifted player of instruments, writer of lyrics, composer of songs and singer—has the prerequisites for being anointed the saving king of Israel—and as such a musician and poet he is the model for the Qumran community in its campaign against the powers of evil. But here the weapons are not the sword, spear and javelin (cf. 1 Sam. 17.45), but the songs of David, whom Psalm 151A portrays as the Jewish Orpheus. That the LXX and the Vulgate, its successor, eliminate this Orphic interpretation of David and that the canonical book of Psalms did not include Psalm 151 at all make it clear that they obviously rejected *this* interpretation of David as musician and

---

4. Kleer, *'Der liebliche Sänger'*, p. 201.
5. Kleer, *'Der liebliche Sänger'*, pp. 204-317.
6. Kleer, *'Der liebliche Sänger'*, p. 313.

poet because of its 'pagan' ambiguity.[7] It is of course an irony of history that just this Orphic interpretation inspired the oldest known reception of the figure of David in painting. With this oldest representation found in Dura-Europos, I want to begin our journey through the history of the reception of this motif, in which I want to view five paradigms in order to formulate a few questions at the close about the role of the Bible in the formation of cultural and religious identity.

2. *The Murals in the Synagogue of Dura-Europos (Third Century)*

In the synagogue of Dura-Europos, which was newly built in 245 CE and already covered over in 256 CE for military strategic reasons, there is an Old Testament series of pictures on the walls that shows the earliest known representation of David as a musician and a poet. This interpretation of the picture is, of course, not indisputable, but it still seems to me to be the most likely.

The picture is found inside the synagogue in a prominent place, namely above the Torah niche. This position in and of itself has always elicited doubt as to whether this could be David at all or should not rather be Moses. If one bears in mind the genesis of this picture, then interpreting it as David becomes plausible.

As iconographical and technical analyses have shown, the picture as we now know it evolved in several phases. Admittedly, in their report the excavators provide different interpretations, so that it is not certain how many phases there are; but there is a consensus among the experts that the picture evolved in several phases.[8]

The oldest layer of the picture shows a luxuriant tree or vine; below the tree on the right there is an empty throne with a pillow upon which a diadem is lying, and on the left there is a table (Fig. 1a). This picture

---

7.   Besides Kleer, 'Der liebliche Sänger', pp. 256-57, cf., concerning this theory, especially H.-J. Fabry, '11Q Ps^a und die Kanonizität des Palters', in E. Haag and F.-L. Hossfeld (eds.), *Freude an der Weisung des Herrn: Beiträge zur Theologie der Psalmen* (Festschrift Heinrich Gross; SBB, 13; Stuttgart: Katholisches Bibelwerk, 2nd edn, 1987), pp. 45-67.

8.   Cf. the excavation report, C.H. Kraeling, *The Excavations at Dura-Europos: Final Report*. VIII, Part 1. *The Synagogue* (New Haven: Yale University Press, 1956), pp. 214-27; see also H. Stern, 'The Orpheus in the Synagogue of Dura-Europos', *Journal of the Warbourg and Courtauld Institutes* 21 (1958), pp. 1-6; H.G. Kippenberg, 'Pseudikonographie: Orpheus auf jüdischen Bildern', in *Visible Religion: Annual for Religious Iconography* 7 (1990), pp. 233-45.

was probably inspired by Psalm 80, which describes Israel as the vine planted by Yahweh whose shoots, as Ps. 80.12 says, grew even as far as the Euphrates River. Does the picture in this synagogue, which lies on the Euphrates, not intend to evoke just this very nuance? And since, theologically speaking, Ps. 80.18 also has a royal (messianic?) perspective, the throne and the table could be alluding to this dimension.

In the second phase a coherent pictorial composition has been painted on the first picture into the treetop as if on a background. It shows a lion striding to the left and, above it, a royal figure sitting on a throne flanked by two courtiers (scribes?) standing in front of it (Fig. 1b). Theologically speaking, this could indeed be a royal–messianic re-interpretation of the tree, which, on the one hand, is inspired by Gen. 49.8-12 (the saying about Judah: reference to King David; motifs: lion *and* vine) and which, on the other hand, construes the tree as a messianic metaphor.

To the left of the lion a third hand has then painted a seated figure playing a lyre (Fig. 1c). Like the king enthroned in the treetop, this figure is also wearing an 'Iranian costume: caftan, pants, boots, and with them a *chlamys* as well as a Phrygian cap. Within the clothes symbolism of the entire picture this indicates royal rank'.[9] To the left of this royal lyrist there is a yellow bird, probably an eagle, and to the right of the lion one can see another bird (a duck?). In compositional terms the drawing in of the lyrist has changed the role of the lion: it now belongs to the listeners of the music along with the birds. This constellation of figures, the lyrist and the wild animals that are peacefully listening to him while he plays, is a typical Orphic constellation that has already been pointed out by several authors.

A fourth hand gave the picture its final form as we know it (Fig. 1d).[10] The picture has been split into two frames by an ornamental ribbon. In the bottom half of the picture, two scenes of blessing have been painted: on the right the blessing of Joseph's two sons, Ephraim and Manasseh, by Jacob (cf. Gen. 48) and on the left the blessing of the twelve sons of Jacob (cf. Gen. 49). A group of 13 figures has been added to the top half of the picture. They now surround the king, who is seated on his throne.

---

9. Kippenberg, 'Orpheus', p. 233.

10. Figs. 1a-1c are from Kippenberg, 'Orpheus', pp. 244-45; Fig. 1d is from V. Zakovitch, *David: From Shepherd to Messiah* (Jerusalem: Goldberg, 1995), p. 204.

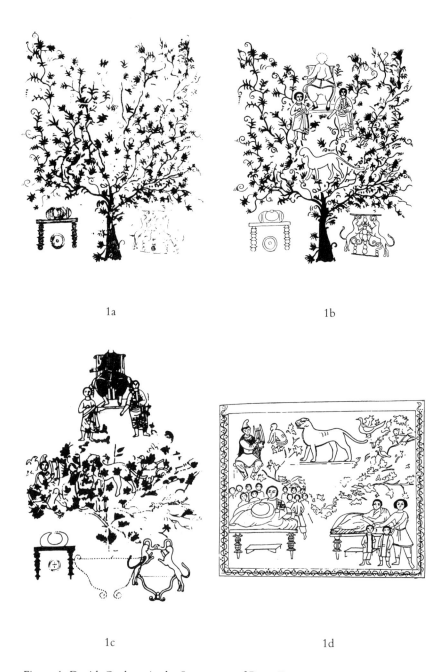

1a　　　　　　　　　　　　　　　　1b

1c　　　　　　　　　　　　　　　　1d

Figure 1. David–Orpheus in the Synagogue of Dura-Europos

In the present context the question is whether it is possible to interpret the Orphic figure as David and what significance *this* David then has in the total composition of the picture.

The notion of David–Orpheus is well documented in certain currents of early Jewish thinking, especially in Hellenistic Judaism. We have already encountered it above in Qumran with Psalm 151A. The floor mosaic discovered in a synagogue in Gaza in 1966, which, according to an inscription, was probably laid on top of another floor mosaic around 508/509, proves that the pictorial motif was native to synagogal art in Israel.[11] The mosaic, which unfortunately was partially destroyed after its discovery (especially around its top part), shows or showed David as king with a crown and nimbus sitting on the throne and playing the lyre with a plectrum, while a lion, a snake and a giraffe listen to him spellbound. The accompanying *titulus*, דויד, reveals that this figure of Orpheus is the royal David.

Before I give my own interpretation of the lyrist, I want to begin by briefly mentioning four other lines of interpretation. In Volume 8 of his 'Final Report' on the excavations at Dura-Europos, which was published in 1956, C.H. Kraeling holds the view that the artist simply took up a pictorial pattern well known at that time in order to foreground the biblical tradition of 2 Samuel 22, according to which David was a gifted musician and poet: 'The artist fell back upon the best-known and most appropriate of the many clichés for musicians as a happy device for portraying David in the rôle assigned to him by 2 Sam. 22'.[12] According to Kraeling, the lyrist is the biblical David, admittedly not as a shepherd, but as a king singing his song of triumph, 2 Sam. 22.

E.R. Goodenough has interpreted the picture not just as a visualization of the biblical material, but as an attempt to integrate elements of the Orphic mystery religion for which Jewish circles in Alexandria, including Philo, among others, had great sympathy: 'Hellenized Jews obviously admired the figure and teachings of Orpheus... It is chiefly important to recognize that whatever the identifications intended by the painter, the Orpheus and King together would have indicated the sense of this mystic ascent'.[13] The lyrist is David–Orpheus; the figure on the throne is God, before whom David–Orpheus is playing.

11. Cf. M. Barasch, 'The David Mosaic of Gaza', *Assaph* 1 (1980), pp. 1-41.

12. Kraeling, *The Excavations*, VIII, p. 225.

13. E.R. Goodenough, *Jewish Symbols in the Greco-Roman Period*, IX (New York: Pantheon Books, 1964), pp. 83-104 (102).

H. Stern has rejected these two attempts at interpretation as inadequate or inapplicable respectively and has instead recommended an interpretation along the following lines:

> For the pagan world, the image of Orpheus charming the beasts was the symbol par excellence of a state of heavenly peace—of the Golden Age. In the synagogue it has been used to illustrate not the actual prophecy of Isaiah but, in a more general sense, the Golden Age of the Messiah. The lion of Judah has simply changed its meaning, and has become the representative of the wild beast tamed by the musician's song. This picture, therefore, only serves to indicate precisely the meaning of the whole fresco, and to make it clear to all.[14]

In opposition to Kraeling and Stern, but in continuity with Goodenough, H.G. Kippenberg has tried to understand the Orpheus picture of Dura-Europos in a logically consistent manner from the perspective of the conceptual world of the Jewish pseudo-Orphic texts.[15] In these texts one finds not only the notions that Orpheus taught monotheism like Moses and that God holds the entire world together by means of his power, but also the idea (advocated by Artapanos, a contemporary of Aristobulos) that Moses was the teacher of Orpheus. According to Kippenberg this Moses–Orpheus correlation of the Jewish Orphic tradition is the backdrop for our picture. The precondition is the idea, which was operative in Judaism at the beginning of the Christian era, especially in apocalyptic and Orphic circles, that there are divine revelations which were hitherto secretly passed on or must be secretly passed on and which are to be disclosed only to a circle of insiders. In a pseudo-Orphic poem quoted by Aristobulos, Orpheus begins his speech with the solemn formula of the mysteries: 'I will speak to those who are entitled to it; close the doors, all you uninitiated. But you listen, Mousaios, you scion of the light-giving moon, for I shall let what is true ring out' (Pseudo-Justin, *Cohortatio ad Gentiles* 15, and, with smaller additions, Eusebius).[16] After this opening, Orpheus develops his monotheistic cosmology and then stops abruptly: 'It is not permitted to say more'.

This is the starting point from which Kippenberg wants to interpret the pictorial composition of Dura-Europos. At that time Orpheus represented

---

14. Stern, 'The Orpheus', p. 4.
15. Kippenberg, 'Orpheus', pp. 236-41.
16. Kippenberg, 'Orpheus', p. 240.

the founder of an esoteric tradition of teachings about salvation. Unlike the Jewish pseudonyms Enoch, Daniel, Ezra, Baruch and others whose names first had to be connected with secrecy, Orpheus had already been associated with such practice and theory for a long time and in a way which was apparent to everyone. Unlike the Jewish pseudonyms his secrecy remained a constant characteristic of his religion and was not suspended in view of the approaching last days... Now I think that from this type of literature one can gain an insight into what expectation in terms of meaning Jewish viewers brought to a picture of Orpheus in their synagogue. Whoever saw Orpheus in the context of a synagogue—whether Jew or not—was supposed to see an ancient piece of wisdom in Jewish law and teaching which had been passed on, hidden from the eyes of the public. He was to share the assumption which the pseudepigrapha also suggested to him (and which was of course far from accepted by everyone): that Orpheus already taught the true religion of Moses and passed it on in secret. From this I would like to draw the conclusion: The picture of Orpheus and pseudo-Orphic material belonged to the context of an esoteric interpretation and reception of the Jewish religion... The Jewish picture of Orpheus therefore testifies to much more than just an external process of adopting pagan picture schemes to express biblical ideas. It documents a particular interpretation and conception of the Jewish tradition... The Jewish pictures of Orpheus interpret the Jewish tradition in their own way: namely as ancient, esoteric truth... The picture of Orpheus is further evidence for a depoliticized interpretation of Jewish traditions, especially the David-tradition.[17]

For my own interpretation I would like to take the observations about the history of the successive growth of the picture *and* its entire composition as well as its position over the Torah niche as my starting point. What is striking about the composition is that a royal figure appears in it twice. That the lyrist is not just the familiar figure of Orpheus (as Stern assumes), but David–Orpheus (in my opinion Kippenberg does not give this element sufficient consideration) is indicated both by the royal clothing and by the given constellation David–lion, which, for those who know the biblical tradition, must evoke the story of the shepherd boy David who defeats the lions *and* plays his lyre. But according to the biblical tradition precisely *this* David is chosen to be king of Israel, which is shown in our picture by the king enthroned in the treetop. Admittedly this is only the biblically, narratively given frame, which, in our composition, constitutes several superimposed layers of meaning for its contemporary viewers:

17. Kippenberg, 'Orpheus', pp. 240-42.

1. The picture already had a royal-theological-messianic perspective *before* the David–Orpheus figure was drawn in. This perspective is then reinforced by the Orpheus motif and its correlation with Isa. 11.1-10; therefore, in agreement with Stern, it should be emphasized that the concept of the 'Golden Age of the Messiah' is evoked here.

2. But at the same time it should be remembered that the messianic figure of Isa. 11.1-10 is a royal personality, who is depicted both as a tree bearing fruit and as a teacher and mediator of God's Torah. In Dura-Europos these are both intended insofar as the enthroned King David is sitting in the treetop and the picture has its place over the Torah niche.

3. The royal David–Orpheus above the Torah niche must be seen within the context of broad and diverse ideas according to which David has a special relationship to the Torah as poet and singer of the psalms. It is not only to be recalled here that the five books of the Psalter were understood to correspond to the five books of the Torah of Moses. Above all we should call to mind the psalm composition Psalms 1–2 that opens the Psalter and with which David as author of the book of psalms invites one to study and to obey the Torah. It even seems to me not out of the question that our picture is intended as an allusion to Ps. 1.3, in which, as is well known, the one praying the psalm is compared to a tree that yields much fruit and provides shade with its treetop of never-fading leaves.

4. It is difficult to decide whether the tree over the Torah niche is not, in the end, supposed to evoke the idea of the Torah itself as the paradisiacal tree of life (cf. Sir. 24, etc.).

Whatever way this picture is to be interpreted in detail, a fundamental insight emerges in hermeneutical terms concerning the reception of the picture, which will be substantiated by the further examples I intend to consider. Here we are not concerned with understanding the picture of David given in the Bible, let alone with understanding a single biblical text. Instead, different individual elements of the Davidic tradition and other elements of Jewish tradition are put together with contemporary, even non-Jewish elements, in such a way as to create a cultural and religious horizon for the addressees of the picture into which they can and should integrate themselves.

3. *The David Cycle of San Ambrogio in Milan (Fourth Century)*

The wooden double door of the middle entrance of the basilica of San Ambrogio in Milan, whose scheme was probably designed by St Ambrose himself, presents the oldest David cycle in Christian art.[18] Unfortunately the door, which was made towards the end of the fourth century, was reworked around 1750, and some reliefs were replaced, so that the initial scheme can be reconstructed only by means of the pieces of the original door preserved in the museum of the basilica; there is, however, consensus among researchers about the reconstruction. Each door leaf has five panels of reliefs, namely three short and two tall picture panels each. The short panels show one scene each, the tall panels two scenes each. As a result, there are seven scenes for each of the leaves (Fig. 2) of which the first, at the bottom, and the seventh, at the top, do not depict a Davidic motif but rather mark the christological horizon within which the David sequence is to be read.

On the two bottom panels (it is true that they may only date from the restoration of the eighteenth century, but there is no reason not to assume that they follow the motifs of their predecessors) two monsters are fighting each other, whereas the two uppermost panels show two hovering angels holding in their hands a victory wreath with the (Constantinian) monogram of Christ. Thus the line for interpreting the sequence is given: we are dealing with the victorious battle against the evil powers. This battle is decided by Christ—in typological correspondence to David, whose battle against evil is depicted in the other panels. These pictures of David are inspired by 1 Sam. 16–17, Sir. 47.1-11 and probably also by Psalm 151 (LXX and Vulgate).

The two double scenes of the bottom half of the door (Fig. 3) show the anointing of the shepherd boy David who, in the midst of his seven brothers, is being anointed king over Israel (in Saul's place) by Samuel. The sequence of scenes begins here programmatically with the presentation of David as the victorious combatant. The scene on the left (B) shows the shepherd David in the middle of his flock, brandishing a club and chasing after an animal, probably a lion, which has carried off a lamb in its mouth as prey (the scene has only been preserved in fragments). In the corresponding scene on the right (I), David is sitting

---

18. Concerning their genesis and interpretation, see the still fundamental investigation of A. Goldschmidt, *Die Kirchenthür des heiligen Ambrosius in Mailand: Ein Denkmal frühchristlicher Skulptur* (Strasbourg: Heitz, 1902).

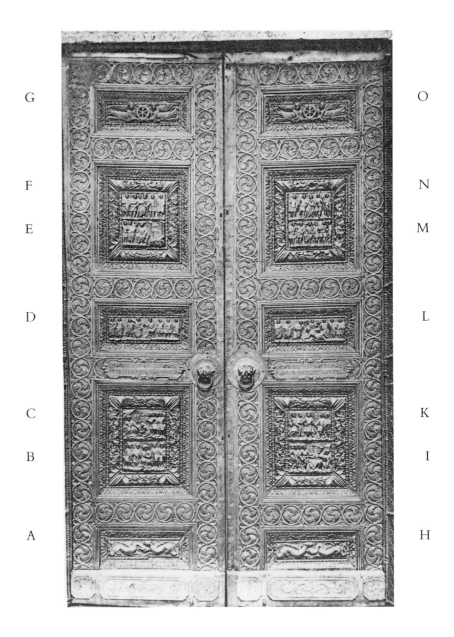

Figure 2. Wooden double door, middle entrance, basilica of San Ambrogio, Milan

K

I

C

B

Figure 3. Bottom half of wooden double door, San Ambrogio, Milan

between two trees and is resting his feet on a lion, lying in front of him. A bear is timidly and meekly creeping up from the right. In the background on the right, two sheep suggest the herd. The picture therefore shows David as ruler of the dangerous powers symbolized by the lion and the bear, and it does so by taking up David's self-recommendation in 1 Sam. 17.34-36, before the fight with Goliath:

> Then David told Saul: 'Your servant used to tend sheep for his father. Whenever a lion or bear came to carry off a sheep from the flock, I went after it and attacked it and rescued the prey from its mouth. And if it turned against me, I would seize it by the jaw, strike it, and kill it. Your servant has killed both a lion and a bear, and this uncircumcised Philistine will be as one of them, because he has insulted the armies of the living God'.

In the scene 'David as ruler of the wild animals', a figure is approaching on the left who is obviously addressing David; it is probably the messenger whom, according to 1 Samuel 16, David's father Jesse sends into the field to fetch David so that Samuel can anoint him king—the event depicted in the two scenes C and K. These two double pictures therefore characterize David as a shepherd who protects his flock from predators—and is thus suited to be a royal shepherd of his threatened people. This line of interpretation is further developed in the two picture sequences above these. This series is of particular importance in this context because the lyrist David is shown here in a powerfully expressive composition.

Following 1 Samuel 16–17, the picture series is arranged in a successive, linear way, namely from the middle on the left to the top on the left and then onward from the top on the right to the middle on the right: D shows how Jesse leads his son David to King Saul, who is sitting on his throne, so that David can expel the evil spirit from Saul by playing the lyre, which is then shown in E (Fig. 4; for the context D + E, cf. the text sequence 1 Sam. 16.20-23). It is true that the present composition of E has been enlarged or replaced to a great extent (originally figures probably stood in place of the group of buildings), yet the motifs that interest us are clear: Saul (the mitre on his head can hardly be original) is sitting on his throne, which is shaped like the throne in the previous scene D. The evil spirit, in the form of a snake, coils itself around the right chair leg of the throne. The snake is turning from the middle of the picture to the right, obviously under the influence of the lyre music of David, who is standing to the left of Saul's throne.

This scene is followed by David's battle with Goliath in the sequence FNML. Here the broad treatment of the theme of wearing the appropriate armour is striking, the armour in which or with which David can fight and defeat Goliath. In scene F (Fig. 4) David presents himself to King Saul for the fight against Goliath. This is followed by scene N (Fig. 5) in which Saul clothes him in his own armour, which is similar to the armour worn by Goliath in scene L. In compliance with the biblical narrative in 1 Samuel 17, David obviously then takes off this armour again because, as 1 Samuel 17 says, it was unfamiliar and cumbersome;

F

E

Figure 4. Middle left panel of wooden double door, San Ambrogio, Milan

this is discernible in scene M (Fig. 5) where David is no longer wearing
Saul's armour as in scene N, but his shepherd's tunic—which he also has
on in the final scene L, in which he has defeated Goliath.

N

M

Figure 5. Middle right panel of wooden double door, San Ambrogio, Milan

It is important for the present context that, according to the evidence
of the composition, the scenes are also intended to be read as a sequence
of pictures that are related to each other in a parallel fashion. This technique is already visible in the parallelism of the bottom set of double
pictures where B and I as well as C and K belong together. In my
opinion, the two scenes E and M are related analogously. That in M
David has taken off Saul's battle armour again in order to fight Goliath

as a 'shepherd' corresponds to his battle against Saul's evil demon with
the lyre as his shepherd instrument. It is beyond doubt that at the time
of Ambrose the lyrist David was also understood to be the psalm-singer
David. As a result, the psalms of David were interpreted as songs of battle against the powers of evil, especially if they were seen in a
christological *and* ecclesiological perspective, as they were by Ambrose.
Ambrose, in fact, devoted himself intensely to the study of the Davidic
traditions of the Bible and to the study of the psalms. Repeatedly he
construes the victory of David over Goliath as the victory of Jesus Christ
over the evil powers and enemies of the church. In the process, he uses
the picture scheme of the church door of San Ambrogio down to the
last detail, a scheme which we encounter for the first time on a church
door and

> which in the subsequent Middle Ages up to the end of the 12th century
> was executed over and over again on innumerable portals and expressed
> in different configurations: the victory of Christ over the devil, of good
> over evil, which cannot be gained by force, but only by means of the
> word of God, by entering the church. The sequence of pictures here is
> structured on a completely different basis than the door of St. Sabina. At
> St. Sabina the events of the Gospels were presented for the glorification
> of Christ and the foreshadowing narratives of the Old Testament were
> placed at their side. Here a biblical figure is chosen which serves, in con-
> nection with some symbols, to sensualise an idea in an allegorical-mystical
> way, the idea of the battle and victory of Christian teaching.[19]

4. *The David Cycle of the* Psalterium Aureum *of St Gallen (around 900)*

The 'Golden Psalter' (*Psalterium aureum*), written and illustrated around
900, during the cultural golden age of the monastery of St Gallen, also
presents a David cycle.[20] It belongs to the rare group of those medieval
psalters that neither illustrate individual psalm texts (as, for example, the
Utrecht Psalter and the Stuttgart Psalter) nor place a combination of Old
and New Testament pictures before the psalm (as, for example, the
Psalter of St Louis and the Ingeborg Psalter). The Golden Psalter of St
Gallen focuses entirely on the figure of David, who is at the same time a
prefigurement of Christ as well as a programmatic figure for the Carolingian emperors and kings. It is very likely that the magnificent

19. Goldschmidt, *Die Kirchenthür*, p. 30.
20. Cf. the thorough study, C. Eggenberger, *Psalterium aureum Sancti Galli: Mit-
telalterliche Psalterillustration im Kloster St. Gallen* (Sigmaringen: Jan Thorbecke, 1987).

manuscript was commissioned with 'royal-theological' intent. The sources at St Gallen say nothing about the origin and use of the magnificent psalter which, due to its size and its precious illustrations, stands apart from the ordinary book production of the scriptorium at St Gallen.

> The magnificent mannerism of the manuscript calls for an occasion, and first and foremost the visits of high-ranking guests in the monastery of St. Gallen should be taken into account... The numerous artistic allusions to the monarchy in the scheme of the pictures...indicate that the sought-after occasion could have been the visit of an emperor or king in the monastery of St. Gallen. Two dates are possible: the visit of Charles III the Fat in 833 and the visit of Conrad I in 911.[21]

It is difficult to decide whether the magnificent psalters were placed at the disposal of the guests, so that they could follow along with the divine office of the monks, or whether the splendid text was displayed in order to honour the emperor in a theological-political way with its illustrations. At least this theological-political intent of the Golden Psalter could be the explanation for the focus of the psalter on David as royal poet and singer of the psalms and for the absence of the David–shepherd tradition, especially the absence of the David–Goliath tradition. The intended, close reference of the illustrations to the Carolingian monarchy, particularly obvious in the four-part picture for Psalm 60 (59), which reflects the typical milieu of Carolingian authority with its depiction of standards, horses, armour and palace architecture, can also explain the fact that, out of consideration for the Carolingian court, there is no illumination for Psalm 51 (50), with the account of David's adultery with Bathsheba, although this scene is missing in no other illuminated psalter.

The David sequence of the Golden Psalter consists of twelve pictures, all of which (except the twelfth) are inspired by the biographical information in the heading of the psalm, which describes the (fictive) situation in which David prayed/sang/composed each psalm respectively. The first illumination of the David cycle in the text of the Psalter is placed before Psalm 18 (17) and can be taken to be a kind of summary of David's life, which is then pictured in the subsequent illuminations. The twelfth and last illumination is found before Psalm 69 (68).

The twelfth illumination is the only initial with a figure in the entire manuscript. It is distinguished as the final illumination by showing

---

21. Eggenberger, *Psalterium aureum*, p. 13.

David as king, clothed in precious robes and with a green and gold coloured crown (Fig. 6). It is a picture for meditation that depicts David on the one hand as the prefiguration of the king per se. On the other hand, within the context of Psalm 69 (68), which in many cases (and already in the New Testament) was read christologically, and from the perspective of the prophetic-eschatological programme aimed at in the preceding eleventh illumination (Ezekiel's vision of the *porta clausa* that only the eschatological king may open and enter), this majestic figure of a king is without doubt intended to be a prefiguration of the messianic king, Jesus Christ.

Figure 6. Twelfth illumination, *Psalterium aureum* of St Gallen

The David–Christ typology is also obvious in the first illumination, in which David is depicted at the same time as the prefiguration of the Carolingian kings. This first illumination is inspired by the heading of Psalm 18 (17), to which the picture belongs. From the perspective of biblical research, it is impressive in a twofold sense in that the Golden Psalter waits until this psalm for the first illumination of its David cycle, although there are already several psalms and biographical headings to psalms before this. For one thing, according to present historical knowledge, the so-called Davidization of the psalms started precisely with the secondary allocation of this psalm to David. And for another, the painter of the miniature or his patron designed this first illumination as a summary of the entire David sequence exactly in the way we know this psalm to be passed on again in 2 Samuel 22.

The miniature first translates the psalm heading, which characterizes the psalm as David's song of thanksgiving for being rescued from the grasp of his enemies. The illumination shows David on his throne in royal vestments under an arcade (Fig. 7). With the long fleur-de-lis staff in his right hand, he is pointing at three warriors clad in scale armour, lying in the left corner of the picture, as if he were pushing the three fatally wounded figures, who represent the enemies of David named in the heading, into the depths. On the right side of the picture, there are again three figures to whom David is pointing with his left hand. These three figures are wearing tunics with robes and swords; the front one is presenting his sword to David as a sign of his loyalty. On the above right side in the arcade, which is painted with a crimson-coloured background, the hand of God can be seen—a pictorial summary of the miraculous rescue by the hand of God that David himself narrates in the psalm (cf. especially Ps. 18.17-18). The fact that the miniature not only depicts the annihilation of the enemies but also the homage or voluntary submission of the three figures on the right goes beyond the psalm heading, but it is inspired by the text of the psalm itself, which in vv. 44-46 presents David, the one rescued from his enemies, at the same time as king over peoples and clans who obey his dictates and pay him homage.

Through the manner of its representation the miniature points beyond the biblical life of David in two ways. First, David is meant to suggest the eschatological judge of the world, Jesus Christ. David is enthroned in the pose of the judge who differentiates between the evil figures on his left and the good on his right, in the way this occurs in the New Testament imagery of the Final Judgment—and also in the way this is depicted in many paintings of the Last Judgment. A manuscript kept in Zürich confirms that there was also such a painting on the west wall of the Minster of St Gallen.

Figure 7. First illumination, *Psalterium aureum* of St Gallen

Secondly, this David–Christ is depicted at the same time as a Carolingian emperor. Iconographic analysis shows that the composition of the miniature relies heavily upon pictures of dedication and royal pictures that were especially popular at the court school of Charles the Bald. David's royal attire, his fleur-de-lis crown and the throne with the heads of animals as the border of the backrest are Carolingian as well. The crimson background also accentuates the connection to the role of king or emperor, since crimson is the colour reserved for the emperor— or for David as well as Christ. Of course, in the case of the David–Christ of our miniature, it is not a question of a particular Carolingian ruler. Instead, it is the way the Carolingians understood their office that becomes evident here: they called themselves David and gave their surroundings corresponding Old Testament names.[22] They understood

22. Concerning David as a figure with whom medieval rulers identified, cf.

themselves to be David's successors and 'vicars' of Christ—and to be mediators of salvation, which the Golden Psalter depicts on the title page (*frontispicium*) with recourse to the motif of David as royal poet and singer of the psalms. In the present context this illumination matters the most. But its purpose and function can be understood only if it is seen and interpreted within the framework of the 12-part David cycle that is painted in the psalter itself.

The frontispiece, which appears on a page after an empty page and measures 26.5 × 19.3 cm (the figure of David is 10.5 cm high), is a unique composition in a number of ways. This picture of David

> is *the* masterpiece of the school of painting at the monastery of St. Gallen of the Carolingian period... Individual figures were indeed taken from available material, but not a single one was slavishly copied and all of them underwent fundamental modifications so that they could be fit into the composition. Individual examples did influence the composition as a whole, yet the St. Gallen illuminator formulated the idea of the picture, the content of the illumination on his own, though supported by the spiritual director of the school of painting and by the patron, probably the abbot of the monastery, and borne by the atmosphere of the great intellectual flowering of the monastery at the time the manuscript was produced. For the first time the representative frontispiece of a psalter is not embedded in a historical connection; rather it is raised into timelessness, indeed into the last days: David...is enthroned in this illumination as musician and liturgist, as mediator between God and humans.[23]

The illumination shows David on a box-shaped throne (Fig. 8). He is holding a long, plucked string instrument in his left hand, similar to the way kings otherwise hold their sceptres. He has placed the fingers of his left hand on the strings of the instrument while holding the pick (plectrum) in his right hand in such a way that it is obvious he is just pausing in his playing of the music. He is sitting on his throne, yet his whole posture, especially the spread-apart position of his legs and the slanted position of the footstool, give the impression that at any minute he could jump up and join the dancing movements of his four attendants. David is looking up to the left at an angel whose right hand is pointing to him. This gaze at the angel is an expression of keen attentiveness to

especially H. Steger, *David rex et propheta: König David als vorbildliche Verkörperung des Herrschers und Dichters im Mittelalter, nach Bilddarstellungen des achten bis zwölften Jahrhunderts* (Erlanger Beiträge zur Sprach- und Kunstwissenschaft, 6; Nürnberg: Hans Carl, 1961), pp. 125-32.

23. Eggenberger, *Psalterium aureum*, p. 53.

the divine inspiration mediated by the angel, as the source of David's
music and psalm writing. That David, here on his throne, is flanked by
two dancers playing bifurcated cymbals and two veil-dancers reverts
compositionally to models; it is possible that the number of attendants,
namely four, signalizes the cosmos-ordering power of the imperial
David–Christ. But that musicians dance on both sides of the enthroned
David is singular and is probably intended to lend the scene a liturgical
dimension insofar as it alludes to the cultic atmosphere of the biblical
narratives about the return of the ark by David.

Figure 8. Frontispiece, *Psalterium aureum* of St Gallen

The illumination portrays the inspirational, indeed virtually ecstatic power that is conveyed by David as the royal musician and singer to his surroundings. By means of the composition of the frame of his picture, the illuminator has given this event a transcendent meaning that is indeed beyond time. The scene takes place on the one hand under the architectonic motif of the apsidal arch of an early Christian basilica, which in its turn has the form of an antique temple arch. On the other hand, in a basilica this arch opens into the sanctuary, so that David is at the same time enthroned in this room whose sanctity is even more emphasized by the crimson colour.

David thus becomes an imperial figure in which the Carolingian royal theology is consolidated, also in its superiority over the priestly office: David is *rex et sacerdos* for his kingdom. And at the same time, through the iconographical assimilation of Byzantine models, Carolingian imperial rule distinguishes itself from the Byzantine claim to power. Indeed, that the illumination points to the enthroned David *rex et sacerdos* by means of the divine hand on the top right side may also be interpreted as a sign of divine installation and confirmation.

5. *The David Cycle of the Bamberg Psalm Commentary of Peter Lombard (Twelfth Century)*

A further example of a David cycle in which we encounter the motif of the *shepherd* David playing music is found in a manuscript that was produced in Bamberg around 1160–70 and contains the Psalm commentary of Peter Lombard, which was widespread in early scholasticism as a work of reform.[24] This is a seven-page series of coloured pen-and-ink drawings that was specifically placed before the commentary as a theological-political programme on the tension-filled relationship of emperor and pope or secular and ecclesiastical authority. By means of borders the illuminated pages are organized into three frames, which, in their turn, contain one or two scenes. The interpretation of the pictures is

24. Cf. the fundamental study, S. Wittekind, *Kommentar mit Bildern: Zur Ausstattung mittelalterlicher Psalmenkommentare und Verwendung der Davidgeschichte in Texten und Bildern am Beispiel des Psalmenkommentars des Petrus Lombardus* (Bamberg, Staatsbibliothek, Msc. Bibl. 59; EHS, 28.212; Frankfurt: Peter Lang, 1994), and the investigation, G. Suckale-Redlefsen, *Der Buchschmuck zum Psalmenkommentar des Petrus Lombardus in Bamberg* (Bamberg, Staatsbibliothek, Msc. Bibl. 59; Wiesbaden: Reichert, 1986).

intentionally steered by means of Latin *tituli* (in hexameter) and by the inscription of names for people and places; moreover, there are many bands of writing with Bible quotations that are also meant to underscore the intended programme.

The cycle itself can be divided into two parts. David is the main figure in both parts, but the first part, pages 1-4, actually has Saul's reign as its theme, whereas the second part, pages 5-7, reflects the reign of David. One can also read the first part, which ends with the death of Saul, as the story of the rise of the shepherd David to become Saul's successor. Here the generally harmonious prevailing tone is striking and is expressed in particular through the scene showing the bond of friendship between Jonathan and David and the depiction of the wedding between Michal and David, which fills an entire page.

In our context the first two pages are important (Fig. 9) because they, again, parallel the motif of David playing the harp with the fight against Goliath. This time the parallel is emphasized in a special way by the formal composition of the three picture frames that correspond to each other. The two top frames each present two scenes that belong together. Page 1 shows David as the 'good' shepherd of his flock, who first holds his flock spellbound with his harp music, and then tears the snatched-up lamb out of the jaws of the lion or, as the case may be, tears the lion apart. Parallel to this, page 2 shows Samuel being instructed by an angel to anoint David king and then carrying out this instruction.

The two middle panels show the following: on page 1 Saul, who has been seized by an evil spirit and has gone mad as a result, is lashing out in all directions with his sword; on page 2 there is the wildly blaspheming Goliath. Compositionally speaking, both frames have in common that the figure representing evil (Saul or Goliath) is on the right side of the illumination and thrusts his weapon into the written border above. Moreover, they are standing among groups of figures that are each formed analogously; on the left there is in each frame a group from which one single figure breaks away, and on the right there is another single figure (page 1) or another group (page 2).

The two bottom frames place the taming of Saul's evil spirit by the harp-playing David parallel to the victory over Goliath, whom David beheads with Goliath's own sword. As was the case with the top frames, each of these two bottom frames has a further scene that has a close connection to the other scene. The bond of friendship between Jonathan and David follows the taming of Saul's evil spirit, and the presentation

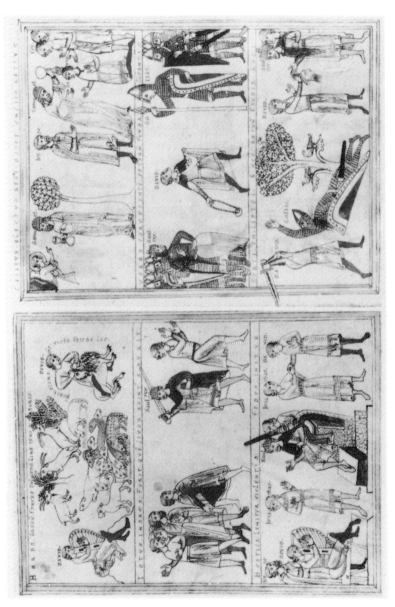

Figure 9. The Bamberg Psalm Commentary of Peter Lombard

of the head of Goliath follows the beheading of Goliath. These scenes are designed analogously by means of the frontal positions of Jonathan and David or David and Saul and through similar gesticulations.

As far as the composition is concerned, a dual possibility for the interpretation of the six frames of these two illuminated pages emerges. On the one hand, each page is to be read by itself from top to bottom and the *tituli* are to be taken into consideration as well; on the other, the pages are to be read in a parallel fashion so that they interpret each another.

The picture sequence of the first page portrays the power of David's music, and it does so in two senses: for one, David's harp playing drives away Saul's violent madness, and for another, it creates community and harmony. This interpretation follows completely the line of the medieval commentaries on the corresponding passages of the books of Samuel. The twofold effect of David's music is underscored by the *titulus* of the third frame, showing David playing the harp before the enthroned Saul on the left and the bond of friendship between Jonathan and David on the right, *hostica lenitur violentia fedus initur*; that is, 'the hostile violence is mitigated, the alliance has been initiated'. The fight against violence and the power of David's music to create harmony are depicted in the upper frame and interpreted by the *titulus* and another gloss. The scene on the left shows David as a shepherd boy, sitting on a hill playing the harp; a part of his herd listens to his music intently, several animals are peacefully and contentedly grazing, and three goats are eating shrubs with great relish. The *titulus* gives the following commentary on the scene: *herba gregum fauces dulcedo lire tenet aures*; that is, 'the herbs are for the gullet of the herd, the sweetness of the lyre holds the ears under its spell'. The scene on the right in which David tears the lion apart is interpreted as proof of God's power by the gloss: *brachia plena deo victe fatere leo*, 'admit, conquered lion, that the arms [of David] are strong through God'. The attribution of David's strength to God is, moreover, in accord with 1 Sam. 17.37, where David credits Yahweh with his power over the lion. And analogously 1 Sam. 16.18 connects David's skill in playing the lyre to the fact that Yahweh was with him. Thus the picture sequence of the three frames of page 1 must be read as illustrating that the power of David's music to mitigate violence and create community, as witnessed in his playing before the king, is the work of God himself.

The picture sequence of the three frames of page 2, which depict

David's victory over Goliath as a result of his anointing by Samuel, has the same tenor. This close connection is not present in the biblical narrative; there the anointing occurs *before* the narrative about David playing the lyre at King Saul's court. Through this new emphasis, the fight with Goliath is depicted as a battle of David's God against the blasphemous Goliath, and this even more so here than in the biblical narrative. The *titulus* of the middle frame also emphasizes this aspect where it states: *verba coruscantem prosternit funda gigantem*, 'the sling knocks the word-brandishing giant down'.

Since both picture sequences also interpret one another as a result of the compositional parallelism that I have sketched above, it follows that David's musical charism and his anointing are correlated and that, in an analogous way, his lyre-playing before Saul, which overcomes violence, and his victory over Goliath correspond to each other.

In our context we must of course ask this further question: what message is intended as a result of the fact that this series of illuminations in the Bamberg Manuscript was placed precisely before the psalm commentary of Peter Lombard by order of the Bishop of Bamberg, Eberhard II, who was chancellor of the Chancellory of the Reich under Frederick I, and who tried to mediate in the relationship between the pope and the emperor, that is, between ecclesiastical and secular authority—which was still extremely tense even after the investiture controversy?

First of all, it should be borne in mind that this David cycle does not preface a Psalter or stand in a Bible. Instead it is placed at the beginning of a book of study that reform-minded circles, especially bishops who were politically involved in church and Reich matters, accepted and propagated in the second half of the twelfth century as a 'modern' (at least at that time) consensus-seeking textbook of the University of Paris. These reform groups were trying to redefine their self-image and their understanding of office in the tension-filled arena of secular and ecclesiastical authority by means of the book of Psalms, which could very well be read as a theo-political book, and David as author of the Psalms, together with the 'modern' theology formulated in the psalm commentary of Peter Lombard—alongside the appeal to set in motion a reform of the church that daily renews religious life from the inside through devotion to the psalms and study of the Psalter. In the opinion of the Reichsbishop of Bamberg, Eberhard II, the David cycle he and his theological team of advisors constructed was obviously well suited to this purpose. Since the preparation of the manuscript and of the David cycle belongs to the period in which Emperor Frederick I repeatedly stayed in Bamberg to discuss topical questions of imperial politics with Bishop Eberhard, and especially to consult him on the conflict with the pope, it cannot be ruled out that the David cycle also intentionally contributed to reflecting this political context.

> By not being inserted into the text, but standing before it, the picture cycle can also be viewed without taking the text into consideration. Since it assumes a prominent position among the Bamberg cathedral manuscripts because of its ornamentation, it is likely that it was used as a representative, showpiece manuscript for important guests... The picture cycle is tailored to courtly circles and to the emperor himself, for the narrative-courtly characteristics of the scenic design make it entertaining for a secular audience. And since it is told of Frederick I that he was interested in stories about rulers of bygone days, it is conceivable that he turned to this appealing depiction of the story of King David or was supposed to turn to it. From the perspective of the secular ruler or of the court... David...is considered to be literally an ideal knight and a good king. His playing the harp and his fighting the lion...acquire a new meaning before the background of contemporary epic poems as proofs of the chivalry of the future king which also underscore his suitability in accordance with the courtly system of values.[25]

The generally positive relationship between the *shepherd* David and the *king* Saul is notable in the first part of the cycle, of which I could interpret only pages 1 and 2. The figure of David is ambiguous here. First of all, as has already been mentioned, David is the embodiment of the chivalrous ideal. He represents a type of spiritual rule which, in its dialectic of piety and pastoral care on the one hand (the harp-playing David who sings psalms) and combative intervention against the enemies of the Reich on the other hand (David fighting against Goliath), supports the welfare of secular rule. In terms of Reich and church politics the 'message' of this part of the David cycle is thus clear: with the aid of the figure of the music-making shepherd David, the manuscript speaks up for a constructive cooperation of the spiritual with the worldly power, whereby it admittedly gives precedence to spiritual power. 'Not only a high regard for modern theological ideas is therefore expressed in the unequalled, rich pictorial ornamentation of the Lombard manuscript, but in the end the ecclesiastical or spiritual formation of all rule...is asserted and confirmed'.[26]

25. Wittekind, *Kommentar*, pp. 222-23
26. Wittekind, *Kommentar*, p. 225.

6. David as Musician in the Portrayals of Rembrandt and his School (Seventeenth Century)

As a final example of the reception of the theme of David as musician, I want to discuss two portrayals of the biblical theme, 'David plays the harp before Saul', by Rembrandt or, respectively, by his school (around 1629/1630 and 1655 respectively).[27] Their significance will become clear when we set them apart from the tendency to play down the biblical traditions of David the musician and poet, which begins at about the same time, in particular in sixteenth-century Germany. This belittlement was at work when David became the patron saint of the Meistersingers, groups of singers and music colleges, which ultimately led to David's appearing as the personification of music per se on organ brochures and the title pages of books of musical notation. The expressive power of the Rembrandt pictures becomes discernible when we perceive this and also how Rembrandt, with these paintings, broke away from the earlier 'historical pictures', in which this motif was always part of a larger David sequence. Rembrandt turned the motif into an independent theme because he wanted to portray the drama of the encounter of people, the tension of human emotions and the mysterious, enigmatic conflict of historical protagonists.

Rembrandt's new programme is easily discernible when we compare his two pictures with Lucas van Leyden's[28] view, whose etching, completed around 1508/1509 (Fig. 10), Rembrandt knew personally.

> This is a full-length historical picture whose protagonists, David and Saul, take up the forestage before the backdrop of the courtiers who are pointing and participating in the scene. David, nicely dressed, but looking like a shapeless, witless oaf, and conscious of himself while carefully observing the effect of his harp playing, is standing before King Saul. Saul is cowering on his throne, his face averted. The large, sad, wild eyes, the half-opened mouth, the fiercely clenched fists, one of which is gripping a spear, and the feet apparently shifted out of position by a cramp all betray the man's inner conflict between hate and love which will be decided by the music. One senses how the etcher moves in on his subject and seeks

---

27. Concerning the following, cf. C. Tümpel, *Rembrandt: Mythos und Methode* (Königstein: Langenwiesche, 1986), pp. 49-54; I. Smidt-Dörrenberg, *David und Saul: Variationen über ein Thema von Rembrandt* (Vienna: Bergland, 1969).

28. Cf. M.J. Friedländer, *Lucas van Leyden* (Berlin: W. de Gruyter, 1963).

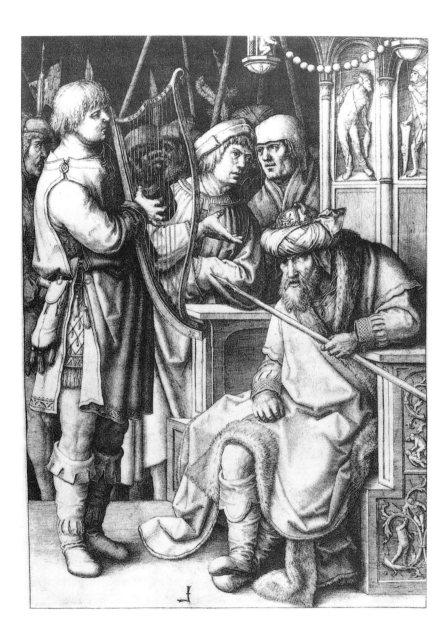

Figure 10. Lucas van Leyden (1508/1509), *David Plays the Harp before Saul*

to make the dramatic event clear by means of the physiognomical intensity of the large heads and by the hands which jut out brightly from the
shaded areas'.[29]

In contrast to the (rare) medieval representations of the scene and to
the portrayal we looked at in the sequence on the door of San Ambrogio, it is an innovation here that the evil spirit no longer appears as a
demon, let alone as the devil in the form of a snake; instead, the evil is
portrayed as a mood, as a disease or even, in the end, as a painful
longing.

Rembrandt takes up this approach and designs the relationship
between King Saul and the shepherd boy, David, who is playing the
harp in front of him, as a tragic spiritual conflict in which David is the
threatened, and the powerful figure at the same time. The biblical
background for this is 1 Sam. 18.10-11 and 1 Sam. 19.9-10. Rembrandt
painted the first of the two pictures around 1629 (see Fig. 1 in the article
by Esler, above).

> The shepherd boy is playing the harp at the feet of the grim king, who
> has been seized by an evil spirit, to alleviate his melancholia. The
> clenched fist with which Saul is holding a spear is at the centre of the
> painting... This fist hence expresses the entire wrath and displeasure of
> the king who is beset with melancholy, envy and jealousy. The deep
> wrinkles on his forehead, piercing eyes and a pouting mouth betray the
> mood of the king. In contrast, David, kneeling in the left corner as his
> subject, is completely immersed in his playing. Actually we only see the
> frame of the harp and the two hands which are plucking the strings in a
> relaxed manner.[30]

In contrast to his model, van Leyden, Rembrandt leaves out all the
minor characters and concentrates on the two main figures, Saul and
David. Two worlds confront each other in Saul and David. Saul appears
in the glaring light as the embodiment of the evil power that is strikingly
concentrated in his fist grasping the spear, which constitutes the centre
of the painting and which, in its sinisterness, could explode at any
moment—paradoxically precisely against the one who alone can heal
him from his melancholy and viciousness. In contrast, David is placed in
the shadows, his profile is blurred, and only his left hand, which is
playing the harp, stands out brightly and in three dimensions. 'He is

29. G. Bandmann, *Melancholie und Musik: Ikonographische Studien* (Cologne:
Westdeutscher Verlag, 1960).

30. Tümpel, *Rembrandt*, p. 54.

more sound than figure... He is deeply immersed in his playing, enveloped in an atmosphere which isolates and protects him and which remains inaccessible to Saul'.[31]

In the second picture, painted in the Rembrandt school around 1655 (see Fig. 2 in Esler's article), the tragic drama of the conflict is heightened even more. In the picture Saul and David are now only half-figures. The opposition of the two worlds they represent is depicted very intensely in the contrast of their hands and their gazes. The two figures, which are of unequal size, are separated from each other by a dark expanse that appears to be insuperable. Only the sound of David's music seems to be capable of leaping across this hiatus, as is intimated by Saul's tears, which he is wiping from his eyes with the curtain. Yet this is only an inner emotion, not a cure. Saul's piercing gaze, his hand on the spear and his whole posture shrinking back into itself, such that he is almost in danger of falling over forward, make it clear that his rule is finished, even though he is still holding or trying to cling to its insignia. In contrast, how different the little David is in his red shepherd tunic, devoting himself completely to the music that he summons forth from the harp with his delicately formed hands. As in Rembrandt's first picture, David and his instrument form a compositional whole. David the musician and Saul the tyrant are like two world models that are competing with each other and whose tragic intertwining can be sensed in the picture: 'The two figures seem to be suspended as if on a scale held by an invisible hand; soon the higher pan will fall and the lower one rise, Saul will be on the bottom, David on top. And this, too, one senses'.[32] Here David is not just simply a harpist; the way he plays his instrument and intently listens to it makes him not only the embodiment of the healing powers of music but also the symbolic figure for a political idea that trusts in charism and prevails against the concept of power represented by Saul. After all, by means of their recourse to Old Testament figures and materials, the Dutch painters of the period in which Rembrandt and his school painted our two pictures justified and inspired in a biblical way the struggle for the political independence of the Protestant Netherlands against the Catholic Spaniards. It is obvious that Saul's replacement by the young David was a particularly explosive issue.

---

31. Smidt-Dörrenberg, *David und Saul*, p. 20.
32. Smidt-Dörrenberg, *David und Saul*, p. 13.

7. *Conclusions*

I will now break off our journey through the history of the reception of the biblical figure of David as musician and poet and close with questions that are extremely important *for the discussion*. What role did the biblical sources play in all this? Why and, in particular, for what purpose were they taken up and reshaped? Which previously available pictorial expectations were taken up in each case? Which cultural and political roles of the Bible have actually become apparent in the process? How can we more precisely specify the relation of text and picture which arises when a *known* motif and its later reworking in a *new* picture interact in such a way?

For the time being I wish to give only three short general answers to these questions:

1. The pictures are not supposed to be interpretations of any biblical texts. Rather, the biblical texts are used to constitute and evoke a religious, cultural, political or anthropological horizon for interpretation in which the viewers of the picture should situate themselves and their community and from which they should understand themselves. In the process, the recourse to the Bible is supposed to have a justifying and motivating function.

2. A subtle fusion of biblical and contemporary levels, that is, of past and present, occurs in the pictures. This lends the pictures a dynamic structure and demands from viewers a creative examination of the *sujet*, even if only 'somehow' known, *and* of the associations, intentionally suggested by the pictures, that do not come from the Bible but from the different historical periods. The tension between the 'biblical' and the 'nonbiblical' aspects should and can also address the viewer in his or her emotional faculties.

3. A biblical motif that is taken up or reshaped time and again, and anew in the history of its reception, as is the case with the motif of David as musician and poet, can thus become a cultural and political model that influences individual and collective action, and also does this independent of the Jewish or Christian context of the Bible.

J.M.W. Turner: Interpreter of the Bible

David Jasper

> They are all gone into the world of light!
> And I alone sit lingering here.

If indeed it is the case, as has been recently suggested,[1] that the Bible has exerted more cultural influence on the West than any other single document, it is also the case that the place of the Bible within culture has always been and remains strange, unique and equivocal. In the particular sphere of literature, T.S. Eliot remarked long ago that 'the Bible has had a *literary* influence upon English literature *not* because it has been considered as literature, but because it has been considered as the report of the Word of God'.[2] Insofar as this is the case, the Bible has been a problem for culture even while it has often lain at the heart of its self-expression in art and literature. The great religions of the Bible have often elevated and equally often, perhaps understandably, banned the powerful images of art that have found inspiration in the drama of biblical narrative, while culture and society, even when its laws and customs have virtually demanded a practice of worship that centres upon the scriptural text, has produced art that enters into an often highly critical dialogue with the Bible, daring to claim a priority that would see the Bible as a commentary upon the art rather than vice versa. With J.M.W. Turner (1775–1851) we encounter an art that is profoundly expressive of the ways in which European Romanticism was beginning to see the world and our place within it, and that challenges the claims of the Bible to dictate our vision. Turner's great biblical landscapes radically express a culture in nineteenth-century England which, often in spite of itself, continued to celebrate Scripture and to question the foundations that grant it authority and power.

---

1. The Bible and Culture Collective, *The Postmodern Bible* (New Haven: Yale University Press, 1995), p. 1.
2. T.S. Eliot, 'Religion and Literature' (1935), in *Selected Essays* (London: Faber & Faber, 3rd edn, 1969), pp. 388-401 (390).

Although literary critics are now more or less accepted by the academy of biblical scholars as bringing valuable insights into the reading of the Bible through the study of novels, plays, poetry and letters, art historians have remained resolutely excluded despite the wealth of biblical art in the West.[3] No doubt this is partly a consequence of the particular preoccupations of art history itself, and one or two of the more significant contributions to biblical interpretation from the world of art have come from critics who would not claim to have specialized training in art intepretation. From the work of such scholars as Mieke Bal, who describes him as possibly 'Holland's most interesting biblical scholar',[4] Rembrandt has become recognized as an important figure in biblical criticism, but work on other artists who have visualized the Bible has been quite slow to emerge. In spite of the huge critical literature on J.M.W. Turner, including a journal dedicated wholly to his art, almost nothing has been said about him as a biblical interpreter, working in a Romantic age when biblical criticism was hugely energetic and inventive. Even the catalogue of the recent exhibition at the McMullen Museum of Art in Boston College, entitled *J.M.W. Turner and the Romantic Vision of the Holy Land and the Bible* (1996) does little more than allude to Turner's extraordinary translation of biblical narratives into paintings—his transformation of the word into colour. For Turner tries to understand the Bible not so much through historical reference, incident or object but through colour, or what has been described as 'historical colouring'. In his *Studies in the Louvre Sketchbook*, Turner comments on Titian's *Entombment*, describing its power through 'colour and pathos of effect', its vision of Jesus and the figures around him being effected by colour and light. He concludes:

> Thus the Breadth is made by the three primitive colours breaking each other, and are connected by the figure in vermilion to the one in crimson striped drapery, which balances all the breadth of the left of the picture by its brilliancy. Thus the body of Jesus has the look of death without the affected leaden colour often resorted unto... The drapery of the Body is the highest light or more properly the first that strikes the eye.[5]

3. One honourable exception to this is Jane Dillenberger in works like *Image and Spirit in Sacred and Secular Art* (New York: Crossroad, 1990).

4. Mieke Bal, 'Dealing/With/Women', in Regina Schwartz (ed.), *The Book and the Text: The Bible and Literary Theory* (Oxford: Basil Blackwell, 1990), p. 34.

5. J.M.W. Turner, *Studies in the Louvre Sketchbook*, quoted in Mordechai Omer, *J.M.W. Turner and the Romantic Vision of the Holy Land and the Bible* (Boston: Boston College Press, 1996), p. 24.

Turner interprets the Bible through space and more particularly colour. Thus this greatest of English Romantic artists is also a neglected critic of the Bible, and this essay seeks to redress this neglect, linking the culture of the visual arts with our understanding and interpretation of Scripture.

Turner was notoriously inarticulate. When he was Professor of Perspective at the Royal Academy from 1807 to 1837, the only appreciative members of his audience were his father and the artist Thomas Stothard, who was completely deaf and came only to see Turner's drawings and diagrams. Turner's own paintings, particularly in his later years, were beyond his own powers of explanation and interpretation. Indeed, what in his art becomes a strength increasingly defies language and definition: when a purchaser, James Lenox, expressed disappointment at the indistinctness of Turner's *Staffa: Fingal's Cave* (1832), the painter retorted, 'You should tell him that indistinctness is my *forte*'.[6]

Turner, however, though of humble origins, was widely read, as a boy becoming familiar with the work of the poets Mark Akenside, James Thomson and later Thomas Campbell, but most significantly studying Homer, Virgil and the Bible. Throughout his long career, Turner repeatedly painted biblical scenes, choosing as his subject for his first oil painting that he exhibited at the Royal Academy, *The Fifth Plague of Egypt* (1800). It was painted in the Grand Manner after the style of Poussin, and, like many of Turner's works, was accompanied by a quotation in the Academy catalogue, in this instance from the Bible itself.

> And Moses stretched forth his hands towards heaven, and the Lord sent thunder and hail, and the fire ran along the ground (Exod. 9.23).

The fact that the picture portrays the *seventh* plague and not the fifth (which was the plague on cattle—Exod. 9.1-7) indicates that Turner was not remotely concerned with biblical accuracy. In addition, the Gothic predilections of its purchaser William Beckford, author of the novel *Vathek* and builder of Fonthill Abbey, suggest the artistic line between Turner and the huge, and in their day immensely popular, apocalyptic canvasses of John Martin and John Danby, from whom Turner himself was later to draw for his own last paintings. What is significant in his highly original painting, which focuses upon the huge white Pyramid throwing a strange, lurid light on the surrounding city— a kind of ancient Egyptian *Götterdämmerung*—is its development of the

6. Graham Reynolds, *Turner* (London: Thames & Hudson, 1969), pp. 153-56.

tradition of landscape painting after Claude and Poussin with epic 'historical' themes drawn from the Bible. But Turner's corpus of painting also draws upon a wide range of classical history and mythology. *The Fifth Plague of Egypt* was followed by the *Holy Family* (1803), *The Destruction of Sodom* (1805), and continued as late as *Pilate Washing his Hands* (1830) and *Shadrach, Meshach and Abednego* (1832), paintings which owe a great deal to Turner's study of Rembrandt's biblical art. At the same time, his epic landscapes include 'historical' paintings from *Snowstorm: Hannibal and his Army Crossing the Alps* (1812) to numerous studies of the ships of Lord Nelson's navy in action at Trafalgar, to the elegiac *Fighting 'Temeraire'* (1838), but also 'mythical' scenes from his early reading in Homer and Virgil. In particular Turner was fascinated by the story of Aeneas and Dido, the tragic queen of Carthage.

For Turner, the narratives of the Bible, and in particular the Old Testament, were part, albeit an important part, of a much wider canon of Western literature and history—including contemporary events such as the burning of the Houses of Parliament on 16 October 1834— which stimulated his development of the tradition of landscape painting. In his apocalyptic studies of disasters, there is no difference between the storms that afflict Egypt during the Exodus and the snowstorms that dominate his image of Hannibal crossing the Alps. This latter painting was accompanied in the Royal Academy catalogue entry for 1812 with lines from Turner's own poem, *Fallacies of Hope*, which links the catastrophes that afflict the ancient world with the state of modern Europe during the long Napoleonic wars.

> While the fierce archer of the downward year
> Stains Italy's blanch'd barrier with storms.
> In vain each pass, ensanguin'd deep with dead,
> Or rocky fragments, wide destruction roll'd
> Still on Campania's fertile plains—he thought,
> But the loud breezes sob'd, 'Capua's joys beware!'

In Turner's landscapes of this early period he aims at a single, overall effect. Buildings and figures are blurred or lost and all human activity remains unresolved in the immediacy of overwhelming natural disaster. In *Modern Painters* (1843–60), a work more or less dedicated to the defence of Turner's landscape art, John Ruskin returns repeatedly to the artist's simultaneous grasp of the whole of what he is doing. The imaginative artist, Ruskin maintains, 'owns no laws. He defies all restraint and cuts down all hedges. There is nothing within the limits of natural possibility that he dares not do, or that he allows the necessity of doing'. Turner, he says, strictly speaking does not *think* at all.

> If he thought, he would instantly go wrong; it is only the clumsy and uninventive artist who thinks. All these changes come into his head involuntarily; an entirely imperative dream, crying, 'Thus it must be', has taken possession of him; he can see, and do, no otherwise than as the dream directs.[7]

This dream was fed, in Turner's vision, by the Bible as part of the whole of our cultural experience dominated by the eternal, implacable forces of nature. But if, in the hands of critics and thinkers like Herder, Eichhorn and Coleridge, the need for a modern mythology and the recognition of the poetic value and historical content of the Bible gave rise not only to new forms of biblical criticism but to nothing less than the modern conception of history,[8] in Turner's art, as it was to develop in his later years, we find a very different, and perhaps ultimately a far more radical refiguring of the canon of Scripture, one in which the coherence is premised on neither a view of history nor on narrative, but on colour and light.

In 1828, Turner turned to the legend of Regulus for a classical harbour scene reminiscent of his earlier Carthaginian paintings. Regulus, whose suffering Augustine compares to Christian martyrdom in *The City of God,* was punished by the Carthaginians by having his eyelids cut off for refusing to engage in peace negotiations with the Romans after the defeat of Carthage. Turner paints his picture looking directly into the glare of the setting sun, the rays of which burn a passage down the centre of the painting with intense reflection that renders indistinct the figures in the foreground. In other words, we are seeing the scene as if we were Regulus himself—the painting literally enacts the excruciating experience of its subject: the canvas *is* its subject. Turner achieves the same effect far more radically in his later biblical painting *The Angel Standing in the Sun* (1846) (see Plate 1). To this title Turner added two quotations. The first is from Rev. 19.17-18:

7.   John Ruskin, *Modern Painters,* quoted in Philip Davis (ed.), *Selected Writings* (London: J.M. Dent, 1995), pp. 70-71, 77.

8.   See Friedrich Meinecke, *Historism: The Rise of a New Historical Outlook* (trans. J.E. Anderson; London: Routledge, 1972); E.S. Shaffer, *'Kubla Khan' and the Fall of Jerusalem* (Cambridge: Cambridge University Press, 1975).

> And I saw an angel standing in the sun; and he cried with a loud voice, saying to all the fowls that fly in the midst of heaven, Come and gather yourselves together unto the supper of the great God;
>
> That ye may eat the flesh of kings, and the flesh of captains, and the flesh of mighty men, and the flesh of horses, and the flesh of all men, both free and bond, both small and great.

The second is from Samuel Rogers's fragmentary epic *Columbus* (1810):

> The morning march that flashes to the sun;
> The feast of vultures when the day is done.

In Revelation this feast stands in grim contrast to the wedding feast of the Lamb, and looks back to the prophecy of the defeat of Gog in Ezek. 39.17-20, and perhaps the apocalyptic statement in the Gospel of Matthew which relates to the coming of the Son of Man: 'For wheresoever the carcass is, there will the eagles be gathered together' (Mt. 24.28; see also, Lk. 17.37).[9] In Turner's painting the angel with raised sword emerges from a vortex of dazzling light that begins as white, gradually shading to yellow and finally red. The angel and the light are one. Around the rim of the vortex flit, indistinctly, the birds of prey. In the foreground, and equally indistinct, are various biblical figures, among whom may be identified Judith holding aloft the severed head of Holofernes, and perhaps Adam and Eve lamenting the death of Cain. As in *Regulus*, the blinding light literally blurs, for us, these figures associated in the Bible with murder and treachery so that the very light itself consumes them. In the first edition of *Modern Painters*, Ruskin identified Turner himself as 'like the great angel of the Apocalypse... clad in a cloud and with a rainbow over his head and with sun and stars given into his hand'.[10] The passage was omitted from later editions as it was felt to be verging on the blasphemous.

Whether Turner intended to portray himself as the angel is neither likely nor pertinent. What we see in this picture—or rather, barely see, as we are blinded by the picture and thus prevented from clearly 'seeing' it at all—is a devouring of the Bible by light itself, a revelation, as in the texts of Scripture, too intense for interpretation. The very brilliance of the painting holds us in the experience of looking so that we fail

---

9.   See further, G.B. Caird, *The Revelation of St John the Divine* (BNTC; London: A. & C. Black, 1966), pp. 247-48.

10.   *The Library Edition of the Works of Ruskin*, III (ed. E.T. Cook and A. Wedderburn; London: George Allen, 1903–12), p. 254 note.

properly to 'see' its subject. Yet still art historians struggle to decipher its motifs,[11] just as biblical critics struggle to decipher Scripture. What Turner offers is a vision of the resistance of Scripture to interpretation, a challenge to hermeneutics born out of a Romantic art that refuses to tolerate the fragmentation of the whole into parts, and which 'sees' the Bible as a unique whole within a 'canon' that is nothing less than all things. Thus Ruskin describes a Turner drawing ('with the same words by which I describe nature'): 'Look at it generally, and it is all symmetry and arrangement. Look at it in its parts, and it is all inextricable confusion.'[12]

As the critical reading of the Bible became increasingly immersed in questions of history, Turner's later art, though frequently returning to biblical themes, becomes both less historical and less concerned with its subject as such. Although he continued to give his paintings very precise titles, Turner's art becomes more abstract, and more concerned with experience as defined not by the specifics of objects and events but by colour and movement. In his middle years his works frequently began 'without form and void',[13] and in private, away from the publicity of the Royal Academy, he was painting pictures that are almost entirely abstract studies of colour, anticipating in a remarkable way the twentieth-century expressionistic art of painters like Mark Rothko and Willem de Kooning in his last years. A.J. Finberg, Turner's biographer,[14] entitled them simply 'Colour Beginnings'. In these works the visible world is represented not by forms and figures, but by the experience of colour, which becomes equally constitutive of 'reality'. History, objects, shapes, are subordinated to immaterial vehicles such as smoke or steam which, by their very nature, affect the way in which we see things. At the same time, though granting a powerful spatial effect, these pictures render highly ambiguous the nature of spatial relationships—interpretation is invited and endlessly denied. *What* these paintings are is both puzzling, and finally impossible to define.

11.   See, for example, Sheila M. Smith, 'Contemporary Politics and "The Eternal Word" in Turner's Undine and Angel Standing in the Sun', *Turner Studies* 5.1 (1986), pp. 40-49; Reynolds, *Turner*, pp. 200-203.

12.   Ruskin, *Modern Painters*, in Davis (ed.), *Selected Writings*, p. 19.

13.   Gen. 1.2; see Reynolds, *Turner*, pp. 141-42.

14.   A.J. Finberg, *The Life of J.M.W. Turner* (Oxford: Oxford University Press, 1961 [1939]).

For, in the end, they are simply themselves. In trying to look *through* the canvas, we fail to see the colours themselves, and to recognize Turner's total absorption in the act of the picture itself as it is defined by the flow of paint and colour, the way it dries and the manner in which layers merge and combine.

If one transfers this powerful immediacy of the 'Colour Beginnings' to the experience of Turner's later biblical paintings, one begins to realize his extraordinary and almost completely unrecognized contribution to scriptural interpretation, and his vision of the Bible as both a unified canon, and yet within the total experience of Western culture.

In 1843, long after the 'Colour Beginnings' of his middle years, Turner was presented with a copy of Goethe's *Theory of Colours* (*Zur Farbenlehre* [1810]) by his friend, the painter Charles Lock Eastlake, who had translated it into English in 1840. Turner studied Goethe's work thoroughly, making detailed annotations in his copy. Though critical of it, Turner responded readily to Goethe's scientific analysis of colour, just as he himself had concentrated on the same subject with considerable theoretical acumen, though far less articulately, as Professor of Perspective at the Royal Academy.

It has been suggested that Goethe proposes a Critique of the Senses by analogy with Kant's *Critique of Pure Reason*. In the Preface to the *Theory of Colours* he suggests that

> Colours are the actions of light, actions and sufferings. In this sense, we can expect to learn about light from them. Colours and light stand in the most precise relationship to one another; but we must think of both as belonging to the whole of Nature for it is she, as a whole, who wants to reveal herself concretely in this way to the sense organ of the eye.[15]

The immediate sensual impression of light and colour may give rise to an interpretative or evaluative response, constituting what we describe as feeling. Goethe was convinced that meaning is essentially sensuous, the phenomena of light and colour being operative under conditions that are at once physical, psychological and aesthetic.[16] The act of constructing the form of a painting through observation (rather than, for example, through association with previously 'constructed' objects or events) is, Turner asserts in a marginal note to Goethe, 'the object of

15. Quoted in R.H. Stephenson, *Goethe's Conception of Knowledge and Science* (Edinburgh: Edinburgh University Press, 1995), p. 49.

16. See further, Michael Bockemühl, *J.M.W. Turner. 1775–1851: The World of Light and Colour* (Cologne: Benedikt Taschen, 1993), p. 84.

Paintg [*sic*]'. Begin with the painting, not with its 'object'. In the text upon which this is a comment, Goethe had written:

> If the totality of colour is presented to the eye from outside in the form of an object, it will be pleasing to the eye, because it thereby encounters the sum of its own activity as reality.[17]

This goes far to explain why Turner's later paintings require such enormous energy of the viewer. They yield little or nothing to the casual glance and have, at best, a highly complex relationship with forms that would be familiar to us. Ships, bodies, buildings become lines, blurs or single brush-strokes, even while Turner continues to give his paintings very precise titles. But from realistic depictions he concentrates more and more on the phenomena of colour and light as effects in nature. We speak of being blinded by light—just as Regulus is blinded by the setting sun, or the angel standing in the sun literally consumes the figures destined for the great supper of the birds. Yet, at the same time, as light yields to colour, so, after the artist, we begin to perceive, and construct, a world of shapes and forms, and to interpret their interrelated nature. At this point, Goethe is crucial: 'It is precisely that which strikes uneducated people as nature in a work of art that is not nature (from without), but man (from within)'.

What has this got to do with our understanding of the canon of Scripture? Let us return for a moment to Turner's earlier epic paintings of biblical scenes. As in all his landscape painting (and quite unlike his great contemporary, John Constable), Turner continually dissolves depth and concentrates rather upon the effects of light and colour, the shading of one colour into another. It was not that he was careless of perspective—far from it. But if Constable, with his far narrower range, leads us into the depths of his views, Turner keeps us on the surface, struggling to make sense of the picture itself as a powerful, immediate phenomenon forming itself in the mind through the very technique of the artist. Such 'representation of reality' relates to Erich Auerbach's classic essay on the form of biblical narrative, 'Odysseus' Scar', in *Mimesis: The Representation of Reality in Western Literature* (1946).

> If the text of the Biblical narrative, then, is so greatly in need of interpretation on the basis of its own content, its claim to absolute authority forces it still further in the same direction. Far from seeking, like Homer, merely to make us forget our own reality for a few hours, it seeks to

17. Quoted in Bockemühl, *J.M.W. Turner*, p. 84.

overcome our reality: we are to fit our own life into its world, feel ourselves to be elements in its structure of universal history. This becomes
increasingly difficult the further our historical environment is removed
from that of the Biblical books; and if these nevertheless maintain their
claim to absolute authority, it is inevitable that they themselves be
adapted through interpretative transformation.[18]

In Auerbach's reading of the narrative of the Sacrifice of Isaac (Gen.
22.1-19) is stressed the 'unexpressed "background" quality' of the
telling, its multiplicity of meanings requiring yet defying interpretation.
The story is 'preoccupied with the problematic', and offers little or
nothing to the reader by way of 'depth'—no depth of character, no
depth of landscape, yet the surface of the narrative is mysteriously
fraught with background.

   To move from Auerbach's reading of the Genesis narrative to
Turner's later art is but a short journey. The eye is attracted to the
painting itself—indeed to the very paint—and to the implied narrative
of the swirls of light and colour. If Constable is at pains to paint an
instant of time (*The Haywain*, when it was first exhibited at the Royal
Academy in 1821, was entitled *Landscape: Noon*), Turner's paintings
invariably imply a story, a narrative that stretches before and after the
picture itself and is suggested in the visual experience of movement and
speed in the lines of paint. At the same time, his work strikes you with
an impact of utter immediacy—one sees, and *feels* the moment in the
dramatic experience (just as one *feels* the impending blow of Abraham's
knife in Gen. 22.10), and the very confusion and dramatic anxiety of
this moment defy rational comprehension. Turner said of *Snowstorm—
Steam-boat off a Harbour's Mouth Making Signals in Shallow Water, and
Going by the Lead* (1842):

> I did not paint it to be understood, but I wished to show what such a
> scene was like: I got the sailors to lash me to the mast to observe it; I was
> lashed for four hours, and I did not expect to escape, but I felt bound to
> record it, if I did. But no one had any right to like the picture.[19]

A painting neither liked nor understood: translate this now to
Turner's two late biblical pieces, redolent with tragedy and painted after
his close reading of Goethe's *Zur Farbenlehre*. *Shade and Darkness: The*

   18. Erich Auerbach, *Mimesis* (trans. Willard R. Trask; Princeton, NJ: Princeton
University Press, 1968), p. 15.
   19. Quoted in Graham Reynolds, *Turner* (London: Thames and Hudson, 1968),
p. 190.

Evening of the Deluge (Plate 1), and *Light and Colour (Goethe's Theory): The Morning after the Deluge—Moses Writing the Book of Genesis* (Plate 2) were exhibited at the Royal Academy in 1843. Both paintings, which were conceived as a pair, were described by Turner with verses from the *Fallacies of Hope*. The lines for *Shade and Darkness* are as follows:

> The moon put forth her sign of woe unheeded;
> But disobedience slept; the dark'ning Deluge closed around,
> And the last token came; the giant framework floated,
> The roused beasts forsook their nightly shelters screaming,
> And the beasts waded to the ark.

And for *Light and Colour*:

> The ark stood firm on Ararat; th'returning Sun
> Exhaled earth's humid bubbles, and emulous of light,
> Reflected her lost forms, each in prismatic guise
> Hope's harbinger, ephemeral as the summer fly
> Which rises, flits, expands and dies.

They were not the first time that Turner had painted the theme of the deluge. He had done so in 1813, followed by John Martin, with a picture entitled *The Deluge*, which was shown at the Royal Academy in 1837. But, it has been suggested,[20] the titles followed the paintings after a process of interpretation, Turner painting *towards* his theme rather than following 'realistic preconditions of representation'. The painting itself gives rise to interpretation, rather than the image providing a premise for the picture. In other words, Turner was not so much painting *from* the biblical narrative, as discovering the narrative in the process of painting.

Goethe believed that the earth's rocks originated in the covering of waters at the Flood. Turner's paintings add to his poetic reference to the origin of the Deluge in human 'disobedience' an awareness of the contemporary debates on the scientific significance of the Flood story. In *Shade and Darkness*, the figures, mostly of animals, and suggested shape of the Ark in the very centre of the picture, suggest the Genesis narrative, but allow neither precise interpretation nor grant specific points of perspective, impelling an endlessly restless viewing of the painting as a whole. Never coming to rest in the parts, the eye travels across the whole canvas in a 'narrative' that finally can be appropriated, if at all, only in one complete viewing of the whole: a narrative act that is one

20. Bockemühl, *J.M.W. Turner*, p. 88.

and holistic. Furthermore, this act is motivated not by shape and form so much as by the movement of colour itself in a statement that travels from dark to light rather than vice versa. What the viewer experiences, then, is not a remembrance of the word of the Bible, but a creative act that realizes, without final interpretation, the experience that gives rise to the Deluge narrative.

The second painting offers almost the reverse of the first, moving *from* the light in a narrative of colours—a dramatic enactment of the rainbow itself—after Goethe's theory of colours rather than, in the first instance, the biblical text, with its symbolic explanation of the rainbow as 'God's promise'. Even less representative than *Shade and Darkness*, *Light and Colour* presents an arc of colour that defies the consolidation of any structure except the shady figure of Moses 'writing the Book of Genesis', and a snake-like line at the very centre of the picture that suggests the serpent. In the words of Michael Bockemühl:

> If one starts with the most intensive yellow, orange and red follow; then blue, abruptly isolated in the upper right-hand corner and facing the most intensive yellow; then bright yellow again, orange, red, and black. The central zone of green, the secondary colour from blue and yellow, does not lie within the circle: the 'original contrast' of the creation of colour, yellow and blue, face each other in this pattern of movement. It is out of this contrast that every colour emerges ('Goethe's Theory'). Colour does not merely depict colour. Colour is colour. Wherever colour can appear in pictorial form in accordance with its own laws of manifestation, there it reveals its nature as reality.[21]

In this demonstration picture, Turner evokes, scientifically, the biblical act of creation and promise, with, mysteriously and without interpretation, the biblical motifs of the serpent and writing of the Pentateuch. If Goethe (and the Bible) saw light as benevolent, and its colours as indicative of the divine promise, Turner saw it as indifferent and the dominant medium for whatever theological moments may take place, almost superimposed upon it.

'Earth's humid bubbles' are evident in the bottom right-hand part of the sphere of colour, the result of the sun's heat and light drawing up the moisture of the Flood from the earth's surface in bubbles that reflect 'in prismatic guise' the rainbow of colours that are the sign of God's promise, but are as fleeting and momentary in their existence as the summer fly. With typical pessimism Turner turns the biblical narrative

21. Bockemühl, *J.M.W. Turner*, pp. 92-93.

of promise into a story of indifference—all is merely change in the circle of emerging colours, a narrative of the significance of the moment that anticipates future nineteenth-century debates between science and religion after Darwin.

Turner then places biblical origins—the genesis of light and colour, the promise of the 'rainbow', the sin associated with the serpent and the writing, by Moses, of the first book of the Bible—within a pictorial exploration of the associative properties of colour. The two paintings are within the tradition of biblical historical epics that Turner had been painting all his life since *The Fifth Plague of Egypt*, but now encapsulated within an associative scientific theory of light and colour which, after Goethe, recognizes that merely spatial metaphors are quite misleading if they are assumed to be accurately descriptive of nature.[22] According to Goethe, light appears on the spectrum as a reflection utterly dependent upon chance circumstances:

> If the darkness of endless space is seen through an atmospheric haze illuminated by daylight, then the colour blue appears. The sky, as observed from high mountains during the day, appears royal blue, since the quantity of fine haze floating in front of endless, dark space is but small; as soon as one descends into the valleys, the blue becomes lighter in hue, finally turning completely into a white-blue in certain regions and with increasing haze.[23]

Turner followed Goethe in making watercolour experiments in 'Colour Circles',[24] exploring the spectrum. In his Deluge pictures, these experiments are expanded into biblical themes, where the observation of *forms* is almost entirely determined by the gradations of colour, and in the second picture the only clear forms—of Moses and the serpent—are *imposed* on the enclosed world of light and colour as alien, unassimilable objects in a swirling, ephemeral environment. The bubbles of air in the right-hand bottom corner of the painting *might* be suggestive of a crowd of human heads, but there is no particular reason that this should be so.

In these two great paintings, Turner draws together many of the preoccupations of a lifetime spent painting epic landscapes. The one a study of darkening colours, the other of dazzling light, they both explore the

---

22. See Stephenson, *Goethe's Conception*, Chapter 5: 'Rewriting Nature: The Language of Science'.

23. Johann Wolfgang von Goethe, *Theory of Colours*; quoted in Bockemühl, *J.M.W. Turner*, p. 88.

24. Now in the British Museum.

effect on objects of looking directly at light, so that all is almost consumed by light. Specifics are lost in a visual experience that can only be grasped as a whole, and within which the particularities of form become matters of interpretation by reference to the text of Genesis: we 'imagine' we recognize the animals, the Ark, the heads of people. The biblical history—in the solitary figure of the 'historian' Moses—is imposed on the relentless action of the light.

Turner's tragic view of life in his last years presents us with a 'reading' of the Bible that has achieved little recognition in the history of biblical interpretation. Pessimistic, even cynical, he places the biblical narratives of 'salvation history' within the context of scientific theories of light drawn from Goethe and from experiments in reflection and perspective that he conducted in his Royal Academy lectures. Analogously with Kant's critical philosophy, Turner abandons any simple notion that objects and their forms can be known or defined independently of the observers and the conditions of light under which they are observed: light blinds as well as reveals. The biblical *narrative* and the sequential movement of its history are dissolved in a vision which, in taking all as a momentary vision, grants priority to no particular moment, and therefore denies the development of history as anything other than a blind succession of events 'ephemeral as the summer fly', which rises, flits, expands and dies. It is not merely that Turner's art acknowledges the inadequacy both of the human ability to construct meaningful history, and of language to convey 'man's ideas of God' in contrast to 'the license of affirmation in our Western theology'.[25] Rather, the whole canon of the Bible is absorbed into traditions of landscape painting that make no distinction between the mythical and the historical, and also into contemporary scientific theory that is transforming not only how we understand the world and ourselves, but how we perceive and appropriate things.

Turner painted neither to be liked nor understood, and the 'dark clue' of his later paintings, as Ruskin described his tragic insight, was little understood by his contemporaries. As the individual parts of scattered biblical references in his canvasses disappear in the demands of the whole, so he refuses to allow the Bible to be seen in its specific parts, and therefore denies access to processes of interpretation. Rather, the whole remains, yet as a whole reveals a tendency towards dissolution

25. Matthew Arnold, *Literature and Dogma* (Smith, Elder & Co., 1873), Chapter 1, 'Religion Given'.

that absorbs the individual tendencies of the parts. Unlike, for instance, Rembrandt, to whose biblical art Turner was in many ways indebted,[26] Turner does not paint *from* the Bible but *towards* it, on a surface that refuses to yield a depth of reality—one rarely moves upon the surface colour—but implies a mystery within the physicality of light itself.

Oddly enough, as Auerbach has suggested in his literary reading of Genesis 22, this mystery may return to something very like the biblical text itself, particularly the text of the Old Testament narratives. In Turner's art, the canon of Scripture is released from the formal demands of the authoritative 'canon'. On the one hand, he undercuts a literalist or fundamentalist reading that holds a reading of the Bible in the grip of religious assumptions that never allow it the fluidity that is the very nature of Turner's world of light and colour. On the other hand, the Bible is not subjected to the critical attentions of a historical criticism that tends to reduce it to an accumulation of parts in a historical quest for 'the truth', which the nineteenth century discovered to be elusive and, ultimately, self-destructive. But neither, finally, was Turner's Bible subjected to the Romantic storytelling of, above all, Renan, since for Turner there was no prioritizing, no heroic portraiture, no azure Galilaean skies. There were not even the moral claims made later in the century by Matthew Arnold when, for him, the Bible becomes a literary phenomenon within the cultural experience of the West.

Turner's place in the history of the Bible is strangely unacknowledged. In his last great paintings, he returns our reading of Scripture to the utterly primal experience recorded in Genesis: 'Let there be light'. The light both blinds and reveals in paintings like *The Angel Standing in the Sun* and the two Deluge canvasses, suggesting Scripture grasped momentarily as a whole, yet somehow without form, and therefore open to endless interpretation. When we look straight into the light in this picture, it is not quite clear if we are looking at Judith and Holofernes or Salome and John the Baptist, or even Samson and Delilah. Interpretation of these pictures, and therefore of the Bible itself, emerges not from prior recognition or theological position, but moves towards it in a literal, if vague, refiguring of images. Yet, at the same time, in the flux of creative light, certain images are imposed on the surface of the picture—above all the serpent, often chained, or the figure of Moses writing Scripture itself. The Bible, then, emerges on two levels—the one clearly stated with a pessimism that amounts to

26. See, for example, *Pilate Washing his Hands* (1830).

cynicism; the other suggested through the circle of colour, somehow still present though elusive of all interpretative quests, in the glare of scientific theory, alongside classical mythologies and history, and never yielding to more than the surface of the paint, the text of the picture itself. In Turner, '...il n'y a pas de hors-texte'.[27]

27. Jacques Derrida, *Of Grammatology* (trans. Gayatri Chakravorty-Spivak; Baltimore: The Johns Hopkins University Press, 1976), p.158.

Semiotics in Stained Glass:
Edward Burne-Jones's Song of Songs

Fiona C. Black and J. Cheryl Exum

Working on different projects on the Song of Songs,[1] also known as the Song of Solomon and as Canticles, we were both very interested to discover that there was a stained-glass window depicting the Song at the church of St Helen in nearby Darley Dale.[2] The window was designed by the Pre-Raphaelite artist Edward Burne-Jones.[3] Stained-glass windows in churches have a long history as a medium through which people learned Bible stories and through which artists represented their interpretations of biblical stories in visual form, filling gaps and often compressing the biblical story by including events that take place before or after the scene the window represents. But a *Song of Songs* in stained glass? What sort of Song of Songs was Burne-Jones offering his Victorian, and now twentieth- and almost twenty-first-century, viewers?— literate viewers in contrast to the churchgoers of centuries past, but probably not well-versed in a book as unusual in the Bible as the Song of Songs.[4] How to represent the Song—with its erotic subject, its

---

1. Exum is writing a commentary on the Song of Songs for the Old Testament Library series (Louisville, KY: Westminster/John Knox Press), and Black, a PhD thesis on 'The Grotesque Body in the Song of Songs'.

2. We would like to thank the parish church of St Helen's, and, in particular, the Revd Robert Quarton for patiently arranging our repeated visits to study the window and for permission to reproduce a photograph of it. We are also grateful to Reyahn King of the Birmingham Museums and Art Gallery for allowing us to consult the eight cartoons for the window in the Gallery's collection.

3. The tracery is not of Burne-Jones's creation, but was most likely designed by Philip Webb, whose designs of animals and angels often appear in windows by Morris, Marshall, Faulkner & Co. (or Morris & Co.).

4. The debate over the canonical status of the Song of Songs is well documented; see *m. Yad.* 3.5; *m. 'Ed.* 5.3; *t. Yad.* 2.14; *b. Meg.* 7a; *Cant. R.* 1.1.10; Sid Z. Leiman, *The Canonization of Hebrew Scripture: The Talmudic and Midrashic Evidence* (Transactions of the Connecticut Academy of Arts and Sciences, 47; Hamden: Archon, 1976), pp. 120-26, 132; see also the discussions in Roland M. Murphy, *The*

intimate descriptions of the protagonists' bodies, and its lack of specific religious content—in a stained-glass church window anyway? Our curiosity was naturally piqued; it seemed the ideal topic for a Colloquium dealing with biblical and cultural studies.

Two features of our investigation, in particular, locate it within the wide ambit of cultural studies. One is its interdisciplinary nature, its blurring of the artificial boundaries between the academic study of the biblical text and the reader-oriented interpretation of a modern work of art. The other is its interest in what real people do with cultural artefacts. Burne-Jones is not a theoretical reader, either implied or ideal, but rather a real one, reading within a specific and somewhat elitist Victorian context. His visual representation of the Song of Songs is a *reading*.[5] In discussing it, we are not interested in arguing for some 'correct', 'original' reading of the biblical version and then looking at how Burne-Jones 'got it right' or 'got it wrong'. Instead we want to establish influence in both directions. Whereas biblical studies might conceivably ask how the Bible has influenced Burne-Jones, cultural studies invites us to invert the question and ask how Burne-Jones's window might influence the Song of Songs, that is, our interpretation of it.[6] The simple existence of this article in a volume aimed largely at a biblical studies audience brings Burne-Jones's window into the arena of biblical studies. More important for us is the fact that we will take what we have learned from Burne-Jones into our further work on this text. In writing this essay, we are aware of participating in the same process of hybridization Burne-Jones contributed to when he rendered a biblical book in stained glass for a church setting: we are taking the cultural object he produced (on commission) for a church to produce a different effect in the realm of academic discourse.

In this essay, we want to read the stained-glass window at Darley Dale in the context of Burne-Jones's work, in the context of the source text, the biblical Song of Songs, and as an object of investigation in its own

Song of Songs (Hermeneia; Minneapolis: Fortress Press, 1990), pp. 5-7; Marvin H. Pope, *Song of Songs: A New Translation with Introduction and Commentary* (AB, 7C; Garden City, NY: Doubleday, 1977), pp. 18-19.

5.   Works of art do tell a story; see especially Mieke Bal, *Reading 'Rembrandt': Beyond the Word–Image Opposition* (Cambridge: Cambridge University Press, 1991).

6.   We are reminded of the way David Lodge caricatures this idea in his novel, *Small World*, where he has a character writing a postmodern dissertation on T.S. Eliot's influence on Shakespeare.

right. We propose to read it semiotically, by which we mean viewing it as if, like a text, it has a story to tell. Burne-Jones's window is ideally suited to this kind of investigation. Not only is it sequential (there are 12 panels) but, more importantly, it is already semiotic: each panel is accompanied by a text from the Song, in the King James Version. As a result, we do not have to wonder what scene in the Song a particular panel is meant to represent. Without the textual identification, matching the panels to specific verses of the Song would be a difficult, if not impossible, task. For viewers not familiar with the order of the verses in the source text, however, the sequence in which the panels should be 'read' is not evident, since only the text is provided, but not chapter and verse reference. Even when the sequence is established by identifying the chapter and verse reference for each caption, there are disjunctions, and there will be more than one way of 'reading' the 'story' the window tells, as we will argue below.

Cultural studies emphasizes the subjective and the individual in criticism; it both draws attention to and calls for the engagement of the critic in the process of analysis.[7] While talking about the 'message' of Burne-Jones's stained-glass version of the Song of Songs and about possible responses on the part of viewers in general, we (the authors of this essay) are always in the background as informed readers/viewers seeking to decode the window's potential meanings. This becomes especially clear by the end of the essay, where we talk about the influence of the window on our own biblical scholarship and about what we see as possible wider implications of Burne-Jones's version of the Song for biblical studies.

Edward Burne-Jones and the Window at St Helen's, Darley Dale

St Helen's is a parish church of the Church of England, probably built in the thirteenth century.[8] Its namesake is St Helen, mother of Constantine, who is represented in a small stained-glass window in the south

7.   Some participants in the Colloquium asked us how we went about writing a joint paper. Initially we had planned to pursue two distinct readings, but through writing and discussion came to the common view expressed here. This process was both complex and serendipitous.

8.   Like many English churches, St Helen's has several 'layers' of building. The date for its inception is provided by Nicholas Pevsner (*Derbyshire* [London: Penguin Books, 1953], p. 109), though some claims are made for the church having Norman origins, at least as a worship site (most notably in the existence of a Norman font

transept next to the Burne-Jones window. Burne-Jones's connection with the church came about through Raphael Gillum, the person to whom the window is dedicated.[9] Colonel William James Gillum, Raphael's great-nephew, commissioned the memorial window from Morris, Marshall, Faulkner & Co.[10] in either 1861 or 1862, and Burne-Jones, who was a partner in this firm, completed the designs in 1862.[11] Colonel Gillum had ties with members of the Pre-Raphaelite Brotherhood, in particular Madox Brown[12] and William Morris,[13] and no doubt approached the firm to do the work both because of these connections

and some Norman architectural decoration, the latter now dislodged and displayed in the portico).

9.   The inscription in the corner of the bottom right frame reads, 'In Mem. Raphael Gillum OB [*obiit*] AD 1860. AET [*aetatis*] 90'.

10.   Pevsner attributes the manufacture of the window to Powell & Sons (*Derbyshire*, p. 109), but his information about the window is not overly reliable. Martin Harrison ('Church Decoration and Stained Glass', in Linda Parry [ed.], *William Morris* [London: Philip Wilson Publishers, 1996; published in conjunction with the exhibition, *William Morris 1834–1896*], pp. 106-35 [119]) confirms Morris, Marshall, Faulkner & Co.'s manufacture.

11.   The date of the window has been disputed (see, for example, A. Charles Sewter, *The Stained Glass of William Morris and his Circle* [2 vols.; New Haven: Yale University Press, 1974], II [catalogue], p. 60). Gillum's death marks its creation at least at 1860, but it was likely not finished and installed in that year. Warrington Taylor (business manager of Morris for some time) confirms its date at 1862 (Harrison, 'Church Decoration', p. 119). The cartoons for the window are almost universally attributed to Burne-Jones (Pevsner disagrees; 'Colonel Gillum and the Pre-Raphaelites', *The Burlington Magazine* 95 [1953], pp. 78-81 [81]). It is interesting, however, that in many sources, notably the biography by his wife (Georgiana Burne-Jones, *Memorials of Sir Edward Burne-Jones* [2 vols.; London: Lund Humphries, 1993]), they are never mentioned. Moreover, the window does not appear in the account books in either 1860 or 1862 for either of the firms for which Burne-Jones worked. One source, while maintaining that the cartoons are Burne-Jones's, observes the parallels between at least one of them and Morris's work (Harrison, 'Church Decoration', p. 119). There is, however, enough similarity between the work of both artists and mutual borrowing of ideas and designs, especially within their company, to explain this. Further, the omission of the window in various sources can be explained by the sheer volume of designs that Burne-Jones produced.

12.   Gillum was an amateur painter and took lessons informally from Brown (Pevsner, 'Colonel Gillum', p. 78).

13.   Gillum served on the management committee of the Home for Boys, which was started by Morris, and whose members were enlisted to make some of the products (notably furniture) that Morris designed.

and because of the name it was quickly making for itself in the art world. Colonel Gillum's uncle had mining interests in the area and, though he lived and practised medicine in Bath, must have had some association with Darley Dale, as he and his wife are buried in the churchyard at St Helen's.

Burne-Jones began designing windows in the 1850s for Powell & Sons, but soon transferred his interests when Morris, Marshall, Faulkner & Co. was created in 1861.[14] Though Rossetti and Morris (two of the partners) also designed windows, Burne-Jones quickly became the chief producer for the company, both because of his interest in the medium and his obvious talent for design. In his early days, the windows provided the meat of his living, though even when he became more established, he continued designing them, viewing them as pleasant work which paid the bills. By the end of his life, he had produced hundreds of cartoons for windows.[15]

It is difficult to establish who might be responsible for the subject matter of the window at Darley Dale, since there is no record of Gillum's order and the cartoons are mentioned infrequently in biographies of Burne-Jones and studies of his work. One source has concluded that 'Gillum seems the most likely candidate for having suggested the Song of Solomon theme, a paean to earthly love', because of its unusual nature.[16] But since Burne-Jones usually selected the subjects for his projects, and the subject, earthly love, is entirely appropriate to and even characteristic of his work, it is likely that using the Song of Songs was his idea.[17] In any event, the question is not whether or not the Song of Songs was Burne-Jones's choice, but what aspect of it he might choose to capture in his 12-part series on the book.

It is easy to see from Burne-Jones's paintings that a story of two lovers, separated by difficult circumstances, would have appealed to him. Burne-Jones shared with his Pre-Raphaelite counterparts an interest in the medieval period and its age-old theme of unrequited love. Of

14. Soon to become the better known Morris & Co. in 1874–75 (Ralph Watkinson, *Pre-Raphaelite Art and Design* [London: Studio Vista, 1970], p. 174).

15. Between 1872 and 1878, the high point of his career, he made over 270 cartoons (Sewter, *Stained Glass*, p. 46).

16. Harrison, 'Church Decoration', p. 119.

17. Of course, Burne-Jones might have acted on the customer's orders; some of his earlier work naturally depended on commissions, where the customer specified the subject matter and the medium.

specific interest to the painter, then, was not the uniting of the lovers, but the longing and searching, particularly of the lover for his lady, and his difficulty in finding her.[18] Picture after picture reveals a couple yearning for the impossible, as the viewer knows from the subject of the paintings (*Orpheus and Eurydice, Pyramus and Thisbe, Tristram and Yseult, Phyllis and Demophoön*), or only hints at requited love after desperate seeking (the *Pygmalion* series, *The Briar Rose* series, *King Cophetua and the Beggar Maid, Cupid and Psyche*). A text like the Song of Songs was ideal for Burne-Jones. In it are expressions of longing and seeking and of the frustration of not finding. Burne-Jones gives preference to these aspects of the Song and virtually ignores the text's often explicit references to the uniting of the lovers. The seeking is prolonged for ten frames and finally culminates in a panel showing the couple together at last.

Burne-Jones's attitude towards love may be explained in part by his own life experience, as one might expect. His letters and the biography written by his wife reveal a melancholic man who had anxieties about his health and his success as an artist, parent, husband, and friend. Burne-Jones rarely chose to speak directly on the subject of love, though one or two comments he made are revealing. Jocularity might explain his asking his wife whether, since marriage was like a lottery, it should be outlawed.[19] Other comments, however, suggest a man who realized the impossibility of perfect love and saw marriage as a constant tax from which he sought freedom:

> [I]t is quite possible, and not seldom happens, that people's lives are quite destroyed by what they began in the hope of helping them [i.e. marriage]. There's no getting away from it—it's a constant momentary tax. When one has undertaken to pay house-rent for the remainder of his existence it only comes once a quarter, but in this it's every instant. If people could only get away for a while and have time to think it over, there might often be a chance of recovering ground.[20]

18. Burne-Jones's painting, *Saint Valentine's Morn*, in which a man is outside, looking through the window at his beloved, who is reclining on her couch, is strikingly similar to one of the panels (panel 6) of the window.

19. Burne-Jones, *Memorials*, II, p. 193.

20. Burne-Jones, *Memorials*, II, p. 192. Georgiana explains that this comment is in reference to a model of Burne-Jones's, who was experiencing difficulties in her personal life. Georgiana's view of her marriage and her husband's happiness is, however, heavily slanted, as the omission in her 600-page biography of her husband's six-year affair (among others?) with Mary Zambaco reveals. Burne-Jones referred to this time in his life as the 'desolate years' (Penelope Fitzgerald, *Edward Burne-Jones: A*

Plate 1.   J.M.W. Turner, *Shade and Darkness: The Evening of the Deluge* (1843)
(© Tate Gallery, London)

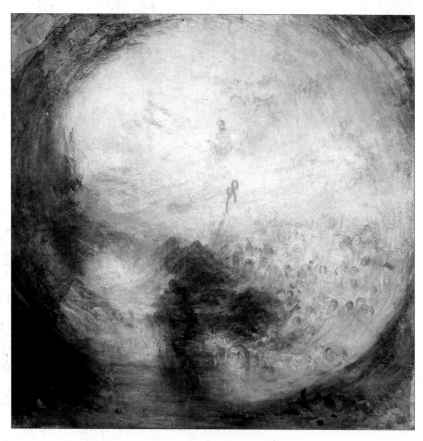

Plate 2.   J.M.W. Turner, *Light and Colour (Goethe's Theory):*
           The Morning after the Deluge (1843)
           (© Tate Gallery, London)

Plate 3. Sir Edward Coley Burne-Jones, 'The Song of Songs which is Solomon's' (stained-glass window at St Helen's Church, Darley Dale, Derbyshire).
Photograph: W. John Lyons

The · watchmen · that · went · a bout · the · city ·
fovnd · me · they · smote · me · they · wovnded · me ·

Plate 4.   Burne-Jones, 'The Song of Song's which is Solomon's', detail (panel 8).
            Photograph: W. John Lyons

Burne-Jones's preference in his work for suggestion over blatant depiction also helps to explain his version of the Song of Songs. Burne-Jones's view of art was that it was not to be didactic, but that it should tell a story in the sense of communicating something of the incommunicable. The objective of art is to please or to exalt, but in depicting subjects that did either or both of these things, Burne-Jones preferred subtlety and suggestion, especially where expression in the face or of the body was concerned. In the matter of love, which is the subject of so much of his work, overt expressions of physicality would have been entirely inappropriate.[21] Physical love in its perfect and complete sense belonged to the realm of the incommunicable (undepictable), and emphasis in art should remain, as in the medieval vision, on the pursuit of love and/or its object rather than fulfilment. Moreover, Burne-Jones could hardly depict in his art the kind of perfect love he could not envision in reality.[22] In the window, the couple's long-awaited union is depicted with a sanitary embrace (she has merely hooked her arm around his), and the final word, the celebration, is not the lovers', but belongs to those who watch them. This is indeed unlike the biblical version of the story. Obviously, in deciding what parts of the Song to represent, Burne-Jones had to be selective. An important question for us is, how does his version of the Song compare with the biblical one?

Biography [London: Michael Joseph, 1975], p. 132).

21. Burne-Jones does depict couples in physical contact, particularly in embrace. It is, however, usually apparent that the embrace is imperfect—about to end because it is unable to be sustained—as bodies twisting away or pathetic expressions show.

22. In discussion of the *Briar Rose* (Sleeping Beauty) paintings, notably the last in the series, he says, 'I want it to stop with the Princess asleep and tell no more, to leave all the afterwards to the invention and imagination of the people, and tell them no more' (Burne-Jones, *Memorials*, II, p. 195). He also says, on getting the thorns right in this painting, '... and now my honour will be saved, and the sleeping beauty's honour, which is of more account' (*Memorials*, II, p. 145). In these two statements, we see both the medieval idea of the pursuit of a lady (notably, in protecting a lady's honour) and the understanding that the consummation of that pursuit is not for the realm of his art but beyond it.

The Source Text, the Biblical Song of Songs

We said above that we want to read Burne-Jones's Song of Songs in the context of the source text. But since influence works in both directions, we also want to read the biblical Song of Songs in the context of the window, asking how Burne-Jones's version might lead us to consider new and different ways of viewing the source text. Related problems of 'reading' bring certain issues to the forefront of interpretation of both source text and metatext. Crucial issues in the interpretation of the source text—the question of unity and the related question of plot—are also key issues in reading the window, and this is surely not fortuitous. Is the source text of one piece? And what is it about?

The unity of the biblical Song of Songs is a subject on which there is no consensus, and probably never will be. Some commentators see the Song as a loose collection of poems arranged in no particular order.[23] Those who see the Song as an artistic unity (either compositional or redactional) do not agree on the number or extent of the individual songs that comprise it.[24] The problem with formalistic approaches that find evidence of a conscious poetic design in the strategic repetitions of key words, motifs, and in other formal patterns, such as chiasmus and inclusio, is that there is no end to the number of formal features one

---

23. E.g. Pope, *Song of Songs*, p. 54; Wilhelm Rudolph, *Das Buch Ruth, Das Hohe Lied, Die Klagelieder* (KAT, 17; Gütersloh: Gerd Mohn, 1962), pp. 98-100; Oswald Loretz, *Gotteswort und menschliche Erfahrung: Eine Auslegung der Bücher Jona, Rut, Hoheslied und Qohelet* (Freiburg: Herder, 1963), p. 75; Gillis Gerleman, *Ruth, Das Hohelied* (Neukirchen–Vluyn: Neukirchener Verlag, 1965), p. 59; Robert Gordis, *The Song of Songs and Lamentations* (rev. and augmented edn; New York: Ktav, 1974), pp. 16-18; Marcia Falk, *Love Lyrics from the Bible: A Translation and Literary Study of the Song of Songs* (Sheffield: Almond Press, 1982), pp. 66-67; John G. Snaith, *The Song of Songs* (New Century Bible Commentary; Grand Rapids: Eerdmans, 1993), pp. 6-8; Athalya Brenner, *The Song of Songs* (OTG; Sheffield: JSOT Press, 1989), p. 39.

24. For the argument that the Song is composed of six poems (1.2–2.6; 2.7–3.5; 3.6–5.1; 5.2–6.3; 6.4–8.3; and 8.4-14) in which the first and last form a frame within which the second, third, fourth, and fifth appear in an ABA´B´ pattern, see J. Cheryl Exum, 'A Literary and Structural Analysis of the Song of Songs', *ZAW* 85 (1973), pp. 47-79. Cf. the studies of William H. Shea, 'The Chiastic Structure of the Song of Songs', *ZAW* 92 (1980), pp. 378-95; Edwin C. Webster, 'Pattern in the Song of Songs', *JSOT* 22 (1982), pp. 73-93; Francis Landy, *Paradoxes of Paradise: Identity and Difference in the Song of Songs* (Sheffield: Almond Press, 1983), pp. 33-57.

could isolate and find meaningful. (Thus different readers will rely on different formal features to isolate different poems.)[25] Another limitation of the formalistic approach is that it fails to consider what difference poetic structure and unity, or lack of them, make to the reading process. Can real readers perceive the formal intricacies—the chiasms, inclusios, and other complex structures—that scholars find in the Song? Perhaps on a subliminal level, the way we perceive the structural intricacies of a musical composition even if we cannot read the score. What readers will certainly recognize, however, is the presence of repetition. Our awareness that the Song repeats both longer and shorter poetic units, that it keeps returning to the same themes, discourages us from seeking a clearly developed plot. There have, to be sure, been dramatic theories of the Song, but they falter on this very issue of plot, which they inevitably must provide from outside the textual world.[26] The Song is a poetic text of great lyrical power and beauty, which is not lost on readers, even in translation. When we read poetry, we revel in words and images; we normally do not expect the kind of linear unfolding of events that produces a plot. The poetic movement of the Song, ever forward and then returning to itself, reflects the repetitive pattern of seeking and finding in which the lovers engage, which is the basic pattern of sexual love: longing–satisfaction–renewed longing–and so on. There may be artistic unity, but there is no real plot.

Or is there? In creative tension with the recognition that the Song unfolds repetitively and not linearly is the powerful readerly tendency to read sequentially and to make sense of a literary work as a whole; in other words, to read for the plot.[27] When we read a biblical 'book' like

25. Interestingly, where the Song is concerned, structural studies have not tended to go so far as most formalistic analyses of biblical texts in seeing form as semantically meaningful; that is, in making claims about the *meaning* of the Song based on its formal features. We suspect the poetic nature of the Song, discussed below, is what inhibits this process.

26. E.g. Franz Delitzsch, *Commentary on the Song of Songs and Ecclesiastes* (trans. M.G. Easton; Grand Rapids: Eerdmans, n.d.); Leroy Waterman, *The Song of Songs, Translated and Interpreted as a Dramatic Poem* (Ann Arbor: University of Michigan Press, 1948); Arvid Bruno, *Das Hohe Lied, Das Buch Hiob: Ein rhythmische und textkritische Untersuchung nebst einer Einführung in das Hohe Lied* (Stockholm: Almqvist & Wiksell, 1956); Michael D. Goulder, *The Song of Fourteen Songs* (JSOTSup, 36; Sheffield: JSOT Press, 1986).

27. See Peter Brooks, *Reading for the Plot: Design and Intention in Narrative* (New York: Random House, 1984).

the Song, we typically start at the beginning and read through to the end. We are unlikely to say to ourselves, 'I am reading fragments with no connections'; rather we naturalize events in such a way as to fit them into our understanding of the way the world works, either the real world or the fictional world of the text.[28] We create connections as we read, revising them, abandoning them and adopting others when necessary. We tend, for example, to think that the protagonists are the same two people throughout the Song. We can create a plot of sorts, revolving around the lovers' success at overcoming the obstacles that keep them apart.

The questions of the Song's unity and its structure are different, though they are related. A structure may be created from originally unrelated poems because of similarity of theme, key words, and other common features. Unity is created when we posit the same protagonists, and, further, when we relate all the experiences described in the Song to these protagonists. It makes a decisive difference for interpretation whether one sees the Song as a collection of unrelated love poems, featuring different protagonists and exhibiting different attitudes toward love, or as a unity in which the protagonists and their love for each other remain the same throughout. Without minimizing the vastly different conclusions they lead to, we would argue for the validity of both views of the Song as against the necessity of choosing one. In our opinion, both interpretive paths need to be followed because, like the proverbial mountain that needs to be climbed, they are there. It is not a question of which is the right reading procedure, since both are well established.[29]

In this essay, we are using the source text as an analogy to the window, for inherent and inherited questions of unity and plot, even if a different unity and plot, reappear in Burne-Jones's window, where the

28. See Jonathan Culler, *Structuralist Poetics: Structuralism, Linguistics, and the Study of Literature* (Ithaca, NY: Cornell University Press, 1975), p. 146 and *passim*.

29. One of the other poetical books of the Bible, Psalms, offers an interesting analogy. It is generally regarded as an anthology, but it also has a literary design, an artistic structure, that is closely bound up with its theological message; see Frank-Lothar Hossfeld and Erich Zenger, *Die Psalmen: Psalm 1–50* (NEB, 29; Würzburg: Echter Verlag, 1993); Matthias Millard, *Die Komposition des Psalters: Ein formgeschichtlicher Ansatz* (FAT, 9; Tübingen: Mohr Siebeck, 1994); see also the discussion among Hossfeld and Zenger, Millard, and Rendtorff in *BibInt* 4 (1996). On the one hand, people can and do start reading the Psalter anywhere, and at random. On the other, we can read it sequentially, looking for connections and finding them.

individual frames are analogous to the individual poems of the source
text. One could say that there is no pattern to the window, but leaving
the frames to stand alone is very much like leaving the individual poems
of the biblical Song to stand alone. In our opinion, this is unsatisfactory
because it never allows the reader or viewer to gain an appreciation of
the whole as something greater than the sum of its parts.

Even if Burne-Jones was not working from a unified source text, one
could argue that he has created a unified work out of it. Burne-Jones's
selection of verses from the source text is not haphazard; it is clear from
the scenes he has chosen that he did not open the Bible and put his
finger randomly on verses of the Song of Songs which he then represented. As we shall see, most of his panels come from the two dream
sequences in Song 3.1-5 and 5.2–6.3, and this has serious implications
for the kind of Song of Songs he gives us. Nevertheless, it remains the
case that the structure of his Song of Songs is not immediately apparent,
and thus the window poses for us similar questions about how to read
the work as a whole as the source text posed. The window is a unity in
a sense that the source text is not, for Burne-Jones gives us the same
protagonists throughout. The woman and man are fair-haired in all of
the frames; she wears a white night-dress and a red or green outer garment in many of them; he wears a crown, and in two of the four panels
in which he appears he is wearing the same royal robes and sports red
boots (all medieval attire).[30] The situation would be entirely different if,
for example, some of the panels showed a black-haired protagonist and
some a blonde or redhead. The window also has a pattern in that the
order of the frames is not entirely arbitrary; some of them represent
contiguous events in the source text. But like the source text, the window does not unfold in a strictly linear fashion. Whereas some of the
frames follow the order of the source text, others disrupt it. What is
most arbitrary, of course, is the selection of scenes represented. What
kind of Song of Songs does this particular selection of parts make?

Burne-Jones's Song of Songs

Following the title of the book in the King James Version, which is a
direct translation of the Hebrew, Burne-Jones titles each column of his

---

30. Other features add to this unity: the background of a red fence appears in
three panels and grey brickwork is present in almost all of the frames; the panels are
separated and surrounded by writing that is consistent in style.

window, 'The Song of Songs Wh[ich] Is Solomon's'.[31] This heading serves to make Solomon, as he is sometimes thought to be, the male protagonist of the Song. He wears a crown, symbol of his royal status, in all frames in which he appears. The final frame announces the marriage of the couple by means of the citation from Song 3.11 about Solomon's wedding. Each column has four panels arranged in tiers,[32] with the following citations from the biblical text (Plate 3):

1. As the apple tree among the trees of the wood so is my beloved among the sons [= Song 2.3]

2. My mother's children were angry with me they made me keeper of the vineyards [= Song 1.6]

3. Behold he standeth behind our wall he looketh forth at the windows shewing himself through the lattice [= Song 2.9]

4. By night on my bed I sought him whom my soul loveth I sought him but I found him not [= Song 3.1]

5. I charge you O daughters of Jerusalem if ye find my beloved that ye tell him that I am sick of love [= Song 5.8]

6. I sleep but my heart waketh It is the voice of my beloved that knocketh [= Song 5.2]

7. I opened to my beloved but my beloved had withdrawn himself and was gone [= Song 5.6]

8. The watchmen that went about the city found me they smote me they wounded me [= Song 5.7]

9. As the lily among thorns so is my love among the daughters [= Song 2.2]

10. Whither is thy beloved gone O thou fairest among women [= Song 6.1]

11. Who is this that cometh up from the wilderness leaning upon her beloved [= Song 8.5]

12. Go forth O ye daughters of Zion and behold King Solomon [= Song 3.11]

31. Literally, 'the song of songs which is to/for Solomon', and not evidence of Solomonic authorship. The ascription of authorship of the Song is a traditional one; legend has it that Solomon wrote the Song when he was a young man, because young men's thoughts are about love; he wrote Proverbs in middle age, when practical thoughts occupied him; and he wrote Ecclesiastes as an old man, when he was disillusioned with life.

32. The window is described in Sewter (*Stained Glass*, p. 60) as '3 lts [lights] and tracery, each main lt with 4 panels arranged in tiers'; this is also the arrangement that follows most closely the sequence of the biblical text.

The panels that are out of textual sequence are the top three panels and the 'last' (bottom right) one (panels 1, 5, 9 and 12). The left and right top panels (1 and 9) are clearly companion pieces. They share a couplet of the biblical text, in which she praises him and he praises her in kind: 'As the apple tree among the trees of the wood, so is my beloved among the sons' / 'As the lily among thorns so is my love among the daughters'. Apple trees appear in the frame with him and she is surrounded by lilies and holding a lily in her hand.[33] The figures are facing each other (even if they are not looking at each other),[34] representing visually their antiphonal responses in the biblical version. The last panel (12), referring as it does to the couple's marriage, makes an appropriate closure to the story the window tells. Interestingly, some commentators who have rearranged the Song also put ch. 3, about Solomon's wedding, at the end in order to have what they consider a suitable ending.[35]

The top middle panel, addressing the daughters of Jerusalem (panel 5), plays a distinct role. It fits the 'plot' sequence we will discuss below, but is actually out of sequence when compared to the source text. Its position in the top row is especially appropriate, however, for the result is that all the speaking characters of the source text are represented in the top row of panels: the woman, the man, and the daughters of Jerusalem.[36] The top middle panel is also noteworthy because it is identical with the last panel, a panel also out of textual sequence.

What 'story' emerges if we read the panels of the window roughly

33. In the source text the man and the woman are also associated with gazelles and doves. Burne-Jones has also utilized these descriptions: above Solomon in panel 1, there is a gazelle gazing through a window, an activity associated with the male lover (panels 3 and 6), and above the woman in panel 9, a dove rests on a branch. Two crowns, one on top of the other appear over the middle panel 5, symbolizing the royal status of the couple, both of whom are wearing crowns in frames 1 and 9.

34. And they are separated by a panel depicting the daughters of Jerusalem; see below.

35. See, for example, J. Angénieux, 'Le cantique des cantiques en huit chants à refrains alternants', *ETL* 44 (1968), pp. 87-140 (107); Helmut Schmökel, *Heilige Hochzeit und Hoheslied: Abhandlungen für die Kunde des Morgenlandes*, as cited in Pope, *Song of Songs*, pp. 42-44.

36. Some commentators assign a speaking part in Song 8.8-9 to the woman's brothers, but there is no need to posit another speaking voice; see Exum, 'Literary and Structural Analysis', pp. 75-76. The woman, the man and the daughters of Jerusalem are certainly the major characters.

following the order suggested by the textual citations? In panel 1, Solomon, wearing his crown and royal robes, is writing in a book, perhaps composing the Song of Solomon. It is his book, but it is in her voice. Just as her voice predominates in the source text, so in the window frames all the words are hers except in the last four frames (possibly three, if we ascribe the words of Song 3.11, beneath the last frame, to her).

In panel 2, she begins her tale. This panel is an amusingly inaccurate rendition of the source text. No doubt the misunderstanding came about from the King James translation of Hebrew $b^e n\hat{e}$ as 'children' and not sons.[37] The result is a picture of three women that looks more like Cinderella and her two ugly stepsisters than a woman whose 'mother's sons' respond to her in heated emotion (Song 1.6).[38] Moreover, in the source text the brothers make the woman a keeper of vineyards—strenuous, outdoor, 'manly' work—but here she is using a wine-press in a domestic scene. The bare feet are a nice touch, befitting the Cinderella image. Indeed, we think this frame encourages viewers to expect a Cinderella plot line: fair young woman persecuted by cruel stepsisters will, after some difficulty, find her kingly prince and live happily ever after, as the final frames might suggest. The sisters do not show up again as the obstacle to the heroine's happiness, for they play no role in the source text, but they have served to alert the viewer that true love's realization will not be easy.

Panels 3 and 4 look as if they might represent the same moment in time. In panel 3, Solomon looks in the woman's window, while in panel 4, she seems to be listening to him. But the text accompanying panel 4 tells us otherwise: she cannot find him, and so this must be a different occasion. In panel 5, therefore, she enlists the aid of the daughters of Jerusalem, adjuring them, if they find him, to tell him of her desire (we think viewers will recognize that 'sick of love' is archaic language for 'lovesick' and does not mean that she is fed up with the

37. $b^e n\hat{e}$ can refer to children in general (e.g. $b^e n\hat{e}$ $yi\acute{s}r\bar{a}'\bar{e}l$ = the Israelites, or, as the KJV has it, 'children of Israel') and not just sons, but in a case like this, where there is no warrant for taking it as a reference to such a mixed group, we should understand it in its most natural sense as 'brothers'. It is noteworthy, however, that she calls them 'mother's sons' and not 'brothers' (the father is absent, and brothers are referred to by means of a circumlocution).

38. The precise meaning of the Hebrew in 1.6 is obscure. Do they burn in anger or with desire?

whole thing). Though panel 5 is out of textual sequence, it fits well between panels 4 and 6, for it is part of an account that begins with the woman in her bed, seeking her lover. There are two such accounts, commonly referred to as 'dream sequences', in the source text, one in Song 3.1-5 and the other in Song 5.2–6.3. In the source text, the verse cited in panel 5 (Song 5.8) belongs to the second dream sequence. If the textual order were followed, panel 5, citing Song 5.8, would appear after panel 8, which cites Song 5.7. Burne-Jones has moved it between the two dream sequences (panel 4 from the first, 3.1, and panel 6 from the second, 5.2), in effect compressing the two dream sequences of the source text into one.

So the bedroom scene of desire continues in panel 6. The compression of the two dream sequences is further served by the white nightdress the woman wears in frames 4 and 6 (also 10). From a perspective inside the room, we see Solomon peeking through a window in the door (which makes this scene the reverse of panel 3, where he is peeking through the lattice, and our perspective is from outside, with him, and not inside, with her). The peeking man and the listening woman of panels 3 and 4 are brought together in this panel. This time she responds because she actually has heard him seeking her. But when she opens the door in the next panel, he is gone. When she goes out in the city to seek him, she is found and attacked by the watchmen, of whom only one is shown (panel 8). The entire middle column of panels derives from the dream sequence in Song 5.2–6.3, and it is continued in the next column in panel 10.[39]

> I sleep but my heart waketh; it is the voice of my beloved that knocketh, 5.2 (panel 6);
> I opened to my beloved but my beloved had withdrawn himself and was gone, 5.6 (panel 7);
> The watchmen that went about the city found me; they smote me, they wounded me, 5.7 (panel 8);
> I charge you, O daughters of Jerusalem, if ye find my beloved that ye tell him that I am sick of love, 5.8 (panel 5);
> Whither is thy beloved gone, O thou fairest among women?, 6.1 (panel 10).

39. Following Exum, 'Literary and Structural Analysis', pp. 50-53, we take 6.1 as part of the dialogue between the woman and the daughters of Jerusalem in 5.2–6.3.

In panel 10 the woman is wearing her nightdress without her robe (which the source text tells us the watchmen took from her, Song 5.7). As in panel 8, she is crouched on the ground and her arm is raised; only here her raised hand pulls at the skirt of one of the women before whom she kneels in an attitude of supplication. In the source text, the daughters of Jerusalem offer to help the woman in her search, but their offer is left out in the citation under this scene in the window, which leaves open the question of the role of these women in Burne-Jones's version. Are they likely to become helpful companions in the woman's search for her lover, or do they do no more than offer sympathy? There is a kind of balance between this panel and panel 2, the panel occupying the corresponding position in the first column: in these two panels, the woman appears with other women, whereas elsewhere she is either alone or pictured with Solomon.[40] In panel 2, the other women are hostile ('my mother's children were angry with me; they made me keeper of the vineyards'). Is panel 10 meant to represent a sympathetic group of women as a counterbalance to the mean sisters (this is, after all, not the first time that the daughters of Jerusalem are called on)? Or are these other women, since they do not offer to further love's cause, more like the sisters than not?[41] Depending on how we choose to interpret the scene, panel 10 can either be a positive step in the right direction (preparing for panel 11, the uniting of the couple), since the group of women will help in the search, or it can represent a dead end (leaving

40. It is also possible that some viewers will identify one of these five women (probably the centre one) as the female protagonist herself, as in, for example, Dante Gabriel Rossetti's painting, *The Beloved*, where the protagonist is featured at the centre of a group of women who are most likely the daughters of Jerusalem. The identification of the protagonist as one of the daughters would give rise to other interpretive possibilities for the window. For example, if the female lover appears in the last panel, then she has the last look and her presence in the final panel balances Solomon's in the first panel. In panel 5, she could be among the women she is addressing in the caption, in which case the daughters would no longer be separating the couple, as we argue below.

41. In looking at the window we could not decide from the body language and expressions of the three women whether the panel depicts a group disposed to help or to hinder; in particular, the woman in red on the left seemed to us to be scowling, although her arm is outstretched. In the cartoon for this panel, however, her expression appears sympathetic. With few exceptions, the facial expressions of the figures in the window—and especially of the daughters of Jerusalem in panels 5 and 12—are rather nondescript. Burne-Jones was criticized for overly stylizing his subjects, particularly their expressions.

the Cinderella story to continue, with the unhelpful daughters, like the stepsisters in the corresponding panel 2 and the watchman in panel 8, presenting obstacles in the path to true love).

The two final scenes suggest—rather demurely—the sought-after union of the lovers. The first (panel 11) shows the woman, also wearing a crown, walking arm in arm with Solomon. In this panel the woman is finally permitted one moment of contact (though it is barely that) with her lover. Burne-Jones does not depict the culmination of her longing in any kind of amorous posture, neither does he select anything from the source text that might reveal her joy at being united with Solomon (such as, 'I am my beloved's and my beloved is mine'). According to the window, the couple's longed-for union will be achieved through a marriage that is very much in the public eye, as the next and final panel underscores. The last citation from the source text in the window alludes to the marriage ('Go forth, O ye daughters of Zion, and behold King Solomon'); in the source text it is followed by the words, 'with the crown with which his mother crowned him on the day of his wedding, on the day of the gladness of his heart' (Song 3.11).[42] But instead of giving us Solomon and his bride, Burne-Jones's last panel depicts the daughters of Zion, who are exhorted to be onlookers, to 'behold King Solomon', doubtless in celebration of the happy event. (Zion is another name for Jerusalem, and we saw these women before in panel 5.)

The daughters play instruments, and presumably look upon the king, but where are the lovers, and, in particular, where has the woman gone?[43] Her voice, so dominant in most of the story, is now silent (or directs attention away from itself, if she is the speaker of these final words). The subject of the daughters' attention is the king, bringing the viewer back full circle to panel 1, to Solomon, to his book, and, once again, to her narration.

---

42. The two final panels (and thus probably also the marriage in Burne-Jones's mind) are connected by means of the phrase, 'who is this coming up from the wilderness', which appears in Song 8.5 in reference to the woman, and in Song 3.6 (where Solomon's wedding day is described), possibly also in reference to the woman (see Exum, 'Literary and Structural Analysis', p. 65 and n. 50).

43. It is possible that Burne-Jones had in mind giving the couple a private moment, and thus in the final panel he has the viewers look away and view the daughters instead. But in that case, it seems strange that he would call upon the daughters to look. The difference between what seems to be represented in the window and what is actually represented comes up again in panel 8, the woman and the watchman (see below).

As in the source text, the window seems to focus on the woman. She appears in eight panels, and the words are all hers except those of the final panels (9, 10, 11 and possibly 12). Solomon speaks only once (panel 9) and appears in only four frames. He is as elusive a lover in the window as in the biblical text. Yet it is Solomon who first appears and he who is last spoken of, as if the story was never the woman's to begin with. Moreover, he is the object of panels in which he is not actually depicted: in panel 4, the woman listens for him; in panel 5, she pleads for a message to be given to him; in panel 7, she looks for him; in panel 10, the woman is asked about him; and in panel 12, the daughters are told to look upon him. By appearance or implication, then, he makes his presence known in 9 out of 12 panels. Even the companion panels 1 and 9 reverse the textual order of Song 2.2 and 2.3 in order to foreground him. Is the window thus her story or his? On this point, Burne-Jones's Song of Songs is as complex and challenging as the biblical version, where the question of whether the text gives expression to a male or a female voice (or both) has only recently become a pressing one, with significant implications for interpretation.[44]

What should we make of Burne-Jones's visual presentation of textual events? As we indicated above, his selection of material is not haphazard. He has consistently chosen to represent encounters sought but missed. What he gives us is a Song of Songs marked by frustration, by seeking but not finding, with what may be read as a happy ending attached. Out of a biblical book arguably devoted to mutual desire, he has included the only unambiguously negative elements, the anger of the 'mother's children' (1.6) and the beating of the woman by the watchmen (5.7). Omitted are the *waṣfs* (the descriptions of the lovers' bodies from head to foot or foot to head) and the veiled descriptions of and allusions to sexual intercourse that appear scattered throughout the biblical Song. Of the many words of praise and mutual devotion spoken by the lovers, Burne-Jones has used only the one couplet, 2.2-3, for the captions to panels 1 and 9, and, with the exception of the 'portraits' of the lovers in these panels, he has not used any parts of the source text that do not tell a story. He concentrates on the dream sequences (Song 3.1-5; 5.2-8), which have more of a plot line than any other parts of the biblical Song. The dream sequences, moreover, are the very parts of the biblical Song

44. See Athalya Brenner and Fokkelien van Dijk-Hemmes, *On Gendering Texts: Female and Male Voices in the Hebrew Bible* (Biblical Interpretation Series, 1; Leiden: E.J. Brill, 1993), pp. 72-81.

that describe in some detail the search for the elusive lover, a recurrent theme in Burne-Jones's work.

Given his preference for the medieval vision of love, with its emphasis on seeking and longing rather than finding, it is easy to see why these parts of the source text so appealed to Burne-Jones that he forged out of them a (more or less loose) plot by compressing the dream sequences into one long and difficult search (seven panels out of twelve) that finally ends in union. Burne-Jones has replaced the source text's ambiguous ending, 'Flee, my love!' (8.14), with the marriage of Solomon in ch. 3, though only if one knows the source text will the reference to marriage in the final panel be evident. The happiness of the ending seems forced, again in keeping with the theme of many of Burne-Jones's paintings.

Any Way You Look at It

The reading of the window we have offered follows a particular order, one suggested by the order of citations as they appear in the source text. Indeed, we relied on the source text to fill 'gaps' in the window's story; for example, it was our knowledge of the source text that enabled us to recognize the allusion to marriage in the final frame. As we noted above, however, the window does not strictly follow the order of the source text; Burne-Jones's 'plot', such as it is, is not that of the biblical Song of Songs. Our reading, then, was not simply informed by the source text; it also accommodated Burne-Jones's rearrangement of the source text, with one exception, panel 9 ('As the lily among thorns, so is my love among the daughters', Song 2.2). To produce a plot by reading the frames consecutively, we had to 'skip' this frame—to skip it as contributing to the plot, but not to ignore it: we viewed it as part of a different pattern, a kind of framing device or superscription at the top of the window, where it clearly forms a companion piece to the first panel ('As the apple tree among the trees of the wood, so is my beloved among the sons', Song 2.3).

To read the top panels across (as presenting the main characters of the source text: the man, the daughters of Jerusalem, and the woman) and, at the same time, to incorporate two of them in our sequential reading for the plot is a rather sophisticated readerly manoeuvre, and not one that will necessarily occur to most viewers. Our reading is clearly an educated, or competent, one. We approached the window from the outset as viewers well versed in the source text and as viewers motivated by a desire to find a plot. Because the window is sequential and textual, it invites viewers to read it as a story, and we found the invitation irresistible.

But what of viewers, probably the majority, who do not know the source text and who do not read the panels in the sequence we described?[45] There will surely be viewers who see no connections between some of the panels, who decide there is no plot, or only the loosest of plots. It is likely, we think, that viewers will see some connection between panels 3, 4, 6 and 7, where the man is at the woman's lattice or door and she listens and opens the door for him. But the relation of these to the beating scene in panel 8 may not be readily apparent, and panel 10, where a group of women ask the woman 'whither is thy beloved gone', actually provides a better sequel to panel 7, where the woman reports that her 'beloved had withdrawn himself and was gone'. Will viewers recognize the group of women in panel 10 as the daughters of Zion or Jerusalem (the speakers of these lines in the source text)? The group is made up of only three women, whereas the panels in which the daughters are addressed depict five women, and they appear in the same stereotyped pose.

Especially interesting to us is the fact that, without a knowledge of the source text, viewers are unlikely to recognize that the bottom right panel refers to Solomon's marriage. They may, of course, decide that a marriage has taken place on the basis of panel 11, the one frame in which the lovers, both wearing crowns, appear together. But given the position of this panel, it would be hard to take marriage as closure, since the last panel, with its dedicatory inscription, is about the daughters of Zion/Jerusalem and Solomon.

Viewers not familiar with the source text may find it difficult to piece together a story with a clearly developed plot simply on the basis of Burne-Jones's window, but, in our opinion, no matter how you look at it, the overall impression the window gives is that the path to love is

---

45. Since the textual citations are available to anyone who studies the window closely, we are not considering here how the window might be perceived by viewers who only look but do not read the text. It should be noted, however, that viewers of the window in St Helen's may have difficulty reading the accompanying text unless they come quite close to the window to study it. It is not especially easy to decipher the writing from many vantage points in the church.

strewn with obstacles.[46] As is the case with many of his paintings, most of Burne-Jones's panels represent the search for the elusive object of desire, the quest but not the attainment. If we consider the panels individually, exactly half of them depict seeking or unfulfilled desire (3, 4, 5, 6, 7, 10). The man seeks entry to the woman's chamber but never succeeds (3, 6); she listens for him (4, 6), opens the door to find that he has gone (7), appeals to the daughters of Jerusalem, if they find him, to tell him of her desire (5), and even undergoes a beating in her search for him (8). Two panels are not simply about the unattainability of true love but go further to portray the desiring subject as the object of anger or abuse (2 and 8). There are only a few scenes where it could be said that love is satisfied. In two of the panels (1 and 9) the lovers, seemingly at peace, engage in mutual praise. They are united in only one panel (11), however. The daughters of Jerusalem, and not either of the lovers, are depicted in two panels (5 and 12). If the window were a celebration of love, as readers conclude almost unanimously about the source text, we might expect the couple to be together in more panels.

Readers not guided by the source text in ordering the panels might draw connections between frames that appear to address each other. For example, in both frames 1 and 9 and 3 and 7, the lovers, though they are not together, are facing each other. Frame 3 shows Solomon at the lattice, and frame 7 has the woman opening the door as if to welcome him, only to find the darkness of the night. The impression of an encounter missed that we get here typifies the experience of reading the whole. The top left and right panels (1 and 9), which we have already described as companion pieces, both look and sound as if they should be read in conjunction. The lovers recite each other's praises and each is turned in the direction of the other, but between them, keeping them apart forever in the fixity of stained glass, are the daughters of Jerusalem. One might presume that the woman talks of being 'lovesick' in the citation to this frame because the daughters separate her from her lover. Here too we have reason to wonder about the role of the daughters in Burne-Jones's version: are they sympathetic to the lovers or an obstacle to love's fulfilment? The daughters of Jerusalem have a way of intruding, ever so delicately, either on our reading or on the couple's union: at the beginning, if one considers the top row (panels 1, 5 and 9), by separating the couple, and at the end, where the happy couple, united at

---

46. The situation with the source text is similar: readers may not agree about its unity and plot but recognize that the parts deal with the same subject matter, love.

last (panel 11), yields the position of honour in the window to those pesky daughters (panel 12, with the mention of Solomon's name, as we noted above, also serving to bring viewers back, full circle, to the first frame).

Burne-Jones's Song of Songs in stained glass is, like the text upon which it is based, a complex artistic creation, and we could not hope to exhaust the possibilities of 'reading' it. Other viewers will undoubtedly see things we have not noticed. There is one other way of reading a work like this we would like to discuss, however, not only because we think it is a fairly common one but also because it led us to unexpected conclusions about how to read the source text. Some viewers may be drawn to interpret the whole window in the light of one of its parts. Looking at the window as a whole without trying to establish its semiotic integrity, a viewer may be struck by a specific panel, finding in it the key to the whole, even to the extent of ignoring or underplaying other panels.[47] For example, a viewer might be drawn to panel 11, where the couple appear together as king and queen, and decide that the window's story concludes happily in marriage, a suitable Victorian ending, and that the window is therefore a paean to love. There may be vicissitudes, but they are not really serious, since all ends well. This is Solomon's song, as the three superscriptions inform us, and he and his queen, standing imposingly in the top corners, inspire confidence in their tranquillity. Another reading in the light of one particular panel could take us in a very different direction, however, and this is what happened to us.

What We'd Rather Not See

By far the most disturbing image in the window is that of panel 8, where the woman is beaten by the watchman (Plate 4). This panel arrests attention both by virtue of its position in the centre of the bottom row,[48] and because its dynamic quality and violent nature contrast

---

47. It also happens in the reading process that readers will find one aspect of a story so significant that they will use it as their key to understanding the whole, unless convinced otherwise by the story's development or by competing interpretations.

48. The window is located in a small chapel in the south transept, which does not currently have any pews or chairs in front of it. When viewers stand or kneel in front of it, their eyes are likely to rest comfortably on the bottom row.

sharply with the panels around it. The watchman's figure is larger in size than the figures in the surrounding panels, and this makes the panel seem closer to the viewer.[49] The image is a surprising picture to find in its ecclesiastical context and for this reason, too, it holds the viewer's attention.[50]

For some, the panel might be the first impression they get of the window. Who is this woman? Why is she being attacked? If this panel stood alone, viewers would have difficulty identifying it as part of any well-known biblical story. Stained-glass windows might represent biblical stories of violence or struggle, such as Cain and Abel in conflict, or Jacob wrestling with the angel, but this picture of a man attacking a woman is difficult to negotiate. In context, however, the frame can be satisfactorily accounted for and viewers may thus find its presence less troubling (or possibly even see the event as justified). But the violence does not go away.

Interestingly this panel, in which we witness a beating, is one of the few in which Solomon is neither pictured nor spoken about.[51] But although this may distance him from the violence, it does not absolve him of responsibility for it. Viewers well versed in the source text will know that the watchmen find the woman because she is out in the streets looking for her lover; other viewers will have to supply this connection.

Why would Burne-Jones incorporate this piece? If an artist wanted to capture some of the beauty and emotional appeal of the book, the beating would doubtless be a part of the text to leave out. Perhaps it is Burne-Jones's greatest example of the trials of true love, the climax of the seeking before the denouement of the finding and union. Or perhaps it marks for him a measure of the risk and pain of loving.

Whereas Burne-Jones obviously felt that the inclusion of the beating was important to his story, it seems either that he was not entirely

49. The woman's figure is also large, but she is crouched on the ground, and thus the watchman looks larger than she is.

50. Many of the frames are unusual—a woman in bed, a man looking through her window—but this makes an especially startling impression because of its violent nature.

51. The other two are panel 9, where Solomon is apparently the speaker of the accompanying text, and panel 2, the only other scene representing hostility toward the woman.

comfortable with it or that he did not feel he could represent it explicitly. The citation under the picture, 'they smote me, they wounded me', is far more severe than what the panel actually shows. The woman lies crouched in a defensive position, but the watchman leaning over her is not delivering any blows. He grabs her wrist with his left hand and shines in her face a lantern, which he holds with his right. The visual impact of the clenched fist pointed at the woman's face is so strong that viewers at first might not recognize the lantern for what it is, and thus take the scene as more violent than it is.[52] But the fact is, Burne-Jones's watchman cannot beat the woman without either letting go of her or putting down the lantern. So Burne-Jones has both drawn attention to the beating exactly as it is mentioned in the source text (he could easily have omitted the words, 'they smote me, they wounded me'), and toned it down by making it difficult for his watchman to carry it out. We could ask, at what point does Burne-Jones capture the scene? Has the beating already happened, and now the watchman hoists his victim to her feet, inspecting the effects of his rough treatment? Or is the beating about to happen now that he has pushed her to the ground? Burne-Jones's inclusion of the scene is problematic in itself, but the nature of his depiction of it raises just as many questions.

The beating, it turns out, is just as problematic in the source text. Readers may not be surprised at the woman's night-time perambulations, or at her contact with the watchmen. After all, she has searched for her lover in the streets and squares once before (Song 3.2-4), where she even sought the watchmen's help, which, as it turns out, was neither given nor necessary ('scarcely had I passed them when I found him whom I love', 3.4). It is a completely unexpected outcome, however, that in Song 5.7 the woman is beaten and her mantle taken from her for the same behaviour of which we read earlier. What makes the beating especially problematic, and disturbing, is the fact that the text offers no reason or justification for it. If, for example, the text read, 'the watchmen beat me because a woman should not go about the city alone at night', we could at least account for it in terms of social norms of the time. But as it stands, it is hard to know what to make of the enigmatic scene.

52. It is easier to make out the lantern in the reproduction (Plate 4) than in the church window itself. We both had the experience of seeing the large, clearly articulated clenched fist first and only later recognizing the lantern, for its handle cannot be seen.

Not surprisingly, commentators have difficulty with the passage. Many ignore the event entirely, while some, acknowledging the violence, attempt to find reasons for it, and these are frequently weak. Roland Murphy, for example, suggests that 'perhaps her failure to discover the man at once (as in 3.4) is enough to account for this graphic detail of physical beating'.[53] Sometimes commentators try to address the scene, but actually skirt the issue, as, for example, John Snaith does when he notes that this treatment is 'quite unsuitable for the police'.[54] Ancient Near Eastern parallels are sometimes appealed to in an effort to make sense of the beating, but the assumption of a mythological background (even if we accepted it) does not account for what happens at this point in this text.[55] Perhaps things are not what they seem. Athalya Brenner tries to reassure us: 'Love brings pain as well as joy, but this pain does not have far-reaching physical and social consequences...'; the woman is beaten, she notes, but 'not sexually molested for her immodesty'.[56] Still others explain (away) the difficulty in 5.7 by appealing to the event's presence in a 'dream sequence'.[57] It has been suggested that the beating represents a barrier between the dreamer's subconscious and conscious, either as anxiety over the loss of her virginity[58] or her impending exposure.[59] Whatever the interpretation, the result of restricting the beating to its posited oneiric context is to downplay its gravity. Moreover, even in this context, the difficulty still persists: why would the woman's fantasy about her lover's approach and her response, already aborted when her lover disappears, continue to the point of violence to the dreamer? Is this a woman's fantasy, the kind of dream a

53. Murphy, *Song of Songs*, p. 171.

54. Snaith, *Song of Songs*, p. 76.

55. E.g. Inanna's Descent to the Underworld.

56. Brenner, *Song of Songs*, p. 83.

57. Song 3.1-5 and 5.2-8 are commonly referred to as dream sequences because they both begin with the woman in her bed at night; but the text never states that she is dreaming and it is quite possible to imagine that she is lying in bed awake, thinking about her lover.

58. D. Garrett, *The New American Commentary: An Exegetical and Theological Exposition of Holy Scripture. Proverbs, Ecclesiastes, Song of Songs* (Nashville: Broadman Press, 1993), pp. 409, 412. Garrett notes: 'Metaphorically, then, it is not any person who assaults her; it is her own virginity. This is an experience in which the man paradoxically has no part' (p. 412).

59. Ilana Pardes, *Countertraditions in the Hebrew Bible: A Feminist Approach* (Cambridge, MA: Harvard University Press, 1992), p. 137.

woman would have, or is it—and the entire biblical Song—a male fantasy representing what a male author might like to think a woman dreams about?[60] Is our inability to account for this scene a result of our unwillingness to consider what is most disturbing about it?

Looking through the Window at the Source Text

Our close association over many months with Burne-Jones's beautiful, yet disquieting, window has inevitably cast the source text in a new light for us. We said above that major issues in the interpretation of the source text are also issues in the reading of the window: the question of unity and the related question of plot. There are, of course, important differences; interpreting the biblical Song of Songs is certainly a more complicated matter because we know so much less about it. In particular, we know Burne-Jones's source text but we have no way of knowing what sources the author or redactor of the biblical Song of Songs used.[61] Whereas the absence of real evidence convinces us that critical interpretation should approach the biblical Song both as a collection of unrelated love poems and as a unity in which we can discover a plot,[62] we know that Burne-Jones's panels are not unrelated. Unlike the biblical text, the window is the composition of one 'author' (though Burne-Jones left it for Morris to translate his cartoons into stained glass), composed at one time (within the space of one year at most), and produced for one window space in one building. Even so, the arrangement of the panels—that is, the order in which they should be 'read'—is not, we have argued, immediately apparent, nor is the plot something viewers will necessarily agree on. In these respects the window is like the biblical Song, and exploring different ways of viewing it has reinforced for us the importance of the role that the reader or viewer plays in interpretation. Viewers who read for the plot will find one; viewers

60. See, e.g., David J.A. Clines, 'Why Is There a Song of Songs and What Does It Do to You If You Read It?', in *Interested Parties: The Ideology of Writers and Readers of the Hebrew Bible* (Gender, Culture, Theory, 1; Sheffield: Sheffield Academic Press, 1996), pp. 94-121.

61. Egyptian parallels are illuminating (see Michael V. Fox, *The Song of Songs and the Ancient Egyptian Love Songs* [Madison: University of Wisconsin Press, 1985]), but there is no reason to conclude that they must have been models for the Song.

62. We think it likely that the redactor/author of the biblical Song of Songs based the composition upon existing love songs, arranging them and probably adding to them in such a way as to create an artistic whole.

who see only a loose connection between the panels and read them randomly will not find a plot, though they may get a sense of thematic unity from the repeated depictions of the unrealized desire for the beloved; viewers who read the whole window in the light of one panel will create a story of sorts based on their reaction to that panel. We see no benefit in trying to argue for the superiority of one approach over the others, since each of them yields valuable insights into aspects of the story that the others do not address at all.

In his representation of the biblical Song in stained glass, Burne-Jones has emphasized one aspect of the source text, its longing and unfulfillment. Of all the possibilities offered by the source text, he has chosen to represent something that most commentators overlook, its disturbing images that challenge the overall message about love's delights. The anger of the woman's siblings and her beating by the watchmen are details that do not fit the conventional understanding of the Song of Songs as a celebration of mutual desire and fulfillment. They are details that biblical interpretation usually overlooks or smoothes over. But they do not go away, and our inability to account for them raises questions about our interpretive assumptions and prejudices.

Another example of such a detail that does not fit the way most readers would like to interpret the biblical Song of Songs is the ending, where the woman says: 'Flee, my love, be like a gazelle or a young stag upon the mountains of spices'. The verb used here indicates motion away from the speaker. Is she sending him away? It is difficult to say, since spice mountains is a metaphor used of the woman herself. There is no closure with the lovers together for all time, and the ending is not entirely satisfying, but by and large interpreters have tended to gloss over the problem. Some translations strain the sense of the Hebrew in order to obtain a more satisfying ending. The New Revised Standard Version, for example, translates, 'Make haste, my beloved, and be like a gazelle or a young stag upon the mountains of spices!', as if she were calling him to her.[63] Burne-Jones's closure, where the couple is united, is more satisfying than that of the source text, but still ambiguous (is it really a happy ending?), and that ambiguity draws our renewed attention to the ambiguity of the source text.

63. Cf. Murphy, *Song of Songs*, p. 200: 'She invites him to "flee" to the mountains of spice, i.e., to herself'. See also the discussion of various proposals for understanding the verb in Pope, *Song of Songs*, pp. 697-700.

Burne-Jones's window has sent us back to the source text with a heightened sense of the disruptive power of these details for traditional sanguine readings of this text. What would happen to the place of honour held by the biblical Song of Songs if, rather than suppressing these recalcitrant details, we foregrounded them? What Burne-Jones's window has most impressed upon us is the importance of a counterreading of the biblical text in which the picture of love is not so rosy as most commentators would have it. When we look at Burne-Jones's Song of Songs in stained glass, we see not only a beautifully executed, visually striking and complex work of art but also a challenge to biblical interpretation to reassess its comfortable assumptions about the biblical book and to re-examine what it has been reluctant to see.

The Use of the Song of Songs in J.S. Bach's Church Cantatas

John W. Rogerson

'Noch bei der höchstvollendeten Reproduktion fällt eines aus: das Hier und Jetzt des Kunstwerks—sein einmaliges Dasein an dem Orte, an dem es sich befindet'.[1] Walter Benjamin's observations on the consequences of the mass reproduction of works of graphic art are also applicable to musical compositions whose original setting was religious worship. Even to hear such works performed in a concert hall rather than as part of worship is to lose touch with a complex of conventions shared and pre-supposed by composer, musicians and listeners. Yet such works of art contain sufficient latent meaning for them to be able to survive trans-plantation into a world in which culture has become commercialized and politicized. In such a world, where powerful interests control and exploit popular culture in order to promote dubious values, falsify the truth and create humankind in their own image, great works of art, even in reproduced form, give access to intimations of possibilities that call humankind to vocations more worthy of humanity. The role of the Bible in such works of art is reciprocal. It shapes and is shaped by the traditions and institutions in which it is taken seriously. This can be illustrated by the use of the Song of Songs in Bach's Church Cantatas.

In two of the roughly 200 Church Cantatas composed by J.S. Bach for Lutheran worship, principally in St Thomas's Church, Leipzig, the Song of Songs features prominently. The Cantatas are numbers 49, 'Ich geh und suche mit Verlangen' ('I go and search with longing') and 140, 'Wachet auf, ruft uns die Stimme' ('Sleepers wake, loud sounds the warning'). Although the latter Cantata is by far the better known, the former is an unusual and remarkable Cantata in its own right, apart from the way in which it uses the Song of Songs.

1. 'Even the most perfect reproduction lacks something: the here and now of the work of art—its unique existence at the place where it [originally] finds itself.' Walter Benjamin, 'Das Kunstwerk im Zeitalter seiner technischen Reproduzier-barkeit' (Zweiter Fassung), in R. Tiedemann *et al.* (eds.), *Walter Benjamin Gesam-melte Schriften* (Frankfurt-am-Main: Suhrkamp Verlag, 1991), VII.1, p. 352.

Cantata 49 was composed for the Twentieth Sunday after Trinity and first performed on 3 November 1726 at St Thomas's.[2] Unusually, Bach had no choir available for the occasion (this was also the case for another Cantata for the same Sunday in the Church year, Cantata 162, 'Ach! ich sehe, itzt, da ich zur Hochzeit gehe') and this affected the shape of the Cantata. The Gospel reading set for this Sunday was Mt. 22.1-14, the Parable of the Royal Wedding, and this parable supplied the key to the interpretation and use of material from Song of Songs.

In the parable a king arranges a wedding feast in honour of his son, but the guests decline to attend. The king therefore sends out servants to find replacement guests, and also sends his armies to destroy towns that have ill-treated his servants. Finally, the banquet hall is filled with guests. One of them, however, who is not wearing the appropriate wedding garment, is cast out of the feast into outer darkness. The unknown librettist handled the parable with great freedom, and interpreted the sending out of the king's servants to look for guests in terms of a personal search by Christ for a bride (representing the individual believer) to invite to the marriage feast. The incident of the marriage garment is transformed into an aria by the bride, who affirms that she is clothed by the righteousness of Christ's salvation. The Cantata thus expresses the Lutheran pietist themes of God's search for humankind in order to offer salvation through faith in Christ, the outcome of which is an intimate and mystical relationship between Christ and the believer.

In the absence of a choir and thus of an opening chorus, Bach began the Cantata with a Sinfonia for solo organ and orchestra adapted from an earlier work.[3] The Sinfonia has a festive note, which is appropriate to the theme of a marriage. The opening aria is for a bass soloist representing Christ, and it describes his search for his bride in language using allusions to Song 1.7 and 2.14:

> Ich geh und suche mit Verlangen
> Dich, meine Taube, schönste Braut.
> Sag an, wo bist du hingegangen,
> Daß dich mein Auge nicht mehr schaut?[4]

---

2.   See Alfred Dürr, *Die Kantaten von Johann Sebastian Bach* (Kassel: Bärenreiter Verlag; Munich: Deutscher Taschenbuch Verlag, 6th edn, 1985), p. 660.

3.   Dürr, *Kantaten*, p. 660.

4.   'I go and search with longing / For you, my dove, my fairest bride. / Tell me, where have you gone / That my eye no longer beholds you?'

There then follows the first of two recitatives in duet form, in which the soul is represented by a soprano. The bass soloist declares that his marriage feast is ready and that all that is lacking is his bride. The opening words of the first aria, 'Ich geh und suche…' are repeated, and the meeting of bride and bridegroom is indicated by the intertwining of the dialogue and music of the two soloists. The words are allusions to Song 1.2, 4.8 and 4.16, with a reversal in the last example from the woman inviting the man to a meal to Christ inviting the soul to a meal. The intimacy of the relationship is expressed in the sharing of words as much as possible:

> Komm, Schönste [soprano: Schönster], komm und laß dich küssen,
> Du sollst mein [sop.: Laß mich dein] fettes Mahl genießen
> Komm, liebe Braut, und [sop.: Mein Bräutigum! ich] eile nun.
> [Bass and sop.] Die Hochzeitkleider anzutun.[5]

Figure 1. Cantata 49, BWV 49, 3rd movement, bars 17–32

5. 'Come fairest (sop. fairest) / come and let me kiss you, / You shall enjoy my (sop. Let me enjoy your) sumptuous meal / Come my dear bride and (sop. My bridegroom! I) hasten now / To put on the wedding garments.'

The fourth number in the Cantata is an aria by the soprano, which begins with words adapted from Song 1.15, 'Sjhe [*sic*] / meine Freundin / du bist schöne' and 2.1, 'Ich bin ein Blumen zu Saron':[6]

> Ich bin herrlich, ich bin schön.[7]

In what follows in the aria, the festal garments being worn by the bride are those of Christ's righteousness, and the following, and second recitative in the form of a duet owes its allusions to the parable of the wedding feast rather than the Song of Songs.

In the final, and remarkable, number, Bach had to deal with the problem that, without a choir, he could not end the Cantata in the usual way, with the choir singing a verse from a chorale. He solved the problem by combining three things. The organ was given a brilliant solo part, as was the bass soloist, while the soprano sang in slow time the final verse of Philipp Nicolai's hymn 'Wie schön leuchtet der Morgenstern':

> Wie bin ich doch so herzlich froh,
> Daß mein Schatz ist das A und O,
> Der Anfang und das Ende.
> Er wird mich doch zu seinem Preis
> Aufnehmen in das Paradeis:
> Des klopf ich in die Hände.
> Amen! Amen!
> Komm, du schöne Freudenkrone, bleib nicht lange!
> Deiner wart ich mit Verlangen.[8]

Here, the unknown librettist linked the end of the Cantata back to its beginning via the word 'Verlangen' ('Ich geh und suche mit Verlangen'). At the same time, themes were employed from Song of Songs, not in a direct way, but via the influence of Song of Songs on a text such as Rev. 3.20: 'Sihe / ich stehe fur der Tür / und klopffe an'. That text, which probably admonishes rather than invites the hearer to admit the Christ who knocks on the door, echoes Song 5.2, 'Da ist die stim meins Freundes der anklopffet. Thu mir auff liebe Freundin meine

---

6. The translation is that of Luther's 1545 Bible, with the original spellings retained. See D. Martin Luther, *Die gantze Heilige Schrifft* (ed. Hans Volz; 3 vols.; Munich: Deutscher Taschenbuch Verlag, 1974).

7. 'I am glorious, I am fair'.

8. 'How truly glad am I indeed / That my treasure is the A and O / The beginning and the end. / He will indeed, to his great praise / Receive me into paradise: / For this I'll clap my hands. / Amen! Amen! / Come, fair crown of gladness, wait no more! / You with great longing I await.'

schwester / meine Taube / meine frome'. In the Cantata the words combined with those of the soprano are

> Dich hab ich je und je geliebet,
> Und darum zieh ich dich zu mir.
> Ich komme bald,
> Ich stehe vor der Tür,
> Mach auf, mein Aufenthalt!
> Dich hab ich je und je geliebet,
> Und darum zieh ich dich zu mir.[9]

In these words there is an allusion to Jer. 31.3, 'Jch hab dich je vnd je geliebet / darumb hab ich dich zu mir gezogen'.

Figure 2. Cantata 49, BWV 49, extract from 6th movement

In the treatment of the Parable of the Wedding Feast, it is the dramatic and dialogic nature of the Song of Songs that provides the scheme for the whole construction. The traditional Christological interpretation of the text is adapted to the pietist understanding of Christianity as an intimate and mystical relationship between Christ and the individual believer. The whole effect is enhanced by the fact that music is a medium in which it is possible to have two or more voices simultaneously singing different words set to differing melodic lines which, however, may include imitation. Bach uses this possibility to great effect in three of the six numbers, in two of which there are allusions to the

9. You have I loved eternally, / And therefore draw you unto me. / I come soon, / I stand at the door, / Open up, my abode! / You have I loved eternally, / And therefore draw you unto me.

Song of Songs. The medium of the sung Cantata therefore adds a dimension to the use of the Song of Songs that would not be possible for spoken dialogue, and which in any case is appropriate to the claim of the text that it is a song.

Cantata 140 was composed for the Twenty-seventh Sunday after Trinity, a Sunday that occurs only if Easter is exceptionally early, and it would appear that this Sunday occurred only in 1731 and 1742 in Bach's Leipzig period.[10] The Cantata was performed on 25 November 1731 but has become so popular in recent times as to be linked with the last Sunday before Advent. The Gospel reading for this Sunday was Mt. 25.1-13, the Parable of the Wise and Foolish Virgins and the unknown librettist[11] used as a basic framework for the Cantata the three-verse hymn by Philipp Nicolai (1598), 'Wachet auf, ruft uns die Stimme', which is loosely based upon the parable, and which provides the words for numbers 1, 4 and 7. However, the fact that the parable concerns a wedding enabled the librettist to insert as numbers 2 and 3 and 5 and 6 two recitatives, and two arias in the form of duets, in which words are intertwined between the soprano and bass soloists as in Cantata 49. There are many allusions to the Song of Songs.

In the first recitative, sung by a tenor acting as a kind of narrator, the daughters of Sion are warned of the approach of the bridegroom. However, this is no ordinary bridegroom making a prosaic journey from one house to another. Song 2.8-9, 'Sihe / Er kompt vnd hüpffet auff den Bergen / vnd springet auff den Hügeln. Mein Freund ist gleich einem Rehe oder jungen Hirss' appears in the recitative as

> Der Bräutgam kommt, der einem Rehe
> Und jungen Hirsche gleich
> Auf denen Hügeln springt
> Und euch das Mahl der Hochzeit bringt.[12]

---

10. The Lutheran practice, like that of the *Book of Common Prayer* of the Church of England, is to have a fixed 'Sunday next before Advent' and to omit any Sunday after Trinity for which there is no space. Thus, if Easter Sunday falls on 25 April there will be only 22 Sundays after Trinity.

11. It has been surmised that the librettist was Picander, that is, Christian Friedrich Henrici (1700–64); see W Siegmund-Schultze, *Johann Sebastian Bach* (Leipzig: Verlag Philipp Reclam, 1976), p. 140. The similarity of the treatment of Song of Songs in Cantatas 49 and 140 raises the question whether the two Cantatas had the same librettist.

12. 'The bridegroom comes, who like a buck / And a young stag / Upon the hills does leap / To bring to you the wedding feast.'

Here, it seems, the rustic imagery of the coming of the beloved has been transformed into metaphors for the coming of a heavenly bridegroom.

This is not the only allusion to Song of Songs in the recitative. 'Ihr Töchter Zions, kommt heraus' ('Let Zion's daughter gaze with joy') and 'In euer Mutter Haus' ('in goodly fellowship') can be compared with Song 3.11, 'Gehet er aus vnd schawet an / jr töchter Zion' and 3.4, 'Bis ich jn bringe in meiner Mutter haus'.

The first of the duets contains no allusion to the Song of Songs, but with the second recitative allusions abound. The text of the recitative is as follows:

> So geh herein zu mir,
> Du mir erwählte Braut!
> Ich habe mich mit dir
> Von Ewigkeit vertraut.
> Dich will ich auf mein Herz,
> Auf meinem Arm gleich wie ein Siegel setzen
> Und dein betrübtes Aug ergötzen.
> Vergiß, o Seele, nun,
> Die Angst, den Schmerz,
> Den du erdulden müssen;
> Auf meiner Linken sollst du ruhn,
> Und meine Rechte soll dich küssen.[13]

Lines 5 and 6 can be compared with Song 8.6, 'Setze mich wie ein Siegel auff dein Herz / vnd wie ein siegel auff deinen Arm' while the last two lines are clearly taken from 8.3 (compare 2.6), 'Seine Linke ligt vnter meinem Heubt / vnd seine Rechte hertzet mich'.

In the final aria, the second duet, the soprano and bass begin by singing alternately the following words from Song 6.2, 'Mein Freund ist mein / und ich bin sein' ('My love is thine! Yea, I am thine!'). They then sing together, 'Die Liebe soll nichts scheiden' ('Our love shall stand for ever'), which has no direct correspondence in Song of Songs but which could be a summary of 8.7, 'Das auch viel Wasser nicht mügen die Liebe auslesschen / noch die ströme sie erseuffen'.

---

13. 'So come within to me / You, my chosen bride. / I have myself to you / Eternally betrothed. / You will I on my heart, / And on my arm like a seal engrave / And your troubled eye delight. / Forget now, O dear soul, / The fear, the pain, / That you have to endure; / On my left arm shall you rest, / And my right arm will enfold you.'

Figure 3. Cantata 140, BWV 140, 7th movement, bars 8–12

The voices are now intertwined as in Cantata 49 in the next words, which allude to the latter part of Song 6.2, 'der unter den Rosen sich weidet':

Ich will [Bass: Du sollst] mit dir [Bass: mir] in Himmels Rosen weiden[14]

The intimacy of the lovers is expressed not only in the sharing of words, but in the melodic imitation in the two parts.

The Cantata closes with the final verse of the hymn.

The Song of Songs is one of the most sublime parts of the Hebrew Bible. Bach wrote some of his most sublime music in order to express its theme of unalloyed love in theological terms.

14. 'I will (Bass: you will) with you (Bass: me) in heaven's roses pasture'.

Figure 4. Cantata 140, BWV 140, 7th movement, bars 46–55

Ecce Vir,
or, Gendering the Son of Man

David J.A. Clines

Biblical into Cultural Studies is to me a slogan for the transformation of
biblical studies. It implies a frame of reference and a set of questions
from outside the Bible itself, so that it is not the Bible that sets the
agenda but the culture in which its interpreters find themselves.

Has it ever been any different? we might well ask. Has there ever
been a time when biblical studies were pure and simple? I do not suppose so. When the questions we brought to the Bible were of its historical setting or of the growth of its compositions, was it the Bible that
was prompting those questions, or was it not the intellectual climate of
the time, the culture? Or when Gregory the Great dictated his *Morals* on
the book of Job or Calvin preached his *Sermons*, were they not culturally
determined as much as biblically?

What is different today is, as I see it, no more than a self-conscious-
ness about the culture. We are bound to be more aware than ever
before of the cultural influences on our reading of the Bible. I see three
reasons for the current insistence on the cultural context of our biblical
studies. Many of our contemporaries feel they have had experience of
several different cultures within their own lifetime, the tempo of global-
ization brings us unavoidably into constant contact with cultural differences, and in our Western liberal culture at least we have become
committed to esteeming the importance of cultural location and to
sensitizing ourselves to recognizing cultural difference. We cannot help
seeing biblical studies as a subset of cultural studies.

Is everything cultural studies, then? Yes, I suppose so, not only the
humanities but law and economics and the hard sciences and medicine.
But if that is so, what is the point of the label 'cultural studies'? Mainly
its shock value, its novelty. There are not many physicists who would
readily agree that physics is a branch of cultural studies,[1] nor many

1. The latest illustration I have seen of this is an account of the Royal Society's

biblical scholars who see themselves as millhands in the cultural industrial complex. So, until it becomes obvious and taken for granted, we need colloquia and papers to press the point, in manifold modulations.

Where this paper fits into the project 'Biblical Studies/Cultural Studies', as I conceive it, is that the question of gender and gender-representation in literary texts is one that is brought to the surface by our contemporary culture. I did not fasten on the topic of this paper because I am by long habit a biblical scholar, but because gender is on the agenda, so to say. Or, to be more personal, I am writing this paper because one day, feeling a little marginalized by the impact of feminist biblical criticism, I asked Cheryl Exum, in the words of Peter, What shall this 'man' do?, feeling sure that feminist criticism could be no business of mine. I got a one-word answer: Masculinity; and I have gone in the strength of that word forty days and forty nights.

As I have discovered, it was a subject that needed taking up in biblical studies. It was a stunning example of the unthinking androcentrism of biblical scholars that it had not occurred to anyone much to ask what was typically male about their primary texts;[2] they just assumed that 'human' and 'masculine' were coterminous. Once one recognized what a canard that was, a rich vein of research opened up almost of its own accord. I began with a paper on David the Man,[3] followed it with analyses of masculinity in the Psalms ('The Book of Psalms, Where Men Are Men: On the Gender of Hebrew Piety') and in Job ('Loingirding and

---

1992 report on Risk. Engineers saw busy roads with low death tolls as objectively safe, and were maddened by the social scientists' claim that risk is just as much a cultural construct. Though the road accident death rate for children in Britain is less than half what it was in the 1920s (scientific objectivity), there can be little doubt that the roads are perceived as more dangerous (cultural subjectivity). I was reading 'Why Talk of Risk is Full of Hazards', in *The Times Higher Education Supplement* 1271 (14 March 1997), p. 18. The Royal Society has just held last week another such symposium, on Science, Policy and Risk, hoping yet again to get engineers and social scientists to see eye to eye.

2.   And then Stephen Moore came along with *God's Gym: Divine Male Bodies of the Bible* (London: Routledge, 1996)..

3.   Now published as 'David the Man: The Construction of Masculinity in the Hebrew Bible', in David J.A. Clines, *Interested Parties: The Ideology of Writers and Readers of the Hebrew Bible* (JSOTSup, 205; Gender, Culture, Theory, 1; Sheffield: Sheffield Academic Press, 1995), Chapter 10, pp. 212-43.

Other Male Activities in the Book of Job').[4] When this paper is finished, I shall be thinking about the next in the series, for the World Congress of Jewish Studies; invited to read a paper in the section on Feminist Biblical Studies (though I am no woman), I decided, with the help of my colleagues, who saw what a dangerous game I was playing, it had better be 'Masculinity's Debt to Feminist Biblical Criticism'. And when I have thought about the masculinity of Paul and the prophets and maybe also the Proverbs, I shall try to make a book, which I have already entitled in my head, *Play the Man!* The 'play' signifies that masculinity is a role, and the imperative verb with its exclamation mark denotes the force of the social constraint upon biological males to exhibit prescribed male behaviour.

That is the background to the present paper, the concern of which is to analyse the way masculinity is constructed in the figure of Jesus in the Gospels. Needless to say, I am not interested here in the historical Jesus, but in the literary portraiture; and I am not undertaking to develop distinctive profiles for the masculinity of Jesus according to the various Gospels. My personal interest (though this is not the topic of the present essay) is in the influence of the biblical texts upon its readers of various historical periods, principally our own, so my concern with the figure of Jesus is not with the differing representations of the character devised by the evangelists but with the effects of the composite portrait.[5] What I expect the present paper will show is the prominence of traditional male characteristics in the character Jesus. In previous papers, I identified them variously as strength, violence, bonding, womanlessness, solitariness, musicality, beauty, persuasive speech, honour, binary thinking, objectifying. For this paper, I want to work inductively, from the evidence of the texts, but prompted at the same time to look for the categories that have shown up in the previous studies.

I should observe how rarely the question of Jesus' maleness seems to have been treated in the scholarly literature, appending below the only bibliography I can discover on the subject.[6]

---

4.   Both are available in pre-publication form at http://www.shef.ac.uk/~biblst/BibsStaff/BibsResearch/DJACcurrres/DJACcurrres.html.

5.   Stephen Moore kindly warns me that in ignoring the differences among the Gospels I am infringing the last taboo in Gospels criticism. My defence is that as a cultural critic I am interested in the reception of the Jesus story, not in its origins.

6.   As yet I have read none of these. Most promising seems to be J. Timmerman, 'The Sexuality of Jesus and the Human Vocation', in James B. Nelson and

1. *The Masculinity of Jesus*

a. *Jesus the Strong*
It is fundamental for the traditional male to be strong.[7] Weakness is not a desirable male trait in traditional societies; even in our own less traditional and more egalitarian society, lack of physical strength in a boy or a man is still deplored to a degree it is not in a girl or a woman.

Not to worry. Jesus is strong. His strength is never described in the Gospels in physical terms—unlike the extrabiblical texts in Stephen Moore's article in the present volume. But his strength is never far from sight, and it is never of course said to be spiritual[8] or moral. In Mark, before we ever catch sight of Jesus, we know about his strength; in fact, that is *all* we know about him from John the Baptist: the burden of his announcement was, 'There comes after me one who is *stronger* than me'. The reader is invited to contemplate a heroic figure who is still off-stage. John the Baptist is a mighty man himself: an angel has told his father that he will be another Samson, 'mighty in the sight of the Lord, and shall drink neither wine nor strong drink' (Lk. 1.15), and he has himself been doing 'mighty works' (Mt. 14.2; Mk 6.14). But Jesus will be stronger still, a super-Samson. His deeds of healing (? and others) are often called 'his mighty works' (Mt. 11.20, 21, 23; 13.58; Mk 6.5; Lk. 10.13; 19.37); even his own countrymen acknowledge his strength, asking, 'Whence has this man these mighty works?' (Mt. 13.54;

Sandra P. Longfellow (eds.), *Sexuality and the Sacred: Sources for Theological Reflection* (Louisville, KY: Westminster/John Knox Press, 1994). Least promising is John Piper and Wayne A. Grudem (eds.), *Recovering Biblical Manhood and Womanhood: A Response to Evangelical Feminism* (Wheaton, IL: Crossway Books, 1991), since I know one of the editors, having had a big row with him on the day the Americans bombed Libya, as God's appointed world policemen, he claimed. I shall be interested in Vivian Clark, 'Was Jesus Christ a Man's Man? When a Man Seeks the Ultimate Model for Manliness, to Whom Should He Go?', *Christianity Today* 27.4 (1983), pp. 16-18, and Thomas K. Hearn, 'Jesus Was A Sissy After All', *Christian Century* 87 (1970), pp. 191-93. I can find no other bibliography, despite assiduous searching on the ATLA database.

7. We might note the Pauline injunction: 'Watch ye, stand fast in the faith, quit you like men, be strong (ἀνδρίζεσθε, κραταιοῦσθε)' (1 Cor. 16.13).

8. It is interesting that the KJV, conflating the phrase about Jesus with that about John in Lk. 1.80, translates ἐκραταιοῦτο as 'waxed strong in spirit' (2.40)—as if the physical strength the text appears to allude to can be no concern of the evangelist.

Mk 6.2). On the road to Emmaus, too, Jesus' companions describe him
as 'a prophet mighty in word and deed' (Lk. 24.19). Jesus sees himself as
a strong man, stronger even than Beelzebub, and so superhuman in
strength: No one can get into a strong man's house, he says, and spoil
his goods, unless he first binds the strong man (Mt. 21.29; Mk 3.27).
Does he imagine himself here not as Samson, but as the even stronger
Delilah who is binding the strong man?

   I should have really said, Big and strong. Little boys are encouraged,
especially by their mothers, who have their own investments in masculinity, to eat up their cornflakes so that they will grow up *big and
strong*. Being small and strong is nowhere near so desirable. Is Jesus 'big'
too? It is not commonly said, but a key sentence from the beginning of
Luke may come to mind: 'He shall be great, and shall be called the Son
of the Highest: and the Lord God shall give unto him the throne of his
father David' (1.32). This is followed up, at least initially, by 2.40 'And
the child [Jesus] grew and became strong (ἐκραταιοῦτο)' (almost the
same phrase has been already used of the Samson figure, John the Baptist, in 1.80). Jesus is nowhere explicitly 'big' or 'great', but before we
dropped this line of thought we would have to go further and examine
the language of domination and power, Κύριος and ἐξουσία and
δύναμις and the like—but that is another project.

b. *Jesus the Violent*

Being strong is not an end in itself. The purpose of being strong as a
man, and especially of being stronger than other men, is to be able to
overcome them and, if need be, kill them. The name for strength in
action, in traditional male terms, is violence. And the name for the violent action of men in groups is war.

   Jesus is a traditional male, and he participates in violence in the ways
open to him given the historical and social setting supplied for him by
the Gospel accounts. I am not now thinking of the debates about
whether Jesus, the historical Jesus, was a revolutionary or not.[9] My
interest here is solely in the literary portrait of Jesus in the Gospels.

   The familiar view is that Jesus is a man of peace. Michel Desjardins

---

   9.   See, for example, Richard A. Horsley, *Jesus and the Spiral of Violence: Popular
Jewish Resistance in Roman Palestine* (Minneapolis: Augsburg–Fortress, 1993); *idem*,
'Ethics and Exegesis: "Love your enemies" and the Doctrine of Non-Violence',
JAAR 54 (1986), pp. 3-31; Josephine Massyngbaerde Ford, *My Enemy Is my Guest:
Jesus and Violence in Luke* (Maryknoll, NY: Orbis Books, 1984).

has recently pointed out that this is only half the story, and that the New Testament is 'suffused with violence': 'Jesus and his followers can be found accepting, condoning, and even inciting violence'.[10] It is not generally (though it is occasionally) physical violence, but it is violence all the same. As Desjardins puts it, 'A sword is not always a sword, and all battles are not alike'. The sword that cuts off the ear of the high priest's slave is not the sword that will pierce Mary's heart (Lk. 2.35). But the language is the language of violence, the ethic is the ethic of war—and, we must add, the violence is the violence of men.

In Luke, while Jesus is still an infant, we are assured, ominously, that '[T]his child is marked for the fall and rising of many in Israel, for a sign that is spoken against' (Lk. 2.34). Jesus, by his own account of himself, did not 'come' in the cause of peace: 'I came not to send peace, but a sword' (Mt. 10.34; cf. Lk. 12.51). It is as if the character Jesus realizes he is bound to be misunderstood on this matter: 'Think not', he says, 'that I have come to bring peace'—as if the gentle Jesus, meek and mild, is a stereotype he is already worried about. It is domestic tension he has in mind here, not armed conflict, but his metaphors do seem to leak a little into the real world of physical violence. We might even infer that the Jesus band roams the countryside armed. In Luke his disciples certainly take him literally when he urges them to sell their clothes to buy arms (22.36)—though they still seem to have their garments. In Matthew and Mark, however, though they have not been encouraged to lay in weapons for a last stand, there seems to be nothing strange in their carrying a weapon: 'one of them drew his sword', as if it might have been any one of them (Mt. 26.51; Mk 14.47). By any account, the swords in Gethsemane are real enough, and one at least of them is sharp enough to cut off an ear (Mt. 26.51; Jn 18.10).

There is at least one other scene of physical violence in the Jesus story. The 'triumphal' entry into Jerusalem has itself been seen as an act of violence,[11] but the incident with the money changers on the following day is a much more obvious example. He overturns the tables of the changers of money and the seats of the pigeon sellers (Mt. 21.12; Mk 11.15). In John, he makes a whip to drive the merchants and the animals out. It may be a good cause, but it is certainly violence.

What is far more evident in the figure of Jesus is the violence of his

---

10. Michel Desjardins, *Peace, Violence and the New Testament* (The Biblical Seminar, 46; Sheffield: Sheffield Academic Press, 1997), pp. 62, 66.

11. Cf. Desjardins, *Peace, Violence*, p. 75.

language. Cursing, for example, is violent language, for it invokes physical violence. There are 'woes' to towns (Mt. 11.21), a woe to the world because of temptation and to the man by whom it comes (18.7), to scribes and Pharisees (23.14, 15, 16, 23, 25, 27, 29), to the man who betrays Jesus (26.24). There is the cursing of the fig tree (21.19-20). And there is the threat of future punishment, like the casting of worthless servants into outer darkness where there is weeping and gnashing of teeth (25.30; cf. 8.12; 22.13).

c. *Jesus the Powerful and Persuasive Speaker*
When I was studying masculinity in the David story, I came to realize that persuasive speech was in ancient Israel a typical mark of male behaviour. A servant of Saul describes David, to Saul and the readers before we ever meet David, by what I judge to be typical characteristics of a traditional male: he is a mighty man of valour (גבור חיל), a warrior (איש מלחמה), intelligent in speech (נבון דבר), a beautiful man (איש תאר), and skilful in playing (ידע נגן) (1 Sam. 16.18). David's intelligence in speech is evidenced on several occasions: for example, when he persuades Saul that he is capable of withstanding Goliath (1 Sam. 17.34-36), when he explains to Saul why he did not kill him in the cave (24.10-15), and when he asks Saul why he continues to pursue him (26.18-20) and brings Saul to admit that he has done wrong (26.21).

These are all effective examples of the power of words, not in any magical sense,[12] but as instruments of control. To be master of persuasion is to have another form of power, which is not an alternative to, and far less a denatured version of, physical strength, but part of the repertory of the powerful male.

The Jesus of the Gospels is nothing if not a powerful and persuasive speaker. In the story, it is he who has all the punchlines. Many narratives about him are told entirely for the sake of the 'pronouncement' with which he concludes an interchange, making a definitive statement or defeating his opponents' arguments. Some of the earliest writing about Jesus (such as 'Q'), so they say, was nothing other than a collection of his 'sayings', which evidently brought to their collectors and readers a kind of satisfaction and enjoyment at the verbal prowess of their hero.

Simply to illustrate the point, I open Mark, and take note of the first

12. I am not claiming that, since I find the analysis of A.C. Thiselton convincing ('The Supposed Power of Words in the Biblical Writings', *JTS* NS 25 [1974], pp. 282-99).

ten speeches of Jesus. (1) He says just one line to Simon and Andrew, 'Follow me'; it is so effective that 'immediately they left their nets and followed him' (1.17-18). (2) A man with an unclean spirit resists him, Jesus rebukes him with a word of power, and the unclean spirit comes out of the man (1.24-26). (3) The third is a less authoritative word, almost like normal conversation: Simon and others say everyone is looking for him, and he responds by saying, 'Let us go on to the next towns, that I may preach there also'. So he goes throughout Galilee (1.36-39). (4) A leper says, 'If you will, you can make me clean', and he says just those words, 'I will; be clean', and 'immediately the leprosy left him' (1.40-42). Jesus thereupon 'growls' (ἐμβριμησάμενος) at him that he say nothing to anyone, the term signifying apparently the forcefulness of his speech.[13] It is true that in this case Jesus' charge is ignored by the man; here, I suppose I would say that Jesus is being forceful rather than successful. (5) Jesus says to a man with paralysis, 'Your sins are forgiven' (2.5)—a textbook example of a performative utterance, which by any account has to be among the most powerful forms of speech. Speech that is itself an action has a strange potent quality, deconstructing as it does the familiar dichotomy of words versus deeds. (6) Jesus responds to the unspoken criticism of 'scribes' with an adept rhetorical flourish: 'Which is easier to say, "Your sins are forgiven", or "Rise, take up your pallet and walk"?' (2.9). This is one of those wonderful Gospel logia that mean less the more you look into them.[14] Jesus' opponents are questioning whether Jesus has any right to pronounce sins forgiven. Jesus the rhetor astonishes them (v. 12) by (a) changing the subject from legitimacy to 'ease' (what has 'ease' got to do with it?)[15] and (b) by answering their question with a question. Before they can catch their breath, he reverts to the question of legitimacy, switching addressees in mid-sentence ('So that you [plur.] may know that the son of man has

13. So Robert H. Gundry, *Mark: A Commentary on his Apology for the Cross* (Grand Rapids: Eerdmans, 1993), p. 96.

14. My favourite example is 'Render to Caesar the things that are Caesar's, and to God the things that are God's' (Mt. 22.21). What has Caesar that is not God's?

15. Hugh Anderson thinks Jesus' opponents will regard the forgiveness of sins as easier since it is not subject to verification (so too Gundry, *Mark*, p. 114), whereas from Mark's point of view it is 'both prior and more difficult' (*The Gospel of Mark* [NCB; London: Marshall, Morgan & Scott, 1971), p. 101. Having tried it, I find that both sentences are equally easy to say, and I have always understood Jesus to mean that it is a matter of indifference which he says. But that of course diverts attention from the question of legitimacy.

authority...I say to you [sing.], "Arise, take up your pallet"' (v. 10). Which the paralysed man promptly does. (7) To Levi he says laconically, 'Follow me', and he does (2.13). Jesus doesn't even promise to make him a tax collector of men (he had told Simon and Andrew they would still be fishermen, of a sort, 1.17). (8) Jesus hears that the 'scribes' are criticizing him for eating with 'sinners' and tax collectors, and puts a sudden end to the criticism, and to the story, with a proverb-like utterance: 'Those who are well have no need of a physician, but those who are sick' (2.17). (9) The next episode is likewise a vehicle for a pronouncement by Jesus. Why do Jesus' disciples not fast? The rhetor replies: 'Can the guests fast while the bridegroom is with them?' (2.19). And more wisdom follows, on new wine in old skins. There is no response from his critics. (10) The Pharisees ask why his disciples are unlawfully plucking grain on the sabbath. They too are silenced by Jesus' speech, first by a precedent from Scripture, secondly by yet another ad hoc proverb: 'The sabbath was made for humans, not humans for the sabbath' (2.25-28).

Perhaps this is a not a wholly representative sample of Jesus' speeches. But even this little collection by itself is proof enough that Jesus is represented in the Gospels as a powerful and persuasive speaker, to whom his critics tend to respond with silence and his audience with amazement.[16]

My point here is that this man who is so powerful with words is a typical male. Men get what they want by talking, arguing, being clever in speech, being authoritative, putting down opponents—all in the public arena, where women's voices are seldom heard. I would like the leisure to search for examples in the Gospels where it is *women's* speech that brings controversy to an end, where people do as women bid them, where women's cleverness with words defeats opponents. All that I know of women's words at the moment suggests that women do not typically find themselves playing such roles. Here are some characteristic words of women: (1) The haemorrhaging woman 'said to herself, "If I only touch his garment, I shall be well"' (Mt. 9.21; Mk 5.28). This is a word of faith, but not of authority, and it is not even heard by anyone else. (2) The adulterous woman in John 8, when asked who condemns her, says 'No one, Lord', but that is not a word of enough force to

16. On the latter, see most recently, Timothy Dwyer, *The Motif of Wonder in the Gospel of Mark* (JSNTSup, 128; Sheffield: Sheffield Academic Press, 1996).

conclude the story: it remains for Jesus to bring the episode to a conclusion with 'Neither do I; go and sin no more' (8.11). (3) Herodias says to her daughter, '[Ask for] the head of John the Baptist on a plate'. Now *that* is a powerful sentence, and it is effective, since the daughter 'came in immediately with haste to the king' and asked for the head (Mk 6.24-25). But it *is* a transaction between women. A woman can be authoritative with another woman, but a woman must 'ask' a man. (4) An episode in the Lazarus story in John 11 concludes with a strong statement by Martha. Jesus has said, 'I am the resurrection and the life... Do you believe this?' (v. 26), and she responds with a 'fully fledged confession of faith'[17] that sounds like a liturgical ecclesiastical formula: 'I believe that you are the Christ, the Son of God, he who is coming into the world' (v. 27). It is a rare theologically acceptable speech for a woman; when Peter says something equivalent he is rewarded with the Petrine declaration 'On this rock'; one fantasizes the possibility of an alternative, Marthan, papacy founded on her confession. (5) Elizabeth seems to have some power in speech. When her friends and relatives assume that her child will be named Zechariah after his father, she resists with 'Not so! He shall be called John'. But it is not her word that resolves matters. It waits upon the word of her dumb husband, who writes on his tablet, 'His name is John' (Lk. 1.59-63). (6) The final case is my exception that proves the rule. It is the speech of a woman that upstages Jesus. He says, 'It is not fair to take the children's bread and throw it to the dogs' (Mt. 15.26), one of his rather typical ad hoc proverbs. But the Canaanite woman, playing the role that we have come to expect of *Jesus*,[18] defeats him with her riposte: 'Yes, Lord, but even the dogs eat the crumbs that fall from their master's table'. Jesus acknowledges her victory with his 'Be it done for you as you desire', and the narrator chimes in with 'And her daughter was healed instantly' (v. 28).[19]

17. George R. Beasley-Murray, *John* (WBC, 36; Waco, TX: Word Books, 1987), p. 192.

18. As J. Martin C. Scott says ('Matthew 15.21-28: A Test-Case for Jesus' Manners', *JSNT* 63 [1996], pp. 21-44 [42]). In structuralist terms, Scott notes, Jesus is the 'opponent' and the woman is the 'helper' (p. 43).

19. In other places, women speak in order to ask for help (the Canaanite woman, Mt. 15.25; the widow to the judge, Lk. 18.3; Martha to Jesus, implicitly asking him to restore Lazarus, Jn 11.21), for a favour (Zebedee's wife for her sons, Mt. 20.20; Mary Magdalene for herself, Jn 20.17) or to share in rejoicing (the woman with the lost coin, Lk. 15.9), to pass on a message (Martha to Mary,

362 Biblical Studies/Cultural Studies

I am not of course arguing that in 'real life' women cannot speak as powerfully and persuasively as men; just that in our traditional literature such as the Gospels they do not.

d. *Jesus the Male Bonder*

Male bonding is a feature of male behaviour that has been attested throughout history but that has only recently been given a name.[20] The ideology of such male friendship has been analysed as containing these elements: loyalty to one another, a dyadic relationship with an exclusive tendency, a commitment to a common cause, and a valuing of the friendship above all other relationships. In such a friendship there is not necessarily a strong emotional element; the bond may be more instrumental and functional than affective.[21]

Jn 11.28; Mary Magdalene to the disciples, Jn 20.2, 18), to congratulate another woman (Elizabeth to Mary, Lk. 1. 42-44), to reproach (Mary to the young Jesus, Lk. 2.48 [but she is put down by Jesus]; Martha to Jesus, Lk. 10.40 [but she is put in her place by Jesus]; the high priest's serving woman to Peter, Mk 14.67 [but she is resisted by Peter]), to ask for information (Mary to the angel, Lk. 1.34) or to agree (Mary to the angel's announcement, Lk. 1.38) or to answer a question (Mary Magdalene to the angels, Jn 20.13), to greet (Mary Magdalene to Jesus, Jn 20.16), and to praise God (Mary, Lk. 1.46-55—the longest speech of a woman in the Gospels)—or else speak to themselves (Elizabeth, Lk. 1.25; the haemorrhaging woman, Mt. 9.21).

20. The term seems to have been first used by Lionel Tiger, in his *Men in Groups* (London: Thomas Nelson & Sons, 1969). See also Y.A. Cohen, 'Patterns of Friendship', in Y.A. Cohen (ed.), *Social Structure and Personality* (New York: Holt, Rinehart & Winston, 1961); E. Wolf, 'Kinship, Friendship and Patron–Client Relationships in Complex Societies', in M. Banton (ed.), *The Social Anthropology of Complex Societies* (London: Tavistock, 1966), pp. 3-27. Among recent studies of male bonding in literary texts may be mentioned those of Donald J. Geiner, *Women Enter the Wilderness: Male Bonding and the American Novel of the 1980s* (Columbia, SC: University of South Carolina Press, 1991), advancing the questionable theory that in the last decade the tendency in (white, male) American novels has been for male bonding to be less exclusive of women; Anne J. Cruz, 'Homo ex machina? Male Bonding in Calderón's *A secreto agravio, secreta vengenza*', *Forum for Modern Language Studies* 25 (1989), pp. 154-66.

21. 'Male bonding is not a vehicle for male–male emotional relationships, but rather is a substitute for them' (Joseph H. Pleck, *The Myth of Masculinity* [Cambridge, MA; The MIT Press, 1981], p. 150). Cf. also Drury Sherrod, 'The Bonds of Men: Problems and Possibilities in Close Male Relationships', in Harry Brod (ed.), *The Making of Masculinities: The New Men's Studies* (London: Routledge, 1987), pp. 213-39 (217): '[w]omen seem to look for intimate confidantes, while men seek for partners for adventure'.

By these norms, Jesus is the quintessential male bonder. Very soon after we first meet him in Mark, for example, he is gathering male companions (1.16-20). The men he attracts to himself have no time for anything else than their relationship with him: they leave everything to follow him—their nets, their ship, their counting table (Mt. 4.20, 22; 9.9). Peter speaks for all the disciples when he says, 'We have forsaken all, and followed you' (Mt. 19.27). They 'deny' themselves (Lk 9.23) and invest all their energies in his mission. Men say to him that they will follow him wherever he goes (Mt. 8.19). He has an immediate charm for other men: the moment he speaks to them they 'immediately' have eyes for him alone (Mk 1.18). He takes an instant liking to a man: when he sees the wealthy prince, we read: 'He loved him, and said to him, One thing you lack; go and sell all you have and give it to the poor...and come...follow me' (Mk 10.21). Men undertake to die for him (Jn 13.37). He for his part regards them as his family, gesturing to them with the words, 'Look! my mother and my brothers' (Mt. 12.49; Mk 3.34). And he makes the classic statement of buddyhood ('mateship' as we call it in Australia): 'No one can be my disciple if he does not hate his father and mother and wife and children and brothers and sisters— and his own life!' (Lk. 14.26).[22]

Wherever we read in the Gospels, more or less, Jesus is accompanied by his male band.[23] His disciples are mentioned in the Gospels almost half as often as Jesus is himself (by a somewhat crude measurement, according to which 'disciple[s]' occurs 236 times and 'Jesus' 566 times). There are occasions, indeed, when Jesus is alone, as at the temptation; but mostly he moves around the country in the company of his band, and, if you are thinking of inviting him to a wedding, it is apparently bad form not to invite his companions also; they and Jesus are a kind of 'item' (Jn 2.2).

Jesus' relationships with other men seem to be cemented at parties. He is evidently a convivial man. By his own admission, 'The son of man came eating and drinking' (Mt. 11.19), as if that is how, in a way, he would quite like to be known and remembered.[24] He is notorious for

22. See Michael Theobald, 'Jesus und seine Jünger: Ein problematisches Gruppenbild', *Theologische Quartalschrift* 173 (1993), pp. 219-26.

23. There are indeed some women among his followers (e.g. Mt. 27.55; Mk 15.41; Lk. 8.1-3; 23.27, 49, 55), but they do not belong to the inner circle, and they are comparatively rarely mentioned.

24. In similar vein, Luther, having the responsibility for the Reformation laid at

the flexibility of his companionship; Matthew as narrator reports that he is a friend of taxmen and 'sinners' (Mt. 9.10-11; 11.19), and Jesus himself acknowledges that the word on the street is that he is 'a glutton and a winebibber' (Mt. 11.19). He does spend a lot of time at the table (at Matthew's house, Lk. 5.29; at Simon's house, Mt. 26.6; Lk. 7.36-40; at Lazarus's house, John 12; at the Cana wedding, John 3; the Last Supper, Mt. 26.18-26); and these seem to be pretty lavish affairs (a big reception with a great crowd at Matthew's) and sodden to boot (six waterpots of wine *after* the bought-in wine has run out, at Cana). According to one scholar at least, 'party animal' is the most appropriate designation for the Jesus of the Gospels.[25] Let it not be overlooked that these feasts and meals are probably all male events. There are, indeed, two women at one of the meals—Mary and Martha in the house of Lazarus—but one of them serves and the other anoints him; it is the man of the house who 'sits at the table with him' (Jn 12.2). At another meal (or is it the same one?), an unnamed woman—who is not a diner at the table—anoints him (Mt. 26.6; Mk 14.3). And while the mother of Jesus is at the feast at Cana, it is not, apparently, by invitation: he and his disciples were 'called' (Jn 2.2) but she was just 'there' (2.1).

In all these male relationships, there is no evident erotic element. Jesus 'loves' the wealthy prince (Mk 10.21) and Lazarus (Jn 11.5) and especially the nameless disciple known only as 'the one Jesus loved' (Jn 13.23; 19.26; 20.2; 21.7, 20), who also leans on him when reclining at table (Jn 13.23; 21.20). Despite the language[26] and despite the intimate physical contact, what we seem to have depicted is a network of homosocial rather than homosexual relationships.[27] There is however one fact

his door, protested that he had done nothing but sit and drink beer with Philip Melanchthon.

25. Leif Vaage, *Atlanta Constitution*, 30 September 1989, quoted by Luke Timothy Johnson, *The Real Jesus: The Misguided Quest for the Historical Jesus and the Truth of the Traditional Gospels* (San Francisco: HarperSanFranscisco, 1996), p. 15; needless to say, Johnson does not hold with this description in the slightest, regarding it as 'deliberately intended to shock and, in the fashion of naughty schoolchildren, draw attention'.

26. Jesus also 'loves' Martha 'and her sister' (Jn 11.5).

27. See Eve Kosofsky Sedgwick for the distinction between the homosocial, which includes all same-sex relations, and the homosexual, which denotes only that segment of the homosocial that is distinguished by genital sexuality (*Between Men: English Literature and Male Homosocial Desire* [New York: Columbia University Press, 1985]). Not all accept the distinction, however; cf. Robert K. Martin, *Hero, Captain*

that gives us pause: in the ancient world, and certainly in Greece, while non-sexual male friendship is well attested, male bonding friends tended to be peers—as were also Jonathan and David. Homosexual love was more typical of the assymetrical relationship between an older lover and a younger beloved.[28] The interesting thing is that Jesus is never portrayed as the equal of his companions; though they are 'brothers' to one another, on a more or less equal footing[29] (e.g. Lk. 22.32), he is always their leader. Rarely he calls them his 'friends' (Lk. 12.4; Jn 15.14, 15).[30]

There is one other aspect of male bonding that I have not yet referred to. It is that there is typically in such bonding a dyadic element, an exclusive friendship such as those of Gilgamesh and Enkidu, David and Jonathan, and many others—as Hammond and Jablow have so interestingly drawn attention to in their paper on 'Gilgamesh and the Sundance Kid: The Myth of Male Friendship'.[31] Jesus has a wide range of male friends, both an outer and an inner circle, and although there are leaders among them like Peter, we read of no special buddy of Jesus until we get to the second half of the fourth Gospel: though he is never named, we are left in no doubt that he has a different kind of relationship with Jesus from that of the other disciples. The first time we meet him, he is simply 'one of his disciples, whom Jesus loved' (Jn 13.23)—as if there might well be other disciples whom Jesus 'loves' in the same sense. But then in 20.2, Mary runs 'to Peter and to the other disciple whom Jesus loved'—and we know that that is his sobriquet, if not to the disciples generally, then to the fourth evangelist. So too at 21.7. And when we

<hr />

and Stranger: Male Friendship, Social Critique, and Literary Form in the Sea Novels of Herman Melville (Chapel Hill: University of North Carolina Press, 1986), p. 13. The distinction between male friendship and homosexuality, though always problematic, has been clearly enough recognized in other ages than our own; cf. for example Alan Bray, 'Homosexuality and the Signs of Male Friendship in Elizabethan England', *History Workshop* 29 (1990), pp. 1-19.

28. Cf. Kenneth J. Dover, *Greek Homosexuality* (Cambridge, MA: Harvard University Press, 1978).

29. Jesus' 'brothers' in Jn 7.5, 10 are not his disciples; they are distinguished from the disciples in 2.12.

30. A little curiously, he says in Jn 15.15 that henceforth he will call them not servants but friends; but we have never heard him calling his companions servants.

31. Dorothy Hammond and Alta Jablow, 'Gilgamesh and the Sundance Kid: The Myth of Male Friendship', in Brod (ed.), *The Making of Masculinities*, pp. 241-58.

read at 21.20 that 'the disciple whom Jesus loved' also 'leant on his breast at supper'—as a matter of course, though the verb is aorist—then we know for sure that this is Jesus' special buddy, his bonded other.[32] And we wish we knew more.[33]

e. *Jesus the Womanless*

It is widely recognized that one of the concomitants of strong male bonding is a relative minimizing of cross-sex relationships. The male Jesus, true to type, is everywhere surrounded by male friends; it is therefore not surprising that Jesus gets on well without women.

There is of course a tendency in current literature, some of it quite scholarly, to insist on how well Jesus treats women; and there is no doubt some truth in this position, more, that is, than at first meets the (male) eye, trained as it is to screen out those it does not recognize as its own kind. The issue here, however, is not whether or not Jesus treats women well, but whether he needs them. There are men ('men's men') even of our own day who have been brought up in a male world and much prefer the company of men to women, who can nevertheless be very charming and gallant to women, can even, better than that, recognize their rights and go so far as to proclaim themselves feminists, in their own small way—and yet have no place for women in their lives and get along fine without women.

Jesus is such a womanless man, and he shows it first and foremost by not being married. No matter his reasons, or *the* reasons, perhaps we should say, for he himself never seems to think about it (or could being a eunuch for the sake of the kingdom be a clue?). It is actually a very ostentatious way of signalling, Women? Who needs them? He is not a woman-hater, and he actually 'loves' Martha and her sister (what was her name?) (Jn 11.5; he has remembered it in 20.16), though he is a bit severe with his mother (2.4). He can be kind, perhaps even affectionate, to ill women (Mt. 9.20; 15.22; Lk. 8.2) and, on principle, it seems, to

32. I know that Meg Davies thinks that the 'beloved disciple' is not a real person but a fictional idealization of what disciples should be (*Rhetoric and Reference in the Fourth Gospel* [JSNTSup, 69; Sheffield: JSOT Press, 1992]). Historically speaking, she may well be right, but, as I say, I am not thinking of the historical.

33. To develop this theme further, see H. Attridge, 'Masculine Fellowship in the Acts of Thomas', in Birger A. Pearson, A. Thomas Kraabel and George W.E. Nickelsburg (eds.), *The Future of Early Christianity: Essays in Honor of Helmut Koester* (Minneapolis: Fortress Press, 1991).

socially unacceptable women (John 4; 8). He is touched by a woman
(Mary in Jn 12.3) who adores him (Mt. 26.7-13; Mk 14.3-9; Lk. 7.36-
50), and he obviously inspires loyalty in the 'many' women who go so
far as to follow him from Galilee to Jerusalem (Mt. 27.55). Some
wealthy women idolize him (Lk. 8.3). And he has one in depth conversation with a woman by a well in John 4.[34]

But he has no wife, no female friend; he does not live in a family with
a mother and sisters and aunts and female cousins. He is an itinerant
preacher, and his male disciples have taken their place—they are his
family (Mt. 12.49). And he is a self-sufficient male.

f. *Jesus the Binary Thinker*

I am arguing that binary or oppositional thinking is a typically male
mode of thought. I believe that it is an intellectual expression of the
male aggressiveness that has been commented on above. As far as I can
tell, not many people have adopted this viewpoint, which I believe I
inherited from Hélène Cixous; but I find it very intriguing to work
with the possibility that a fundamental structural element in everyday
and academic thought alike might be essentially gendered.[35]

The project of deconstruction of binary oppositions must be brought
into the discussion at this point. Derrida has shown, and it would be a
brave person who denied it now, that the whole edifice of Western
intellectual thought has been built upon a set of binary categories, such

34. On Jesus and women, see also Brian Grenier, 'Jesus and Women', *St Mark's
Review* 119 (1984), pp. 13-21; Ronald W. Graham, 'Women in the Ministry of Jesus
and in the Early Church', *Lexington Theological Quarterly* 18 (1983), pp. 1-42; Stuart
L. Love, 'The Place of Women in Public Settings in Matthew's Gospel: A Sociolog-
ical Inquiry', *BTB* 24 (1994), pp. 52-65; Julie M. Hopkins, *Towards a Feminist
Christology: Jesus of Nazareth, European Women and the Christological Crisis* (Kampen:
Kok, 1995); Carla Ricci, *Mary Magdalene and Many Others: Women Who Followed
Jesus* (Minneapolis: Augsburg–Fortress, 1994); Ingrid Rosa Kitzberger, 'Mary of
Bethany and Mary of Magdala—Two Female Characters in the Johannine Passion
Narrative: A Feminist, Narrative-Critical Reader-Response', *NTS* 41 (1995), pp.
564-86; Hisako Kinukawa, *Women and Jesus in Mark: A Japanese Feminist Perspective*
(Maryknoll, NY: Orbis Books, 1994).

35. I already built upon this concept in my paper, 'Beyond Synchronic/ Diachronic', in Johannes C. de Moor (ed.), *Synchronic or Diachronic? A Debate on Method
in Old Testament Exegesis* (Oudtestamentische Studiën, 34; Leiden: E.J. Brill, 1995),
pp. 52-71, as well as in my 'Loin-girding and Other Male Activities in the Book of
Job' (Society of Biblical Literature International Meeting, Dublin, July 1996).

as nature/nurture, mind/body.[36] Derrida's ambition has been to show that such categories are less watertight than has been supposed, and to envisage the removal of the security of these familiar categories. If now we add that the construction of binaries has been an essentially male project—like the Western intellectual tradition in general—we can contemplate the future emergence of a different conceptuality that is more representatively human.

There is no denying, however, the force and the drama in oppositional thinking. I take another example, from the world of education, where Kieran Egan has argued that the binary oppositions typically enshrined in stories (the simple contrasts of heroes and villains, of fear and security, courage and cowardice, and so on) suggest a most effective way of teaching. The best learning experiences, he proposes, are those that begin with a conflict or a tension or a binary contrast. The opposition creates in the pupils a desire for resolution, which can ultimately be effected by the skilful teacher. Meantime the pupils' interest, attention and involvement is assured.[37] Egan does not suggest that his approach is a gendered one, but I would not be surprised if what I am calling a male mode of thinking should also be an intriguing and exciting one. There is more excitement in conflict than in networking.

What of Jesus? Is he a male binary thinker? This is a question that could be pursued on the level of rhetoric or on a more structural level. Though there is a plethora of studies on rhetoric in the New Testament, I can find nothing of much help to me. But I do not find it too difficult to collect examples from the Gospels of what I would call binary thinking. Here is a sample from the early chapters of Matthew:

> Whoever is not with me is against me (12.30).
> You have heard it said, but I say to you ... (5.33-34, etc.).
> Not to abolish but to fulfil (Mt. 5.17).
> Let what you say be simply Yes or No (5.37).
> The wise builder and the foolish builder (7.24-26).

36. Here is a longer list of such binary oppositions we find so fundamental to thought: necessary/contingent, essence/accident, objective/subjective, reason/emotion, literal/metaphorical, precise/fuzzy, history/fiction, content/form, central/marginal, positive/negative, object/representation, text/interpretation, original/copy, text/context, conscious/unconscious, transcendent/immanent, presence/absence, male/female.

37. *Teaching as Story Telling: An Alternative Approach to Teaching and the Curriculum* (London: Routledge, 1988). I am grateful to Heather McKay for telling me about this book.

Those who are well need no doctor, but those who are sick (9.12).
There is nothing covered that will not be revealed (10.26).
He who finds his life will lose it (10.39).
Hidden from the wise and revealed to infants (11.25).
Mercy and not sacrifice (12.7).
The good man out of his good treasure brings forth good, and the evil
       man out of his evil treasure brings forth evil (12.35).
To him who has will be given, from him who has not will be taken away
      (13.12).

Those are more rhetorically shaped binary oppositions. On the structural level, Jesus makes great play with oppositions such as these that occur in the same chapters of Matthew:

earth / heaven
sheep / wolves
teacher / disciple
body / soul
light / dark
acknowledge / deny
peace / sword
good tree / bad tree
wheat / tares
evildoers / righteous

I should also note that I do not think that Jesus is entirely a victim of binary thinking, since it is also characteristic of him to confuse traditional categories. Sometimes his refusal to align himself with binary oppositions amounts to what I understand as a deconstruction of them.[38] Here is a collection of such cases from the same chapters of Matthew:

Love your enemies (5.44).
Leave the dead to bury their dead (8.22).
Not dead but sleeping (9.24).
My yoke is easy and my burden light (11.30).
If Satan casts out Satan, he is divided against himself (12.26).
Seeing they do not see and hearing they do not hear (13.13).

All the same, I think it is true to say that Jesus thinks largely in binary categories. That is part of the force of his rhetoric, and that is in part why he is so sure of himself. Jesus is no postmodernist, whatever some

---

38. I have studied Jesus as deconstructionist in my paper, 'Ethics as Deconstruction, and, The Ethics of Deconstruction', in John W. Rogerson, Margaret Davies and M. Daniel Carroll R. (eds.), *The Bible in Ethics: The Second Sheffield Colloquium* (JSOTSup, 207; Sheffield: Sheffield Academic Press, 1995), pp. 77-106.

might like to think. He believes in absolutes, though not necessarily the absolutes of his opponents. But by and large, he works with the same categories as his contemporaries (how could he not, and still be intelligible to them?). Above all (for the purposes of this paper) he thinks and speaks as a traditional male, setting one binary against another.

2. *The Masculinity of the Modern West*

So much for the masculinity of Jesus. In order to understand him, and especially in order to evaluate his masculinity, we need to be aware of what masculinity might mean in our own culture. This is not the place where I can embark upon a full-scale analysis of contemporary masculinity, which is bound to be diverse and complicated by the complexities of modern societies. But in order to say something at all, I have recourse to one influential analysis that has been advanced as appropriate for our modern Western culture.[39] Five major themes in the construction of masculinity have been noted.

39. The typology is that of J.A. Doyle, *The Male Experience* (Dubuque, IA: William C. Brown, 2nd edn, 1989), cited by Julia T. Wood, *Gendered Lives: Communication, Gender, and Culture* (Belmont, CA: Wadsworth Publishing Company, 1994), pp. 77-81. See also Pleck, *The Myth of Masculinity*.

There are other important dimensions to the study of masculinity of which this essay cannot, of necessity, take account. One is that of *change* in Western masculinity and of the processes by which the prevailing norms have developed. See, for example, Michael Roper and John Tosh (eds.), *Manful Assertions: Masculinities in Britain since 1800* (London: Routledge, 1991); J.A. Mangan and James Walvin (eds.), *Manliness and Morality: Middle-Class Masculinity in Britain and America 1800–1940* (Manchester: Manchester University Press, 1987); Clyde W. Franklin, II, *The Changing Definition of Masculinity* (New York: Plenum Press, 1984); Michael S. Kimmel, *Changing Men: New Directions in Research on Men and Masculinity* (Newbury Park, CA: Sage Publications, 1987). Cf. also the reviews introduced by Michael Roper, 'Recent Books on Masculinity', *History Workshop* 29 (1990), pp. 184-93; and the review forum in *Victorian Studies* 36 (1993), pp. 207-26: James Eli Adams, 'The Banality of Transgression? Recent Works on Masculinity' (pp. 207-13); Ed Cohen, 'Mar(r)king Men' (pp. 215-210); Mary Poovey, 'Exploring Masculinities' (pp. 223-26).

Another significant dimension is *theorizing* masculinity; see especially Peter Middleton, *The Inward Gaze: Masculinity and Subjectivity in Modern Culture* (London: Routledge, 1992); and Joseph A. Boone and Michael Cadden (eds.), *Engendering Men: The Question of Male Feminist Criticism* (London: Routledge, 1990).

A third dimension is the challenge to the concept of masculinity itself posed by a

1. The primary rule is: Don't be female. J.A. Doyle calls this the 'negative touchstone' of men's role. Whatever women do is *ipso facto* what a real man must not do.[40]

2. The second rule is: Be successful. Men are trained to be 'success objects',[41] and their worth as husbands, friends and simply as men is determined by their successfulness. 'The object, a boy soon gathers, is not to be liked but to be envied...not to be part of a group but to distinguish himself from the others in the group.'[42]

3. The third rule is: Be aggressive. From childhood, boys are encouraged to be tough, to fight, and not to run away. Competitive sport emphasizes these values, and in many cultures military training reinforces them.[43]

4. The fourth demand is: Be sexual. Men are supposed to be sexually experienced, and to be always interested in sex.[44] 'Sex isn't a free choice when you have to perform to be a man.'[45]

5. Fifthly, the rule for men is: Be self-reliant. 'Men are supposed to be confident, independent and autonomous...A "real man" doesn't need others, particularly women. He depends on himself, takes care of himself, and relies on nobody.'[46]

deconstructive approach to the opposition male/female. See especially Jeff Hearn, *Men in the Public Eye: The Construction and Deconstruction of Public Men and Public Patriarchies* (London: Routledge, 1992), esp. pp. 1-9.

40. Cf. Arthur Brittan, *Masculinity and Power* (Oxford: Basil Blackwell, 1989), p. 3: 'Masculinity...does not exist in isolation from femininity—it will always be an expression of the current image that men have of themselves in relation to women'.

41. W. Farrell, 'Men as Success Objects', *Utne Reader* (May/June 1991), pp. 81-84.

42. Alfie Kohn, *No Contest: The Case against Competition* (Boston: Houghton Mifflin, 1986), p. 168.

43. See also Brittan, *Masculinity and Power*, Chapter 4, 'Masculinity and Competitiveness' (pp. 77-107).

44. Cf. W. Gaylin, *The Male Ego* (New York: Viking; London: Penguin Books, 1992).

45. Wood, *Gendered Lives*, p. 81.

46. Wood, *Gendered Lives*, p. 81. This is not of course the only analysis of the male role that can be and has been made. Catharine Stimpson, for example, identifies three ways in which 'real men' define themselves: they earn money in the public labour force and so support their families; they have formal power over the women and children in those families; they are heterosexual with the women they dominate and bully other men who are not heterosexual (Catharine R. Stimpson, 'Foreword'

Obviously, there is nothing natural or God-given about these roles.
Masculinity, like femininity, is a social construction, the product of historical processes, as much a human construct as the pyramids or pewter
(as Catharine Stimpson puts it).[47] To be masculine, as she says, is 'to
have a particular psychological identity, social role, cultural script, place
in the labor force, and sense of the sacred'[48]—and all of those elements
are socially constructed.

Different societies write different scripts for their men, so it is a priori
likely that maleness in the modern West does not closely resemble maleness in ancient societies such as the world in which Jesus lived. And we
had better be open to the possibility of a plurality of masculinities. Perhaps his society legitimated more than one way of being a man—though
perhaps not, since social pressures tend toward uniformity rather than
diversity.[49] More significant is the fact that not all males, in whatever
culture, conform with the social norms. The norms may privilege
young, heterosexual, strong and physical men, for example, and those
who cannot be so characterized will be deviants from socially acceptable
maleness. But they will still be males. We can expect, then, to find in
our texts, as well as in our own society, representations of conflicting

to Brod [ed.], *The Making of Masculinities*, p. xiii). And here is another much-cited
account of the typical male: 'Someone who: is aggressive, independent, unemo-
tional, or hides his emotions; is objective, easily influenced, dominant, likes maths
and science; is not excitable in a minor crisis; is active, competitive, logical, worldly,
skilled in business, direct, knows the ways of the world; is someone whose feelings
are not easily hurt; is adventurous, makes decisions easily, never cries, acts as a
leader; is self-confident; is not uncomfortable about being aggressive; is ambitious,
able to separate feelings from ideas; is not dependent, nor conceited about his
appearance; thinks men are superior to women, and talks freely about sex with men'
(Fay Fransella and Kay Frost, *On Being a Woman: A Review of Research on How
Women See Themselves* [London: Tavistock, 1977, pp. 43-44], cited by Ann Oakley,
Subject Women [Oxford: Martin Robertson, 1981], p. 64).

47. Stimpson, 'Foreword' to Brod (ed.), *The Making of Masculinities*, p. xiii.

48. Stimpson, 'Foreword' to Brod (ed.), *The Making of Masculinities*, p. xii.

49. Even in a period of rapid social change such as our own, the blueprint of
gender stereotypes remains remarkably constant; cf. Wood, *Gendered Lives*, p. 21;
F. Cancian, 'Love and the Rise of Capitalism', in B. Risman and P. Schwartz (eds.),
Gender in Intimate Relationships (Belmont, CA: Wadsworth, 1989), pp. 12-25. Of
course, it is all too easy to slip into various intellectual sins over this matter of defining masculinity; David H.J. Morgan, for example, warns against the errors of essentialism, reductionism and reification (*Discovering Men* [Critical Studies on Men and
Masculinities, 3; London: Routledge, 1992], pp. 41-43).

masculinities. That is an issue that I will need to explore further, asking, for example, whether there is anything in the characterization of Jesus that breaches the typical masculinity of his period.

For the moment, however, I can do no more than stick with my own analysis of Jesus' masculinity, and compare and contrast it with what I have just outlined above.

3. *Conflict and Coherence of Masculinities: His and Ours*

If it is a key to modern masculinity that it defines itself over against femininity, there is an obvious conflict with ancient masculinity. As I argued in relation to the case of David, it seems that in ancient societies the spheres of men and women were so distinct, and their cultural scripts so divergent, that neither defined itself over against the other. If our culture represents the 'feminization' of society, as has been argued,[50] it makes sense that males now tend to define themselves oppositionally, having lost a distinct idea of their own role. I can see no point in the Jesus story in which his masculinity is defined in reference to its binary opposite, femininity.

A second striking conflict between ancient and modern masculinities is in the matter of sexuality. If men of our time are scripted to be sexual, to be interested in sex and to be active sexually, it is very interesting to observe the absence of sex and the erotic in the Gospels. Can it be that contemporary absorption in sex coheres with a masculinity that is not so sure of itself, that is troubled about self-definition and functionality? If sex is as much a way of finding oneself as finding the other, might finding oneself be a peculiarly modern desire, one that is not shared by the world of the text?[51]

---

50. Such 'feminization' has been seen, historically, most clearly by its opponents, such as the Boy Scout movement. See, for example, Joseph H. Pleck, 'The Theory of Male Sex-Role Identity: Its Rise and Fall, 1936 to the Present', in Brod (ed.), *The Making of Masculinities*, pp. 21–38 (23); Michael S. Kimmel, 'The Contemporary "Crisis" of Masculinity in Historical Perspective', in Brod (ed.), *The Making of Masculinities*, pp. 121–53 (143-49); Michael Messner, 'The Meaning of Success: The Athletic Experience and the Development of Male Identity', in Brod (ed.), *The Making of Masculinities*, pp. 193–209 (196).

51. Cf. Robert Nozik, 'Sexuality', in Anne Minas (ed.), *Gender Basics: Feminist Perspectives on Women and Men* (Belmont, CA: Wadsworth, 1993), pp. 302-306: 'It is

In other respects, there are interesting coherences between the analysis of modern masculinity proffered above and what I have identified in the portraiture of Jesus. Being aggressive is the most obvious parallel, being self-reliant (including independence of women) is the most interesting, and being successful is the most promising. I will take up only the last, and that very briefly. There is a lot in the Gospels about meekness and humility, and Jesus seems at times idealistic, naive and unpolitical. Success is often thought to be the polar opposite of his motivations. Nonetheless, he is goal-oriented, and he has high stakes to play for. He envisages himself as the key player in the kingdom of heaven, and offers his disciples privileges in that kingdom (Mt. 19.22; Lk. 22.30). He is the only route to the Father (Jn 14.6), no one knows the Father except himself and those to whom he reveals him (Mt. 11.27; Lk. 10.22). He sees himself as ruler of an otherworldly kingdom (Jn 18.36), and as having overcome the ordinary world (Jn 16.33). He may not be a success in the conventional sense, though he is important enough to be feared by the authorities (Mt. 26.5). But he is out to win, on a daily basis and as a life goal; and win he does, according to the Gospel story. He is a man's man, by any standard, ancient or modern.

4. *Conclusion*

I need to make my own position clear at the end. Just because Jesus is male, indefeasibly and unmistakably male, does not mean that there is something wrong with him. There are those of us in the world who are male, even if not entirely indefeasibly and unmistakably, and we do not intend to be wrongfooted on that account alone. So I would not like it to be thought I have said that because Jesus is male he is somehow bad. What is bad is if people think Jesus is human rather than male, that he speaks as a human being *simpliciter* and not in the name of masculinity.

But I need to say also that, for my part, just because something is male I do not necessarily approve of it. My response to the maleness of Jesus ranges right across a spectrum: for example, the violence and domineering aspect of his behaviour and speech I find troublesome, whereas his tendency to binary thinking does not faze me, since, I have to admit, that is my own default mode. I simply do not wish to be constrained by

not only the other person who is known more deeply in sex. One knows one's own self better in experiencing what it is capable of ' (p. 303).

the masculinity of Jesus, and I want to urge that it is a defect or limitation in him that he is a traditional man, which is to say (a) he is unaware of his masculinity, (b) he is unaware that masculinity is only one way of being human, (c) he is not a woman also. I speak of course, as I have done throughout, of the fictional character Jesus, the Jesus of the Gospels.

Ugly Thoughts:
On the Face and Physique
of the Historical Jesus[1]

Stephen D. Moore

The Abattoir

'I'm finished', groaned Jesus, gratefully giving up the ghost. Late that night his father came to claim the body. Never one to stand on ceremony, he went to work there and then in the tomb. First he skinned the corpse. After he had laboriously removed the body hair by scraping, he scrubbed the skin clean, sighing all the while at the punctures and tears that marred it. Then he smoothed it with pumice and dressed it with chalk. Perspiring profusely now, he carefully cut it into rectangular sheets, stacked and folded them meticulously, and sewed them along the crease. Leaving the book on the slab, he wearily vacated the tomb before sunrise, dragging the flayed corpse in his wake. Soon afterwards this blank book was found by two of Jesus' disciples (as it was meant to be), one of whom recognized it for the remains of his master and lovingly bore it away. Years later he would use it to write the first draft of his Gospel.

This tale, too, refuses to remain buried. This is now the third time that I've told it. Always with variations, of course. The last time it was the Beloved Disciple himself who manufactured the book. He had arrived with Peter at the tomb

---

1. A less-developed version of this essay (amounting to the bones without the meat, meager though the latter still is) was presented to the Johannine Literature Section of the Society of Biblical Literature at its 1996 Annual Meeting in New Orleans and is scheduled for publication in Fernando F. Segovia (ed.), *More Interpretations Than the World Can Contain: Readers and Readings of the Fourth Gospel* (Atlanta: Scholars Press). Various colleagues have contributed to the essay's development. David Brakke, Yael Feldman, Susan Graham, Hugh Pyper and Elliot Wolfson supplied many succulent scraps (not all of which I have been able to ingest), while Obery Hendricks spooned out some slightly bitter medicine (which I am still struggling to swallow).

and seen only the linen wrappings lying there, together with the face cloth, all of them covered with a tiny elegant script written in bright red ink: Ἐν ἀρχῇ ἦν ὁ λόγος, καὶ ὁ λόγος ἦν πρὸς τὸν θεόν, καὶ θεὸς ἦν ὁ λόγος... *Tenderly the disciple had gathered the grave cloths, burying his tear-streaked face in them and inhaling the scent of death that still clung to them. He had slept in the linen wrappings for many years, the face cloth under his head. Finally, when the writing had begun to fade, he had reluctantly cut the moldering rags into crude rectangular sheets, stacked them roughly in order, folded them in two, and stitched them along the crease, thereby producing the first Christian codex.*

The first time the tale imposed itself on me, however, I was standing not in the tomb but by the cross. And the cross in question was not John's pink cross with the padded patibulum and rubber nails but Mark's cruel, crimson cross with the red-hot, razor-sharp spikes. Here is what I saw:

> Writ(h)ing in pain on his cross, Jesus can at last be read: 'Truly this man was God's son' (Mk 15.39). He is in the process of becoming a book. Nailed, grafted onto the tree, Jesus' body is becoming one with the wood. His flesh, torn and beaten to a pulp, joined by violence to the wood, is slowly being changed into processed woodpulp, into paper, as the centurion looks on. As tree and budding book, Jesus is putting forth leaves, the leaves of a gospel book, whose opening sentence the centurion has just read: Ἀρχὴ τοῦ εὐαγγελίου Ἰησοῦ Χριστοῦ υἱοῦ θεοῦ...
>
> Doubled over in pain, folded like a stack of leaves, Jesus is bound to a hard wooden spine. Graphted onto the tree, he is leafing his body, in order to readturn as a book. He will spend three days in the tome. But in death his voice will acquire the volume that it lacked in life.

And in death his body will also acquire the beauty that it (most likely) lacked in life, a beauty generally found only in books. Or in glossy magazines, or on TV, which is all very much to the point, as you shall see.

But will it be biblical/cultural studies? If not, I've wandered into the wrong volume. What might this / mean, anyway? North Americans would sound it out as slash—'biblical studies slash cultural studies'—whereas Britons would prefer the less violent stroke— 'biblical studies stroke cultural studies'. These titular imperatives notwithstanding, I suspect it's cultural studies, not biblical studies, that's doing most of the slashing/stroking in this volume. If forced to choose, however, I'd prefer to see biblical studies stroked to arousal by cultural studies rather than gutted by it. For me, cultural studies is primarily a pretext to bring biblical studies into contact with contemporary culture, to let biblical studies at its driest, dustiest and most ecclesiastical experience the touch of popular culture in particular. Alternately bland and bizarre, the latter already has a Bible in its pocket anyway, its spine comfortably pressed up against a copy of the TV

Guide. *Not that I'm interested in* idealizing *popular culture; it fatigues and nauseates me as often as it fascinates me. But it envelops me enough to impel me to acknowledge it. What the present essay aims to acknowledge, for example, is that although fewer people than ever know what Jesus is supposed to have said, many remain reasonably sure that they at least know what he looked like. Jesus' face is a (pop-)cultural icon, and has been for quite some time. As such, his image speaks louder than his words.*

The Beauty Parlor

What are we to make of the Fourth Gospel today? Is it not at once the most essential—and most inessential—of the canonical gospels? At the close of the twentieth century, no less than at the close of the fourth, does the Johannine Jesus not remain the bench-mark of christological orthodoxy for all the mainline Christian churches? But what of the roles of the Johannine Jesus(es) within the critical-scholarly communities?

To the extent that our discipline began as an attempt to wrench the historical Jesus free from the suffocating embrace of the Christ of faith, it appears that we have found our stride once again as New Testament critics. A renewed quest for the historical Jesus rages even as I write. Many of us have joined in the manhunt for the Jew of Nazareth, many more of us cheering or yelling obscenities from the sidelines. Startled eyes turn as the hysterical Jesus suspects are dragged into the church by the triumphant band of scholars. To the dubious congregation in the pews, each Jesus seems more unlikely than the last. 'Did you at any time claim to be the Christ, the Son of the living God?' each is asked in turn. 'I did not', most of them reply. But if the congregation is in shock, we are in our element. For this we were born, to testify to the truth, most especially the truth about this Jesus, called Christ. And what could be less relevant to this truth than the Gospel according to Saint John?

Hardened as we are by historical Jesus research, it is hard not to smile superciliously if we contemplate the great controversies that shook Christendom in the fourth century, the heresiarch Arius, for example, daring to claim that the pre-existent Christ was not an eternal being after all, but merely a superior creature created *ex nihilo* by the Father as an instrument for the creation of the cosmos. Which is simply to say that by the fourth century the Fourth Gospel was calling the shots, establishing the parameters of permissible debate on the identity of the enigmatic Nazarene more than any other early Christian document, while the early imperial church yawned, stretched itself, and lumbered unsteadily to its sandaled feet to tower imperiously over the earth. The fourth century was the century of the Fourth Gospel, and the same can be said of every century since then, as far as Christian orthodoxy has been concerned. Several centuries of critical biblical scholarship has done remarkably little to change that, which is why the Jesus Seminar was formed.

I'm eager to add my squawk to the current cacophony of commentary on the Jesus Seminar, hence this sudden swerve. Ten years or so ago, a small group of colleagues and I comprised the Literary Facets Seminar, one of several sideshows that met alongside the Jesus Seminar, under the ringmastership of Robert W. Funk. At the 1988 Spring Meeting of the Seminars in Sonoma, perched on kindergarten chairs and surrounded by alphabet charts and children's art in the grade-school classroom that had been assigned to us, our group read papers on postmodernism to each other and to a lone misdirected local who gradually came to realize that we were not the Jesus Seminar. The Postmodern Bible *was conceived in that classroom.*

The contrast between the Johannine Jesus and the Jesus Seminar's Jesus could not, of course, be more dramatic. Johannine scholars like to say that the Jesus who speaks in the Fourth Gospel is not the historical Jesus but the risen Lord. As such, the Johannine Jesus is, from his very first appearance in this Gospel, a Jesus risen from the dead even before he has died, a Jesus always already resurrected. Valentinus and his school seem to have grasped this intuitively. A fragment attributed to Valentinus by Clement of Alexandria (*Miscellanies* 3.59.3) states: 'Jesus digested divinity: he ate and drank in a special way, without excreting his solids. He had such a great capacity for continence that the nourishment within him was not corrupted [i.e. did not become excrement], for he did not experience corruption.'[2] Valentinus rightly refuses to be thrown off the scent by the fact that this is also a body that, on the Fourth Evangelist's own account, is susceptible to exhaustion (4.6) and capable of being cut open (19.34; 20.25, 27). For a risen body is of necessity incorruptible, in life no less than in death.

---

2.   This fascinating fragment is what lies behind the present paper, actually. Chancing upon it, I was assailed by a desire to create a sanctuary for it. And so I began to build this essay. The translation of the fragment is Bentley Layton's in *The Gnostic Scriptures: A New Translation with Annotations and Introductions* (The Anchor Bible Reference Library; New York: Doubleday, 1987), p. 239.

Contrast the worm-ridden corpse of Jesus that the Jesus Seminar claims to have exhumed. In a recent issue of *The Fourth R*, the Seminar's popular periodical, we read that Gerd Lüdemann, controversial author of *Die Auferstehung Jesu* and guest speaker at the Seminar's Spring 1995 meeting, 'argued in a public address that the body of Jesus undoubtedly decayed in the usual way', and that the Fellows of the Seminar 'approved this thesis overwhelmingly'.[3] 'They found that Jesus' corpse probably rotted in some unknown grave', the report continues.[4] We should not be unduly alarmed by their grisly discovery; history, after all, is written with a gravedigger's spade. Compare the French historian Michelet, who, having witnessed the opening of his wife's grave, wrote in a journal entry of 4 September 1839:

> Severe ordeal. Alas! I scarcely saw anything but worms. It is said: 'returned to the earth'. It is a figure of speech. The corpse's inanimate substance reanimates a living substance. That aspect is hideous to the eye, harsh as Christian humiliation...[5]

In later years, as though condemned to remain poised forever on the lip of his wife's opened grave, Michelet would characterize his own life's work, and that of historians in general, as one of unending exhumation.

What might the decomposed body of Jesus have looked like in life? Appearing human, all too human, in death, should he not likewise have appeared human, all too human, in life? As it happens, the same century that presents us with the spectacle of a cruelly constipated Christ, the Valentinian Jesus without an anus, also presents us with the specter of a physically repulsive Christ.

I find this ugly Jesus strangely alluring. As a research topic, indeed, the face and physique of the 'earthly' Jesus holds an almost irresistible attraction for me. What could be more immanent, more mundane than this Jewish peasant's physical aspect? And yet, as absolutely unknowable, is it not also somehow ineffable?

---

3.   Anon., 'The Jesus Seminar Spring 1995 Meeting', *The Fourth R* 8.2 (1995), pp. 10-11 (10).

4.   Anon., 'The Jesus Seminar Spring 1995 Meeting', p. 10.

5.   Jules Michelet, *Mother Death: The Journals of Jules Michelet 1815–1850* (ed. and trans. Edward K. Kaplan; Amherst: University of Massachusetts Press, 1984), pp. 89-90. I find myself curiously incapable of commenting on this searing passage. It is not that I have nothing to say, but rather that I do not trust myself to begin.

The apparition first rears its ugly head briefly in Justin Martyr's *First Apology* (50) and later in Irenaeus's *Against Heresies* (3.19.2; 4.33.12; cf. 2.22.4), although Clement of Alexandria seems to have been the first to grasp it firmly by the horns. Justin and Irenaeus had taken Isa. 53.2-3 at its word; so, too, does Clement: 'And that the Lord Himself was uncomely in aspect, the Spirit testifies by Esaias: "And we saw Him, and He had no form nor comeliness; but his form was mean, inferior to men"' (*The Instructor* 3.1).[6] Subsequently Clement will cite the same proof text in the course of explaining how certain individuals can be just 'even should they happen to be ugly in their persons' (*Miscellanies* 2.5). Tertullian and Hippolytus will each appeal to this Isaian passage also as they propound the doctrine of the two advents. 'We affirm two characters of the Christ demonstrated by the prophets, and as many advents of His forenoted', writes Tertullian. Whereas the second advent will be incomparably glorious, the first was 'in humility', 'not even in his aspect comely'—and the quotation follows: 'And we saw Him, and he had not attractiveness of grace; but His mien was unhonoured', and so on (*Answer to the Jews* 14; cf. *idem, Against Marcion* 3.7; Hippolytus, *Treatise on Christ and Antichrist* 44). Elsewhere, too, Tertullian will concede that Jesus was 'inglorious in countenance and aspect, just as Isaiah...had fore-announced' (*On Idolatry* 18; cf. *idem, Against Praxeas* 11), and so will Cyprian (*Treatises* 12.2.13), Novatian (*Concerning the Trinity* 9), Lactantius (*The Divine Institutes* 4.16), and Augustine (e.g. *Exposition of Psalm 127* 8).[7] The most notable allusion to the ugly Christ, however, occurs

6.   Here and in what follows, the translation is from the *Ante-Nicene Fathers* series. The apologetic contortions that these blunt statements induced in certain of the devout editors and translators of the series merit a study in themselves. See, e.g., Vol. II, p. 272 n. 1, which is appended to the sentence from *The Instructor* quoted above: 'But see also Ps. xiv. 2, which was often cited by the ancients to prove the reverse. Both may be reconciled: he was a fair and comely child like his father David; but as 'the man of sorrows', he became old in looks, and his countenance was marred. For David's beauty, see 1 Sam. xvi. 12. For our Lord's at twelve years of age, when the virgin was seeking her child, Canticles v. 7-16. For his appearance at three and thirty, when the Jews only ventured to credit him with less than fifty years, John viii. 57.'

7.   In the *Acts of Peter* (c. 180–90 CE), too, we read of Jesus 'beauteous, yet appearing among us as poor and ugly', while in the *Acts of John* (late second century?) we read that the polymorphous Jesus 'sometimes appeared to [John] as a small man with no good looks' (trans. from *New Testament Apocrypha*, rev. edn).

in Origen. In the course of his interminable refutation of Celsus, Origen attributes the following statement to him:

> Since a divine Spirit inhabited the body [of Jesus], it must certainly have been different from that of other beings, in respect of grandeur, or beauty, or strength, or voice, or impressiveness, or persuasiveness. For it is impossible that He, to whom was imparted some divine quality beyond other beings, should not differ from others; whereas this person did not differ in any respect from another, but was, as they report, little, and ill-favoured, and ignoble (*Against Celsus* 6.75; cf. 1.69).

To which Origen indignantly replies:

> There are, indeed, admitted to be recorded some statements respecting the body of Jesus having been 'ill-favoured'; not, however, 'ignoble', as has been stated, nor is there any certain evidence that he was 'little'. The language of Isaiah runs as follows, who prophesied regarding Him that He would come and visit the multitude, not in comeliness of form, nor in any surpassing beauty: '… He has no form nor glory, and we beheld Him, and He had no form nor beauty; but His form was without honour, and inferior to the sons of men' (*Against Celsus* 6.75; cf. 1.54; 4.16; 7.16; *Commentary on Matthew* 12.29).

As will by now be readily apparent, this recurrent portrait of the incarnate Christ as physically ill-favored hangs principally from Isaiah 53.2.

Robert Eisler notwithstanding. On first looking into Eisler's The Messiah Jesus and John the Baptist According to Flavius Josephus's Recently Rediscovered 'Capture of Jerusalem' and the Other Jewish and Christian Sources,[8] *I found myself plunged into a parallel universe, one in which the* Testimonium Flavianum, *for example—the christianized passage on Jesus in Josephus's* Antiquities of the Jews *(18.3.3 §63)—comes replete with a head-to-toe description:*

> *[H]e was a man of simple appearance, mature age, dark skin, short growth, three cubits tall [about four-and-a-half feet], hunchbacked, with a long face, a long nose, eyebrows meeting above the nose, so that the spectators could take fright, with scanty hair, (but) having a line in the middle of the head after the fashion of the Naziraeans, and with an undeveloped beard.*

Eisler 'reconstructed' this stark sketch from an eclectic group of arcane sources, notably an expansive Old Russian version of The Jewish War, *blended with further 'quotations' from Josephus found in certain Byzantine chroniclers, and the enigmatic, difficult-to-date document known as* The Letter of Lentulus on the Appearance of Christ. *Eisler was convinced that the description derived*

---

8.   Trans. Alexander Haggerty Krappe; New York: The Dial Press, 1931.

ultimately from an official record of Jesus' trial, one to which Josephus had access, but which was subsequently expunged both from The Jewish War and the Antiquities of the Jews by Christian censors.

These eyebrows that meet and greet each other above the long nose of this Jesus look familiar. I've seen them before. They also grace the face of Paul in that famous physical description of him in the Acts of Paul and Thecla (3.2)—'a man small of stature, with a bald head and crooked legs, in a good state of body, with eyebrows meeting and nose somewhat hooked, full of friendliness; for now he appeared like a man, and now he had the face of an angel'.[9] This description has drawn cruel comments from modern scholars. Abraham J. Malherbe has assembled a litany of them: 'hardly flattering'... 'naiv-unheroisch'... 'plain'... 'ugly and small'... 'ein Mann von numinoser Hässlichkeit'... 'the typical portrait of a Jew', and so on.[10] But these ethnocentric moderns have missed the Apostle's true beauty, according to Malherbe. First, he quotes a passage from Archilochus, which was popular in the second century: 'I love not a tall general nor a straddling one, nor one proud of his hair nor one part-shaven; for me a man should be short and bowlegged to behold, set firm on his feet, full of heart' (Fragment 58, LCL translation). This rehabilitates Paul's bandy legs. Then he quotes Suetonius's description of his idol Augustus: 'His teeth were wide apart, small, and well-kept; his hair was slightly curly and inclining to golden; his eyebrows met. His ears were of moderate size, and his nose projected a little at the top and then bent slightly inward. His complexion was between dark and fair. He was short of stature...' (Augustus 79.2, LCL translation). This rehabilitates Paul's meeting eyebrows, hooked nose, and small stature, argues Malherbe, since Suetonius regularly had recourse to physiognomic stereo-types to provide physical descriptions of his ideal political leaders. Meeting eyebrows were widely regarded as a sign of beauty, as the Greco–Roman physio-gnomic manuals and other contemporary texts testify (for me, too, meeting eye-brows are a cause of admiration, or outright fascination, especially on an otherwise hairless face), while a hooked nose was deemed a mark of royalty, and small stature a sign that someone was quick. The evidence duly laid out on the dressing table that has been dragged into the courtroom for the occasion, Malherbe rests his case: 'It is clear by now that Paul's hooked nose, bowed legs, and meeting eyebrows were not unflattering features in the context in which the Acts was written'.[11]

9. Translation from *New Testament Apocrypha*, rev. edn.

10. 'A Physical Description of Paul', *HTR* 79 (1986), pp. 170-75 (170-71).

11. Malherbe, 'A Physical Description of Paul', p. 174. Bruce J. Malina and Jerome H. Neyrey largely concur with Malherbe's conclusion in their own analysis

Could Malherbe provide a similar makeover for Eisler's short, stooped, long-faced, long-nosed Christ, transform him through sheer erudition from a nerd into a stud? I suspect he would have his work cut out for him (even with the promising foundation provided by the meeting eyebrows). For certain of this Jesus' other features are found on such frightful faces as that of the Antichrist, as represented in Jewish lore. 'We learn... that the Antichrist has a long nose', notes Joan Massyngbaerde Ford in her intriguing article, 'The Physical Features of the Antichrist',[12] which builds on J.M. Rosenstiehl's collection of 17 related descriptions of the Antichrist found in late Jewish apocalyptic and rabbinic literature,[13] arguing that these descriptions can be readily deciphered using the ancient physiognomic handbooks as codebooks. Even a cursory glance at Ford's essay, replete with physiognomic lore, would likely cause the self-esteem of Eisler's Jesus to plummet dismally: 'One notes that a curved body and shoulders are a sign of malignancy, envy, avarice... [T]oo large a face denotes foolishness, a boorish man... [B]aldness is not a good sign. Too little hair on the head, a few hairs scattered here and there...indicate an incorrigible character.'[14] Fairer by far are the features ascribed to Jesus in the immensely influential description of him composed by John of Damascus in the eighth century in the shadow of the iconoclastic controversy; they include an olive complexion, a strong nose, curly hair, a dark beard, and—what else?—eyebrows that meet and embrace, thereby becoming one.[15] The moral is plain, not to say ugly: Beauty bespeaks goodness.

Origen himself suggests that his ill-favored Christ has stumbled directly out of the pages of the Old Testament: 'But now, as neither the Gospels nor the apostolic writings indicate that "He had no form nor beauty", it is evident that we must accept the declaration of the prophets as true of Christ...' (*Against Celsius* 6.76). Even the 'report' that Jesus was 'little' seems to hinge on Isa. 53.2; 'He is like a little boy [*puerulus*]', is how Tertullian renders its opening words (*Against Marcion* 3.17;

---

of this description (*Portraits of Paul: An Archaeology of Ancient Personality* [Louisville, KY: Westminster/John Knox Press, 1996], pp. 127-48.)

12. Joan Massyngbaerde Ford, 'The Physical Features of the Antichrist', *JSP* 14 (1996), pp. 23-41 (37).

13. 'Le Portrait de l'Antichrist', in M. Philonenko *et al.* (eds.), *Pseudépigraphes de l'Ancien Testament et Manuscrits de la Mer Morte* (Cahiers d'Histoire et de Philosophie Religieuses, 41; Paris: Presses Universitaires de France, 1967), pp. 45-60.

14. Ford, 'The Physical Features of the Antichrist', pp. 33, 34, 38.

15. See Cornelius Russel, 'Byzantine and Romanesque Art and Architecture', in Gilbert Cope (ed.), *Christianity and the Visual Arts* (London: The Faith Press, 1964), p. 28.

cf. *idem*, *Against Praxeas* 11). But Tertullian, in particular, also likes to trot out Ps. 22.6 (21.7 LXX) hard on the heels of the Isaian passage: 'He pronounces Himself "a worm, and not a man, an ignominy of man, and the refuse of the People". Which evidences of ignobility suit the First Advent, just as those of sublimity do the Second...' (*Against Marcion* 3.17; cf. 3.7; *idem*, *On the Flesh of Christ* 15). In sum, 'His body did not reach even to human beauty, to say nothing of heavenly glory' (*On the Flesh of Christ* 9).

At first blush, there would seem to be something singularly un-Johannine about this homely, not to say ugly, Jesus. Note, for example, that the Jesus Seminarian whose historical Jesus is the least Johannine, the least divine, the least sublime, is also the Seminarian whose historical Jesus is the least attractive. I speak of Burton Mack.[16] Mack himself has even admitted to not liking his Jesus particularly,[17] although he apparently does not have his physical appearance in mind. Yet, as I shall argue below, Mack's countercultural Jesus and that of the Jesus Seminar generally positively cries out for an unprepossessing physique and an unattractive face, to say the least. John Meier's Jesus is closer by far than Mack's to mainstream christological orthodoxy, which is to say Johannine orthodoxy (although not of course identical with it). Is it merely by

16. Mack has had a long association with the Seminar, but seems to have now retired from it. His name was on the official roster of Charter Fellows of the Seminar published in the first issue of *Forum* (1.1 [1985], p. 30), the Seminar's academic journal. But his name is mysteriously absent from the roster of current Fellows in the Seminar's popular bestseller, *The Five Gospels* (see Robert W. Funk, Roy W. Hoover and The Jesus Seminar, *The Five Gospels: The Search for the Authentic Words of Jesus* [New York: Macmillan, 1993], pp. 533-37). It was during my brief career as a Jesus Seminar groupie that I first laid eyes on Mack. It's always interesting finally to behold a scholar hitherto known only as an implied author, a paper persona. Interesting but also intrusive, somehow, when you come to read that writer again. Even when I'm reading a trashy novel (and I read a great many more than I should), I always try to avoid peeking at the photograph of the author on the inside back cover.

17. In the course of *The Jesus Summit: The Historical Jesus and Contemporary Faith*, a teleconference broadcast by The Episcopal Cathedral Teleconferencing Network on 19 February 1994. In his tongue-in-cheek performance on this video, Mack manages to make John Dominic Crossan look like a thorough traditionalist (no mean feat), and to make Marcus Borg, the third star of the show, look like a schoolboy in short pants. Culturally I feel a profound affinity with Crossan (same rural Irish roots, same rural Irish accent, same abortive affair with a religious order), but Mack's principled irreverence has always inspired me.

chance that the Jesus who gazes past us from the jacket of the second volume of Meier's *A Marginal Jew* (see Fig. 1) is a Jesus whose face is oddly arresting, possessed of sharp, striking features, an exceptionally handsome man who has more than fulfilled the physical promise exhibited by the unusually attractive boy who graced the cover of the first volume of Meier's magnum opus (see Fig. 2)?[18]

Figure 1. Jacket illustration by Marco Ventura for John P. Meier, *A Marginal Jew: Rethinking the Historical Jesus*. II. *Mentor, Message, and Miracles* (The Anchor Bible Reference Library; New York: Doubleday, 1994)

18. John P. Meier, *A Marginal Jew: Rethinking the Historical Jesus*. I. *The Roots of the Problem and the Person*; II. *Mentor, Message, and Miracles* (The Anchor Bible Reference Library; New York: Doubleday, 1991–94). Volume 3 has yet to appear as I write.

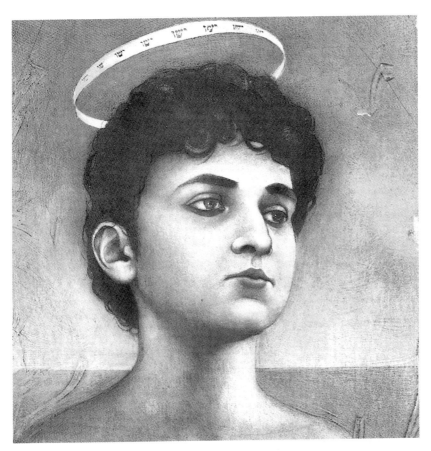

Figure 2. Jacket illustration by Joel Peter Johnson for John P. Meier, *A Marginal Jew: Rethinking the Historical Jesus*. I. *The Roots of the Problem and the Person* (The Anchor Bible Reference Library; New York: Doubleday, 1991)

Why would a historian choose to illustrate his critical investigation of the historical Jesus with highly intrusive fictitious images of his subject? Is it possible to read Meier's ongoing historical narrative and not visualize its protagonist first as the boy and then as the man on the jacket? As one reads, Meier's 'historical' Jesus is being played by two actors, one young, the other mature, but both undeniably handsome—as in any docudrama 'based on a true story'.

And what of the cover of E.P. Sanders's recent Penguin paperback, The Historical Figure of Jesus?[19] *What are we to make of this other figure (hardly*

19. New York: Penguin Books, 1995.

*historical) who coolly returns our curious stare, this broad-shouldered, regular-fea-
tured young man with the flowing auburn hair, large brown eyes and sensuous
lips? The rear cover identifies the figure as a detail from an early seventeenth-
century painting by Pacecco de Rosa,* Christ Blessing Children.[20] *The children
have been excised from this reprint. Deep in self-absorption, the figure hardly
seems to notice. Did Sanders himself select this stereotypical image of Jesus, so
reaffirming of popular piety, on the one hand, and the identification of virtue and
beauty, on the other? Or did the cover designer choose it for him? What role does
Sanders imagine this image to have in relation to his historical portrait of Jesus?
Is the visual portrait meant to illustrate the verbal portrait? Or is the relationship
between word and image wholly contingent instead? Would any depiction of
Jesus have done? Or just any standard depiction of him, as a more-or-less
handsome Caucasian male?*

Contrast the image of Jesus that adorns the cover of Crossan's Jesus: A
Revolutionary Biography.[21] *Dating from the early fourth century this time,
this Jesus too is bearded and curly haired. Yet he is not handsome, at least by
late twentieth-century Western standards. Badly in need of a Malherbean makeover, his face droops like a bloodhound's and he has big bags under his eyes.
And whereas Meier and Sanders leave us guessing about their own views on the
Jesuses that grace their jackets, Crossan devotes a whole page to elucidating the
links between the Jesus on the cover and the Jesus between the covers, going so far
as to claim that the former is an 'iconographic miniature' of the latter*[22]*—not
because of his face, however, but because of his dress, which he takes to be that of
a Cynic philosopher. Even Crossan has no conceptual apparatus with which to
reflect on Jesus' face and physique.*[23]

---

20. The original 1993 edition featured an entirely different jacket design (as my
colleague Meg Davies reminds me), centered on an image from the Catacombs of
Christ as the Good Shepherd. Youthful, short-haired, clean shaven and pink-
skinned, Jesus looks relaxed and attractive in a rather revealing shepherd's smock and
appears to be preaching to a captive audience of sheep and birds.

21. John Dominic Crossan, *Jesus: A Revolutionary Biography* (San Francisco:
HarperSanFrancisco, 1994).

22. Crossan, *Jesus*, p. v.

23. Then there's the grim Christ Pantocrator who dominates the cover of N.T.
Wright's *Christian Origins and the Question of God. II. Jesus and the Victory of God*
(Minneapolis: Fortress Press, 1997), and his even gloomier cousin, the other Christ
Pantocrator whose scowling visage casts a dark shadow over the cover of Ben
Witherington III's *The Jesus Quest: The Third Search for the Jew of Nazareth* (Downer's
Grove, IL: InterVarsity Press, 1995), not to mention the less lugubrious Jesuses who
grace the covers of Luke T. Johnson's *The Real Jesus: The Misguided Quest for the*

Curiously enough, Meier is not entirely silent on the matter of Jesus' physical aspect. Jesus' trade, that of τέκτων, *which Meier aptly translates as 'wood-worker', 'involved no little sweat and muscle power', he claims. 'The airy weak-ling often presented to us in pious paintings and Hollywood movies would hardly have survived the rigors of being Nazareth's* τέκτων *from his youth to his early thirties.'[24] What might Meier's modest espousal of a more manly Jesus look like magnified into a book? Cut to Bruce Barton's* The Man Nobody Knows,[25] *a life of Jesus whose chapter titles alone constitute a treasure trove for the connoisseur of Christian curiosities: 'The Leader', 'The Outdoor Man', 'The Sociable Man', 'His Method', 'His Advertisements', 'The Founder of Modern Business'… Barton's book is a belated product of that peculiar Victorian movement known as 'muscular Christianity'.[26] The best-known expression of muscular Christianity is Thomas Hughes's novel,* Tom Brown's Schooldays, *but it is to his own boyhood in Sunday school that Barton traces his arousal from dogmatic slumber:*

> The kindly lady who could never seem to find her glasses would have been terribly shocked if she had known what was going on inside the little boy's mind.
>
> 'You must love Jesus', she said every Sunday…
>
> Love Jesus! The little boy looked up at the picture which hung on the Sunday-school wall. It showed a pale young man with flabby forearms and a sad expression. The young man had red whiskers.
>
> Then the little boy looked across to the other wall. There was Daniel, good old Daniel, standing off the lions. The little boy liked Daniel. He liked David, too, with the little sling that landed a stone square on the forehead of Goliath. And Moses, with his rod and his big brass snake. They were winners—those three. He wondered if David could whip Jeffries. Samson could! Say, that would have been a fight!
>
> But Jesus! Jesus was the 'lamb of God'. The little boy did not know what that meant, but it sounded like Mary's little lamb. Something for girls—sissified…
>
> Years went by and the little boy grew up and became a businessman.

Historical Jesus and the Truth of the Traditional Gospels (San Francisco: HarperSan-Francisco, 1996) and Marcus Borg's successive Jesus books… Can these books, too, be judged by their covers?

24. Meier, *A Marginal Jew*, I, p. 281.

25. Bruce Barton, *The Man Nobody Knows* (London: Constable, 1925).

26. On the latter see Norman Vance, *The Sinews of the Spirit: The Ideal of Chris-tian Manliness in Victorian Literature and Religious Thought* (Cambridge: Cambridge University Press, 1985); Donald Hall (ed.), *Muscular Christianity: Embodying the Vic-torian Age* (Cambridge: Cambridge University Press, 1994).

He began to wonder about Jesus.

He said to himself: 'Only strong magnetic men inspire great enthusiasm and build great organizations. Yet Jesus built the greatest organization of all. It is extraordinary'.

The more sermons the man heard and the more books he read the more mystified he became.

One day he decided to wipe his mind clean of books and sermons.

He said, 'I will read what the men who knew Jesus personally said about him. I will read about him as though he were a new historical character, about whom I had never heard anything at all.'

The man was amazed.

A physical weakling! Where did they get that idea? Jesus pushed a plane and swung an adze; he was a successful carpenter. He slept outdoors and spent his days walking around his favourite lake. His muscles were so strong that when he drove the money-changers out, nobody dared to oppose him![27]

The latter scene is one that Barton particularly relishes. Later he dwells at length upon this spectacular show of strength. A five-page imaginary replay of the scene culminates in the following revelation:

There was, in his eyes, a flaming moral purpose; and greed and oppression have always shrivelled before such fire. But with the majesty of his glance there was something else which counted powerfully in his favour. As his right arm rose and fell, striking its blows with that little whip, the sleeve fell back to reveal muscles that were hard as iron. No one who watched him in action had any doubt that he was fully capable of taking care of himself. No flabby priest or money-changer cared to try conclusions with that arm.[28]

For Barton, this is the pivotal scene in Jesus' ministry, revealing much more than the bulge of Jesus' biceps. It reveals the sort of man he was, or rather that he was a man, the kind of man Barton himself presumably would want to be.

How interesting that Jesus' aggressive action in the Temple should also be of central significance to at least two of the leading contemporary Jesus scholars, namely Sanders and Crossan. That Jesus created some sort of violent disturbance in the Temple area is, for Sanders, one of the few virtually indubitable things that we can know about his public career. For Sanders, no less than for Barton, the event is an epiphany. It is central to Sanders's reconstruction of Jesus' self-understanding.[29] Crossan, although more skeptical than Sanders generally, is

27. Barton, *The Man Nobody Knows*, pp. 1-3.

28. Barton, *The Man Nobody Knows*, p. 33.

29. See E.P. Sanders, *Jesus and Judaism* (Philadelphia: Fortress Press, 1985), pp. 11, 61-76, and *idem*, *The Historical Figure of Jesus*, pp. 10-11, 252-69.

also certain that Jesus caused a ruckus in the Temple. That action is central to Crossan's explanation of why Jesus was executed, and fully in keeping with Crossan's construal of Jesus' character.[30] *Reading Crossan and Sanders side by side with Barton, however, makes me wonder whether all three men might not be animated by the same impulse; whether what is overtly the case with regard to Barton might not be covertly the case with regard to Crossan and Sanders; whether they, like him, are not intent on (re)constructing a Jesus who, if nothing else, was at least a 'man', and as such eminently equipped for violent behavior, that perennial hallmark of masculinity. If so, the comically macho Jesus who marches through Barton's singularly unscholarly pages, shoulders squared, 'fine features' (a favorite Bartonian phrase) set in an expression of grim determination as he contemplates the work of salvation (man's work, needless to say), is also tiptoeing more shyly through Crossan's and Sanders's more scholarly pages, no less an idealized figure inviting the (male?) reader's identification, no less an embodiment of imagined masculine virtue.*

Meier's dust-jacket Jesus seems to radiate an inner glow, even a divine glow. Lit up from within, he is recognizably Johannine, for the Fourth Gospel, more than any other New Testament Gospel, is the Gospel of the incandescent Christ. And when one ventures outside the fenced enclosure of critical scholarship altogether, which is to say fully into the realm of popularized Johannism, Jesus' flesh fairly glows in the dark. Witness, for example, Anne Rice's sketch of Jesus' face in *Memnoch the Devil*, Volume 5 of her bestselling *Vampire Chronicles*:

> I looked up, and in the midst of the flood of light I saw again the balustrade, and against it stood a single form.
>
> It was a tall figure who stood with his hands on the railing, looking over it and down. This appeared to be a man. He turned around and looked at me and reached out to receive me.
>
> His hair and eyes were dark, brownish, his face perfectly symmetrical and flawless, his gaze intense; and the grasp of his fingers very tight.
>
> I drew in my breath. I felt my body in all its solidity and fragility as his fingers clung to me. I was on the verge of death. I might have ceased to

30. See John Dominic Crossan, *The Historical Jesus: The Life of a Mediterranean Jewish Peasant* (San Francisco: HarperSanFrancisco, 1991), pp. xii, 355-60, and *idem*, *Jesus*, pp. 130-33. What about Meier? We shall have to await his third volume for his definitive pronouncement on the incident. What is already apparent is that he, too, believes it occurred. See, e.g., his 'Reflections on Jesus-of-History Research Today', in James H. Charlesworth (ed.), *Jesus' Jewishness: Exploring the Place of Jesus in Early Judaism* (New York: Crossroad, 1991), pp. 84-107 (101); cf. Meier, *A Marginal Jew*, I, p. 175.

breathe at that moment, or ceased to move with the commitment to life
and might have died!

This being drew me towards himself, a light flooding from him that
mingled with the light behind him and all around him, so his face grew
brighter yet more distinct and more detailed. I saw the pores of his darkening golden skin, I saw the cracks in his lips, the shadow of the hair that
had been shaved from his face.[31]

This is the Jesus that the public demands. This is the Johannine Jesus, as
popularly conceived.

*Rice's gorgeous Jesus reaches out to receive me along with Memnoch, and the
grip of his fingers is indeed very tight. We have met before, you see, although not
in a celestial mansion. Once again I am 13 or 14, visiting my grandfather's cot-
tage on the Limerick–Tipperary border. Straw-bestrewn flagstone floor, hellish
fire over which a huge blackened pot bubbles, monstrous slabs of bacon suspended
from hooks under the thatch. My father and grandfather are engaged in an extra-
ordinarily prolonged exchange about the weather. The conversation switches to
cattle, then to hurling, at which point it becomes passionate. In an agony of boredom I cast around for something to read. All I can find is a crushed copy of* Ben
Hur *propping up a corner of the dresser. I start to skim distractedly through it,
gradually slowing down as the plot begins to grip me. As I am dragged in chains
through Galilee with the unlucky Ben Hur, a familiar figure comes out to meet
me at the tiny hamlet of Nazareth. Familiar yet unfamiliar; never before has he
looked so good:*

> Thereupon a youth who came up with Joseph, but had stood behind him
> unobserved, laid down an axe he had been carrying, and, going to the
> great stone standing by the well, took from it a pitcher of water. The
> action was so quiet that before the guards could interfere, had they been
> disposed to, he was stooping over the prisoner, and offering him a drink.
>
> The hand laid kindly upon his shoulder awoke the unfortunate Judah,
> and, looking up, he saw a face he never forgot—the face of a boy about
> his own age, shaded by locks of yellowish bright chestnut hair; a face
> lighted by dark-blue eyes, at the same time so soft, so appealing, so full of

---

31. Anne Rice, *The Vampire Chronicles*. V. *Memnoch the Devil* (New York: Alfred
A. Knopf, 1995), pp. 168-69. Rice's Jesus, physically at least, can count Renan's
Jesus among his fine-featured forebears. Of Jesus, Renan wrote: 'His amiable character, accompanied doubtless by one of those lovely faces [*une de ces ravissantes figures*]
which sometimes appear in the Jewish race, threw around him a fascination from
which no one in the midst of these kindly and simple populations could escape' (*The
Life of Jesus* [ET; Great Minds Series; Buffalo: Prometheus Books, 1991 (1863)],
p. 63).

love and holy purpose, that they had all the power of command and will. The spirit of the Jew, hardened though it was by days and nights of suffering, and so embittered by wrong that his dreams of revenge took in all the world, melted under the stranger's look, and became as a child's. He put his lips to the pitcher, and drank long and deep. Not a word was said to him, nor did he say a word.[32]

I read on, entranced. Later that same afternoon, he appears to me again (and, of course, to Ben Hur), this time on the banks of the Jordan:

...a form slightly above the average in stature, and slender, even delicate. His action was calm and deliberate, like that habitual to men much given to serious thought upon grave subjects; and it well became his costume, which was an undergarment full-sleeved and reaching to the ankles, and an outer robe called the talith; on his left arm he carried the usual handkerchief for the head, the red fillet swinging loose down his side. Except the fillet and a narrow border of blue at the lower edge of the talith, his attire was of linen yellowed with dust and road stains. Possibly the exception should be extended to the tassels, which were blue and white, as prescribed by law for Rabbis. His sandals were of the simplest kind. He was without scrip or girdle or staff.

These points of appearance, however, the...beholders observed briefly, and rather as accessories to the head and face of the man, which—especially the latter—were the real sources of the spell they caught in common...

The head was open to the cloudless sky, except as it was draped with hair long and slightly waved, and parted in the middle, and auburn in tint, with a tendency to reddish-golden where most strongly touched by the sun. Under the broad, low forehead, under black, well-arched brows, beamed eyes dark-blue and large, and softened to exceeding tenderness by lashes of great length sometimes seen on children, but seldom, if ever, on men. As to the other features, it would have been difficult to decide whether they were Greek or Jewish. The delicacy of the nostrils and mouth was unusual to the latter type; and when it was taken into account with the gentleness of the eyes, the pallor of the complexion, the fine texture of the hair, and the softness of the beard, which fell in waves over his throat to his breast, never a soldier but would have laughed at him in encounter, never a woman who would not have confided in him at sight, never a child that would not, with quick instinct, have given him its hand and whole artless trust: nor might any one have said he was not beautiful.[33]

32. Lew Wallace, *Ben Hur* (London: Collins, 1954 [1880]), p. 118.

33. Wallace, *Ben Hur*, pp. 405-406.

It would still be a decade or more before I would give myself wholly to Jesus, before I would 'invite him in'. But my initial infatuation with him undoubtedly dated from that drowsy Sunday afternoon in my grandfather's overheated kitchen. In retrospect I think I fell for his looks.

And what of Lew Wallace himself—husband, father, soldier supreme (ascending to the rank of Major-General in the Union army during the American Civil War), and first Governor of the new Union state of New Mexico? The Collins edition of Ben Hur *(whose biographical introduction yielded up these interesting facts) has an artist's sketch of Wallace as a frontispiece, bellicose, beetle-browed and bearded. Whence the extraordinary tenderness with which he writes about Jesus? Whence the extraordinary tenderness with which I have heard so many other rugged men speak of Jesus, and speak to him, when I moved in charismatic Christian circles? The (inevitable?) homoeroticism of the male believer's intimate relationship to the male Christ, the socially sanctioned worship of one man by another, institutionalized same-sex love on an incalculable scale—this is a topic that I would like to examine on another occasion.*

The Johannine Jesus was abandoned early on by the Jesus Seminar, but later appeared to it in October 1994 while it was gathered behind closed doors in a hotel ballroom in Santa Rosa, California, greatly alarming it. Movie director Paul Verhoeven (*Robocop, Total Recall, Basic Instinct, Showgirls, Starship Troopers*), a long-time fellow of the seminar, was reading an outline of the screenplay for his forthcoming Jesus movie to the assembly.[34] According to the testimony of one eyewitness, however, 'the faces of his fellow seminarians slowly froze' as he read. 'For it became clear that despite eight years of faithful attendance at the Jesus Seminar, he hadn't been paying much attention.'[35] Verhoeven's chief scriptural source for his screenplay was none other than the Fourth Gospel. Basing himself on John's narrative framework, but jettisoning John's miracles, Verhoeven outlined a gripping drama of a courageous Jewish visionary, who, having earned the enmity of the authorities by running riot in the Temple, is forced to become a fugitive. 'When Verhoeven finished, there was a long silence. Then, speaking practically all at once, the seminar's participants took him to task. He was pandering

34. *Robo-Jesus?* Well why not? *Robocop* is all about death and resurrection, after all. Savagely executed by his enemies, the hero is raised to new life in an indestructible body, thanks to the miracle of science.

35. Charlotte Allen, 'Away with the Manger: Scholars Tackle the Historical Jesus', *Lingua Franca* (January/February 1995), pp. 1, 22-30 (27).

to fundamentalists by relying on John's Gospel.'[36] Verhoeven defended himself by pointing out the obvious, namely that the Jesus Seminar's Jesus was simply not the stuff of film. 'You'd have a man walking about from marketplace to marketplace saying aphorisms... That isn't much of a movie.'[37]

One suspects that Verhoeven's Jesus will cut a handsome figure, should he ever make it to the silver screen. We probably shouldn't expect to see Wallace Shawn in the role,[38] nor even Sean Penn.

Well, maybe Sean Penn. Have you seen Dead Man Walking? *Penn almost succeeds in becoming Jesus in the final sequence. Hemmed in by guards, he proceeds in regal slow-motion to the death chamber to the accompaniment of mournful music, his eyes already fixed on eternity. The anguished visage of Susan Sarandon, become Veronica, bobs above his left shoulder—Death Row as the Via Dolorosa. Upon reaching the place of execution, he is strapped to a black upright cross, incredibly, arms outstretched. He utters his last words from this high-tech cross—a prayer addressed to the father of one of his victims, 'Forgive me, for I knew not what I did', or words to that effect—and soon after yields up his spirit. Sarandon, meanwhile, maintains her look of tearful love throughout, now no longer Veronica but the Magdalen, or even the Virgin.*

On second thoughts, do we really need another blue-eyed cinematic Christ? We've seen such a long procession of pale-eyed Galileans over the years, Willem Dafoe in The Last Temptation of Christ *(1988) dispiritedly bringing up the rear. It was* Jesus of Nazareth *(1977), however, that set a daunting new standard for blue-eyed biblical characters. Not content with a blue-eyed Jesus (played by Robert Powell), director Franco Zeffirelli threw in a blue-eyed John the Baptist (Michael York) for good measure, a gesture all the more telling given Zefferelli's painstaking quest for authenticity in this film, his abandonment of fake beards, American accents (he recognizes that first-century Mediterranean people spoke with English accents instead), freshly starched peasant robes, cardboard architecture, and other hallowed features of the Hollywood Bible epic.*

I had my historical Jesus class watch Jesus of Nazareth *once at the Kansas state university where I previously taught. Afterwards students were asked to write a review of the film. Several of the reviewers commented on Powell's ice-blue eyes, although not as a glaring anachronism. 'They were just as I'd always*

36. Allen, 'Away with the Manger', p. 28.
37. Allen, 'Away with the Manger', p. 28.
38. 'Wallace who?' I hear you say. Well, you try naming a well-known male Hollywood actor under 50 who is decidedly plain and homely looking. Excluding comedians, that is. John Goodman as Jesus?

imagined Jesus' eyes would be', wrote one. But another reviewer noted that Powell's teeth protruded slightly, and wondered why he had been selected for the role.[39] *Yet another objected to Powell's stringy hair and skeletal physique: 'The real Jesus would have had neat hair and a good build'.*

Also while at this same university, I found a mysterious pamphlet in my pigeonhole one morning. It bore the alluring title, 'Jesus: The Most Beautiful Man I Have Ever Seen'. It told how Jesus had appeared to the author late one evening in his pickup truck as he paused on the shoulder of the highway on the outskirts of Lubbock, Texas, to pray in tongues and read aloud from the opening chapter of the book of Revelation. The author was fortunate enough to have a tape recorder with him at the time (a camcorder would have been even better, of course) and so was able to record Christ's message to the world. The pamphlet ended with a 1-900 number, but when I called, it had already been disconnected. My mail at Sheffield pales dreadfully by comparison.

Had I not moved to England, however, I might never have learned that Elvis expired while contemplating the face of Jesus. There it was in the Culture section of last week's Sunday Times. *Elvis exited this life while seated on a lavishly padded lavatory seat at Graceland (his one-piece sequined jumpsuit pulled down around his knees, adds a friend, although that may be a legendary embellishment). Open in his lap at the time was a book entitled* The Scientific Search for the Face of Jesus. *'A mere coincidence?' asks the author of the article. He doesn't think so, apparently, for 'Elvis has become the kitsch Christ of an American—and, therefore, global—peasant religion', most conspicuously for the First Presleytarian Church of Elvis the Divine, whose members offer up daily prayers to the King and engage in ritual consumption of his favorite banana pudding.*[40] *But is it the young, beautiful Elvis or the aging, obese Elvis who is*

39. This reviewer is by no means alone in deeming divinity and dental perfection to be ontologically linked. Reviewing *The Last Temptation of Christ* for the *National Review* (16 September 1988) John Simon remarked: 'Willem Dafoe, if you like your Jesus as a Zen hippie, is good enough, and very nice looking, and wouldn't you think that the Son of God would have better teeth?' (quoted in W. Barnes Tatum, 'Jesus at the Movies', *The Fourth R* 11 [1998], pp. 3-10 [8]).

40. Bryan Appleyard, 'Bloated Victim', *The Sunday Times*, 13 July 1997, Section 11, p. 1. You can visit First Presleytarian's website at http://www.elemental music.co.uk/alabama3firstprs.htm (I learned this from Bill Scott, who himself has made the pilgrimage). These arcane electronic addresses are to contemporary cults as incantatory formulae were to ancient cults: gateways to the abode of the gods. Further on Elvis and religion, see Gilbert B. Rodman, *Elvis after Elvis: The Posthumous Career of a Living Legend* (New York: Routledge, 1996), esp. pp. 111-22; Mark Gottdiener, 'Dead Elvis as Other Jesus', in Vernon Chadwick (ed.), *In Search of*

the object of veneration for millions? The recent defeat of the ungracefully aging Elvis by the youthful Elvis in the much-publicized battle between the two for a coveted place on a US commemorative postage stamp strongly suggests that it is Elvis the Beautiful who is King in the minds of most of his devotees.

Of course, there is no intrinsic reason why the Johannine Jesus should be visualized as gloriously good-looking; John's claim, after all, is that the enfleshed Word's innate glory was invisible to all save a select few, and that this glory, when he chose to reveal it, was to be seen not in his face but in his deeds.[41] Furthermore, it is probably safe to surmise that the Fourth Gospel supplied the safety net for the second-century apologists' tightrope assertion that Jesus was physically ugly—the Fourth

Elvis: Music, Race, Art, Religion (Boulder, CO: Westview Press, 1997), pp. 189-200.

41. Most contemporary Christians, however, seem to find it infinitely easier to imagine the monomaniacal announcements of the Johannine Jesus—'I am the Light of the World', 'I am the Way, the Truth and the Light', etc.—issuing from a pair of well-formed lips, barely concealing a set of gleaming white teeth, and attached to a handsome face, which in turn is attached to a lean, well-proportioned body, than to imagine the same unlikely words issuing from a dreadfully deformed mouth, barely concealing a set of ruinously decayed teeth, and so on. The age-old inclination to equate looks with worth, which, in antiquity, crystallized in the physiognomic handbooks of the second to the fourth centuries CE (see Elizabeth C. Evans, *Physiognomics in the Ancient World* [Transactions of the American Philosophical Society, 59.5; Philadelphia: American Philosophical Society, 1969], p. 5), finds its quintessential expression in our own time in the US-led global entertainment industry (comprising the Hollywood film industry, television and popular music), aided and abetted by the advertising and fashion industries (see Naomi Wolf, *The Beauty Myth* [London: Chatto & Windus, 1990]; Robin Tolmach Lakoff and Raquel L. Scherr, *Face Value: The Politics of Beauty* [London: Routledge & Kegan Paul, 1984]; Wendy Chapkis, *Beauty Secrets: Women and the Politics of Appearance* [Boston: South End Press, 1986]; Susan Bordo, *Unbearable Weight: Feminism, Western Culture, and the Body* [Berkeley: University of California Press, 1993]; 'Part III: Marketing Femininity', in Alison M. Jaggar [ed.], *Living with Contradictions: Controversies in Feminist Social Ethics* [Boulder, CO: Westview Press, 1994], pp. 143-262). The ultimate product of this 'global culture machine', as Chapkis aptly styles it (*Beauty Secrets*, p. 37), is an idealized human couple, heterosexual of course, and also beautiful in accordance with an aesthetic code that is simultaneously white and Western, a new Adam and Eve. (The old physiognomy snubbed Eve, lavishing its attention on Adam. The new physiognomy focuses mainly on Eve, although Adam, too, comes under its purview [see 'Men and Beauty', in Lakoff and Scherr, *Face Value*, pp. 209-44].) And it is in the image of this Adam, this Adonis, that Jesus is currently being remade, or made over, in the minds of millions of his adorers, his nose straightened, his teeth whitened, his body nipped, tucked and toned.

Gospel especially as read through the lens provided by the hymn to the
kenotic Christ preserved in Phil. 2.6-11. For if the pre-existent Son of
God elected to empty himself, to become flesh and dwell among us,
why should he not have gone all the way and taken on flesh that was
inglorious rather than glorious, becoming as ugly, precisely, as sin? The
assertion that Jesus was ugly made theological sense only within the
framework of a pre-existence christology, a framework whose central
strut was the Fourth Gospel. Before this framework was firmly in place,
Christian authors seem not to have known what to do with Isa. 53.2; it
is the only verse from Isa. 53.1-9 not to be quoted in the literature that
now makes up our New Testament. But by the end of the second century, as we have seen, it is cited fearlessly and repeatedly by the apologists and other Christian theologians.

To return to the question raised earlier, what might the decomposed
corpse of Jesus, that worm-ridden horror exhumed by the Jesus Seminar, have looked like in life? What sort of body should we expect the
Seminar's Jesus to have, given his resolutely countercultural tendencies,
an affront not only to the dominant social values of his own age but to
ours as well (as evidenced by his unsuitability for a Hollywood career)?
The answer, it seems to me, is that we should expect this Jesus to possess
a visage and physique that the prevalent aesthetic canons of our culture
would deem unattractive or downright ugly. This would be a face and
physique that could not be played by Leonardo DiCaprio, or George
Clooney, or even by Daniel Day Lewis, that would be ineligible to
guest-star on *Baywatch* or *Melrose Place*, that would be unfit to appear on
Entertainment Tonight, that advertisers would shudder even to think of
placing in proximity to their products—the same face and physique that
were revealed to the second-century apologists. And if we are all but
incapable of seeing this face and physique at the close of the twentieth
century, it is because we have allowed ourselves to become dazzled by
the Gospel of the Incandescent Christ. Somehow, without ever quite
showing him, the Fourth Gospel has taken the subversively ugly
Nazarene and, like a primetime docudrama, represented him as a radi-
antly handsome hero.

The Asylum

*Joshua Josephson awoke before dawn, only gradually becoming aware of where he
was, like one who has slept the sleep of the dead. The suffocating mound of
myrrh and aloes under which he had slipped into unconsciousness had dissolved,*

he realized with a surge of relief, although its cloying scent lingered in the cold morning. He unglued his eyes and his relief increased. The terrible, entombing boulder had been rolled away from his door, he knew not how nor by whom. It had left a deep rut in the hospital corridor, a trail of ripped linoleum and ruined tiles.

He eased himself out of bed and padded gingerly to the bathroom on bandaged feet. Nervously he peered at his dim reflection in the mirror. It was worse even than he had feared. The face that gazed fearfully back at him was breath-takingly—no, blandly—beautiful, each feature perfect (painfully so), the flesh faintly pellucid. The face glowed gently in the dull light. It was not his own face.

He heard the echo of running feet in the corridor and excited male voices at the outer door. That would be Peter and his weird friend whatshisname, the one that nobody liked. He waited until the voices had retreated down the hall, merging with the dawn chorus of muffled screams that had begun to seep from the locked wards.

He limped out of the bathroom. Mary was standing with her back to him con-templating the empty bed, its shroud and face napkin crumpled and bloodstained, the medicine tray balanced on her right hand. Her crisp white uniform shimmered in the soft light. 'Mary', he said, a little too loudly. She turned with a cry of surprise, the tray teetering precariously. 'Jesus! You scared the pants off me'. Calmly resigned he waited for his newly numinous countenance to have its awful effect on her, for her to falter, to pale, or to stutter, but she gave him his medicine without comment, barely glancing at his face.

Afterwards he sat in the garden immersed in the brilliant blue scroll of the sky, delicately deciphering its gilt script. And knew what he was about to become. Already he could feel time lengthening impossibly. By noon eternity would have begun.

Life of Brian Research

Philip R. Davies

And his name shall be called in Israel, The house of him that hath his shoe loosed (Deut. 25.10).

I

I have long been of the conviction that Monty Python's *Life of Brian* is an indispensable foundation to any student's career in New Testament studies. In my view, it not only reflects a higher level of historical and biblical research than nearly all exemplars of the Hollywood genre which count among its targets, but also engages with a number of basic scholarly historical and theological issues. I do not claim that the makers of this film (hereafter named jointly and severally as 'Monty Python') have fully apprehended the significance of their contribution to 'Life of Jesus' research, nor that they intended their contribution to be taken with scholarly seriousness. But their authorial intent is of course entirely irrelevant in the application of Viewer-Response Criticism, and it seems in any case perfectly proper that a master parodist should be in turn parodied (in a fashion) by being subjected to an academic analysis. If Monty Python wishes to make fun of what is serious, why should one not make something serious out of what is fun?[1]

In the first part of this paper, then, I want to construct a relatively serious foundation for a 'Life of Brian' by showing the abundant evidence of historical and biblical research reflected in the script of this film.[2] The evidence is sufficiently extensive to exclude the possibility of happy coincidence, forcing the conclusion that Monty Python, whether

---

1. As has been done in many books and articles on the book of Jonah, for example.
2. The best version of the script (abbreviated) I can currently find (several *Life of Brian* items have mysteriously disappeared from the Web in recent months) can be located at http//bau2.uibk.ac.at/sg/python/Scripts/LifeOfBrian/MontyPythonsLife ofBrian.

real or implied film-maker, is a biblical scholar, however temporarily. The second part of the paper will then deal with the theological strategies of this theological film.

II

The evidence of Monty Python's historical research may be divided into two groups: information culled from ancient non-biblical sources, and allusions to New Testament passages or New Testament scholarship.

The Use of Nonbiblical Ancient Sources

1. *Two Cases from Josephus*

The depiction of resistance to Roman occupation and rule of Judah is divided in *Life of Brian* among various liberation parties, representing a minority of the population and in rivalry with each other. Such a depiction can easily be mistaken for a crude parody of the 'liberation' groups dedicated to terrorist activity that have populated the politics of the late twentieth century. It is certainly also in contrast to the Hollywood cliché that the war was entirely between Romans and Jews (in which it is customary to use Americans actors to play Jews and British actors to play Romans) and not at all between Jews and Jews; and that Roman occupation was widely resisted by the Jews. But the major historical source for these events is *The Jewish War* of Flavius Josephus (written towards the end of the first century CE). As has frequently been noted, Josephus blames the war fundamentally on the disharmony within the Jewish nation, leading to civil war (Greek: *stasis*), and his account underlines two points: that the Romans were not widely disliked, but rather that the nation as a whole was dragged into the war by hotheads; and that at least the latter phases of the war saw rival factions attacking each other, doing the Romans' work for them.[3] I quote, for specific illustration, from Book 5.11.4:

3. The scholarly literature on Josephus's presentation of the Jewish War is extensive, and much of it suggests that this Flavian client was attempting to minimize the Jewish hatred of Rome and the extent of Jewish commitment to the revolt. However, the fact remains that Josephus constitutes the film-maker's major resource for this conflict because (a) it is practically the only narrative source for this conflict and (b) it is composed in a way that would make any Hollywood scriptwriter proud.

> There were now three treacherous factions in the city, each one sepa-
> rated from the others. Eleazar and his group, who were keeping the first-
> fruits festival, attacked John in a state of drunkenness. John's followers
> plundered the populace and zealously went after Simon. Simon had his
> provisions supplied from the city, unlike the rebels, and so when John
> was attacked from both sides, he had his men turning in both directions,
> throwing javelins from the porticoes at the citizens attacking him from
> below, while using siege engines against those he was attacking in the
> Temple itself. Whenever he was free from the attentions of those above
> (which happened frequently, when they got drunk or tired), he charged
> out with a large force against Simon and his group, attacking whatever
> areas of the city he could get to, setting on fire the buildings where corn
> and other provisions were stored. Simon did the same thing: when John
> retreated, he took over attacking the city, as if deliberately to do the
> Romans' work for them.

'O most wretched city', exclaims Josephus at this scenario, 'what misery
as great as this did you suffer from the Romans, when they came to
purify you from your internecine hatred?'

The description given by Josephus of the internal fighting is echoed
by Tacitus (*History* 5.12.4), and, while Monty Python's account does
not extend as far as the events of the war, his depiction of the fragmentation and mutual loathing of Jewish resistance groups is in accord
with that evidence. Josephus also goes out of his way to argue in *The
Jewish War* that the Jews by and large did not wish the war with Rome,
but were led into it by hotheads. That impression is conveyed by the
Life of Brian.[4]

There is one other episode to consider in this connection. Towards
the end of the film a brigade of Jewish resistance fighters commit mass
suicide in front of the crucified victims. This scene, again, is capable of
being superficially interpreted as a parody of Japanese suicide squads
(whose actions have been influential in some terrorist attacks of recent
times).[5] But a much more relevant basis is a reference to the end of the
siege of Masada, where a group of Jewish terrorists[6] killed themselves

---

4.   Josephus's depiction of the Romans is complicated. He understandably
commends their noble and fair dealings with the Jews during the war, because matters were then conducted by his patrons; but he also accuses individual Roman
governors of incompetence and malice. There are degrees of correspondence
between this attitude and that of *Life of Brian*, but not complete agreement.

5.   The dress and manner of the suicide squad in fact exploits a clear Japanese
intertext.

6.   The remains of pig bones at Masada have not yet been integrated into the

rather than be captured. The incident is widely celebrated in the modern State of Israel, where the slogan 'Masada shall not fall again' has been coined. However, in one of the more delightful ironies that history offers, the immortality of the defeated terrorists is secured solely by the eloquence and dramatic skills (not to mention fictional elaboration) of the Quisling Josephus, to whom the defenders of Masada were generally an object of loathing. The speeches of their leader Eleazar, recorded in *War* 7.8.6-7, induced them to commit mass suicide rather than submit to the Romans, finding, finally, no longer any object on which to turn their violence but themselves.

It is, of course, true that in his entire account of the war and the long history that precedes it, Josephus has his own axes to grind: he has his own personal involvement to exculpate, his aristocratic-priestly class to exonerate and his Flavian family to extol.[7] Josephus is very obviously exercising his own prejudice against terrorism and supporting his thesis that the Jewish people as a whole did not wish for the war. But scholarly debate over the extent of Josephus's reliability is not precisely the issue; rather I wish to point out that Josephus's portrait is substantially reproduced in *Life of Brian*.

2. *Two Cases from Rabbinic Literature*

It could be argued, if taken in isolation, that the previous example is the result of coincidence rather than research. However, in the second example that possibility can be ruled out. In the stoning episode, the elderly man who is about to be executed for blasphemy claims that he merely used the name 'Jehovah' in praise of a piece of fish. Most viewers, no doubt, imagine that blasphemy in the ancient Jewish world involves saying something detrimental to the deity, or perhaps claiming divinity, as implied in Mark's account of Jesus' trial (see Mk 14.62-63). But the ensuing antics of the priest make it clear that naming the deity is the issue. This is in accordance with Mishnaic ruling.

---

prevailing historical construction, partly because their discovery was never publicized.

7.   Among the wealth of literature on this topic, the following may be consulted: D.M. Rhoads, *Israel in Revolution: 6–74* C.E. *A Political History Based on the Writings of Josephus* (Philadelphia: Fortress Press, 1976); P. Bilde, 'The Causes of the Jewish War According to Josephus', *JSJ* 10 (1979), pp. 179-202; T. Rajak, *Josephus: The Historian and his Society* (London: Gerald Duckworth, 1983); M.D. Goodman, *The Ruling Class of Judaea: The Origin of the Jewish Revolt against Rome A.D. 66–70* (Cambridge: Cambridge University Press, 1987).

> The blasphemer is not culpable unless he pronounces the Name itself...
> when sentence was to be given they did not declare him guilty of death
> with the substituted name, but they sent out all the people and asked the
> chief among the witnesses and said to him: 'Say expressly what thou
> heardest', and he says it; and the judges stand up on their feet and rend
> their garments, and they may not mend them again. And the second wit-
> ness says, 'I also heard the like', and the third says 'I also heard the like'.[8]

A second use of rabbinic texts, or at least a tradition represented in rabbinic texts, is making Brian the son of a Roman legionary. The legend
that Jesus had such a parentage is found at several places,[9] and the name
attached to the soldier is 'ben Pantera'; 'Yossi Pantera' is a name by
which Jesus is still sometimes known and referred in to certain non-
Christian circles.

3. *Onomastics*

The cleverest of all historical allusions (but also the one that I regard as
most susceptible to an explanation of coincidence) is in the perversion
of 'peacemakers' to 'cheesemakers' during the 'sermon on the mount'.
The city of Jerusalem at the time of Jesus was divided by a north–south
valley, running along the western wall of the Temple mount and separating the Temple hill from the upper city. Nowadays it is marked by a
much more shallow depression called (in Arabic) the *wad*. The name
given to this valley in antiquity is *Tyropoean*, which is widely understood
to derive from the Greek word 'cheesemaker'. The origin of the name
remains a puzzle, though one possible implication is the existence of a
dairy industry in the very heart of ancient Jerusalem.

The Use of New Testament Allusions

References to events described in the New Testament are obviously
abundant in a story set in that time and place; nothing much will be
proved by a rehearsal of the entire list. A few instances will therefore

8.	*M. Sanh.* 7.5 (trans. H. Danby, *The Mishnah* [Oxford: Oxford University
Press, 1933], p. 392).

9.	For a collection of the texts, see G. Dalman, *Jesus Christ in the Talmud,
Midrash, Zohar and the Liturgy of the Synagogue: Texts and Translations* (Cambridge:
Deighton Bell and Co.; New York: George Bell & Sons, 1893 [repr.; New York:
Arno Press, 1973]), especially p. 5 (*b. Šab.* 104b; *b. Sanh.* 67a) and 17 (*Targum Sheni*
to Esther 7.9). The discusssion of the name Pandera is on pp. 19-25, where Dalman
dates the origin of the name to the second century CE.

suffice. Having pursued their messiah Brian back to his lodgings, the crowd call for him, and at the appearance of his mother comes the cry, 'Behold his mother', a scarcely avoidable reference to Jn 19.27 ('Then he said to the disciple, "Behold, your mother!" And from that hour the disciple took her to his own home').

Just previously, a crowd had pursued Brian, and, seeking to identify him as Messiah, selected a gourd and a sandal as 'signs' of his Messiahship. There are 24 references to a messianic 'sign' in the Gospels (and numerous scholarly monographs about it), and frequently the 'sign' is asked for by crowds or opponents (Mt. 12.38: 'Then some of the scribes and Pharisees said to him, "Teacher, we wish to see a sign from you"'; or Lk. 21.7: 'And they asked him, "Teacher, when will this be, and what will be the sign when this is about to take place?"'). Jesus usually refuses such a sign (Mk 8.12: 'And he sighed deeply in his spirit, and said, "Why does this generation seek a sign? Truly, I say to you, no sign shall be given to this generation"'), but just once offers them the 'sign of Jonah', but without explaining what this sign is or what it is a sign of (Lk. 11.29: 'there shall no sign be given except the sign of Jonah the prophet'). Similarly, Brian responds by refusing a sign, though neither the tenor nor the wording of this response are offered with appropriate dominical dignity. And one of the signs, accepted though not given, is also meaningless. Or is it? A 'sign of Jonah' it may be nonetheless, for in the King James version of Jon. 4.6-10 the sign to Jonah is—a gourd.

The episode of Simon of Cyrene is also worked into the *Life of Brian*, and it is worth remarking because it alludes to something more. The incident, recorded briefly in each of the Synoptics (Mk 15.21; Mt. 27.32; Lk. 23.26) reads (Lukan version): 'And as they led him away, they seized a Simon of Cyrene, who was coming in from the country, and laid the cross on him, to carry it behind Jesus'. The Python version, celebrating the resourcefulness of human nature (see below) has a do-gooder volunteering rather than being compelled, who with the hasty departure of the intended victim finds himself facing crucifixion instead. It is a predictable comic midrash, but theologically informed viewers will be aware of several traditions, both Christian and Muslim, holding that Jesus was not crucified but another in his place.[10]

---

10. The notion that another was substituted was held by Gnostics such as Basilides; cf. the *Gospel of Barnabas* for the same opinion. The Qur'an (Sura 4.157-58) merely asserts that the crucifixion was an appearance only.

But the most striking of New Testament allusions, which the average Bible reader is less likely to have spotted, is the sequence in which Brian climbs to a high point and is taken into outer space (an episode I shall return to later). The jumping off should have been fatal, but Brian is rescued by a group of extra-terrestrial aliens. The text that seems to me to underlie this is the final temptation (Mt. 4.5-6; cf. Lk. 4.9-11):

> Then the devil took him to the holy city, and set him on the pinnacle of the Temple, and said to him, 'If you are the Son of God, throw yourself down; for it is written, "He will give his angels charge of you", and "On their hands they will bear you up, lest you strike your foot against a stone" '.

I shall return to the theological significance of this episode presently. For the present, I merely note that Monty Python's use of the New Testament betrays a more knowledgeable and even sophisticated use of the material than a superficial appreciation of its parodic humour realizes.

III

The nature of the film's relationship to historical research and to the New Testament offer an adequate pretext for exploring Monty Python's *Life of Brian* as a theological text. The second part of my essay is, accordingly, an analysis of the *Life of Brian* as a *Life of Jesus*. The basis for such an analysis must be the superficial observation that Brian both *is* Jesus and is clearly *not* Jesus. The device itself has contributed to the success of the film, allowing it to escape a certain amount of criticism for blasphemy or poor taste and thus to purvey its humour to a wider audience. But whether or not Monty Python was aware of it, the device has roots going back to the foundations of Christianity itself.

Christology (or Brianology)

'He comes to us', said Schweitzer famously of his historical Jesus, 'as One unknown'.[11] This is a perspective abandoned by most subsequent scholarly Jesus biographers, whose subject only too often appears as a familiar, if lightly disguised, image of themselves, be they a cynical Irish

---

11. A. Schweitzer, *The Quest of the Historical Jesus: A Critical Study of its Progress from Reimarus to Wrede* (London: A. & C. Black, 3rd edn, 1954), p. 401.

peasant (Dominic Crossan), a reforming Presbyterian (Sanders) or an itinerant charismatic Jewish healer (Vermes).[12]

The treatment of Jesus in film has generally been of a different order, because of the susceptibilities of audiences, pressure groups, censors and the like. While scholarly biographies may at the most speculate on the human motives of this man–god figure, film-makers, however much they wish to humanize Jesus, must not abandon the element of divinity. It is statistically certain that an American mass cinema audience, whose favour is a prerequisite of the big budget movie, must comprise a large number of believers in the divinity of Christ, and, with or without prompting from such as the Christian Coalition or the Catholic Church, will condemn any depiction that makes their icon too human. Even *The Last Temptation of Christ*, one target of such viewers (or more frequently, non-viewers), does not dispense with the (nonbiblical) icon of the Sacred Heart.

The treatment of Jesus in Monty Python's *Life of Brian* brilliantly succeeds in resolving the dilemma of Jesus' dual nature at the theological–doctrinal level. The figure bearing the name of Jesus *is* emphatically a stranger, and a suitably divine one. His nativity is not that upon which the three wise men stumble, nor is his mother recognizable as the beloved pantomime dame.[13] His stable is already a media event, of which ordinary humans are an excluded or at best remote audience. Similarly, the staging of Jesus' other appearance, delivering the 'sermon

12. J.D. Crossan, *The Historical Jesus: The Life of a Mediterranean Jewish Peasant* (Edinburgh T. & T. Clark, 1991); E.P. Sanders, *The Historical Figure of Jesus* (London: Allen Lane, 1993); Geza Vermes, *Jesus the Jew: A Historian's Reading of the Gospels* (London: SCM Press, 2nd edn, 1973).

13. Even sophisticated non-British cultural critics may be unaware of the British tradition in which, at the most dismal time of the year in January and early February (i.e. a little earlier than *Mardi Gras*), entertainment celebrities repair to theatres across the country to perform in such traditional offerings as *Cinderella* or *Aladdin* or *Dick Whittington*. These pantomimes include such stock transvestite figures as the 'principal boy' (whose requirement is an attractive pair of female legs) and the 'dame' (usually the hero's mother), played by a man, and traditionally performing at some point a partial striptease to reveal voluminous underwear. That Monty Python should invoke this parodic (not to say carnivalistic) genre in the person of Brian's mother (Terry Jones) is entirely appropriate, since the pantomime character functions culturally in some respects like the Virgin in Mediterranean cultures, and indeed might well have some roots in a parody of the Virgin, the archtypal Hero's Mother.

on the mount', maintains a distance between him and the human race. The reason may have to do partly with his non-visibility, as in the corresponding scene in *Ben Hur*, where Jesus' face is hidden in a camera shot that looks from behind his back towards the admiring crowd. But rather more important is the implication of remoteness from humanity.

Thus, in the 'sermon on the mount' scene in *Life of Brian*, the camera looks towards (though not *at*) the preaching Jesus from the back of the crowd, and Jesus is scarcely seen, his voice so inaudible that his words are garbled as they reach the back of the crowd and the camera. 'Peacemakers' becomes 'cheesemakers'. In a stark reversal of focus, the camera is set not on the speaker, but on a crowd gathered for amusement and out of boredom rather than from spiritual hunger. The contrast between preaching and reception is brutal enough: while peacemaking is being proclaimed, fighting breaks out over the most trivial matter, and the dominical words are immediately exegeted by the rabbinical device of *kelal upherat*[14] into a statement about the dairy industry. Monty Python's Jesus is offered as someone out of touch with ordinary humans, psychologically as well as physically, since his principles of non-violence clearly do not strike much of a chord with any of his compatriots. Brian, however, is the opposite, suffering rather from too much contact with other humans, and indeed representing the essential comic vulnerability of the human being which is the core of Python's anthropology.

The remoteness of Jesus from the life of ordinary humans is also conveyed by the case of the ex-cripple, where we are offered the dominical version of 'workfare'. A cripple has a job, of which his cure has deprived him. However much the message is overlaid with traces of human corruptibility and resourcefulness (also key characteristics of humanity in Monty Python's book), the distance between the values of the gospel (in which both a historical Jesus and his modern disciples are implicated) and those of the human implied audience of the film are again set against each other, and worldly wisdom wins over heavenly. The contrast is particularly sharply expressed in the potentially difficult subject of crucifixion. Rather than skirt round this central offence, Monty Python prepares for it by showing human connivance in punishment, first from

---

14. *Kelal upherat* is one of the seven rules (*middot*) ascribed to Hillel (and extended to thirteen by R. Ishmael). For the list, see *Sifra* 3a; *t. Sanh.* 7.11; *Abot deRabbi Nathan* 37. The phrase means 'general and particular' and connotes the device of extending a verse pertaining to one member of a class so as to cover the entire class.

a politically right-wing internee hanging on a prison wall and proclaiming the virtues of 'law and order', then by a crucifixion willingly and jokingly accepted by the victims when they are accidentally offered freedom as an alternative; and finally by the victorious celebration of the bright side of life in the closing scene. As one character sums it up, 'crucifixion is a doddle'.

What Monty Python has done is to split the cultural icon of Jesus into two parts. The one bears the name of Jesus and the other the name of Brian. The former represents the icon of most filmed Jesuses, who must be recognizably divine, while the latter constitutes the icon of most scholarly written Jesuses, who must be human and have a personality. If the contrast between the two is a little too neat (as I acknowledge), nevertheless the human–divine Jesus has always been a problem for Christian theology. The Nestorian controversy instigated a debate about whether the second person of the trinity has one or two natures, and the division was never healed, because the earthly body of Christ remains split over the issue. In recent times, and in a slightly different mode, Rudolf Bultmann famously severed the 'Jesus of history' from the 'Christ of faith'. In the shadow of two famous dichotomies, then, Monty Python divides the two natures into two persons, and assigns divinity to the one (who is the 'historical' Jesus, divinity advertised early on by the Christmas card nativity scene) and humanity to the other ('who shall be called Brian'). One is the divine figure seen through the eyes of post-Easter resurrection faith (namely, the icon of conventional Christian piety), the other a flesh and blood, historically conditioned human being. Because Jesus in the *Life of Brian* conforms to the stereotype of filmed Jesuses, and because Brian bears an entirely incongruous non-Semitic name, the formal dissociation of Brian from his counterpart is straightforward, even when every filmgoer realizes that Brian *is* indeed a Jesus in human drag and that we are watching Monty Python's *Life of Jesus*. The entrenched difficulty of combining in a twentieth-century Bible epic (and in Christian belief) a divine Christ with a human Jesus has effectively created two figures, and Monty Python formalizes that dichotomy. The viewer, however, *necessarily recombines the figures*.

It is Brian, then, who represents the human nature of the dichotomized Messiah. And what sort of a humanity does he bear? He is indeed 'meek and mild': always the victim, rarely if ever the instigator. He is the true 'man for others' whether these others are his mother, his colleagues in the revolutionary gang, his female companion or a crowd of messianic followers. All of these, of course, in turn betray him as thoroughly as Judas did. He is never the real leader, but rather that parodic leader, the stooge. He is the disciple of others, even when having messiahship foisted on him and when being betrayed by his own band of revolutionaries. His response to potential followers is not 'follow me' but the exact opposite, and bluntly expressed at that. Not a man really to be followed, then, and one not at all desirous of disciples. His inability to accept any initiative and his willingness to be led into even the most dubious of causes displays a benevolence towards fellow humans that induces sympathy in the audience. And perhaps self-identification as well: the humanity of Brian is in many respects the humanity not only of all the characters in the film, but of many of the audience, for whom *imitatio Briani* is almost inevitable.[15]

Anthropology

I mean 'anthropology' in the traditional theological sense of a doctrine of human nature. According to the gospel as preached by Christian orthodoxy, human nature has fallen into sin and requires redeeming by divine grace. This construction does not correspond to Pythonesque anthropology. A fundamental characteristic of the Monty Python portrait of human nature is benevolence. Such benevolence means that oppression is borne with a smile, whether one is hanging on a prison wall and blessing the Romans for introducing good order, or hanging on a cross celebrating the bright side of life. Even the oppressor oppresses rather benevolently, preferring to throw someone repeatedly to the floor in a symbolic gesture of brutality, or oblige writers of graffiti to 'do lines' in correct Latin. The benevolence of the Romans is carefully brought to our attention through the mouths of their would-be resisters: aqueducts, roads, peace, irrigation, wine, baths, education.[16] A certain sympathy towards imperial government is hard to overlook, perhaps because of its striking absence from any American-made movie.[17]

---

15. For the benefit of non-British readers, I should underline the fact that the film's implied viewers are British. But space does not permit an excursus into the British psyche here.

16. The rehearsal of Roman benefactions in *Life of Brian* is not actually entirely accurate: irrigation, wine and education were not introduced by Romans to Judaea.

17. The American Hollywood movie *is* American imperialism at its most effective.

Americans have not run an empire: rather, they exercise direct *political* influence through the occasional military intervention, through selective foreign aid, intelligence operations, bullying and economic clout. Their films, however, rarely if ever condone imperialism. The British, on the other hand, and especially the public-school class from whom Monty Python comes, are content to poke gentle fun at its administrators, without condemning the system itself. The gifts of the Romans to the Jews point to the gifts of the British empire to large areas of the planet.

Monty Python's definition of the original sin from which humans need to be redeemed is sheer incompetence, which increases as one moves up the scale of authority. In true parodic fashion, moral authority also decreases as one moves from the person in the crowd to the lisping Roman governor.[18] Roman incompetence is also evident in the failure to discover fugitives, in the inability of Pilate to maintain dignity, let alone order, in front of sniggering Roman soldiers and jeering Jewish crowds. The stoning of an accidentally blaspheming priest is a further illustration of the impotence of authority in the face of a *massa perditionis*. The crowd, which plays such a part in the New Testament biographies as a foil for dominical exploits—hearing, receiving, or just gathering (14 times in Matthew, 24 in Mark, 15 in Luke, and 9 in John)—is the hero in the *Life of Brian*, stealing the initiative in listening to sermons, in stoning, in heckling the teller of parables, in creating a messiah, in ridiculing the Roman governor and his crudely-named friend, Bigus Dickus.

Finally, human nature is resourceful, always bordering, indeed, on petty criminal behaviour. Such a trait is identified in the would-be cross bearer who leaves his pious helper to take his place, as well as in the ex-cripple still trying to make a beggar's living. It also ensures that the efforts to save Brian from execution are frustrated, for what Pythonesque human would not claim to be Mickey Mouse if it would get him off a cross?

Salvation

Now, from benevolence, fallibility and resourcefulness no human authority can turn humanity, nor any messiah deliver it. Monty Python's humanity is irredeemable and furthermore has no wish to be

18. Speech defect is a almost a hallmark of Pythonesque anthropology; recall the stammering Michael Palin in *A Fish Called Wanda*.

redeemed. The audience is expected to find itself drawn into the same opinion. There *is* no real evil in a Pythonesque world. If the Jesus of the New Testament exposes to humans the possibilities of perfection, Monty Python exposes to us a mischievous and lovable human condition, without a single unforgivable character. There is an anti-gospel here, conscious or not. No sooner is any kind of return to a pre-sinning Eden mooted than it is lampooned. The nearest to a vision of ideal world we are offered is a loyal female companion and a Roman administration that brings untold material benefits. Messiahs are not created or begotten; they have messiahship thrust upon them by a superstitious and feckless humanity. Nor can divine truth be imparted to them through parables, for the audience do not have ears to hear, wanting to know about the parable that Brian suddenly finds himself obliged to deliver ('And when he was alone, they that were about him with the twelve asked of him the parable', Mk 4.10). In the case presented by Monty Python, Brian parabolizes out of a desire not to communicate but to throw off pursuit, and the impression is given that he understands, and cares about, what he is saying even less than his listeners. His parables remain 'mysteries' (Mk 4.11).

In short, the proper Pythonesque human response to acts of messianic charity, to the offer of redemption, is uttered by Brian to the ex-leper: 'There is no pleasing some people', he says: and the reply? 'That's what *he* said'. What is lampooned in the *Life of Brian* is not redemption or salvation but the wish for it.

'My Father's House'

There is one scene in which Brian has one of those otherworldly journeys beloved of apocalyptic literature. The episode represents, of course, yet another parody of the Hollywood genre repertory, this time, extra terrestrials. ET and his friends are present in the Gospels' own Lives of Jesus as angels, one of whom had a hand (?) in his conception, and others who looked after him in the desert after his temptations. The transcendental world from which the son of God came is always present in the Gospels, whether in teaching (parables of the kingdom) or in vision (transfiguration) or in ascension. That which represents ultimate reality in the Gospels, however, becomes a human fantasy (of a fairly tacky kind) in the film, whose view of human existence allows for no extra-human dimension. This episode, depicted as a cartoon sequence, converts the transcendent reality into space-fiction, something culturally received as unreal—though perhaps this analysis is already obsolete with the encroachment of the millennium and the popularity of *The X Files* with its slogan, 'the truth is out there'. With such a sentiment, *Life of Brian* emphatically does not agree. Humans are the measure of all things and gods are Toons.

Conclusion

Technically, this has been a viewer-response exegesis of the *Life of Brian*. I have indeed suggested that some of the features identified point to deliberate authorial intention. But some are probably coincidental. In the end, this is a reading by a particular member of the cinema audience, wearing the floppy hat of a secular biblical scholar with a small Union Jack stitched to it.

The idea of the parodic, which Mikhail Bakhtin's work has made fashionable, can so obviously be applied to Monty Python's *Life of Brian* that I have refrained from doing so at length or programmatically. I wish, however, to make one final, and serious comment on the tradition. The mediaeval mystery play, encouraged by the church and eagerly accepted by the populace as another day off work, represents not only an opportunity for parody but an interplay of cultures. The dominant (hegemonic) culture, that of the church, offered to the mediaeval world a complete account of human existence, from Fall through redemption to ultimate judgment, locating the individual within a web of diabolic temptation, ultimate hell fire or heavenly bliss, and the saving instrumentality of church authority. That this all-embracing myth did not succeed in imposing a Christian lifestyle on many ordinary mortals (nor even on ecclesiastics) may be taken for granted. But the mediaeval church was in conflict not only with human fecklessness of the kind that *Life of Brian* celebrates, but also with an inherited set of values that was essentially what we would call 'pagan'. Many of the religious practices of this paganism were Christianized. However, the underlying non-Christian mentality has never departed. It has always expressed itself in various forms, literary and artistic. The *Life of Brian* does not merely parody the life of Jesus and certain conventional forms of Christian piety. It also affirms a different set of values. I do not know that such a serious intention was ever contemplated; but every good cultural critic knows that you cannot parody without exposing yourself. To a cultural critic (especially a deconstructively-minded one interested in overturning hierarchies of discourse), the ideology of the *Life of Brian* is as interesting and potentially valuable as those that the various *Lives of Jesus* try to impose on the Christian Messiah.

Life of Brian's main flaw, in my view, is revealed in the final scene. Hanging on a cross singing 'Always look on the bright side of life' is funny so long as the viewer forgets what crucifixion was actually like. The scene just would not work with nails and blood as it does with rope. As one of my newer colleagues has remarked: 'no pain, no gain'.[19] Is there ultimately a deep flaw in the anthropology of *Life of Brian*? Probably. But I have deliberately taken its ideology more seriously than Monty Python intended. It is, after all, a countertext, just like the book of Ecclesiastes. As such, it deserves a place in the cultural canon of Christian and post-Christian theology as much as it does in the canon of cult films.

19. Stephen Moore, *God's Gym: Divine Male Bodies of the Bible* (London: Routledge, 1996).

Stereotyping the Other:
The 'Pharisees' in the Gospel According to Matthew[1]

Margaret Davies

Twentieth-century 'cultural studies' embraces such a wide and complex spectrum of contemporary living that no aspect of our existence is entirely irrelevant to its concern. Popular music, art, fashion and advertising through festivals, magazines, newspapers, TV, radio and the Internet are as important as 'high art', so that a distinction between the two is all but disappearing. Attempts at discussing 'cultural' aspects of our lives in our post-traditional capitalist social, educational, legal, economic and political contexts require our reflections on details and possible generalizations that are difficult either to define or encompass. The writings of Raymond Williams, for example, represent endeavours to avoid reductionist simplicities. In this context, my writing a short article about 'characterization' in the New Testament Gospel according to Matthew, in regard to cultural stereotyping in its own time and in ours, is an expression of hubris. Nevertheless, and in spite of the nemesis it invites, I shall take up insights from contemporary literary criticism in order to highlight some aspects of the topic.

One of the difficulties we experience when we read ancient narratives, especially ancient didactic narratives like the New Testament Gospels, is that their depictions of characters are much less complex than those to which we have become accustomed in contemporary fiction, historical narrative and biography. Seymour Chatman describes the differences as qualitative rather than quantitative:

> The difference between modern characters like Leopold Bloom or Marcel and Prince Charming or Ivan are so great as to be qualitative rather than quantitative. Not only are the traits more numerous, but they tend not to 'add up', or more germanely 'break down', that is, reduce to any single aspect or pattern... What gives the modern fictional character the

---

1. A stereotype is a solid metallic plate for printing, cast from a plastic mould of movable types. Figuratively, it refers to a fixed, unchanging image.

particular kind of illusion acceptable to modern taste is precisely the
heterogeneity or even scatter of his personality.[2]

What Chatman means by 'character trait' is a system of interdependent
habits persisting through time. But contemporary depictions of a character often encompass contradictory traits or exhibit traits that do not per-
sist through the whole of a character's life, so that such a character is less
than wholly consistent and is complex.[3] Moreover, attributing a trait to
a character may not determine the development of the plot. So, for
example, a narrator may depict a character as jealous of someone else,
but readers do not automatically expect the jealous character to harm
the object of her jealousy.[4] Again, Rimmon-Kenan notes the absence of
direct definitions in contemporary fiction:

> In the present day, when suggestiveness and indeterminacy are preferred
> to closure and definiteness and when emphasis is put on the active role of
> the reader, the explicitness and guiding capacity of direct definition are
> often considered drawbacks rather than advantages. As a result, definition
> is less frequently used in twentieth century fiction and indirect definition
> tends to predominate.[5]

In other words, a character is not introduced with a defining adjective
like 'good' or 'honest' or 'hypocrite' which fixes the dominant trait
through which we will read the character. On the contrary, we have to
infer the character from indirect presentations like 'actions' and these
presentations may not 'add up'.

2.   Seymour Chatman, *Story and Discourse: Narrative Structure in Fiction and Film*
(Ithaca, NY: Cornell University Press, 1978), p. 112.
3.   Chatman, *Story and Discourse*, p. 113.
4.   Chatman, *Story and Discourse*, p. 114.
5.   S. Rimmon-Kenan, *Narrative Fiction: Contemporary Poetics* (New Accents;
London: Routledge, 1989), p. 61. See also B. Hochman, *Character in Literature*
(Ithaca, NY: Cornell University Press, 1985); S. Bar-Efrat, *Narrative Art in the Bible*
(Bible and Literature, 17; Sheffield, Sheffield Academic Press, 1989), especially
Chapter 2. In New Testament studies, the Gospel according to Luke and the Acts of
the Apostles have been the focus for scholarly studies of character depiction, espe-
cially from the perspective of reader-response criticism. See, for example,
R.L. Brawley, *Centering on God: Method and Message in Luke–Acts* (Louisville, KY:
Westminster/John Knox Press, 1990); D.B. Gowler, *Host, Guest, Enemy and Friend:
Portraits of the Pharisees in Luke and Acts* (New York, Peter Lang, 1991); J.A. Darr,
On Character Building: The Reader and the Rhetoric of Characterization in Luke–Acts
(Louisville, KY: Westminster/John Knox Press, 1992).

Chatman, in calling 'the contemplation of character' 'the predominant pleasure in modern art narrative', suggests that this represents our cultural contruction of 'the convention of the uniqueness of the individual'.[6] It is now part of our proverbial wisdom to recognize that contemporary Western culture is individualistic, and Mary Douglas's heuristic diagram of group and grid separates societies in which the group takes precedence over the individual from societies like ours in which the individual takes precedence over the group.[7]

Chatman also suggests that character traits are socially invented signs which are not perfect designations of 'what is going on' but rather expressions of particular cultural concerns. So he interprets, for example, traits like 'devoted' or 'patient' as mediaeval church articulations of Christian concerns, and traits like 'introverted' as contemporary articulations of psychological concerns.

For reasons of space, I shall confine my study to the depiction of 'Pharisees' in the Gospel according to Matthew.[8] I shall focus on three features that distinguish contemporary and ancient didactic narrative depictions of character: (1) simple rather than complex characterization; (2) group rather than individual characterization; (3) distinctive cultural character traits.

1. *Simple rather than Complex Characterization*

I shall consider the Matthaean portrait of 'Pharisees' in the light of two cultural traditions that could have influenced Matthaean characterization:

---

6. Chatman, *Story and Discourse*, p. 113.

7. Mary Douglas, *In the Active Voice* (London: Routlege & Kegan Paul, 1982), pp. 183-254.

8. Matthew and/or Mark and Luke sometimes agree in their references to 'Pharisees': Mt. 9.11, 14; 12.2, 14; 15.1; 16.1, 6; 19.3; 22.15; 23.23, 25, 26, 27. But Mark and/or Luke sometimes have 'scribes' where Matthew has 'Pharisees': Mt. 12.24; 21.45; 22.15, 34, 41. Luke sometimes has 'lawyer' when Matthew has 'scribes and Pharisees': Mt. 23.4, 13, 29, 34. Luke sometimes has 'Pharisees' when Matthew has 'scribes and Pharisees': Mt. 23.23, 25, 26, 27. Matthew also has 'Pharisees' in passages without parallel in the other Gospels: 5.20; 9.34; 12.38; 15.12; 23.2, 15; 27.62. See K.G.C. Newport, *The Sources and Sitz im Leben of Matthew 23* (JSNTSup, 117; Sheffield: Sheffield Academic Press, 1995), which argues that Mt. 23 represents a pre-Matthaean source. Whatever the source, however, ch. 23 now forms part of the whole Gospel, and there are contradictions within ch. 23, as well as between ch. 23 and the rest of the narrative. See below.

classical and Hellenistic Greek, and prophetic denunciations of Israel and its leaders in the Jewish Scriptures.

a. *Classical and Hellenistic Greek Characterization*
Plato's and Aristotle's explorations of the cardinal virtues—practical wisdom, justice, temperance and courage—insist that these virtues form a unity and that the virtuous person expresses all of them. From their perspective, it is impossible to act justly without being courageous and temperate, and without the practical wisdom that discerns what acting justly involves.[9] Hence these virtues cannot be in conflict either within a person or within a city. Of course, they recognized ethical conflicts within and between the cities of their own times, but were concerned to reform the cities for this reason. Moreover, while the Stoic tradition did separate what is good from what people desire and insisted on the complete subjugation of human desires, the Platonic and Aristotelean traditions explore ways in which the virtues and only the virtues could bring about human flourishing because the desire for happiness is formed through virtuous activity. Aristotle's *Nicomachean Ethics* characterizes the virtues as 'the mean' between vices of excess and vices of defect. So, for example, 'courage' is the 'mean' between the vice of excess, 'rashness', and the vice of defect, 'cowardice'.[10] This description, however, fails to capture the work's subtlety and breadth of discussions about how to live well, for example, in book 4.

Aristotle's pupil, Theophrastus, wrote a book, usually called *Characters*, although it is more accurately called *Character Traits*,[11] which developed Aristotle's discussions of vices into vivid depictions of character traits (dissembling, flattering, idle chattering, boorishness, obsequeousness, shamelessness, garrulity, rumour-mongering, sponging, penny-pinching, obnoxiousness, untimeliness, overzealousness, absent-mindedness, grouchiness, superstitious, griping, mistrustful, squalid,

---

9.   See A. MacIntyre, *After Virtue* (London: Gerald Duckworth, 1981), p. 132 and Chapter 12.

10.   Book 2.8. And see C. Pelling (ed.), *Characterization and Individuality in Greek Literature* (Oxford: Clarendon Press, 1990), which shows that, although classical tragedy integrates character traits, characters are not reducible to types. Nevertheless, in ethical discourse, integration works together with the purpose of providing examples to impede individual differences.

11.   χαρακτηρ is an engraved mark, impress or stamp, and, figuratively, a distinctive personal mark or character trait. In Greek, ἠθος means 'character'.

tasteless, pettily ambitious, ungenerous, fraudulent, arrogant, cowardly, authoritarian, juvenile, slandering, or being patronizing scoundrels, defrauding). These characterizations both reflected and influenced depictions of characters in Greek and Roman comedy, and also influenced seventeenth- and eighteenth-century European literature.[12] In philosophy, the second century CE Hellenistic writer Plutarch took up this tradition in his essays on vicious character traits (*On Garrulity, How to Tell a Flatterer from a Friend, On Superstition, On Meddling, On the Love of Money, On Extravagant Self-Praise*). Moreover, the portayal of character traits in fiction and history seems to have formed part of educational training in rhetoric.[13] In these ways, 'character traits' became divorced from Plato's and Aristotle's analyses and arguments about virtues and vices. In effect, vicious character traits could be attached by name to any rival philosophical or teaching group.

So, for example, some of Plato's characterizations of the Sophists became detached, standard, stereotypical traits, used of other groups in philosophical didactic literature from various schools: merchants selling their teaching for gain,[14] deceivers,[15] those who do not practise what they preach,[16] disputatious quibblers.[17] This last character trait, disputatious quibbling, is what is meant by the English 'sophistry'.

In the Gospel according to Matthew, the character Jesus is depicted attributing the character trait 'hypocrite' to the 'Pharisees'. Jesus' seven woes are addressed to 'scribes and Pharisees, hypocrites' (23.13, 15, 23, 25, 26, 27, 29), and the section is introduced in 23.2-3 by Jesus' teaching the crowds and his disciples: 'The scribes and Pharisees sit on Moses' seat; so practise and observe whatever they tell you, but not what they

---

12. See J.W. Smeed, *The Theophrastan 'Character': The History of a Literary Genre* (Oxford: Clarendon Press, 1985).

13. Aristotle, *Rhetoric* 2.12-14; Cicero, *Topica* 83; Quintillian, 1.9.3. See C. Gill, 'The Question of Character Development: Plutarch and Tacitus', *Classical Quarterly* 33 (1983), pp. 469-87.

14. Plato, *Sophist* 223b, 224a-d, 231d; Philo, *Vit. Mos.* 2.212; Dio Chrysostom, *Orations* 54.1; 1 Tim. 6.5; Tit. 1.11. See R.J. Karris, 'The Background and Significance of the Polemic of the Pastoral Epistles', *JBL* 92 (1973), pp. 549-64.

15. Plato, *Sophist* 234-35; Philo, *Migr. Abr.* 76, 83; Dio Chrysostom, *Orations* 4.33, 35, 37; 2 Tim. 3.33.

16. Plato, *Sophist* 226a, 231e, 232b, 234c; Philo, *Migr. Abr.* 171; Seneca, *Epist. Moral.* 108.36; 2 Tim. 3.5; Tit. 1.16; 3.8-9.

17. Plato, *Sophist* 226a, 231e, 232b; Philo, *Migr. Abr.* 171; Dio Chrysostom, *Orations* 12.5-15; 1 Tim. 1.4, 6; 4.2; 6.4; 2 Tim. 2.14, 16, 23; Tit. 1.10; 3.9.

do; for they preach but do not practise'. The English word 'hypocrite' is a transliteration of the Greek word ὑποκριτης, which in classical Greek means 'one who answers'. It was used to refer to actors. In Hellenistic ethical discourse, however, it took on the connotation 'pretender, dissembler'.[18] The only clear instances of the word in the Septuagint occur in Job 34.30 and 36.13. The Gospel according to Matthew, then, takes up this Hellenistic tradition to characterize the 'Pharisees' through direct definition in the discourse of its reliable character Jesus, and suggests that they are 'hypocrites' because they do not practise what they preach.

Another accusation attributed to Jesus in 23.5-7 fills out the picture of their 'hypocrisy' by asserting that 'Pharisees' 'love to be called rabbi by people' and that their other pious acts are performed to gain honour among the general population. Elsewhere, the narrative depicts Jesus as accepting honorific titles from people: rabbi (26.25, 49); lord (e.g. 8.2, 6, 21; 10.24-25; 14.28, 30, etc.); Christ, son of David (16.16; 21.9); and in 23.10 he is said to claim the title 'guide'. In some of these instances, however, an impression of Jesus' diffidence is created by his commanding suppliants who had been healed to tell no one (8.4; 9.30; 12.16), or by his reinterpretation of the title's significance in terms of dishonour rather than honour (16.16-23; cf. 20.25-28), or by the narrator's attributing the motive of compassion to him (9.36; cf. 8.17; 14.14; 15.32; 20.34). In the story of Jesus' public ride into Jerusalem (21.1-11), his action is defined as 'humble' and the crowds are said to recognize him not only as the son of David but also as the prophet. In other words, the narrative seems deliberately to offset any impression that Jesus sought honour from other people, while, at the same time, suggesting that these titles are correctly attributed to Jesus.

Other accusations of 'hypocrisy' interpret the term by presenting 'Pharisees' as disputatious quibblers (23.16-22), and as using piety to cover extortion and rapacity (23.25-28). Further epithets are also used directly to define the 'Pharisees' and to consolidate the portrait of them as deceptive teachers: 'sons of Gehenna', that is, belonging to Gehenna, the place of eschatological punishment (23.15); 'blind guides' (23.16; cf. 15.14); 'fools and blind people' (23.17); 'snakes, brood of serpents', that is, deceivers (23.33; cf. 12.34 attributed to Jesus, and 3.7 attributed to John). The epithet 'fool'[19] is particularly striking because earlier teaching

18. E.g. Lucian, *Alexander* 4; Vettius Valens 42.25.
19. Plato depicts the Sophist as an ignorant imitator, *Sophist* 200d, 267e, 268c-d. In the Septuagint, occasionally people are called 'fools': Deut. 32.6; Ps. 94.8;

attributed to Jesus in 5.22 warns that 'whoever says "you fool" shall be liable to the Gehenna of fire'. This earlier teaching condemns name-calling and encourages reconciliation (5.21-26). The Matthaean character Jesus, therefore, is depicted, presumably inadvertently, as breaking his own rules. Moreover, there is an obvious contradiction between Jesus' command that people should follow 'Pharisaic' teaching (23.3) and his descriptions of their teaching as deceptive and disputatious.

There are, however, these similarities between Plato's characterization of the 'Sophist' through the mouth of his character 'the Stranger' and the Matthaean characterization of the 'Pharisees' through the mouth of his character 'Jesus'. But the Matthaean Jesus is also depicted as directly defining the 'Pharisees' through epithets. Luke Johnson's study,[20] section 5, seeks to set all the New Testament's slanderous statements about Jewish groups in the literary context of contemporary slanders against alien groups, focusing on the writings of Epictetus, Plutarch, Philostratus and Lucian in the Hellenistic tradition, and Josephus, Philo, the Mishnah, *4 Ezra*, the *Psalms of Solomon* and the Dead Sea Scrolls in the Jewish tradition, and recognizing their shared conventions. He concludes that the language is connotive rather than denotive. Moreover, although the word 'polemic' is used throughout the study, as if these literary characterizations were aimed at real, historical adversaries and rivals, Johnson also notes that, in literature, characterizations of 'bad people' can serve the didactic purpose of reinforcing the characterizations of 'good people' by providing an exact negative counter-image to cause the reader's revulsion. That is, the purpose may not be polemical but didactic. So, the 'Pharisees' in the Matthaean text are represented as the counter-image of the character 'Jesus' (see below, section 3).[21]

Jer. 5.21; and very occasionally leaders are called 'fools': Isa. 19.11; 32.5-6; and the depiction of 'the fool' is a theme of Ecclesiasticus; cf. 4.27; 8.17, etc.

20. 'The New Testament's Anti-Jewish Slander and the Conventions of Ancient Polemic', *JBL* 108 (1989), pp. 419-41 (esp. 441).

21. Sections 2 and 3 of Johnson's article usefully highlight the diversity of first century CE Judaism and of the messianic movement. M.S. Taylor, *Anti-Judaism and Early Christian Identity: A Critique of the Scholarly Consensus* (Studia Post-Biblica, 46; Leiden: E.J. Brill, 1995), questions the consensus among patristic scholars who use various models of social 'conflict' to explain Christian anti-Jewish writings, and who ignore the theoretical and theological contexts in which anti-Judaism appears. Moreover, she demonstrates the Patristic writings' literary dependence both on pagan anti-Judaism and on Christian traditions of biblical interpretation, and convincingly

b. *Prophetic Denunciations in the Jewish Scriptures*

That the Gospel according to Matthew represents Jesus as a prophetic figure (13.57-58; 21.46), even providing parallels between Jesus and Moses,[22] is generally recognized. The form of Jesus' address to the 'Pharisees' in 23.13-36 as a series of woes imitates prophetic woes against Israel and its leaders in the Jewish Scriptures (e.g. Isa. 5, 8, 23; Zech. 11.17). This presentation, however, causes some tension in the narrative. Teaching attributed to Jesus in 7.1-6 warns people against judging other people and against trying to force their insight upon those who are not interested. But Jesus' seven woes against the 'scribes and Pharisees' and his woes against towns and cities (11.20-24, cf. 23.37-39) are set in contexts in which these groups had neither asked Jesus' advice nor directly challenged him.

Elsewhere in the narrative there are other echoes of prophetic denunciations. In Mt. 21.13, allusions to Isa. 56.7 and Jer. 7.11 are placed on the lips of Jesus as an interpretation of his prophetic actions in driving out of the Temple those who bought and sold, and in turning over the tables of money-changers and the seats of pigeon sellers.[23] Jeremiah 23.1 accuses 'the shepherds', that is, the rulers, of destroying and scattering the sheep of the Lord's pasture (cf. Mt. 9.36). Isaiah's oracle about the people's 'blindness' (6.9-10) is quoted by Jesus (Mt. 13.10-16) against

argues for understanding 'Jews' in these writings as 'symbolic figures' who are made to play a role in Christian theological concerns. See also R. Radford Reuther, *Faith and Fratricide: The Theological Roots of Anti-Semitism* (New York: Seabury, 1974).

22. E.g. Mt. 2.1-18, Jesus' escape from the ruler's attempt to kill him, cf. Exod. 1.8–2.10; Mt. 5–7, Jesus' sermon on the mount, cf. Exod. 20.21–23.33; Mt. 8–9, Jesus' ten miracles, cf. Exod. 7–12; Mt. 17.1-8, Jesus' transfiguration, cf. Exod. 34.29-35; and see most recently Dale Allison, *The New Moses: A Matthaean Typology* (Minneapolis: Augsburg Fortress, 1993).

23. The quotation of Jer. 7.11 is often interpreted as Jesus' condemnation of those who supposedly made extortionate profits through Temple trade, but that is not the significance of the reference in Jer. 7.11. Rather Jer. 7 accuses people of irreligious and unethical behaviour and of going to the Temple and saying 'we are delivered' while continuing these 'abominations'. That is, they are said to treat the Temple as if it is a cave of robbers, and they are reminded of God's destruction of the temple at Shiloh for the same reason. Similarly, the Matthaean narrative presents Jesus' condemnation of people's religious infidelity and social injustice, and their failure to amend their ways while worshipping at the Temple therefore means that they treat the Temple like a cave of robbers. The depiction of Jesus' actions in the Temple, therefore, is best understood as symbolic, in the light of his prediction of the Temple's destruction in 23.27–24.2.

the crowds, and another oracle of Isaiah (29.13), which develops the same imagery, is quoted by Jesus against the 'Pharisees' (15.8-9). Here, the stated reason for Jesus' calling the 'Pharisees' 'blind', that they dishonour parents for the sake of their tradition, again causes tension in the narrative, however, since elsewhere teaching attributed to Jesus can be construed as dishonouring parents (Mt. 8.21-22; 10.34-37; 12.46-50).

c. *Characterization through the Depiction of Actions and the Attribution of Motives*

The Matthaean characterization of the 'Pharisees' through the direct definitions and arguments attributed to Jesus, therefore, repeats conventional characterizations of alien teachers in Hellenistic literature and conventional characterizations of unfaithful people and their leaders in the Jewish Scripture's prophetic books. And these characterizations are attributed to Jesus, the narrative's main protagonist. How far, however, are these character traits, attributed to the 'Pharisees' by Jesus, supported in the narrative depiction of their actions and motives? They are supported in a general way by presenting Jesus as a superior teacher who is always depicted winning disputes.[24] The 'Pharisees' appear in these accounts as mere quibblers. Moreover, Jesus is always given the last word, even when obvious questions or replies are suggested by the rhetoric of the text. For example, Jesus' enigmatic 'render to Caesar the things that are Caesar's and to God the things that are God's' (Mt. 21.21) prompts the questions: what is Caesar's, what is God's and how are the two related? But the narrator concludes the story: 'When they heard it, they marvelled; and they left him and went away' (21.22), so distracting readers into marvelling and going on to the next story. Again, Mt. 12.9-14 relates a story of Jesus' healing by word on the sabbath a man with a withered hand. But the justification of Jesus' actions attributed to him prompts questions: what relevance has rescuing a sheep from a pit, where to leave it could threaten its life, to the healing of a man's non-life-threatening withered hand; what does 'it is lawful to do good on the sabbath' mean; and how does Jesus' healing by word break the sabbath command that forbids work? The narrator's conclusion: 'And the Pharisees went out and took counsel against him, how to destroy him' pictures the 'Pharisees' as so inept that they are unable to

---

24. Mt. 9.11-13; 12.1-45; 15.1-20; 16.1-4; 19.3-9; 21.33-45; 22.15-22, 34-46.

ask obvious questions and, instead, have to resort to other methods for the destruction of this brilliant rival.

The description of their purpose, 'to destroy him', however, is ambiguous. Does it mean that they planned to destroy his reputation as a teacher and healer who attracted crowds? The context seems to suggest so, since they are next depicted trying to undermine Jesus' credibility by construing his exorcisms as miracles performed through the power, not of God, but of 'Beelzebul the prince of demons' (12.24). Once more, however, Jesus is represented getting the better of them in argument (12.25-45).

The narrator also intensifies the negative portrait of the 'Pharisees' by attributing unworthy motives to them. In 16.1, together with the 'Sadducees', they are said to 'test' Jesus with a request for a sign, trying to force him to meet their own (mistaken) expectations, which are left unfulfilled. In 19.3, they are said to 'test' him with a socially difficult question about the grounds for divorce, but Jesus' reply is represented as leaving them speechless, in spite of the tension between 'let not a person put asunder' and the exception clause in 19.9, which could be construed as an expression of the husband's 'hardness of heart'. Again in 22.15, the 'Pharisees' are said to have 'taken counsel how to entangle him in his talk' and to have sent their disciples with the Herodians to ask him a politically sensitive question about Roman tax. In each case, the failure of their schemes serves to enhance Jesus' stature.

Does the narrative anywhere, however, depict the 'Pharisees' as acting in a way that would warrant Jesus' accusation that they are 'full of extortion and rapacity' (23.25)? The dispute about their dedicating wealth to the Temple (15.1-20) does not justify the accusation since they could not gain in that way. Moreover, the woe that assumes they tithe herbs (23.23-24) represents their going beyond what is required by the law in acts of generosity, actually endorsed by Jesus. Nowhere, therefore, is this accusation of extortionate behaviour warranted by depictions of their behaviour in the narrative. Again, does the narrative represent the 'Pharisees' as acting in a way that would support Jesus' accusation that they 'neglect justice, mercy and faith' (23.23)? Perhaps the attempts to test Jesus could be construed as unjust. And their criticisms of the disciples' picking grain on the sabbath in order to satisfy hunger is explicitly reckoned unmerciful by Jesus (12.1-8), as is their criticism of Jesus' eating with tax-collectors and sinners (9.11-13). But how are we to coordinate the narrative construction of Jesus' own actions as expressions of mercy with the visions and statements, attributed to Jesus, of the actions of the son of the human being at the eschatological judgment, which include his repudiation, exclusion from the kingdom and destruction of people (e.g. 7.21-23; 13.41-42; 25.12, 26-30, 41-46)? That 'Pharisees' lack 'faith', however, seems to be warranted by the account of their accusation that Jesus casts out demons by Beelzebul (12.22-32). But here, Jesus' argument against them in 12.27 suggests that their practice is good but their teaching bad, which contradicts Jesus' statement in 23.3.

Finally, is the accusation against the 'Pharisees', attributed to Jesus in 23.31, that they are 'sons of those who killed the prophets', that is, sons as people who do what their fathers do, justified by the narrative depictions of their actions? A similar accusation is attributed to Jesus in the parable of the tenants in the vineyard, according to which the tenants killed the owner's son, a reference to Jesus' impending execution (22.37-39). In 22.45, the 'Pharisees' are said to have perceived that Jesus was speaking of them in this parable. But the narrative makes no reference to the 'Pharisees' in connexion with Jesus' arrest, trials and crucifixion. As commentators have repeatedly noticed, after ch. 23, they are mentioned only once, in 27.62, as among those who requested that a guard be placed at Jesus' grave, and they are not mentioned in the subsequent story about the bribing of the guard (28.11-15). In the narrative, therefore, Jesus' characterization of the 'Pharisees' as murderers is not instantiated through accounts of their actions.

In summary, some of the accusations against the 'Pharisees' attributed to Jesus are warranted by narrative accounts of their activities: their foolishness, and lack of mercy, justice and faith; but others are not: that their preaching is good enough to be followed in practise while they fail to practise it themselves, that they are full of extortion and rapacity, and that they killed Jesus.[25]

---

25. Sean Freyne's article, 'Vilifying the Other and Defining the Self: Matthew's and John's Anti-Jewish Polemic in Focus', in J. Neusner and E.S. Frerichs (eds.), *To See Ourselves as Others See Us: Christians, Jews and Others in Late Antiquity* (Chico, CA: Scholars Press, 1985), pp. 117-43, usefully highlights parallels between the criticisms of the 'Pharisees' in Mt. 23 and the criticisms of Jesus' disciples elsewhere in the narrative (see Appendix B, p. 143). G.M. Smiga, *Pain and Polemic: Anti-Judaism in the Gospels* (New York: Paulist Press, 1992), understands the Gospels in the light of prophetic conventions, but also tries to answer the question: what evaluative stance does the text make regarding Judaism? In relation to the Matthaean narrative, the study argues that this Gospel presents the followers of Jesus as the true Israel,

2. *Group rather than Individual Characterization*

The individualism of contemporary Western culture, epitomized by British Prime Minister Thatcher's declaration that there is no such thing as society, has affected characterizations in our literature in the ways suggested by Chatman and Rimmon-Kenan. But when we read the New Testament Gospels, we find that many of the characterizations are of groups, not of individuals. In the Gospel according to Matthew, repeatedly we find references to 'the crowd(s)' (e.g. 4.25; 5.1; 7.28; 8.1, 18, etc.), 'the people' (e.g. 1.21; 2.6; 4.16, 23, etc.), 'this generation' (e.g. 11.16; 12.39-45; 16.4, etc.), 'the disciples' (e.g. 5.1; 8.21, 23; 9.10, 14, 19, 37, etc.), 'the Pharisees' (e.g. 3.7; 5.20; 9.11, 14, 34, etc.), 'the scribes' (e.g. 2.4; 5.20; 7.29; 8.19, etc.), 'the Herodians' (22.6), 'the Sadducees' (e.g. 3.7; 16.1, 6, 11, 12, etc.), 'the chief priests' (e.g. 2.4;

denying all other claims to that role. In this way, the promises made to Israel by God in the Jewish Scriptures become promises to Jesus' followers, while the castigations of unfaithful Israelites inform the characterizations of the 'Pharisees' and other Jewish groups. Smiga uses the word 'polemic' because he envisages the text as directed against historical opponents. The study also supposes that it is important to ask whether the statements made about the 'Pharisees' are historically convincing. On this question, which I consider important but outside the scope of this article, see E.P. Sanders, *Jesus and Judaism* (London: SCM Press, 1985); *idem, The Jewish Law from Jesus to the Mishnah* (London: SCM Press; Philadelphia: Trinity Press International, 1990), and *idem, Judaism: Practice and Belief 63BCE–66CE* (London: SCM Press; Philadelphia: Trinity Press International, 1992); G. Vermes, *Jesus and the World of Judaism* (London: SCM Press, 1983); M. Goodman, *The Ruling Class of Judaea: The Origins of the Jewish Revolt against Rome* (Cambridge: Cambridge University Press, 1987). Unfortunately, J.D.G. Dunn, 'The Question of Anti-Semitism in the NT Writings of the Period', in J.D.G. Dunn (ed.) *Jews and Christians: The Parting of the Ways AD 70 to 135* (Tübingen: J.C.B. Mohr [Paul Siebeck], 1992), pp. 177-211, perpetuates a simplistic redaction-critical construction of a purported community situation from the text in order to support the view that the First Gospel is a Jewish work and therefore cannot be an expression of anti-Judaism or anti-Semitism in the limited way in which it is defined. The Matthaean 'Pharisees and their scribes' are identified with the Yavneh rabbis. But never is a question raised about the actual content of Matthaean accusations in comparison with any possible reconstructions of the teachings of the Yavneh rabbis. See also B. Przybylski, 'The Setting of Matthaean Anti-Judaism', on which Dunn's essay largely depends, in P. Richardson (ed.), *Anti-Judaism in Early Christianity. I. Paul and the Gospels* (Waterloo: ON: Wilfred Laurier University, 1986), pp. 181-200; and J.A. Overton, *Matthew's Gospel and Formative Judaism: The Social World of Matthaean Judaism* (Minneapolis: Fortress Press, 1990).

16.21; 20.18, etc.), 'the soldiers' (27.27), 'the guards' (27.66; 28.4, 11, 12), 'the Jews' (28.15, and in the expression 'the king of the Jews', 2.2; 27.11, 29, 37), 'the Gentiles' (e.g. 4.15; 5.47; 6.7, 32, etc.), the inhabitants of whole cities and towns (11.21, 23; 23.37-39). When these groups are represented as acting or speaking, they do so in chorus. For the most part, they are not individuated either by action or by name. There are, however, some exceptions. Among the chief priests, the high priest is named Caiaphas, and individual speech and action are attributed to him (26.57, 62, 63, 65, 66). Among the crowds, suppliants for Jesus' healings and exorcisms are characterized by their ailments, their requests and their responses, but they are not named (e.g. chs. 8–9). Among the Gentiles, the unnamed centurion and the unnamed Canaanite woman are depicted requesting Jesus to heal their dependents from a distance and justifying his acquiescence (8.5-13; 15.21-28). Among the soldiers, the statement, 'Truly this was a son of God', is attributed to their centurion (27.54). But, even in these cases, we read nothing about them after they have played their limited parts in relation to Jesus.

Only in the case of disciples is a full list of their names supplied (10.2-4), with the addition of Joseph of Arimathaea in 27.57. Sometimes a smaller group of disciples is distinguished from the larger group, on the mountain (17.1-3, Peter, James and John), and in Gethsemane (26.36-46, Peter and the sons of Zebedee), but often no distinctions are made among them. Judas, however, is singled out. He is introduced as the disciple who handed Jesus over (10.4) and this definite description moulds readers' construction of him for the rest of the story. He is then presented as a conventionally 'bad character' in his desire for money (26.15) and his deceptive speech (26.25). He is described as handing Jesus over by leading the armed crowd to Gethsemane, and by identifying Jesus to the crowd with a greeting and a kiss, deceptive acts (26.48-49). Unusually, however, his character is developed by relating his repentance, expressed in his confession of sin at betraying innocent blood and his return of the money, and then, when his actions fail to change the course of events, by his despairing suicide (27.3-10). The story serves both to emphasize Jesus' innocence and to discourage readers from betraying Jesus.

By contrast, the character of Peter is not developed. Rather, he is the representative disciple of 'little faith' (8.26; 14.31; 16.8; cf. 17.17, 20; 6.30). The story of his confession that Jesus is the Christ and the blessing with which Jesus responds is immediately followed by the account of his repudiation of Jesus' mission and Jesus' dismissal of him as Satan (16.16-23). The depiction of his only partially successful attempt to join Jesus in walking over the stormy sea prefigures his denials of association with Jesus (14.28-33; 26.58, 69-75). Unlike Judas, Peter is not described revoking his denials. And in the final story of the resurrected Jesus' meeting with his disciple-missionaries, Peter is among those who are said to have doubted (28.17). Consistently, as the representative disciple, Peter is presented as a person of 'little faith'.

We would write neither a historical biography nor a historical or fictional narrative with these group depictions and choruses, nor would we portray individuals as one-dimensional 'types', because we are interested in individual particularities, complexities and developments. The Gospel according to Matthew expresses an ancient cultural concern with groups, and attention is drawn to the group 'Pharisees' without indicating their individual components. Even when individuals are distinguished, their lives are not presented in all their individual complexity. In the case of Judas, for example, the only motive for betraying Jesus attributed to him is his desire for money. Moreover, Jesus is represented as a type of persecuted prophet, a loyal son and slave of God, so that others can follow him. This means, of course, that our biographies, historical narratives, and even our novels, are very much longer than this Gospel.

3. *Distinctive Cultural Character Traits*

I suggested earlier that, in the Matthaean didactic narrative, the 'Pharisees' represent the negative counter-image of Jesus. For example, Jesus' sermon on the mount in chs. 5–7 gives a general impression of his teaching and the rest of the narrative presents his practising what he preaches, in spite of the contradictions noted earlier. The 'Pharisees', then, are represented as not practising what they preach (23.3). Other characterizations of the 'Pharisees' in ch. 23 also represent counter-images. They are said 'to bind heavy burdens' on people (23.4) and Jesus is said to invite people to accept his light burden (11.28-30). Of course, this burden is 'light' only for people so dedicated to God's purpose that all self-concern, even concern for self-preservation, is absent (e.g. 6.3, 19-34; 16.24-26; 26.39, 42, 52-56). Again, the 'Pharisees' are said to use pious practices to bring honour to themselves (23.5-7), in contrast to Jesus, who is said to be gentle and humble in heart (11.29; 21.5; cf. 5.5;

6.1-18; 18.2-3; 23.12; Ps. 27.11).[26] In the Matthaean discourses and narrative, 'humility' is construed as non-judgmental and forgiving behaviour to other people (18.10-35; 6.12, 14-15; 7.1-5; 9.1-13) but also as involving a powerless social position (18.1-4; 20.20-28) such as actual poverty creates (8.20; 10.9; 19.16-30). The 'Pharisees' are given the counter-image of extortionate rapacity (23.25). Similarly, Jesus is represented as merciful and the 'Pharisees' as unmerciful (9.9-13; 12.1-8). The depiction of Jesus' last days, culminating in his crucifixion (chs. 26–27), illustrates what happens to people who do not seek to be honoured by other people but trust solely in God (cf. 16.21-28), and who eschew violent retaliation when threatened by brutal assault (5.38-48; 20.25-28; 26.51-53). The 'Pharisees' provide the counter-image: murderers (23.29-36). In the context of persecution, 'endurance' is highlighted as a necessary virtue (10.22; 24.13).

The character traits that are advocated by this narrative, therefore, are gentleness, humility, mercy, extraordinary generosity, endurance, non-violent resistance, selfless service to others, complete and unalloyed dedication to God and his kingdom. This fills out what 'justice or righteousness' is conceived to involve (e.g. 5.6, 10, 20; 6.1, 33, etc.). Moreover, the narrative creates the impression that it is impossible to live in this way without God's inspiration (3.11, 15-17; 28.19). The characterization of the 'Pharisees' serves as a counter-image to these character traits. In a very short didactic narrative, written in a cultural context in which groups took priority over individuals, the 'Pharisees' are constructed for a didactic purpose, as the negative stereotype that clarifies the positive. That the constructions of neither the negative characters nor the positive character are wholly consistent makes the rhetoric less compelling than it might have been.

26. 'Gentleness' is a virtue valued in ancient Greek philosophical literature and in the LXX, e.g. Plato, *Laws* 867b, 888a, 930a; Aristotle, *Nicomachean Ethics* 1125b26; Num. 12.3 of Moses; Pss. 25.9; 34.2; Zech. 9.9, quoted in Mt. 21.5. It informs the English 'gentleman', for example, in Jane Austen's portrait of Mr Knightley in *Emma*. 'Humility' in ancient Greek literature carries both a positive (e.g. Plato, *Laws* 716a) and a negative connotation (e.g. Plato, *Laws* 791d), but only a positive connotation in the LXX (e.g. 1 Sam. 18.23 of David; Ps. 10.18; Isa. 11.4 of the Messiah).

Conclusion

Chatman and Rimmon-Kenan highlight the differences between ancient narrative characterizations, which we would call stereotypes, and modern narrative characterizations, which are complex and which do not 'break down' into a single dominant trait. But literary critics concern themselves primarily with 'high' culture rather than 'low'. Characterizations in contemporary popular fiction, like romances and detective stories, are often stereotypical, and so are some radio, television and newspaper presentations of social and political groups. And the 'sound-bites' of political rhetoric depend on stereotyping.

Moreover, perhaps all of us begin by thinking and talking in stereotypical categories, in order to clarify our experiences. Stereotyping can be useful in learning to make initial distinctions and has always formed part of our didactic literature aimed at children. What is distinctive about our cultural individualism, however, is that we recognize this and guard against allowing these categories to become rigid. Our individualism gives us a sense that 'justice' requires a just appreciation of individual complexities, and has led to legislation that outlaws slandering and discriminating against ethnic and gender groups.

The Gospel according to Matthew became part of the Christian churches' New Testament and therefore a classic text of Western culture. And just as Plato's depictions of the 'Sophists' became detached from Platonic discussions about practical wisdom, so the Matthaean negative stereotypes of 'Pharisees' became detached from their positive counter-image. In *Our Mutual Friend*, Dickens placed the following speech in the mouth of his Jewish character, Mr Riah:

> It is not, in Christian countries, with the Jews as with other peoples. Men say, 'This is a bad Greek, but there are good Greeks. This is a bad Turk, but there are good Turks.' Not so with the Jews. Men find the bad among us easily enough—among what peoples are the bad not easily found?—but they take the worst of us as samples of the best; they take the lowest of us as presentations of the highest; and they say, 'All Jews are alike'. If, doing what I was content to do here, because I was grateful for the past and have small need of money now, I had been a Christian, I could have done it, compromising no one but my individual self. But doing it as a Jew, I could not choose but compromise the Jews of all

conditions and all countries. It is a little hard upon us, but it is the truth.[27]

The new racism, fuelled by European imperialism's contempt for peoples who were dominated from the eighteenth century onwards, and by popular nationalism, was combined with the New Testament stereotypes of Jews, including the Matthaean portrait of 'Pharisees', to warrant pogroms against Jews in nineteenth- and twentieth-century Europe. And when the capitalist economic system brought not increased prosperity but depression in the 1920s and 1930s, these stereotypes helped to give credance to the propaganda that led to the Holocaust. In the 1990s, the stereotyping and the persecutions are still with us, and now include stereotypes of Christianity's old enemy, Islam. Is individualism's recognition of the complexities of characters a sufficiently dominant perception in our culture to prevent further disastrous consequences following from political and cultural stereotyping?[28]

The neglect of the Matthaean ideal type in its portrait of Jesus is also understandable in the light of our cultural individualism. We value the individual competitive virtues: individual self-interest, self-fulfilment, self-expression, self-sufficiency. Acquisitiveness is encouraged rather than generosity. Cooperative virtues like mercy and selfless service to others begin to look like vices. Humility forms no part of our perception of the strong leader. In a rapidly changing world, adaptability seems better than fidelity and endurance. Nevertheless, calling institutions 'trusts' assumes people's unselfish trustworthiness, and even economic 'confidence' assumes institutions' reliability and constancy, although it is difficult to resist reading these terms ironically. There are contemporary

27. London: Collins (1990), p. 680, first published 1865. Mr Riah is constructed as a gentle and generous character, a 'fairy godmother', in contrast to the rapacious Christian, Mr Fledgeby. Mr Riah also contrasts with the earlier portrait of the Jewish Fagin in *Oliver Twist*. George Eliot's *Daniel Deronda* (published 1876) creates a more psychologically complex Jewish character. Eliot wrote about the book: 'Precisely because I felt that the usual attitude of Christians towards Jews is—I hardly know whether to say more impious or more stupid when viewed in the light of their professed principles, I therefore felt urged to treat Jews with such sympathy and understanding as my nature and knowledge could attain to' (a letter quoted by Barbara Hardy in the introduction to the Penguin edition, 1967, p. 13).

28. A letter published in *The Observer*, 13 October 1996, suggests that, if we are to ban anti-Jewish writings, the first to go should be the New Testament Gospels. And see especially the sociological study, M. Maffesoli, *The Time of the Tribes: The Decline of Individualism in Mass Societies* (ET; London: Sage, 1996).

people who encourage apparently powerless groups to gain influence through mutual support and endurance, but these groups we now see as free associations of individuals rather than as 'natural'. The demise of large industries and the close communities that used to work in them means that common experiences and living conditions in compact geographical areas no longer exist. Some associations, however, suggest that, if we are to leave a habitable world to our descendants, we shall have to abandon narrow self-interest and rediscover the cooperative virtues in our relations with other peoples of the contemporary world and across generations.

Almost Cultural Studies?
Reflections on the 'New Perspective' on Paul

R. Barry Matlock

It is a fair guess that Pauline studies is, in terms of methods and approaches, the most conservative enclave of biblical criticism. I say this with little fear of wresting the dubious honor from other, more deserving hands, and my reasoning runs something like this: as a result of the Christian reflexes that still seem to typify the ('mainstream') discipline, the 'new fangled' sorts of criticism are much more readily turned loose on the Old Testament/Hebrew Bible than the New Testament, which makes New Testament studies as a whole more conservative than the Old Testament counterpart; the Gospels have going for them both their narrative character (facilitating the application of 'new' literary readings, as in 'new critical', which is to say 'old'—'new fangled' is a relative term) and their perennially interesting central figure, Jesus (on account of whom Gospel criticism can always be counted on to generate some heat, if not light—witness the Jesus Seminar); and since the General Epistles are largely ignored and Revelation comes more or less under the Old Testament rule (anything goes), that leaves Pauline studies, as I said, bringing up the rear. Now whether this is down to limitations in the source material or in scholarly imagination, or some combination of both, is subject to debate; but at any rate, one does not expect Pauline studies to be a particularly prominent site of the transposition of 'Biblical into Cultural Studies'.

So what does one do when one's main area is Paul and one is called upon to contribute in some small way to a colloquium on just such a disciplinary transposition? What I propose to do here is to suggest some ways in which contemporary 'new perspective' discussion in Pauline studies carries, at least implicitly, concerns relevant to cultural studies. Granted, this cultural studies potential will, for the most part, be of a relatively low order theoretically: the significance of cultural location in biblical reading will be seen to be the most obvious bridge between familiar Pauline interpretation and cultural studies. I can also point,

though, to a recent effort by a cultural critic (predictably, an 'interloper' into Pauline studies!) to develop and extend the 'new perspective' into an explicit reading of Paul as himself a cultural critic; here, the matter of the construction of 'identity' will be seen to belong quite properly to the reading of Paul. (Perhaps I can simply say that my modest engagement with cultural studies via Pauline criticism might serve as a softening-up move for others, revealing how even 'real biblical scholarship' itself already takes us to the borders of cultural studies, if not beyond!)

The 'New Perspective' in Ironic Perspective

William James described with considerable insight 'the classic stages of a theory's career. First…a new theory is attacked as absurd; then it is admitted to be true, but obvious and insignificant; finally it is seen to be so important that its adversaries claim that they themselves discovered it'.[1] That this description came to my attention in a more recent application of it to the fortunes of Thomas S. Kuhn's theory of scientific paradigms and revolutions is apposite, for in recent years Pauline studies has proudly marked a 'paradigm shift' of its own, known broadly as 'the new perspective on Paul', a shift associated in particular with Krister Stendahl and E.P. Sanders.[2] When sufficient distance is achieved from this interpretive sea change in reading Paul, perhaps it will be seen that it, too, suffered such a fate or enjoyed such a fortune, a movement from an initial urge toward dismissal of the perspective on the part of many, to an effort to reveal the degree to which the 'new' agenda was anticipated and preceded by earlier work and thus represents nothing really new at all, to, in the end, a quiet assumption of the heart of this new perspective.

1. W. James, *Pragmatism* (ed. F. Bowers and I.K. Skrupskelis; The Works of William James; Cambridge, MA: Harvard University Press, 1975), p. 95.
2. R.J. Bernstein, *Beyond Objectivism and Relativism: Science, Hermeneutics, and Praxis* (Philadelphia: University of Pennsylvania Press, 1983), p. 51. For such reference to a 'paradigm shift' in Pauline studies, see, e.g., D.J. Moo, 'Paul and the Law in the Last Ten Years', *SJT* 40 (1987), pp. 287-307 (287). The pivotal works of Stendahl and Sanders here are K. Stendahl, 'The Apostle Paul and the Introspective Conscience of the West', *HTR* 56 (1963), pp. 199-215, reprinted with other relevant studies in *idem*, *Paul among Jews and Gentiles and Other Essays* (Philadelphia: Fortress Press, 1976); E.P. Sanders, *Paul and Palestinian Judaism: A Comparison of Patterns of Religion* (Philadelphia: Fortress Press, 1977).

Where we might now stand on such a trajectory—let alone where my own effort here fits in—is difficult to say. Things have yet to settle down to a clear, singular consensus (which is, these days, perhaps too much to hope for in biblical studies anyway, if it ever was a realistic goal). Still, we seem to be far enough along to achieve some degree of perspective on the 'new perspective'. Moreover, it is imperative that self-reflective questions be raised, and a significant part of this disciplinary stocktaking ought well to be hermeneutical (indeed, cultural). There is no need to rehearse the matter of the embeddedness in its own time of the 'old perspective', the Reformation's 'new look' at Paul—indeed, as we will note, this has been a staple theme in 'new perspective' argument. But the ways in which our own contemporary new readings of Paul are implicated in our time—inasmuch as this is transparent to us—will, in the nature of the case, be less familiar (a matter, furthermore, on which the 'new perspective', given its rhetoric, is less eager to dwell).

For my purposes, I must assume a degree of familiarity with the 'new perspective' on Paul.[3] I will, though, give the briefest of characterizations. First, it might be helpful to point out that, at least according to my usage here, the 'new perspective' signifies not a singular, settled position but a broad family of related interpretive tendencies. And 'new' though it may be, its concerns are still broadly traditional, that is, theological (particularly soteriological). We might describe the perspective as resting on two 'pillars', two fundamental axioms: that Paul was not really about individual sin, guilt and forgiveness, but rather that communal and social concerns to do with Jewish and Gentile relations, practical concerns arising from Paul's mission, were his primary context and focus; and that the Judaism of Paul's day was not a 'legalistic' religion of meritorious 'works-righteousness', so that Paul's 'opponents', and his position over against them, must be reassessed.[4] Notice that each

3. A minimal remedial reading list would include at least Stendahl's 'Introspective Conscience' essay, a selection from Sanders (his 'Jesus, Paul and Judaism', *ANRW*, II.25.1 [1982], pp. 390-450, nicely summarizes his work on these three entities), and J.D.G. Dunn, 'The New Perspective on Paul', *BJRL* 65 (1983), pp. 95-122, reprinted in his *Jesus, Paul and the Law* (Louisville, KY: Westminster/John Knox Press, 1990), pp. 183-214 .

4. On such a twofold description, cf. Moo, 'Paul and the Law in the Last Ten Years', pp. 287-89; similarly, e.g., D.A. Hagner, 'Paul and Judaism: The Jewish Matrix of Early Christianity: Issues in the Current Debate', *Bulletin for Biblical Research* 3 (1993), pp. 111-30 (111-13). This characterization is readily confirmed in

Biblical Studies/Cultural Studies

axiom begins in a negative: the new perspective defines itself polemically over against what it typically identifies as the 'Lutheran' reading of Paul, this negative self-definition providing the real unity for what is otherwise an internally divided and still developing set of views. If we may take this new perspective broadly as an ongoing research program, the questions it brings, particularly to Paul's Epistles to the Galatians and Romans, concern Paul's overall argumentative context: is there, in Paul, a principled contrast between 'doing' (the law) and 'believing' (the gospel), or is the contrast between an 'exclusive' (a Jewish law) and an 'inclusive' (a *universally* accessible faith) approach to God's saving prerogatives? Larger interpretive issues concern, on the one hand, Paul's relative continuity and/or discontinuity with his own religious past and its traditional expectations and Scripture readings, and, on the other, the structure of his thought (in particular, its division into two strands, the 'juristic' and the 'participatory') and the meaning and relative place of Paul's 'righteousness/justification by faith' language.

A defining moment in the interpretive shift we are considering is Krister Stendahl's justly famous essay, 'The Apostle Paul and the Introspective Conscience of the West'.[5] Stendahl's title itself, in its juxtaposition of Paul and 'the West', implicitly suggests cultural studies import in terms of the significance to biblical reading of social and cultural location. His reading emphasizes the unfortunate interpretive consequences of the individualistic and subjectivistic tendencies of 'modern' reading of Paul as defined by the tradition of Augustine ('the first modern man'), Luther (that 'truly Augustinian monk'), and the Protestant Reformation (the cradle of modernity).[6] Paul was actually concerned with proper Christian–Jewish relations. Of the many matters touched upon in E.P. Sanders's *Paul and Palestinian Judaism*, nothing dominates the whole so much as the exposure of typical Christian readings of Judaism, particularly those beholden to the tradition critiqued by Stendahl,

---

the literature; we may regard Stendahl as serving more to make the former point (about Paul's salvation-historical context) and Sanders the latter (about the Judaism of Paul's day)—though each figure is relevant to the other point as well. Other fine surveys of the interpretive debate include, in brief, J.M.G. Barclay, 'Paul and the Law: Observations on Some Recent Debates', *Themelios* 12 (1986), pp. 5-15, and, at length, S. Westerholm, *Israel's Law and the Church's Faith: Paul and his Recent Interpreters* (Grand Rapids: Eerdmans, 1988).

    5.   Stendahl, *Paul*, pp. 78-96.
    6.   Stendahl, *Paul*, pp. 83, 85.

as self-serving caricatures (an insight against which Sanders's Paul is careful not to offend), again, implicitly a matter of reading location. To these we may add the perspective of James Dunn, who follows up Stendahl and Sanders by working to make the new Paul fit more closely the new perspective on Pauline interpretation (our individualism has hidden Paul's corporateness from us) and Judaism (Paul critiques Judaism as it actually was). According to Dunn's reading, Paul's own characteristic struggle is actually against nationalism, against ethnocentrism, against racial bigotry—implicitly making Paul himself something of a 'cultural critic'.

But the cultural studies legacy of the new perspective on Paul is not without its ambiguities, its ironic turns. This is evident at those many moments when the debate itself goes hermeneutical. Typically, those associated with the new perspective have wanted not merely to present their new picture of Paul but also to say just where, how, and *why* the old picture went wrong. The history, or *story*, of interpretation is told with a very strong *moral* offering a self-consciously *hermeneutical* lesson.

Stendahl plays heavily on the irony that, at the very point where Western interpreters have felt most near to Paul, they are in fact most distant:

> In Protestant Christianity—which, however, at this point has its roots in Augustine and in the piety of the Middle Ages—the Pauline awareness of sin has been interpreted in the light of Luther's struggle with his conscience. But it is exactly at that point that we can discern the most drastic difference between Luther and Paul...[7]

But having thus emphasized the significance of perspectival reading, Stendahl does not become an advocate of 'reading from this place' (to borrow a recent title),[8] but instead he notoriously promotes 'reading from no place'. He concludes his exposé of Western misdirection of interpretive energies with the pronouncement: 'Few things are more liberating and creative in modern theology than a clear distinction between the "original" and the "translation" in any age, our own included'.[9] As his programmatic hermeneutical piece 'Contemporary Biblical Theology' has it (commenting here on Karl Barth):

---

7. Stendahl, *Paul*, p. 79.
8. F.F. Segovia and M.A. Tolbert (eds.), *Reading from This Place* (2 vols.; Minneapolis: Fortress Press, 1994, 1995).
9. Stendahl, *Paul*, p. 96.

> To say that the Reformers interpreted Paul by equating the problem of
> the Judaizers and the Torah in Paul with the problem of work–righ-
> teousness in late medieval piety and that this ingenious translation or
> application of Pauline theology may be 80 per cent correct but left 20 per
> cent of Paul inexplicable—and consequently distorted in a certain sense
> the true picture of Pauline thought—to say this is to call attention to a
> problem which could not be detected, let alone criticized, by Barth or
> any truly Barthian exegete. Thus biblical theology along this line is
> admittedly incapable of enough patience and enthusiasm for keeping alive
> the tension between what the text meant and what it means. There are
> no criteria by which they can be kept apart; what is intended as a com-
> mentary [i.e. Barth's *Romans*] turns out to be a theological tractate,
> expanding in contemporary terms what Paul should have said about the
> subject matter as understood by the commentator.[10]

Thus, to depart hermeneutically from Stendahl's 'two stage' method
(what the text meant, what the text means) is both to be doomed to
interpretive failure and to an interpretive inability even to perceive the
problem—one would be unable both to see the real Paul and to see that
one could not see the real Paul—blinded, presumably, as one would be
by the perspective of the present.

To Stendahl we may add hermeneutical statements from Sanders and
Dunn. Sanders complains of the traditional Protestant interpretation of
Paul and Judaism that it is an example of 'the writing of theology as if it
were history', and he later declares: 'I have been engaged for some years
in the effort to free history and exegesis from the control of theology'.[11]
'Augustine, Luther, and Barth…all read Paul through their own
spectacles and interpreted him in ways appropriate to their own
circumstances', whereas it is Sanders's aim 'not to use Paul to address the
present situation, but rather to try to reconstruct what he thought, and
why he thought it, and to do so in the categories of his own time and
place'.[12] We, presumably, are now able to remove our spectacles, or at
least to render them transparent and distortion-free, interpreting thus to

10. K. Stendahl, 'Biblical Theology, Contemporary', in *IDB*, I, pp. 418-32
(420).

11. Sanders, *Paul and Palestinian Judaism*, p. 57; *idem*, *Jesus and Judaism*
(Philadelphia: Fortress Press, 1985), p. 333 (Sanders goes on to explain that he is not
guilty of any such control of history and exegesis by theology, since his own liberal,
modern, secularized Protestantism is able to sit rather loosely with respect to Jesus
[p. 334]).

12. E.P. Sanders, *Paul* (Past Masters; Oxford: Oxford University Press, 1991),
p. 18.

no particular circumstances or situation (our own perspective being excluded as only getting in the way of our access to Paul).

Finally, in similar vein James Dunn declares: 'Luther read Paul and the situation confronting Paul through the grid of his own experience... Now, however, in the light of Sanders' contribution the scales have fallen from many eyes.'[13] No lesser language than that of Paul's own conversion is borrowed to express how we, with unclouded vision, have finally seen the light (a no doubt tongue-in-cheek analogy perhaps telling in more ways than it intends[14]).

Thus encouraged by the debate itself to take a hermeneutical view, I shall proceed to make a series of ironic observations on this recent shift in interpretation. (As to what my ironic emplotment of the story says about *my* interests, that matter I will leave to others.)

The Objective Stance

The first irony to observe is the very claim to objectivity so often stated or implied. The susceptibility of the two axioms of the new perspective to analysis as arising from, or at least as being in keeping with, contemporary concerns makes the stance of objectivity look immediately suspect, given the insistent denials we have witnessed that any such modernizing is going on. For indeed, we moderns are not typically concerned so much about sin and guilt and forgiveness as we are about notions of community, so that *our* theological climate is reflected here; and we need hardly mention how our renewed interest in Jewish–Christian dialogue, standing where we stand in time, exerts its own influence over new perspective debate.[15]

13.   J.D.G. Dunn, *The Partings of the Ways between Christianity and Judaism and their Significance for the Character of Christianity* (London: SCM Press; Philadelphia: Trinity Press International, 1991), p. 14.

14.   Note the use made by Kuhn of 'conversion' language, Thomas S. Kuhn, *The Structure of Scientific Revolutions* (Chicago: University of Chicago Press, 2nd edn, 1970), pp. 144-59; cf. P. Hoyningen-Huene, *Reconstructing Scientific Revolutions: Thomas S. Kuhn's Philosophy of Science* (trans. A.T. Levine; Chicago: University of Chicago Press, 1993), pp. 257-58.

15.   What I allude to here in brief I find spelled out more fully in a recent study which, though doing its own distinctive thing, is at points nicely complementary to my own, but came into my hands only after I had completed the first part of the present study and planned the final part (on Daniel Boyarin, with whom also, I found, this study fruitfully engages): J.M.G. Barclay, ' "Neither Jew Nor Greek":

It is certainly not as though these interpreters are blind to, or lack interest in, the contemporary significance of their new look at Paul; precisely the reverse is the case.[16] Yet they are, rhetorically, caught in their own web. For in figuring the interpreter's own perspective as itself in some sense the problem, they have restricted their own work to the terms of a 'modernist' critical rhetoric that is both easily undermined and begs to be.[17] (To take this irony one step further, this 'modern' rhetoric, turned with admittedly great effect against the Reformation's reading of Paul, was first used by the Reformers themselves, in the rhetoric of *sola scriptura*, to install *their* new Paul—which means the Reformers are caught in *their* own web as well, the same as that which ensnares their latter-day counter-reformers.)

The way we have tended to do history of interpretation here is revealing—the way we like to tell the story.[18] The preferred tone is triumphalist, the theme upward progress, converging on us (as it happens). We somehow do not wish to say that traditional readings of Paul simply no longer serve for our time, that we need other readings. The tradition is *wrong*, and we know why—we mean that absolutely, that is, we are able to occupy a position from which we can measure prior readings

Multiculturalism and the New Perspective on Paul', in M.G. Brett (ed.), *Ethnicity and the Bible* (Leiden: E.J. Brill, 1996), pp. 197-214 (see pp. 203-205). I thank John for alerting me to his essay on a visit to Sheffield and for sending me a copy.

16. All three follow up their work on Paul with work having an ecumenical aspect (though historically focused on early Judaism and Jewish/Christian relations): cf. Stendahl's two essays on 'Judaism and Christianity', repr. in his *Meanings: The Bible as Document and as Guide* (Philadelphia: Fortress Press, 1984), pp. 205-32; the three volumes on *Jewish and Christian Self-Definition* edited by Sanders *et al.* (London: SCM Press, 1980–82); and Dunn (ed.), *Jews and Christians: The Parting of the Ways, A.D. 70–135* (WUNT, 66; Tübingen: J.C.B. Mohr [Paul Siebeck], 1992).

17. For such a restriction, note Sanders's apparent discomfort with a possibly more 'activist' construal of his efforts in *Paul and Palestinian Judaism*, where, pointedly denying a concern with anti-Semitism in biblical scholarship, he suggests his own preferred terms for how his work should be construed: 'As I see it, the view which is here under attack is held because it is thought to correspond to the evidence, and I attack it because I think is does not' (p. xiii). On 'modern' hermeneutics, see A.K.M. Adam, *Making Sense of New Testament Theology: 'Modern' Problems and Prospects* (Studies in American Biblical Hermeneutics, 11; Macon, GA: Mercer University Press, 1995).

18. On matters touched on here, see my 'Biblical Criticism and the Rhetoric of Inquiry', *BibInt* 5 (1997), pp. 133-59 (esp. pp. 141, 147-48, 151-52).

against 'the real thing'.[19] Ironically—but not surprisingly—we are much readier to borrow the Kuhnian language of a 'paradigm shift' to describe the significance of our own revolutionary work than to reflect on the implications of such language in terms of the circularity of our critique of the former paradigm from our vantage point within the new. Thus, alongside a self-serving emphasis on the difference a change of 'perspective' can make, and the need thus to 'convert' and join those who have made the interpretive shift, we have a realist rhetoric of non-perspectival, that is 'critical', interpretation of former interpretation, where apparently the shift does not exert an influence on our reading of other readings.

To add an ironic footnote to the irony of the claim to objectivity, *compliments* are, of course, no more 'scientific' than insults. Yet a certain urge to say nice things about early Judaism often seems to be present. An example may be taken from James H. Charlesworth in a recent monograph: in the midst of a plea for greater scientific objectivity, where Charlesworth states axiomatically that 'the historian is called on to describe not to prescribe', he reflects on proper terminology for treating the Judaism of Paul's time, weeding out offensive or misleading terms.[20] Among these, 'Late Judaism' is to be replaced by 'Early Judaism', and about this, I expect, there is already unanimity—but note Charlesworth's explanation:

> ['Early Judaism'] has the connotation of being alive with refreshing new insights: we find here highly-developed and sophisticated metaphysical speculation, and introspective perceptions into the psychological complexities of being human... Early Jews were brilliantly alive with penetrating speculations into almost every facet of our world and universe.[21]

Descriptive, not prescriptive?

Now my point in drawing attention to this is not that I do not like to see Judaism complimented; nor am I urging interpreters to be more 'scientific'. Rather, I am taking this very 'urge to compliment' as indicating that there is more at play here than mere 'science'. And our

19. Granted, Stendahl said not that the Reformers were wrong but that they were, say, '80 per cent correct', but it may be questioned whether this kind allowance (which at any rate is more or less taken back as soon as it is given) is really borne out by his interpretive stance toward this traditional reading of Paul.

20. J.H. Charlesworth, *The Old Testament Pseudepigrapha and the New Testament* (SNTSMS, 54; Cambridge: Cambridge University Press, 1985), p. 58.

21. Charlesworth, *The Old Testament Pseudepigrapha and the New Testament*, p. 59.

impulsive denials of this are simply part of the story.

Furthermore, as an ironic footnote to this ironic footnote, such compliments often appear cynical and even condescending. Surely the pseudepigraphal literature that Charlesworth has particularly in mind, though certainly still of interest and value in a number of ways, presents at innumerable points for Charlesworth the same mixture of the quaint and the bizarre as it does for everyone else. Does Charlesworth really consult these Early Jewish texts for contemporary guidance ('refreshing new insights', 'highly-developed, sophisticated, and penetrating specula-tions') on the matters treated there? The 'urge to compliment', then, can come off, in the end, as rather insulting (hence my pausing to make a point of the matter).[22]

A Residual Biblicism

Having begun to take an ironic look at the new perspective, we can proceed through several more turns of the screw, and in so doing the cultural studies potential of the new perspective is rendered by degrees more ambiguous, more diluted, more attenuated. The irony now to be observed is not unrelated to the ironic claim to objectivity. By 'residual biblicism' I mean the apparent desire to have Paul affirm our own deepest values, to find ready to hand in this biblical witness that which we may now affirm for ourselves. (Logically, this point particularly con-cerns Christian interpretation of Paul—indeed, the 'new perspective' is a contemporary Protestant interpretive movement, a reformation of its own Reformation heritage.) Thus Paul is at times sounding surprisingly liberal, Western and pluralist—and that after all the warnings of his

22. Charlesworth is, admittedly, a rather obvious example of what I would nevertheless suggest are wider tendencies. At an earlier stage with the present study (in oral presentation in Sheffield, June 1994), I spoke of 'political correctness' as typifying the new perspective at such points as this and as further confirming its contemporaneousness, its reflection of current concerns; I would now refrain from using the term, as it has clearly emerged as a buzz-word for the political right. Bar-clay, '"Neither Jew Nor Greek"', pp. 205-206, uses the term 'multiculturalism' in a similar connection. Whatever the term, I (like Barclay) would commend the move toward multicultural sensitivity and dialogue; yet here I want to make a negative point (but not the negative one made by the political right, which is of the 'there goes the neighborhood' variety): what is going on in this vein in reading Paul and Judaism is, as I suggest above, at times somewhat shallow and even, in a roundabout way, offensive (thus working at cross purposes with the wider cultural impulse).

distance from us (leaving us to ask once more whether Luther's Paul comes to grief more for his failure to fit the twentieth century than the first, whether, ironically, the new perspective's hermeneutical moralizing could as well be turned on itself).[23]

Now, I do not really wish simply to repeat Stendahl's 'original versus translation' scheme, and it is not in my interest to chide interpreters when their readings can be placed in some kind of intimate relationship with contemporary contexts of aims and values, contemporary 'interpretive communities'. Indeed, this irony is what it is in light of the pointed and specific denials that anything such is going on. (Apart from this polemical context, my own intuition that this sort of thing is only ever what goes on would prohibit me from making much of this ironic biblicism.)

There are subtle shades here. Some positions within the new perspective, where Paul comes off *as is* exactly as we might want him to (for example, as never critiquing Judaism and the law *as such*, but only opposing a nationalistic and sectarian exclusivism), seem on their very face biblicistic. That is, they read right off the biblical page self-affirmative views, and it seems difficult not to have one's suspicions raised—by the self-same suspicious reflex that the new perspective itself exercises—that perhaps there is the *need* to do this (in the sense of a need for direct biblical *authorization*). But even where other readings of Paul allow some degree of tension between Paul and contemporary Christian convictions, such readings do not simply on that account escape connection with the present, for wherever they are found they are enabled simply by other strategies or possibilities of relating biblical interpretation to contemporary praxis—other 'interpretive communities'. What is more, an important rival to this 'universalistic Paul', the 'dogmatic Paul', according to which view Paul offers no real reason for his shift from life within the law to faith in Jesus Christ, so that Paul emerges as (apparently) making an arbitrary leap, is susceptible of analysis as finding resonance in contemporary sensibilities. For here Paul, though admittedly exclusivistic in his avowal of Jesus, *is so in such a way as to leave Judaism untouched in its own right*. If for Paul the difference between Christianity and Judaism (leaving aside the anachronism of

23. An example of such an unexpectedly pluralist Paul might be found in the 'two covenants' reading associated with Stendahl, according to which Pauline Christianity and Judaism each go their own mutually affirming way.

speaking thus of two discrete religions at that time) is at bottom arbitrary, so much the better for us, because that is the way we as moderns would prefer to have it, too. True, Paul's instinctive pastoral attempts to offer secondary rationales for his change of heart hide his arbitrariness from *him*; but not from us.[24]

History and exegesis (those reified and rarefied entities), if emancipated from theology, do not then find themselves with their destinies in their own hands, as it were. They never find themselves, in fact, in anyone's hands but ours, with all that this entails. Exegetical and historical debate, then, may often be seen as concealing more fundamental issues left unspoken, unaddressed, and unresolved. (Here one such issue might be the very place of the Bible in contemporary theology, ethics, and politics.[25]) With the (reputed) demise of theology, the introspective conscience of Pauline studies will still have matters over which to wring its worried hands.

A Certain Covert Protestantism

As we have noted, criticism of Protestantism's record of handling early Judaism is central to the new perspective, a critique of Christian caricatures of Judaism that was long overdue.[26] Ironically, though, it often seems uncannily as though the same old Protestant debates are being played out, only now a favorable verdict is being passed down on Judaism. Judaism suddenly finds itself shifted from one side of the equation to the other, but the same set of values works the scales, the same Protestant reflexes animate the interpretive debate. This is one of the most biting ironies of the whole story before us.

A couple other voices on this score may help me make my (otherwise perhaps controversial) point. First, from Philip Alexander, in a review of

24. Those familiar with the interpretive debate will be readily able to assign the points of view hinted at in this paragraph to individual scholars; I do not name names, not to be underhanded, but out of a sense for the oversimplification present in my characterization.

25. Jennifer Glancy and I noticed here a partial overlapping of our contributions to the Colloquium.

26. Sanders in particular, of course, is associated with this critique; he builds self-consciously on the classic essay by G.F. Moore, 'Christian Writers on Judaism', *HTR* 14 (1921), pp. 197-254, as well as on the work of such Jewish scholars as C.G. Montefiore, S. Schechter, H.J. Schoeps and S. Sandmel (the critique was not so much long overdue, then, as far too long in taking hold).

Sanders's *Jesus and Judaism*:

> Sanders continues [his] attack…on the Christian caricature of Pharisaic and Rabbinic Judaism as 'legalism'. He has no difficulty in exposing the *odium theologicum* that lies behind some supposedly critical New Testament scholarship, and in showing that notions of divine love, grace and forgiveness are not foreign to the Pharisees and the Rabbis. This is music to the reviewer's ears. But perhaps Sanders has not identified the point at issue here with total accuracy. His answer to the charge of 'legalism' seems, in effect, to be that Rabbinic Judaism, despite appearances, is really a religion of 'grace'. But does this not involve a tacit acceptance of a major element in his opponent's position—the assumption that 'grace' is superior to 'law'? The correct response to the charge must surely be: And what is wrong with 'legalism', once we have got rid of abusive language about 'hypocrisy' and 'mere externalism'? It is neither religiously nor philosophically self-evident that a 'legalistic' view of the world is inferior to one based on 'grace'. If we fail to take a firm stand on this point we run the risk of seriously misdescribing Pharisaic and Rabbinic Judaism, and of trying to make it over into a pale reflection of Protestant Christianity.[27]

(Dunn might seem in danger of the latter in such comments as: 'Paul is wholly at one with his fellow Jews in asserting that justification is *by faith*'.[28])

Similarly if less gently, and serving to illustrate Alexander's point, Jacob Neusner, in an article review of Sanders's recent work on the Pharisees and early Judaism, closes with some highly personal comments on 'Sanders' Protestant theological apologetic for a Judaism in the Liberal Protestant model'.[29] He cites a lengthy excerpt in which Sanders, commenting on Sabbath observance and its negative treatment in Jesus and Paul, says that 'the assumption that they attacked "ritual" implies

27. P. Alexander, review of *Jesus and Judaism*, by E.P. Sanders, in *JJS* 37 (1986), pp. 103-106 (105).

28. Dunn, 'The New Perspective on Paul', in *Jesus, Paul and the Law*, p. 190. In highlighting this comment, I do not intend to give aid to the caricatures of Judaism that Dunn rightly joins Sanders in exposing. But 'justification by faith' has become a watchword for Protestantism, not Judaism in its own self-description, and one expects there to be some reason for this, pointing to *some kind* of *difference*. To smooth over such difference *by stretching one's own perspective to cover all* invites precisely the counter-charge suggested here of imperialism and condescension, of misplaced 'generosity'.

29. J. Neusner, 'Mr. Sanders' Pharisees and Mine: A Response to E.P. Sanders, *Jewish Law from Jesus to the Mishnah*', *SJT* 44 (1991), pp. 73-95 (92).

that rest on the sabbath should be considered "ritual". It was instead commemorative (of God's rest) and ethical (not only men, but also women, servants, animals, and the land itself were allowed to rest)'.[30] To Neusner, this is 'theologically condescending',

> because Sanders affirms that, if the Pharisees practiced 'ritual', then they, and the Judaism that claims descent from them, would be subject to condemnation by Jesus and Paul... As a believing Jew, I practice Judaism, and I do not appreciate—or require—a defense that dismisses as unimportant or inauthentic what in my faith is very important indeed: the observance of rituals of various kinds. They are mine because they are the Torah's. I do not propose to apologize for them, I do not wish to explain them away. I do not reduce them to their ethical significance. 'Commemorative' and 'ethical' indeed!... Nor do I value a defence of my religion that implicitly throughout and explicitly at many points accepts at face value what another religion values and rejects what my religion deems authentic service to the living God. In the end Sanders wants to defend Judaism by his re-presentation of Pharisaism in a form that, in his view, Christianity can have affirmed then and should appreciate today—and therefore now cease to denigrate. That approved Judaism turns out to be a Judaism in the model of Christianity (in Sanders's pattern). [His] 'Judaism' represented as *kosher* to Liberal Protestantism is only a caricature and an offence.[31]

Both these respondents are careful to acknowledge Sanders's good intentions, but nevertheless both point to undesired consequences, and suggest unconscious motivations, of Sanders's interpretation. And a

---

30. Sanders, *Jewish Law*, p. 245, cited in Neusner, 'Mr. Sanders' Pharisees', p. 93.

31. Neusner, 'Mr. Sanders' Pharisees', pp. 94-95. The irony presently under review struck me from my earliest encounter with Sanders's work on Paul and Judaism. The point has not gone entirely unnoticed in critical responses to Sanders, as Alexander and Neusner testify (though it has not received sufficient attention or response, I believe). Concerning Sanders's earlier *Paul and Palestinian Judaism*, A.J. Saldarini, in a review in *JBL* 98 (1979), pp. 299-303 (300), hints at 'Christian theological interests' lying behind Sanders's treatment of rabbinic Judaism; similarly, Jacob Neusner, in 'The Use of the Later Rabbinic Evidence for the Study of Paul', in William Scott Green (ed.), *Approaches to Ancient Judaism*, II (BJS, 9; Chico, CA: Scholars Press, 1980), pp. 43-63, claims that Sanders puts to the Jewish material 'questions of Pauline-Lutheran theology' (p. 51; cf. pp. 47, 49, 50, 53-56, 60). Sanders replies in the same volume ('Puzzling Out Rabbinic Judaism,' pp. 65-79 [65-69]), denying that he approaches the material with such extrinsic values; Sanders does not seem, though, to take up the real substance and force of Neusner's objection on this matter (contrast Neusner, pp. 53-56, with Sanders, pp. 73-75), an objection which Neusner puts more pointedly in the text cited here.

further irony that seems to be implied in Neusner's critique, when he speaks of 'Christianity *in Sanders's pattern*', is that that liberal Protestantism which casts its shadow unwittingly over early Judaism does the same for those strands of Christianity that alike fall foul of its strictures. In this way, a seemingly ecumenical gesture might have a sharply exclusionary rebound.

On Perspective

A final cluster of ironies revolves around the whole matter of 'perspective', Paul's *and* ours. I will attempt to get at a couple of points through a pair of citations from a recent treatment of many of the issues surrounding the new perspective, Stephen Westerholm's *Israel's Law and the Church's Faith*:

> The methodological error has often been committed in the past of concluding that, since Paul contrasts grace and works and argues for salvation by grace, his opponents (and, ultimately, Judaism) must have worked with the same distinction but argued for salvation by works. Clearly this distorts Judaism, which never thought that divine grace was incompatible with divine requirements. But we become guilty of a similar methodological error if we conclude that, since Paul's opponents did not distinguish between grace and requirements, Paul himself could not have done so either… The methodological point is crucial. Paul must not be allowed to be our main witness for Judaism, nor must Judaism, or the position of Paul's opponents, determine the limits within which Paul is to be interpreted… Paul moves the whole discussion onto a different level… Forced to explain (as his opponents were not) both the law's inadequacy and the distinction between the path of faith and that of the law, Paul characterized the law and the gospel in terms crucial to his case, but foreign to the understanding of his opponents.[32]

And elsewhere in the same work:

> [T]he insights of the 'new perspective' must not be lost to view. Paul's convictions need to be identified; they must also be recognized as Christian theology. When Paul's conclusion that the path of the law is dependent on human works is used to posit a rabbinic doctrine of salvation by works, and when his claim that God's grace in Christ excludes human boasting is used to portray rabbinic Jews as self-righteous boasters, the results (in Johnsonian terms) are 'pernicious as well as false'. When, moreover, the doctrine of merit perceived by Luther in the Catholicism

---

32. Westerholm, *Israel's Law*, p. 150.

of his day is read into the Judaism of the first Christian centuries, the
results are worthless for historical study. Students who want to know
how a rabbinic Jew perceived humanity's place in God's world will read
Paul with caution and Luther not at all. On the other hand, students who
want to understand Paul but feel they have nothing to learn from a Martin Luther should consider a career in metallurgy. Exegesis is learned
from the masters.[33]

One small irony here is that an interpreter reading Paul in recognizable
continuity with Luther is more successful at shaking loose the debate
over Paul from the ongoing Reformation debates than some of his rival
'new perspectivists' are.

Another more significant irony concerns the shift in perspective of
criticism generally. As Westerholm notes, *Paul is doing Christian theology.*
That is, *Paul has himself experienced a paradigm shift.* The question *then*
becomes: Through whose eyes do *we* see the debate *Paul* is engaged in?
Once upon a time interpreters may have simply (more or less unconsciously) assumed Paul's critique of non-Christian Judaism as their
own—that is, the reader was, quite unproblematically, doing Christian
theology right along with Paul. This was 'the norm'. Now, perhaps, we
feel drawn to give priority to Judaism's story (or stories) of itself. This
inexorable process of secularization of biblical reading is, in fact, precisely an instance of what I am arguing—the beholdeness of interpretation to perspective, a beholdeness not just inevitable (where we might
lament) but (at least potentially) productive, as the new perspective
indeed wishes to claim for itself, and which we may readily grant
(though, admittedly, where one is thinking perspectivally notions like
'productive' and 'progress' become somewhat problematic in the
abstract).

But there is more (questions of biblicism re-emerge here). For *our*
shifting apprehension of *Paul's* shift is often such as to render *both* invisible to us. Frequently, as I have argued, the new perspective variously
obscures or erases Pauline *difference* from Judaism (creating good Protestants all around, while insisting that Paul's critical perspective on Judaism must be seen to match Judaism on its own terms), failing all the
while to make clear its own stance toward Paul's stance (we are presumably just doing what we have always done—stating the facts about Paul,
seeing Judaism as it is). Often we affect to keep to a neutral description
of two parties in (some sort of) opposition, without ever quite having

33. Westerholm, *Israel's Law*, p. 173.

them opposed or ourselves entering into that opposition, while still wishing at points to question the *legitimacy* of Paul's (apparently) revisionist appropriation of his tradition.[34]

What I have described above as two larger interpretive issues carried by the contemporary debate on Paul, namely, Paul's continuity and discontinuity with his own tradition and the structure of Paul's thought relative to this, have taken on in recent years a characteristically modern form in the 'new perspective' (though one ought really to note that these questions in some form characterize interpretation of Paul since Paul). But we should probably not congratulate ourselves *too* much about this. For when I say 'characteristically modern' I mean just that— covered with the imprint of our own time and its concerns (or, to cite James once more, 'the trail of the human serpent is...over everything'[35]). So much of our recent discussion of Paul comes down to this: was Paul *reasonable* (and we mean that *absolutely*) in his change of perspective, and could he *reasonably* have expected other Jews to follow? The conclusion that some are eager to draw and others anxious to avoid is that Paul is arbitrary, that is, unreasonable. The spectre of reason as somehow 'relative' to alternative, 'incommensurable' perspectives, where it rises for us at all, only leaves us cold—ironic, given how much of *identity*, Jewish and Christian alike, is bound up in this interpretive debate over Paul. Ultimately, the question presses itself: could we help telling our own story through Paul even if we tried? And in the present, 'postmodern' critical climate, it becomes strange to us, perhaps, that we ever did try. As an index to *this* paradigm shift, and to what could come of the cultural studies potential of the new perspective given the will to exploit it to the full, I turn briefly in the end to the recent work of Daniel Boyarin.

34. A further irony is at times apparent. For the modern, critical period, to be 'critical' is precisely to offer a view from 'outside', a view not beholden to the perspective of that which is the *object* of critical analysis. But in this case, although Paul might on some readings be described as taking such a critical view of his own Jewish tradition, only the 'insider' (that is, non-Christian) view of Judaism is allowed critical weight. By contrast, Paul's own apparent efforts at self-definition are exposed as secondary rationalizations, ideological mystifications laid over what *we* know to be 'the real Paul'.

35. James, *Pragmatism*, p. 37.

A Cultural Reading of Paul

Daniel Boyarin's *A Radical Jew* does not quite stand alone as an example of a cultural reading of Paul (though neither is the field particularly crowded).[36] I have chosen to highlight this as opposed to any other example especially because of its self-conscious development of the new perspective: Paul's discourse on the Law and Judaism is seen to be 'forever caught in a paradox of identity and difference'.[37] It is impossible to do justice to Boyarin's challenging and suggestive reading of Paul here. I will simply offer Boyarin as an extended example of a 'cultural reading', highlighting his hermeneutical self-positioning, his distinctive approach to Paul, and the links he draws between Pauline and contemporary cultural politics.[38]

36. D. Boyarin, *A Radical Jew: Paul and the Politics of Identity* (Contraversions: Critical Studies in Jewish Literature, Culture, and Society; Berkeley: University of California Press, 1994). Other varied examples of 'cultural readings' of Paul would include E.A. Castelli, *Imitating Paul: A Discourse of Power* (Louisville, KY: Westminster/John Knox Press, 1991) and R. Jewett, *Paul the Apostle to America: Cultural Trends and Pauline Scholarship* (Louisville, KY: Westminster/John Knox Press, 1994) (Jewett also interacts with the new perspective). In the present essay, I exaggerate, of course, in suggesting that it is all 'the same old thing' in Pauline studies (nor have we exhausted all the interest in 'the same old thing'!). Thus at the Colloquium Philip Esler rightly named a number of contemporary scholars applying 'social-scientific' research to Paul as further examples of 'cultural readings'; but while I certainly acknowledge that these are fresh attempts to explore new directions, I am not sure the label 'cultural studies' quite applies (which is no insult, of course, but only a question of the definition of a term that is admittedly up for grabs)—though the work of Dale Martin could well be included here: cf. D.B. Martin, *The Corinthian Body* (New Haven: Yale University Press, 1995), and note Boyarin's enthusiastic review (*JBL/CRBR Online Reviews* [http://scholar.cc.emory.edu/scripts/jbl-crbr/reviews.html], 7/96).

37. Boyarin, *A Radical Jew*, p. 204.

38. I have chosen to be largely descriptive here (raising critical questions only briefly in the end relative to 'cultural studies'), in order to introduce Boyarin's work on Paul and to commend it to others; see also Barclay, 'Neither Jew Nor Greek', pp. 206-14. In the introduction to the present paper I alluded to Boyarin (a talmudist) as 'an "interloper" into Pauline studies' (cf. Boyarin, *A Radical Jew*, pp. ix-xi, 1, 12), meaning by this that, predictably, the mold of Pauline studies, where cultural studies is concerned, had to be broken from the outside. Actually, though, Boyarin's engagement with Paul and with recent Pauline scholarship is so competent and insightful that he could only be regarded as an 'outsider' in a (in this case negligible)

First, Boyarin's interpretive self-understanding, which stands out in its contrast to the 'modernist' impulses of the new perspective suggested above:

> Here...you have a talmudist and postmodern Jewish cultural critic reading Paul. I think that my particular perspective as a practicing Jewish, non-Christian, critical but sympathetic reader of Paul conduces me to ways of understanding his work that are necessarily different from the ways of readers of other cultural stances. This text fits into the tradition, then, of what has come to be called cultural readings of the Bible, readings that are openly informed by the cultural knowledge and subject-positions of their producers.[39]

Reading Paul himself as 'a Jewish cultural critic' who poses 'a challenge to Jews now', Boyarin asks 'in what ways [Paul's] critique is important and valid for Jews today, and indeed in what ways the questions that Paul raises about culture are important and valid for everyone'.[40] 'Paul represents in his person and thematizes in his discourse, paradoxes not only of Jewish identity, but...of all identity as such.'[41] 'Are the specificities of human identity, the differences, of value, or are they only an obstacle in the striving for justice and liberation? What I want to know is what Paul is saying to me, a male Jew, and how I must respond to it.'[42] 'Rather than seeing Paul as a text and my task that of a philologist, I see us engaged across the centuries in a common enterprise of cultural criticism.'[43] 'I am concerned...to register the response of an actively practicing (post)modern rabbinic Jew to both Paul and Pauline interpretation, particularly insofar as these (especially the latter) have often been inimical to my religious/ethnic group and practice.'[44]

The choice of a 'starting point' or 'key' to Paul 'is primarily a theological, ethical, political decision, not a "scientific" one'; Boyarin thus prefers readings that 'render the Pauline corpus more or less coherent' and that prove 'useful in appropriating the Pauline texts

---

disciplinary sense. Such boundary crossing as Boyarin engages in is always risky, vulnerable to a disciplinary closing of ranks; one hopes his effort will receive the attention it clearly deserves.

39. Boyarin, *A Radical Jew*, p. 1.
40. Boyarin, *A Radical Jew*, pp. 2-3.
41. Boyarin, *A Radical Jew*, p. 3.
42. Boyarin, *A Radical Jew*, p. 3.
43. Boyarin, *A Radical Jew*, pp. 3-4.
44. Boyarin, *A Radical Jew*, p. 4.

today'.[45] The interpretive goal is not *the* correct reading, but *a* valid reading.[46] 'Perhaps not surprisingly, this book is part of the movement to thoroughly discredit the Reformation interpretation of Paul and particularly the description of Judaism on which it is based. I go further than some of the scholars in arguing that not only is this reading unsupportable in scholarly terms, but that it is an ethical scandal as well...'[47]

Boyarin's portrait of Paul makes no claim to know 'what really happened' or 'what was actually going on in the mind of Paul', but is rather, he asserts, 'a highly politicized intervention in biblical interpretation and, I hope, more than that as well', a political reading of Paul accompanied by 'a highly political account of different interpretations of Paul from the perspective of a Jew committed to the significance and continuation of Jewish culture and particularity'.[48] Through an incisive account of recent new perspective debate, in which Boyarin emphasizes the need for a reading of Paul that does not 'slander Judaism', he associates his own approach most closely with the tradition of F.C. Baur ('Paul the universalizing critic of Jewish particularity') as refined through the recent work of James Dunn ('Paul the universalizing critic of Jewish ethnocentrism'), figured by Boyarin as 'Paul the cultural critic'.[49] For Boyarin, the key Pauline document is his Epistle to the Galatians; the key texts, 3.26-29 and 4.21-31.[50] Boyarin's two chapters on Galatians particularly reveal his nearness to yet independence from Dunn:

> I wish to establish the plausibility of two claims: (1) that the social gospel was central to Paul's ministry, i.e., that the eradication of human difference and hierarchy was its central theme, and (2) that the dyad of flesh

---

45. Boyarin, *A Radical Jew*, p. 6; on this dual preference and Boyarin's hermeneutics generally, see pp. 39-40, 54, 130-35, 183, 190, 199, 213-14, 218, 261 nn. 4, 5, 262 n. 6, 270 n. 50, 293-94 nn. 21, 23, 316 n. 20, 322-23 n. 53, 325 n. 13.

46. See Boyarin, *A Radical Jew*, p. 261 n. 5.

47. Boyarin, *A Radical Jew*, p. 11; see n. 17 above. As Boyarin remarks elsewhere: 'Postmodern hermeneutics has often been claimed as an escape from moral responsibility. I would claim the exact opposite. Interpretation can no longer serve as a cover for moral and political irresponsibility, since we know that hermeneutical choices are always being made by interpreters. There may be interpretations that the text excludes; it almost never demands only one reading' (pp. 213-14).

48. Boyarin, *A Radical Jew*, pp. 39-40.

49. Boyarin, *A Radical Jew*, pp. 40-56; 11-12.

50. Boyarin, *A Radical Jew*, pp. 22-25, 266 n. 20; 32-36, 269 n. 42.

and spirit was the vehicle by which this transformation was to take place.[51]

The second of these two claims introduces what is distinctive in Boyarin's reading of Paul. '[T]he hermeneutical key to Paul' is 'his allegorical hermeneutic and a cultural politics which grow out of the hermeneutical/intellectual and religious/moral world that he inhabits, the world of Hellenized Judaism of the first century'.[52]

> Paul was motivated by a Hellenistic desire for the One, which among other things produced an ideal of a universal human essence, beyond difference and hierarchy. This universal humanity, however, was predicated (and still is) on the dualism of the flesh and the spirit, such that while the body is particular, marked through practice as Jew or Greek, and through anatomy as male or female, the spirit is universal... Paul's anthropological dualism was matched by a hermeneutical dualism as well. Just as the human being is divided into a fleshy and a spiritual component, so also is language itself. It is composed of outer, material signs and inner, spiritual significations.[53]

Boyarin reads Paul, with Philo and others, as partaking of a diffuse and eclectic Hellenistic Jewish middle-Platonism, the source of his intimately interrelated anthropological and hermeneutical dualisms of letter or flesh and spirit.

Paul's Christian theology represents a supersession of historical Israel as carnal, a carnality aided by and expressed in a literal reading of scripture, of circumcision, of 'Israel'.

> [T]he premise of this book is that for Paul the term *flesh* enters into a rich metaphorical and metonymic semantic field bounded on the one hand by the metaphorical usages already current in biblical parlance and on the other hand by the dualism of spirit and flesh current in the milieu of Hellenistic—that is, first-century—Judaism. It was the working out and through of these multiple semantic possibilities that generated Paul's major semantic innovations. Flesh is the penis and physical kinship; it is the site of sexuality, wherein lies the origin of sin; it is also the site of genealogy, wherein lies the ethnocentrism of Judaism as Paul encountered it. All of these could be opposed, Paul came to see, by a spiritual or ideal set of counterparts which would enable the escape from the two elements of human life that Paul felt most disturbing: desire and ethnicity... Paul came to oppose the Law because of the way that it literally—

51. Boyarin, *A Radical Jew*, p. 107; see pp. 106-57.
52. Boyarin, *A Radical Jew*, p. 6.
53. Boyarin, *A Radical Jew*, p. 7.

Biblical Studies/Cultural Studies

that is, carnally—insisted on the priority and importance of the flesh, of procreation and kinship, symbolized by the mark in the flesh, par excellence, the penis.[54]

'What concerned Paul…was the literal observance of the Law insofar as it frustrated what Paul took to be the moral and religious necessity of humankind, namely to erase all distinction between ethnos and ethnos, sex and sex and become one in Christ's spiritual body', and Paul's 'genius' lies in his having found in the 'dualist ideology' of his culture a solution to this theological problem.[55] For Paul, ' "true Jewishness" ends up having nothing to do with family connection (descent from Abraham according to the flesh), history (having the Law), or maintaining the cultural/religious practices of the historical Jewish community (circumcision), but paradoxically consists of participating in a universalism, an allegory that dissolves those essences and meanings entirely'.[56]

Boyarin links Paul to the present via a tightly-knit chain of interpretive reasoning. On such cultural matters as gender and ethnicity, Boyarin 'assum[es] that in some fundamental ways Paul has set the agenda…*for both Jews and Christians* until this day'.[57] Paul's allegoresis, hermeneutical and anthropological, is an expression of 'a profound yearning for univocity', for 'the One', for an idealized universal humanity (typically figured in the continuous 'phallogocentric' Western tradition as male and European).[58] 'It is no accident, then, that the discourses of misogyny and anti-Judaism are profoundly implicated in projects of allegorical reading of the Bible', given that the 'metalinguistic practice' of 'allegorical interpretation' is 'not a local intervention in the meaning of texts but a global discourse on the meaning of language and the human body and especially on human difference'.[59] The 'hermeneutic system' of 'midrash' which characterized the Rabbis 'seems precisely to refuse that dualism, eschewing the inner–outer, visible–invisible, body–soul dichotomies of allegorical reading… Midrash and platonic allegory are alternate techniques of the body.'[60] Boyarin's 'central thesis' is 'that the allegorization of the sign "Israel" in Paul is part and parcel of the

54. Boyarin, *A Radical Jew*, pp. 68-69; cf. pp. 78-81, 86-95.
55. Boyarin, *A Radical Jew*, p. 85.
56. Boyarin, *A Radical Jew*, pp. 94-95, commenting on Rom. 2.28-29.
57. Boyarin, *A Radical Jew*, p. 4.
58. Boyarin, *A Radical Jew*, p. 16.
59. Boyarin, *A Radical Jew*, p. 17.
60. Boyarin, *A Radical Jew*, p. 14.

very conception of difference within which Paul was to found his discourse on gender as well'.[61] Paul yearns for the 'erasure' of gender and ethnicity, and 'allegoresis, the ultimate hermeneutical mode of logocentric discourse, unites both gender and ethnic identity as the secondary and devalued terms of the same binary opposition' (flesh/spirit).[62]

The Pauline linkage between the Law and sin (Rom. 7 and elsewhere) is a reflex of the celibate Paul's Hellenistic revulsion from sexuality: here the Law is problematic in its command to procreate, a command whose enticement to lust (and thus break the Law) ends in fallenness and death. This Law is 'fleshy' both in terms of its literal sense and in its having to do with 'the flesh'. 'In the new life of the spirit, however, even that most fleshly commandment to procreate will be understood in its spiritual sense, namely, as a commandment to spiritual procreation, to that which bears fruit for God and not for death', and so, 'literally by being not under Law, that is by not being obligated to procreate, the Christian is freed from the dominion of sinful passion, that is free to remove sexuality from her person, and thus able to free herself from being under sin'.[63] But embodied Jewish commitment to circumcision and genealogy is thus spiritualized out of existence; similarly, embodied female difference is sacrificed to Paul's yearning for a higher spiritual androgyny, above fleshy, corporeal gender and sexuality—in subsequent Christian tradition, offering a form of equality to celibate women (an 'equality' figured as maleness), but at the cost of sexuality and maternity.[64] Ironically, the very spiritualizing dualism that promises release from the divisions and inequities of race and gender is itself responsible for the devaluation of 'the Jew' and 'Woman'.[65]

---

61. Boyarin, *A Radical Jew*, p. 22.
62. Boyarin, *A Radical Jew*, p. 24.
63. Boyarin, *A Radical Jew*, pp. 167, 169.
64. See Boyarin, *A Radical Jew*, pp. 176-79, 180-200.
65. Boyarin traces Paul's allegorization of 'the Jew' through that Protestant theological tradition according to which 'the Jew' is the symbol of inferior religion or debased human nature (in this case against the Pauline grain), and his critique of this tradition (*A Radical Jew*, pp. 209-219), focused on Bultmann, Käsemann and, more recently, Robert G. Hamerton-Kelly, is withering; it also provides an interesting hermeneutical moment: 'Even granting the undecidability of texts, the multivariate nature of hermeneutics, and my own personal investments that lead me to read one way and not another, I find it hard to imagine that anyone who is not already inclined toward Hamerton-Kelly's hatred of Judaism will find his paraphrase in

In his final chapter, 'Answering the Mail', Boyarin states 'that Paul's letters are letters addressed to us—to me, as a (post)modern Jew', and so Boyarin concludes 'with a highly personal and engaged, perhaps not always completely satisfactory, attempt to answer Paul's letters to me. How can I ethically construct a particular identity which is extremely precious to me without falling into ethnocentrism or racism of one kind or another?'[66]

> Paul's universalism seems to conduce to coercive politico-cultural systems that engage in more or less violent projects of the absorption of cultural specificities into the dominant one. Yet Jews cannot ignore the force of Paul's critique just because of its negative effects, for uncritical devotion to ethnic particularity has equally negative effects.[67]

'My thesis is that rabbinic Judaism and Pauline Christianity as two different hermeneutic systems for reading the Bible generate two diametrically opposed, but mirror-like, forms of racism—and also two dialectical possibilites of anti-racism... The genius of Christianity is its concern for all of the peoples of the world; the genius of rabbinic Judaism is its ability to leave other people alone.'[68]

Drawing on recent discussion of 'essentialism versus constructionism' in identity theory, Boyarin combines the two: 'Claims for essence are legitimation strategies for identity politics and, as such, are attacked at great peril to causes of difference and liberation of differences'.[69] Genealogy serves this purpose for Jewish identity. But is this 'racist'? Boyarin makes a crucial distinction between the political position of a dominated minority and a dominating majority: 'the very things appealed to in order to legitimate the subaltern identity are appealed to as well by dominating groups in order to exploit the dominated. The

Paul's language...' (p. 218; cf. in another connection: 'Zionism is a particular reading of Jewish culture and especially of the Bible. I do not, and could not, given my hermeneutic theories, argue that it is a wrong reading or that there is a right reading that can be countered to it. I do argue, however, that it is not the only reading' [p. 246]; one might question whether the categories 'wrong' and 'right' are as off-limits, even on 'postmodern' assumptions, as Boyarin suggests). The recent post-structuralist use of 'Jew' or 'Woman' as a disembodied symbol for all 'difference' or 'otherness' is held to be a similar, though well-meaning, allegorical move (pp. 219-27).

66. Boyarin, *A Radical Jew*, pp. 228-29.
67. Boyarin, *A Radical Jew*, p. 228.
68. Boyarin, *A Radical Jew*, pp. 232-33.
69. Boyarin, *A Radical Jew*, p. 238.

valence of the claim shifts from negative to positive with the political status of the group making the claim'.[70] Power makes all the difference, then. Boyarin takes up the challenge of Paul's universalizing critique of the divisive effects of 'racial identity' and argues, in the end, that Paul's critique hit the wrong target: it is not identity based on genealogy, but on autochthony, that is to be opposed.[71] Finally, in a critique of aspects of Zionism and the Israeli State against the backdrop of other manifestations of hegemonic nationalisms in the contemporary world, Boyarin makes a plea for 'diasporizing identity' and for 'deterritorializing Judaism':

> The dialectic between Paul and the Rabbis can be recuperated for cultural critique. When Christianity is the hegemonic power in Europe and the United States, then the resistance of Jews to being universalized can be a critical force and model for the resistance of all peoples to being Europeanized out of particular bodily existence. When, however, an ethnocentric Judaism becomes a temporal, hegemonic political force, it becomes absolutely, vitally necessary to accept Paul's critical challenge—although not his universalizing, disembodying solution—and develop an equally passionate concern for all human beings... Somewhere in this dialectic a synthesis must be found, one that will allow for stubborn hanging on to ethnic, cultural specificity but in a context of deeply felt and enacted human solidarity. For that synthesis, Diaspora provides the model, and only in conditions of Diaspora can such a resolution even be attempted.[72]

The heights to which Boyarin takes Paul, compared to the more down to earth norm (positively dusty, actually), makes for an exhilarating (and sometimes dizzying) ride. In addition to Paul's relevance to contemporary identity politics of race and gender, he is seen ultimately to contribute to current political dialogue on the 'new world order'. The expanded sense of what a reading of Paul might open out into is a much needed challenge to Pauline studies.

I initially suggested that the most obvious opening to 'cultural studies' granted by familiar Pauline scholarship is the significance of cultural location in reading Paul—a matter relevant both for Paul and for his readers (in that the constructions of the former by the latter either—

70. Boyarin, *A Radical Jew*, pp. 241-42; Boyarin finds this distinction in both Foucault and Sanders (pp. 241, 250-51)—must be true then!
71. See Boyarin, *A Radical Jew*, p. 253.
72. Boyarin, *A Radical Jew*, pp. 256-57.

depending on whom you ask—conceal the 'real' Paul or else reveal
'Paul' in whatever shape he assumes). Boyarin extends 'cultural reading'
far beyond this.[73] In fact, he offers a cultural reading in both of the two
senses sometimes distinguished, the 'culturalist' and the '(post)
structuralist'.[74] The 'culturalist' reading yields a Paul consciously engaged in a principled political critique of his Jewish contemporaries
(here Boyarin makes explicit what is often implicit in the 'new perspective'). The 'poststructuralist' reading goes behind the back of this other
Paul, probing his allegorical discursive and signifying practices, of which
Paul proves to be a victim (so that Paul is explicitly construed as a
'cultural critic' only to be exposed as a deeply flawed one).[75] That is, the
latter reading undermines, subverts, *deconstructs* the former (by the same
token, the former sets up the latter). This irony must be my parting one,
but just here large questions might be raised, questions that both
appropriately address Boyarin at the level of the broad sweep of his
reading and that address more broadly the enterprise of cultural criticism
itself.[76] If Boyarin's thesis is to meet resistance anywhere, it will surely
be just here, in his move to a 'poststructuralist' reading. What justifies
such a move, in general and in this particular case? Can resistance be
entirely put down to a nostalgic clinging to the notion of a free and
unified human self (which we, as good 'postmoderns', are supposed to
be beyond)? Do we not rightly retain some sense that the ethically
significant level is that of consciously held principles and intentional

73. Though he typically uses the term itself to refer to this kind of awareness of
reading location; cf. Boyarin, *A Radical Jew*, pp. 1, 32, 40, 204.

74. For the distinction between 'culturalist' and '(post)structuralist' approaches,
drawn from Stuart Hall, see A. Easthope, 'Cultural Studies 1: United Kingdom', in
M. Groden and M. Kreisworth (eds.), *The Johns Hopkins Guide to Literary Theory and
Criticism* (Baltimore: The Johns Hopkins University Press, 1994), p. 178: 'The former, based on the work of Raymond Williams and the liberal humanist inheritance,
conceives the human subject (whether individual or collective) as freely able to
make up meanings for itself and rework social institutions, while the latter, deriving
from structuralism and poststructuralism, envisages the subject as an identity or position determined within social and ideological structures of which he or she is an
effect.'

75. This further move distinguishes Boyarin's cultural reading from that of, say,
Jewett, *Paul, The Apostle to America*.

76. I have only questions here, not answers (though one might well perceive a
drift to the following); these questions are not meant to detract from Boyarin, but
are offered in a spirit of constructive dialogue.

purposive action, the level at which we hold each other accountable? How determinative are our tacit conceptions of language and the silent workings of signification? Cannot discursive practices and political convictions combine in varied, complex and reciprocal ways (rather than the former making the latter an inevitability)? Can we simply figure Pauline Christianity as allegorical and rabbinic Judaism as midrashic—and regard the outcome as predictable?

But then do we not rightly sense, after all, some relation of reading practices to politics? And to what does the sort of ironic unmasking or depth-reading Boyarin employs owe its beguiling power, if and where it possesses such? Can we rhetoricize the choice of one or the other of the two modes of cultural reading (the 'culturalist' reading more suited, perhaps, to reformation, the 'poststructuralist' to revolution)? That is, can we relativize the move to our stance toward the object in question (in this case, Paul)? Can we rhetoricize the relation of discourse and politics—for Paul and for us?[77] And might a 'poststructuralist' critical reading wield its rhetorical power in such a way as to constitute a new scientism?

77. Boyarin resists attributing Paul's 'allegorical' discourse to '*mere* rhetoric', wishing rather to *explain* Paul (see pp. 35, 68, 109, 269 n. 42)—quite unpostmodern on both counts. See my 'Sins of the Flesh and Suspicious Minds: Dunn's New Theology of Paul', forthcoming in *JSNT* (note particularly on 'the flesh', where Boyarin is building on Dunn).

House Readings and Field Readings:
The Discourse of Slavery and Biblical/Cultural Studies

Jennifer A. Glancy

A headline in *The New York Times*, 10 May 1996: 'Bible Backed Slavery, Says a Lawmaker'. In the context of a debate over whether the Confederate flag should fly over the Alabama State Capitol, a first-term Republican State Senator named Charles Davidson wrote a speech defending the institution of slavery. According to Davidson, 'white, black, Hispanic and Indian slave owners' loved and cared for their slaves, who were the ultimate beneficiaries of the slave system. In addition, Davidson revived the argument that the Bible vindicated slavery; his textual allusions included Lev. 25.44 and 1 Tim. 6.1. 'The issue is not race', he said. 'It's Southern heritage. I'm on a one-man crusade to get the truth out about what our Southern heritage is all about.' Martha Foy, representing the Republican National Committee, expressed her 'shock' at Davidson's speech. The measure to approve official display of the Confederate flag was tabled, thus precluding Davidson from actually delivering his speech.[1] Criticism over Davidson's role in the incident caused him to drop out of a race for the US House of Representatives.[2]

This brief news item serves as a catalyst in my thinking about the convergence of biblical and cultural studies. Drawing on the political appropriation of biblical texts pertaining to slavery, this article considers two articulations of the conjuncture of biblical and cultural studies. The first approach follows the mandate of cultural studies to take the panoply of cultural productions as its subject matter, whether those productions are artistic, mercantile, pious, or, as in this case, political.[3] (These are

1. 'Bible Backed Slavery, Says a Lawmaker', *The New York Times* (10 May 1996, A20), column 4.

2. 'Ala. State Sen. Forced to Quit U.S. House Race After Defending Slavery', *Jet* 90 (27 May 1996), p. 4.

3. While some formulations of cultural studies focus on popular culture, to delimit the scope of inquiry in this way is to 'repeat and reproduce the boundary between high and popular culture' (Antony Easthope, *Literary into Cultural Studies*

not, of course, mutually exclusive categories.) Interpretation is political. This is true of all interpretation, regardless of its location: classroom, conference, journal. At least in the United States, however, biblical interpretation remains political in another, more overt sense. The Bible is a cultural icon, and both major political parties remain publicly deferential to biblical authority. As biblical and cultural studies converge, the function of the Bible in constructing and maintaining ideologies dominant in the US today emerges as an important area of investigation.

The second articulation of the conjuncture of biblical and cultural studies that I will consider is the movement to include a wider range of voices in the academic conversation of biblical studies. This movement acknowledges that, within the academy, a disparate if intersecting set of social locations informs and influences the readings of biblical scholars; it also acknowledges the legitimacy of readings and ways of reading of those who are not members of the guild of biblical scholars. Recent works by Fernando Segovia and Daniel Patte exemplify this trend within the field of biblical studies. I will argue that political readings of the biblical discourse on slavery point to some useful limits on the celebration of polyphonic hermeneutics.

House Readings

> Let all who are under the yoke of slavery regard their masters as worthy of all honor, so that the name of God and the teaching may not be blasphemed. Those who have believing masters must not be disrespectful to them on the ground that they are members of the church; rather they must serve them all the more, since those who benefit by their service are believers and beloved. Teach and urge these duties... (1 Tim. 6.1-2, NRSV).

A state legislator in Alabama plans to give a speech defending the tradition of slavery in the American South, highlighting what he claims is biblical support for the institution of bond labor. When *The New York Times* picks up the story, the headline is not 'Contemporary Legislator Dares to Defend Slavery', nor is it 'Lawmaker Cites Bible in Political Debate'. Rather, the headline focuses on the legislator's assertion that the 'Bible backed slavery'. What is newsworthy here? Does *The Times*

[London: Routledge, 1991], p. 108). See also the treatment of 'culture' in Raymond Williams, *Keywords: A Vocabulary of Culture and Society* (New York: Oxford University Press, 1976), pp. 76-82.

really dispute Senator Davidson's claim that a variety of biblical texts in some sense 'back slavery'? What would constitute a 'good' reading of 1 Tim. 6.1-2? As I read this brief news item, I try to reconstruct its implicit logic:

1. the Bible is normative for those of the Judeo–Christian tradition, perhaps even infallible;
2. slavery is wrong;
3. therefore, the Bible cannot 'back' slavery.

This logic is familiar to me from my own classroom. In a seminar I have taught on slavery and Christianity, many students cannot accept that the Bible (for them, a univocal and relatively uncomplicated text) tolerates slavery. Therefore, they are willing to argue, *the text must mean something other than what it obviously says.*

We could try to reconstruct some other underlying logic to the story in *The Times*. For example:

1. the Bible supports slavery;
2. slavery is wrong and offends against US democratic ideals;
3. we reject the Bible as a political guide.

In such a case, we would anticipate a headline focusing on the anomaly of an elected official citing the Bible in political debate. However, to challenge biblical authority is dangerous today in American politics. One may quibble with particular readings of the Bible, but in the context of political discourse, a more general rejection of biblical authority is not a viable option.

While I cannot share the surprise implicit in *The Times*'s headline over the assertion that biblical authority supported slavery, neither do I share Senator Davidson's hermeneutical perspective. Meaning is use, according to Wittgenstein's dictum,[4] and Davidson's interpretation of biblical teaching about slavery is inseparable from its use justifying the degradation of human beings in slavery. In the course of a discussion of the

---

4.　'[T]he meaning of a word is its use in language' (Ludwig Wittgenstein, *Philosophical Investigations* [trans. G.E.M. Anscombe; New York: Macmillan, 3rd edn, 1968], p. 20). See also Frank P. Ramsey, *Philosophical Papers* (ed. D.H. Mellor; Cambridge: Cambridge University Press, 1990): '[T]he meaning of a sentence is to be defined by reference to the actions to which asserting it would lead…' (p. 51). Wittgenstein names Ramsey (who died in 1930) as one of the two greatest influences on his abandonment of the project of the *Tractatus*.

scope of cultural studies, Raymond Williams writes that we 'cannot understand an intellectual or artistic project without also understanding its formation; that the relation between a project and a formation is always decisive'.[5] Davidson tells us that his motivation for revisiting the issue of slavery is his one-man mission to convey 'the truth' about 'our Southern heritage'. Consideration of that context may help us, then, as we assess Davidson's biblical interpretation.

Davidson denies that race motivates his defense of Southern heritage, but at the same time he trivializes the violence African-Americans experienced under slavery with an allegation that contemporary housing projects stand witness to a hundred times the rates of rape and murder as were present in slavery. (Aside from methodological questions about Davidson's cliometrics, one notices that Davidson seems to be able to conceive of persons of African descent living only in slavery or in housing projects.) As Ronald Reagan once said, in his youth there was no race problem. The nexus of Davidson's racism and his interpretation of biblical texts as justification of *American* slavery should alert us to the more fundamental problem of the role of biblical allusion and authority in political discourse. After all, Davidson argues not only that the Bible approved of slavery in the ancient world; he extends that to an argument that the Bible therefore legitimates slavery in later and radically different historical circumstances. Davidson claims that those who find the legacy of American slavery morally reprehensible 'are obviously bitter and hateful against God and his word, because they reject what God says and embrace what mere humans say concerning slavery'.[6]

Biblical slavery is an embarrassment to many who claim the Bible as a normative text or collection. Davidson cites 1 Tim. 6.1-2, one of a number of passages in deutero-Pauline letters that direct slaves to submit themselves to their masters (Eph. 6.5-8; Col. 3.22-25; Tit. 2.9-10; see also 1 Pet. 2.18-25). Some commentators displace the difficulties of these passages by explaining them on the basis of Greco-Roman literary prototypes. In the Hermeneia commentary on Colossians, for example, Eduard Lohse writes, 'These rules for the household are not, insofar as their content is considered, "a genuinely Christian creation" and thus they cannot, without further ado, be considered to be "applied

5. Raymond Williams, *The Politics of Modernism: Against the New Conformists* (New York: Verso, 1989), p. 151.

6. 'Ala. State Sen.', p. 4.

kerygma" '.[7] Alternatively, or additionally, commentators imply that the authors of the deutero-Pauline epistles had no choice but to advocate submission to the authority of slaveowners. Ralph P. Martin writes of Col. 3.22-25:

> If this tone of advice seems pedestrian and accommodating, we should respect the limitations of what could be said in urging both slaves and owners to maintain the social order. The incitement to revolt would have been suicidal, as the earlier slave uprisings, led by Spartacus in 73–71 BCE, had shown.[8]

Martin does not consider the possibility that the author of Colossians could simply avoid the question of slaves' obligations to masters, or that there could be alternatives to submission other than revolt. Perhaps more striking from a theological perspective is his repudiation of the possibility that a Christian author could or should give 'suicidal' advice. From a certain perspective, Jesus' injunction to his followers to take up their crosses is an invitation to suicide, as is the glorification of martyrdom throughout the book of Revelation.[9] Despite the tension biblical scholars exhibit when they turn to the slavery passages of the deutero-Pauline epistles, however, their interpretations of these writings support the contention that, in some sense, the Bible backs slavery.[10]

7. Eduard Lohse, *Colossians and Philemon: A Commentary on the Epistles to the Colossians and to Philemon* (Hermeneia; Philadelphia: Fortress Press, 1971), pp. 154-55 n. 4. Material in quotation marks attributed to Karl Heinrich Rengstorf.

8. Ralph P. Martin, *Ephesians, Colossians, and Philemon* (Interpretation; Atlanta: John Knox Press, 1991), pp. 128-29.

9. See Tina Pippin, *Death and Desire: The Rhetoric of Gender in the Apocalypse of John* (Louisville, KY: Westminster/John Knox Press, 1992).

10. Louis Montrose suggests that 'new historicism' tends to focus on the cultural politics of the past, while 'cultural criticism' tends to focus on contemporary cultural politics. Thus, a new historicist writing about Shakespeare would write about cultural issues in Elizabethan England, while a cultural critic would write about the uses of Shakespeare today. It seems to me that whatever boundary exists between new historicism and cultural studies is a permeable one, although I also think the question of this boundary deserves further consideration by biblical critics interested in either the new historicism or cultural studies. The present article focuses on modern uses of the discourse of biblical slavery, but I think it could be within the purview of cultural studies to consider the cultural production of those texts, as well as their cultural implications in the ancient world. See Louis Montrose, 'New Historicism', in Stephen Greenblatt and Giles Gunn (eds.), *Redrawing the Boundaries: The Transformation of English and American Literary Studies* (New York: MLA, 1992), pp. 392-418. For a relevant example of the usefulness of cultural studies in the analysis of

In the nineteenth-century debate over the abolition of slavery in the US, both proslavery and antislavery forces invoked biblical authority to bolster their causes. Proslavery forces relied on direct exegesis of particular passages; antislavery forces avoided discussion of particular texts and cited instead general underlying truths that they found in their reading of Scripture.[11] Certain claims of the proslavery forces were hermeneutically egregious, especially their claim that Africans are cursed descendants of either Cain or Ham. Thornton Stringfellow, a Baptist minister from Virginia, cited Gen. 9.25-27 as he claimed, 'Here, language is used, showing the *favor* which God would exercise to the posterity of Shem and Japheth, while they were holding the posterity of Ham in a state of *abject bondage*' (emphasis in original).[12] Other than this notorious hypothesis situating the enslavement of Africans in an ancient curse, the proslavery forces were in fact able to marshal a range of textual evidence to support their claim that the Bible was tolerant of slavery, and even supported the institution. In debates with abolitionists, proslavery clerics would quote chapter and verse from both Old and New Testaments, and challenge their opponents to quote even a single biblical verse that referred to slavery that unequivocally condemned the institution. Abolitionists regularly bypassed this challenge.

Eugene D. Genovese, who has written extensively on the slave system of the American South, writes of the hermeneutical debate:

> Regrettably, such formidable southern theologians…sustained themselves in scriptural exegesis with the abolitionists. Orthodox theologians demonstrated that neither the Old nor the New Testament condemned slavery as sinful. The abolitionists, displaying no small amount of intellectual dishonesty, never succeeded in making the Word say what they said it did, and eventually they had to spurn the Word for the Spirit. In consequence, they virtually reduced the Holy Spirit to the spirit (the conscience) of individuals. I do not say that an antislavery Christian theology

historical instances of cultural change, see Homi K. Bhaba's discussion of the obstacles encountered by missionaries in India when they tried to preach the gospel, in Bhaba, *The Location of Culture* (London: Routledge, 1994), pp. 33-34.

11. Larry R. Morrison, 'The Religious Defense of American Slavery before 1830', *Journal of Religious Thought* 37 (1980), pp. 16-29; John. R. McKivigan, *The War against Proslavery Religion: Abolitionism and the Northern Churches, 1830–1865* (Ithaca, NY: Cornell University Press, 1984), pp. 30-31.

12. Thornton Stringfellow, 'A Scriptural View of Slavery', reprinted in Eric L. McKitrick (ed.), *Slavery Defended: The Views of the Old South* (Englewood Cliffs, NJ: Prentice–Hall, 1963), pp. 86-98, esp. pp. 86-87.

remains an impossibility... But as a historian, I do insist that the abolitionists failed to construct one...[13]

Like Senator Davidson, Genovese concludes that the 'Bible backed slavery'. Davidson's biblical interpretation assumes the Bible's normativity
in moral and political discourse. Genovese, who is not tied to upholding
the cultural authority of the Bible, identifies the biblical position on
slavery as a flaw of Christianity. His evaluation of the quality of Christian debate over slavery in the nineteenth century points to the intellectual distortions that arise when the Bible dictates the parameters of cultural discourse: 'Not always skillfully or even honestly, the abolitionists
interpreted the Bible as antislavery, and we may thank God and the big
battalions that, whatever their sins against intellectual integrity, they
prevailed.'[14]

While antislavery forces questioned the use of the Bible by proslavery
forces, they gave their consent to the authority of the same volume,
locating the moral problem not in the Bible but in their opponents:
'They have turned our Bible into a smith shop whence consecrated
hands bring fetters for the feet and manacles for the mind. They make
the Old and New Testament a pair of handcuffs; and the whole book a
straight jacket for the soul!'[15] Trapped within the debate, Christians who
fought over the slavery question were unable to recognize that the Bible
itself, or at least its use as an arbiter of cultural practice, was the source
of ambivalence and embarrassment.[16]

---

13. Eugene D. Genovese, *The Southern Front: History and Politics in the Cultural
War* (Columbia, MO: University of Missouri Press, 1995), pp. 10-11. Genovese
ranks among the most influential historians of slavery; for decades, an intellectual
and political commitment to Marxism informed his work. *The Southern Front* represents a retreat from that commitment for reasons he confronts in an epilogue, where
he attributes some measure of guilt for atrocities committed by socialist and com-
munist regimes to American leftists. Readers of the volume may be surprised by the
extent to which Genovese's emotional reaction against his past informs the spirit of
this work, especially in light of his vituperative attack on the expression of 'feelings'
in 'objective' scholarly work (pp. 6-7).

14. Genovese, *Southern Front*, p. 131.

15. J. Blanchard and N.L. Rice, *A Debate on Slavery: Held in the City of Cincinnati, on the First, Second, Third, and Sixth Days of October, 1845* (Cincinnati: Wm. H.
Moore, 1846; repr.; Detroit: Negro History Press, n.d.).

16. This is not entirely true. The Garrisonian abolitionists challenged the infal-
libility of the Bible. However, to the extent to which the public perceived the
Garrisonians as inimical to biblical authority, their influence was diminished. On the

Senator Davidson located his defense of slavery in the context of what he called a one-man crusade to disseminate the truth about Southern heritage. The narrative of a Southern heritage has been a deliberate fiction throughout the twentieth century. D.W. Griffiths's *Birth of a Nation* supplied a genealogy for the Ku Klux Klan. Margaret Mitchell created a nostalgic plantation world where elderly servants were grateful to be in the presence of their owners; white men were too busy courting white women to rape black women. *Gone with the Wind*, along with other plantation epics, has perpetuated an image of genteel Southern life that generations of Americans (at least white Americans) have found both convincing and comforting. There are, however, other possible stories to tell about Southern history, from legends of slaves who organized slave revolts to biographies of the many Southerners (both white and black) who fought on the side of the Union in the Civil War. Davidson's rhetorical claim that he is disseminating 'the truth' about Southern heritage implies that Southern cultural traits pre-exist their representation.[17] However, as Stuart Hall argues, cultural identities are constructed 'within, not outside representation'.

> Though they seem to invoke an origin in a historical past with which they continue to correspond, actually identities are about questions of using the resources of history, language and culture in the process of becoming rather than being: not 'who we are' or 'where we come from', so much as what we might become, how we have been represented and how that bears on how we might represent ourselves…not the so-called return to roots but a coming-to-terms with our 'routes'.[18]

The fictive and poetic qualities of tradition and identity in no way lessen their effectiveness.[19] Tradition, like the Bible, functions as part of the cultural apparatuses that sustain dominant ideologies in the US.

Antonio Gramsci was instrumental in articulating the variety of ways

---

whole, more moderate antislavery rhetoric helped sway public opinion in the North against the institution of slavery.

17. Bhaba warns that the 'representation of difference must not be hastily read as the reflection of *pre-given* ethnic or cultural traits set in the fixed tablet of tradition', *Location*, p. 2.

18. Stuart Hall, 'Introduction: Who Needs "Identity"?', in Stuart Hall and Paul du Gay, *Questions of Cultural Identity* (London: Sage, 1996), pp. 1-17 (4).

19. By describing tradition and identity as 'poetic', I hope to imply that we are not simply handed our identities or traditions, but that in interesting ways we *make* them.

that cultural forces (from the family to the arts) create a climate of consent that binds individuals and communities to a social order. Imprisoned by the Fascists in Italy, Gramsci studied the mechanisms by which political powers gain and reproduce their hegemony.[20] For Gramsci, hegemony 'is not limited to matters of political control but seeks to describe a more general predominance which includes, as one of its key features, a particular way of seeing the world and human nature and relationships'.[21] Gramsci recognized that certain organs of the State exerted control by coercion—the police, say, or the military. However, he understood that the threat of coercion is more effective as a crisis tactic than as the ordinary apparatus of social control. He argued that State and civil society are inseparable, and that civil society exercises its control through a variety of cultural apparatuses that operate not through coercion but through consent. Families, religious bodies, the media, schools and other cultural institutions elaborate and reiterate a vision of society that advances the interests of dominant powers. Hegemonic thinking unites interests that would otherwise be at odds. Inasmuch as individuals and groups within society participate in this vision, civil society has managed to exert control without the overt exercise of violence.[22] Working out of a Marxist background, Gramsci nonetheless emphasized the role of non-economic cultural forces in the ordering of society. He understood that hegemony was both an unstable and a conflictual achievement, always contested by emergent groups in society.[23]

20. The standard collection of Gramsci's writings in English remains the *Selections from the Prison Notebooks* (trans. Geoffrey N. Smith and Quintin Hoare; New York: International Publishers, 1971). As one might infer from the title, these writings are occasional and often fragmentary.

21. Summary of Gramsci's understanding of hegemony in Williams, *Keywords*, p. 117.

22. Louis Althusser developed Gramsci's ideas in 'Ideology and Ideological State Apparatuses (Notes towards an Investigation)', in *Lenin and Philosophy and Other Essays* (trans. Ben Brewster; New York: Monthly Review Press, 1971), pp. 127-86. Although I have been influenced by Althusser, I find the larger framework of his thinking to be problematic, especially his ahistoricism and his faith in a clear division between ideology and science. For an accessible critique of Althusser, see Terry Eagleton, *Ideology: An Introduction* (New York: Verso, 1991), pp. 136-53.

23. For a helpful discussion of Gramsci's continuing (or even increasing) significance for postmodern thought, see Marcia Landy, *Film, Politics, and Gramsci* (Minneapolis: University of Minnesota Press, 1994).

Articulation of theory in Gramsci's writings is inseparable from his investigations into Italian realities. He cannot describe the particular forms that hegemonic struggles will take in other historical and geographical circumstances; however, he does point to the real power that cultural productions and texts can exercise. The appropriation of the Bible in political discourse is a moment in a cultural struggle for hegemony—as is the invocation of regional tradition, or even a debate over whether the Confederate flag should fly over the statehouses of Southern capitals. Americans who may be utterly unacquainted with the Bible as text nonetheless consent in some vague way to its moral normativity. Senator Davidson's reliance on the Bible to bolster his argument for the vindication of the institution of slavery illustrates the difficulty that arises in contesting the authority of ideological apparatuses. Davidson's interpretation slips from the recognition that biblical texts do not challenge the institution of slavery in their own times to the implication that the Bible therefore legitimates slavery, and in an ahistorical manner. When the direct applicability of biblical teachings to today's circumstances is *assumed*, interpreters are put in the awkward and disingenuous position of denying that the 'Bible backed slavery'. What is at stake, however, is not a particular reading of the Bible on any single social issue, but the role of the Bible in ideological struggles in American political life.

Davidson's speech seemed to backfire, causing him to drop out of a race for the US House of Representatives. However, his campaign to spread the word of Southern heritage brought him 15 minutes of fame, which in turn allowed him to reach far more people with his ideas than he might have anticipated. Of greater relevance, by seeming to locate the moral problem solely in Davidson's speech and not in the biblical texts he quoted, *The New York Times* illustrates the unimpeachable status of the Bible as a moral and cultural authority in the US today.

Field Readings

Fernando Segovia and Daniel Patte have recently set forth theories of reading that focus on the interplay between the interpreter's social location and his or her construction of meaning. Both theorists suggest that biblical critics need to honor the interpretations of 'ordinary' readers as valid. Gramsci's analysis of the role of intellectuals in cultural struggles for hegemony offers a framework in which to evaluate these recent forays by biblical critics into cultural studies. The discussion continues by considering Senator Davidson and his political reading of biblical slavery as an everyday intellectual offering an 'ordinary' reading.

In Gramsci's formulation, the agents of cultural change are intellectuals. In the struggle for hegemony, intellectuals participate as cultural workers advancing the interests not only of the left but also of the right. His understanding of intellectuals is slippery, but several points are clear:

1.   'All men are intellectuals...but not all men have in society the function of intellectuals.' Each person 'carries on some form of intellectual activity, that is, he is a "philosopher", an artist...he participates in a particular conception of the world, has a conscious line of moral conduct, and therefore contributes to sustain a conception of the world or to modify it'.[24]

2.   Traditional intellectuals locate themselves in the historical lineage of intellectuals, and thereby disguise the nature of their ties to dominant powers in society. Intellectuals construct for themselves a 'social utopia by which...[they] think of themselves as "independent", autonomous, endowed with a character of their own, etc.'.[25]

3.   'Organic' intellectuals are those members of emergent social groups who help to articulate a conception of the world that reflects the group's experience and helps the group to negotiate a position in society. Note: although Gramsci primarily linked organic intellectuals to economic classes, he understood that other cultural factors (such as regional location and urban or rural ties) shaped group affinities.

Gramsci does not use 'common sense' to refer to practical insights into everyday life. Rather, 'common sense' refers to a person's unreflective understanding of the world in which she or he lives. 'Common sense' includes knowledge of tactics necessary to make one's way through life; it also includes misconceptions, accretions from earlier cultural moments, subordination of original insights to hegemonic categories. Common sense is incoherent, reflecting piecemeal the ideas gleaned from participating in a variety of social and cultural environments. In other words, it is not reliable. But Gramsci's claim that everyone is an intellectual, a philosopher, highlights his respect for common

---

24. Gramsci, *Selections*, p. 9.
25. Gramsci, *Selections*, p. 8.

sense as the grounds of a more critical understanding of the world. Common sense contains much that is true, much that is useful. In order to help people understand their realities so that they can begin to shape them, Gramsci believes that education is necessary. But the starting point for such an education is common sense:

> In the teaching of philosophy which is aimed...at giving him [the student] a cultural formation and helping him to elaborate his own thought critically so as to be able to participate in an ideological and cultural community, it is necessary to take as one's starting point what the student already knows... And since one presupposes a certain average cultural and intellectual level among the students, who in all probability have hitherto only acquired scattered and fragmentary bits of information and have no methodological and critical preparation, one cannot but start in the first place from common sense...[26]

In many ways this articulation of common sense serves as a positive introduction to the hermeneutical proposals advanced by Segovia and Patte. Gramsci acknowledges each person as an intellectual and a philosopher. Segovia states that for 'cultural studies...all readers and critics are theologians',[27] while Patte focuses on the 'legitimacy' of readings by ordinary readers. Gramsci writes, 'In acquiring one's conception of the world one always belongs to a particular grouping which is that of all the social elements which share the same mode of thinking and acting. We are all conformists of some conformism or other...'[28] Likewise, Segovia and Patte emphasize that one's social location and cultural attachments form the grounds of interpretive activity. Gramsci's notion of common sense has a critical edge, however; common sense is as likely to lead a person to accept her circumstances as inevitable as it is to lead her see how to change those circumstances. For Gramsci, education is a necessary moment, helping everyday intellectuals become 'organic intellectuals' who are able to articulate the interests of their social groupings and to make alliances with others in society who share common interests. Without this critical edge, deference to the productions of common sense would simply reify existing realities.

26. Gramsci, *Selections*, pp. 424-25.

27. Fernando F. Segovia, 'Cultural Studies and Contemporary Biblical Criticism', in Fernando F. Segovia and Mary Ann Tolbert (eds.), *Reading from This Place* (2 vols.; Minneapolis: Fortress, 1995), II, pp. 1-17, esp. p. 12.

28. Gramsci, *Selections*, p. 324.

Segovia sets forth an agenda for the conjuncture of biblical and cultural studies in his introductions to the first two (of a projected three) volumes of *Reading from This Place*.[29] These volumes include the papers from two conferences held at Vanderbilt University that were coordinated by Segovia and Mary Ann Tolbert. The volumes reflect the increasing diversity of social locations represented in the guild of biblical scholars, and highlight the influence of social location on the interpretive process.[30] Segovia's understanding of cultural studies is consistent with a trend to equate cultural studies with the 'theory and politics of identity and difference'.[31] His essays situate the emergence of cultural studies in an overview of biblical studies in the late twentieth century. The story he tells is familiar: in the 1970s new movements in literary criticism and social scientific criticism began to displace, or at least compete with, historical criticism. These various critical movements share the myth of the disinterested reader who sets aside his or her particular concerns when interpreting the text; meaning is not contingent on the location of the interpreter. Against these movements Segovia sets cultural studies, 'a joint critical study of texts and readers, perspectives and ideologies'.[32]

29. Segovia and Tolbert (eds.), *Reading from This Place*. Volume 1 covers 'Social Location and Biblical Interpretation in the United States'; Volume 2 covers 'Social Location and Biblical Interpretation in Global Perspective'.

30. I will primarily direct my remarks to Segovia's position papers on cultural studies. However, several questions about the conference and the larger project of cultural studies remain. First, does the arrangement of papers construct a 'problematic chain of equivalences, between, say, women, people of color in the US, people from the third world, lesbians, gay men...[that falsely implies] these groups are caught in the webs of postmodernity in analogous ways'? (Lata Mani, 'Cultural Theory, Colonial Texts: Reading Eyewitness Accounts of Widow Burning', in Lawrence Grossberg, Cary Nelson and Paul A. Treichler [eds.], *Cultural Studies* [New York: Routledge, 1992], pp. 392-408, esp. p. 393.) Secondly, how do we evaluate the participation of Two Thirds world scholars in a conference primarily designed for the edification of First World American scholars? What efforts are made to avoid viewing these scholars as 'natives' and 'providers of knowledge about their nations and cultures'? (Questions raised in another context by Rey Chow, *Writing Diaspora: Tactics of Intervention in Contemporary Cultural Studies* [Bloomington: Indiana University Press, 1993], p. 99.)

31. Lawrence Grossberg, 'Identity and Cultural Studies: Is That All There Is?', in Hall and du Gay (eds.), *Questions*, pp. 87-107, esp. p. 87. Grossberg's article is a critique of the conflation of cultural studies with the study of identity/difference.

32. Fernando F. Segovia, '"And They Began to Speak in Other Tongues":

Segovia understands that readers read in all their historical specificity: 'Different readers see themselves not only as using different interpretive models and reading strategies but also as reading in different ways in the light of the multilevel social groupings that they represent and to which they belong.'[33] Furthermore, every interpretation, every historical reconstruction, is a construct reflecting the position of a flesh-and-blood reader. Meaning is situated in the interchange between 'a socially and historically conditioned text and a socially and historically conditioned reader'.[34] This understanding of meaning renders 'the question of validity in interpretation as a problematic, since even the very criteria used for judgment and evaluation are seen...as themselves constructions on the part of real readers and hence as emerging from and formulated within specific social locations and agendas'.[35] Segovia insists that cultural studies cannot demand any special training for readers, since all readings, 'high or low, academic or popular, trained or untrained', are equally constructs.[36] Cultural critics are to regard readings emanating from marginal communities, such as base Christian communities or millennarian groups, just as they regard readings emanating from conventional scholars within the field of biblical studies: as social constructs reflecting the complex cultural locations of their authors.

Towards the end of his essay, 'Cultural Studies and Contemporary Biblical Criticism', Segovia raises a series of problems with the agenda he has proposed for cultural studies, promising to return to these problems on a later occasion. One question he raises is this: 'If no master narrative is to be posited or desired, how does one deal with the continued abuse of the oppressed by the oppressor, the weak by the strong,

---

Competing Modes of Discourse in Contemporary Biblical Criticism', in Segovia and Tolbert (eds.), *Reading from This Place*, I, pp. 1-32, esp. p. 25.

33. Segovia, ' "And They Began" ', p. 31.

34. Segovia, 'Cultural Studies', p. 8.

35. Segovia, 'Cultural Studies', p. 11.

36. Segovia, 'Cultural Studies', p. 12. In a footnote Segovia denies that he sees education as 'unnecessary and superfluous', identifying it instead as essential for movements of liberation. He goes on, however, to say that 'education and scholarship—a high socioeducational level—represent no privileged access to the meaning of a text...but are simply another constitutive factor of human identity affecting all reading and interpretation, and in this sense are no different from any other such factor' (p. 12 n. 20). Perhaps Segovia will clarify his understanding of this issue in the projected third volume of this series, which is to deal with pedagogy.

the subaltern by the dominant?'[37] How does one deal, that is, with an interpretation of biblical texts on slavery that claims the Bible legitimates the practice of American slaveholding? If the criteria by which we judge interpretive validity develop in the same cultural matrices as the interpretations we thereby evaluate, on what grounds do we disqualify any interpretation? Senator Davidson's interpretation of biblical texts on slavery reflects his own social location, or at least the story he has created about that social location in his narrative of Southern heritage.[38] Senator Davidson might even claim a marginalized status for himself, since the narrative of a Southern heritage imagines the South as a victimized geographic region occupied by an imperial power (the North, or the Union): '*no one has a monopoly on oppositional identity.* The new social movements structured around race, gender, and sexuality are neither inherently progressive or reactionary...'[39]

Senator Davidson, we might say, is an 'ordinary' reader, one who has not formed his readings in the crucible of the biblical field, who does not rely on the tools of the biblical field. His readings reflect his social location, or at least, his *interpreted* social context.[40] But his readings also

37. Segovia, 'Cultural Studies', p. 17.

38. In an article prepared for the Vanderbilt conference, Mary Ann Tolbert raises the question: 'what do we mean by "right," "legitimate," and "valid" in the context of biblical interpretation?' She sketches two readings of Mk 13.9-27, one a historical reconstruction of the interpretation of first-century Christians, and the other a version of a contemporary and conservative interpretation. After rejecting historical soundness as the chief criterion of interpretive legitimacy or validity, she notes that many scholars who would embrace liberationist readings would reject the readings of more conservative congregations. By what criteria, she asks, do we designate 'one modern community's appropriation of the Bible commendable and another's not?' Tolbert recognizes many of the interpretive problems I am struggling with here. However, she ultimately seems to conflate the question of validity in biblical interpretation and the validity of the Bible itself (Mary Ann Tolbert, 'When Resistance Becomes Repression: Mark 13.9-27 and the Poetics of Location', in Segovia and Tolbert [eds.], *Reading from This Place*, II, pp. 331-46, esp. pp. 339 and 343-46).

39. Kobena Mercer, ' "1968": Periodizing Politics and Identity', in Grossberg, Nelson and Treichler (eds.), *Cultural Studies*, pp. 424-49, esp. p. 426.

40. 'How can one explain the difference between the reading of the Bible in the base communities and the reading of the Bible by popular Pentecostals who live in the same social context?' asks Paulo Fernando Carneiro de Andrade. He answers that 'the "social context" that characterizes the reading of the text must be always understood as "interpreted social context" ' (P.F.C. de Andrade, 'Reading the Bible

correspond to textual elements that express acceptance of the institution of slavery. According to recent work by Daniel Patte on the ethics of biblical interpretation, those trained in the biblical field should accept the basic legitimacy of ordinary readings, and even assist ordinary readers in developing and defending their readings: 'the different readings proposed by ordinary readers should be welcomed and *affirmed* as legitimate by critical readers, whose task would be to discover the meaning-producing dimension of the text that is reflected by this reading'.[41]

Patte argues that critical readings are simply refined versions of ordinary readings.[42] He concludes that '*the goal of critical exegesis is the bringing to critical understanding of an ordinary reading*'.[43] Even the readings of fundamentalist evangelical interpreters are legitimate, Patte says, although he finds the attempt to *universalize* such interpretations to be illegitimate (as he would find any attempt to offer a universalizing interpretation). Patte suggests that critical readers have much to learn from ordinary evangelical readers about the power-authority of the text, which precedes and grounds the interpretive process.

Finally, Patte proposes that 'we ask each of the various legitimate interpretations the following questions: What is its relative value? Is it helpful? Is it harmful? Who benefits? Who is hurt?'[44] We could apply these questions to the entire process of interpretation that Patte outlines. For example, would it be helpful or harmful for a critical reader to work with an ordinary reader such as Senator Davidson to help him articulate and defend his interpretation more clearly? And for whom would it be helpful or harmful? For when we turn to the real world, we will find many ordinary readers who share Davidson's agenda. Is it beneficial or harmful to emphasize the meaning-authority of the biblical text when we remember what the Bible actually says about slavery (not to mention issues of gender and sexuality)? And for whom would it be beneficial or

in the Ecclesial Base Communities of Latin America: The Meaning of Social Context', in Segovia and Tolbert [eds.], *Reading from This Place*, II, pp. 237-49, esp. pp. 246-47).

41. Daniel Patte does not locate his 'ethics of interpretation' in the rubric of cultural studies; I include this discussion here because Patte's project coheres with the critical agenda Segovia has articulated explicitly for cultural studies. Daniel Patte, *Ethics of Biblical Interpretation: A Reevaluation* (Louisville, KY: Westminster/John Knox Press, 1995), p. 11; emphasis his.

42. An insight that I find both valid and significant.

43. Patte, *Ethics*, p. 74; emphasis his.

44. Patte, *Ethics*, p. 125.

harmful? Patte's stated purpose in his ethics of interpretation is to include in the conversation of biblical studies the voices of those who have often been excluded: the voices of women and ethnic minorities, for example, but also the voices of ordinary people sitting in the pews of their churches. Those ordinary people, however, are not necessarily without power. Although they may not have voices at meetings of the Society of Biblical Literature, they do have voices that are heard in letters to the editor, local politics, the Internet, and a variety of other locations. Assuming the basic legitimacy of a reading such as Davidson's and abetting its development seem to me a curious project, yet it seems to be the very project that Patte advocates.

The proposals advanced by Segovia and Patte raise fundamental questions for the conjuncture of biblical and cultural studies. Cultural studies analyzes the productions of popular culture, often turning a critical eye towards those productions and their function in society. Segovia and Patte, however, simply *assume* the basic legitimacy of the ordinary readings they advocate. Gramsci acknowledges each person as an intellectual, yet also notes that the 'common sense' that is the basis of most people's intellectual interactions with the world is an uneven mix of insights, prejudices, contradictions, and images imposed by hegemonic discourse. The lack of this critical edge in the acceptance of 'ordinary' readings perpetuates those prejudices, contradictions, and hegemonic impositions. A cultural studies agenda that defers to popular readings without *emphasizing* the effects of those readings in the social sphere is in danger of repeating and confirming the liabilities of those readings.

Senator Davidson is not a scholarly construct, but a real reader attempting to draw on the cultural authority of the Bible to promote his regressive political position. This authority transcends any particular interpretation of the Bible, and is thus a formidable weapon in ideological discourse. In the absence of other interpretive criteria, *power* determines which interpretations will gain a hearing: the power to manipulate the press, the power of those with access to the airwaves or the Internet, the power to convince racists that their racism has theological merit. We might raise, therefore, the pragmatic question: what does Davidson's biblical interpretation allow him *to do?* Davidson's biblical interpretation (like many other instances of biblical interpretation outside our ivy-covered towers) relies on the cultural authority of the Bible to persuade people to consent to a particular ordering of society. A pragmatic approach bypasses the question of truth or validity in interpretation and focuses instead on the consequences of adopting a particular interpretation, or indeed on the consequences of relying on biblical authority in political discourse.

The Bible John Murders and Media Discourse, 1969–1996

William T. Scott

1. *Preliminary Considerations*

a. *Metatheoretical Issues*

It should perhaps be obligatory for all scholars to begin each contribution to the literature with a clear statement of where their work stands on the two fundamental axes that structure debates about understanding and interpretation. These are present in all epochs, but are particularly foregrounded in these distempered times currently labelled 'postmodernity'.

Not surprisingly, this obligation is most obvious in the work of the hermeneutic, meta-interpretative disciplines, which offer texts-for-interpretation about texts (perhaps themselves interpretative texts about texts, and so on). Of these, two are particularly burdened with the need to justify transcendent textual interpretation, law and religion, most especially when these institutionalized practices are book-based, and operate in literate cultures.

The first axis may be presented as a continuum from the universalizing tendency at one extreme to the relativizing and particularizing tendency at the other. Scholars undisturbed by the blasts of critical theory might consider themselves to be concerned with making significant generalizations, ideally, establishing immutable laws, about the phenomena they study. This they might claim to do by discovering whatever salient similarities and commonalities, even uniformities, underlie the superficially diverse particularities displayed by members of all classes of phenomena. (Note that these remarks apply equally to the object and theory levels of our efforts to understand the world and our experiences.)

The concern for essences and uniformities immanent in heterodox reality shifts our attention to the other axis, where broadly positive and negative approaches are arrayed. The universalizing (also 'totalizing' or 'foundationalist') approach summarized above is, typically, positive, in several respects:

1. it assumes and reifies stable reality—a real text and real recoverable meaning, for example;

2. it assumes that the transparent truth about these texts and their embodied meanings can be both identified and uttered reliably as well as validly, such that everybody, everywhere, always must, by force of reason or persuasion, experience these perennially true meanings uniformly;

3. it assumes that extending our enlightenment in all spheres of experience, not just the study of scriptural and other texts is not only possible, but a good thing…and so on.

Just as the universalizing and the positive/positivist tendencies intertwine, so too do their opposing tendencies. Here, destabilizing exceptions, changes and deviations are emphasized in opposition to the normative forces at the other extreme, in order to resist specific foundationalist interpretations and statements. More fundamentally, the very possibility of identifying the truth and telling it validly or reliably—the possibility of understanding—may be denied outright in such work.

The radical relativism so noticeable in much of critical theory, and in much cultural studies work, illustrates one problematic outcome of the attitudes to understanding summarized here. Relatedly, and as part of the oppositionalist agenda, mainstream scholarship—along with other structures of understanding—is particularly indicted for the twin crimes of merely reifying the status quo, thus serving its beneficiaries, and of doing so behind the pretence of disinterestedly pursuing truths/the Truth.

The two continua, or irreconcilable polarities as some still enamoured of structuralist digitizing would insist, can be arrayed as in Figure 1. This is offered as a simple map that all of us (*sic*) contributing to gatherings such as this might agree that we navigate by, and on which we should declare our current coordinates, so that others may make sense of the sense we are attempting to make.

In shorthand terms, at the top of the vertical axis we might locate all the key terms of the enlightenment and modernity, such as: reality, truth, trust, progress, optimism, logic and reason, agreement, collaboration. At the opposite extreme, we find the conceptual currency of what has become known as postmodernism, more broadly critical theory,

with which cultural studies has strong affinities, such as: artefactuality/
falsity, illusion/error, suspicion, stasis/decline, pessimism (of the intellect
and/or the will), rhetoric/deceit, coercion.

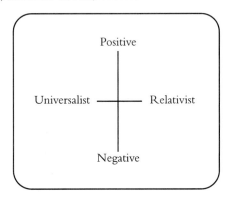

Figure 1. Modernity–Postmodernity: Two Continua

Similarly, at the left of the horizontal axis we locate interest in laws,
or at least strong generalizations, the possibility of a common human
nature and shared experience, including understanding in all senses, an
emphasis on stable uniformities in the world and in ourselves. By contrast, at the right of the axis we find an emphasis on exceptions, deviations and misfits of all sorts, discontinuities, breakdowns and barriers,
misunderstanding and confusion, unpredictable change. In slogan terms,
we here add to Ricoeur's 'hermeneutics of suspicion' and Lyotard's
'incredulity toward metanarratives', the insistence on resistant reading,
reading for absences, subversion of author-ity, and all the other centri-
petal tactics whereby normativity in life or in scholarship has been
assailed, to an unprecedented extent in our dystopian times.

Conventional scholarship starts from and returns to the top left, having toured the other quartiles, particularly bottom right. Here, putative
generalizations are subjected to the falsifiability test, while, top right,
alternative hypotheses and evidence are generated. Critical theory, in its
various forms, generally orientates to and from the bottom right quar-
tile, although, in its most militant form, it moves bottom left, postulat-
ing the universal impossibility of ever knowing anything, of ever being
understood, indeed, of postulation itself.

On the enabling assumption that the continua really are continua and
not sheerly disjoined polarities, the present essay will be orientated to
and from the top left. It will presume to use core elements of broadly
received scholarship in the hope of making better rather than worse

sense, in this case of the way in which a series of murders was presented to 'the public' by 'the media'.

In answer to the question 'why?', with its implication of sleeping with the enemy and, typically, its deeper claim that there are no valid criteria for any such hermeneutic effort (or any other intervention in the real world and its problems), one might reply 'why not ?', and point to the disabling nihilism—although rarely silence—that awaits persistent denial of both knowability and effability. The late Paul Feyerabend's assertion (Feyerabend 1968) that the only real principle at work in the knowledge-generating business is 'Anything goes' notoriously leads to the practical outcome that everything stays, there being no basis for critique (his own excepted, of course). Similarly, Derrida offers many reminders that his strictures require that which they deny, not least somehow efficacious writing, if we are to make necessarily fleeting sense (hence the reminders) of that denial.

To engage further in the ludic pastime of paradoxification, we might counter such counter-principles, and their myriad congeners mustered under the self-effacing banners of postmodernism, just by adopting them. We thereby access the right to proceed as if their very opposite were true, mirroring those who write against writing, theorizing against theorizing, and so on. As ever, those who are uncomfortable with this seeming capitulation to the hydra-headed enemy usually demonized as a WASP patriarch will stop at this point, there being nothing to say and no way of saying it in any case, as we knew from the outset. (One of the best brief accounts of the broad perspective being turned back on itself here, and one of particular relevance to biblical scholarship, is Moore 1994, but there are many other contributors to a frequently fractious and mischief-rich literature.)

b. *Cultural Relativism/Relativity*

The study that follows considers aspects of a particular set of texts and their cultural context, and speculates as to whether or not such a text would 'mean' in similar ways now. In particular, it questions whether or not a reporter could nowadays take for granted the knowledge of, and attitudes to, the Bible assumed in these texts, along with other key assumptions, such as the existence of a community partly formed by these cultural possessions. The moral certitude and assertiveness displayed was, it is argued, grounded in these cultural conditions. As these no longer exist, the style and certainly the content of the reporting are no longer possible. From the contemporary perspective, we must therefore reconstruct something of the original context in order to make the same sense of the texts that the audience at the time would have made.

This essay thus raises a particularly acute version of the tensions starkly caricatured in the opening section above, a version sometimes referred to as 'the anthropologist's problem', which we may generalize as follows. The anthropologist's chosen task is to enter an alien culture as free of presuppositions as possible, and, almost re-enacting the process of primary socialization, to find out the contents of its constituent institutions, for example, religious beliefs, traditions, social mores and practices enacting the essentials of life everywhere, such as families, marriage, conflict-management, and so on. The ambient language is both one of the social institutions to be investigated, and, as a repository of the community's accumulated experiences, a tool necessary for the asking of questions that the anthropologist needs to ask.

Clearly, the summary just given reveals that presuppositions are irreducibly present when we approach even the most 'exotic' or seemingly undisturbed culture, among them the idea that a more rather than less organic, functionally integrated, way of life will normally be there awaiting the investigator's analytic and descriptive skills. This particular presupposition is evident even in recent work, such as that of Macdonald (1993) or Maffesoli (1996), studying the fractured and variously partial microcultures that those of us inhabiting modern/Western societies also belong to, albeit self-consciously and often ironically.

The extreme relativist, whether an anthropologist or a general-purpose sceptic, contends that an alien culture (or, indeed, an alien mind within 'the same' culture) is not only unknown prior to investigation (or so deemed, by the minimum presupposition principle) but truly unknowable, ever, to any outsider. To know *that*, of course, the extreme relativist has to know at least two cultures well enough to have convinced herself that Culture A is wholly different from Culture B, precisely the possibility being denied. She also has to assume the possibility of knowing, if not in general then at least in this regard, for herself and for the rest of us receiving, somehow, her message.

To complete the declaration of credentials, then, the work that follows will assume that we can adequately recreate a cultural context within which certain powerful mass media texts functioned in ways that we can also describe accurately, and that we can make comparisons and contrasts with the ways in which these and other texts functioned when they, and the story they helped to carry and create, re-appeared a generation later. The key point will be that the cultural circumstances into which the story and its accumulated texts re-emerged are significantly different, and so the texts work differently, but in ways that we can identify and calibrate. Notably, the awareness of and respect for biblical knowledge and associated values, on which the earlier texts rely, have substantially vanished.

To use the useful distinction of Hollis and Lukes, relativity in the sense of selective contextualization will thus be adopted rather than the extreme and disabling relativism so characteristic of critical and cultural studies: we will travel between top left and top right in Figure 1, attempting to make the 'best text', in Dworkin's phrase, we can of the text we are studying.

2. Background

Almost thirty years ago, in Glasgow, Scotland, three murders took place over a period of about a year, the last occurring on 30 October 1969. Each of the victims was a married woman who had been enjoying an evening, without her husband, at a famous dance hall in the city. The evening—a Thursday—was well known as one when wedding rings would be temporarily removed by men and women alike, and flirtation, titillation and more might be available. There was and is no suggestion that any of the women who died was there for extramarital sex. However, the reputation of those Thursday evenings was known to many, but mentioned explicitly by few, even in the many media reports that appeared as the story evolved. Such restraint would be unlikely now, to make an obvious relativizing point.

One witness had shared a taxi with the likely killer and his last victim, who was her sister. She told police, in her very detailed evidence about the man's demeanour and appearance, that he had made use of at least one biblical quotation (never finally tracked down), having been asked if his claimed agnosticism meant that he was an atheist. The man had also referred to dance halls as 'dens of iniquity', and spoken of the 'adulterous' people who used them. Lastly, he had spoken of his strict upbringing, and displayed many of the nonverbal characteristics recognized locally, and more widely, as typical of repressive Presbyterian rectitude.

The suspect was swiftly dubbed 'Bible John' by the press, when these scanty scraps of evidence were revealed, and he has been so referred to in almost all reporting then and since. Before that, he had occasionally been referred to in the media as 'the ladykiller', a somewhat ghoulish borrowing of an everyday expression for the sort of man he had been described as being (charming, highly-mannered, etc.). The term had also been given additional currency by the success of a popular film of that title.

This, in passing, is an illustration of the tendency, in media discourse, to establish a 'hook' term for a running story. Ideally, a hook should be short, and already familiar to the public, who can use it to contextualize each new development as it arises. Recent examples in British culture have been 'sleaze', which immediately calls up an extensive catalogue of financial and/or sexual failings on the part of public figures, mainly politicians. Another is 'Camillagate', a raunchy royal rompings saga featuring the heir to the British throne and a lady also married to someone else at the material time. (Note the durability of the original Watergate hook, of which this use involving the name of Mrs Camilla Parker-Bowles is one of many since the original apartment block address came to stand for an entire set of events, actions, attitudes and values, also almost 30 years ago. An obvious question is what sense is made of such constructions by those who remember or know nothing of the events that led to Richard Nixon's disgrace.)

Another crucial piece of media shorthand used in the Bible John story was the 'artist's impression' portrait (shortly to be improved by the then new Identikit representation). This was constructed with the aid of the same witness in the main, and gives the suspect a curiously serene, almost Christ-like persona. Perhaps the artist's depiction was influenced by the newly-coined name for the suspect and the other information summarized above, all of which were dominating the media in the days following the last murder. Certainly, unlike the blank, expressionless face usually presented for identification purposes, this face has 'a look': it gazes with a hint of self-assured contempt.

Bible John's image, and the associated, imagined person, dominated posters and billboards, front pages and television screens for many months. As we will see below, John's media persona became, in the particular cultural context, a powerful element in the search for the killer. This amounted to one of the most extensive manhunts ever conducted by the local police, who were aided not only by a description even more detailed than was revealed to the public (he had very distinctive front teeth, for example, and that was the first detail that detectives looked at with each new suspect) but by exceptional public interest and involvement. However, the culprit was never caught.

During 1995, the local police force, in the ongoing process of transferring paper files to computer, found themselves reconsidering this case, particularly given that DNA testing of semen samples found on the last victim's clothing, still stored in the archives, had become available since the original investigation. In addition, one individual who had been a strong suspect and had committed suicide in 1980 at the age of 41, had re-emerged in the minds of officers still fascinated by the case as a candidate for such attempted matching. On 1 February 1996, the man's body was exhumed, amid intense publicity, and taken away for analysis, first in Glasgow and then in Cambridge. After nearly six months of tests, on extremely unpromising material it should be stressed, the tests proved inconclusive. The body was reburied, and with it, perhaps, the still unsolved case of Bible John.

Figure 2. Artist's impression of Bible John (*The Herald*, Glasgow)

3. *Text and Context*

The main text to be examined in this essay is a television broadcast, transmitted by BBC Scotland at the height of the public interest in the case. Parts of the text are transcribed at the end of this article. Before considering that, however, a number of general concepts and concerns remain to be dealt with.

The power of naming is well understood and respected in all cultures, and is one of the most important of the many taboos and restrictions that bear upon language use. Naming a child is not simply a matter of family or cultural tradition, of taste or fashion: few of us court bad luck, second-hand opprobrium or ridicule for our children, and even our dogs. We need not fall into facile linguistic determinism in noting that the broader notion of labelling an object or whatever, especially with a single morphological unit, somehow institutionalizes and legitimates the existence of what might in fact be illusory: we still speak of 'the ether', for example, and many other useful concepts that only exist through talk and/or writing. (This is but one aspect of the creative power of language, a power that can be used destructively, of course.)

Where individuals are concerned, one's given name (even if John Smith, or the equivalent) is a crucial part of one's identity, self-identity as well as public and social identity; so also are nicknames, pet names and the rest. When uttered by a person in authority in threatening circumstances, one's full set of names carries great semiotic effect, as do any attendant titles which may be available. Name in the sense of one's good name, or having a name for some skill or talent calls up other senses that confirm the importance of names, particularly in mediated cultures where stardom, celebrity and villain status are so much part of our voyeuristic cultural consumption.

Therefore, while names are arbitrary strings of signifiers, as Shakespeare reminded us somewhat more elegantly, they are also conventional, constructed in response to what is current in the interpretative community. John Smith, for example, really is the name of many people, but is also used as an alternative to Mr Average, and even as a self-advertising false identity. In the case of Bible John, his use of the Christian name was probably just that, a conventional means of disguise that simultaneously advertised to other participants his own participation in the game of suspended identities.

The name Bible John also has particular resonances. The legendary figure of Prester John, and the many priests who would be known as Father John, provide familiar phonological analogies for the construction. In addition, there was a tradition locally and no doubt elsewhere of referring to enthusiastic lay Christians as Bible Jack, and so on, as part of the widespread process where given names are adapted or added to for satirical or other semantic effect. The journalist who first labelled the elusive killer 'Bible John' was, therefore, exploiting, in the usual way that all communicators must, the potential of what was already shared for making new information intelligible in convenient and ready form.

This raises once again the issue touched upon in earlier remarks about relativism/relativity. At one extreme we may imagine a perfectly whole, sealed and crystalline culture, where everybody of adult age and in possession of normal faculties has equal and identical possession of a uniform stock of cultural capital, including the language and other semiotic resources through which social life is enacted. There would be little need for social life in these circumstances of high redundancy, in information-theoretic terms, less for communication, given that everybody knows everything (and knows that about everybody else, etc.) already. At the other extreme, we can imagine a high entropy society, where difference and change are maximized person to person, situation to situation, moment to moment. We can imagine such a volatile and unstable society in principle, but it is difficult to conceive of the detailed life experiences of its unfortunate inhabitants. Such utter derangement denies not only sociality but, perhaps hence, sanity.

Somewhere between the two extremes, the banal conclusion is that real individuals and their social being, above all what they know as communicatively competent performers of that social being, negotiate positions. Notoriously, in the so-called hot or dynamic societies, this is hard work. We yield to the nostalgic notion that previous generations enjoyed a more stable and nourishingly organic solidarity, that the core of shared values, beliefs and lifestyle practices was larger, more widely dispersed in the community, more respected in every sense, that there were stable 'places' and people knew theirs, so were less 'disturbed', and so on. Most nationalist movements, irredentist or not, have constructed some such lost golden age, but even societies we judge to be relatively undisturbed and unpoliticized tell tales of past glory and present decline. Debates about education, and all other forms of public communication in countries such as Britain and the USA often invoke the need to instill, foster and protect the content of the somehow identified shared core. In the USA, with its history of deliberate assimilation programmes for diverse minorities (many members of which remain stubbornly 'hyphenated' Americans), the work of Hirsch and others on the knowledge, values and attitudes one should possess in order to be a fully competent participant in the culture has been especially controversial. That it is a political matter involving the exercise of power through the various institutions and media of communication, including schools and churches, is evident.

For our purposes, these wider debates about what our compatriots, or co-culturalists, know or ought to know need not be explored in any more detail. What is given here is sufficient to serve as a framework in which to raise the question of religious, and biblical, knowledge in the community that received the original Bible John reporting, and in the descendant community in which the story was relaunched.

Since the mid-sixteenth century, Scotland has been, in religious terms, 'Reformed'. The strongly Calvinist brand of Protestantism associated with John Knox weakened and diversified over the centuries, but some of its essential features maintained a grip on the minds of many, affecting public institutions and practices in numerous ways. In terms of international politics, the doctrine of divine election even extended to Scotland's destined role as the world's finest example of Reformation, both in church and society (see Stevenson 1988 on 'the marriage with God').

A characteristically schizoid combination of God-fearing righteousness and homicidal wrath is an enduring theme in Scottish literature, for example in Stevenson's *Dr Jekyll and Mr Hyde*, or Galt's *The Sins and Confessions of a Justified Sinner*. Many other writings deal with the contradictions, typically polarized, that emerge from the notion of a predestined distinction between the saved and the damned, the rational and the irrational, and so on. Burns's great, ironic poem, *Holy Wilie's Prayer*, is but one exploration of this Manichean tendency, the prevalence of which in Scottish culture is considered so fundamental that one critic has written of the Caledonian antisyzygy (Smith 1919). Tellingly, one Burns story known to most Scots is his quasi-legal trial by church elders for immorality, and the subsequent punishment of being forced to sit in the 'sin-bin' of the local church during Sunday services.

At a more mundane level, Sabbatarian restrictions were still powerful, even in the large cities, as late as the 1950s. They are complied with to this day in parts of the country where the various sorts of Free Church, which split with the mainstream, Presbyterian Church of Scotland early in the last century, survive.

By the mid-1960s, the great majority of the population remained more or less associated with the Church of Scotland. However, as elsewhere, the second half of the twentieth century has seen a catastrophic decline in membership (especially new communicants) and attendance. I. Smith writes: 'Historically, the post-war period is particularly startling due to the rapidity of decline, unprecedented both in absolute terms and growth rate' (1992: 4). He adds later: 'The unabated decline in the stock of Church of Scotland members since 1957 primarily reflects falling inflow rates among young people' (1992: 12).

By the end of the 1960s, then, the ambient culture, certainly for the relatively young people who featured in the Bible John murders, was one in which, to use Matthew Arnold's image, the sea of faith was retreating noticeably. However, it was also one in which the mores, including the linguistic customs and practices, of previous generations lived on, albeit etiolated and no doubt ironicized, but still part of the linguistic currency. Most adults at the time would have had acquired their familiarity with these cultural tokens in their considerable exposure to biblical and otherwise religious discourse, at school, Sunday school or other 'faith-related' groups such as youth organizations and evangelical 'missions' and 'crusades', in addition to whatever church-going they had experienced in childhood.

Religious broadcasting was also still taken for granted, and was by no means restricted to Sundays. Given the decline in active participation noted above (which also affected the other major denomination, Roman Catholicism), 'the God-slot' on television or *Thought for the Day* on BBC radio were for many the only direct link they retained with religious experience and knowledge, once fundamental to the culture around them, and still recognized, in various senses, not least in the details of a suspected murderer's speech, and in the great weight placed upon these by police, reporters, and public.

4. *A Text Resurrected*

The main text from the period of the murders that is of interest here is an extract from a television news feature, broadcast after the third murder, when public interest in the man later titled—debatably—'Scotland's first serial killer' was at its height, and his oddly serene image (publicly endorsed as an extremely good likeness) was everywhere (see script below).

Visually, the film borrows heavily from film noir conventions, and from the detective film genre. Black and white broadcasting was the only format available at the time, but the darkness and starkness of the imagery here is deliberately exaggerated in the 'reconstruction' sections, and in the passages where the reporter addresses John directly. Light sources are shot so as to emphasize the glaring and bleary quality of such illumination as there is in the subfusc world the viewer is shown. This is a shadow world, the habitat of morally—and otherwise—dubious individuals consorting in dance halls, secreting themselves in taxis—something of a luxury for most Scots at that time, only used for very particular reasons—and suchlike.

The doom-laden and somewhat menacing atmosphere is greatly enhanced by the voice of the reporter, firstly in its timbre and resonance. It is the voice of respectability, of decency and dependable normality, the voice of reason. Many middle-aged male actors, in countless series and soap operas, have provided versions of this acoustic centre of gravity/gravitas. The speaker intones, in a clearly hortatory or suasive mode. If all preaching is suasive, then this is a form of preaching, directed personally to the man he addresses using the Christian name, John. Unlike the politician delivering the televised fireside chat, almost conversational in style and delivered straight to the viewer quasi-individually, this text is delivered to an unknown individual person. We the viewers/listeners eavesdrop, providing an 'over-the-shoulder' supporting chorus, as the reporter strives to persuade the individual to come in from the shadow world.

There is specific reference to, and exploitation of, the most infamous detail known about the man, his familiarity with passages from the Bible. Leviticus 20, which provides strictures against whoring, adultery, incest, and so on, is mentioned as one text that he may know. The other is Exodus 2, the story of Moses, with its theme of the stranger in a strange land. The reporter's climactic rhetorical ploy, however, is not to mine either of these sources for meanings that might have moved his target appropriately. He turns to Jer. 23.24: ' "Can any hide himself in secret places that I shall not see him?" saith the Lord. "Do I not fill heaven and earth?" saith the Lord'. These words, and the accompanying images suggestive of the all-seeing eye that the spectatorial powers of the camera provide to the viewer (not unlike the judgmental role Burns maneouvres his readers into in the poem mentioned above), are aimed at exacerbating whatever guilt and isolation the fugitive may have been feeling. If, of course, he was motivated by some debased remnant of the Calvinist mindset, believing himself chosen as God's instrument in the war against whores and adulterers, that argumentative strategy would have had little chance of success. It is perhaps the very likelihood that the killer was a man with a clean conscience that gave the story such fascination for people living lives still shaped by a belief system that endowed a diverse cast of authority figures with the right to be right, especially in their manifest conformity to the laws of God and 'man'. That a seemingly 'churchy' and respectable person could perpetrate such crimes in such a milieu was shocking in the extreme to that public.

Certainly, such a piece of current affairs broadcasting is difficult to imagine in current circumstances. When the body of the suspect, John McInnes, was exhumed on 1 February 1996, little of the religious and moral resonances around the story, so powerful at the time, were reactivated by the media professionals, who were nonetheless aware of the lingering fascination that older people still retained. That emotionality was partially recreated by showing the archive film discussed here. However, the reporting of the exhumation and related information was considerably less theatrical.

The dramatic charge created by the combination of a triple murder and a respectable suspect who also knew his Bible is simply no longer possible. Even in a country such as the UK, with its tiny annual rate of murders-per-thousand of population, we are much more hardened to such crimes than previously, particularly after Hungerford or Dunblane. These have many rivals in both peace and war situations brought to us ever more dysphemistically, and often live, by the ever more global and efficient media, and so few of us would give much time to the story examined here.

Also, it is difficult to imagine a modern reporter attempting such a theatrical, moralistic and confidently *grounded* piece. This last point returns us to issues raised above. The reporter who scripted and planned the text seems very confident of speaking for and in the presence of a community that shared certain categories of knowledge and experience, and whose emotional reactions to the combination of 'ingredients' mentioned above he could equally confidently assume (in both senses) and exploit. Neither that confidence nor the assumption is imaginable today. Indeed, what appears to be a personal intervention by the journalist in negotiating directly with, and playing upon the emotions of, the suspect might even be considered a breach of professional ethics.

Screenshots taken from television broadcast, BBC Scotland, October 1969

Transcript from 'Reporting Scotland' on Bible John Murders—
Leslie Anderson Reporting, February 1996 (1969 material in italic).

Hugh Cochrane:	*John, if your name is John. John, if you're out there now, watching and listening, maybe it's time to come in out of the glare for your own good. The police want to talk to you, wherever you are you should know that.*
Leslie Anderson:	It was at the Barrowland Ballroom that the story of Bible John began. Helen Puttock and her sister Jean left the dance hall accompanied by two men. One went to catch a bus, the other, called John, went with the sisters in a taxi. During the drive, and before that, as they walked to Glasgow Cross, the reddish-haired man allegedly made references to the Bible. Jean left the taxi, Helen and the man continued. The next morning she was found brutally murdered, sparking what was then the largest manhunt ever mounted by Scottish police.
Detective:	*I would say that this man is possibly a loner. He lives, I would think, with a relative. He's a personable man, good looking. He possibly occupies some place in society where he has a little authority.*
Telephone rings.	
Policeman answers:	*Marine Division CID murder room.*
Voice on telephone:	*Is that the Bible John enquiry room?*
Policeman:	*Yes it is.*
Voice on telephone:	*I think I've seen this fellow you're looking for, you know, this Bible John.*
Leslie Anderson:	Hundreds of men had the finger of suspicion pointed at them as the public was gripped by the hunt for Bible John.
Hugh Cochrane:	*A man on a taxi journey to Edinburgh innocently quotes the Bible to the driver and finds himself deposited at Police Headquarters as a suspect.*
Detective:	*Any tall red-haired men with a Bible going to church on a Sunday morning, there's a call arrives here.*
Hugh Cochrane:	*You are still hoping that you've got a million pair of eyes working for you?*

Detective:	*Well you say a million pair of eyes, Mr Cochrane, I would like to think perhaps ten million pair of eyes.*
Leslie Anderson:	The hunt stretched across the world as sightings of Bible John were reported from as far away as Australia.
Hugh Cochrane:	The quest impinges on the life of ordinary people nearly everywhere. Day in, day out, something new. Faces in the busy streets being studied closely. Twenty-six years on, that quest for Bible John may at last be over.
Hugh Cochrane:	*John, it seems probable that you may know Leviticus, Chapter 20 and Exodus, Chapter 2, but do you remember Jeremiah 23 verse 24? ' "Can any hide himself in secret places that I shall not see him", saith the Lord'.*

(Acknowledgments to BBC Scotland)

BIBLIOGRAPHY

Bodine, W.A. (ed.)
   1995   *Discourse Analysis of Biblical Literature: What It Is and What It Offers* (Semeia Studies; Atlanta: Society of Biblical Literature).
Derrida, J.
   1985   'Des Tours de Babel', in J.F. Graham (ed.), *Difference in Translation* (trans. J. Graham; Ithaca, NY: Cornell University Press); reprinted in *Semeia* 54 (1992): 3-35.
Feyerabend, P.K.
   1968   *Against Method* (London: Verso).
Hollis M., and S. Lukes
   1982   *Rationality and Relativism* (Oxford: Basil Blackwell).
Jobling D., and S.D. Moore (eds.)
   1992   *Poststructuralism as Exegesis* (Semeia, 54; Atlanta: Scholars Press).
Macdonald, S.
   1993   *Inside European Identities* (Providence, RI; London: Berg).
Maffesoli, M.
   1996   *The Time of the Tribes: The Decline of Individualism in Mass Society* (London: Sage).
Moore, S.D.
   1994   *Poststructuralism and the New Testament: Derrida and Foucault at the Foot of the Cross* (Minneapolis: Fortress Press).
Patrick, D., and A. Scult
   1990   *Rhetoric and Biblical Interpretation* (Sheffield: Almond Press).
Porter, S.E., and T.H. Olbricht (eds.)
   1993   *Rhetoric and the New Testament: Essays from the 1992 Heidelberg Conference* (Sheffield: Sheffield Academic Press).

Smith, G.G.
  1919   *Scottish Literature: Character and Influence* (London: Macmillan).
Smith, I.
  1992   *The Economics of Church Decline: The Case of the Church of Scotland* (Discussion Paper Series, 9210; St Andrews: Department of Economics, University of St Andrews).
Stevenson, D.
  1988   *The Covenanters: The National Covenant and Scotland* (Edinburgh: The Saltire Society).

INDEX OF AUTHORS

JOURNAL FOR THE STUDY OF THE OLD TESTAMENT
SUPPLEMENT SERIES